An Introduction to Geographical and Urban Economics
A Spiky World

A comprehensive introduction to both urban and geographical economics: the two dominant approaches used to explain the distribution of economic activity across space. This fully revised and up-to-date third edition gives a full account of the ever-expanding body of knowledge and insights on urban and geographical economics, with an increased emphasis on analytical concepts and empirical methods, reflecting developments in the literature since the last edition. The authors provide both state-of-the-art theories and empirics, introducing new data, methods and models for this edition, including a whole chapter dedicated to measurement issues and empirical methods. Written in a style that is accessible to students who are new to the field, this textbook also includes more advanced concepts that will interest experienced researchers. Unrivalled in its scope and depth, this title is perfect for readers seeking to understand the uneven spatial distribution of economic activity between and within countries.

Steven Brakman is Professor of International Economics at the Faculty of Economics and Business at the Rijksuniversiteit Groningen. He is a research fellow of the CESifo Institute in Munich, and co-editor of the *Journal of Regional Science.* He is academic partner of the Netherlands Bureau for Economic Policy Analysis, and member of the programme committee of Statistics Netherlands.

Harry Garretsen is Professor of International Economics and Business at the Rijksuniversiteit Groningen, and a visiting fellow at the University of Cambridge. Garretsen has published widely in books and leading international journals on urban, geographical, international economics and also on economics and leadership. He has also been active in giving policy advice on these topics. His editorial board activities include the *Journal of Economic Geography, Journal of Regional Science, Cambridge Journal of the Regions, Economy and Society,* and *Leadership Quarterly.*

Charles van Marrewijk is Professor of Economics and Head of Research at Universiteit Utrecht School of Economics, The Netherlands. He has published widely for leading international journals and publishers on spatial economics (including international, urban, regional, and geographical economics) and development economics (including economic growth, agglomeration, and globalization).

An Introduction to Geographical and Urban Economics

A Spiky World

Steven Brakman

University of Groningen

Harry Garretsen

University of Groningen

Charles van Marrewijk

Utrecht University

CAMBRIDGE
UNIVERSITY PRESS

CAMBRIDGE
UNIVERSITY PRESS

University Printing House, Cambridge CB2 8BS, United Kingdom

One Liberty Plaza, 20th Floor, New York, NY 10006, USA

477 Williamstown Road, Port Melbourne, VIC 3207, Australia

314-321, 3rd Floor, Plot 3, Splendor Forum, Jasola District Centre, New Delhi - 110025, India

79 Anson Road, #06-04/06, Singapore 079906

Cambridge University Press is part of the University of Cambridge.

It furthers the University's mission by disseminating knowledge in the pursuit of education, learning and research at the highest international levels of excellence.

www.cambridge.org
Information on this title: www.cambridge.org/9781108407366
DOI: 10.1017/9781108290234

First published (as *An Introduction to Geographical Economics*) 2001
Second edition (as *The New Introduction to Geographical Economics*) 2009

A catalogue record for this publication is available from the British Library

ISBN 978-1-108-41849-2 Hardback
ISBN 978-1-108-40736-6 Paperback

Additional resources for this publication at www.cambridge.org/brakman3

Contents

Figures

Tables

Boxes

Technical Notes

Exercises

Preface

The purpose of our book is to offer an introduction to urban and geographical economics, the two dominant approaches in mainstream economics to explain the distribution of economic activity across space. The fact that we offer an 'introduction' does not mean that we avoid models or shy away from more advanced or difficult concepts; it indicates that we have attempted to write a book that is both accessible to readers and students who are new to the field but also of interest to fellow researchers. This book builds upon the first and second editions of 2001 and 2009, respectively. At the same time, this book is rather different from its two predecessors. Apart from an ever expanding body of knowledge and insights on urban and geographical economics that needs to be covered, the present version of the book is also different because it puts much greater emphasis on analytical concepts and empirical methods, which reflects the developments in the literature since the time of writing the 2009 edition. In addition, the new book pays far more attention to urban economics to the extent that we have decided to incorporate 'urban economics' in the title of our book.

To help the reader in learning and understanding the basics of modern urban and geographical economics, each chapter offers a set of questions as well as technical notes and special interest boxes to guide the reader through the material. In addition, there is a website that goes along with the book where answers to the questions are given, additional material is discussed, and where a simulation of the core model of geographical economics can help the reader to enhance her understanding of the main mechanisms involved. The website also gives access to 'ready-made' versions of the long list of tables and figures that appear in the book.

The book is in four parts. Part I (Chapters 1–3) introduces the spiky world in which we live and deals with the basic empirical facts and methods that guide the subsequent analysis of the spiky or uneven allocation of human and economic activity across the globe, both between and within countries. Parts II and III are the core of the book. Part II (Chapters 4–6) deals with the main theories and empirics of urban economics and Part III (Chapters 7–9) does the same for geographical economics. Part IV of the book (Chapters 10 and 11) uses some of the main insights on urban and geographical economics in applying them to the topics of economic development and policy making. Of course we feel that the book is best read and studied as a whole from the front to the back cover by studying Chapters 1–11 sequentially. But for an actual course in which one would like to focus on the essentials of urban and geographical economics only, the reading menu could simply start with Chapter 1 and continue the course with Parts II and III. Similarly, a focus on either urban or geographical economics would base the essential reading on either Part II or Part III, in particular if the course material consists partly of a number of key book chapters and partly of state-of-the-art research papers (many of which are already briefly introduced in the book). On the other hand, a course that zooms in on the empirics and applications of urban and geographical economics could consist of Part I, Chapters 6 and 9 and Part IV.

The (changes in) composition and content of the book are in no small part the result of the fact that we ourselves have used the book in various (advanced) undergraduate and graduate courses in the last decade or so. The 2009 edition has been used for courses at the universities of Utrecht, Rotterdam (Erasmus), Groningen, Suzhou, and Cambridge. Our own teaching experiences and also the feedback we got from scores of students helped to shape the new book. We also benefited from the feedback we received from various fellow lecturers and researchers across the globe. We owe them our thanks. We are also grateful to our research colleagues with whom we worked on various papers and projects on urban and geographical economics, the results of which proved a real source of inspiration for the new book.

We also want to thank Cambridge University Press (CUP) and especially 'our' CUP editors, Phil Good and Charles Howell, for not only giving us the opportunity to produce a third and rather different version of the book, but also for encouragement and patience. Likewise, we are grateful to Malcolm Todd who went through the whole manuscript and spotted and corrected many mistakes and also improved the use of English. Any remaining errors are, of course, our own. Michiel Gerritse was a real help in commenting on the manuscript and Thomas van den Berg provided excellent research assistance and input for the accompanying website. It is now 20 years since we started to work on the first edition of the book. Much has changed but not the continued support of our families and friends. Writing a book like this eats up a lot of time, and is also a spiky experience in itself, sudden and uneven bursts of activity and dead-lines that have to be met during and also outside the regular academic calendar and working hours. In the end we very much enjoyed the experience of making the new book and we really hope the same goes for our readers.

Finally, we want to dedicate the book to the memory of Dirk Stelder (1953–2017), fellow traveller in urban and geographical economics. His work does not only show up clearly and in a very visible manner in Chapter 9, but as a lecturer Dirk was strongly involved over a large number of years in setting-up and teaching the first and second editions of our book to many cohorts of students of international economics and economic geography at the University of Groningen.

Steven Brakman, Harry Garretsen, Charles van Marrewijk
Groningen and Utrecht

PART I
Empirical Foundations

··

Never judge a book by its cover, as the saying goes. But for this book the cover already gives a fairly good idea about the book's aim and contents! Our book is about the uneven distribution of human and economic activity across space. This unevenness shows itself through the fact that human and economic activity is strongly concentrated or spiky. Most of the human and economic activity is restricted to a relatively few locations or places. The fact that we live in a spiky word manifests itself at multiple levels of aggregation or geographical scales, that is within and between cities, regions, and also countries. Before we turn to the economic explanations for the spiky world via an in-depth discussion of urban and geographical economics, Part I of the book provides the empirical foundations for this inquiry by presenting a wide range of stylized facts on the spatial distribution of human and economic activity. This is the topic of Chapter 1. Although the focus of our book is on urban and geographical economics as a guide to understand the spiky world in which we live, Chapter 2 discusses alternative explanations for spikiness based on the role of physical geography, history, and institutions. In Chapter 3 we introduce various measures of spatial concentration or inequality and also briefly delve into the empirical methods and issues that are useful to keep in mind and include in the reader's toolkit when trying to answer the question of what the main determinants of economic spikiness are in the remainder of the book.

1 A Spiky World

LEARNING OBJECTIVES

- Show that economic activity is unevenly distributed over space; this is what we call Spikiness.
- Show that Spikiness is visible on different levels of aggregation; at the global, country, and regional level.
- Show that Spikiness has a long history.
- Show that Spikiness and economic performance are highly correlated. This book explains this correlation.

What came before … (the 2001 and 2009 editions of our book)

This book follows in the footsteps of Brakman, Garretsen, and van Marrewijk (2001, 2009). In retrospect, the 2001 book came out when geographical economics (also known as new economic geography) was probably at its peak research-wise. Ten years after Krugman (1991) launched the core model of geographical economics, the 2001 book focused strongly on the key ingredients of this model and its first extensions. It paid far less attention to empirical research and alternative approaches to understanding the spiky world. The 2009 book made up for this, aided by a decade of burgeoning research, as far as the empirics of geographical economics was concerned. The 2009 edition of our book did, however, still pay less attention to the other main approach in mainstream economics to dealing with a spiky world: urban economics. The 2020 version of our book tries to remedy this by spending a large part of the book on urban economics while maintaining the two, in our view, basic strengths of the first two editions, an extensive discussion of geographical economics as well as, also compared to other books or monographs, a strong focus on examples, data, and empirical research. This means that the new edition of our book is in many ways similar to, but at the same time rather different from the first and second editions. Apart from a more balanced treatment of urban versus geographical economics, another main difference is that we pay more attention to (even a whole chapter, see Chapter 3) measurement issues and empirical methods. This last choice reflects the fact that, if anything, the strongest progress in urban and geographical economics between 2009 and 2019 has been on the empirical side, and in particular on the use of new research designs and data sets.

When writing a book like ours, choices have to be made regarding the topics to focus on and also, given the target audience, what the analytical depth of the book should be. Given our choice to focus on the basic modern models and empirics of urban and geographical economics, we pay less attention to some other topics in the field of spatial economics, like transportation economics or the economics of housing. For those interested in the state of the art of spatial economics more generally, we refer interested readers to the comprehensive and up-to-date survey by Proost and Thisse (forthcoming). Given that our book aims to offer an *introduction* to urban and geographical economics, we also keep the discussion of the latest development in spatial economics, the so-called 'quantitative spatial economics' approach, rather minimal. In this approach many of the basic mechanisms upon which urban and geographical economics is grounded are combined into a single framework with rich (but also technically rather advanced) empirically quantifiable models that can address a whole range of questions regarding (changes in) the determinants of the spiky world. See Redding and Rossi-Hansberg (2016) for a short non-technical introduction[1] or the survey by Proost and Thisse (forthcoming, section 5.2) for details.

The decision to pay more attention to urban economics in the third edition of our book also reflects the fact that in the last decade or so the research in urban economics has flourished relative to research in geographical economics. As will become clear from this new version of our book, the main models, mechanisms, measures, and methods of urban and geographical economics are by now so much intertwined that they should not be treated separately, but should be seen as representing complementary approaches to analyse and understand the spiky world. In doing so, we are also better able to deal simultaneously with urban, regional, and international dimensions of the spiky world. The urban implications are naturally more at home in urban economics, whereas geographical economics, with its firm footing in international trade theory, offers a more natural platform to analyse the *relations* between different locations, such as the uneven spatial distribution of human and economic activity within countries but also across the globe (Head, Mayer, and Ottaviano, 2017).

The fact that we try to pack urban and geographical economics alongside a more extensive discussion of examples and empirical methods into a single book also implies that we cannot cover all topics that could be included in a book like

---

[1] See Redding and Rossi-Hansberg (2017) for an advanced introduction to quantitative spatial economics.

this. Compared to the 2009 book, we trimmed down the parts on international economics, and did the same for alternative approaches to urban and geographical economics, like economic geography or regional science. We also updated the book. We did so not only by including many studies that saw the light after 2009, but also by updating and extending the data and examples used. And even though geographical economics is still at the heart of the book, its discussion is now more concise and restricted to basically only Part III of the book whereas the previous two editions largely dealt with geographical economics only. The shift to focus more on other topics and notably more on urban economics is in our view also a fair reflection of the fact that urban economics has gained more prominence vis-à-vis geographical economics since the days when we wrote the 2001 and 2009 books.

What hopefully remains true for the third edition is that it is of interest to students and scholars not only from urban and geographical economics but also from international economics and business, economic geography, and regional science. The fact that we offer an 'introduction' does not imply we avoid models or shy away from more difficult concepts. It indicates that we have attempted to write a book that is also accessible to readers who are new to the fields of urban and geographical economics. Although we discuss and use various modelling approaches, we have also tried to keep the required technicalities to a minimum in the new book. Whenever needed we make use of technical notes to give background information on derivations and the like. Similarly, we make ample use of special interest boxes to highlight certain topics and insights.

1.1   Introduction

As the title of the book signals, this book is about *urban and geographical economics*.

The urban economics literature uses micro-economic forces to better understand spatial phenomena at the urban level, both within cities and between cities. Think, for example, why different types of economic activities are in different parts of the city, why rents are higher in the city centre, how population density varies across the city, why certain ethnic or income groups are segregated in different parts of the city, or why different cities are specializing in certain types of activities (manufacturing, finance, entertainment, and so on).

The geographical economics literature uses micro-foundations to better understand macro-economic forces at the regional level and the role of economic interactions for determining these macro-economic variables.[2] The key question is to

---

[2] We introduced the term 'geographical economics' in 2001 in the first version of our book (Brakman, Garretsen, and van Marrewijk, 2001), as an alternative for the dated term 'new economic geography'. The term 'geographical economics' better reflects that the models are about introducing geography in economic models, rather than the other way around. This is the central topic of Chapter 7.

determine what kind of interactions of economic variables (transport costs, elasticity of demand, and share of income spent on mobile activity) are responsible for the agglomeration of economic activities, or not. From a historical point of view, this literature tries to better understand how agglomeration of economic activity has evolved over time.

The premise of this book is that it is appropriate to analyse these two strands of literature in a similar framework because of the fractal nature of spatial economic forces: similar powers are at work at different spatial scales, giving rise to similar patterns of uneven distribution and interaction. This first chapter, entitled *A Spiky World*, introduces this fractal nature by analysing the distribution of people and economic activities at different spatial scales or levels of aggregation.[3]

The remainder of this chapter is organized as follows. Section 1.2 provides an overview of the large number of people on our planet. Section 1.3 analyses uneven distributions at the global level, section 1.4 at the country level, and section 1.5 within countries. Next, section 1.6 provides a historical overview of urban development, section 1.7 of more recent urban development, and section 1.8 of the link between urbanization and income levels. Section 1.9 introduces two regularities (regarding distribution and interaction). Finally, section 1.10 concludes with an overview of the remainder of the book.

1.2   Many People

As of 11:30 a.m. coordinated universal time on 3 January 2019 there were 7,674,551,061 people alive on planet Earth according to www.worldometers.info/world-population/, which provides a world population clock and detailed information per second on births, deaths, and population for countries and the world as a whole based on the United Nations Population Division (2017, medium variant) data. On that day and time, the world population increased by about 108,000 people, the result of 185,000 births minus 77,000 deaths.

Average population density in the world in 2018 is about 58 persons per square kilometre. If you are part of a family with two children and land were evenly distributed, your family could have about 7 hectares (or 17 acres) at its disposal. Most of our readers will probably look around in amazement to conclude that they do not own an area close to this size. The reason is simple: the world population

---

[3] The idea that the 'world is spiky' and the visualizations (see the book cover) that go along with this idea are due to the work by Richard Florida (http://martinprosperity.org/author/richard-florida/), who coined the phrase 'spiky world' in his books and in a 2005 article in *The Atlantic Monthly* to counteract the then influential idea by the American journalist Thomas Friedman that modern-day globalization would lead to a flat world where agglomeration and geography would become ever less relevant.

is unevenly distributed as people tend to cluster together across space, and the question is why?

There are many reasons why people cluster together. Sociological: you like to interact with other human beings. Psychological: you are afraid to be alone. Historical: your grandfather already lived where you live now. Cultural: the setting here is unlike anywhere else in the world. Geographical: the scenery is breathtaking and the beach is wonderful. The focus in this book is on the economic rationale behind clustering or agglomeration.

In a sense an economic motive behind population clustering might be a prerequisite for other motives as psychological, sociological, cultural, and historical motives may have largely developed in response to an economic motive that brought people together to live in villages and cities. Before analysing some details of urban development in section 1.6, we first briefly describe some of the characteristics of clustering of economies at a regional scale.

1.3   Global Regions

The World Bank provides a lot of information at the country level in the World Development Indicators online (www.worldbank.org). We use this information as a basis for discussion throughout this book. For presentation and discussion purposes it is sometimes useful to group countries together in bigger regions. Based on historical, cultural, and geographic information, the World Bank identifies seven main regions, as listed in Table 1.1. The East Asia and Pacific (EAP) region consists of 32 countries and includes such diverse countries as China, Japan, Indonesia, and Australia. The Europe & Central Asia (ECA) region consists of 49 countries, including the core European countries, such as France, Germany, and the UK, and Central Asian countries, such as Kazakhstan and Russia. The Latin America & Caribbean

Table 1.1 Overview of the World Bank regions

Code	Region	Examples of countries included	#
EAP	East Asia and Pacific	China, Japan, Indonesia, Australia	32
ECA	Europe & Central Asia	UK, Germany, France, Russia	49
LAC	Latin America & Caribbean	Brazil, Mexico, Argentina	35
MNA	Middle East & North Africa	Egypt, S Arabia, Algeria	21
NAM	North America	USA, Canada	3
SAS	South Asia	India, Pakistan, Bangladesh	8
SSA	Sub-Saharan Africa	Nigeria, S Africa, Ethiopia	48

Source: World Development Indicators online; # = number of countries.

(LAC) region consists of 35 countries. It includes virtually all American countries south of the USA, such as Mexico, Brazil, and Argentina. From a geographical point of view, a cut at Panama would have been understandable. The World Bank decided to include Mexico and the Central American countries in the LAC region in view of the historical and cultural links. Therefore, the North American (NAM) region consists of only three countries: USA, Canada, and Bermuda. The Middle East & North Africa (MNA) region is the link between Europe and Africa and consists of 21 countries, including Egypt, Saudi Arabia, and Algeria, and thus stretches partly over the African and Asian continents. The remainder of Africa (48 countries) is grouped together in the Sub-Saharan Africa (SSA) region. It includes Nigeria, South Africa, and Ethiopia. The final region is South Asia (SAS), which consists of eight countries, including India, Pakistan, and Bangladesh.

Table 1.2 provides some information on selected variables for the World Bank regions. The top part of the table reports the share of the world total (in per cent) for land area, population, and income. The key aspect to focus on is the wide variation in these numbers. South Asia, for example, is home to 23.7 per cent of the world population, but only generates 8.9 per cent of the world income using only 3.7 per cent of the world land area. Similarly, Sub-Saharan Africa consists of 18.2 per cent of the world land area, is home to 13.9 per cent of the world population, but only generates 3.1 per cent of the world income. North America, on the other hand, consists of 14.1 per cent of the world land area and can generate 17.1 per cent of the world income with only 4.8 per cent of the world population. These variations are partially reflected in the bottom part of Table 1.2, which provides indices (in per cent) for the World Bank regions relative to the world average for selected variables.

World average income per capita in 2016 was $16,171 (PPP current international $), but the variation between global regions is large. The average person in Sub-Saharan Africa earns only 22 per cent of the world average income level, while the average person in North America earns 354 per cent, or almost 16 times as much. Similarly, the average person in South Asia earns 37 per cent of the world average income, while people in Europe and Central Asia earn five times as much (192 per cent).

The average person in the world has 0.19 hectares of arable land available (1,942 m^2). The variation at the global region level ranges from 55 per cent of the world average in East Asia and Pacific to 283 per cent in North America, or five times as much. Note that the low score in Sub-Saharan Africa for income per capita cannot be explained by a lack of arable land available as this is above the world average (110 per cent). Moreover, the amount of arable land available in South Asia is low (61 per cent), as it is in East Asia and Pacific. Perhaps it would be wise to take the fertility of land into consideration, as these are the only two global regions above the world average population density of 57.4 people per km^2, namely 164 per cent in East Asia and Pacific and an enormous 645 per cent in South Asia. The latter is 19 times higher than the population density in North America.

Table 1.2 Selected characteristics of World Bank regions, 2016

	EAP	ECA	LAC	MNA	NAM	SAS	SSA	World level
Share of world total (per cent)								
Land area	18.8	21.2	15.4	8.7	14.1	3.7	18.2	129.7 million
Population	30.9	12.3	8.6	5.9	4.8	23.7	13.9	7,442 million
Income	32.5	23.5	7.9	7.1	17.1	8.9	3.1	120.4 trillion
Index relative to world average (per cent)								
Income per capita	105	192	92	121	354	37	22	16,171
Arable land	55	192	143	64	283	61	110	0.19
Population density	164	58	55	68	34	645	76	57.4
CO_2 emissions	127	139	62	124	329	29	17	5.0
Urban population	106	131	147	119	151	62	70	54.3
Exports	99	145	76	133	48	63	97	28.6
Death rate	94	133	78	65	106	93	124	7.6
Birth rate	72	65	90	122	64	108	193	19.1
Population growth	57	19	98	160	36	118	239	11.4
Life expectancy	105	108	105	102	110	95	83	71.9

Source: data from World Development Indicators online, most recent in period 2014–2016; land area in km²; income and income per capita in GNI PPP current international $; arable land in hectare per person; density in people per km²; emissions in metric tons per capita; urban population as percentage of total; exports of goods and services as percentage of GDP; death rate and birth rate are crude per 1,000 people; population growth (crude natural) = birth – death; life expectancy at birth in years; for region abbreviations: see Table 1.1.

How polluting are the different global regions? If we take CO_2 emissions per capita as an indicator, then the average person in the world emits 5.0 metric tons per year. This is below the world average in Sub-Saharan Africa (17 per cent), South Asia (29 per cent), and Latin America (62 per cent). Perhaps not surprisingly, these are also the regions where income per capita is below the world average. This helps explain why pollution per person is highest in North America at 329 per cent of the world average, or 19.5 times as high as in Sub-Saharan Africa.

The share of the population living in cities (urban population) is 54.3 per cent for the world. This is below the world average in South Asia and Sub-Saharan Africa. It is particularly high in North America, Europe, and Latin America. The variation, however, is less extreme than for most of the other variables, namely only 2.4 times higher in North America than in South Asia. The same holds for the exports of goods and services (relative to income), which is 28.6 per cent of income for the world and is three times higher in Europe than it is in North America.

The last four variables in Table 1.2 are related to demographics. The world aver-age crude birth rate is 19.1 per 1,000 people, which is lowest in North America (64 per cent of the world average) and highest in Sub-Saharan Africa (193 per cent, or three times higher). The world average crude death rate is 7.6 per 1,000 people, which is lowest in the Middle East & North Africa (65 per cent of the world aver-age) and highest in Europe (133 per cent, or twice as high). Note that the death rate in Europe is high because of its aging population, while it is high in Sub-Saharan Africa for medical and sanitation reasons. The combination of birth rates and death rates leads to the (natural) population growth rates also reported in Table 1.2 (which thus excludes migration flows). The world average crude population growth rate in 2016 was 11.4 per 1,000 people (or 1.14 per cent). It was lowest in Europe (19 per cent of the world average) and highest in Sub-Saharan Africa (239 per cent, or 12.4 times higher). Finally, the world average life expectancy at birth in 2016 was 71.9 years. Here the variation is less extreme, ranging from 83 per cent of the world average (59.9 years) in Sub-Saharan Africa to 110 per cent (79.1 years) in North America (1.3 times higher).

We emphasize in this section the variation of economic and population vari-ables at the global regional level using the seven main regions identified by the World Bank. Even at this highly aggregated scale we note that the distribution of population and economic activity is highly uneven, with relatively empty areas as well as densely populated areas and with large variations in income levels per person. We now go one geographical step further by looking at variations at the country level.

1.4   Countries

As the central piece left over after the break-up of the Soviet Union, the Russian Federation, henceforth Russia for short, is still by far the largest country in the world in terms of land area. With 16.4 million km², or 12.6 per cent of the world total, Russia is about 75 per cent larger than China, the world's second-largest country. Other large countries are Canada, the USA, and Brazil. Because of the most frequently used methods for projecting the world globe on a flat piece of paper, most people tend to underestimate the size of the African land area. To avoid this problem and get a better indication of the land area at different locations Figure 1.1a provides a simple equilateral projection of bubbles proportional to a country's total land area, where the centre of the bubble is located at the country's geographic centre. For discussion purposes, the figure displays individual country data and at the same time groups the countries together in the seven regions of the World Bank. Figure 1.1a clearly illustrates the size of the African continent as many African countries are large in area. Taken together, the African countries account for more than 23 per cent of the world's total area. If we realize that Russia (for its land area at least) and Kazakhstan are in Asia, we also note that Europe is rather small in total land area (the sum of the other bubbles is not so large).

Two Asian countries, China and India, clearly stand out in terms of total population. Together they have 2.7 billion inhabitants in 2016, or about 36 per cent of the world total population, where China takes care of 18.5 per cent and India of 17.8 per cent. The USA, ranked third with 323 million inhabitants, has only about 4.3 per cent of the world population (less than a quarter of India's population). Other Asian countries also have large populations, such as (ordered): Indonesia, Pakistan, Bangladesh, Japan, the Philippines, and Vietnam. Note that we do not include Russia in this list of Asian countries, even though its largest land mass is in the Asian continent, because the largest share of its population is on the European continent. Figure 1.1*b* illustrates the distribution of the world's population across the globe. When we compare it with Figure 1.1*a* on the distribution of land area we notice that the Americas shrink substantially, while Asia (in contrast) becomes much more important. This holds in particular for South Asia and the countries in East Asia and Southeast Asia.

Figure 1.1*c* focuses on the economic power of countries as measured by GDP corrected for purchasing power parity (PPP). With $21.3 trillion, China is the world's largest economy in 2016; this represents about 17.7 per cent of the world total. The USA is the second largest economy as it generates 15.8 per cent of the world total. India is third (with 7.2 per cent) and Japan fourth (with 4.6 per cent). When we compare panel *c* of Figure 1.1 (on income) with panels *a* and *b* (on land area and population) we note that the African and South Asian bubbles shrink substantially, while the European bubbles become larger. All Sub-Saharan African countries taken together, for example, only generate 3.1 per cent of the world's income level (even after correcting for low prices), which is less than the income level generated in Germany alone (3.4 per cent). If we combine the income generated in the 28 European Union countries, we arrive at 17.2 per cent of the world total, which is second only to China (and larger than the USA). Our next step in this section is to focus on relative measures at the country level related to land area, population, and income, by analysing population density and income per capita.

Figure 1.2 illustrates the enormous differences in population density in 2016 at the country level. The figure is constructed as follows. First, we rank the 215 included countries (which represent about 99.5 per cent of the world population) from lowest population density to highest population density.[4] Second, we calculate a percentage rank for each country, starting from 0 for the country with the lowest density (Greenland) to 100 for the country with the highest density (Macao)

---

[4] The largest missing country / region is Taiwan (population 23.5 million) as it is not part of the United Nations.

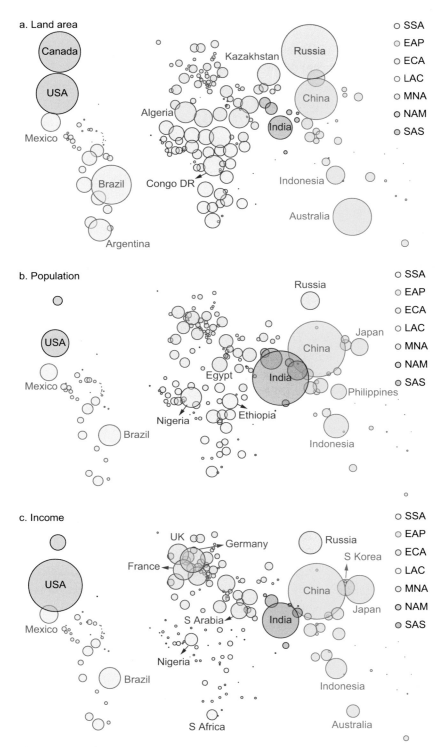

Figure 1.1 Land area, population, and income at the country level, 2016
Source: created using World Bank Development Indicators data, see main text for details; bubbles proportional to land area, population, and income (current GNI PPP) located at the geographic centre (CIA world fact book; except USA at centre of 48 contiguous states), equilateral projection; 196 countries included; see Table 1.1 for the World Bank region abbreviations.

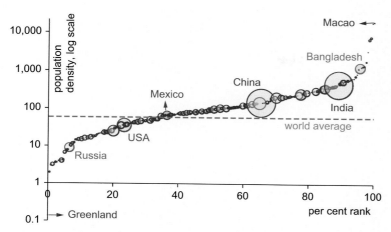

Figure 1.2 Differences in population density at the country level; log scale, 2016
Source: created using World Bank Development Indicators data; population density in people per km²; 215 countries/regions included; bubbles proportional to population in 2016.

with steps of $100/(n-1)$, where n is the number of included countries (215 in this case). Third, we create a scatter plot of percentage rank versus population density (in logs) using a bubble diagram, where the size of a bubble is proportional to a country's population size as an indicator of the relative importance of that country.

The world's average population density is 57 people per km². The lowest density is in Greenland, with only 0.14 people per km² (the world average population density is about 419 times higher). Because of its small size (about 56,000 inhabitants), the Greenland bubble is only visible in Figure 1.2 because we identified it with an arrow. The first bubble that is visible in the figure is the small dot for Mongolia, which has the second-lowest population density of almost 2 people per km² (and a population of about 3 million). Population density is, for example, below the world average in Russia (almost 9 people per km², or about 15 per cent of the world average) and the USA (35 people per km², or about 62 per cent of the world average). It is about equal to the world average in Mexico and above the world average in many Asian countries, like China (147 people per km²), India (445 people per km²), and Bangladesh (1,252 people per km², almost 22 times the world average). The highest population density is reached in Macao, namely an astounding 20,204 people per km² (or 352 times the world average). It is almost as high in the small principality of Monaco (19,250 people per km²). In short, the variation in population density at the country level is enormous, with density in Monaco about 148,000 times higher than in Greenland!

Figure 1.3 provides similar information to Figure 1.2, but this time by showing differences in income per capita in 2016 (corrected for differences in prices) at the country level (again using a log scale). Data for some small countries/regions are lacking, so only 187 observations are included. Together these observations account for about 98.6 per cent of the world population (down from 99.5 per cent

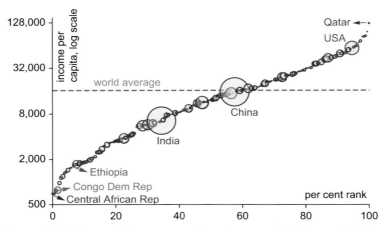

Figure 1.3 Differences in income per capita at the country level; log scale, 2016
Source: created using World Bank Development Indicators data; income per capita is GNI PPP in current international $; 187 countries / regions included; 2015 data used for S Sudan, Oman, Bahrain, and Qatar; 2014 data used for Vanuatu and Venezuela; other data from 2016; bubbles proportional to population in 2016.

in Figure 1.2). Average income per capita for the world in 2016 was $16,171. The lowest income levels are in Central Africa and Liberia ($700 in both countries), followed by Burundi ($770) and the Democratic Republic of Congo ($780). All four countries are in Sub-Saharan Africa and have an income level per capita less than 5 per cent of the world average. Income levels are, for example, also below the world average in Ethiopia ($1,730, or about 11 per cent of the world average) and in India ($6,490, or about 40 per cent of the world average). It is about equal to the world average in China ($15,407) and above the world average for many European countries and the USA ($58,700, or about 3.6 times the world average). The highest per capita income level is generated in the small oil state of Qatar ($124,760, or about 7.7 times the world average). It is also high (above $70,000) for some other small oil states and open trading (or gambling) economies, like (in descending order): Macao, Singapore, Brunei, and United Arab Emirates. For all these countries, income per capita is thus about 100 times higher than for the four poor African economies mentioned above (Central Africa, Liberia, Burundi, and DR Congo). We thus observe that the variation in income per capita levels at the country level is also enormous.

1.5   Within-Country Variation

After analysing the variation of a range of economic variables at the global region level in section 1.3 and variation of income and population at the country level in section 1.4, we again go another geographical step further by looking at variation within countries. As this section is for illustration purposes only, we concentrate on one variable (population density) for one country (USA). We proceed in three steps: (i) we show variation of population density for 'states' in the USA, (ii) we show variation of population density for counties in the state of Texas, and (iii) we show the distribution and size of 'cities' within the USA.

1.5.1 Variation Within the USA

The US Census Bureau collects detailed information for the 50 American states plus Puerto Rico and Washington DC (District of Columbia). Together we refer to these 52 entities as 'states' for convenience. Figure 1.4 illustrates the differences in population density (using a log scale) for these 'states' in 2010, the most recent year available. The average population density in the USA is 33.7 people per km². As (probably) expected, the lowest population density is in Alaska (0.5 people per km², or only 1.4 per cent of the USA average) and the highest population density is in the District of Columbia (3,806 people per km², or 113 times the USA average). This means that population density in the District of Columbia is 8,214 times higher than in Alaska. Although many people are attracted to the wonders of the wild (and oil) in Alaska, there are apparently important reasons for not locating there in large numbers.

One can, of course, object to including Washington DC in the list of 'states' as it is a city, rather than a proper state. However, even if we exclude the District of Columbia from our list the variation in population density is still enormous. The second most densely populated 'state' in Figure 1.4 is New Jersey, which has a

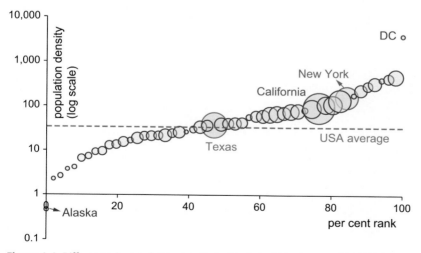

Figure 1.4 Differences in population density for 'states' within the USA; log scale, 2010
Source: created using data from US Census Bureau (www.census.gov); density in people per km² land area; bubbles proportional to population size; 52 'states' includes – see main text; DC = District of Columbia.

population density of 462 people per km² and is about 1,000 times more densely populated than Alaska. For illustration purposes, Figure 1.4 also identifies the position of the three largest states in terms of total population (California, Texas, and New York). Of these three states, the population density in Texas is close to the USA average (namely 37.2 people per km²), while that of the other two states is higher (namely 92 people per km² for California and 159 for New York).

1.5.2 Variation Within Texas

The US Census Bureau subdivides the 52 'states' analysed in section 1.5.1 into 3,221 counties. On average, each state thus consists of 62 counties with a population of almost 96,000 people. For some 'states' the actual number of counties is low: it is 1 for the District of Columbia, 3 for Delaware, and 5 for both Hawaii and Rhode Island. For eight states the number of counties is 100 or more, including Georgia (159 counties) and Texas, which has the most counties (254). The actual population in the counties in 2010 varies from 82 in Loving County, Texas to 9.8 million in Los Angeles County, California. Since Texas is a large state with a population density close to the USA average and the largest number of counties, we proceed with the next step by analysing variation in population density for the counties within the state of Texas.

Figure 1.5 illustrates the differences in population density for counties within the state of Texas in 2010, again using a log scale. This time we observe a regularity not noted before, namely that the bubbles tend to get bigger if we move from left to right in the figure. The largest share of the population therefore tends to live in a few densely populated areas. Indeed, the top five *most* densely populated

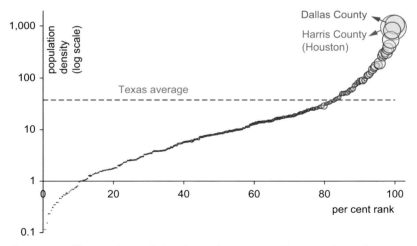

Figure 1.5 Differences in population density for counties within Texas; log scale, 2010
Source: created using data from US Census Bureau (www.census.gov); density in people per km² land area; bubbles proportional to population size; 254 counties included.

counties in Texas take care of more than 56 per cent of the population, whereas the 50 per cent *least* densely populated counties (127 counties) take care of only about 4.2 per cent of the population.

The average population density in Texas is 37.2 people per km^2. The lowest population density is in Loving County, which was home to 82 people in 2010 and has a land area of 1,733 km^2 in the Western part of Texas, leading to a density of 0.04 people per km^2 (or 0.1 per cent of the Texas average). This county is not visible in Figure 1.5 as the vertical scale starts at 0.1. The first visible point is second-ranked Kennedy County with a population of 416 and a density of 0.12 people per km^2. The highest population density is in Dallas County, with a population of 2.4 million and a density of 1,049 people per km^2 (or 28 times the Texas average), followed by Harris County (Houston), with a population of 4.1 million and a density of 928 people per km^2 (or 25 times the Texas average). The variation of population density at the county level within Texas is thus enormous, with density in Dallas County 27,180 times higher than in Loving County.

If we extend the analysis to include all counties in the USA then the variation rises even more since the lowest density is still in Loving County, Texas but the highest density is now in New York County, New York, home to a population of 1.6 million with a density of 26,822 people per km^2 (or about 695,000 times higher than Loving County). The next section analyses the distribution of the population across the USA in more detail.

1.5.3   Urban Locations in the USA

Sections 1.5.1 and 1.5.2 have illustrated the enormous differences in population density within the USA. We now illustrate *where* Americans are mainly located. The 2010 US Census identifies 3,592 *urban locations*, consisting of 497 'Urban Areas' (population 50,000 or more) and 3,095 'Urban Clusters' (population between 2,500 and 50,000). Taken together, the urban locations account for about 253 million people or some 82 per cent of the total American population. Most Americans thus live in urban locations. For the remainder of this section we ignore the 57 urban locations in Alaska, Hawaii, and Puerto Rico and concentrate on the 3,535 remaining urban locations.

The distribution of the American population and the size of the urban locations is illustrated in Figure 1.6 using longitude and latitude information to determine a location's position (equilateral projection) and bubbles proportional to population size to illustrate the size of a location. For reference, the size and location of the seven largest Urban Areas is indicated separately in the figure. The largest Urban Area is New York – Newark (18.4 million), followed by Los Angeles – Long Beach – Anaheim (12.2 million), Chicago (8.6 million), Miami (5.5 million), Philadelphia (5.4 million), Dallas – Fort Worth – Arlington (5.1 million), and Houston (4.9 million). Taken together, these seven locations account for more than 60 million

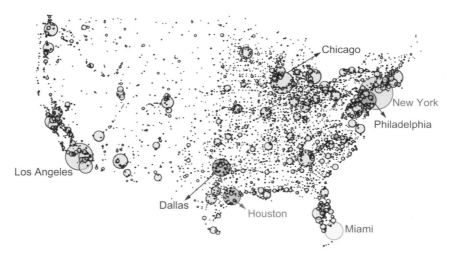

Figure 1.6 Distribution and size of urban locations in the USA, 2010
Source: created using data from US Census Bureau (www.census.gov); 3,535 locations included; equilateral projection; bubbles proportional to population size; 48 contiguous states only.

people and almost 20 per cent of the American population. Evidently, people like to cluster together in big cities / agglomerations. We analyse the economic forces underlying this tendency to cluster together throughout this book. We continue our introduction of the stylized facts for our 'spiky world' in the next section with a brief overview of the history of urban development.

1.6   Urban Development in History

Recent evidence shows that our Neanderthal ancestors were already engaged in human building projects as long as 175,000 years ago, when they created large mysterious cave structures about 300 metres from the cave entrance (Jaubert et al., 2016).[5] It is, of course, a long way to go from these early structures to something that we would now call a city. There is an ongoing debate about what constitutes a city (involving trade, self-sufficiency, and plumbing) and what is thus the world's oldest city, either continuously inhabited, or not (see Compton, 2015, also for the discussion below). It is clear, however, that city development is related to the agricultural revolution, which started in the Fertile Crescent around 8500 BC. The oldest city is thus located somewhere in the Fertile Crescent. Familiar names are Damascus (Syria) and Jericho (Palestine), with early settlements dating as far back as 9000 BC (but not continuous settlements). Less familiar is Byblos

---

[5] This section is partially based on Brakman, Garretsen, and van Marrewijk (2016).

(Lebanon), founded in 7000 BC, with continuous habitation since 5000 BC. Or possibly Aleppo (Syria), with settlement dating back only to 6000 BC but evidence of wandering nomadic domestic camps up to 5,000 years earlier.

Another issue that creates occasional controversy is the question: what is the largest city in the world? Various sources arrive, of course, at slightly different answers, but we base our review on the influential work of Chandler (1987), who uses a range of methods to estimate the size of a city and includes the surrounding suburban or urbanized area. Figure 1.7 illustrates the evolution of the size of the largest city for the past 5,000 years using a log scale. Memphis (Egypt) was probably the largest city in 3000 BC, with a modest population size (according to modern standards) of 30,000 inhabitants. Ur (Iraq) took over some 1,000 years later with a population of around 65,000 people, followed by Babylon (Iraq) around 600 BC with 200,000 people.[6] Figure 1.7 shows that the size of the world's largest city started to rise particularly fast after 1200 AD. There are five Chinese cities in Figure 1.7, starting with Xi'an (or Chang'an, Shaanxi province), followed by Kaifeng (Henan province), Hangzhou (Zhejiang province), Nanjing (Jiangsu

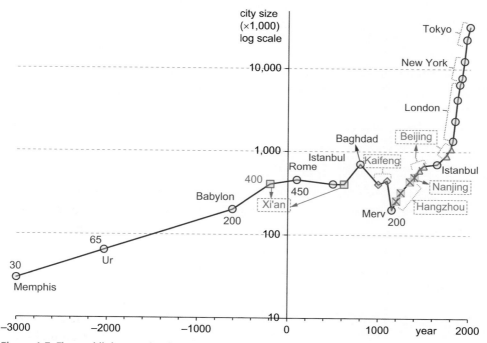

Figure 1.7 The world's largest city since 3000 BC
Source: based on data from Chandler (1987), updated for Tokyo metropolis in 2015; Chinese cities in dotted boxes with larger text size and different markers; non-Chinese cities with circular markers.

---

[6] We are skipping a few cities in the first 2,000 years of Figure 1.7 that took over the 'largest city' banner, but without clear information on the number of inhabitants.

province), and Beijing, which was the first city to cross the one million threshold. Beijing was first replaced by London (first city to reach five million), then by New York (first city to reach ten million), and ultimately by Tokyo (first city to reach 20 million and 30 million).

1.7   Recent Urban Development

Today more than half of the world population lives in cities, but this is a relatively recent phenomenon. In 1960 about 34 per cent of the world population lived in cities, rising to 53 per cent in 2014 and crossing the 50 per cent threshold only in 2011; see Figure 1.8. As one might expect, there is a high positive correlation between the share of the rural population and the share of income or employment generated in agricultural activities. Since the latter is negatively correlated with general development levels (as measured by income), there is a positive correlation between income levels and urbanization. This is illustrated in Figure 1.8 for the high-income OECD member countries, where the share of the urban population was 64 per cent in 1960 (almost twice the world average), rising to 81 per cent in 2014 (28 percentage points higher than the world average).

Figure 1.8 also depicts urbanization developments in China and India, by far the two largest countries in terms of total population, and in Latin America (LAC) and Sub-Saharan Africa (SSA; referred to as Africa in the discussion below). In 1960, the degree of urbanization was similar and substantially below the world average in China, India, and Africa, namely around 15–18 per cent. It was substantially

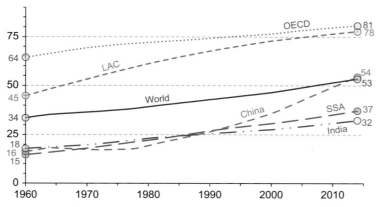

Figure 1.8 Urbanization since 1960
Source: based on data from World Development Indicators online; urbanization: urban population (% of total); OECD = high-income Organization for Economic Cooperation and Development countries; SSA = developing Sub-Saharan Africa; LAC = developing Latin America and Caribbean.

higher in 1960 in Latin America, about 45 per cent (which is higher than the world average).

The developments over time are rather diverse. Latin America almost closes the gap with the OECD countries as the urban population share rises steadily to 78 per cent in 2014. In India the developments are stable: the urban population share rises steadily every year and reaches 32 per cent in 2014. In Africa the urbanization process is also relatively stable, but urbanization is more rapid than in India: the urban population share more than doubles to 37 per cent in 2014. The urbanization rate is higher in Africa than in India from 1985 onwards. In China, the developments are much more dramatic (see also below). Initially the urban population share rises from 1960 to 1964 (from 16.2 to 18.3 per cent), but then it declines until 1972 (to 17.2 per cent) and slowly crawls back until 1977 (to 17.5 per cent). From 1979 on the urban population share starts to rise quickly (more than 0.7 percentage points per year) and even more strongly from 1996 onward (more than 1.0 percentage point per year), reaching 54 per cent in 2014 and surpassing the world average in 2013.

Figure 1.9 shows the impact on the absolute number of people living in cities (panel *a*) and in rural areas (panel *b*). For the high-income OECD countries, the urban population rose by 86 per cent or 400 million people in the period 1960–2014 (from 463 to 863 million), while the rural population declined by 20 per cent or 50 million people (from 257 to 207 million). A similar process is observed in Latin America, where the urban population rose rapidly from 80 to 408 million and the rural population is almost stagnant (a slight increase only of 19 million people). The Indian urban population also rose rapidly, by 420 per cent or 339 million people (from 81 to 419 million). In contrast to the OECD countries and Latin America, however, the rural population also increased rapidly, by

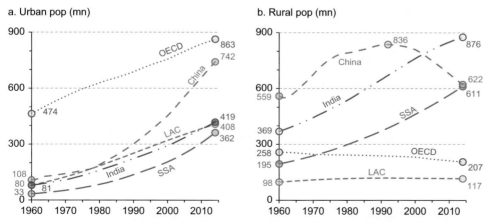

Figure 1.9 Urban and rural population since 1960, millions
Source: see Figure 1.8.

137 per cent or 507 million people (from 369 to 876 million). In absolute terms, the population increase in India is thus larger in the villages than in the cities. Similar observations hold for Africa, where the urban population rose by 329 million (about a 10-fold rise) and the rural population even more, namely by 416 million people (from 195 to 611 million). Together India and Africa are responsible for 69 per cent of the worldwide increase in the rural population (of 1.4 billion people), while taking care of only 23 per cent of the rise of the worldwide urban population (of 2.9 billion people).

China is responsible for the most spectacular urbanization process, as it takes care of the largest urban population increase in this period, namely by 587 per cent or 634 million people (from 108 to 742 million). The increase in the number of people living in Chinese cities is thus higher than the total population of the European Union in 2015 and about twice the population of the USA in 2015. In the Chinese rural areas, the population increased only by 11 per cent or 63 million people (from 559 to 622 million). Those numbers are distorted, however, by the fact that there was a peak of 836 million people in the Chinese rural population in 1991 (meaning an increase of 50 per cent or 277 million people in the period 1960–1991) and a substantial decline since then (a fall of 26 per cent or 215 million people in the period 1991–2014). Under the simple assumption that the Chinese natural population growth is the same in the cities and the rural areas, the implied migration flow from the villages towards the cities in China is 461 million people in the period 1960–2014.[7] If the natural growth rate is higher in the rural areas, the implied migration flows are even larger.

1.8 Urbanization and Income Per Capita

As briefly suggested in section 1.7, the degree of urbanization tends to go hand in hand with rising levels of income per capita. The World Bank collects information on urbanization, income, and population. The degree of urbanization is then measured as the share of the population living in urban areas.[8] The relationship between urbanization and income per capita in 2016 is illustrated in Figure 1.10.

The lowest degree of urbanization (8.4 per cent) is reached in Trinidad and Tobago, with a fairly high level of income per capita ($31,770) and a small population (1.4 million). The second-lowest degree of urbanization (12.4 per cent)

---

[7] This includes 'migration' of people for villages that pass the threshold of becoming a city.
[8] Data are provided by national statistical offices (with varying definitions of urban areas), but collected and smoothed by the UN Population Division.

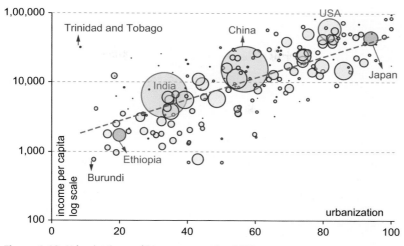

Figure 1.10 Urbanization and income per capita, 2016
Source: created using World Bank Development Indicators online; income per capita: GNI PPP (current int. dollar); urbanization: urban population (% of total); bubbles proportional to size of population; 180 countries included.

is reached in Burundi, with a low level of income per capita ($770) and a population of 10.5 million. The lowest urbanization rate (19.9 per cent) for the first 'sizeable' country (above 100 million people) is Ethiopia, with a low income level of $1,730.

There are four countries in Figure 1.10 with 100 per cent of the population living in cities, namely Nauru, Hong Kong, Singapore, and Macao. The average population for these four countries is 3.4 million and the population-weighted average income level is $72,000.[9] The first 'sizeable' country with a high urbanization rate (93.9 per cent) is Japan, with an income level of $43,540 per capita.

The above examples suggest that highly urbanized countries tend to have higher levels of income per capita. Using recent data for 180 countries, Figure 1.10 shows that this is indeed the case. Examples of large countries identified in the figure are: India (population 1,324 million, urbanization 33.1 per cent, and income per capita $6,490), China (population 1,379 million, urbanization of 56.8 per cent, and income per capita of $15,470), and the USA (population 323 million, urbanization 81.8 per cent, and income per capita $58,700). The regression line in Figure 1.10 suggests that a one percentage point higher degree of urbanization is associated with about 3.55 per cent higher income per capita levels. The line explains about 49 per cent of the variation in log income per capita (see Chapter 3). Before providing a brief overview of the book in section 1.10 we conclude with a brief description of empirical regularities.

---

[9] Lowest income is for Nauru ($17,510 per capita), which has a population of only 10,000.

1.9 Two Regularities

This section discusses two regularities in the unequal distribution of people and economic activity across space, namely (i) regarding the distribution pattern of centres of economic activity across cities (Zipf's Law) and (ii) regarding the interactions between these centres of activity across countries (the gravity equation).[10]

1.9.1 Distribution Pattern (Zipf's Law)

The regularity in the distribution pattern, known as Zipf's Law, is most easily illustrated using a concrete example. Take the largest city in India. In 2010, the most recent year for which we have reliable data, this was Mumbai (formerly Bombay), with about 13.8 million inhabitants. Give this city rank number 1. Then take the second largest city (Delhi, with about 12.6 million inhabitants) and give this rank number 2. The third largest city (Bangalore, with 5.4 million inhabitants) is given rank number 3, and so on. The data above are derived from the 2011 Indian census, which concluded that there are more than 1.2 billion Indians. Arranging the data for the 180 largest Indian cities this way, you now take the natural logarithm of the population size and of the city's (rank–0.5).[11] When the latter are plotted in a scatter diagram, the outcome is an almost perfect straight line; see Figure 1.11.[12]

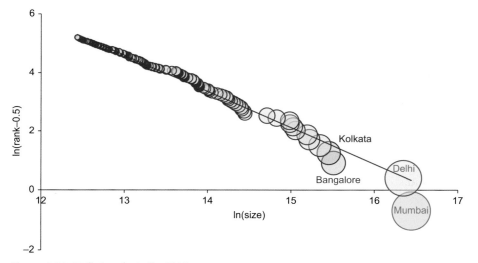

Figure 1.11 Zipf's Law for India, 2010
Source: van Marrewijk (2017); bubbles proportional to population size.

---

[10] This section is partially based on van Marrewijk (2017, ch. 16).

[11] We take the natural log of (rank–0.5) rather than simply the rank for technical reasons as it leads to an unbiased estimate of the slope coefficient; see Gabaix and Ibragimov (2011). The reported high significance is based on an estimated standard error using their methodology.

[12] The discussion in the text is based on city limits. Similar results hold when we analyse agglomerations, in which case there are 55 agglomerations with more than one million people, Mumbai is the largest agglomeration with 21.9 million people, the slope of the line is -1.23 and 97 per cent of the variance is explained. Data are then from www.populationdata.net.

Obviously, there is a negative relationship between population size and rank by construction. The puzzling feature is why this is an almost perfect log-linear straight line. A simple linear regression of the data plotted in Figure 1.11 gives:

$$ln\left(rank - \frac{1}{2}\right) = 20.66 - 1.24\,ln\left(population\right) \qquad 1.1$$

The coefficient is highly significant and the regression explains a whopping 98.3 per cent of the variance in city size. Based on this estimate, we would predict the size of the population of urban agglomeration number 100, for example, to be 437,000 people. This is close to the actual size of number 100 (Jhansi), with a population of 449,000. This regularity in the distribution of city sizes holds not only for India, but also for the USA, Brazil, France, China, Russia, and many other countries. Apparently, hitherto poorly understood economic forces play an important role in determining the size distribution of cities, regardless of the economic structure, organization, wealth, and history of a nation. Ever since George Kingsley Zipf (1949) presented evidence on this regularity, scientists have been searching for an adequate explanation.[13]

1.9.2 Interaction (Gravity Equation)

There is also a pattern in the interaction between centres of economic activity. It is known as the 'gravity equation', and is related to Zipf's Law (see Head and Mayer, 2014 for a survey). The gravity equation is also most easily illustrated using a simple example, for which we focus on the trade flows of Germany, the dominant European economy. Trade is measured as the sum of exports from and imports to Germany in billions of US dollars. In 2015 the Netherlands was the largest trade partner for Germany, with a value of $216 billion. The second largest trade partner was France ($194 billion), followed by the USA ($177 billion), China, UK, Italy, Poland, Austria, Belgium, Switzerland, and the Czech Republic.

The 'local' flavour of this top trade partner list is immediately evident. Except for the USA and China (the world's largest economies) the most important German trade partners are in its vicinity. Germany has eight direct neighbours, seven of which are listed above.[14] These neighbours, some of which are tiny in terms of economic size, are more important for German trade flows than the mighty Japanese economy, which only ranks 17th as trade partner with a trade value of $35 billion. This is only one step up from Germany's last direct neighbour Denmark, which is ranked 18th with a trade value of $33 billion. Indeed, Denmark is about as important for German trade flows as Japan even though the Japanese economy is about 19 times larger than the Danish economy. Similarly, the Netherlands is more

---

[13] Strictly speaking, 'Zipf's Law' applies if the estimated coefficient in equation 1.1 is equal to minus one. For other significant parameters, a 'power law' or the 'rank-size rule' holds, see Chapter 5.

[14] Luxembourg is combined with Belgium in trade data, hence for trade flows there are only eight neighbours.

important for German trade flows than the USA and China, even though these economies are about 21 times larger than the Dutch economy.

Trade of goods and services from one country to another involves time, effort, and hence costs. Goods must be physically loaded and unloaded, transported by truck, train, ship, or plane, packed, insured, traced, and so on before they reach their destination. There they must be unpacked, checked, assembled, and displayed before they can be sold to the consumer or as intermediate goods to another firm. A distribution and maintenance network must be established, and the exporter will have to familiarize herself with the (legal) rules and procedures in another country, usually in another language and embedded in a different culture. All of this involves costs, which tend to increase with 'distance'. As indicated above, this can be both physical distance, which may be hampered or alleviated by geographical phenomena such as mountain ranges or easy access to good waterways, and political, cultural, or social distance, which also require time and effort before one can successfully engage in international business.

We use the term 'transport costs' as a shorthand notation for both types of distance described above. As these costs increase it will become more difficult to trade goods and services between nations. As a proxy for transport costs we calculated the 'weighted distance to Germany' for all German export markets, using the average distance between the main population centres in both countries. Also taking into consideration the economic size of the trade partner as measured by a country's income level (GDP PPP), a simple regression yields the following result:[15]

$$ln(trade) = 3.9925 + 1.0605 \times ln(GDP) - 1.0613 \times ln(distance) \qquad 1.2$$

This simple relationship, which explains 88.4 per cent of the variance in German export size, is illustrated with respect to the distance to the German market in Figure 1.12, that is after correcting the size of the trade flow for the size of the destination market using the estimated coefficient of equation 1.2. The top left corner is dominated by neighbours and other countries close to Germany. The slope of the regression line in the figure is –1.0613 as given in equation 1.2. This empirical relationship is known as the 'gravity equation' and was first applied to international trade flows between countries by Jan Tinbergen (1962) and holds quite generally for all countries. The relationship is influenced by wealth and the overall development level of trading partners, as well as cultural, political, and social organization in a proper historical context of the trading countries involved, such as whether trading countries share a common language or a common border, have a colonial history together, and so on. The main objective of our book is to

---

[15] The regression is based on 184 German trade partners for which relevant data are available.

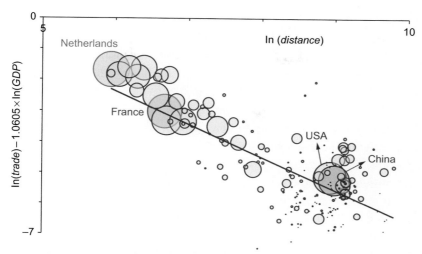

Figure 1.12 German trade and distance, 2015
Source: van Marrewijk (2017) using data from International Trade Centre (www.intracen.org; *trade =*
(export+import) in USD bn), World Bank (GDP PPP, current USD bn), and CEPII (www.cepii.fr; weighted
distance in km); bubbles proportional to share of trade flows; 184 trade partners included; the slope of
the line is −1.0613.

provide a better understanding of the unequal distribution of economic activity
across space and its regularities in terms of distribution pattern, like Zipf's Law,
and interaction, like the gravity equation.

1.10   Overview of the Book

The various examples and discussions presented in this chapter paint a clear picture. People and economic activity are unevenly distributed across space, with
strong agglomeration in some important centres. We really live in a *spiky world*.
We illustrated this phenomenon at different spatial scales using global regions,
countries, and regions within countries. Moreover, the distribution across space is
not random but often displays remarkably stable and uniform patterns across time
and across various levels of geographical aggregation, global, national, regional,
and urban. These observations suggest that similar spatial economic forces are
relevant for explaining clustering phenomena and the regularities of distribution
and interaction across space.

The remainder of this book, which consists of four parts, presents a common
structural approach at the urban and regional level to better understand the main
economic forces at work that were introduced and illustrated in Chapter 1. We now
provide a brief overview of the four parts and their chapters.

Part I Empirical Foundations (Chapters 1–3)

We start in Part I with some empirical facts and foundations to guide our analysis of the spiky world in the rest of the book. Chapter 1 thus highlighted the fact that the world is indeed 'spiky' (unevenly distributed) for various variables at different spatial scales, indicating clustering of economic activities in a limited number of locations. We also briefly discussed two interaction regularities. Chapter 2 introduces some factors that play a role in determining the spikiness analysed in Chapter 1. We distinguish between so-called first nature forces and second nature forces for understanding the spatial distribution of economic activity. In this terminology, first nature refers to the role of physical geography (climate, mountains, rivers, and so on) and second nature refers to the role of human and economic interactions. In Chapter 2 we focus on the second nature explanations that are largely 'non-economic' and originate in for instance history and politics. These interactions also imply a man-made clustering of economic activities but they are different from the explanation offered by urban and geographical economics that form the thrust of our book. Before we can analyse the forces of agglomeration emphasized by urban and geographical economics in the remainder of this book, Chapter 3 provides an overview of the main empirical methods used for analysing spatial phenomena, including a discussion of the main problems facing empirical research and how these can be solved.

Part II Urban Economics (Chapters 4–6)

The second part of the book analyses spatial economic organization at the urban level. We start in Chapter 4 with the organization of space within cities in a unified framework in which economic agents choose the optimal location within the urban area. This allows us to determine rent curves, analyse different transport methods, determine land use, building heights, population density, and so on. We continue in Chapter 5 by analysing urban systems and hierarchy based on power law regularities (see section 1.9.1). We also analyse the dynamics of cities within the distribution, where some cities successfully replace declining sectors while others do not. We conclude in Chapter 6 with a general discussion of the empirics of agglomeration economies, the main force to explain why cities vary in size and economic structure that urban economics has to offer.

Part III Geographical Economics (Chapters 7–9)

The third part of the book analyses spatial economic organization at the regional level. The key aspect of this part is a better understanding of the role of economic interaction in the agglomeration process (the second nature forces mentioned above). Chapter 7 introduces the core model of geographical economics in which the size of each location is determined endogenously based on inter-regional labour mobility. Chapter 8 extends this framework to alternative models based on mobile human capital or intermediate goods and analyses systems of cities. Chapter 9 evaluates the empirical relevance of geographical economics models.

Part IV Development and Policy (Chapters 10 and 11)

The fourth and final part of the book consists of two chapters. In Chapter 10 we focus on the role of geography for economic growth and development in a broader perspective based on the insights generated from an urban and geographical economics perspective in previous chapters. Chapter 11 concludes with a discussion of the main policy implications of urban and geographical economics, including space-based policies and clusters.

Exercises

Question 1.1 Uneven Distribution

In this chapter we illustrate the uneven distribution of human activity across space at various geographic scales (global, country, and province/state), for example by looking at population density. Can you think of other – measurable – indicators to illustrate the uneven distribution of human activity? Provide some data to illustrate your indicator.

Question 1.2 Income and Prices

According to World Bank data China's GDP at market prices (in current US dollars) was $10,355 billion in 2014. In that same year the GDP at market prices (in current US dollars) in the USA was $17,419 billion.

Your neighbour argues that China has been the biggest economy in the world since 2014. Could she be right, or not? Explain why, or why not.

Question 1.3 Zipf

Collect information on the population size of a range of cities in a large country (such that you have at least 40 observations). Determine to what extent Zipf's Law holds using the methodology of section 1.9.1 and evaluate your findings.

Question 1.4 Trade and Gravity

Collect information for your country (or a substantial neighbouring country) regarding trade flows (exports and/or imports) to all other countries in the world using International Trade Center data (see intracen.org). Also collect information on the size of income (GDP) of these countries (for example using World Bank data; see worldbank.org) and the bilateral distance between your country and all other countries using CEPII data (see cepii.fr). Reproduce the gravity equation of section 1.9.2 as follows:

a   Estimate the gravity equation using *only* trade and distance data. What is the share of explained variance (R^2) and what is the estimated coefficient for distance?

b   Estimate the gravity equation using trade and distance data while also controlling for destination income levels. What is the share of explained variance (R^2) and what is the estimated coefficient for distance?

c   Comment on your findings.

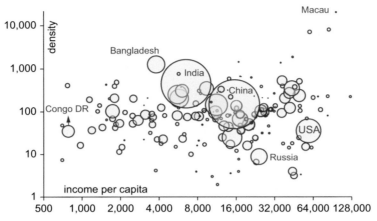

Figure Q1.1 Income per capita and population density at the country level, 2016
Source: created using World Bank Development Indicators online; income per capita in GNI PPP (current international dollars); density in people per km²; bubbles proportional to population; 186 countries included.

Question 1.5 Income and Population Density

You are invited to participate in a panel discussion for a broad audience regarding the relationship between population and development. One participant presents information at the country level gathered from the World Bank Development Indicators (see Figure Q1.1) for income per capita (GNI PPP in current international dollars, log scale), population density (people per km², log scale), and population size (size of bubbles). She basically argues that there is a negative relationship between income per capita and population density. As an example she lists Bangladesh, India, China, and the USA; four important countries where income per capita levels rise as population density falls.

Using the information provided above and the knowledge you gained in Chapter 1, write a brief *essay* for an educated lay audience (such as readers of *The Economist*) that highlights your position on the connection between income levels and population density.

2 Geo-Human Interaction

LEARNING OBJECTIVES

- To know the distinction between first nature and second nature forces for understanding spikiness.
- To understand the impact of biogeographic components, such as climate system, distance from the equator, and access to waterways, on spikiness.
- To understand the role of man-made institutions versus biogeographic conditions in explaining spikiness.
- To understand how agricultural and institutional knowledge is incorporated in the worldwide migration flows and how this helps to explain current spikiness.

2.1 Introduction

Chapter 1 illustrates in various ways how the distribution of economic activity and population is unevenly distributed or *spiky*.[1] In this chapter we introduce some factors that play a role in explaining this spikiness. The title of the chapter is *geo-human interaction*, where *geo* is short for (physical) geography. It indicates that two types of fundamental forces play a role for understanding the spikiness. Krugman (1993) labelled these forces 'first nature' and 'second nature', where *first nature* refers to the role of physical geography (climate, mountains, rivers, and so on) and *second nature* refers to the role of man-made human and economic interactions that shape the spatial distribution of economic activity. We analyse these forces in more detail in the remaining chapters of this book.

This chapter starts with a simple discussion of the first nature and second nature forces, an idea of their power of explanation, and how these forces interact with one another. When it comes to the second nature forces, it should be emphasized from the outset that they come in two flavours. The first concerns the man-made *economic* interactions that can give rise to a spiky world. This is the topic of Parts

---

[1] Parts of this chapter are based on van Marrewijk, Brakman, and Swart (2018); see ch. 3 and ch. 4 in that book for further details.

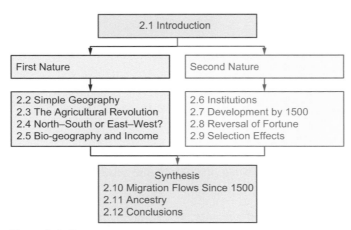

Figure 2.1 Chapter structure

II and III of the book in our discussion of urban and geographical economics respectively. Here, we confine ourselves to the man-made or human but (largely) 'non-economic' interactions that can result in an uneven spatial distribution in the second half of Chapter 2. With the first nature and the human or 'non-economic' determinants out of the way, the remainder of the book can focus on the second nature theories and empirics that form the underpinning of the economic interactions that help to shape the spiky world.

The main structure of this chapter is illustrated in Figure 2.1. We start in sections 2.2 to 2.5 with a discussion of first nature forces. We show that bio-geographic forces can explain a substantial part of current variations in prosperity. We continue in sections 2.6 to 2.9 with a discussion of some second nature forces, with a focus on the importance of institutions for economic development. We show that man-made institutions are also important for explaining current prosperity. We conclude in sections 2.10 to 2.12 with a synthesis of these first nature and second nature forces by showing how these forces combined with human migration flows are better able to explain current economic activity. In short, the chapter argues that first nature forces interact with second nature forces to determine the spikiness illustrated in Chapter 1, hence the title of the chapter: geo-human interaction.

We start our analysis of first nature forces in section 2.2 with a discussion of a simple relationship between per capita income levels and bio-geographic factors, like distance to the equator, climate zone, and having access to the sea. We continue with an analysis of the *deep roots* of economic development based on the work of Jared Diamond (1997). We highlight the importance of the agricultural revolution for the development of mankind in section 2.3. This involved the domestication of plants and animals, which enables the transition from a hunter-gatherer society to a farmer society. We show that bio-geographic factors, such as the availability of the domesticable plants and animals, are important for explaining the timing of the agricultural revolution, as is the role of humans through the spread of knowledge facilitated by these factors, see section 2.4. We conclude our discussion of first nature determinants of the spiky world in section 2.5 with an overview of the ability of bio-geographic forces to explain current levels of economic development, in particular for the *old world*, which excludes the Americas and Oceania from the analysis. We explain in section 2.11 why it is appropriate to exclude the Americas and Oceania.

We start our analysis of second nature forces in section 2.6 with an overview of the role of institutions in explaining economic development. Next, we show in section 2.7 that bio-geographic conditions can help explain human development levels for the whole world up to the year 1500. Up to this point bio-geographic conditions have been important for explaining income per capita levels. We question this importance based on the *reversal of fortune* discussion in sections 2.8 and 2.9. In this discussion, some researchers argue that the role of man-made institutions is more important than the role of bio-geographic factors. To support this claim, they point at initially rich countries in 1500 (such as Peru) that have become relatively poor 500 years later because of *bad* institutions imposed by European powers, and vice versa for initially poor countries in 1500 (such as the USA). Hence the name reversal of fortune. We point out sample selection effects associated with this discussion and note that the reversal of fortune is not observed if European countries are included in the sample and is reversed (hence initially rich countries tend to be richer today) for countries that were not former European colonies or for indigenous countries (with more than 50 per cent of the current population descending from people who already lived in the country in 1500).

We conclude with a synthesis of the interaction between the first nature and second nature forces, or *geo-human interaction*, that have been introduced in Chapter 2. First, in section 2.10 by discussing the size and consequences of international migration flows in the period 1500–2000 for the structure of the present-day population of a country. Second, in section 2.11 by showing how the agricultural and institutional knowledge that is incorporated in the people and descendants of these migration flows is important for explaining current income per capita levels for the whole world, including Oceania and the Americas. We thus conclude in section 2.12 that bio-geographic factors are important for determining income levels today, either directly or indirectly through geo-human interaction.

2.2 Simple Geography

The distance from the equator to a country can be measured by the absolute value in degrees latitude from its geographic centre. A simple, but effective illustration of the relationship between geography and income is provided in Figure 2.2. Using

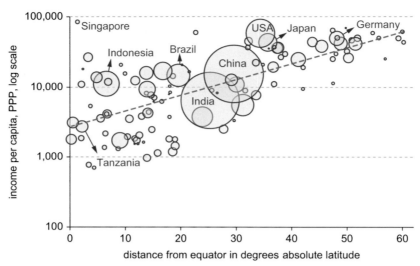

Figure 2.2 Absolute latitude and income per capita, 2016
Source: latitude data from Olsson and Hibbs (2005); income per capita GNI PPP (current international
$) and population from World Development Indicators online; bubbles proportional to population size;
straight line is a regression line.

data for 2016, the figure shows that, on average, income per capita levels increase
the further away you move from the equator. Tanzania, for example, is close to
the equator (2.15 degrees) and has a modest PPP income level of $2,740. Germany,
on the other hand, is much further away from the equator (48.16 degrees) and has
a high income level of $49,690. The same holds for other high-income countries
in the North, such as the USA and Japan. It also holds when we go to the South,
with higher income levels for Australia and South Africa. Not all countries close
to the equator are poor. A clear example is Singapore at 1.36 degrees and with a
high income level of $85,020. This city-state is a thriving harbour benefiting from
many international connections, as discussed below (see also Box 2.1). Why do
countries close to the equator tend to perform worse economically? The tropical
climate zones, which are concentrated around the equator, are thought to be a
primary reason for the poor economic performance of countries located there.
Let's have a closer look at this aspect of the geography of population and income.

Your geographic location on the globe has consequences for the climate you
live in. It can be hot or cold, wet or arid, windy or calm and all of this may vary
substantially over the year, or not. Climate zones can be identified based on the
Köppen classification system, which uses up to three letters to characterize a climate; see the explanation in Table 2.1. The *Af* climate is thus tropical – fully
humid, the *As* climate is tropical – dry summers, the *BSk* climate is dry – steppe –
cold arid, the *Cwa* climate is mild temperate – dry winter – hot summer, and so
on. The various relevant combinations together lead to 31 different climates; see
Figure 2.3 for a recent global overview of main types. The detail was also a bit too

Table 2.1 The Köppen climate classification letters

First letter		Second letter		Third letter	
A	Tropical	f	Fully humid	h	Hot arid
B	Dry	m	Monsoon	k	Cold arid
C	Mild temperate	s	Dry summer	a	Hot summer
D	Snow	w	Dry winter	b	Warm summer
E	Polar	W	Desert	c	Cool summer
		S	Steppe	d	Cold summer
		T	Tundra		
		F	Frost		

Source: Chen and Chen (2013).

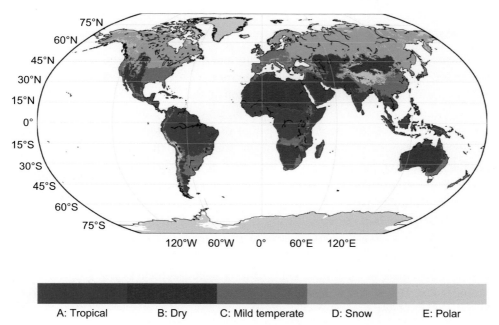

Figure 2.3 The Köppen climate classification system for 1901–2010
Source: Chen and Chen (2013); see http://hanschen.org/koppen/ and Table 2.1 for further explanation; the resolution is 0.5 degrees latitude/longitude.

much for Sachs, Mellinger, and Gallup (2001) to handle when they wanted to summarize the geography of population and income, so they grouped them together into five major types:

- Tropical – subtropical
- Desert – steppe
- Temperate – snow

- Highland
- Polar

Since there are virtually no people living in the polar climate this leaves us with four main climate types, which we henceforth refer to as tropical, desert, temperate, and highland, for short.

In this section we interact the four main climate types with another important geographical aspect of prosperity, namely that coastal regions usually do better than inland areas because of their easy access to sea trade. This was already noted by Adam Smith (1776) in a by now well-known quote in the first book of *The Wealth of Nations*:

> As by means of water-carriage a more extensive market is opened to every sort of industry than what land-carriage alone can afford it, so it is upon the sea-coast, and along the banks of navigable rivers, that industry of every kind naturally begins to subdivide and improve itself, and it is frequently not till a long time after that those improvements extend themselves to the inland parts of the country.

To illustrate the interaction between geography, population, and income Sachs, Mellinger, and Gallup (2001) used information on a country's income level, the distribution of its population across the country, the climate zones, and the extent to which an area is near to the sea. They do this by dividing the world map into five-minute by five-minute sections (equal to about 100 km^2 at the equator). For each section they determine the size of the population, the level of gross national product (GNP) per capita (based on the relevant country's national average), and the GNP density (income per km^2). They also determine for each section to which of the four climate zones it belongs and whether the section is near to the sea or not. The latter is done by labelling a section *Near* if it is within 100 km of a seacoast or a sea-navigable waterway (a river, lake, or canal in which oceangoing vessels can operate) and labelling it *Far* if it is not. In combination with the four climate zones we thus have eight different geographical types: Tropical-Near, Tropical-Far, Desert-Near, Desert-Far, Temperate-Near, Temperate-Far, Highland-Near, and Highland-Far.

Sachs, Mellinger, and Gallup (2001) then report for each of the eight types the land area, population, and GNP as a percentage of the world total. In terms of climate zones: the largest area is for the Temperate zone (39.2 per cent), followed by Desert (29.6), Tropical (19.9), and Highland (7.3); the largest population is in Tropical (40.3), followed by Temperate (34.9), Desert (18.0), and Highland (6.8); the largest GNP is in Temperate (67.2), followed by Tropical (17.4), Desert (10.1), and Highland (5.3). In terms of Near or Far from the coast: the land area of Near is smaller (17.3 per cent), but it has about the same population level as Far (49.4) and much higher GNP (67.5).

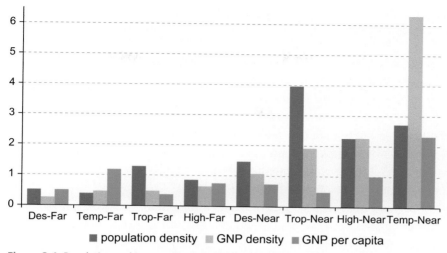

Figure 2.4 Population and income density relative to the world average
Source: based on Sachs et al. (2001); Trop = Tropical; Des = Desert; Temp = Temperate; High = Highland.

Based on this information we calculated the population density, GNP density, and GNP per capita level for each of the eight geographical types relative to the world average, as illustrated in Figure 2.4 (ordered by GNP density). Even for such broad geographical types the figure shows enormous differences in income level per km^2 (GNP density). It is above the world average for all Near types and below the world average for all Far types. It is by far the highest for the Temperate Zone Near the coast (6.3 times the world average, or almost 25 times as high as for the Desert Zone Far from the coast). The Temperate Zone Near the coast also has the highest income per capita level (2.3 times the world average or more than six times higher than for the Tropical Zone Far from the coast). The highest population density is for the Tropical Zone Near the coast (almost four times the world average, or more than 10 times that of the Temperate Zone Far from the coast). The above shows that being Near to the coast gives large benefits in terms of income per capita and income density. It also shows that being in the Tropical zone leads to high population density (note that it is also above the world average Far from the coast), but low income per capita. The next section starts to analyse possible deep roots for these observations.

2.3   The Agricultural Revolution

By about 11,000 BC Homo Sapiens was spread around the globe, the glaciers had retreated, resulting in a warmer and wetter climate, and technologies for harvesting, transporting, preparing, and storing cereals were in place; see Olsson and

BOX 2.1 Singapore, Lee Kuan Yew, and Air Conditioning

In March 2014 Lee Kuan Yew passed away at the age of 91 years.[2] Born when Singapore was a British colony, Mr Lee studied in London and Cambridge. He returned to Singapore after World War II, where he co-founded the People's Action Party (PAP) and became the first prime minister in 1959 when Singapore won self-government from Britain. He led Singapore to a federation with Malaysia in 1963 and was heart-broken when the country was expelled and became independent in 1965. Mr Lee was prime minister until 1990 and remained an important influence until shortly before his death.

Under Mr Lee's guidance Singapore became an economic success story.[3] In 1960 GDP per capita in Singapore was 83 per cent of the world average in that year. By 2013 it was 465 per cent of the world average, an astounding relative income rise of more than 7 percentage points per year for more than five decades; see Figure 2.5. The rise is even more remarkable since Singapore is in the tropics, very close to the equator, has no natural resources (no oil or precious metals; it initially even lacked its own water supply) and nonetheless currently has a higher income per capita than the USA; see Figure 2.2. Its success is built on a record of honest and pragmatic government and its ideal location as a harbour, making trade relations with other nations the source of its prosperity.[4] At the end

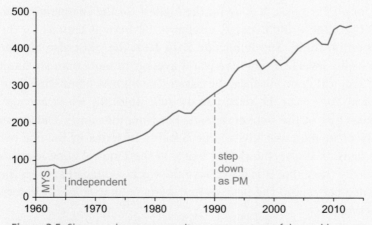

Figure 2.5 Singapore income per capita as a percentage of the world average
Source: created using World Development Indicators; income is GDP in constant 2005 USD; MYS = Malaysia.

---

[2] Information is taken from *The Economist* (2014a, 2014b).
[3] Dutchman Albert Winsemius played an important role as Chief Economic Advisor from 1961 to 1984.
[4] At the personal level Mr Lee could be relentless; he used defamation suits to tame the press and sometimes to bankrupt his opponents.

BOX 2.1 (cont.)

of the second millennium Mr Lee himself, however, saw things differently; see *The Economist* (2014a):

> In some ways, Mr Lee was a bit of a crank. Among a number of 20th century luminaries asked by the *Wall Street Journal* in 1999 to pick the most influential invention of the millennium, he alone shunned the printing press, electricity, the internal combustion engine and the internet and chose the air-conditioner. He explained that, before air-con, people living in the tropics were at a disadvantage because the heat and humidity damaged the quality of their work.

This inspired journalist Cherian George to start a website (www.airconditioned nation.com) and write a book entitled 'The air-conditioned nation: essays on the politics of comfort and control' as a metaphor for the comfort Mr Lee brought to his people at the expense of the control he took.

Hibbs (2005). These conditions enabled the start of the Agricultural Revolution, where the domestication of plants and animals allowed for the transition from a hunter-gatherer lifestyle to the more efficient sedentary agriculture. The domestication of a species is defined as (Smith, 1998): 'the human creation of a new plant or animal – one that is identifiably different from its wild ancestors and extant wild relatives ... [which] ... has been changed so much that it has lost its ability to survive in the wild'. This transition started independently in at least five different places in the world with a time difference of at least 6,000 years; see Figure 2.6 for an overview. One of the questions we address is why this revolution occurs so much earlier in some places than in others.

The first transition occurs in the Fertile Crescent / Near East, consisting of parts of present-day Israel, Lebanon, Syria, Jordan, and Iraq. For plants (wheat, pea, and olive) around 8500 BC and for animals (sheep and goat) around 8000 BC. The second transition occurs about 1,000 years later in China (around 7500 BC; plants: rice and millet; animals: pig and silkworm). The third and fourth transitions take place 4,000 years later (around 3500 BC) in Mesoamerica (plants: corn, beans, squash; animals: turkey) and Andes & Amazonia (plants: potato and manioc; animals: llama and guinea pig). The fifth transition occurs another 1,000 years later (around 2500 BC) in the Eastern United States (plants: sunflower and goosefoot; animals: none).

There are in addition four – disputed – places for the independent origin of domestication. Although it is clear that local plants (and in one case animals) were domesticated, this may only have occurred after the adoption of so-called

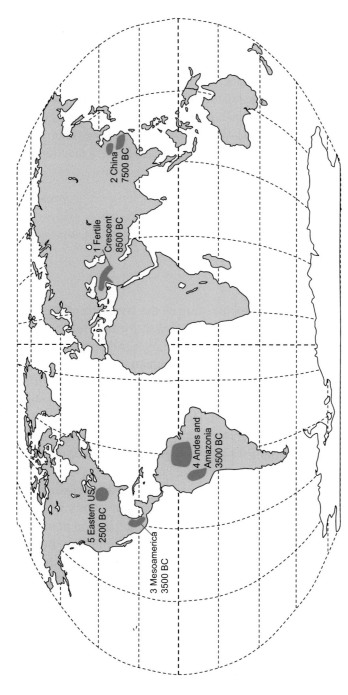

Figure 2.6 Centres of origin of food production
Source: based on Diamond (1997), Figure 5.1.

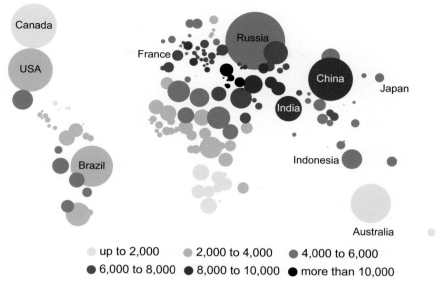

Figure 2.7 Start of agricultural transition, number of years ago
Source: author construction; agricultural transition from Putterman and Weil (2010); bubbles are proportional to a country's land area, located at the geographic centre (CIA world fact book), equilateral projection.[5]

founder crops from elsewhere. These places are Sahel (5000 BC; plants: sorghum and African rice; animals: guinea fowl), Tropical West Africa (3000 BC; African yams and oil palm), Ethiopia (timing unclear; coffee and teff), and New Guinea (7000 BC; sugar cane and banana). Three other important locations where local domestication surely only followed the arrival of founder crops are Western Europe (6000–3500 BC; poppy and oat), the Indus valley (7000 BC; plants: sesame and eggplant; animals: humped cattle), and Egypt (6000 BC; plants: sycamore fig and chufa; animals: donkey and cat).

As the above description clearly shows, the population of a certain location may benefit from the start of an agricultural transition even without making the first step itself. Through human interaction and trade contacts, knowledge about the domestication of plants and animals and their benefits spread from one location to another location, and so on. Indeed, this spread of knowledge allowed pretty much all of Europe, most of Northern Africa, and all of Southwest Asia to go through an agricultural transition thousands of years before the Americas, based on adoption rather than invention. This is illustrated in Figure 2.7 and further discussed in Section 2.4.

---

[5] Except for USA (which is at the geographic centre of the 48 contiguous states) and Russia (which is at the population-weighted geographic centre).

2.4   North–South or East–West?

One of the most important benefits of human interaction, through trade, invest-ment, and knowledge flows, is that you can enjoy the fruits of inventions and human ingenuity originating from one location at very low costs at another loca-tion. To use a popular phrase, this avoids the need for 'reinventing the wheel' at high cost and effort (see below). The domestication of plants and animals has important benefits that spread beyond the inventor's use by adoption elsewhere. Jared Diamond notes that there is a great difference between the speeds at which domestication spread in the Americas compared to that in Eurasia.[6] In his calcu-lations the llama spread from Peru to North Ecuador at a speed of about 0.2 miles per year and corn and beans spread from Mexico to the Southwest of the US at less than 0.3 miles per year. In contrast, all sorts of domesticated plants and animals spread quite rapidly from the Fertile Crescent to Europe, Egypt, and the Indus val-ley of India at an average rate of about 0.7 miles per year (and from the Philippines to Polynesia at about 3.2 miles per year).

One of the most important consequences of the quick spread of crops from the Fertile Crescent is that the domestication is based on just one wild variant of the original species, indicating a single domestication that was adopted at all other locations, from Spain and France to Egypt and India. After all, if farmers have a productive crop available they will not trouble themselves with finding a wild relative and re-domesticating it. In contrast, there is ample evidence of crops domesticated at least twice at different locations in the Americas, such as lima

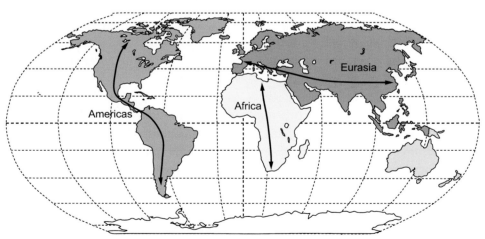

Figure 2.8 Major orientation of the continents
Source: Figure 1.11 in Brakman et al. (2009).

---

[6] This section is largely based on Diamond (1997, ch. 10).

beans, common beans, and chili peppers in Mesoamerica and South America, as well as squash and goosefoot in both Mesoamerica and the Eastern US. This double domestication at two different locations indicates that the speed of spreading from the earliest location was so slow as not to prevent a second domestication at the other location.

The main reason for the slow speed of spreading domesticated plants and animals in the Americas and Africa compared to Eurasia lies in the *orientation* of the continents either along the North–South or East–West axis, as illustrated in Figure 2.8. In the Americas the distance from North to South is about 9,000 miles and the widest distance from East to West is 3,000 miles (the narrowest distance is 40 miles in Panama). The major orientation of the Americas is thus North–South. The same holds, although less extreme, for Africa. In contrast, the major orientation of Eurasia is from East to West along 10,000 miles. Locations at the same latitude have the same daylight and seasonal variation and tend to have similar vegetation, temperature, and rainfall. Local circumstances thus tend to be rather similar when you go from East to West. In contrast, locations at different latitudes have different daylight and seasonal variation and tend to have different vegetation, temperature, and rainfall. Local circumstances thus tend to be rather different when you go from North to South. Since plants have adapted to the local circumstances for germination, growth, and disease resistance, it is much easier to spread (knowledge of) domesticated crops from East to West than it is to spread from North to South.

After food production arose in the Fertile Crescent around 8500 BC it spread for thousands of miles to Greece, Cyprus, and the Indian subcontinent by 6500 BC, Egypt by 6000 BC, Central Europe by 5400 BC, Spain by 5200 BC, and Britain around 3500 BC; see Figure 2.7. In contrast, many domesticated plants and animals did not spread from Mesoamerica to the Andes, even though the distance between Mexico's highlands and Ecuador's is only 1,200 miles and the local conditions are quite similar. The reason is that the spread would have to go from North to South or vice versa through the hot lowlands of Central America unsuitable for those crops. Thus, no llamas, guinea pigs, or potatoes reached Mexico from the Andes and no turkeys reached the Andes from Mexico. For the same reason, Fertile Crescent crops quickly spread to Egypt and reached the cool highlands of Ethiopia but never reached South Africa's perfectly suitable Mediterranean climate because of the 2,000 miles of tropical conditions in between these two locations. Agriculture could thrive in South Africa only after European settlers brought with them the whole Fertile Crescent package in the seventeenth century.

Associated with the human interaction through trade, investment, and knowledge flows incorporated in domesticated plants and animals is the spread of technological advancement. Originating from within or near the Fertile Crescent, the knowledge of writing, metalworking, milking, fruit trees, and beer and wine production spread far and wide. The same holds for the invention of the wheel, which has obvious advantages for transportation purposes although its invention is not that simple; see Wolchover (2012). Once successful at one location in Eurasia, it spread quickly from there. In the Americas, however, the wheels invented in pre-historic Mexico never spread to the Andes region.

2.5   Bio-geography and Income

The above discussion summarizes part of Jared Diamond's argument that the inhabitants of Eurasia enjoyed a series of bio-geographic advantages that allowed for an early transition from a hunter-gatherer society to farming and a rapid spread of knowledge. Building on this transition, population rose rapidly and more complicated social structures were possible. This in turn allowed for specialized crafts to develop, leading to technological innovation with long-term consequences for comparative development. Among the advantages of Eurasia were the large size of its land mass, the diversity of animals and plants available for domestication, and its East–West instead of North–South orientation.

To what extent is current income per capita explained by the bio-geographic conditions discussed above? Many people have pointed out the importance of bio-geographic conditions prior to Diamond. In their overview article Spolaore and Wacziarg (2013) mention Machiavelli, Montesquieu, Marshall, Myrdal, and more. They also distinguish between a direct channel, where bio-geographic conditions have a direct impact on current productivity and development, and an indirect channel, where these conditions built up to sustained advantages over a longer period (with Jared Diamond as one of the representatives). We discuss these issues in the remaining sections of this chapter.

Olsson and Hibbs (2005) provide a first test of Diamond's work. We base our discussion on an update of their work by Spolaore and Wacziarg (2013); see Table 2.2. We start with the explanatory power of four simple bio-geographic factors, namely (i) absolute latitude, (ii) percentage land area in the tropics, (iii) landlocked dummy (equal to one if the country has no direct access to a sea or ocean), and (iv) an island dummy (equal to one if the country is an island). Column (1) of Table 2.2 shows that for the world these factors explain about 44 per cent of the variance in current income levels. The higher the absolute latitude (so the further North or South from the equator) the higher current income. Current income is higher for island countries (with easier trade contacts across the sea) and lower for landlocked countries. The percentage of land area in the tropics is not significant. Column (2) of Table 2.2 repeats the analysis of column (1) for a selection of countries, which we refer to as the Olsson-Hibbs sample (OH in the table). This sample excludes neo-European countries (Australia, Canada, New Zealand, and the USA) and countries whose current income level is primarily based on extractive wealth (mainly oil production based on foreign technology and skilled labour). It is thought to be a better representation of the true bio-geographic forces and the explained variance rises to about 55 per cent.

The remaining columns of Table 2.2 try to estimate more directly the impact of Diamond's bio-geographic conditions. They are grouped together into two components, namely geographic conditions and biological conditions. The geographic conditions are based on the first principal component of absolute latitude, climate suitability to agriculture, rate of East–West orientation, and size of landmass in million km². The biological conditions are based on the first principal component of the number of annual or perennial wild grasses and the number of domesticable big mammals. Since absolute latitude is part of the geographic conditions it is no longer included separately in the analysis in columns (3)–(6). When entered separately, both geographic conditions and biological conditions are highly significant in determining current income levels; see columns (3) and (4) of Table 2.2 (note that the percentage of land area in the tropics becomes negatively significant in column (4), basically because it picks up the importance of the excluded variable absolute latitude [which is not incorporated in the geographic conditions

Table 2.2 Bio-geography and current income

Dependent variable: log per capita income, 2005 (PWT 6.3), OLS estimates

Variable	(1) World	(2) OH[#]	(3) OH[#]	(4) OH[#]	(5) OH[#]	(6) Old world
Absolute latitude	0.044***	0.052***				
Percentage land area in the tropics	−0.049	0.209	−0.410	−0.650**	−0.421	−0.448
Landlocked dummy	−0.742***	−0.518***	−0.499**	−0.572**	−0.505**	−0.226
Island dummy	0.643**	0.306	0.920***	0.560**	0.952***	1.306***
Geographic conditions[a]			0.706***		0.768***	0.780***
Biological conditions[b]				0.585***	−0.074	0.086
Observations	155	102	102	102	102	83
Adjusted R^2	0.440	0.546	0.521	0.449	0.516	0.641

Source: Spolaore and Wacziarg (2013, Table 1); constant and t-statistics not reported.
[#] OH = Olsson-Hibbs sample; this excludes Australia, Canada, New Zealand, USA, and countries whose current income is based primarily on extractive wealth; see Olsson and Hibbs (2005). Shaded cells with ***, ** and * are significant at the 1, 5, and 10 per cent levels, respectively.

[a] First principal component of absolute latitude, climate suitability to agriculture, rate of East–West orientation, and size of landmass in million km².
[b] First principal component of the number of annual or perennial wild grasses and the number of domesticable big mammals.

for this column]). When entered together, see column (5), the geographic conditions appear to be more important than the biological conditions (which are not significant). The last column (6) restricts attention further by including only the countries of the Old World (excluding the Americas and Oceania). The explanatory power of the bio-geographic conditions in this case further improves to more than 64 per cent of the variance.

The above analysis shows that bio-geographic conditions still play an important role in explaining current income levels, either through their direct impact on current productivity or through their indirect impact on accumulating knowledge. Empirical estimates seem to indicate that the impact of geographic factors is stronger, or longer-lasting, than the impact of biological factors. This probably reflects the fact that it is harder to change the geographic factors than the biological factors. After all, you cannot relocate a country to alter its absolute latitude or climate, but you can import biological species from other parts of the world that may be useful at this location even though they do not originate locally.

2.6 Institutions

We briefly discussed in sections 2.3 to 2.5 how bio-geographic advantages may lead some regions to an early start of economic development based on the Agricultural Revolution and how the orientation of the continents may speed up or slow down knowledge transfers. As emphasized by Jared Diamond, the domestication of plants and animals enables the formation of villages and cities with specialization of economic activities and the development of rules and regulations beneficial to economic growth. This process is thus nurturing the formation of human institutions. What do we mean by this? According to leading authority (and Nobel prize winner for economics) Douglass North (1990, p. 3): 'Institutions are the rules of the game in a society or, more formally, are the humanly devised constraints that shape human interaction.' As emphasized by Acemoglu and Robinson (2010), this definition highlights that institutions are created by humans (unlike geographic factors) to provide constraints on human behaviour working through incentives.

The above broad definition implies that all aspects of human behaviour and human interaction are somehow influenced by institutions. Economic research in this area tries to find connections between institutional characteristics and economic outcomes. We can think of the methods for collective decision making, property rights, entry barriers, education, and so on. All these aspects are, indeed, correlated with economic outcomes.

The evolution of institutions is complex and determined by the current institutions, political power (both by law and in fact; *de jure* and *de facto*), and the distribution of resources. Acemoglu and Robinson (2010) discuss some examples of how *de jure* changes may not lead to *de facto* changes and vice versa. They even discuss examples of how *de jure* changes accompanied by *de facto* changes may not alter the economic outcome (Bolivia, 1952), simply because one extractive elite is replaced by another based on the same principles (which they label the 'fighting fire with fire' phenomenon in Sub-Saharan Africa). It is clear that economic institutions change slowly over time.

Cross-country differences in economic prosperity are, of course, related to differences in the amounts of physical capital, human capital, natural resources, technology, and knowledge. We can view these as the *proximate* causes of prosperity. Acemoglu and Robinson (2010) argue that the *fundamental* cause for the differences in prosperity lies in the way a country organizes itself to mobilize the proximate causes, in the rules and regulations, in the institutions (p. 1): 'we argue that the main determinant of differences in prosperity across countries are differences in economic institutions'. To make their case, they need a source of exogenous differences in institutions for which they refer to earlier work on the *reversal of fortune*. We analyse this work in section 2.8 and argue that it is related to migration flows in section 2.11. Before we can do that, however, we need to establish a benchmark for the level of economic development in 1500, which is before both the reversal of fortune and the large migration flows. We do that in section 2.7. The size of world-wide migration flows is analysed in section 2.10. In Chapter 10, we will return to the question of how important institutions, as opposed or next to geography, are to understanding international differences in the level of economic development.

2.7   Development by 1500

As we will discuss below in sections 2.10 and 2.11, the worldwide migration flows into the Americas, Oceania, and parts of Africa in the past 500 years have had important consequences for the level of economic development of the receiving nations. This makes it worthwhile to briefly investigate what the level of economic development was before these migration flows started, say around 1500 AD. Associated with this investigation is another problem: how do we estimate the level of economic development 500 years ago? Economic historians have tackled this question for quite some time. Reliable estimates are only available for a limited number of countries or regions. More importantly, it appears that until around 1500 the 'Malthusian theory' was still empirically valid; see Ashraf and Galor (2011). This theory argues that technological progress and resource expansion primarily lead to a rise in an area's population and not to a rise in income per capita. Therefore, economists tend to use estimates of population densities in countries or regions as an early indicator of economic development. These estimates are also more widely available (and probably more reliable) than the early income per capita estimates.[7]

Bio-geographic factors are, indeed, correlated with population density in 1500 (see column (2) of Table 2.3), but some (such as the number of wild grasses and domesticable big mammals) mainly through their influence on the timing of the adoption of agriculture; see Ashraf and Galor (2011). The first step taken in Table 2.3 is therefore to determine the influence of bio-geographic factors on the timing of the agricultural transition (column (1); this is a first-stage regression). Most of the effects are highly significant and together they account for 71 per cent of the variance in the date of adoption. The next step taken in Table 2.3 is then to determine the influence of the number of years since the agricultural transition on population density in 1500, both using OLS (column 3) and IV (instrumental variables, column 4). The estimated effects are positive (population density rises as the number of years since the agricultural transition rises) and economically significant.[8] Building on their Neolithic advantages countries with early adoption of agriculture thus create a technological lead that gives them an economic advantage by 1500. Note, however, that although these effects are economically significant and explain about 40 per cent of the variance of population density (see column (3) of Table 2.3), this still leaves enough room for other factors to be important for explaining the remaining 60 per cent.

Table 2.3 Geography and development in 1500

Dependent variable	Years since agricultural transition	Population density in 1500		
	(1)	(2)	(3)	(4)
Estimator	OLS	OLS	OLS	IV
Absolute latitude	−0.074***	−0.022	0.027**	0.020*
Percentage land area in the tropics	−1.052**	0.997**	1.464***	1.636***
Landlocked dummy	−0.585**	0.384	0.532	0.702***
Island dummy	−1.085***	0.072	0.391	0.508
# wild grasses	0.017	0.030		
# domesticable big mammals	0.554***	0.258***		
Years since agricultural transition			0.426***	0.584***
Observations	100	100	98	98
Adjusted R^2	0.707	0.439	0.393	–

Source: Spolaore and Wacziarg (2013, Table 2); constant and t-statistics not reported.
Shaded cells with ***, **, and * are significant at the 1, 5, and 10 per cent levels, respectively.

---

[7] The discussion in this section is largely based on Spolaore and Wacziarg (2013).
[8] A one standard deviation increase in the years of agriculture results in a 63 per cent standard deviation change in log population density in 1500.

2.8 Reversal of Fortune

There are, of course, many crucial human interactions involved in raising the level of economic development for a nation. In this section we just want to point out the importance of *institutions* in this process; see section 2.6. Countries with better institutions, such as more secure property rights, less distortionary policies, and a more reliable government, create an environment in which people have a bigger incentive to invest in physical capital, in themselves through education (human capital), and in research and innovation (to develop new goods and services) since it is more likely that they can reap the fruit of their own efforts and investments. Therefore, in the longer run better institutions lead to higher levels of economic development. Our discussion is based on the work of Acemoglu, Johnson, and Robinson (2001, 2002; AJR in the remainder of this section). They focus on the current economic consequences of colonization by European countries for former European colonies through differences in institutions. Their main argument runs roughly as follows.

- First, there were different types of colonization policies. Some colonies were regarded as 'extractive states', such as the Congo, colonized by Belgium. In those cases, the colonial power did not provide checks and balances for the government or sufficient protection of private property. Other colonies were regarded as 'Neo-Europes', possible destinations for migration and settlement. Examples are Australia, New Zealand, Canada, and the USA. In those cases, the colonial power imposed the same 'good' institutions as at home.
- Second, the colonization strategy was influenced by the feasibility of settlement. If the disease environment was unfavourable, such as in the tropics where malaria and yellow fewer resulted in high settler mortality, the formation of extractive states rather than Neo-Europes is more likely.
- Third, institutions change slowly over time. So, the colonial state and institutions persisted even after independence.

Because of the three premises above, high settler mortality influenced the likelihood of settlement, which influenced the likelihood of extractive institutions, which influenced the quality of current institutions, which influences current economic performance.

To get an indication on potential settler mortality, AJR gathered information on the number of deaths per 1,000 soldiers measured by the number of replacements for European troops in different locations, mostly in the period from 1818 to 1848. The variation is enormous, ranging from less than nine replacements in Australia and New Zealand to more than 1,000 for Gambia, Mali, and Nigeria. To get an indication of the quality of current institutions, AJR gathered information on the average protection against expropriation risk in the period 1985–95. We combine this with current income per capita levels (GNI per capita PPP in constant 2011 international $, most recent available in the period 2011–13). Panel *a* of Figure 2.9 shows that there is indeed a strong negative association between the current income level and settler mortality in the nineteenth century. Similarly, panel *b* of Figure 2.9 shows that there is a negative association between settler mortality and the current level of institutional quality. Note that Figure 2.9 depicts the information for two groups of countries, namely the countries included in the AJR sample to be discussed in Table 2.4 and other countries; see also section 2.9.[9]

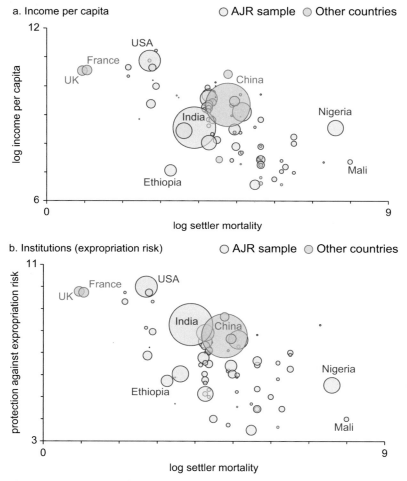

Figure 2.9 European settler mortality, current institutions, and income per capita
Source: based on data from Acemoglu et al. (2001) and World Development Indicators online; income per capita is GNI PPP in constant 2011 USD (most recent observation in 2011–13); European settler mortality per thousand; expropriation risk = risk of expropriation of private foreign investment by government (index from 0 to 10 where a higher score means lower risk); 84 observations in panel *a* and 72 in panel *b*.

---

[9] Three countries are excluded in panel *a* for lack of current income per capita data, namely Argentina in the AJR sample and Djibouti and Myanmar in the other countries sample; in panel *b* 10 of the other countries are missing for lack of protection against expropriation data.

Table 2.4 Institutions and development

Panel *a* Second stage; dependent variable: log GDP per capita

	AJR sample (1)	AJR sample, colonial dummies (2)
Institutions (expropriation risk)	0.94***	1.10***
British colonial dummy		−0.78**
French colonial dummy		−0.12

Panel *b* First stage; dependent variable: institutions (protection against expropriation risk)

Log settler mortality	−0.61***	−0.53***
British colonial dummy		0.63*
French colonial dummy		0.05
R^2	0.27	0.31
Observations	64	64

Source: Acemoglu et al. (2001, Tables 4 and 5); t-statistics not reported.
Shaded cells with ***, **, and * are significant at the 1, 5, and 10 per cent levels, respectively.

The main results are summarized in Table 2.4 using two-stage regressions. Panel *b* shows the first-stage influence of settler mortality on the quality of institutions, where higher settler mortality leads to significantly worse institutions. Panel *a* shows the second-stage influence of institutions on current income per capita, where better institutions lead to significantly higher income levels. According to the estimates, the difference in institutional quality between Chile and Nigeria, for example, lead to an estimated sevenfold difference in income per capita (Acemoglu et al., 2001).

Column (2) of Table 2.4 adds dummy variables for British and French colonies, with colonies from other nations as the omitted group. It has been pointed out that British colonies tend to have better institutions and perform better; see La Porta et al. (1998). As column (2) shows, however, it is important to control for settler mortality: Britain colonized places where settlements were possible, leading to better institutions, which in turn resulted in better performance.

Table 2.5 summarizes two simple versions of a more controversial aspect of AJR's work, known as the 'reversal of fortune' phenomenon; see Acemoglu et al. (2002). Here the main argument is as follows. European colonies that were relatively rich in 1500, such as the Mughals in India and the Aztecs and Incas in the Americas, were confronted with worse institutions after colonization than previously poor places, such as North America, Australia, and New Zealand. Because of the institutional reversal we observe a reversal of fortune in terms of income per capita: previously rich places become relatively poor and vice versa. AJR argue explicitly that their findings are indicative of institutional quality as the crucial variable for determining prosperity and are not supported by a simple geography

Table 2.5 Reversal of fortune

Dependent variable: Log per capita income 1995; estimator OLS

	AJR base sample	AJR base sample
Urbanization in 1500	−0.078***	
Log population density in 1500		−0.38***
Observations	41	91
R^2	0.19	0.34

Source: Acemoglu et al. (2002, Tables III and V); t-statistics not reported.
Shaded cells with ***, **, and * are significant at the 1, 5, and 10 per cent levels, respectively.

hypothesis on the prosperity of nations, since geographic variables that do not change over time cannot explain a reversal in relative incomes.

AJR use two indicators of economic prosperity in 1500, namely the degree of urbanization and population density, and analyse their influence on current income levels. Column (1) of Table 2.5 focuses on urbanization. It shows that countries with a higher urbanization level in 1500 tend to have a lower income level today. There are only 41 observations and the share of current income variance explained is 19 per cent. Although AJR prefer urbanization as an indicator of prosperity in 1500 they also use population density estimates since this is correlated with urbanization and available for more countries (91 instead of 41). Column (2) of Table 2.5 shows that countries with a high population density in 1500 tend to have a lower income level today, another indicator of the reversal of fortune that explains 34 per cent of the variance in current income.

2.9 Selection Effects

One can raise various objections to the reversal of fortune phenomenon discussed in section 2.8. First, one may wonder how appropriate it is to compare economic development per capita today, which is measured relatively precisely in real dollars, with economic development measured relatively imprecisely by urbanization or population density 500 years ago. Second, the standard neo-classical growth model also gives rise to convergence, or a reversal of fortune without any need for a change in institutional quality. Third, perhaps countries with high economic development have good institutions because of the way we measure institutional quality, namely ex post with a tendency to interpret evidence on institutional quality in rich countries as 'better' (otherwise they would not have been rich). Fourth and the topic of the remainder of this section, the selection of countries to be included in the analysis plays a crucial role; see Spolaore and Wacziarg (2013).

Table 2.6 Selection effects

Dependent variable: Log per capita income 2005; estimator OLS

Panel *a*: Including European countries

	Whole world	Europe only	Not former European colony	Indigenous countries
	(1)	(2)	(3)	(4)
Log pop dens 1500	0.027	0.117	0.170**	0.193**
Beta coefficient (%)	3.3	22.8	22.3	20
Observations	171	35	73	138
Adjusted R^2	0.001	0.052	0.050	0.040

Panel *b*: Excluding European countries

	Whole world	Former European colony	Not former European colony	Indigenous countries
	(5)	(6)	(7)	(8)
Log pop dens 1500	−0.246***	−0.393***	−0.030	−0.117
Beta coefficient (%)	−27.8	−47.9	−3.1	−11.7
Observations	136	98	38	103
Adjusted R^2	0.077	0.229	0.001	0.014

Source: Spolaore and Wacziarg (2013, Table 3); t-statistics not reported; indigenous countries have more than half of the current population descended from people who lived there in 1500; see section 2.10 for details.
Shaded cells with ***, **, and * are significant at the 1, 5, and 10 per cent levels, respectively.

The main selection effects are summarized in Table 2.6. The beta coefficients in the table indicate by how many standard deviations a dependent variable will change per standard deviation increase in the exogenous variable.[10] Spolaore and Wacziarg use extended information for a broader sample of countries and updated to 2005 in terms of 'current' income per capita. Panel *b* column (6) shows that the reversal of fortune effect holds if we restrict attention to former European colonies (a negative and significant coefficient). This also holds for the world if we exclude European countries (column 5). The effect does not hold, however, for countries that were not former European colonies (column 7), and for non-European indigenous states (column 8). An 'indigenous state' is defined as a country where more than half of the current population descended from people who lived there in 1500; see also section 2.10.

---
[10] Based on a regression where all exogenous variables are standardized to have a variance of one.

Panel *a* of Table 2.6 shows that when Europe is included there is no evidence of a reversal of fortune. The effect is not significant for the world (column 1) and if we restrict attention to European countries only (column 2). The effect is significant and *positive*, thus indicative of persistence rather than a reversal of fortune, if we exclude former European colonies (column 3) or only look at indigenous countries (column 4). Spolaore and Wacziarg (2013) note on page 335: 'In other words, the reversal of fortune is a feature of samples that exclude Europe and is driven largely by countries inhabited by populations that moved there after the discovery of the New World, and now constitute large portions of these countries' populations – either European colonizers (e.g. in North America and Oceania) or African slaves (e.g. in the Caribbean).'

The estimates thus suggest that the composition of a country's population may play a role in determining the prosperity of nations. After all, when people move to other countries, such as Europeans settling in North America or Africans forcibly transported to Brazil, they bring with them their human capital and all aspects of their country's culture and history; see Glaeser et al. (2004). Before we discuss the potential contribution of these migration flows to economic development today in section 2.11 we first analyse the size and impact of these migration flows in section 2.10.

2.10   Migration Flows Since 1500

Putterman and Weil (2010) are the first to provide a structural and detailed account of the migration flows in the world in the past five centuries. They use information for 172 countries, together comprising almost the entire world population. We are interested in determining to what extent the current population living in a country descend from people who already lived there in 1500 and from ethnicities from other countries. The 1500 benchmark date is taken as the starting point of the era of European colonization of other continents, which resulted in large-scale population movements. We refer to both the direct and indirect consequences of these movements as 'migration' flows; the term therefore includes voluntary migration, the transport of slaves, and forced relocation. If a person migrated recently from one country to another the direct consequence for the current population is just one additional person. If a person migrated from one country to another several decades or even centuries ago, the consequences for the current population add up indirectly as well through their offspring (their children, grandchildren, and so on). Putterman and Weil use detailed country-level studies and genetic information to estimate both the direct and indirect consequences of migration flows.

To analyse the consequences of the main migration flows since 1500, we (i) use the detailed 172-country data of Putterman and Weil which we (ii) combine with the current population size for these countries, and then (iii) group together in larger global regions for illustration purposes. The World Bank identifies seven global regions based on geography, history, and development: see Table 2.7. We further subdivide two of those regions. First, we subdivide the large East Asia and Pacific region (31.3 per cent of the world population) into three parts: East Asia (including China, Korea, and Japan), Southeast Asia (including Indonesia and the Philippines), and Pacific (including Australia and New Zealand). Second, we subdivide the Europe and Central Asia region into Europe and Central Asia (including Russia) separately. We thus have ten different global regions.[11]

Figure 2.10 illustrates the consequences of the migration flows since 1500 for the ten global regions, while further detail is provided in Table 2.8. First, we note that the population of only three global regions currently consists largely of non-indigenous population, namely North America (97 per cent), Pacific (94 per cent), and Latin America (68 per cent). Of the 351 million people currently living in North America, for example, only 11 million descend from people who lived there

Table 2.7 Global regions

World Bank regions – further subdivided

Region	code	population million	%	million	%	# countries
East Asia and Pacific	EAP	2,225	31.3			36
Pacific	PAC			31	0.4	17
East Asia	EAS			1,570	22.1	7
Southeast Asia	SEA			624	8.8	12
Europe and Central Asia	ECA	899	12.7			57
Europe	EUR			542	7.6	45
Central Asia	CAS			357	5.0	12
Latin America and Caribbean	LAC	615	8.7			41
Middle East & North Africa	MENA	403	5.7			21
North America	NAM	351	4.9			3
South Asia	SAS	1,671	23.5			8
Sub-Saharan Africa	SSA	937	13.2			48
Total		7,101	100			214

Source: based on World Bank Development Indicators classification, 2015.

---

[11] As a United Nations organization the World Bank does not include Taiwan in its global regions. We have included it in the East Asia region.

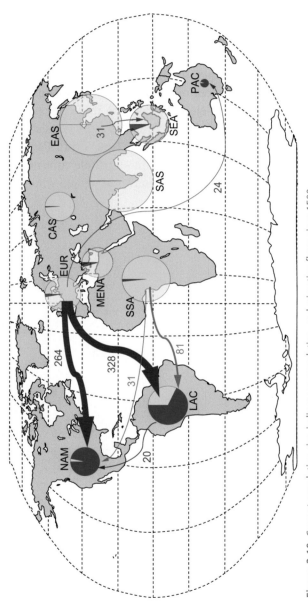

Figure 2.10 Current population size, indigenous population, and migration flows since 1500

Source: own calculations based on data from Putterman and Weil (2010) and World Bank Development indicators; region abbreviations: see Table 2.7; bubbles proportional to population size in 2013; light-shaded area is indigenous population (descended from people who lived in the region in 1500); dark-shaded area is non-indigenous population; weight of migration line is proportional to size of population flow (in millions); only flows of 15 million or more people are shown, see Table 2.8 for further details.

Table 2.8 Global migration flows in the past five centuries

Region-wide global migration flows in the past five centuries (millions of people)

Lives in					Originates from						
	CAS	EAS	EUR	LAC	MENA	NAM	PAC	SAS	SEA	SSA	sum
CAS	352	1	3	0	1	0	0	0	0	0	357
EAS	0	1,593	0	0	0	0	0	0	0	0	1,593
EUR	7	0	524	0	4	0	0	2	1	1	540
LAC	1	2	328	196	3	0	0	1	0	81	613
MENA	4	0	5	0	378	0	0	3	0	7	398
NAM	6	8	264	20	2	11	0	4	5	31	351
PAC	0	1	24	0	1	0	2	1	1	0	28
SAS	4	0	0	0	0	0	0	1,666	0	0	1,670
SEA	0	31	0	0	0	0	0	4	589	0	624
SSA	0	0	12	0	1	0	0	2	0	909	925
Origin	375	1,636	1,160	216	389	11	2	1,684	596	1,030	7,099

As percentage of total world population

	CAS	EAS	EUR	LAC	MENA	NAM	PAC	SAS	SEA	SSA	
Origin	5.3	23.0	16.3	3.0	5.5	0.2	0.0	23.7	8.4	14.5	100

Source: calculations based on the Putterman and Weil (2010) migration matrix and population in 2013; 172 countries included; CAS = Central Asia; EAS = East Asia; EUR = Europe; LAC = Latin America and the Caribbean; MENA = Middle East and North Africa; NAM = North America; PAC = Pacific; SAS = South Asia; SEA = Southeast Asia; SSA = Sub-Saharan Africa.

in 1500. For the remaining seven global regions the non-indigenous population is less than 6 per cent (even 0 per cent for East Asia). To the extent that migration flows have an impact on current development this therefore has an impact only for the Americas and Pacific. There are a few exceptions at the country level. In contrast to the largely non-indigenous population in the Pacific and Latin America, more than half of the population *is* indigenous in Fiji, Bolivia, Ecuador, Guatemala, Honduras, Mexico, and Peru. Except for Mexico, which benefits from being in the neighbourhood of North America, all these countries with a high indigenous population have a lower income per capita than their region average.[12] Similarly, in contrast to the largely indigenous population in Sub-Saharan Africa and Southeast Asia, there are only two countries where the non-indigenous population is more than half, namely Mauritius and Singapore. Both these countries have a (substantially) higher income level than their region average.

---

[12] GDP per capita in 2013 (measured in constant 2011 PPP dollars).

Second, we note that by far the largest global regional migration flows originate from Europe. Of the 1,160 million people currently alive originating from Europe in 1500 only 524 million live inside Europe; see Table 2.8. The remaining 636 million moved to Latin America (328 million), North America (264 million), Pacific (24 million), and other regions. Sub-Saharan Africa is a distant second global region for the origin of migration flows. Of the 1,030 million people currently alive originating from Sub-Saharan Africa in 1500, most live inside Sub-Saharan Africa (909 million), while 81 million migrated to Latin America and 31 million to North America. The only remaining migration flow we would like to mention is from East Asia to Southeast Asia (31 million).

2.11   Ancestry

We now briefly discuss the historical influence of geographic *locations* as well as the historical legacy of the *populations* inhabiting these locations for current economic development. We use two measures of early economic development, namely *state history* and the number of *years of agriculture*; see Putterman and Weil (2010). The state history variable measures the history of the state. That is, the extent to which what we now consider as a country had a history of a supra-tribal government, what the geographic scope of that government was, and whether this was indigenous or by an outside power in the fifteen centuries prior to 1500. It discounts the past by reducing the weight for each half century by 5 per cent. Ethiopia, for example, achieves the maximum value of one; China reaches 0.906; Spain reaches 0.562; while the USA has a value of zero. The number of years since the agricultural transition was already discussed in section 2.7. It is measured in thousands, with, for example, a highest value of 10.5 for Israel; a value of 9 for China; a value of 4 for Ecuador; a value of 3.5 for Ivory Coast; and a value of one for Haiti.

We examine state history and years of agriculture both in their original form and adjusted to take account of migration flows since 1500. We label these variables *ancestry-adjusted* state history and *ancestry-adjusted* years of agriculture. The principle for the adjustment is simple: migrants bring with them the state history and years of agriculture of their old country to their new country. The historical influences of state history and years of agriculture on current development is thus incorporated in the migrants and (partially) passed on to their offspring. The adjustment is a population-weighted average of the historical experiences of the entire population. If, for example, the population of country A consists of 90 per cent population from country A with a state history of 0.6 and of 10 per cent population from country B with a state history of 0.2 then the ancestry-adjusted state history of country A is: $0.9 \times 0.6 + 0.1 \times 0.2 = 0.56$. Similarly for years of agriculture.

Figure 2.11 illustrates the differences between years of agriculture and ancestry-adjusted years of agriculture. For many countries there is hardly any difference

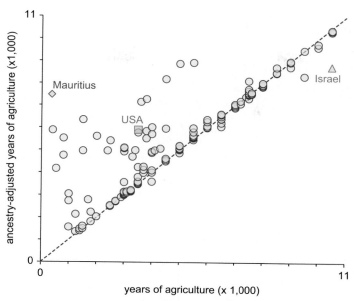

Figure 2.11 Years of agriculture and ancestry-adjusted years of agriculture
Source: own calculations based on Putterman and Weil (2010) data; the dotted line is a 45° line.

between these two variables: the observations are close to the 45° line. Most of these countries are in one of the seven global regions largely consisting of indigenous population; see section 2.10. For a range of other countries, mostly in the Americas and the Pacific, the ancestry-adjusted years of agriculture is much higher than without the adjustment. An example is the USA, where the ancestry-adjusted years of agriculture is 5.9 instead of 3.5. Occasionally this also holds for countries outside these regions, such as Mauritius (7.5 instead of 0.4) and Singapore (8.2 instead of 4.5, not shown). Only in two cases are the ancestry-adjusted variables significantly lower than the original variables, namely for Israel (8.8 instead of 10.5) and Kuwait (8.3 instead of 9.5, not shown).

The importance of adjusting for migration flows for the historical influence on current economic development is summarized in Table 2.9. All regressions estimate current income levels and include four geographic components, namely absolute latitude, percentage land area in the tropics, landlocked dummy, and an island dummy. The two measures of early economic development, state history and years of agriculture, are then added to the regression in turn, both in their original form and ancestry-adjusted. In their original form both variables are insignificant (columns 1 and 3). When using ancestry-adjusted variables, however, both measures of early development are highly significant and economically important (columns 2 and 4). A one standard deviation increase in years of agriculture raises the log of income by 17 per cent, while a one standard deviation increase in state history raises this by 22 per cent; see Putterman and Weil (2010). These results indicate that economic development today is at least partially based on the characteristics of

Table 2.9 Ancestry-adjusted geography, state history, and development

Dependent variable: Log per capita income 2005; estimator OLS; beta coefficient in parentheses

Main regressor	Years of agriculture	Ancestry-adjusted years of agriculture	State history	Ancestry-adjusted state history
	(1)	(2)	(3)	(4)
Years of agriculture	0.019			
	(3.8)			
Ancestry-adjusted years of agriculture		0.099**		
		(17.2)		
State history			0.074	
			(1.5)	
Ancestry-adjusted state history				1.217***
				(21.6)
Absolute latitude	0.042***	0.040***	0.047***	0.046***
Percentage land area in the tropics	−0.188	−0.148	0.061	0.269
Landlocked dummy	−0.753***	−0.671***	−0.697***	−0.555***
Island dummy	0.681**	0.562***	0.531**	0.503**
Observations	150	148	136	135
Adjusted R^2	0.475	0.523	0.558	0.588

Source: based on Spolaore and Wacziarg (2013, Table 5); t-statistics and constant not reported. Shaded cells with ***, **, and * are significant at the 1, 5, and 10 per cent levels, respectively.

human populations. The people who migrated voluntarily and forcibly to another country brought with them their characteristics, human capital, and familiarity with certain types of institutions and norms of behaviour. All these aspects seem to be important for explaining current levels of economic development.

2.12   Conclusions

We live in a spiky world with large differences between countries and regions in terms of population, density, and economic prosperity. A first force in explaining this spikiness at the global level is based on the deep roots of economic development as explained by bio-geographic factors. A second force is based on the role of human interactions within and between locations of economic activity. We argue that these two forces interact to partially explain the uneven allocation of economic activity and also the uneven level of economic development, as already observed in Chapter 1, hence the title geo-human interaction.

We started with a discussion to show that simple geographic forces play a role in understanding differences in current prosperity and income. We then analysed the importance of the Agricultural Revolution, which allowed for a transition from a hunter-gatherer society to a farmer society. The uneven distribution of domesticable plants and animals gave some regions a head start, in particular the Near East, Europe, and North Africa. We explained how the spread of agricultural knowledge is easier East–West than North–South and how this benefits the Eurasian continent relative to Africa and the Americas. These bio-geographic circumstances thus play an important role in explaining the start of the transition to farming at any location.

We proceeded by analysing the importance of geo-human interaction for explaining current prosperity in four steps. First, by pointing out the connections between current prosperity and bio-geographic factors in general, particularly for the Old World (excluding Oceania and the Americas). Second, by showing how these factors can help explain the agricultural transition and human development levels for the whole world up to the year 1500. Third, by discussing the role of man-made institutions and selection effects in the reversal of fortune discussion, which is not observed if European countries are included in the analysis and reversed for indigenous countries and countries that were not former European colonies. Fourth, by analysing the role of international migration flows from 1500 to 2000 for the structure of the present-day population of a country and by showing how the institutional knowledge incorporated in these flows helps explain current economic development levels for the whole world, including Oceania and the Americas. Eventually, bio-geographic factors are thus important for economic development levels, either directly or indirectly through geo-human interaction.

In the man-made institutions versus bio-geographical factors analysis associated with the reversal of fortune discussion we noted that bio-geographic factors are crucial in at least two ways.

First, there is a direct effect, since European countries only established 'good' institutions in countries that were conducive to their own well-being; that is countries with similar circumstances, a similar climate, and a lower disease burden. Bio-geography is thus important for determining where to impose the good institutions.

Second, there is a geo-human interaction effect. We discuss in section 2.4 that the transmission of knowledge was easier across the Eurasian axis such that people there could benefit from discoveries and knowledge generated elsewhere, which in turn was important for developing good institutions. After 1500 the Europeans colonized large parts of the world and settled in many places. The parts that had good climatic conditions for benefiting from the earlier developments in Eurasia are: North America, Oceania, South Africa, and parts of

Latin America. Those are the parts that are prosperous today. Either through the institutional structure imposed (which depends to a large extent on the bio-geographic conditions) or from the indirect benefit of transferring thousands of years of accumulated historical knowledge to these places through migration flows.

Notwithstanding the fact, and recall our set-up and discussion of Figure 2.1 at the start of this chapter, that the first nature forces and the second nature forces discussed in Chapter 2 are no doubt relevant and cover part of the explanation for the spiky world (hence their inclusion in our book!), they cover at best only a sub-set of the forces at work. This is because we have so far largely ignored the determinants of spatial unevenness that follow (solely) from the economic interactions of firms, workers, and households.

It is on these economic interactions and the role that markets play in deciding the location choice of firms and households that we focus in the remainder of the book. Our main task when discussing urban and geographical economics will be to explain a spiky world in models that are – deliberately – devoid of the kind of first nature geography, institutions, or selection effects that are the focus of this chapter. The task that the models of urban and geographical economics set themselves is to start with a *flat and homogeneous topography* as a depiction of space and ask what economic interactions or mechanisms are necessary to bring about the well-established spatial facts that are highlighted in Chapter 1. The models of urban and geographical economics give us the answers.

Exercises

Question 2.1 Agricultural Revolution
Explain why, according to Jared Diamond, it is no coincidence that the Agricultural Revolution started in the *Fertile Crescent* and gave *Europe* a head start in development.

Question 2.2 Deep Roots
Which continent was the birthplace of mankind? Briefly explain using two 'deep roots' arguments why this continent is not at the peak of economic development today.

Question 2.3 Malaria
Figure Q2.1 shows the estimated number of malaria cases (in million) and deaths (in thousands), worldwide in the period 2000–2013. It looks like the number of deaths has clearly declined but the number of cases hovers around 200 million. Nonetheless, the World Health Organization (WHO) claims that it has made clear progress since 2000 in reducing the malaria burden both in terms of the number

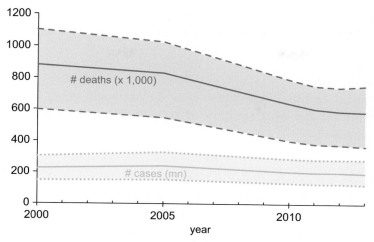

Figure Q2.1 Estimated number of malaria cases and deaths, worldwide
Source: based on Table 8.3, World Health Organization (2014); ranges show lower and upper bound.

of deaths and in the number of cases. Explain how the WHO arrives at this conclusion and briefly indicate if you agree, or not (explain why in both cases).

Question 2.4 Poverty

Figure Q2.2 is taken from the World Bank eAtlas and shows the poverty headcount ratio at $1.25 a day (PPP, % of population). The highest rates are for Liberia and Burundi, namely 83.7 and 81.3 per cent, respectively.

Figure Q2.2 Poverty headcount ratio

In a presentation your colleague argues that the figure shows that the largest number of poor people, measured at an income level of at most $1.25 a day, can be found in Africa. Comment on this statement.

Question 2.5 Reversal of Fortune

What is the 'Reversal of Fortune' hypothesis? How do Acemoglu et al. (2002) measure reversal of fortune and what are some of the problems of their analysis as discussed in this chapter?

Question 2.6 BRIC(S)

The term BRIC countries, which later turned to BRICS countries, was introduced in 2001 by Goldman Sachs to refer to major emerging economies. The term quickly became popular. The included countries are Brazil, Russia, India, China, and South Africa. Figure Q2.3 provides some information on the income developments in these countries using GDP PPP in constant 2011 international dollars with a log

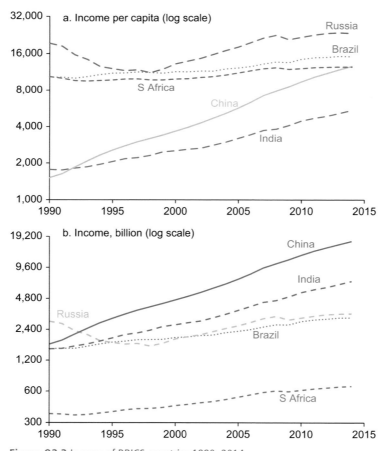

Figure Q2.3 Income of BRICS countries 1990–2014

Table Q2.1 Compounded growth rates (BRICS) over the period 1990–2014 (%)

	Brazil	Russia	India	China	S Africa
GDP per capita	1.6	0.8	4.7	8.8	0.8
GDP	2.9	0.7	6.3	9.6	2.5

scale, both per capita (panel *a*) and in total (panel *b*). Table Q2.1 calculates compounded growth rates (in per cent) over the 24-year period 1990–2014.

Write an *essay* for an interested audience (such as readers of *The Economist*) to explain *why the BRIC / BRICS grouping of countries is or is not appropriate.*

Question 2.7 The World Is Not Flat

The World Development Report (2009) states that 'The economic world is not flat'. Explain this statement by referring to the term 'density'. What is the value of knowing that the world is not flat, from an economic development perspective? Explain.

3 Empirical Methods

LEARNING OBJECTIVES

- To understand how spikiness (the spatial distribution of economic activity) can be defined and measured.
- To know the main inequality and economic concentration measures and their differences with respect to relevant criteria.
- To understand why it is often quite difficult to disentangle cause and effect when trying to understand the spiky world.
- To know the main techniques for addressing the causality issue and being able to apply these techniques to specific examples.

3.1   Introduction

In Chapter 1 we indicated that the world is spiky and that the spikes can be observed at various levels of aggregation: cities, regions, and countries. In Chapter 2 we came across various first nature geography reasons that could help to explain our spiky world, and we also showed how human interactions can be seen as drivers of the stylized facts about the spiky world. The economic reasons for (and consequences of) the spiky world were, however, not yet really discussed. That is the main goal of Parts II and III of our book, on urban and geographical economics, respectively.

Before we can turn to the theory and empirics of urban and geographical economics we have to be more precise on:

- Measures of 'spikiness', and
- The relation between spikiness and economic performance. This involves thorny matters like causality and endogeneity.

As we will see, these two issues are intricate but also relevant.

Measuring spatial unevenness or inequality has a long history that is rooted in measures of income inequality. It is therefore no surprise that many spatial inequality measures are based on income inequality measures, such as the Gini coefficient and entropy measures; see section 3.2. Instead of comparing income between individuals one can compare, for instance, regional income per capita between regions. These standard income inequality measures have a natural application in urban and geographical economics. Some measures, however, are developed specifically to measure spatial inequality, such as the Ellison-Glaeser index and the Duranton-Overman approach; see section 3.3. These measures do not have an equivalent in the area of measurements of income inequality.

How to choose between all these measures? In order to make an informed decision between Gini indices, Herfindahl indices, Krugman indices, entropy measures, Ellison-Glaeser indices, or the Duranton-Overman density approach, we discuss some of the characteristics of these measures. All measures suffer from some type of drawback, such as lack of comparability across sectors or spatial scales and being affected by sector and space definitions (see Duranton and Overman, 2005 for an overview). None of the measures solves all drawbacks: the ideal index does not exist, but it turns out some are better than others for measuring *spikiness*.

Once the spatial concentration of economic activity is established, the relation between the uneven distribution of activity and performance becomes relevant; do clusters of economic activity perform better than peripheral areas? The answer is less straightforward than it seems. Think of the following. Living in a big city enables workers and firms to specialize and become more productive. In a regression this could be revealed by regressing a measure of productivity on a measure of concentration. A positive sign of the estimated regression would indicate such a relationship. However, living in a big city is expensive: think of renting an apartment in New York City versus renting a similar apartment in a small rural area. Could it be that high-skilled and productive people (who earn a relatively high income) move to the big city because they can afford the high rents in New York City and make the city even bigger and more productive? The correlation between concentration and productivity is still positive, but the causality is reversed. It is no longer the case that spatial concentration makes people more productive, but productive people migrate to the big city and make it even bigger.

We also note that information can be missing; we have 'known unknowns' and 'unknown unknowns'. Techniques exist to deal with this, such as the introduction of fixed effects and diff-in-diff estimations. These techniques may correct for missing information. The use of natural experiments can help to solve endogeneity issues. Finally (and importantly in regional economics) regions may influence each other. In many cases assuming that one can analyse a region in isolation is too strong an assumption. If California is experiencing strong economic growth it is likely that this boom spills over to neighbouring states, such that Nevada also benefits. Spatial econometrics is designed to deal with these spatial connections.

This chapter first introduces some of the most often used measures of income and spatial inequality. In addition, we briefly discuss in the second part of the chapter what econometric methods exist to deal with issues that one typically encounters in empirical research as to questions about causality and endogeneity.

3.2   Inequality Measures

We start our analysis with a discussion of the main income inequality measures that can also be used to evaluate spatial inequality. Our notation is as follows. For the spatial dimension, we analyse different economic activities $a = 1,..., A$ in a range of different regions $i = 1,..., R$. If required (for notational reasons), we can also index the regions by $r = 1,..., R$.

Let $y_{i,a}$ denote the size of activity a in region i. We assume that this activity is non-negative, so $y_{i,a} \geq 0$. The total size of activity a in all regions is the sum over all regions: $\sum_i y_{i,a}$. This is equal to the number of regions R times the average size of activity a per region $\bar{y}_a$, that is: $R\bar{y}_a = \sum_i y_{i,a}$. Sometimes, we are interested in the share s of activity a in region i, in which case we divide the size of each activity in a region by the size of the total activity in all regions: $s_{i,a} = y_{i,a} / R\bar{y}_a$. Moreover, we order the shares from small to large, such that $s_{i,a} \leq s_{i+1,a}$ for all $i < R$.[1] If the activity is food production in twelve different regions, our notation implies that the shares $s_{i,a}$ are ordered from the smallest regional food producer to the largest and the sum of the shares equals one: $\sum_i s_{i,a} = 1$.

3.2.1   Desirable Properties of Inequality Measures

There are four desirable properties of income inequality measures which translate easily to desirable properties of measures of spatial inequality.

1. *Symmetry* or *anonymity:* if we swap the observations of two regions there should be no change in the measure of inequality.
2. *Scale independence:* if we double activity in all regions the measure of inequality should not change.
3. *Region size independence:* if the number of regions changes, the measure of inequality should not change, other things being equal.
4. *Transfer principle:* if some activity is transferred from a region with high activity to a region with low activity (while still preserving the order) the measured inequality should decrease (strong form) or not increase (weak form).

Many inequality measures do not satisfy the four properties above and are thus less suitable for empirical evaluation. This holds, for example, for share and ratio

---

[1] Strictly speaking, this implies that the ordering of regions is activity-specific. We do not make this explicit in the equations to avoid cumbersome notation like $s_{i_a}^a$ and to ensure that the equations themselves are clear.

inequality measures, such as the share of the top 10 per cent of regions in total activity or the ratio of the share of the top 10 per cent divided by the share of the bottom 10 per cent. We restrict attention in the remainder of this section to inequality measures that do satisfy the above four criteria, namely the Gini coefficient (see section 3.2.2) and the class of Generalized Entropy measures (see section 3.2.3). The advantages of the Gini coefficient are that it is scaled from zero (perfect equality) to one (perfect inequality) and it represents the views on inequality of a society with general preferences (Sen, 1974). The Generalized Entropy measures have no upper limit (which is a disadvantage for interpretation), but in contrast to the Gini coefficient can be decomposed into population groups (which is an advantage); see also Atkinson (1970) and van Marrewijk (2019).

3.2.2   The Gini Coefficient

The most often used income inequality measure is the *Gini coefficient*; see Gini (1912) and Foster et al. (2013). It can be graphically illustrated by constructing the *Lorenz curve*. For income inequality, this curve depicts the ordered cumulative share of the population on the horizontal axis and cumulative share of income on the vertical axis; see Figure 3.1 for an example. For spatial inequality, the Lorenz curve depicts the ordered cumulative regions on the horizontal axis and the cumulative spatial activity shares on the vertical axis; see Figure 3.2 for an example and the discussion below for details.

We explain the definition of the Gini coefficient using the income distribution of the UK in 2015–2016, depicted in Figure 3.1, as an example. The horizontal axis ranks the population from low to high income; the vertical axis shows the cumulative income in the UK. The Lorenz curve is the curved line depicting the actual

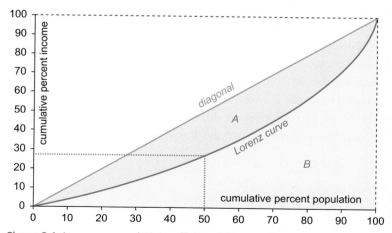

Figure 3.1 Lorenz curve and Gini coefficient: UK income distribution, 2015–16
Source: based on data from https://www.gov.uk/government/statistics, before tax; area *A* and area *B*: see main text.

income distribution. Eyeballing the graph shows that the poorest 50 per cent of people earn about 27 per cent of all income. The diagonal line represents total equality if all people earned the same income level. The Gini coefficient is defined as $A/(A+B)$, where A is the area between the Lorenz curve and the diagonal and B the area below the Lorenz curve. If $A = 0$ the Gini coefficient equals zero, implying total equality in the distribution of employment over the regions in the sample. If B approaches zero the Gini coefficient approaches one. The Gini coefficient thus ranges from zero to one, with higher values indicating inequality. In the example, the Gini coefficient is about 0.34.

How to calculate the Gini coefficient on the basis of the Lorenz curve? Let the coordinates of the Lorenz curve be denoted by (h_i, v_i), with h for horizontal and v for vertical. In the spatial inequality case using the notation above, the Lorenz curve consists of $R+1$ points, starting from $(0,0)$ and adding R regions to reach $(1,1)$ to account for all regions and all economic activity in those regions.[2] If all regions receive the same weight, the size of the horizontal steps is just $1/R$, so the i-th horizontal coordinate is $h_i = i/R$ and the step is $h_i - h_{i-1} = 1/R$. If not all regions receive the same weight, the horizontal step $h_i - h_{i-1}$ is equal to the weight w_i of region i, such that $\sum_{i=1}^{R} w_i = 1$.[3] The size of the vertical step is the share $s_{i,a}$ of the region, so the i-th vertical coordinate is $v_i = \sum_{r=1}^{i} s_{r,a}$. The Gini coefficient is defined in equation 3.1, where the first expression holds in general and the second if all horizontal steps are equal to $1/R$.

$$Gini = 1 - \sum_{i=1}^{R} w_i \left(v_i + v_{i-1} \right) = 1 - \frac{1}{R} \sum_{i=1}^{R} \left(v_i + v_{i-1} \right) \qquad\qquad 3.1$$

An example of a spatial inequality analysis that uses the Gini coefficient is provided in Figure 3.2 which depicts two Lorenz curves of regional employment in the European Union at the so-called NUTS 2 level in 2017. The solid line depicts the Lorenz curve of the employment distribution of the 15–64 year old population, indicative of *total employment*, for 276 regions in 28 European Union countries. The dashed line depicts the Lorenz curve of the employment distribution of the 15–24 year old population, indicative of *youth employment*, for 274 regions in 28 countries.[4] We may wonder, for example if youth employment is more unequally distributed than total employment, or vice versa. A direct comparison of the two Lorenz curves in the figure is inconclusive, because the youth employment curve is first

---

[2] The graphs use percentages and thus go to (100,100).

[3] The weights w_i may, of course, depend on the activity a, but we use the same weights for notational simplicity.

[4] Note that the number of regions is smaller for youth employment than for total employment because of two missing values (one in France and one in Finland). There are several ways to deal with this problem, but we simply compare the Lorenz curves and associated Gini coefficients for the regions for which we have observations.

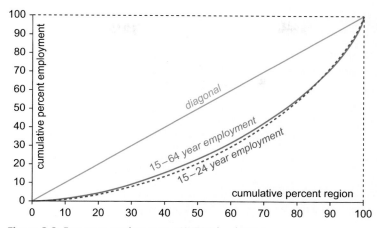

Figure 3.2 European employment at NUTS 2 level, 2017
Source: calculations based on http://ec.europa.eu/eurostat/web/regions/data/database; see main text for details.

below the total employment curve, while it is *above* this curve from about the 88th percentile onwards. This is where the Gini coefficient becomes useful in a spatial setting. Applying equation 3.1 shows that the Gini coefficient for youth employment is 0.4218, which is about 5.6 per cent higher than the Gini coefficient of total employment (equal to 0.3996). On the basis of the Gini coefficient we thus conclude that youth employment is more unequally distributed than total employment.

3.2.3 Generalized Entropy Measures

A disadvantage of the Gini coefficient is that it is not decomposable in its components. If we analyse, for example, global income inequality, we are combining within-country differences and between-country differences. We would therefore like to know the contribution of each component to global income inequality. In this section we briefly discuss the class of Generalized Entropy measures which is decomposable in its components. This class of measures is derived from information theory and defined for all real values α. The essence of the approach is to evaluate the relative deviation of economic activity a in some region i from the average activity $\bar{y}_a$ for all regions (so the ratio $y_{i,a} / \bar{y}_a$) summed over all regions and normalized. The class of measures arises because the relative deviation is then raised to the power α, leading to different evaluations of penalty; see Figure 3.3 for some examples. The figure illustrates that as α rises the influence of large observations rises. The definition for Generalized Entropy $GenEnt_a(\alpha)$ of activity a with parameter α is provided in equation 3.2, where the second equality holds if all weights are equal and the third equality arises from $s_{i,a} = y_{i,a} / R\bar{y}_a$.[5]

---

[5] We use the mnemonic GenEnt rather than GE to avoid confusion with the Ellison-Glaeser index, which we refer to as ElGla rather than EG for the same reason; see section 3.3.2.

Table 3.1 Three special cases of Generalized Entropy

Special case	Name or remark	Formula (for $w_i = 1/R$)
$\alpha = 0$	Mean Log Deviation or Theil L	$\frac{1}{R}\sum_{i=1}^{R} ln\left(\frac{\bar{y}_a}{y_{i,a}}\right) = -\frac{1}{R}\sum_{i=1}^{R} ln\left(Rs_{i,a}\right)$
$\alpha = 1$	Theil or Theil T	$\frac{1}{R}\sum_{i=1}^{R}\left(\frac{y_{i,a}}{\bar{y}_a}\right) ln\left(\frac{y_{i,a}}{\bar{y}_a}\right) = \sum_{i=1}^{R} s_{i,a} ln\left(Rs_{i,a}\right)$
$\alpha = 2$	Related to Herfind-ahl index H_a	$\frac{1}{2R}\left(\sum_{i=1}^{R}\left(\frac{y_{i,a}}{\bar{y}_a}\right)^2 - 1\right) = \frac{1}{2}\left(R\left(\sum_{i=1}^{R} s_{i,a}^2\right) - 1\right) = \frac{1}{2}\left(RH_a - 1\right)$

Note that for $\alpha = 0$ the ratio before the equal sign is $\bar{y}_a / y_{i,a}$ rather than $y_{i,a} / \bar{y}_a$.

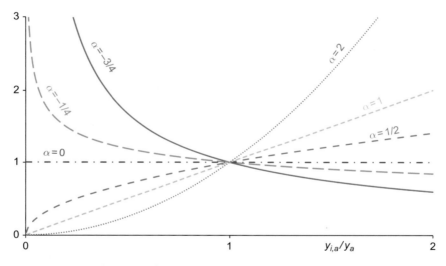

Figure 3.3 Relative deviation functions, related to Generalized Entropy

$$\textbf{\textit{GenEnt}}_a(\alpha) = \frac{1}{\alpha(\alpha-1)}\left[\sum_{i=1}^{R} w_i \left(\frac{y_{i,a}}{\bar{y}_a}\right)^{\alpha} - 1\right] = \frac{1}{\alpha(\alpha-1)}\left(\frac{1}{R}\sum_{i=1}^{R}\left(\frac{y_{i,a}}{\bar{y}_a}\right)^{\alpha} - 1\right)$$

$$= \frac{1}{\alpha(\alpha-1)}\left(\frac{1}{R}\sum_{i=1}^{R}\left(Rs_{i,a}\right)^{\alpha} - 1\right); \alpha \in \mathbb{R} \setminus \{0,1\} \qquad 3.2$$

Table 3.1 provides three important special cases of Generalized Entropy. The cases for $\alpha = 0$ and $\alpha = 1$ are limit cases that can be derived from the general equation 3.2 using L'Hôpital's Rule as α approaches these values; see Technical Note 3.1. The case $\alpha = 0$ is known as the *Mean Log Deviation* (MLD) or *Theil L inequality index* and ranges from zero to infinity. The case $\alpha = 1$ is known as the Theil or Theil T inequality index and ranges from zero to $ln(R)$. The case $\alpha = 2$ is derived by simply substituting this value in equation 3.2 and ranges from zero to $(R-1)/2$. It is a simple transformation of the Herfindahl index H_a used in micro-economics to measure market power: $H_a = \sum_{i=1}^{R} s_{i,a}^2$. The Herfindahl index ranges from a minimum of $1/R$ if economic activity is the same in all regions to one if economic activity is concentrated in one region. We will use this index in section 3.3.

The Generalized Entropy measures are equal to zero if economic activity is the same in all regions for all values of α, while a more unequal distribution implies a rise in the measure of inequality. The upper limit is infinity if $\alpha \leq 0$, while the upper limit is $\left(R^{\alpha-1}-1\right)/\left(\alpha(\alpha-1)\right)$ if $\alpha \in (0,1)\cup(1,\infty)$; see Cowell (2011). A disadvantage of the Theil L and Theil T indices ($\alpha = 0$ and $\alpha = 1$) is that they are not defined if for some regions $y_{i,a} = 0$ (because $\ln(0)$ is not defined). In many empirical situations, however, some regions do not engage in activity a, so zero observations occur in practice. The Theil L and Theil T indices are nonetheless popular because only these two values allow for a decomposition where the within weights sum to a constant (one) and are independent of the between part; see Foster et al. (2013). Suppose regional inequality is the topic of your research and the analysis refers to the European Union. The Theil L and Theil T indices can be decomposed into inequality between European countries (ignoring regional differences) and the within-country regional differences.

Brülhart and Traeger (2005) apply this decomposition using Theil T to analyse concentration patterns in Europe. The decomposition implies: $GenEnt(1) = GenEnt_{be}(1) + GenEnt_{wi}(1)$, where $GenEnt_{be}(1)$ is the between-country inequality, where the formula is applied to the country means. At the country level, the within-country computation applies the formula to the regions of the country as a separate entity. At the European level, $GenEnt_{wi}(1)$ is the within-country inequality using the share of activity a as weights for the calculation. Applying this decomposition Brülhart and Traeger (2005, p. 613) find, for example, that for textiles, clothing, and footwear the within-country concentration has steadily declined, but the between-country concentration relatively increased during the 1980s and 1990s.

Let's return to the example of the regional distribution of employment over NUTS 2 regions in the EU as introduced in section 3.2.2 when discussing the Gini coefficient. Recall that we concluded on the basis of the Gini coefficient that youth employment is more unequally distributed than total employment. Does this conclusion also hold if we base our inequality measure on Generalized Entropy? The answer is: it depends, as Figure 3.4 shows. To calculate Generalized Entropy, we first have to choose a value for α. Figure 3.4 therefore depicts the value of Generalized Entropy for total employment and youth employment for a range of α (from –0.5 to 2.5). We note that for values of α below 1.77 our conclusion from section 3.2.2 still holds and youth employment is more unequally distributed than total employment. For higher values of α, however, the opposite conclusion

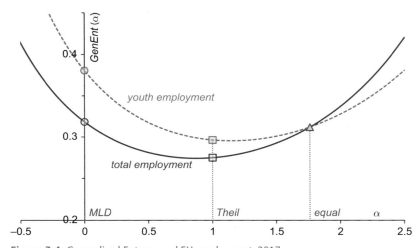

Figure 3.4 Generalized Entropy and EU employment, 2017
Source: see Figure 3.2 for data and main text for details; circles indicate MLD, squares Theil, and triangle equality.

holds. Why? Recall that higher values of α emphasize the influence of large observations (see Figure 3.3), while the Lorenz curve for total employment is below that of youth employment at the upper end of the distribution (see Figure 3.2). Sufficiently large values of α thus emphasize this part of the Lorenz curve and overturn the previously reached conclusion.

Figure 3.4 also shows that the Generalized Entropy formula is well-behaved as it is continuous at the points $\alpha = 0$ and $\alpha = 1$. The disadvantage mentioned above that Theil L and Theil T cannot be computed if some shares are zero is therefore not actually an issue because we can simply take the limit as α approaches either zero or one. Also note that we now have a new problem as two researchers using the same data and methodology can arrive at different conclusions simply because they disagree on the value of α on which their conclusion is based. In the illustration discussed here, however, youth employment is more unequally distributed than total employment for all values of α in the popular range from zero to one, such that most researchers would come to this conclusion. If the switch occurred for a value of α in between zero and one the disagreement would be more hotly debated.

3.3   Economic Concentration Measures

A disadvantage of the inequality measures discussed in section 3.2 when they are applied to measure spatial inequality or spikiness is that these measures have not been designed for this purpose. Indeed, the spatial dimension itself, indicating *where* certain activities are located relative to other activities, is entirely absent from these measures. This section briefly discusses two measures that have been specifically designed for this purpose. To distinguish these from the inequality measures in section 3.2 we label them *economic concentration measures*. We start in section 3.3.1 by listing some desirable properties of concentration measures. We then analyse two key examples: the Ellison-Glaeser index in section 3.3.2 and the Duranton-Overman index in section 3.3.3.

3.3.1 Desirable Properties of Concentration Measures

Based on Combes and Overman (2004) we first list five desirable properties of concentration measures before briefly discussing each property in turn. Economic concentration measures should be:

1. Comparable across sectors
2. Comparable across spatial units
3. Unbiased regarding spatial classification
4. Unbiased regarding sector classification
5. Provide an indication of significance.

Point 1: comparable across sectors. Some sectors, by their very nature, consist of only a limited number of firms while others consists of hundreds of firms. Ellison and Glaeser (1997), for example, note that the US vacuum cleaner industry consists of four dominant firms together representing 75 per cent of total employment. Even if these four dominant firms were not concentrated in any meaningful way, one would find that only four US states together house 75 per cent of all employment in the industry. It would be misleading to conclude that the vacuum cleaner industry is spatially concentrated. Measures should therefore deal with differences between sectors: some consist of many firms, while others only consist of a few firms.

Point 2: comparable across spatial units. Concentration measures should be comparable across different spatial units, such as countries, regions, states, or provinces. Suppose one is interested in comparing the concentration of sectors across US states. This implies that one compares concentration in Rhode Island (very small) to California (very big). In geographical terms California is more than 150 times bigger and includes Silicon Valley, Los Angeles, and San Diego (very dense places). In terms of population, on the other hand, Rhode Island is one of the smallest states (about 1 million people in 2018) but with almost the highest population density (1,006 people per square mile, only second to New Jersey). Comparisons like these can result in artificial differences only because the scale is not comparable.

Point 3: unbiased regarding spatial classification. Standard statistical sources use administrative definitions of spatial units. It is possible that a border between two neighbouring units cuts through a cluster of economic activity that is highly connected. However, many indices treat these spatial units as being independent and it does not matter where these units are placed on the map; as neighbours or far away. This problem is known in the literature as the Modifiable Areal Unit Problem (MAUP). Box 3.1 on 'gerrymandering' briefly analyses why the MAUP is important.

BOX 3.1 Gerrymandering: Why the Modifiable Areal Unit Problem (MAUP) is Important

To illustrate the importance of administrative borders (MAUP) it is instructive to look at the US House of Representatives.

The US congress consists of the House of Representatives (the House) and the Senate. These two legislative bodies have a complicated working relationship, but that is of no concern here. Each State has two senators, but the number of representatives for the House reflects the size of each state; larger States are represented by a larger number of representatives. Each State is subdivided into (single representative) congressional districts that can vote for a representative. The US constitution sets a minimum of thirty thousand inhabitants for a district but no maximum. Given its size California sends 53 representatives to Washington, whereas Wyoming only sends one (each State has at least one representative). Currently there are 435 representatives in the House.

Members of the House stand for election every two years. This implies that members are constantly running for office and trying to raise funds. This makes the electoral process important, and especially the definition of congressional districts because each district chooses a representative in a winner-takes-all system. After each national census (once every ten years) the boundaries of the districts are redrawn to cope with changing populations: some States grow, others shrink. The party that has a majority in a particular State can redraw the district boundaries in such a way that it maximizes the probability of winning the most representatives of the State for itself. This process is called *gerrymandering*, after the Massachusetts Governor Elbridge Gerry. In 1812 he defined odd-shaped districts in order to maximize votes for his party. Manipulating voting outcomes can be done by 'packing' – that is, concentrating the opposition into only a few districts – or 'cracking' – that is, distributing or diluting opponents in as many districts as is optimal in order to maximize the number of representatives for the majority party.

Figure 3.5 provides an example. The left panel represents the State. The squares and circles represent voters. There are 16 circle-voters and 15 square-voters. In this example the State has to vote for 5 representatives (5 districts). By cleverly

BOX 3.1 (cont.)

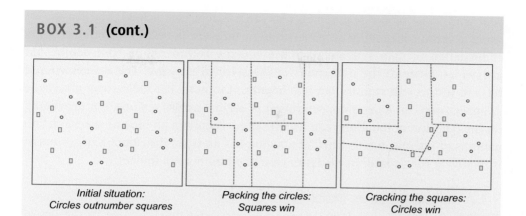

Initial situation:
Circles outnumber squares

Packing the circles:
Squares win

Cracking the squares:
Circles win

Figure 3.5 Gerrymandering

allocating voters to 5 districts of (almost) similar sizes one can manipulate the outcome. In the example, packing results in 3 out of 5 representatives for the squares; cracking results in 3 out of 5 representatives for the circles.

The example relates to voting, but one can easily imagine that the circles and squares represent firms within a 'square' sector or a 'circle' sector. One could be misled into thinking that firms in the square sector dominate the State economy if administrative boundaries for the districts are drawn as in the middle panel.

Point 4: unbiased regarding sector classification. Comparable to the MAUP problem mentioned above, is the problem that one has to classify firms into industries or sectors. This classification can put highly connected firms that have strong mutual connections into different industries or sectors, which could obscure the close ties that possibly exist between firms.

Point 5: provide an indication of significance. All measures result in a number. But how can these numbers be interpreted? In order to conclude that a number is large or small it has to be compared to a benchmark. To put it differently: one wants to know if the observed outcome is significantly different from another outcome or a random outcome.

Neither of the inequality measures (Gini coefficient and Generalized Entropy) that were discussed in section 3.2 satisfy properties 1–4. Only property 5 on significance holds, either by theoretical modelling or by using bootstrap methods.[6] Before the reader gets too excited, the concentration measures discussed below also do not satisfy all properties (the requirements of which have to be specified in more detail in order to become operational in the first place). They do, however,

---

[6] https://www.statsdirect.com/help/nonparametric_methods/gini.htm

deal with some of the requirements to some extent (see below). The reason for using a certain inequality or concentration measure is usually determined by a combination of data availability and pragmatic considerations, but one should always be aware of the limitations of the selected measure. The indices we use refer to sectors and regions, but it is important to note that indices can always be swapped; one can look at concentration of sectors across regions, but depending on the question at hand one can use the same equations to look at specialization patterns of regions, that is whether a region has an equal distribution of sectors or is relatively specialized. In the latter case one has to swap indices.

3.3.2   Ellison–Glaeser Index

The Ellison and Glaeser (1997) index addresses the first problem in the list of section 3.3.1, comparability across sectors, via an approach which they call the *dartboard* approach. The advantage of this measure is that it corrects for sector differences. Some activities are highly specialized (the activity consists of a limited number of firms), while others consist of many firms. If an activity consists, for example, of two firms then at most two regions account for all activity, which could create the illusion of concentration; one should thus not confuse specialization with concentration; see Brakman, Garretsen, and van Marrewijk (2009, ch. 5).[7]

The Ellison-Glaeser index $ElGla_a$ for activity a is based on comparing the share $s_{i,a}$ of activity a in region i with a benchmark share of activities $\bar{s}_i$ in that region, for example based on the distribution over the regions of total manufacturing or total employment. A simple concentration measure C_a for activity a is then the sum of squared deviations (as in econometrics): $C_a = \sum_{i=1}^{R} \left(s_{i,a} - \bar{s}_i \right)^2$. Ellison and Glaeser (1997) show that to turn this simple measure into a usable economic concentration index we have to normalize it both with the distribution of the benchmark activity over regions and with the distribution of plant size locations for activity a. In both cases the Herfindahl index is used.

We start with the distribution of plant size locations for activity a. If we have N firm locations in activity a, indexed by j, and the size of each location is measured by shares $z_{j,a}$ (for example based on sales or employment) such that $\sum_{j=1}^{N} z_{j,a} = 1$ and $z_{j,a} > 0$, then the Herfindahl concentration index H_a for activity a is defined as: $H_a = \sum_{j=1}^{N} z_{j,a}^2$; see section 3.2.3. This index ranges from a minimum of $1/N$ if all locations are of equal size (where N is the number of firm locations) to a

---

[7] A closely related measure is developed by Maurel and Sedillot (1999). The expression $\sum_{i=1}^{R}(s_{i,a} - \bar{s}_i)^2$ is also related to the Isard-Krugman index $\frac{1}{2}\sum_{i=1}^{R} | s_{i,a} - \bar{s}_i |$, where instead of squaring the term in brackets the absolute value of the difference is used such that positive values are not compensated by negative values as both deviations are indicative of the uneven spatial distribution of activity.

maximum of one (which is the limit if the size of one location approaches one). Similarly, we can define the Herfindahl benchmark concentration index $\bar{H}$ over the regions as: $\bar{H} = \sum_{i=1}^{R} \bar{s}_i^2$. Note that this index ranges from a minimum of $1/R$ to one, where the index is now over regions rather than the number of firm locations. The Ellison-Glaeser index $ElGla_a$ for activity a is defined in equation 3.3 and evaluated in more detail below.

$$ElGla_a = \frac{C_a - (1 - \bar{H}) H_a}{(1 - \bar{H})(1 - H_a)} = \frac{\left(\sum_{i=1}^{R} (s_{i,a} - \bar{s}_i)^2\right) - \left(1 - \sum_{i=1}^{R} \bar{s}_i^2\right)\left(\sum_{j=1}^{N} z_{j,a}^2\right)}{\left(1 - \sum_{i=1}^{R} \bar{s}_i^2\right)\left(1 - \sum_{j=1}^{N} z_{j,a}^2\right)} \qquad 3.3$$

Suppose that there is no special reason why firms in activity a would agglomerate in certain regions. In this case, on average, the location of firms in activity a should resemble that of the overall distribution of activity; implying that $\sum_{i=1}^{R} (s_{i,a} - \bar{s}_i)^2$ is close to zero (the minimum value is zero). And vice versa if the distribution is uneven. So, this term is an indication for the unevenness of the spatial distribution of firms in activity a over the regions.

The second term in the numerator of equation 3.3 is $(1 - \bar{H}) H_a = (1 - \sum_{i=1}^{R} \bar{s}_i^2)$ $\left(\sum_{j=1}^{N} z_{j,a}^2\right)$. This expression is proportional to the Herfindahl index H_a of activity a in various regions and is subtracted from the unevenness indicator $\sum_{i=1}^{R} (s_{i,a} - \bar{s}_i)^2$. Suppose that activity a consists of only four equal sized firms, then H_a is relatively large and the subtracted term represents a large correction factor. On the other hand, if an activity a consists of many firms then H_a tends to be small and the correction factor is thus relatively small as well.

This correction related to H_a makes perfect sense. The activity with only four firms would produce high values for $\sum_{i=1}^{R} (s_{i,a} - \bar{s}_i)^2$ if you find a region with a single firm that already captures 25 per cent of all activity, but this is not concentration of activity or a sign of agglomeration tendencies for this activity. It could simply be a random outcome. In order to prevent a researcher from concluding that this activity is agglomerated the correction factor has to be relatively large. For the other activity, say with 100 firms of equal size, the correction should be small, because in this case finding a region with 25 per cent of all activity is indeed indicative of concentration as in this example 25 per cent of the activity corresponds to 25 of the 100 firms.

The activity Herfindahl index H_a is multiplied by $(1 - \bar{H}) = (1 - \sum_{i=1}^{R} \bar{s}_i^2)$. Why? It is possible that the economy we are describing is characterized by natural advantages of certain regions. For example, it may be an island with mountains in the middle such that only the coastal areas are easily occupied. If this is the case $(1 - \sum_{i=1}^{R} \bar{s}_i^2)$ becomes small and H_a gets a smaller weight. This indicates that some concentration is to be expected simply because of natural advantages of certain areas in the economy and the correction can be smaller. The outcome in this island economy is expected to be different from a pure dartboard approach with no natural advantages driving location choices. The opposite is the case if the economy is characterized by an even distribution of activity over all possible regions: in this case $\left(1 - \sum_{i=1}^{R} \bar{s}_i^2\right)$ rises (the maximum value is one).[8]

The corrections in the numerator are necessary to avoid the erroneous conclusion that an activity is concentrated when in fact it is not. The denominator $\left(1 - \bar{H}\right)\left(1 - H_a\right) = \left(1 - \sum_{i=1}^{R} \bar{s}_i^2\right)\left(1 - \sum_{j=1}^{N} z_{j,a}^2\right)$ ensures that the Ellison-Glaeser measure is normalized. The expected value of the Ellison-Glaeser index is zero if the sector distribution mimics that of the benchmark activity. The step forward is that the measure explicitly corrects for the distributional characteristics of the activity relative to a proper benchmark.

3.3.3 Duranton–Overman Density

The Ellison-Glaeser index analysed in section 3.3.2 controls for differences across sectors relative to a benchmark distribution by incorporating the number of firms active in a sector. This requires, of course, additional information. Duranton and Overman (2005, 2008) incorporate more desirable properties from the list of five given in section 3.3.1, again at the cost of requiring additional information. They do not only deal with differences across sectors, but also take care of the issue of comparability across different spatial scales by looking at the location of individual firms.

The main reason that the Duranton-Overman index is unbiased for changes in spatial scales is that it circumvents the use of exogenous (administrative) spatial units altogether. Suppose that a sector is concentrated at a specific location but that an administrative spatial boundary cuts through this agglomeration. All measures discussed so far treat neighbouring spatial units in exactly the same way as more distant spatial units. The fact that an agglomeration is cut by an artificial border becomes blurred. Also, dividing an agglomeration over more spatial units affects the results. A good measure should be able to deal with this issue.

How do Duranton and Overman solve this problem? By making individual *firm* location, rather than the city, region, or country in which this firm is located, the centre of analysis. The approach calculates the bilateral (Euclidian) distance d_{ij} between all pairs of firms. The procedure starts with firm 1 and calculates the distance of this firm to all other firms. Counting the number of firms at a given distance gives the frequency of firms at that distance. The result could be, for

---

[8] The term $\left(1 - \sum_{i=1}^{R} \bar{s}_i^2\right)$ is related to the probability of finding activity in a certain region if firms were randomly distributed over a map that only shows possible locations (see Ellison and Glaeser, 1997, for details).

example, that 30 firms are at a distance of 10 km, 20 at a distance of 13 km, and so on. If there are N firms, then we make $N-1$ bilateral comparisons in the first step, namely of firm 1 relative to the other $N-1$ firms.[9] In the second step, we move to firm 2 and repeat the procedure, again making $N-1$ bilateral comparisons, this time relative to firm 2. The result is another table of frequencies of the number of firms at all distances. Continuing this way, we get a complete table of distances for all possible firm pairs. This is plotted on a graph, with the densities on the vertical axis (rather than frequencies) and on the horizontal axis the distance d between firms. Equation 3.4 provides the definition of the Duranton-Overman density $DurOv_a(d)$ at distance d for activity a. It is based on kernel density estimates using kernel k and bandwidth h; see Box 3.2 for some technical details.

$$DurOv_a(d) = \frac{1}{N(N-1)}\frac{1}{h}\sum_{i=1}^{N-1}\sum_{j=i+1}^{N}k\left(\frac{d-d_{ij}}{h}\right)$$

3.4

To better understand what is happening, the visualization in Figure 3.6 is useful. The figure shows the location of firms in various sectors across China (see for data sources and further details: Brakman, Garretsen, and Zhao, 2017). The dots represent firms in specific sectors and all firms in manufacturing. Panels a–c of Figure 3.6 show three so-called two-digit sectors: Communication, electronic and computer producing (sector 40; electronics), Beverage manufacturing (sector 15; beverages), and Chemical raw materials and chemical products (sector 26; chemicals). The distribution of total manufacturing is depicted in panel d. A quick look at panels a–c in comparison to panel d in Figure 3.6 indicates that firms in sector 40 (electronics) appear to be geographically concentrated, those in sector 15 (beverages) dispersed, and those in sector 26 (chemicals) have a similar pattern to manufacturing as a whole. Clearly, firms in the electronics sector 40 concentrate in three dense clusters: one at the Yangtze river delta (around Shanghai), one at the Pearl river delta (around Hong Kong) and one in the Beijing–Tianjin–Hebei area. The Duranton-Overman procedure should reflect these differences.

The solid lines in the panels of Figure 3.7 depict the Duranton-Overman densities for electronics (panel a), beverages (panel b), and chemicals (panel c) up to a maximum distance of 900 km. The dotted lines in the panels indicate the relevant confidence intervals of the benchmark distribution (see below). It is clear from panel a that there is a high peak in the density of electronic firms around 80 kilometres. In this range electronic firms are highly concentrated (above the

---

[9] The number of firms depends, of course, on the activity a under consideration, but we ignore this in the main text to avoid the cumbersome notation N_a.

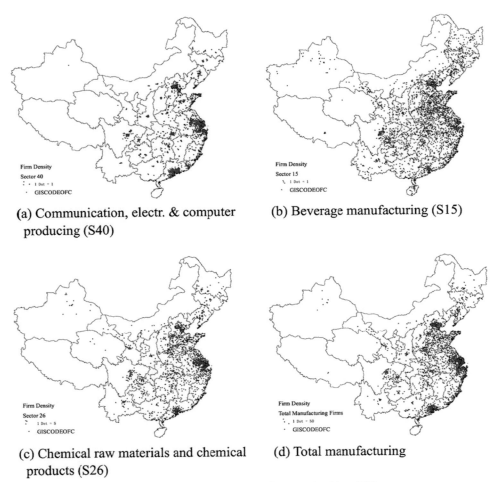

(a) Communication, electr. & computer producing (S40)

(b) Beverage manufacturing (S15)

(c) Chemical raw materials and chemical products (S26)

(d) Total manufacturing

Figure 3.6 The spatial distribution of sectors and manufacturing in China, 2002
Source: Brakman et al. (2017).

benchmark). In contrast, in the range from 200 to 900 kilometre, electronics firms are dispersed (below the benchmark).[10]

The dashed lines in Figure 3.7 show confidence intervals. These tell us whether a particular distribution differs from a random distribution; it is the benchmark or counterfactual. This counterfactual is a hypothetical sector for which firms are randomly reallocated to all possible sites. Assume there are N_m manufacturing firms that define N_m possible sites. Activity a has $N < N_m$ firms. Now, randomly

---

[10] Note that the three electronics clusters (around Hong Kong, Shanghai, and Beijing) are far apart (more than 900 km). If the clusters had been closer to each other this would be visible as multiple peaks in panel a of Figure 3.7. Extending the horizontal axis to 1,100 km would reveal such a second peak.

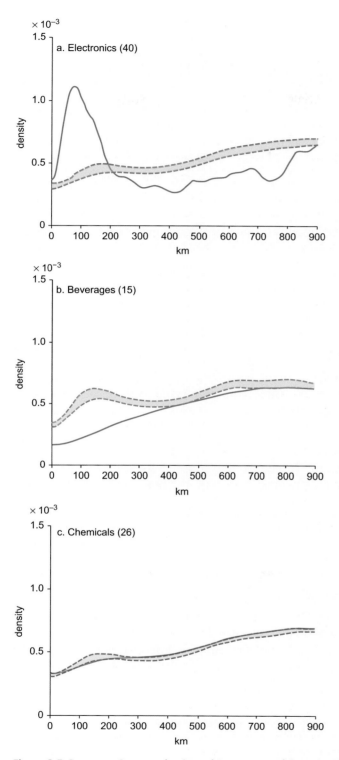

Figure 3.7 Duranton–Overman density and 5 per cent confidence bands for sectors 40, 15, and 26
Source: based on Brakman et al. (2017) using normal kernel; solid line is Duranton–Overman density for respective sector; dotted lines represent the 5 per cent confidence intervals; see main text for details.

BOX 3.2 Duranton–Overman Densities and Kernel Estimates

The solid lines in Figure 3.7 show the densities of firms at various distances. What do we mean by distance and how do we calculate the corresponding densities? For each activity a, with N firms, there are $N(N-1)/2$ bilateral distances between firms. But calculating distances is not as obvious as it sounds. Is it, for example, best to use Euclidean distances (*as the crow flies* distance), or to use travel-time-weighted distances in order to deal with the economically relevant distance? An alternative is to use intervals of distances and count the number of firms that fall within the interval (or bin) of 0 to 5 km, 5 to 10 km, and so on. Using intervals is done frequently and results in histograms. A well-known disadvantage of histograms is that firms with a distance that falls outside the bandwidth of a bin are ignored (they receive a weight of zero), while firms within the bandwidth of a bin receive a constant weight (all are equally important).[11] It seems better to use more subtle ways of weighing firms at various distances.

A solution to the histogram problem is to use so-called kernel smoothing procedures, which give a weight to all the distances of firms. The *kernel* function k is a non-negative function that integrates to one (based, for example, on a uniform, triangular, or normal distribution) used for smoothing; see DiNardo and Tobias (2001) for a detailed discussion of kernel estimates. The bandwidth $h > 0$ is a smoothing parameter that will ideally be chosen to be as small as the data will allow. The choice of the bandwidth involves a trade-off between the bias of the estimator and its variance.[12] Although the procedure seems daunting at first sight, most econometric software packages have kernel estimates built in.

---

select N sites from all possible sites N_m. Do this, for example, 1,000 times. This results in 1,000 density estimates for each distance as defined in equation 3.4. Using these estimates we construct a 90 per cent confidence interval that contains 90 per cent of all values at a particular distance d with the upper bound at the 95th percentile and the lower bound at the 5th percentile. If a density exceeds the upper boundary there is *local* concentration at that distance. If the density is smaller than

---

[11] The bandwidth of a bin is the width of a bin divided by two; it tells you how far to look to the right or the left from the middle of the bin.
[12] If there are p data points, a rule of thumb for the bandwidth h is $(4/3p)^{1/5}\hat{\sigma}$, where $\hat{\sigma}$ is the standard deviation of the sample.

the lower bound there is *local* dispersion at that distance.[13] In panel *a* of Figure 3.7 the peak at 80 km in the electronics sector is clearly above the 95th percentile upper bound, indicating concentration at that distance. Note that this procedure corrects for differences across sectors (point 1 of section 3.3.1).

Turning attention now to panels *b* and *c* of Figure 3.7 which depict the beverages and chemicals sectors in China, respectively, we note that the beverages sector is mostly below the benchmark distribution and never above (it is therefore a dispersed sector), while the distribution for the chemical sector basically coincides with the benchmark distribution (it is neither concentrated nor dispersed). It is reassuring to note that the maps shown in Figure 3.6 are translated into the densities of Figure 3.7 as we expected.

There are many advantages of the Duranton-Overman approach. By using the actual number of firms a correction for sector differences as in the Ellison-Glaeser index is not necessary. Administrative boundaries are not used, so comparing over different spatial scales does not bias the results.[14] What remains is the bias when different sector classifications are used (point 4 of section 3.3.1). On the downside, the method requires detailed information on firm locations. The rapid growth, however, of micro-firm data availability facilitates the use of the Duranton-Overman approach in empirical work.

3.4 An Experiment

Now that we have discussed two inequality and two concentration measures in some detail in sections 3.2 and 3.3 respectively, we will illustrate how they can be used by means of an experiment with 'made up' data.

---

[13] Duranton and Overman (2005) also define *global* concentration and dispersion. Global concentration is the upper limit for which 95 per cent of all draws (over the whole range of distances) is below that upper bound, and vice versa for the lower bound. A sector is defined to be globally concentrated if its density hits the upper limit at least once (over the whole range of distances), and similarly for dispersion (with the added condition that the upper limit is never touched). In principle there are many ways to construct confidence bands such that, say, 5 per cent is globally above or below a band. Duranton and Overman (2005) use the *local* confidence bands to search for a *global* band. The procedure is as follows. Start by constructing an initial global band by connecting all local 1 per cent confidence intervals (over all distances) and draw the band. Next, count how many simulations go beyond this band. If this is more than 5 per cent we take something smaller (stricter) for the local confidence interval, for instance 0.5 per cent, and repeat the procedure until a confidence interval is found that corresponds to 5 per cent of deviations over the entire set of distances that we consider. This is the global 5 per cent confidence interval.
[14] Actually, different spatial scales do not enter the analysis at all.

To do so, we need several activity sectors, at least two levels of aggregation, and real geography. We use three sectors, labelled I, II, and III, five countries, labelled A, B, C, D, and E, and 15 regions (three per country), labelled A_1, A_2, A_3, B_1, B_2, B_3, and so on. The map we use, showing all countries and all regions, is a square land area of length 10 and width 6. In the graphs, we depict the length coordinate on the horizontal axis and the width coordinate on the vertical axis. So these coordinates tell us where, in the square, a firm is located. We then also know in which country and region that firm is located; see below for the relationship with countries and regions.

Our hypothetical economy consists of 20 firms in each sector I, II, and III. How can we distribute firms over the map? We will distribute the firms over the map by randomly drawing coordinates from a statistical distribution. We do have many options to do so. We can draw the horizontal and vertical coordinates from the Normal distribution, the Poisson distribution or an alternative distribution. In this way we can introduce location differences between firms in a sector.

For sector I we use the uniform distribution for both the horizontal and vertical coordinates and we draw 20 horizontal and vertical coordinates from the uniform distribution (for each firm we now know its location). This is illustrated for the horizontal coordinate by the dashed line in Figure 3.8. The procedure for the vertical coordinate is similar (but not drawn in the figure). All outcomes for a horizontal coordinate from 0 to 10 are thus equally likely and the average horizontal coordinate is 5, while the average vertical coordinate is 3. For our geography, sector I is therefore randomly distributed in the sense that there is no location preference for this sector: it does not matter where they are located. In contrast,

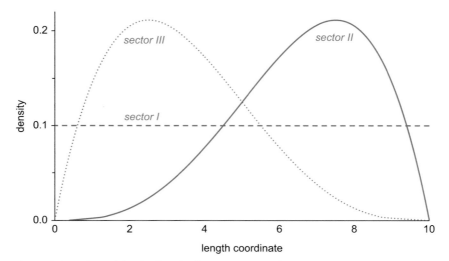

Figure 3.8 Horizontal density function for sectors I, II, and III

firms in sectors II and III have a geographical preference, perhaps based on factor abundance at certain locations or the presence of a location feature (that we do not include in the map, a nearby river for example). This is also illustrated in Figure 3.8, where a high value in the horizontal direction is more likely for sector II and a low value is more likely for sector III.[15] We assume the opposite to hold for the vertical coordinate. As a consequence, the expected values of the coordinates for sector II are $\left(\frac{20}{3},2\right)$ and for sector III are $\left(\frac{10}{3},4\right)$, such that the firms in these sectors are clustered around these points. For simplicity, we assume that the size of economic activity for each firm is the same and identical for the three sectors.[16]

Figure 3.9 illustrates the country/regional distribution in panel a and an example firm distribution in panel b. All regions are equal in size and thus so are the countries. This depiction of geography is of course a bit special, but is of no concern here. The example firm distribution in panel b shows that sector I (the blue circles) is randomly distributed, while sector II (the red squares) is clustered to the southeast and sector III (the green rotated squares) is clustered to the northwest. These distributions are consistent with the statistical distributions from which we draw firms for each sector.

We proceed as follows. First, after we randomly draw 20 firm locations for each sector based on their respective density functions, we calculate some inequality and concentration measures associated with this firm distribution. Second, we repeat this process 1,000 times. Third, we report summary statistics and distributions for the Gini coefficient, Generalized Entropy, and Ellison-Glaeser index. Fourth, we discuss Duranton-Overman densities.

Table 3.2 reports summary statistics for the outcomes of our experiment and Figure 3.10 shows the associated cumulative distributions. Since sector III is the mirror image of sector II we only show results for sectors I and II. Also note that we restrict attention to the Generalized Entropy index for $\alpha = 0.5$ for our discussion.[17] We make five main points.

First, we note that the average and median Gini index for sector II is higher than for sector I at the country and regional level, indicating that sector II

---

[15] More precisely, the beta distribution $\beta(4, 2)$ is scaled from 0 to 10 in the horizontal direction for sector II and from 0 to 6 in the vertical direction for sector III, whereas $\beta(2, 4)$ is scaled from 0 to 10 in the horizontal direction for sector III and from 0 to 6 in the vertical direction for sector II.

[16] The example can be made more complicated in many ways. We can analyse different numbers of firms in different sectors, different size regions, different size countries, different size firms at different locations varied by sector, and so on. Our approach illustrates the main issues as simple as possible.

[17] This is in between the Mean Log Deviation (MLD) and Theil index values for alpha. Note that MLD and Theil are usually not defined since sector shares in regions and countries are frequently equal to zero.

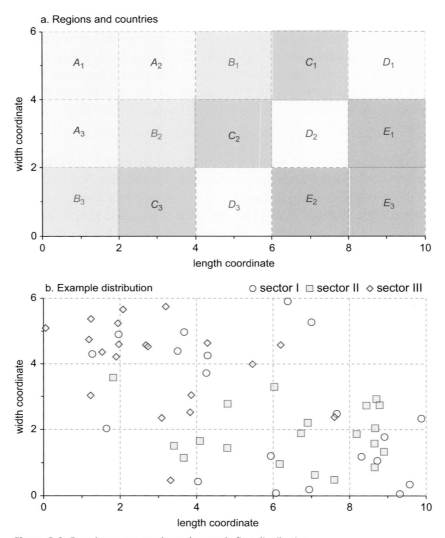

Figure 3.9 Experiment geography and example firm distribution

is more unequally distributed than sector I, as expected on the basis of our experiment.

Second, we note that the Gini index at the regional level is higher than at the country level for the same sector since we ignore geographical variation within the country. Both points are clearly illustrated in panel *a* of Figure 3.10. As a consequence, we cannot compare Gini coefficient results at different levels of geographical aggregation.

Third, we note that the two points above (higher for sector II and higher at the regional level) also hold for the Generalized Entropy measure (although the scale is different). This is clear by comparing panel *b* with panel *a* in Figure 3.10.

Table 3.2 Summary statistics for Gini, Generalized Entropy, and Ellison–Glaeser

	mean	median	minimum	maximum	st dev
a. Regions					
Sector I					
Gini	0.439	0.440	0.167	0.647	0.076
GenEnt (0.5)	0.646	0.655	0.058	1.338	0.193
ElGla	-0.008	-0.010	-0.043	0.072	0.016
Sector II					
Gini	0.648	0.653	0.447	0.813	0.057
GenEnt (0.5)	1.279	1.266	0.666	1.908	0.203
ElGla	0.047	0.045	-0.017	0.151	0.026
b. Countries					
Sector I					
Gini	0.226	0.220	0.000	0.520	0.079
GenEnt (0.5)	0.125	0.096	0.000	0.686	0.113
ElGla	-0.016	-0.021	-0.052	0.120	0.025
Sector II					
Gini	0.493	0.500	0.240	0.740	0.074
GenEnt (0.5)	0.755	0.703	0.139	1.556	0.233
ElGla	0.165	0.157	0.012	0.538	0.067

Source: based on 1,000 simulations, see main text for details; st dev = standard deviation; *GenEnt* (0.5) = Generalized Entropy with $\alpha = 0.5$; *ElGla* = Ellison-Glaeser index.

Fourth, we note that the sectoral correction in the Ellison-Glaeser index does not eliminate the geographical aggregation problem. For a given level of aggregation sector II has a higher index than sector I, as it should because it is more concentrated. The measure is, however, again not comparable between countries and regions for sector II: see panel c of Figure 3.10.

Fifth, we note that the benchmark distribution is important for determining concentration, not geographical randomness. Our experiment is constructed such that sector I is geographically randomly distributed. On the basis of this, one might expect the average value of the Ellison-Glaeser index for sector I to be equal to zero, while in fact it is negative for both countries and regions. This is true because the benchmark distribution of total economic activity is lumpy (concentrated in the southeast for sector II and in the northwest for sector III). Compared to this benchmark sector I is more dispersed, hence the negative average value.

We conclude our experiment with a discussion of Duranton-Overman density as illustrated in Figure 3.11. For sectors I and II the figure is based on a particular

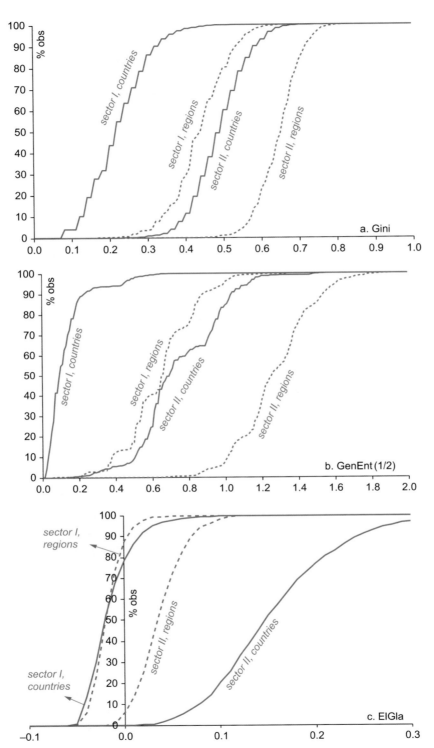

Figure 3.10 Cumulative distribution of Gini, Generalized Entropy, and Ellison–Glaeser
Source: based on 1,000 simulations, see main text for details; step size 0.01; horizontal scales are different.

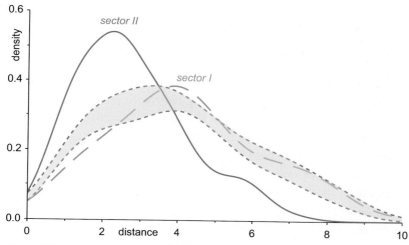

Figure 3.11 Duranton–Overman density
Source: see main text for details; shaded area between dashed lines is 5–95 per cent confidence interval.

outcome of our experiment, while the shaded confidence interval is based on 1,000 simulations as explained in section 3.3.3. It is important to note that in contrast to all previous measures the Duranton-Overman density is *not* an index but a distance-based (density) function, which can be considered a disadvantage. It is also more difficult to calculate (in particular the confidence interval) and requires more information (as already pointed out in section 3.3.3). An evaluation of concentration and dispersion is then based on comparing the density for a sector with the confidence interval. Sector II is clearly more concentrated for small distances (up to 3.45) as the sector density is high above the confidence interval. We see clustering of sector II activities relative to the benchmark at these distances, as expected on the basis of our experiment. For large distances (above 3.90) sector II density is below the benchmark. Sector I, in contrast, is more dispersed for small distances (up to 2.35) as it is below the confidence interval and mostly within the confidence interval from there on (except from 3.70 to 5.10 when it is slightly above). As noted above at point five, it is indicative of sector I dispersion relative to total economic activity.

3.5 Spatial Concentration and Productivity

Once it is established that economic activity is unevenly distributed across space – using inequality and concentration measures as described in the previous sections – the next questions are: *why?* and *so what?* The answers to these questions are obviously related because once we understand why economic activity is clustered for a certain sector, we also better understand the possible implications of clustering. Suppose, for example, that a sector is concentrated geographically to take advantage of natural resources intensively used in the production process, such as the fishing industry located in the vicinity of rich fishing grounds. If new fishermen are added to the location of the existing 'fishing cluster' they try to catch the same fish and thus raise competition for the rest of the cluster. As such they impose a negative externality on the existing cluster. Suppose, on the other hand, that a sector is concentrated geographically to take advantage of forward and backward linkages to nearby firms in the cluster. Backward linkages indicate access to local suppliers of intermediate inputs. Forward linkages indicate access to local firms demanding your outputs. In this case, if new firms enter the cluster they may strengthen the forward and backward linkages, which benefits the cluster as a whole. As such new entrants would now provide a positive externality to the existing cluster. Distinguishing between these possibilities is empirically complicated. We discuss this in more detail in Chapters 6 and 9, where we will encounter empirical examples that try to deal with this issue.

In Chapter 1 we provided an example of the relationship between urbanization and income at the country level. Here, we illustrate this relationship in Figure 3.12 at the city level for the USA. The observations in the figure are actually so-called Metropolitan Statistical Areas (MSAs), which are more or less coherent urban clusters of cities. The largest MSA (more than 24 million people) is labelled *New York* in Figure 3.12, but it actually is the MSA New York – Newark – White Plains, which stretches across parts of the US states New Jersey, New York, and Connecticut. The point of the graph is to illustrate that there is a positive relationship between the (population) size of a location and its income per capita level, both in logs. The dashed line in the graph is a regression line. It indicates that a 10 per cent increase

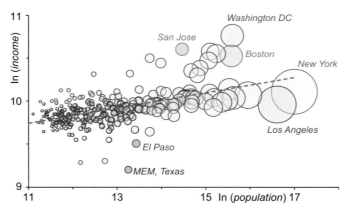

Figure 3.12 Metropolitan Statistical Areas and income per capita, USA, 2010
Source: created using US Census 2010 data; income per capita in USD; 276 metropolitan areas included (Puerto Rico MSAs are excluded); data for 2010; dashed line is a regression line; MEM = McAllen – Edinburg – Mission, Texas; bubbles proportional to population size.

in population leads, on average, to about 9 per cent higher income per capita. The regression explains about 29 per cent of the variance of log income per capita. Some observations, such as Washington DC, San Jose, and Boston, have higher income per capita levels than expected based on the regression. Other observations, such as El Paso and McAllen – Edinburg – Mission (both in Texas), have lower income per capita levels than expected based on the regression.

$$ln\left(w_{it}\right) = \gamma ln\left(pop_{it}\right) + \eta c_{it} + \varepsilon_{it} \qquad\qquad 3.5$$

Figure 3.12 suggests that there is a relationship between concentration of economic activity and income per capita. This can be summarized in a regression like equation 3.5, where i denotes a location (an MSA in the graph). The dependent variable is $ln\left(w_{it}\right)$, the log of wage or income per capita at location i at time t. The explanatory variables are $ln\left(pop_{it}\right)$, which is the log of population size as a measure of urban scale, and a series of control variables $c_{i,t}$. Finally, $\varepsilon_{i,t}$ is an error term and a time index t is added since one may be interested in this relationship over time and not only in a cross-section analysis. The coefficient of interest is γ as it summarizes the relationship between population size and income per capita. Empirical estimates usually find a significant positive value, such as the 0.09 reported above for Figure 3.12; see Box 3.3 for a short digression as to what a 'significant' estimate implies.

BOX 3.3 The Use of p-Values

In empirical analyses it is important to give an indication of which effects are important and which are not when one is interested in the effect of some variable on a phenomenon of interest. In statistical terminology one is interested in what effects are *significant*. This raises all sorts of issues that are routinely covered in textbooks on econometrics. One issue stands out that recently has received a lot of attention: the use of p-values to indicate significance of variables. Before going into some of these problems we have to explain the concept of p-values.

In most empirical research we like to know if something has an effect on something else: does a regional subsidy increase regional growth, and so on. If some regions that receive a subsidy grow, it is important to know if the 'subsidy' indeed has a systematic effect and is not just a fluke of nature. The standard method is the so-called null-hypothesis test. The *null-hypothesis* is the hypothesis that the subsidy treatment does *not* have an effect. Simply observing that subsidies have a positive growth effect in some regions is not enough, the findings should be inconsistent with the null-hypothesis. The p-value gives information on how likely a finding is if the null-hypothesis is valid.

BOX 3.3 (cont.)

A clinical trial example from medicine can explain what the empirical researcher is after when using p-values. Suppose there are 100 sick patients each with a 40 per cent chance of dying and a 60 per cent chance of surviving after five years; 50 patients receive a drug, and 50 a placebo. After five years the survival rates between these two groups are analysed and in the drug-receiving group no one has died. What does this tell us? Under the null-hypothesis that the drug is *not* effective the probability of finding such a result equals $0.6 \times 0.6 \ldots .50$ *times* $.. \times 0.6 = 0.6^{50} \approx 0$. To put it differently, this probability is very small. The null-hypothesis is statistically rejected, and the drug works like a miracle. This is the reason that in empirical analyses low p-values are equivalent with *significance*. A common value to decide whether the effect is significant is $p < 0.05$.

What are the problems that have recently been put forward when using p-values like in our medicine example above?

- To start with, the term significance is ambiguous. In normal English parlance, significant means important. In statistical analyses a significant effect does not have to be important, it only says that *statistically* the effect is present in the data. If a study reports that the influence of higher levels of natural radiation significantly increases the probability of cancer this does not necessarily imply that this type of radiation is an *important* cause for cancer if the probability doubles from, say, 0.00001 to 0.00002, which is still very small.

- The issue of so-called p-hacking is problematic. Suppose we find that a regional subsidy has an effect on regional growth with $p < 0.1$ (meaning that you find this relation in 10 per cent of the cases when the null-hypothesis of no relation is actually true). The null-hypothesis of subsidies having no effect cannot be ruled out. But in practice we include control variables for the presence of airports and ports, the weather, recent elections, national borders, the introduction of the euro, regional monetary policy, and so on. Experimenting with controls until the $p < 0.05$, is called p-hacking. If you torture the data long enough some combination of controls might give you $p < 0.05$. Telling in this respect is a meta-analysis of p-values. A plot of p-values that were published in serious journals shows a peak at $p = 0.05$, which is an indication of selection bias in the results. Meyer, Witteloostuijn, and Beugelsdijk (2017), in an editorial in the *Journal of International Business Studies*, provide for instance a detailed overview of these practices and offer practical guidelines for researchers to prevent p-hacking. Among the recommendations are: in the absence of a clear strategy to find cause and effect one should be careful to discuss statistical findings in terms of cause and

BOX 3.3 (cont.)

effect; null and negative findings are as interesting as positive findings and should be discussed as well; a detailed analyses of outliers is warranted; authors should report actual p-values rather than thresholds and not report asterisks to signal significance; a variety of robustness checks are essential; and so on. They conclude (p. 542): 'Good scientific practice requires that authors assess hypotheses based on a comprehensive assessment using all available evidence, rather than a singular focus on a single test statistic in a specific regression analysis.' It is up to the researcher to truly report how difficult it was to find the sought after effect.

Based on Figure 3.12, it thus seems that larger urban locations are associated with higher average productivity and wages. This suggests that the concentration of economic activity or agglomeration raises productivity. If this conclusion that 'size matters positively' is correct, policy makers may then conclude that stimulating a city's population size and hence urban agglomeration may raise income. Caution is, however, warranted and some fundamental comments are in order.

First, as always, one has to deal with a range of quite well-known econometric issues. Is a (log) linear specification the best choice? Are there possible missing variables? Do the variables represent what one wishes to measure? What estimation method can best be used: OLS or a more sophisticated technique? Answering these questions is important, but they are not specific for urban economics or geographical economics, they are important for all empirical research in economics.

Second, what is cause and what is effect? Equation 3.5 suggests a causal relationship from population size to income per capita, and there are good reasons to expect this to be the case as we will see in the remainder of this book. But the opposite is also possible. It could for instance be that high income levels enable workers to migrate to larger and more expensive cities. These large cities offer good facilities (for example, high-quality services), but are more expensive to live in, such that only people with sufficiently high income levels can afford the high (housing) costs.

Third, it might that there is another omitted variable that drives both urbanization and income per capita. It is possible, for instance, that economic development increases both income levels and urbanization. Urbanization is then simply a by-product of economic development.

Fourth, if a relationship like equation 3.5 exists, the next step is to use it for policy analyses. Does stimulating urbanization also stimulate income? Regional policy is often aimed at backward regions. These regions can be *treated* by administering a policy intervention, such as regional subsidies to stimulate local development. The question is how to measure the effectiveness of the treatment.

Answering these kind of questions is important.[18] Empirical research in the fields of urban and geographical economics on how to answer these questions has made considerable progress recently. In the remaining part of this chapter, we will briefly highlight a few of the useful techniques that have been applied. We briefly touch upon the issues involved below, but our discussion should be sufficient to understand most of the empirical literature discussed in this book and to be aware of some of the important issues for one's own research.[19]

3.5.1   Omitted Variables and Fixed Effects

The correct specification of the relationship between two variables of interest often follows from the model of interest. The exact specification of the relationship depends on the theory at hand. And theory also motivates the choice of variables. As we will see, some theories stress the importance of only the local or own-region market size, while other theories stress market access of a location, that is, the distance of a location to all other markets. The focus here is not how theory might guide the empirical research but how econometric remedies could improve the empirical research given the four 'cautionary comments' stated above.

The *omitted variable* problem deserves special attention as it is almost always present in empirical research. The specification of interest in equation 3.5 is thus between income per capita and population size of cities. It would, however, be naïve to assume that population size is the only variable that affects income. In a comparison across countries it could, for example, be important whether countries have access to a harbour or are landlocked. Countries with a harbour have easy access to the rest of the world enabling international trade flows and a more efficient international division of labour, which raises income. Including an indicator variable that captures the presence of an international harbour can be important. There are many other variables like this and omitting them from the empirical specification leads to biased estimates of γ.[20] The error term then becomes a catch-all for all the omitted effects. The ideal in research is to correct for all these biases in order to get a clean estimate of the parameter γ. In practice this is possible only to a certain extent. Some effects are clearly important, but the information could be missing in statistical sources, not available on the correct spatial scale, or not available for the relevant period etc.

$$ln\left(w_{it}\right) = \gamma ln\left(pop_{it}\right) + \eta c_{it} + L_i + T_t + \varepsilon_{it} \qquad 3.6$$

---

[18] In Chapter 11 we discuss regional policy in detail.

[19] A state-of-the-art discussion can be found in Duranton, Henderson, and Strange (2015), especially Section I on *Empirical Methods*.

[20] Textbooks on econometrics routinely discuss this; see, for instance Wooldridge (2016).

A standard solution to at least address the omitted variables problem is to include so-called *fixed effects* in the model specification. This solution requires a panel data-set. A typical fixed effect is a dummy variable that takes on the value zero or one. Adding fixed effects to equation 3.5 leads to equation 3.6, where L_i is a location fixed effect and T_t is a time fixed effect. The dummy variable L_4, for example, is equal to one if, and only if, the location i is equal to city number 4. It is equal to zero in all other cases. This location-specific fixed effect is thus only operative for the observations of location 4. Similarly, the time fixed effect T_{2018} is only operative for observations in the year 2018. The idea is to capture the fact that locations differ in many ways. They have different institutions, different political systems, different ideas on (local) taxes, and many other differences that could affect wages and urban population.

A fixed effect controls for all these differences that are specific for a location in a general way; the location dummy captures all idiosyncrasies of that particular location relative to the other locations. The assumption is that these differences between locations are constant and do not change over time. The benefit of this solution is that all variables that could affect wages – and are constant over time – are controlled for and no longer lead to a bias in the estimate of parameter γ. The downside of this approach is also evident: the fixed effect is a catch-all variable. This is the reason that in many empirical studies only the use of fixed effects is indicated in the empirical tables and not the coefficients themselves because it is difficult to interpret these coefficients as there is no information on the contribution of the underlying variables separately.

The use of location fixed effects L_i assumes that the location differences are constant over time. However, some factors that could affect wages are not constant over time. The Great Recession that started in 2008, for example, may have affected wages across all locations. To correct or neutralize influences that change over time we can include a time fixed effect T_t just like we did for the location fixed effect L_i. The assumption underlying this time fixed effect is that it is the same for all units of observations, here locations at a specific date.

We have seen that fixed effects have the advantage of neutralizing location- and time-specific unobserved variables in a general way. Some unobserved variables, however, are not constant over time or across locations. Think of changes in taxes after an election. The fixed effects do not capture these elements that change over time as well as across locations. This is, and returning to equation 3.6, why including actual variables that affect wages (besides population size) is a preferred option over the use of fixed effects. In case no reliable information on the variables of interest is available, the fall-back option of including fixed effects is, however, better than not using them at all. Finally, we should qualify our previous statement in the sense that sometimes fixed effects can be interesting in their own right. In De La Roca and Puga (2017), for instance, first a wage equation is estimated as a function of worker and job characteristics using city fixed effects (in this particular regression the city fixed effects capture all elements that affect wages across cities that are not explained by worker and job characteristics). In the second stage they regress the city fixed effects on city sizes in order to capture the effect of city sizes on wages. In Chapter 6 we will discuss this study in more detail. Moreover, from a technical point of view, care should be taken to avoid perfect collinearity with the constant term in the regression if fixed effects (dummies) are included. To avoid perfect collinearity, one location should be dropped with respect to L_i and one year with respect to T_t.[21]

3.5.2 Cause and Effect

As noted above, equation 3.5 suggests a causal relationship from city population size to income per capita, but the reverse is also possible. Both relations are plausible and could be valid at the same time. Technically, we say that we have an explanatory (right-hand side) variable that is endogenous. Let's call this variable x, then x may itself be determined by other exogenous variables, possibly by a missing variable, or it could be partly determined by the independent (left-hand side) variable which would be a case of reverse causation. In this case, the error term in equations 3.5 as well as 3.6 is correlated with the right-hand side explanatory variable x (population size), resulting in biased estimates of γ. A solution in the case of missing variables was discussed in the previous section: use fixed effects.[22] Another solution is to find a so-called *instrumental variable*, which is a variable z that is *not* correlated with the error term, such that $cov(z,\varepsilon) = 0$, but *is* correlated with the endogenous explanatory variable x, such that $cov(z,x) \neq 0$.[23] Loosely formulated, an instrument helps to clean the impact of the endogenous explanatory variable from the part that is affected by the left-hand side or independent variable (or of the effect of a missing variable). In most statistical software packages the application of this method is straightforward.

This is the technical side of solving for the problem of reverse causality. The main 'economic' problem with selecting an instrument is a good and convincing story that motivates the selection of an instrument, a variable that is related to the right-hand side or dependent variable, but not to the error term; the presumed exogeneity of the instrument needs careful motivation and discussion. An example can illustrate this and also serves to illustrate the potential usefulness of

---

[21] In modern statistical software packages (such as R or STATA) this is done by default when fixed effects are generated.

[22] If we can safely assume that the omitted variable does not change over time, first differencing methods can also be used; see Wooldridge (2016, chs. 13, 14).

[23] Remember that $corr(z,e) = cov(z,e) / (sd(z) \times (sd(e))$, where cov is the covariance, corr is the correlation coefficient, and sd the standard deviation. The standard deviation is always positive. Requiring $cov = 0$ is thus equivalent to requiring $corr = 0$.

the instrumental variables themselves. In Combes et al. (2010), for example, the authors are interested in the relationship between wages (different measures are used) and population density in France, using a detailed spatial data set on wages and density. They note, as Adam Smith and Alfred Marshall also observed, that wages are higher in denser populated places because of all sorts of technical or knowledge spillovers, spillovers that are crucially stronger in more densely populated areas hence boosting wages. However, it is also possible that more productive places attract more productive workers and as a result become denser, or that more productive people choose to live in denser places because they can afford it, or that the benefits of dense places accrue especially to high-skilled people (Combes et al., 2010, p. 16). In that case more densely populated areas do not as such make people who locate there more productive and let them earn higher wages, the data merely reflect the fact that more productive people prefer to live and work in more densely populated areas. Whatever the reason for this last observation, this is a classic example of reverse causation.

Combes et al. (2010) suggest two types of instruments to address reverse causation: historical population density variables (by definition historical variables fulfil the condition that $cov(z, \varepsilon) = 0$ because a historical variable is uncorrelated with the current error term) and geological variables such as the nature of soils. The geological variables can be expected to be key drivers of population settlements. Soil quality is important for agricultural productivity and thus is likely to have determined settlement patterns in agricultural France thousands of years ago. It can thus be expected, given the stability of settlements, that these variables are correlated with current density, while it is unlikely that these variables affect current wages (the left-hand side variable), because society has changed from an agricultural economy to a manufacturing and service economy. The pairwise correlation between historical population density variables and current employment density ranges between 0.46 and 0.88. For the soil quality these correlations range between 0.01 and 0.13. The correlation of soil quality with the right-hand side variable is thus lower than that of the historical population density variables, which given the amount of work involved in constructing the soil quality data must have been somewhat of a disappointment for the authors.

The authors present many results, but we show only a few of them in Table 3.3, to illustrate the importance of using instruments. First, note that the use of instruments has an effect on the estimated impact of density on wages as they affect the parameter γ. Second, note that the impact of density is smaller if only historical instruments are used, larger if only soil instruments are used, and smaller again if both instruments are used. After an extensive discussion, the authors prefer estimates in which both types of instruments are used, and conclude that the best estimate is about 0.020. Note that we have shown results for two sets of instruments. The correlation between soil quality instruments and

Table 3.3 Wages in France as a function of density with different instruments

Estimated equation: $ln\left(w_{it}\right) = \gamma ln\left(dens_{it}\right) + \varepsilon_{it}$

		Instruments		
Variable	None	Historical	Soil	Both
ln(dens)	0.033***[a]	0.027***[a]	0.050***[b]	0.020***[c]
Historical instruments				
pop(1831)		Yes	No	Yes
pop(1881)		Yes	No	No
Soil instruments				
Ruggedness		No	Yes	Yes
Depth to rock		No	Yes	No

Source: Combes et al. (2010), [a]Table 1.6, [b] Table 1.7, [c] Table 1.9; *** indicates significance at 1 per cent level; the authors use various ways to define wages (we select results for W^3; these are wages after controlling for sector effects, observable time-varying individual characteristics, and all fixed individual characteristics).

density is lower than the correlations between historical instruments and density. Despite having a good story on the relevance of each group of instruments, the low correlation between the instrument and the right-hand side variable can be problematic; as shown in Wooldridge (2016, p. 469) it can result in biased estimates. So one should always check whether the (endogenous) explanatory variable is correlated with the instrument. It is good practice to include these correlations in a table, as Combes et al. (2010) do. We will return to this seminal study in Chapter 6.

3.5.3 Natural Experiments

Reverse causation and missing variables are major topics in empirical research. In the previous sections we discussed strategies to address some of the issues involved. There is, however, another possible strategy that can be used: the use of *natural* experiments. This is not an experiment in a laboratory setting where the circumstances of the experiment can be carefully organized and controlled in order to assure that only the factor of interest is influencing the outcome. A natural experiment can be thought of as changes in the environment of a group of firms, workers, and locations such that they have to adapt to the new circumstances. One can exploit this change to discriminate between economic agents that are and those that are not affected by the experiment. The group that is affected is the so-called *treatment* group. The group that is *not* affected by the change is the *control* group. Note that even though we do not have a classic lab study, with a perfectly controlled experiment at hand, the terminology in terms of treatment and control group is the same.

Comparing the outcome for these two groups provides us with information on the effects of the environmental change or shock. One should, of course, make sure that the treatment group and control groups are similar except for the treatment and do not differ in other important ways. A natural experiment is ideally an exogenous *shock*. If the shock is truly unexpected the reverse causality problem should not arise. One can think of unexpected floods or hurricanes that might affect housing prices in some areas but not in others, but also the fact that, for example, the Berlin Wall fell in 1989; this too was arguably an unexpected shock. Redding and Sturm (2008) use the fall of the Berlin Wall and the subsequent re-unification to show how regions in Germany that were closer to the old West/East German border – the treatment group – were affected differently by the fall of the wall than regions that were further away from the border.

To evaluate the impact of the change or shock, we need data to compare the situation before and after the shock for both the treatment and control group, which helps us to control for all sorts of systematic differences between the treatment group and the control group. There are four groups in total: the treatment group before and after the change, as well as the control group before and after the change.

We can use the differences between these groups to estimate the effects of the treatment. Figure 3.13 illustrates the basic set-up of this estimation procedure. The variable Y could be some regional development variable, for example regional growth stimulated by central government subsidies aimed at regional infra-structure projects. The central government is interested in whether these subsidies indeed stimulate regional growth. We have a treatment group: the regions that receive infra-structure subsidies. And a control group: regions that do not receive these subsidies. We observe both groups before and after the treatment.

We are interested in the treatment effect $C - D$: the effect of the infra-structure subsidies on the treatment group. From Figure 3.13 it is obvious that we cannot estimate $C - D$ because we cannot observe what would have happened to the treatment group if they had *not* received the treatment; that is, situation D simply does not exist. We can, however, identify the treatment effect if we make a strong assumption: introduce a control group that does not receive the treatment, but has a common trend with the treatment group. This is reflected by lines AE and BD having the same slope: even without the infrastructure subsidies both groups would have grown anyway.

The treatment effect can now easily be calculated as; $\delta = treatment\ effect = (C - E) - (D - E) = (C - E) - (B - A)$. The last equality follows from the assumption that the development of the control group also reflects the development of the treatment group if they had not been treated, that is $(D - E) = (B - A)$.

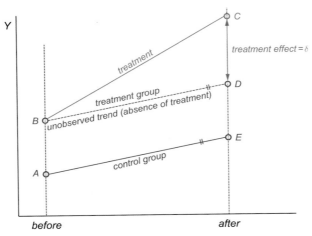

Figure 3.13 Difference-in-difference (DID) estimation

It is therefore crucial for this method to work that one finds a control group that is identical to the treatment group in all respects, except the treatment itself.

$$y_{s,t} = \beta_1 + \beta_2\, Treat_s + \beta_3 After_t + \delta(Treat_s * After_t) + other\ factors + \varepsilon_{s,t} \qquad 3.7$$

The basic estimation set-up is provided in equation 3.7, where y is the variable of interest (for example regional growth), s is the spatial unit (for example states or provinces), t indicates time (before = 0 and after = 1), and *Treat* the treatment status, which takes a value of one for units that are treated in period 2, for example units that receive subsidies, and a value zero otherwise. Sometimes it is easy to specify this as a multiplication of two dummies: one indicating the treated units (for both periods) and the other the period dummy. The treatment effect is captured by δ.

To see this, it is instructive to relate equation 3.7 to Figure 3.13:

$$y_{s,t} = \begin{cases} \beta_1 & Treat_s = 0,\ After_t = 0 & Control\ Group\ before\ treatment = A \\ \beta_1 + \beta_2 & Treat_s = 1,\ After_t = 0 & Treatment\ Group\ before\ treatment = B \\ \beta_1 + \beta_3 & Treat_s = 0,\ After_t = 1 & Control\ Group\ after\ treatment = E \\ \beta_1 + \beta_2 + \beta_3 + \delta & Treat_s = 1,\ After_t = 1 & Treatment\ Group\ after\ Treatment = C \end{cases}$$

This enables us to confirm that:

$$\delta = treatment\ effect = (C - E) - (B - A) = \left[(\beta_1 + \beta_2 + \beta_3 + \delta) - (\beta_1 + \beta_3)\right] - \left[(\beta_1 + \beta_2) - \beta_1\right]$$

This also explains why the estimator δ is called a *difference-in-differences (DID) estimator*; it is the result of two differences: the difference between treated groups versus non-treated groups, and the difference between these groups in both periods (before and after the shock). Note, that *other factors* that might affect regional growth no longer have an influence; they are differenced away. This implies that the missing variable problem no longer needs to be solved and that one does not need to gather information for all variables that are important for, in this case, regional growth.

In Brakman et al. (2012) the DID approach is for instance used to analyse whether the various enlargements of the European Union (EU) affected population growth of cities along the borders that became integrated in the EU. Their key specification is:

$$ShareGrowth_{a,\,t-s,\,t} = L_c + T_t + \beta_1 Border_a + \beta_2 \left(Border_a * Integration_{a,t}\right) + \varepsilon_{a,t}$$

where $ShareGrowth_{a,\,t-s,\,t}$ is the annualized rate of growth (in per cent) in the population share of area a from time period $t-s$ to t; $Border_a$ is a dummy equal to one when an area is a member of the border group as a whole and zero otherwise. The time dummies T_t control for common macro-economic shocks affecting population growth throughout Europe and trends in population growth rates. The location fixed effects L_c take care of unobserved heterogeneity between countries. A typical outcome in this study (see their Table 4, column 1) is $\beta_1 = -0.210$ and $\beta_2 = 0.147$, which indicates that a border location affects city growth along borders negatively, but that border cities along borders that became integrated in the EU compensated this to some extent. In this case the treatment effect is positive.[24]

The same method can be used for policy analysis. Some regions could take part in a special policy programme. The spatial units that take part in the programme form the treatment group, and the other ones are the control group. Using the DID approach can reveal the usefulness of these programmes. In a seminal study Kline and Moretti (2014) analyse a policy experiment of the 1930s in the US where backward regions in the Tennessee Valley received government support. An important share of the discussion in this paper is devoted to finding a relevant control group in order to make the policy comparison worthwhile and to prevent a comparison to a group that is completely different from the treatment group in important ways. This is comparable to finding the effectiveness of a medicine: the treatment group and control groups should be similar except for the use of the medicine. As with the discussion with respect to the fixed effects model, the method works fine if the *other factors* and the fixed effects are indeed constant or fixed across units or time. This need not be the case; we will return to the Kline and Moretti (2014) study in Chapter 11 which specifically deals with the policy implications of urban and geographical economics. In Box 3.4 we briefly discuss some other relevant approaches to deal with (the absence of) control variables.

---

[24] A problem with this particular example, as the authors note, is that the treatment effect might not be unexpected: some anticipation could have happened before the actual integration.

BOX 3.4 When Controls are Missing

We are far from exhaustive in this chapter in discussing possible econometric techniques to deal with the issues that we have highlighted. As an example, an alternative for difference-in-difference could be a so-called regression *discontinuity* approach; see section 3.5.4 for a discussion. The idea is that a treatment can be shown by a 'jump' in a regression line for the outcome variable of interest. Assuming that all other factors that are important for the outcome variable are evolving *smoothly*, the jump must be caused by the treatment.

Another method that has gained popularity in empirical research in urban and geographical economics is that of synthetic controls. Sometimes a convincing control group is missing and the *synthetic control* method allows one to construct a control group out of the available data. The case of the earthquake that struck Kobe in Japan in 1995 is an example; see Dupont and Noy (2015). To find the effect of the earthquake it was necessary to clean the data of all possible other factors that could have affected Kobe if the earthquake had not happened, such as a recession, possible housing market bubbles, government policies, and other variables that could have been important for the development path of Kobe.

So, what would have been the development path of Kobe without the disaster? The method of synthetic controls constructs a hypothetical control group that mimics the growth path of Kobe without the earthquake; a simple extrapolation is not the most likely path as lots of things could have happened to Kobe that need to be taken on board. The method identifies other Japanese prefectures that are similar to Kobe in relevant ways, but were not hit by the earthquake. First one has to identify prefectures that are similar to Kobe, and weigh characteristic variables of these prefectures in such a way that they mimic Kobe in the pre-treatment period. Next, one can use these prefectures and variables to mimic Kobe in the post-treatment period. This gives a development path that could be relevant for Kobe in the absence of the earthquake. The difference between the actual path and the constructed path is assumed to be caused by the disaster. The authors find a persistent effect of the Kobe earthquake.

3.5.4 Regression Discontinuity Design (RDD)

The use of natural experiments to infer causality as discussed in the previous section makes sense when the shock or event that is supposed to set apart the treatment and control group is truly exogenous and also the only aspect in which the two groups differ. As we saw above, spatial events or shocks like natural disasters but also changes to economic integration and the associated borders have been used as examples of (quasi-)natural experiments. With a natural disaster like a flooding or hurricane, the experiment literally falls out of the sky. Researchers in the social and medical sciences do, however, typically not wait for Mother Nature to enable them to conduct such an experiment. Instead they create these conditions themselves via so-called Randomized Control Trials (RCTs). In medicine, the most well-known and straightforward application of RCTs is to test the effectiveness of a medicine by using two groups of trial participants that are identical in all but one respect: the treatment group gets the real medicine and the control group gets a placebo.

The use of RCTs has really taken off in the field of economics at large as well in recent years. In the fields of development economics and labour economics but also urban and geographical economics, RCTs are increasingly used as a research design and as the main strategy to make identification of cause and effect feasible. This is also true for the social sciences at large where both in lab and field experiments, RCTs are by now the leading research design. Like with the natural experiments discussed above, the idea is always to make use of or, as a researcher, deliberately enforce some exogenous variation between otherwise identical groups, be it people, firms, or places.

A related but still different strategy to infer causality is the so-called *regression discontinuity design* (RDD). The main difference from RCTs and natural experiments is that there is no exogenous shock or event that makes for a split between the units or groups of interest. With the RDD, one looks for circumstances or conditions that create a clear discontinuity in terms of some outcome variable across the sample. The classic example, as discussed by Lee and Lemieux (2010, 2014) in their survey of the use of RDDs in economic and the social sciences, is a class of students where every student with an average grade above a certain cut-off gets a scholarship or sizeable reward. The scholarship creates a jump or discontinuity when we plot the average grades of all students against the outcome variable of interest. The RDD aims to show whether we observe a discontinuity exactly at the point where the intervention kicks in; see Figure 3.14 with the assignment variable on the *x*-axis and the outcome variable on the *y*-axis. Ideally, when the intervention is as clear cut as in Figure 3.14 the RDD is basically equivalent to the RCT (and natural experiment) approach in that it yields the possibility of inferring causality.

From the perspective of the current chapter on empirical methods in urban and geographical economics, the point to note is that the RDD can be used with space or geography as the mechanism to invoke the discontinuity, so the RDD then becomes a spatial discontinuity design. A good example is the study by Dachis, Duranton, and Turner (2012) where the impact of the introduction of a land transfer tax in Toronto on the local real estate market is investigated. Instead of a more conventional approach where one would collect data on many local variables, including the tax scheme, and then estimate its possible effect on the dependent variable of interest (here, local housing prices or transactions), Dachis et al. (2012)

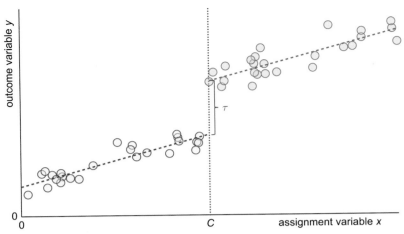

Figure 3.14 The basic idea of regression discontinuity design – RDD
Source: based on Lee and Lemieux (2010, 2014).

opt for an RDD approach. They do so by concentrating their analysis on houses and localities that fall just *in*side the administrative border of the city of Toronto, where the land transfer tax thus applied, as well as on houses and localities that are just *out*side this border, and where thus the tax did not apply. The two sets of localities are deemed equal in nearly all respects (distance to downtown Toronto, jobs, and amenities as well as in other socio-economic respects).

Ideally, think of a line of identical houses along a single street with nearly identical inhabitants where the only difference is that the left side of the street just falls within the Toronto city limits, and house owners thus have to pay the land transfer tax, and the houses on the right side of the street fall just outside the city limits and are thus not subject to this tax. Assuming, as the authors do, that the introduction of the land transfer tax can be seen as an unexpected exogenous shock, they apply the RDD strategy with space (the Toronto tax border) as the mechanism that drives the discontinuity. This is shown in Figure 3.15, where the right line depicts the volume of housing sales transactions in the city of Toronto (*y*-axis) when one moves further away from the border (point 0 on the *x*-axis) inwards into Toronto (*x*-axis). The left line shows also the volume of similar transactions but now, from right to left on the *x*-axis, for areas just next to but marginally *outside* the city of Toronto border to areas that are ever further removed from the city border. The message is clear: there is a marked discontinuity precisely at the city of Toronto border, with housing sales transactions falling most and more sharply for areas in Toronto that are just within the city limits. The paper by Dachis et al. (2012) discusses more examples of an RDD with space as the discontinuity mechanism, and we will briefly return to RDD and this study at the end of Chapter 9.

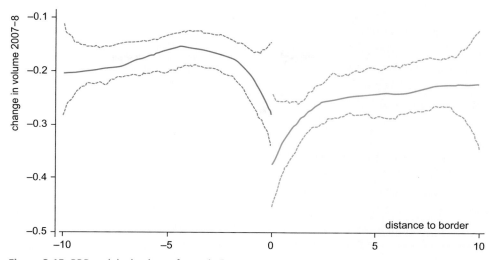

Figure 3.15 RDD and the land transfer tax in Toronto
Source: based on Dachis et al. (2012); thin-dashed lines indicate confidence interval.

3.5.5 Spatial Connections

There are many ways through which individuals, firms, agglomerations and regions can be spatially interconnected. There can be all sorts of spatial spillovers. People that live close together affect each other, both positively (learning from each other) and negatively (congestion), and the same holds for firms and regions. Regions can be each other's destination for products, and a nearby large market could affect our economy positively. There is by now a large literature showing that these interconnections exist, although it is often not clear who interacts with whom and why (see Gibbons et al., 2015 for a detailed discussion). But if these interconnections exist (we analyse this in far more detail in Part III), one has to deal with this from a technical or econometrical point of view.

The toolkit of *spatial econometrics* helps us here. Following the seminal work by Anselin (1988), spatial econometrics applies and extends the toolkit of econometrics to spatial issues. In doing so, it provides an econometric foundation for some of the empirical specifications that we will encounter in later chapters. Let's assume that wages in region j depend positively on the (real) income of other regions, corrected for distance. In the terminology of spatial econometrics such an equation can be estimated as a so-called *spatial lag model*, where (as in non-spatial models with a lagged dependent variable) one seeks to establish whether there is spatial auto-regression in the data. This is captured in equation 3.8 by the $\rho W\left(wages_i\right)$ term, where W is a distance matrix (to be specified by the researcher) identifying the geographical relationships between regions, and ρ is the spatial lag coefficient to be estimated (between -1 and $+1$). For the W matrix one can use all sorts of specifications; e.g. the average of wages of neighbouring regions (giving non-neighbouring regions a weight of zero), or a distance-weighted summation of all regions where more distant regions get a smaller weight. The choices are many. Ideally one should consult an underlying theory for a motivation of a specification of W.

If neighbouring regions are a destination for our products we would expect a positive spatial lag coefficient: higher wages in (nearby) regions i are good news for firms in region j.

$$wage_j = \alpha_0 + \alpha_1\left(control\ variables_j\right) + \rho W\left(wages_i\right) + \varepsilon_j \qquad 3.8$$

Next, we look at the *spatial error model*. By estimating equation 3.9 one tests for the significance of spatial auto-correlation, which is similar to tests for auto-correlation in time series models. Assume that equation 3.9 tries to explain city size. The idea is that city size can be explained by all sorts of fundamental variables, for example a coastal location (one of the control variables), but also by unobserved factors. If the γ-coefficient is significant, there is spatial autocorrelation, implying that an unobserved (not included by a variable) event in city i will have an impact on city-size j. It could be that the attack on the Twin Towers in New York could have had an impact on the growth of nearby cities in New Jersey or Connecticut for instance. The magnitude of this impact depends on the distance between the cities i and j as measured by the distance matrix W.[25]

$$City\ size_j = \alpha_0 + \alpha_1\left(control\ variables_j\right) + \varepsilon_j,\ where\ \varepsilon_j = \gamma W \varepsilon_i + \epsilon_j \qquad 3.9$$

From a technical point of view spatial lags are easy to introduce (see e.g. Elhorst, 2014 for various spatial lag specifications and empirical examples). However, the technique does not solve problems of causality and the exact economic processes that are involved. A strong warning was given by Gibbons and Overman (2012), who wrote an influential article with the telling title 'Mostly Pointless Spatial Econometrics'. Simply introducing all sorts of spatial lags and linkages is 'pointless' without a clear idea of what economic mechanisms drive these spatial connections. In the remainder of this book, and in particular in Part III where we discuss economic models of spatial interdependencies, we provide an in-depth discussion of these mechanisms.

3.6   Conclusions

Chapter 1 showed that the world is spiky. Economic activity is unevenly distributed across space. This is a simple observation. To measure this turns out to be more complicated. Researchers have many options to put indices and numbers on the spikiness described in Chapter 1. We briefly described the Gini index, Entropy measures,

---

[25] Useful information (including spatial econometrics software) is provided by James LeSage (http://www.spatial-econometrics.com/) and also by Paul Elhorst (https://spatial-panels.com/software/). See also Vega and Elhorst (2015).

the Ellison-Glaser index, and the Duranton-Overman density approach. No measure is ideal, but some are better than others. The standard measures – the Gini index, the Entropy measures, and the Herfindahl index – give a quick way to characterize the uneven distribution of activity over space. Often these measures suffice if one only wishes to point out that clustering or agglomerations are present. More sophisticated measures can be used for more serious analyses. The Ellison-Glaeser index corrects for industry differences, dealing with the fact that some industries consist only of a few whereas others consist of many firms. In a serious industry cluster analysis this measure is a preferred option. In addition, the Duranton-Overman method prevents biases from arbitrarily defined administrative spatial units. These measures require more detailed data than more straightforward measures like the Gini coefficient, the Entropy measures, and the Herfindahl index. It is important to realize that all measures have limitations and that, if data availability allows this, a sensitivity analysis by using various measures is always preferred over using just a single measure.

Once it is established how to measure spatial economic inequality or unevenness, the obvious next question is the 'so what' question. Does it matter whether and how economic activity is concentrated? Usually it does, and concentration is positively associated with wages and productivity. But before deriving these conclusions a few far from trivial issues should be taken on board: reverse causation, endogeneity, missing variables, and spatial interactions, just to name a few. In the current literature a few obvious candidates to address the most important of these issues are readily available: the use of fixed effects, instruments, diff-in-diff estimations, regression discontinuity designs, or the use of spatial lags. This chapter briefly introduced these techniques and provided examples of the usefulness of these methods. Once we turn to the empirics of urban and geographical economics, notably in Chapter 6 and Chapter 9 but also in Chapters 10 and 11, the insights on empirical methods as briefly introduced in Chapter 3 will be used. Armed with the stylized facts (Chapter 1 and Chapter 2) of the spiky world and the insights on measurement and empirical methods from the current chapter, we are now well positioned to turn to the core of our book, the theory and empirics of urban and geographical economics in Part II and Part III, respectively.

Technical Note

Technical Note 3.1 Limiting cases of Generalized Entropy using L'Hôpital's Rule
In order to derive the limit expressions of the Generalized Entropy measure in case α is either zero or one, we use L'Hôpital's Rule (for well-defined derivatives) which states that, under some technical conditions, the limit of the ratio of two differentiable functions is equal to the limit of the ratio of the derivatives of these functions, such that: $\lim_{x \to b} \frac{f(x)}{g(x)} = \lim_{x \to b} \frac{f'(x)}{g'(x)}$. Recall that the derivative of

the function $y = a^x$ is equal to $a^x ln(a)$. Applying these rules to the definition of Generalized Entropy, we differentiate the numerator and denominator with respect to α. This gives for the numerator: $\left(\sum_{r=1}^{R} w_r \left(\frac{y_{i,a}}{\overline{y}_a} \right)^{\alpha} \ln \left(\frac{y_{i,a}}{\overline{y}_a} \right) \right)$ and for the denominator $2\alpha - 1$. Applying L'Hôpital's Rule for the cases $\alpha = 0$ and $\alpha = 1$ gives the expressions in Table 3.1 if $w_i = 1 / R$.

Exercises

Question 3.1 Missing Values
Recall the footnote in section 3.2.2 when we analysed the distribution of total- and youth employment in EU NUTS 2 regions: 'Note that the number of regions is smaller for youth employment than for total employment because of two missing values (one in France and one in Finland). There are several ways to deal with this problem, but we simply compare the Lorenz curves and associated Gini coefficients for the regions for which we have observations.'

Discuss some other 'ways to deal with this problem' and their advantages and disadvantages compared to the solution used in Chapter 3.

Question 3.2 Properties of Inequality Measures
In section 3.2.1 the following statement is made: 'Many inequality measures do not satisfy the four properties above and are thus less suitable for empirical evaluation. This holds, for example, for share and ratio inequality measures, such as the share of the top 10 per cent of regions in total activity or the ratio of the share of the top 10 per cent divided by the share of the bottom 10 per cent.'

Discuss which of the four properties are not satisfied for the share of the top 10 per cent of regions, and the ratio of the share of the top 10 per cent divided by the share of the bottom 10 per cent.

Question 3.3 Calculate Indices
On the website you will find a variant of the data depicted in Figure 3.9. Calculate the Gini coefficient, the Herfindahl index, the Krugman index, and the Ellison-Glaeser index with these data.

Question 3.4 Treatment Effect
On the website you will find regional growth data on a hypothetical treatment of some regions with subsidies. Calculate the treatment effect.

Question 3.5 Fixed Effects
Use the data from Question 3.4 and include a region fixed effect. Compare the two results.

PART II
Urban Economics

As stated in Part I of the book, there are two basic explanations for the uneven distribution of economic activity across space, which we dubbed first and second nature explanations. First nature explanations deal with the role of physical geography. We covered this in the first part of Chapter 2. Second nature explanations build around human and economic interactions as the main driver of our spiky world. These interactions can be analysed through various analytical lenses and approaches. Some of them centre around the role and development of history, psychology, or politics. These kinds of human interactions as determinants of the uneven spatial distribution of human and economic activity were covered in the second part of Chapter 2. In Chapter 3 we became more precise in how to measure economic spikiness and which type of methodological or empirical issues a researcher runs into when trying to establish an empirical link between economic spikiness and its possible determinants.

The remainder of our book is concerned with the second nature explanations that arise from economic theory and hence from economic interactions between firms, households, or workers in a market economy. This is really what the book is about. Here we have two basic approaches to choose from: urban economics and geographical economics, respectively Part II and Part III of the book. In Part II we discuss the main insights and ingredients of urban economics in Chapters 4 to 6. To foreshadow our discussions, we will learn that modern urban economics centres around the two key concepts of spatial equilibrium and agglomeration economies. These two concepts help us to better understand how cities are internally shaped and organized, why a system of heterogeneous cities can exist, and also what the main agglomeration economies are that determine where footloose firms and households prefer to locate. In Chapter 4 the focus is on the internal organization of the city: who wants to locate where within a single city. The existence of the city itself is still taken as given. In Chapter 5 we change this by looking more fundamentally into the question of why cities exist to begin with and how we can explain that cities of various sizes and shapes can co-exist. Chapter 6 zooms in on the main determinants of city size and growth by analysing the relevance of agglomeration economies. Many of the tools and insights introduced in Part II turn out to be useful for the rest of the book. In fact, after the reader has finished Part II on urban economics, the main remaining task will be to add the role of economic geography, that is spatial interdependencies between locations. This is done in Part III.

Space Within Cities

LEARNING OBJECTIVES

- To know and understand the concept of a spatial equilibrium and its implications for the choice of a location within cities.
- To see how modern urban economics analysis builds on historical developments, in particular the Von Thünen location model.
- To be able to apply the concept of a spatial equilibrium for deriving the bid–rent curve and the implications of technology for building height and population density.
- To understand whether and how the stylized facts about location choices within a city reflect the standard model of urban economics.

4.1 Introduction

We start our discussion of Part II on urban economics in this chapter by analysing the economic organization of space within cities. The spatial model we construct constitutes the backbone of modern urban economics. Building on the Von Thünen (1826) framework, the foundations were laid by William Alonso, Richard Muth, and Edwin Mills, which explains why the analysis is known as the Alonso-Muth-Mills model. In this framework, Alonso (1964) established the concept of spatial equilibrium, Muth (1969) focused on housing and construction, and Mills (1967, 1972) provided a more complete analysis of the location of economic activity, including production and living space. Glaeser (2008) argues that there are three main actors in urban economics, namely utility-maximizing individuals, profit-maximizing firms, and builders/developers. The latter can be profit maximizing (as below in section 4.9) or entrepreneurial community-builders (Henderson, 1985). For clarity and ease of exposition, which allows us to focus on explaining the main forces of the spatial equilibrium, our discussion is based on a simple monocentric framework with a focus on the decisions of individuals, some attention for builders, and limited attention as yet for firms. Chapter 5 uses a similar framework to analyse the economic organization of space between cities, while Chapter 6 analyses the economics of agglomeration. In both these chapters firms play a more prominent role. For the current chapter, the spatial equilibrium is defined as:

> **Definition – spatial equilibrium (within cities):** In a spatial equilibrium within cities, economic agents do not have an incentive to move to another location *within* the city.

What is it we want to explain? At some level we want to understand the existence of cities, where people cluster together. This surely requires a model in which transport costs play a role to give people an incentive to live in cities. As Mills argues, however, even with transport costs there would be no cities if we had constant returns to scale and homogeneous land, as this would enable very local and very small-scale production wherever we need it to avoid transport costs. Some level of increasing returns to scale or some indivisibilities, in conjunction with transport costs, are therefore inevitable to explain cities. In this chapter we take these issues as given after the discussion of the Von Thünen model in section 4.3. We want to understand the economic organization within cities, taking the city itself as given. Issues that we address include: where to live within the city and what rental rate (for land) to pay at different locations within the city (section 4.4), what the impact is of different (public) transportation methods (section 4.6), how much land to consume and variations in population density (section 4.7), what price for housing is paid at different locations within the city (section 4.9), and what the main impact is of other issues, like heterogeneity and amenities (section 4.10).

We also want to illustrate our findings empirically, for which we use American examples in this chapter. To do so, section 4.2 starts with a brief discussion of American ZIP codes and shows the enormous variation (skewness) in land area, population, and (in particular) population density that we have to explain. Along with other data, this information is also used in section 4.5 when we analyse the variation in average rents paid in different neighbourhoods of New York City and in section 4.8 when we analyse the variation in population density in Indianapolis. These examples are not only useful for illustrating the power of the concept of spatial equilibrium, but also help us to pinpoint what types of issues help us to understand deviations from the predicted pattern: see section 4.10.

4.2 American ZIP Codes

The US Postal Service developed ZIP codes (Zone Improvement Plan) as a geographical tool to deliver the mail more efficiently. Since ZIP codes are a messy kind of geography and change over time, the US Census Bureau decided to develop ZIP Census Tabulation Areas (ZCTA) as an alternative to ZIP codes, starting with the 2000 Census (which we use in the discussion below). In most cases the ZCTA code is equal to the ZIP code, but there are some subtle differences.[1] There are a

---

[1] See http://mcdc.missouri.edu/geography/ZIP-resources.html for all you need to know about ZIP codes and ZCTAs; there are also 3-digit ZCTAs, but we focus attention only on 5-digit ZCTAs.

little more than 43,000 ZCTA codes with a positive land area, of which about 1 per cent do not have inhabitants.

On average, the ZCTAs are fairly large (see Table 4.1): the mean land area is 210 km² and houses 6,445 people. The variation is, however, substantial. The smallest land area is 0.026 km², a part of New York County. The largest land area is (not surprisingly) in Alaska; it is a part of the Yukon-Koyukuk census area of about 288,000 km². Similarly, there are 436 ZCTAs with zero population, while the largest population of almost 114,000 people is reached in a part of Cook County in Illinois. A better indication of what the 'representative' ZCTA looks like is therefore provided by looking at the median values, which are 65 km² for land area and a population of 1,230 people. The skewness in the distribution of population and land area, leading to a much higher mean than median (more than five times as large for population and more than three times for land area), is illustrated in panels *b* and *c* of Figure 4.1.

Table 4.1 US ZCTA summary statistics

Statistics	Population	Land area	Population density
Minimum	0	0.026	0
Maximum	114,124	287,716	66,641
Mean	6,445	210	337
Median	1,230	65	18

Source: calculations based on US Census data 2000, downloaded from the Missouri Census Data Center website (mcdc.missouri.edu); population in number of people, land area in km², and population density in people per km².

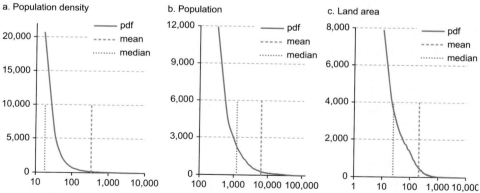

Figure 4.1 USA: ZCTA distributions of population, land area, and population density
Source: calculations based on US Census data 2000, downloaded from the Missouri Census Data Center website (mcdc.missouri.edu); population in number of people, land area in km², and population density in people per km²; horizontal axis for a,b,c is population density, population, and land area, respectively (log scales); vertical axis is always density (smooth histogram); for each variable 400 intervals are constructed of 1/20th the size of the mean.

Using information on population and land area, it is straightforward to calculate population density, which is the average number of people living in a ZCTA per km^2. Again, the variation is substantial, ranging from zero for a range of ZCTAs to 66,641 people per km^2 for the small part of New York County identified above where 1,726 people live. The simple average ZCTA population density is 337 people per km^2. This is, in fact, a highly misleading number, because if we divide the total American population by the total American land area the average population density is about 31 people per km^2. In this respect, the median ZCTA population density of 18 people per km^2 is more representative, although it underestimates the overall average density. Panel *a* of Figure 4.1 illustrates the enormous skewness in population density, leading to a mean value that is almost 17 times larger than the median.

What we want to emphasize at this stage is the enormous variation in population density across the USA. Apparently, some people choose to cluster together at high population densities, while other people decide to live in relatively remote areas. As we discuss in more detail in sections 4.5, 4.7 and 4.8, this also holds for variation in population density *within* urban areas, such as New York and Indianapolis. We analyse how people determine in which city to live or work in Chapter 5 and provide a general overview of the forces of agglomeration in Chapter 6. However, we start our urban economics discussion in this chapter by reviewing the Von Thünen model before analysing location decisions within an urban area.

4.3   The Von Thünen Model

The uneven distribution of economic activity within a country is the starting point for urban economics. The modern analysis of the agglomeration of firms and people in cities or metropolitan areas relies strongly on 'the economics of agglomeration, a term which refers to the decline in average costs as more production occurs within a specified geographical area' (Anas, Arnott, and Small, 1998, p. 1427). In other words, it relies on increasing returns to scale.[2] Before we go into the relevance of scale economies for cities and other forms of agglomeration, we first discuss a model in which there are no increasing returns to scale whatsoever! This model, the so-called *monocentric city* model, originates with Von Thünen (1826) and remains a benchmark model for urban economics to this day.

The monocentric city model assumes the existence of a featureless plane, perfectly flat and homogeneous in all respects. In the midst of this plane there is a single city. Outside the city farmers grow crops which they must sell in the city.

---

[2] This formulation of increasing returns to scale does not say how the decline in a firm's average costs comes about.

There are positive transportation costs associated with getting the farming products to the city, which differ for the various crops, as do the prices for these crops. Von Thünen analyses how the farmers locate themselves across the plane. Each farmer wants to be as close to the city as possible to minimize transport costs. This incentive to be close to the city results in higher land rents near the city than at the edge of the plane. Each farmer thus faces a trade-off between land rents and transport costs.

Von Thünen showed that competition for locations ensures that the resulting equilibrium allocation of land among the farmers is efficient. For every type of crop there is a bid rent curve which indicates, depending on the distance to the city, how much the farmers are willing to pay for the land (see panel *a* of Figure 4.2). Since the bid rent curves differ per crop, as a result of different prices for those crops in the city and different transport costs, the farmers of a particular type of crop are able to outbid their competitors (that is, they are willing to pay more) for any given distance to the city. As we move away from the city centre in panel *a*, we see that first (between points A and B) the flower producers outbid the other two groups of farmers, next (between points B and C) the vegetable producers are willing to pay the highest rents, and finally (between point C and D and thus the farthest removed from the city centre) the grain producers will pay the highest rent. This results in a concentric circle pattern of land use around the city, with every ring consisting of farms that grow the same crop; in sequence: flowers, vegetables, and grain; see panel *b* of Figure 4.2.

Urban economics probably started as a separate discipline in the 1960s. Alonso (1964), who essentially took the Von Thünen model, replaced the city by a central business district (CBD) and the farmers by commuters. The commuters travel back

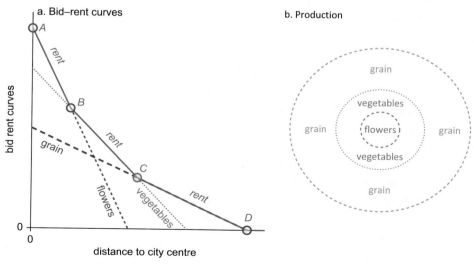

Figure 4.2 The Von Thünen model

and forth to their work at the CBD and each commuter derives utility from space of living but also faces transportation costs. Again, land rents are the highest near the centre and fall with distance. The bid rent approach can thus be applied and competition for land among the commuters implies an efficient allocation of land. The efficiency of land allocation in the monocentric model hinges on the assumption that there are no externalities of location.[3] Combined with Muth (1969) and Mills (1967), the model by Alonso (1964) is still the backbone for much of modern urban economics. We now turn our attention to a more detailed analysis of this model.

4.4   Choosing Location – the Rent Curve

We start our analysis with a simple model to illustrate the use of spatial equilibrium for determining economic variables (in this case, rent) at different locations within a city. We measure the size of the city by the number of people N. We say it is a *closed city model* if the population size is exogenously fixed, while it is an *open city model* if the population size is endogenously determined; see below. We assume that each person uses L units of land (see section 4.7 for a choice of the amount of land to use). As a consequence, the total amount of land we need for the entire city population is NL.

The geographic structure of the city is as simple as possible. It is a monocentric city model in which all individuals work in the CBD and live elsewhere. In this section we focus on the decisions of (identical) individuals and do not worry about builders or firms. The area surrounding the CBD is a featureless plane, implying that all points at the same distance from the city centre will have the same endogenous economic variables in equilibrium, such that this equilibrium is always characterized by concentric circles around the city centre. As a consequence, there is a maximum distance, d_{max} say, that people will be living away from the city centre. The total land area available at that distance is πd_{max}^2 (see Box 4.1 for a reminder of circle geometry), which must be equal to the amount NL needed for the city population as a whole (see the discussion above). Solving $NL = \pi d_{max}^2$ for the value of the maximum distance d_{max} once the size of the city population is known gives: $d_{max} = \sqrt{NL/\pi}$. The circle geometry explains why squares, square roots, and π keep popping up in functions of urban economic theory.

Each individual working in the city centre receives a wage rate and chooses at which distance d from the city centre she lives. Two variables are important for making this decision. First, an individual has to pay transport costs to travel from home (at distance d) to the city centre. These transport costs include actual

---

[3] If there are externalities there will not be a Pareto-efficient allocation of land; see Fujita (1989, part II).

BOX 4.1 Circle Geometry

When we are analysing the organization of space within cities, we frequently have to determine variables such as: (i) the distance d from a particular location l to the CBD, the central business district, or city centre; (ii) the location (and size) of points with a similar distance d to the city centre; (iii) the maximum distance between any two points with a similar distance d to the city centre; and (iv) the number of points within the circle.

There is, of course, a relationship between these four variables, as illustrated in Figure 4.3. Our frame of reference in this chapter will be the distance d from a point to the city centre, as used in the discussion above. It is, therefore, useful to list the other variables above relative to this distance d. More specifically: there are $2\pi d$ points with a similar distance d to the city centre (the circumference, point ii), the maximum distance between any two such points is $2d$ (the diameter, point iii), and there are πd^2 (the area, point iv) points within the circle. The distance of these points from the CBD ranges between zero and d.

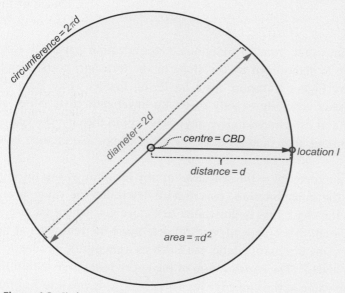

Figure 4.3 Circle geometry

payments, for example for bus or train tickets, and the time opportunity costs for travelling. For both reasons, transport costs rise as the distance to the city centre increases, so $t' > 0$ (see Box 4.2 for notation). Note that transport technology is summarized in the function $t(d)$, which can be taken as given. Second, individuals living at distance d from the city centre have to pay rent per unit of land, L, they occupy, such that total rent payments are $r(d)L$. We do not yet know what this rent function looks like. In fact, this function is *endogenously* determined by the spatial equilibrium described below.

All individuals have the same concave utility function $U(C)$, which depends on consumption only; see equation 4.1. The marginal utility of consumption is positive, so $U' > 0$, but diminishing, so $U'' < 0$. The level of consumption C is equal to the disposable income of each individual, which is equal to the wage rate W minus the transportation costs $t(d)$ and minus the rent costs $r(d)L$; see equation 4.2.[4] Each individual's objective function is therefore to maximize equation 4.1, subject to the budget restriction given in equation 4.2.

$$\max_{c,d} U(C) \tag{4.1}$$

$$C = W - t(d) - r(d)L \tag{4.2}$$

Using two alternative methods, namely the Lagrange multiplier method and direct substitution, Technical Note 4.1 shows that the crucial first-order condition for an optimum is given in equation 4.3:

$$r'(d) = -\frac{t'(d)}{L} < 0 \tag{4.3}$$

This equation indicates that from an individual's optimization perspective the slope of the rent curve is determined by the slope of the transport costs. People are only willing to pay higher transport costs for living further away from the city centre if these higher costs are exactly offset by lower rent costs. Since all individuals are similar and can choose to live anywhere within the city, the *spatial equilibrium* must guarantee that they all have the same disposable income level $W - t(d) - r(d)L$.

To close the model and determine the rent level at any location within the city, we need to (i) specify the transportation costs and (ii) determine the value at any location point within the city.[5] This is illustrated in Figure 4.4, where we use (i) linear transport costs, such that $t(d) = \tau d$, and (ii) determine the rent level at the edge of the city from some alternative land use, such as agricultural production, which provides a rent level $\bar{r}$. The construction of the entire rent curve within the city is now simple. The value at the city edge (at distance d_{max}) is equal to $\bar{r}$. From there on, the slope of the rent gradient must be equal to $-\tau / L$, as given by condition 4.3. This determines the rent level at any location within the city. In particular, it determines the rent level $r(0)$ in the city centre, which is equal to $\bar{r} + \tau d_{max} / L$.

---

[4] Rents are paid to absentee landlords, implying that rents do not affect equilibrium outcomes; see also Chapter 5.

[5] Note that condition 4.3 is a differential equation, which in principle has a continuum number of solutions (see Box 4.3 for a brief discussion).

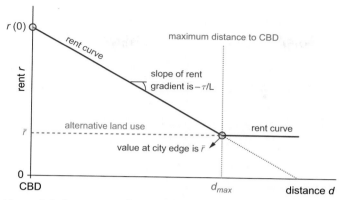

Figure 4.4 Construction of rent curve with linear transport costs

---

BOX 4.2 Notation

If a function $f(x)$ depends on one variable only, we denote the first-order derivative by a prime' and the second-order derivative by a double prime ". If a function $f(x, y)$ depends on more than one variable, we denote the first-order derivative by the relevant sub-index, such as f_x and f_y, and the second-order derivatives by the two relevant sub-indices, such as f_{xx}, f_{xy}, and so on.

Obviously, for large cities d_{max} is higher, so the rent in the city centre is higher. It is common practice to determine the rent level at the edge of the city from some alternative land use. With linear transport costs, the solution to the rent curve is thus $r(d) = r(0) - \dfrac{\tau d}{L} = \bar{r} + \dfrac{\tau}{L}(d_{max} - d)$ for $d \le d_{max}$. From the discussion above on the determination of the city edge d_{max}, an alternative specification involving the population size N is thus: $r(d) = \bar{r} + \dfrac{\tau}{L}\left(\sqrt{NL/\pi} - d\right)$. The general predictions for empirical evaluation are that (i) rents decline with distance to the city centre and (ii) the speed of the decline depends on the transport costs. If we compare two cities at some moment in time or the same city at two different moments in time, we therefore expect the rents to fall more steeply with distance to the city centre if it is more costly or time consuming to get to the city centre.

Substituting the above results for linear transport costs in equation 4.2 allows us to determine the spatial equilibrium consumption level C_{se} for all individuals: $C_{se} = W - \bar{r}L - \tau d_{max} = W - \bar{r}L - \tau\sqrt{NL/\pi}$. The closed city model is now complete and shows that consumption, and thus utility, is rising with the wage rate W and falling with the cost of alternative land use $\bar{r}$, transport costs τ, and size of the city N. In the *open city model*, this consumption level is compared to some benchmark level $\bar{C}$ achieved in another city (or system of cities). The size of the city as measured by the number of people N is then determined by equating C_{se} and $\bar{C}$ and solving for N. The solution is $N = \dfrac{\pi}{L}\left(\dfrac{W - \bar{r} - \bar{C}}{\tau}\right)^2$, which indicates that the size of the city is rising in the wage rate W and falling in transport cost τ, the cost of alternative land use $\bar{r}$, and benchmark consumption level $\bar{C}$. In the remainder of this chapter, we take the size of the city as given.

4.5   The Rent Curve in New York City

To illustrate how the rent curve derived in section 4.4 operates in practice, we provide some information on average rents in 2017 in different neighbourhoods of New York City. Benefiting from an excellent natural harbour along what is now called the Hudson river and with a good location relative to incoming European settlers, the city of New York (known as New Amsterdam prior to 1664) became the gateway to America for several centuries, with the Statue of Liberty as its main symbol since 1886 (a statue donated by France to the United States as a 100-year birthday present). New York City itself consists of five boroughs (Brooklyn, Queens, Manhattan, The Bronx, and Staten Island) and has a population of about 8.5 million, while the *agglomeration* of New York (the metropolitan statistical area) has a population of about 20 million (http://factfinder.census.gov). On both counts, New York is the largest city in the United States. In the mid twentieth century New York was also the largest city in the world, as well as the first agglomeration to surpass ten million people. Today, Tokyo in Japan is the world's largest agglomeration.

The rent curve derived in section 4.4 predicts that rents decline the further away you are from the city centre to compensate for rising transportation costs within the city. We chose City Hall (in Manhattan) to represent the centre of New York City and gathered average rent information for 92 different neighbourhoods of the five boroughs in NYC from the rentjungle website (www.rentjungle.com). There are three neighbourhoods (all in Manhattan) with average rents above $4,000 per month. The highest average rents, almost $5,000 per month, are paid in Carnegie Hill, close to Central Park. The second highest rents are paid in Tribeca (more than $4,800 per month) and the third highest in Central Park (almost $4,500 per month). There are four neighbourhoods with average rents of less than $1,000 per month, namely Port Richmond, Oakwood, Williams Bridge, and Throggs Neck. To relate these rents to the distance from the city centre, we collected coordinate information (longitude and latitude) from the latlong website (www.latlong.net). Next, we calculated the distance of each neighbourhood to the city centre based on these coordinates, which is therefore an 'as the crow flies' distance. For the three neighbourhoods with the highest rents, the average distance to the city centre is 6.0 km and the average rent is $4,769 per month. For the four neighbourhoods with the lowest rents, the average distance to the city centre is 18.6 km and the average rent is $851. This suggests that there is indeed a trade-off between distance to the city centre and rent to be paid.

A more complete picture of this trade-off is provided in Figure 4.5, which shows the relationship between average rent paid and distance to the city centre for all 92 New York neighbourhoods. On the one hand the picture is a success for the model of section 4.4, as there is a clear negative relationship between distance and rents, such that the dashed regression line explains about 52 per cent of the variance in average rents. On the other hand the picture is less successful for this model, as it shows substantial variation in average rents for neighbourhoods at similar distances to the centre. Chinatown and the Garment District, for example, are on average closer to the city centre than Tribeca, Carnegie Hill, and Central Park, but the average rent paid there is 'only' $1,710, or about 36 per cent of the rent paid in these neighbourhoods. We have to keep in mind, of course, that these are average rents per neighbourhood and that it is quite likely that the average floor space and service level provided in the more expensive neighbourhoods is bigger and more complete than in the less expensive neighbourhoods. Note that these space and service issues themselves are not incorporated in the basic model of section 4.4 (but see sections 4.7 and 4.9 on how to incorporate these issues), but there are also other aspects to keep in mind when evaluating the success of our model, in particular natural geography and man-made geography, as we will now discuss in more detail.

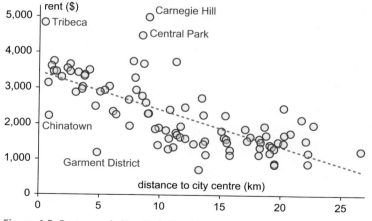

Figure 4.5 Rent curve in New York City, 2017

Source: calculations based on average monthly rents per neighbourhood information on www.rentjungle.com (24 April 2017) and distance calculations based on coordinates obtained from www.latlong.net; 92 neighbourhoods included.

Remember that we assumed in section 4.4 that the 'area surrounding [the city centre] is a featureless plane'. This assumption was made to ensure a free and uninterrupted flow of people and goods. New York is far from a featureless plane. As illustrated in Figure 4.6, which provides a two-dimensional indication of the location relative to natural and man-made geographical features of the neighbourhoods identified in Figure 4.5 and their average rents, there are various waterways and islands creating natural obstacles to the free flow of people and goods. There are man-made bridges and tunnels to partially overcome these obstacles, which by themselves create new disturbances for the flows of people and goods. A closer look at Figure 4.6 also shows that the neighbourhoods are not evenly spaced around the city centre. A large space close to the city centre on the other side of the Hudson river is not incorporated in the neighbourhoods of Figure 4.5 for man-made institutional reasons: these neighbourhoods are located in a different city (Jersey City) and a different state (New Jersey) and for those reasons not included in the analysis above.

Finally, note that a closer look at Figure 4.6 also allows us to understand why rents in Carnegie Hill and Central Park are so high relative to the rents in Tribeca, which is much closer to the city centre. These two neighbourhoods are located right along Central Park, a prime example of a man-made amenity that was created in

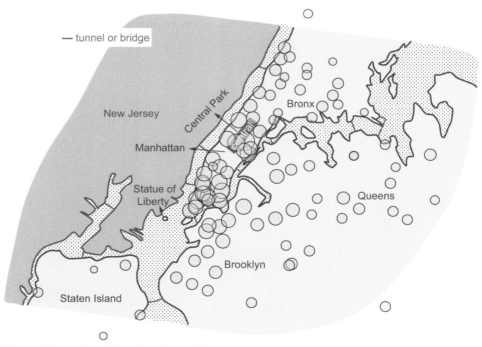

Figure 4.6 Location of New York City neighbourhoods and average rent
Source: see Figure 4.5; size of bubbles proportional to average rent.

the mid nineteenth century and allows people to relax and enjoy nature while living in the city. People who live and work in New York love to live close by Central Park, which drives up rents in the vicinity of the park. We have a closer look at the impact of amenities and other issues in section 4.10. To conclude, we should note that, taking all the aspects of natural and man-made geographical obstacles surrounding New York City into consideration, the main prediction of the basic urban model that rents fall as distance to the city centre rises as illustrated in Figure 4.5 can only be considered a success and an indication of the power of the forces underlying this model. Nonetheless, our next example (discussed in section 4.8) analyses population density in Indianapolis, a location for which the area surrounding the city can more adequately be described as a 'featureless plane'.

4.6 Choosing Transport Method – Steepness of Rent Curve

In the empirical specification of section 4.4 individuals are confronted with a simple, linear transport cost technology and then choose the optimal location within the city. In practice, people have more choices. In this and forthcoming sections we model various other choices as variations of the basic model derived in section 4.4. We start with a choice of transport method as well as location; see Wheaton (1977).

The basic idea is that people choose different means of transportation depending on the distance they have to travel. If a location is close by you will probably walk, which is slow but a pretty good representation of the linear transport costs we used in section 4.4, namely proportional to distance (mostly depending on the opportunity cost of time) and without a fixed cost to get started. If you have to travel somewhat further, you might choose to go by bicycle, which is faster than walking (so you have lower marginal costs) but requires a modest fixed cost for buying the bicycle (and insuring it against theft). If you have to travel a larger distance still, you might choose to go by public transport (bus, metro, or train), which over longer distances is faster than going by bicycle, but requires a larger per-time-period investment to take advantage of year-round fares.[6] Finally, over even longer distances it may be most convenient to buy a car, which is expensive, and drive yourself.

$$t_i(d) = f_i + \tau_i d \qquad\qquad 4.4$$

In this discussion, there are various transport methods $i = 1,..,I$, each with their own technology parameters, leading to total transport cost at a particular

---

[6] Or a fixed cost investment because you first have to walk to the public transport station before you can get started.

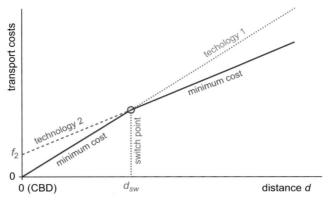

Figure 4.7 Different transport methods and minimum costs

distance level d from the city centre as given in equation 4.4. We assume that the transport methods can be ranked in terms of declining marginal costs τ_i and rising fixed costs f_i, such that $\tau_i > \tau_{i+1}$ and $f_i < f_{i+1}$. An individual now faces two choices, namely which distance d to live away from the city centre and, given this distance, what means of transportation to use. We can solve this optimization problem in two steps, by first determining what means of transportation to use for any given distance from the city centre and then at which location to live.

Figure 4.7 illustrates the first step of the optimization problem if there are two transport methods ($I = 2$) and the fixed cost for transport method 1 is zero ($f_1 = 0$). At any distance d from the city centre, the individual chooses the transport method that minimizes transport costs at that distance (as indicated by the solid *minimum cost* line in the figure). At short distances, individuals choose transport method 1 with high marginal costs and zero fixed costs because that method has the lowest costs. At distance d_{sw} (*sw* for 'switch') in the figure, transport costs for method 1 are the same as for method 2 and the individual is indifferent between using either method. At higher distances, transport costs using method 2 are lower than using method 1, so individuals choose method 2 if the distance to the city centre is higher than the switching distance d_{sw}. In a more general setting with a larger range of transport methods, the switching distance from method i to $i+1$ is determined by the distance $(f_{i+1} - f_i)/(\tau_i - \tau_{i+1})$ and there is a sequence of switching distances.[7] The outcome of the first optimization problem is thus a minimum transport cost level $t(d)$ at all possible distances to the city centre, characterized by an increasing range of switching distances. We use this outcome in equation 4.2 of the model analysed in section 4.4. Note that the switching distances are

---

[7] If there are transport methods for which the ranking hypothesis we use does not hold, they will not be chosen in equilibrium and are therefore irrelevant from an economic perspective.

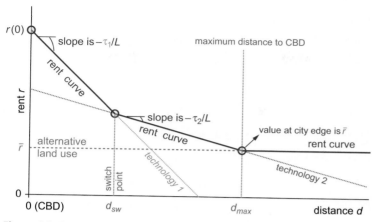

Figure 4.8 Rent curve with different transport technologies

only relevant for the model to the extent that they are below the maximum distance d_{max}.

The second step of the optimization problem uses the outcome of the first step (which transport method to use) as analysed in section 4.4. This means, in particular, that equation 4.3 still holds, such that the slope of the rent curve is still determined by the slope of transport costs: $r'(d) = -t'(d) / L$. The only thing we have to take into consideration now is that this slope is equal to $-\tau_1 / L$ from close to the city centre up to the first switching point, then equal to $-\tau_2 / L$ up to the second switching point, and so on. This is illustrated in Figure 4.8 for the two transport methods analysed in Figure 4.7, assuming that $d_{sw} < d_{max}$. The rent at the edge of the city is again determined by $\bar{r}$, the return to the alternative use of land. From there up to the switch point d_{sw} the slope of the rent curve is equal to $-\tau_2 / L$. At that point, individuals switch to the other transport method and the slope of the rent curve becomes steeper and equal to $-\tau_1 / L$. This allows us to determine the value of the rent curve at the switch point and at the city centre (see question 4.3). This approach allows us to determine the choice of transport methods and enables us to explain why the rent curve tends to become steeper close to the city centre.

4.7   Choosing Land Area – Population Density

We have analysed the choice of where to live within the city in section 4.4 and extended this analysis to include the choice of transport method in section 4.6. In both sections, we have taken the amount of land L occupied per person as given and made it the same for everyone. This is clearly at odds with real-life observations, where the amount of land used per person close to the city centre (where rents are high) is small compared to the amount of land used in locations further

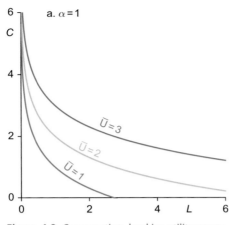 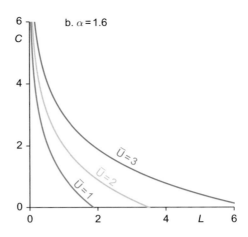

Figure 4.9 Consumption–land iso-utility curves

away from the city centre (where rents are low). We now want to give individuals the choice of where to live in the city (distance d from the city centre) and how much land L to use at that location. To do this, we must make people care about the amount of living space available as well as their consumption level, which enables them to make a trade-off between consumption and land use. This requires an adjustment of the utility function used in section 4.4, which only focused on the utility of consumption (see equation 4.1), to incorporate both consumption and land (see equation 4.5).

To make the exposition of the choice of location and land area as clear as possible, we make two simplifying assumptions. First, we use a specific utility function, as provided in equation 4.5. This additively separable utility function uses a parameter α to represent the importance of land use relative to consumption (the higher α, the higher the importance of land) and gives rise to rather standard iso-utility curves, although they cut the L-axis, as illustrated in Figure 4.9. Second, we focus on only one transport method, which is linear in distance, such that the transport costs are equal to τd; see equation 4.6. Together these two assumptions give rise to a simple analytical solution, as discussed below. The main prediction of the model, namely that the use of land rises with the distance to the city centre, holds quite generally and does not depend on the simplifying assumptions; see Technical Note 4.2.

$$\max_{c,d,L} U(C,L) = C + \alpha ln(L) \qquad\qquad 4.5$$

$$C = W - \tau d - r(d)L \qquad\qquad 4.6$$

The individual's optimization problem is summarized in equations 4.5 and 4.6, where utility (which depends on consumption and the use of land) is maximized by choosing the level of consumption, where to locate in the city, and the use of land, subject to a budget restriction. We can, of course, only make two choices freely, since the third choice is determined by the budget restriction. For example, if we choose the distance d from the city centre and the amount of land L to use then equation 4.6 determines our consumption level. As a result, the solution of our problem is characterized by two first-order conditions as given in equations 4.7 and 4.8; see Technical Note 4.2 for details.

$$r'(d) = -\tau / L \qquad\qquad 4.7$$

$$r(d) = \alpha / L \qquad\qquad 4.8$$

Equation 4.7 is the same as equation 4.3 of section 4.4 (but now with linear transport costs). The rent curve is therefore still determined by the slope of the transport costs, since people are still only willing to pay higher transport costs for living further away from the city centre if these higher costs are offset by lower rent costs. It is reassuring to note that our previously derived result still holds. The only change that we *do* have to be aware of is that the amount of land used at a particular distance to the city centre is no longer constant but changes (and is chosen optimally) as this distance changes.

Equation 4.8 is new and determines the trade-off between rent payments, which is the marginal utility of consumption foregone, and the marginal utility α / L of extra land use. Other things being equal, individuals are willing to pay a higher rent at distance d from the city centre if the parameter α, which reflects the importance of land relative to consumption in the utility function, is higher. Note that our choice of functional form makes equations 4.7 and 4.8 fairly simple, which allows us to find an exact solution.

To find the exact solution, we first solve equation 4.8 to determine $1/L$, the inverse of the amount of land used (an indicator of population density): $1/L = r(d)/\alpha$. Second, we substitute this in equation 4.7 to get the differential equation given in equation 4.9. This equation is discussed in example 2 of Box 4.3 (with $a = -\tau/\alpha$), which also provides its particular solution if we know the rental rate at the city centre, as given in equation 4.10. Finally, to characterize this solution in terms of the relationship between distance to the city centre and either the amount of land used or its inverse, we substitute it back in equation 4.8, as given in equation 4.11.

$$r'(d) = -\frac{\tau}{\alpha} r(d) \qquad\qquad 4.9$$

$$r(d) = r(0) e^{-\frac{\tau}{\alpha}d} \qquad\qquad 4.10$$

$$\frac{1}{L} = \frac{r(d)}{\alpha} = \frac{r(0) e^{-\frac{\tau}{\alpha}d}}{\alpha} \Rightarrow \ln\left(\frac{1}{L}\right) = \ln\left(\frac{r(0)}{\alpha}\right) - \frac{\tau}{\alpha}d \qquad\qquad 4.11$$

BOX 4.3 Differential Equations

Differential equations impose a restriction, in the shape of a functional form, on the derivative of a function. A solution to a differential equation is a function that satisfies this restriction. There are ordinary and partial differential equations, equations of first order and higher orders, and there are general and particular solutions. Here we just give two simple examples, as used in this chapter.

Example 1: $f'(x) = a$, where a is some parameter

We are looking for a function f for which the condition on its derivative given in example 1 holds. A 'guess' solution is the function $f(x) = b + ax$, where b is some other parameter. If we differentiate it, we get $f'(x) = a$, which indeed satisfies the condition. We also note that there are actually infinitely many solutions to the condition imposed in example 1, since the function $f(x) = b + ax$ satisfies this condition for *any* value of b. We say $f(x) = b + ax$ is a *general* solution. To know the *particular* solution under some given circumstances and narrow down the condition imposed in example 1 to only one solution, we need to know the value of the function f at some given point. This is called an initial condition (although in growth theory, for example, it may also be a terminal condition or a limit condition). Suppose we know that the value of f if $x = 0$ is 4. Then this knowledge determines the value of b, which is 4, and the particular solution is $f(x) = 4 + ax$. An example is discussed in section 4.4 with linear transport costs.

Example 2: $g'(x) = ag(x)$, where a is some parameter

This example is already a bit more challenging. We are looking for a function g for which the condition on its derivative given in example 2 holds. A 'guess' solution is the function $g(x) = be^{ax}$, where b is some other parameter. If we differentiate it, we get $g'(x) = abe^{ax} = a(be^{ax}) = ag(x)$, which indeed satisfies the condition in example 2. Again, there are infinitely many solutions to the condition imposed in example 2, since the function $g(x) = be^{ax}$ satisfies this condition for *any* value of b, which is thus the general solution. To know the particular solution under some given circumstances we again have to know some initial condition. For example, if we know the value of g if $x = 0$, then this value is equal to b and the particular solution is $g(x) = g(0)e^{ax}$. An example is discussed in section 4.7. Both examples are straightforward, but the calculus of differential equations can become complicated quite quickly.

Taking natural logs of equation 4.11 provides a simple empirical prediction on the implication of land choice in this spatial equilibrium model: the log of population density falls linearly with distance to the city centre. Alternatively, the log of land used per person rises linearly with distance to the city centre. This type of specification is frequently used in empirical work. The next section illustrates this by analysing population density in Indianapolis.

4.8   Population Density in Indianapolis

Indianapolis is the capital and largest city of Indiana. It was founded in 1821 as the new seat for the government of Indiana. Today, the city itself houses about 853,000 people, while the agglomeration (metropolitan statistical area) consists of about two million people (http://factfinder.census.gov).[8] The city is probably best known for the Indianapolis 500, a 500 mile (805 km) automobile race held over the Memorial Day weekend. The largest employer is Eli Lilly, a large, multinational pharmaceutical company with its headquarters in Indianapolis. The geographical features of the city itself and its surroundings can probably best be described as *flat*. As such, it is a better example of a 'featureless plane' than the example of New York City discussed in section 4.5, although it is located along the small White river. We use Indianapolis as an example to briefly evaluate the empirical validity of equation 4.11 on the relationship between population density and distance to the city centre, as analysed in section 4.7. We do that in two steps. First, we provide information based on the ZIP Census Tabulation Areas (ZCTA) introduced in section 4.2. Second, we provide more detailed grid information on the basis of census blocks.

For our discussion we take the coordinates (latitude and longitude) of Soldiers and Sailors Monument as the centre of Indianapolis. Since the Census Bureau provides internal point coordinates for all ZCTAs, we can use these coordinates to calculate the distance to the centre of Indianapolis 'as the crow flies'. We include all ZCTAs within a 50 km radius in our analysis.[9] Figure 4.10 shows the location of these 148 ZCTAs with bubbles proportional to population size and some of the larger locations away from the city centre, such as Martinsville and Noblesville, identified for reference. We note that the distribution of these locations is more evenly spaced than the neighbourhoods of New York City in Figure 4.6.

The first step of our analysis uses the population information and the land area information for each ZCTA to calculate average population density. The prediction

---

[8] Data for 2015.
[9] More precisely, ZCTAs with a distance of 51 km or more were excluded.

Figure 4.10 Indianapolis ZCTA population within 50 km radius from city centre
Source: calculations based on US Census data 2000, downloaded from the Missouri Census Data Center
website (mcdc.missouri.edu); bubbles proportional to population size; identified roads are interstate
highways and ring road.

of equation 4.11 is that the log of population density declines linearly with distance to the city centre. The outcome of this prediction for ZCTAs within a 50 km radius from the centre of Indianapolis is illustrated in Figure 4.11 using a log scale for the vertical axis depicting population density. There is a clear negative relationship with a fairly good fit. The regression line depicted in the figure explains about 55 per cent of the variance in population density and has a slope of −0.089, which gives an estimated value for τ / α equal to 0.089. We also note that for some observations the deviation from the regression line can be substantial. This holds, for example, for ZCTA 46102, which is part of Boone County, has a very small population of only 40 people and also a very small land area of only 0.026 km², leading to a high population density of 1,544 people per km².

To get a better feel for the implications of the smaller observations with a substantial deviation from the regression line, Figure 4.12 repeats Figure 4.10, but this time with bubbles proportional to population density instead of population

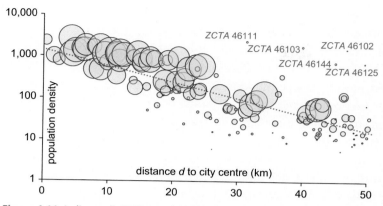

Figure 4.11 Indianapolis ZCTA population density and distance to city centre
Source: see Figure 4.10; population density in people per km²; bubbles proportional to population size;
148 ZCTAs.

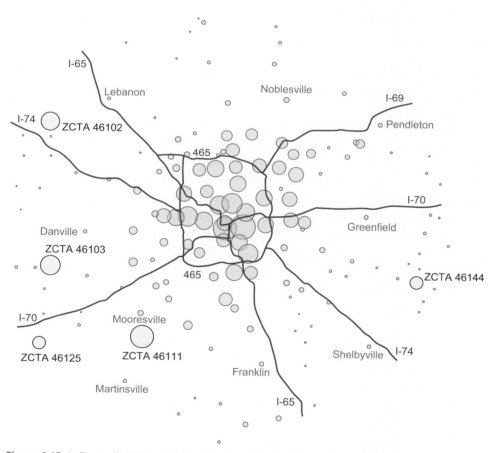

Figure 4.12 Indianapolis ZCTA population density within 50 km radius to city centre
Source: see Figure 4.10; bubbles proportional to population density; roads are interstate highways and
ring road.

size. When we compare the two figures, the observations for five 'outlier' ZCTAs numbered 46102, 46103, 46111, 46125, and 46144, jump out. These five outliers are separately identified in both Figure 4.11 and Figure 4.12. The average population for the outliers is 130 people, or only 1.3 per cent of the overall average. The average land area of the outliers is 0.11 km^2, or only 0.2 per cent of the overall average. This suggests that their outlier status is more based on the boundary peculiarities of the ZCTAs than on the true underlying information on population density. It also suggests we might want to get a better view of the relationship between population density and distance to the city centre based on more detailed information.

The Census Bureau provides much more detailed information on population and land area for the census blocks.[10] For the state of Indiana, for example, there are more than 200,000 of these census blocks. Not all of these blocks have positive population, but all blocks have internal point coordinates, such that we can calculate the distance to the centre of Indianapolis. There are 24,752 blocks with a positive population within a 50 km radius from the city centre. The average population size of these blocks is 60 people and the average land area is 0.295 km^2. We could, of course, construct a similar graph as in Figure 4.11 and evaluate the fit of log population density relative to distance from the city centre for these blocks, but the blocks are even smaller than the ZCTAs and as a consequence the variation in population density is even larger, such that we prefer to use a different procedure based on a geographical approach instead.[11] In the end this leads to a scatter plot provided in Figure 4.14 and discussed at the end of this section.

The approach we want to use to illustrate more detailed variations in population density is based on geographical gridpoints in combination with information taken from the census blocks. We construct gridpoints based on coordinates (latitude and longitude) on the basis of 0.01 decimals. The gridpoint (40.00, −86.00) is an example. Its direct latitude neighbours are (40.01, −86.00) and (39.99, −86.00). We treat all of these gridpoints in the same way. First, we calculate which census blocks are in a 3 km radius of the gridpoint.[12] Second, we use the total population and the total land area of these census blocks to determine the average population density for this gridpoint.[13] Third, we determine which gridpoints are within a

---

[10] Note that we consistently refer to land area. For our calculations we ignored water areas, because most people do not live on the water (and if they do, they tend to be located on the edge of the water to easily access land).

[11] For reference: the maximum population density for the blocks is almost 200,000 people per km^2, the slope of the regression line is −0.071, and the line explains about 24 per cent of the variance in population density.

[12] See question 4.4 for information and graphs using a 2 km radius instead of a 3 km radius.

[13] Our discussion below focuses on gridpoints within a 50 km radius of the city centre, but the construction of average population density at any gridpoint is based on all Indiana census blocks within a 3 km radius.

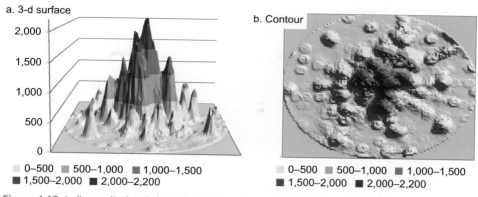

Figure 4.13 Indianapolis detailed grid population density, 50 km radius to city centre
Source: calculations based on US Census data 2000, downloaded from the Missouri Census Data Center website (mcdc.missouri.edu); density in people/km²; based on census blocks in 3 km radius; see main text for details.

50 km radius from the centre of Indianapolis (there are 8,598 such gridpoints), which we use for our further discussion.

The results of these calculations are illustrated in Figure 4.13, where panel *a* provides a 3-d surface plot and panel *b* provides a contour plot. Evidently, there is substantial variation in population density using this method. The average population density of a grid point is 184 people per km² (the median is 39 people), which ranges from almost zero to a maximum of 2,133. The values are clearly higher close to the city centre than at distances further away, but there are also irregular peaks at various distances from the city centre. Comparing the panels of Figure 4.13 with Figure 4.10 we can readily identify some of these local peaks. The contour plot (panel *b*) also shows clear radiant lines of higher population density away from the city centre. We can recognize these as pockets of higher population density along main roads leading into the city centre. Obviously, this raises an endogeneity question. Is the population density higher because of the roads or are the roads there because of the higher population density?

We conclude with Figure 4.14, which shows the relationship between the log of population density and distance to the city centre using gridpoints. There is a clear negative relationship, as illustrated by the regression line (slope is −0.091 and 57 per cent of the variance is explained) and the curvy averages line. Our method has reduced most of the variation at shorter distances (say up to 20 km), but the variation is still substantial at further distances, even if we look at averages. As discussed above, this may be related to man-made geography (such as roads or amenities); see also section 4.10.

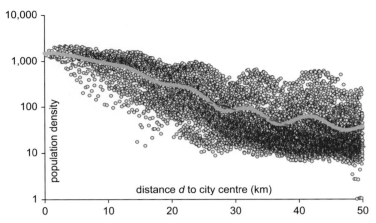

Figure 4.14 Indianapolis gridpoint population density and distance to city centre
Source: see Figure 4.10; the dashed line is a regression line; the curvy line denotes the average population density (at distance steps of 0.1 km) of all gridpoints from distance x to the city centre to distance $x + 2$.

4.9   Choosing Housing – Building Height

An important feature of modern cities is how high the buildings are at the centre of the city relative to distances further away, as well as the building height in the city centre for small cities relative to large cities. The Emporis website (www.emporis .com) provides detailed information on (tall) buildings from around the world. According to the information available on 2 May 2017, the average height of the 200 tallest buildings in the world was 340 metres (median is 316 metres) and the average number of floors was 74 (median is 71).[14] The correlation between building height and the number of floors is high (0.83), such that it is no surprise that the Burj Khalifa in Dubai is both the tallest building (at 828 m) and has the most floors (163). The information is illustrated in Figure 4.15 by providing both the highest building constructed in a given year on the list (bubbles) and the highest building in the world up to that year (solid line). The graph starts in 1965 and thus excludes the four buildings on the list constructed in the USA in the period 1930 to 1932.

Only six buildings on the list were the world's tallest at some point in time, starting with the Chrysler Building in New York (1930) and followed by the Empire State Building (New York, 1931), The Willis Tower (Chicago, 1974), the Petronas Towers (Kuala Lumpur, 1998), Taipei 101 (Taipei, 2004), and the Burj Khalifa (Dubai, 2010). Figure 4.15 suggests that the highest building constructed in a given

---

[14] The website identifies 165 'existing' and 35 'under construction' buildings. Most buildings under construction were scheduled for completion in 2016 or 2017 (except for the Salesforce Tower in San Francisco in 2018 and the China World Trade Center Tower IIIB in Beijing for which no year is given). The statistical differences between these two groups (average and median height and number of floors) are minimal, so we do not analyse them separately.

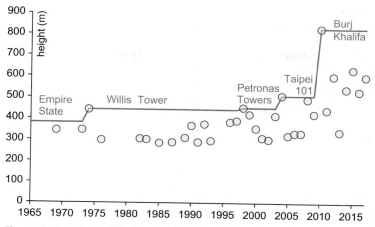

Figure 4.15 Tallest buildings in the world, 2017
Source: based on data from www.emporis.com, downloaded 2 May 2017; circles indicate highest building in the top 200 list constructed in that year; solid line indicates highest building in the world in a given year.

year started to rise around 1985. By far the largest number of tall buildings (96) is located in China (includes Hong Kong), followed at some distance by the USA and Dubai (29 each), the United Arab Emirates (6), and South Korea, Russia, and Saudi Arabia (5 each). Most tall buildings were constructed recently; 141 were completed in 2010 or later. This holds in particular for China, where 79 out of the 96 tallest buildings (82 per cent) were completed in 2010 or later.

We can use a modification of the model analysed in section 4.7 to get a better understanding of the relationship between building height and distance to the city centre. At the same time, this allows us to introduce developers as new entrepreneurs in our model and the trade-offs they face in terms of the use of capital and land depending on the prices they face; see below. The modification follows Muth (1969) and Brueckner (1987) by analysing directly an individual's demand for housing space H measured in square metres, relative to the demand for consumption goods C. Individuals therefore care about the interior living space (rather than the amount of land on which this space is built, see below). To make the analysis as simple as possible, we use the same functional forms as in equations 4.5 and 4.6 by simply using H for housing instead of L for land. Individuals thus maximize $U(C,H) = C + \alpha \ln(H)$, subject to the budget restriction $C = W - \tau d - p(d)H$, where $p(d)$ denotes the price per square metre of housing at a distance d away from the city centre. The first-order conditions for an optimum are, of course, still given by equations 4.7 and 4.8, where we again use H instead of L and $p(d)$ instead of $r(d)$. We therefore have a price for housing gradient determined by the transport costs $[p'(d) = -\tau / H]$ and a trade-off between the utility of housing and consumption $[p(d) = \alpha / H]$. Combining this information gives us a differential equation for the price of housing as in equation 4.9 $[p'(d) = -(\tau / \alpha) p(d)]$, which can be solved as we did in equation 4.10 $[p(d) = p(0)e^{-\tau d/\alpha}]$.

The interesting new aspect of the model is that the supply of housing is provided by entrepreneur-developers using capital K and land L in a concave housing production function $H(K,L)$ with constant returns to scale. For ease of exposition, we use a Cobb-Douglas specification: $H(K,L) = K^{\beta}L^{1-\beta}$. The developers maximize profits, which are equal to the revenue $p(d)H(K,L)$ minus the cost iK associated with the use of capital K and the cost $r(d)L$ associated with the use of land L. The cost of capital is determined by the interest rate i, which is given exogenously. The cost of land is determined by the rental rate $r(d)$, which is determined within the model but taken as given by the developers, as is the price of housing $p(d)$. Because of constant returns to scale production, we can write profits in *intensive* form if we define the capital-land ratio $k = K/L$. This is done in equation 4.12, which provides the objective function for entrepreneurs. A rise in k implies more housing per unit of land, which we take as an indication that the building must be higher, such that we use k as an indicator of building height.

$$\max_{k,L} \left(p(d)k^{\beta} - ik - r(d) \right) L \qquad \qquad 4.12$$

It is clear from equation 4.12 that entrepreneurs can first choose k to maximize profits per unit of land and then choose the optimal amount of land. The first-order condition for the choice of k is given in equation 4.13, which simply equates the marginal product of k with its costs i. The first-order condition for the choice of L is given in equation 4.14. If the revenue per unit of land is higher than the costs $[pk^{\beta} > ik + r]$ she would want to use an infinite amount of land to supply an infinite amount of housing and have infinite profits. This cannot be an economic equilibrium. If revenue per unit of land is strictly less than the costs $[pk^{\beta} < ik + r]$ she would not provide any housing at all, which also cannot be an equilibrium. The equality provided in equation 4.14 is a zero profit condition arising from entry and exit of entrepreneurs in the housing market. It implies that the size of an individual developer (measured by L) is indeterminate, and also irrelevant.

$$\beta p(d)k^{\beta-1} - i = 0 \qquad \qquad 4.13$$

$$p(d)k^{\beta} - ik - r(d) = 0 \qquad \qquad 4.14$$

The two equations above connect the changes in housing price p, which is a function of the distance to the city centre, with changes in the capital–land ratio (indicative of building height) and changes in rental rates. Equation 4.13 allows us to easily solve for the optimal k as a function of the interest rate and the price of housing: $k = A\left(p(d) \right)^{1/(1-\beta)}$, where $A \equiv (\beta/i)^{1/(1-\beta)}$. We can then use this optimal k in equation 4.14 to determine the rental rate at a distance d from the city centre: $r(d) = B\left(p(d) \right)^{1/(1-\beta)}$, with $B \equiv (1-\beta)(\beta/i)^{\beta/(1-\beta)}$ as explained in Technical Note 4.3. Both k and r are therefore power functions of the housing price p, which as

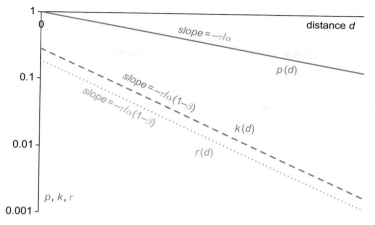

Figure 4.16 Distance to city centre and price of housing, land rent, and capital–land ratio
Note: price of housing at city centre normalized to one; vertical axis has log scale; for p, k, r, and d see main text.

we already know is an exponential function of the distance d to the city centre as illustrated in Figure 4.16 (where we use a log scale on the vertical axis, such that the price of housing is a straight line with slope $-\tau/\alpha$, see also Box 4.3).

Now note that both k and r are functions of p to the power $1/(1-\beta) > 1$, since $\beta \in (0,1)$. This implies that the slope of the capital-land ratio and the rental rate, which are also depicted in Figure 4.16, is steeper than of the housing price p, namely $-\tau/\alpha(1-\beta)$. At distances further away from the city centre rental rates are low, which provides developers a small incentive to invest in capital intensive buildings. Close to the city centre, on the other hand, rental rates are high, which provides developers a clear incentive to save on the use of expensive land by constructing costly, capital intensive, high buildings. As a consequence, this makes land close to the city centre even more valuable, which is reflected by the fact that the rental rate gradient is steeper than the housing price gradient.

Note that the slope of the rental rate becomes steeper if transport costs τ rise and the preference of consumption relative to housing α falls. This is similar to the analysis in section 4.7. We now derived, in addition, that the slope of the rental rate also becomes steeper if β rises (which means $1-\beta$ falls, which in turn means $1/(1-\beta)$ rises). Recall that $H = K^\beta L^{1-\beta}$, such that β can be taken as an indicator of the importance of capital in the production function of housing. The higher this importance, the steeper the slope of the rental rate and the steeper the slope of the capital-land ratio, which is the indicator of building height. If we argue, as seems reasonable, that the importance of capital in construction has been rising over time, this suggests that similar sized cities that were constructed a long time ago (like many European cities) have lower buildings in the city centre than cities that were constructed more recently (like many American cities). Although housing construction functions may currently be similar in Europe and America, the building height of many European cities in the city centre is now still restricted for a range of historical and institutional reasons. The information provided at the beginning of this section on tall buildings suggests that such restrictions are less stringent in many rapidly developing Asian nations, like China and Dubai.

What does the analysis above imply if we compare big and small cities? The answer is straightforward, as long as we remember the (initial) condition for determining the rental rate at some point (going from a general to a particular solution, see Box 4.3). Recall that all functional forms are the same for big and small cities. This implies that the maximum distance to the city centre d_{max} must be bigger for big cities than for small cities. The rental rate at this edge of the city is determined by the alternative use of rent $\bar{r}$, which we take to be the same for both small and big cities. This then allows us to determine the rental rate at the city centre: $ln(r(0)) = \ln(\bar{r}) + \dfrac{\tau d_{max}}{\alpha(1-\beta)}$; see Technical Note 4.3 for details. The rental rate at the city centre is thus higher for big cities, as are (by direct substitution) the price of housing and building height (capital–land ratio k).

4.10 Other Issues

We have constructed the main spatial equilibrium model of location choice within the city in section 4.4 and analysed its implications for the rent curve. We have extended the model in section 4.6 to analyse the impact of different transport methods, in section 4.7 to show the implications of choosing land area, and in section 4.9 to choose the consumption level of housing and its implications for the decisions of entrepreneurs regarding the amount of capital to use, the rental rate, and building height. The ideas developed here have also been used to get a better understanding of a range of important other issues. We briefly discuss a few of these issues in this section, without getting into too much technical detail.

4.10.1 Heterogeneity

So far, all individuals have been the same, earning the same income level, having the same utility function, and making the same types of decisions. On the one hand, this allows us to illustrate the force of the spatial equilibrium by deriving predictions on rental rates, house prices, population density, and so on that can be (reasonably successfully) empirically tested. On the other hand, this prevents us from analysing the consequences of differences between individuals (heterogeneity) for various aspects that are also important at the city level. To illustrate the possibilities in this respect, we discuss a simple example of income heterogeneity as it allows us to understand why rich and poor people may live in different parts of the city.

A similar type of analysis, such as heterogeneity of utility functions or an analysis where derived utility depends on interaction with neighbours, allows us to analyse other types of segregation. Box 4.4 briefly discusses a different type of heterogeneity, namely the changing link between labour market skills and population density.

We use the model specification of section 4.7 as our point of departure, but initially only allow individuals to choose their location at distance d from the city centre (as in section 4.4) and not yet the amount of land to consume (see below). Suppose individuals vary in income level y and maximize utility $U(C,L) = C + \alpha \ln(L(y))$, as in equation 4.5. Note that the amount of land L consumed varies with the income level y, but (for now) we take this function as exogenously given. We assume it rises with income, such that $L' > 0$ and rich people consume more land. Transportation costs are linear with distance (as in section 4.7), but the slope $\tau(y)$ depends on the income level. We assume that opportunity costs rise with income level (Becker, 1965), such that $\tau' > 0$. The disposable income available for consumption for an individual with income level y located at distance d from the city centre is thus: $C = y - \tau(y)d - r(d)L(y)$.

The first-order condition for the optimal choice of distance d gives rise to the same equation on the slope of the rental rate as in equation 4.7, namely $r'(d) = -\tau(y)/L(y)$. The important difference is that the slope is not constant but varies with the income level y, which is not the same for all people. Essentially, this equation thus determines the slope of the rental rate at a particular distance d from a demand perspective. We have to match it with the relevant supply based on the distribution of income, which is given exogenously by some distribution function $G(y)$. The spatial equilibrium can be thought of as a *matching function* $y(d)$ which allocates individuals of a certain income level to a distance d from the city centre such that demand and supply are in equilibrium at all distances d. Substituting this matching function in the slope of the rental rate given above, we get equation 4.15.

$$r'(d) = -\frac{\tau(y(d))}{L(y(d))} \tag{4.15}$$

To appreciate how this equation helps us to understand where individuals with different income levels are located in the city, we differentiate equation 4.15 with respect to distance d and use the fact that the second-order condition for a utility maximum implies that $r'' > 0$ to show that $y'(d) > 0$ if, and only if, the condition in equation 4.16 holds; see Technical Note 4.4 for details.

$$y'(d) > 0 \Leftrightarrow \frac{L'}{L} > \frac{\tau'}{\tau} \tag{4.16}$$

Condition 4.16 implies that rich people live further away from the city centre if their relative willingness to pay for land declines more slowly with distance. Since rich people consume more land they have an incentive to live further away from the city centre where land is cheaper. However, since the opportunity costs associated with transport are higher for rich people, they also have an incentive to live closer to the city centre. The condition shows that the sorting of people in different areas of the city depends on their relative willingness to pay for land compared to the transport opportunity costs. In some cities rich people may live in the suburbs where land is cheap (condition 4.16 holds). In other cities rich people may live in the city centre to avoid high transport costs (condition 4.16 does not hold). It is also possible that condition 4.16 only holds for parts of the relevant domain, in which case (for example) the richest people may live in the city centre, surrounded by a ring of poorer people in the vicinity of the centre, surrounded by a ring of middle-income people in the suburbs (Glaeser, Kahn, and Rappaport, 2008).

We can extend this analysis in various ways. We can, for example, allow people of different income levels to also choose the amount of land they want to occupy, as we did in section 4.7. The core analysis does not change. The first-order conditions for the choice of location and land provided in equations 4.7 and 4.8 still hold $[r' = -\tau / L$ and $r = \alpha / L]$. They can still be combined in a differential equation that needs to be solved as in equation 4.9 $[r' = -(\tau / \alpha) r]$. As in the discussion above, we now have to remember that τ is not constant but depends on the income level y. As a result, solving the differential equation is a little more involved. Moreover, as in the discussion above regarding equation 4.15, we are now looking for a matching function $y(d)$ which allocates people from a certain income level to a distance d from the city centre based on the differential equation

BOX 4.4 Labour Market Skills and Population Density

Labour market skills are another example of economic agent heterogeneity. Among other issues, labour economists analyse the link between labour skills and population density such that they enter the realm of urban economics, as emphasized by David Autor (a leading labour economist) in the 2019 Richard T. Ely Lecture for the American Economic Association in Atlanta.[15] In this box we briefly discuss the empirical connection between skills and density for the USA and how it changes over time. We return to an analysis of (the sorting of) skills in Chapter 5. The discussion below points to external influences for the urban economic system related to technology and globalization. This is also analysed in Chapter 10, while we discuss some policy implications in Chapter 11.

---

[15] The information in this box is based on the lecture itself and the slides available on David Autor's website.

BOX 4.4 (cont.)

Rather than analysing a continuum of skills, we divide the labour force into three broad categories:

- low-skilled labour (several services, transport, and construction workers),
- mid-skilled labour (production workers, clerical, administrative, and sales workers), and
- high-skilled labour (professional, technical, and managerial workers).

Figure 4.17 illustrates the relationship between population density and the three types of labour. In 1980 the share of low-skilled workers fell with population density, while the share for mid-skilled and high-skilled workers rose. This indicates that larger cities with higher population densities had relatively more mid-skilled and high-skilled workers in 1980. There was thus a sorting of mid-skilled and high-skilled workers in larger cities. In 2015, the relationship with population density is the same for low-skilled workers (namely declining, see panel *a* of Figure 4.17) and stronger (rising more rapidly) for high-skilled workers (see panel *c* of Figure 4.17). Remarkably, the relationship for mid-skilled workers has *reversed* by 2015 (switched from rising to declining; see panel *b* of Figure 4.17). Autor (2019) relates this switch to technological changes and globalization issues and discusses several policy implications (see also Chapter 11).

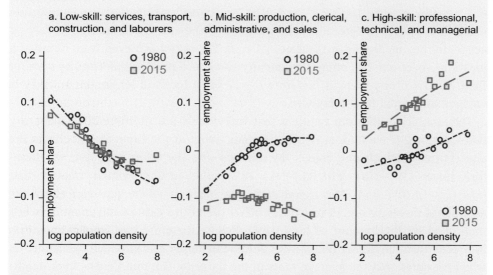

Figure 4.17 Occupation shares of working age adults and population density: USA, 1980 and 2015
Source: based on Autor (2019); employment shares are level relative to 1980 mean.

$r'(d) = -\big(\tau(y(d))/\alpha\big)r(d)$ and the distribution function of the number of people with that income level. As in the above analysis, we can use the second-order conditions to derive (less intuitive) conditions (based on the utility function and the transport cost function τ) to determine the sorting of income levels over the city. As another example, we can identify different transport methods as in section 4.6, such as public transport with low fixed costs and car transport with higher fixed costs, to explain why poorer people may live closer to the city centre and use public transport while rich people may live in the suburbs and use cars. And so on.

4.10.2 Amenities

An amenity is a feature that increases the attractiveness or value of a location. An example is a location close by a public park which can be used for relaxation, exercise, and playing. Other examples are locations in the neighbourhood of shopping malls, good schools, museums, or with easy access to public transport. People tend to enjoy the features of amenities, which should be reflected in their utility functions, usually without paying for it directly. As such, amenities can disturb the spatial equilibrium analysed in this chapter. In Chapter 6 we will try to test for the empirical relevance of urban amenities in the context of the spatial equilibrium model, here we confine ourselves to the way to incorporate amenities into the monocentric city model of this chapter.

We analyse a simple example of the impact of amenities using the basic model of section 4.4. Individuals make location decisions on the basis of the utility of their consumption level $C = W - t(d) - r(d, A)L$. This is the same as equation 4.2, but we now assume $U(C) = C$ and take into consideration that the equilibrium rental rate $r(d, A)$ is determined by distance to the city centre as well as having access to the amenity $(A = 1)$, or not $(A = 0)$. The utility achieved from living at a location where one can enjoy the amenity (such as a park) is modelled as a utility flow A. The utility level is therefore $C + A$ for a location where the amenity is enjoyed and equal to C otherwise.

The spatial equilibrium requires that individuals are indifferent between any two locations. If we look at two individuals living at the same distance from the city centre of which one enjoys the amenity and the other does not, we therefore have: $(W - t(d) - r(d,1)L) + A = W - t(d) - r(d,0)L$, which implies that $(r(d,1) - r(d,0))L = A$. The rental rate at a location where one can enjoy the amenity is therefore higher to exactly offset the utility gain of the amenity (when multiplied by the amount of land used). People therefore pay for the amenities indirectly through higher rental rates. A good example was provided in section 4.5 when we noted that the average rents in the Carnegie Hill and Central Park neighbourhoods of New York City are high because the amenity Central Park is close by. This suggests that we should take information on popular amenities, such as parks, museums, and schools, into consideration when analysing rent curves. We can also turn the question around and estimate the value of an amenity based on how much higher rents people are willing to pay to be in its vicinity (Black, 1999). When we allow people to choose the amount of land to use (as in section 4.7), the higher rental rates in the neighbourhood of amenities translate into higher population densities as people try to partially avoid the higher rental rates.

4.10.3 Miscellaneous

A range of other issues may affect the rent curve or the location of individuals within the city. We have, for example, analysed a monocentric model in which everyone commutes to the city centre, presumably to go to work or to go shopping. In many cases this is a reasonable approximation because the majority of employment and shops is in the city centre. There are, however, also examples of cities which have several main work locations to commute to. Amsterdam, for example, has concentrations of employment in the city centre, the 'Zuidas' (financial) business district, at Schiphol airport, and in the harbour. Similarly, many (expensive) shopping opportunities may be located in the city centre, but other opportunities may be spread out at different locations in shopping malls. The decentralization of employment and shops at other locations in the city interferes, of course, with the implications of our basic model analysed in section 4.4. The good news is that the main structure of the spatial equilibrium model can still be used to better understand the implications of decentralization for the distribution of people and the rent curve in the city, see Fujita and Ogawa (1982), Henderson and Mitra (1996), and Lucas and Rossi-Hansberg (2002). The bad news is that everything becomes more complicated. The related good news is that improved availability of computing power and detailed data allows us to analyse, better understand, and simulate this more complicated reality.

An issue related to both decentralization and amenities is the construction of main infrastructure connections for public and private transport (rail and road); see also section 4.5 for New York City. Having easy access to a highway or ring road that allows you to save on (time) transport costs to commute to work or shops is valuable. As with amenities, this translates to higher rental rates in the vicinity of main roads and higher population densities. The latter was illustrated for Indianapolis in section 4.8 with spikes of population density leading towards the city centre along main roads. The endogeneity problem was also mentioned there. Similarly, easy access to public transportation facilities will interact with the spatial equilibrium. For example, when the Chinese authorities decided to locate the Suzhou North railway station as part of the Beijing–Shanghai high-speed rail connection some 18 km away from the city centre of Suzhou there was not much there when it opened in 2010. Some seven years later firms have located in the vicinity of the station, shopping malls have opened up, and development projects are selling thousands of apartments. This not only allows people to connect to the centre of Suzhou (about 4 million inhabitants) by metro line, but also to travel to the centre of Shanghai (about 24 million inhabitants) by high-speed train in about 30 minutes (a distance of 81 km).[16] As such, this example illustrates that the spatial equilibrium also interacts between cities, as will be analysed in Chapter 5.

A final issue that needs mentioning concerns the role of externalities. These can be related to social issues and to firm productivity. An example of a negative social externality is the desire of some people to *avoid* living in the neighbourhood of people from certain types of origin, social status, cultural background, or religious orientation. An example of a positive social externality is the desire of some people to live in the neighbourhood of certain types of other people, such as the desire to live where rich and famous people live. Obviously, the interaction between externalities and location issues in the spatial equilibrium create complicated endogeneity problems. Why do rich people live here? Because other rich people live here. Externalities related to firm productivity focus on positive technology spillover effects of firms in certain sectors if they are located in the vicinity of other firms in that same sector, or possibly in the vicinity of firms in closely related sectors. This type of agglomeration economics also creates endogeneity problems and is analysed in more detail in Chapter 6.

4.11 Conclusions

The organization of space within cities is mainly driven by the spatial equilibrium forces analysed in this chapter. This implies that a person who is indifferent about living in two different locations within the city must derive the same net utility from these locations. This allows us to explain how rent costs decline away from the city centre as people need to be adequately compensated for higher transportation costs.

We extend the basic framework in various ways. We can incorporate the choice of different transport methods (walking, cycling, public transport, driving a car) to explain the main use of these methods at different locations and why the rent gradient may be steeper close to the city centre. We can incorporate a choice of the amount of land to use, which explains why population density is higher in the city centre. We can incorporate developers who supply housing projects. If land rents are high these developers may choose to substitute capital for land, which leads to higher buildings close to the city centre (and thus higher population density) and provides another incentive for steeper land rents. We can incorporate individual

---

[16] Data for 2010 from the Chinese census. The size of the Shanghai population follows directly from the census information as it is a prefecture level city. The size of the city of Suzhou is less straightforward. The prefecture Suzhou has a population of more than 10 million, but that would overestimate the size of Suzhou. If we focus on the districts that are certainly part of Suzhou we get an estimate of about 4 million.

heterogeneity, which allows us to explain the location of rich and poor people within the city. We can calculate the implied willingness to pay for certain amenities (like parks) by observing rent levels at two similar locations, of which only one has access to the amenity. We can analyse multi-centric rather than mono-centric cities. And so on.

As Anas, Arnott, and Small (1998, p. 1435) point out, a number of stylized facts about the urban spatial structure are in accordance with the monocentric model. First, the population density declines with distance from central business centres. Second, almost every major city in the western world has decentralized in the twentieth century (people have started to locate further away from the city centre), which can be linked to a fall in transport costs. The monocentric model also has some serious limitations. We mention just two. First, the model does not account for the interaction between cities: it cannot deal with urban systems. Second, the model takes the existence and location of the city as given and focuses on the location of farmers/commuters outside of the city. The question why there is a city to begin with is left unanswered. To deal with these limitations, urban economists have long recognized that a theory of cities cannot do without the introduction and theoretical foundation of some type of increasing returns to scale (Duranton, 2006; Glaeser, 2007, pp. 15–16).[17] These can occur at the firm level or at a more aggregated level (the industry level or the national level). The first limitation can be analysed and addressed within urban economics, as we will see in Chapter 5 and Chapter 6, while the second limitation is analysed in Part III on geographical economics, the main alternative to urban economics in understanding the economic interactions that make for our spiky world.

Technical Notes

Technical Note 4.1 Location choice

We can maximize equation 4.1 subject to the budget restriction 4.2 in two ways. First, we can construct a Lagrangian function L using a Lagrange multiplier λ, as in equation (A4.1), and determine the first-order conditions with respect to C and d, as in equations (A4.2) and (A4.3).

$$L = U(C) + \lambda\big((W - t(d) - r(d)L) - C\big) \qquad \text{(A4.1)}$$

$$U'(C) = \lambda \qquad \text{(A4.2)}$$

---

[17] As Glaeser (2007) explains, the Alonso-Muth-Mills model essentially helps to understand the location choice of individuals by assuming constant income and amenities and analysing whether or not housing costs and low transport costs offset each other. Applied to Boston, it explains that an extra mile from the center results in a $1100 drop in housing prices. A drawback of the model is that it assumes monocentric cities, which is often at odds with reality.

$$-\lambda\left(t'\left(d\right)+r'\left(d\right)L\right)=0 \qquad\qquad \text{(A4.3)}$$

Second, we can directly substitute the budget restriction into the utility function, as in equation (A4.4), and maximize only by choice of distance d. That first-order condition is given in equation (A4.5).

$$U\left(\left(W-t\left(d\right)-r\left(d\right)L\right)\right) \qquad\qquad \text{(A4.4)}$$

$$U'\left(C\right)\left(t'\left(d\right)+r'\left(d\right)L\right)=0 \qquad\qquad \text{(A4.5)}$$

The first approach indicates that the value of the Lagrange multiplier is equal to the marginal utility of consumption: see equation (A4.2). Since the marginal utility of consumption is positive, we therefore conclude from the second condition given in equation (A4.3) that there is a relationship between the transportation costs and the rent curve in equilibrium, as given in equation (A4.6). The alternative approach (of direct substitution) arrives, of course, at the same conclusion. In this chapter, the latter approach is usually easier, so we will use it henceforth.

$$r'\left(d\right)=-t'\left(d\right)/L \qquad\qquad \text{(A4.6)}$$

Technical Note 4.2 Land area choice

Suppose the utility function is a concave function $U\left(C,L\right)$ with positive first derivatives, indicating that both consumption and the use of land raise utility. Moreover, suppose that transportation costs are given by the function $t\left(d\right)$. The analysis in section 4.7 is thus a special case of this more general specification. Substituting the budget restriction in the utility function we get $U\left(C,L\right)=U\left(W-t\left(d\right)-r\left(d\right)L,L\right)$. Maximizing utility by choice of d and L gives the following two first-order conditions (where we use short-hand notation when possible):

$$\left(t'+r'L\right)U_{C}=0 \qquad\qquad \text{(A4.7)}$$

$$U_{L}-rU_{C}=0 \qquad\qquad \text{(A4.8)}$$

Equation (A4.7) is the same as equation (A4.5), where we now use U_{C} instead of U' to denote the marginal utility of consumption because the utility function now depends on two variables. We therefore still have $r'=-t'/L<0$, as in section 4.4. Equation (A4.8) is new and determines the trade-off between consumption and the utility of extra land use. In equilibrium, the amount of land consumed at a distance d from the city centre is a function $L\left(d\right)$ of that distance. Our objective is to determine the derivative of this function. To do so, we use the function $L\left(d\right)$ and write equation (A4.7) in its long format:

$$U_{L}-rU_{C}=U_{L}\left(W-t\left(d\right)-r\left(d\right)L\left(d\right),L\left(d\right)\right)-r\left(d\right)U_{C}\left(W-t\left(d\right)-r\left(d\right)L\left(d\right),L\left(d\right)\right)=0$$

Totally differentiating this with respect to distance d and using short notation gives:

$$-r'U_C + r(t' + r'L + rL')U_{CC} - rL'U_{CL} - (t' + r'L + Lr')U_{LC} + L'U_{LL} = 0$$

Note that $t' + r'L = 0$ from first-order condition (A4.7) to simplify. Collect terms for L', the derivative of the land use function, and realize that $U_{CL} = U_{LC}$ to solve for L':

$$L' = \frac{r'U_C}{\left(r^2 U_{CC} - rU_{CL} + U_{LL}\right)} > 0 \tag{A4.9}$$

The denominator of the right-hand-side of equation (A4.9) is negative as it is the second-order condition for an optimal choice of d and L. We already determined that the numerator is negative in Technical Note 4.1. The derivative of $L(d)$ is therefore positive and we have determined quite generally that the use of land increases as the distance to the city centre rises. Note, finally, that if the utility function is given by $U(C,L) = C + \alpha \ln(L)$, as in equation 4.5, then equation (A4.8) simplifies to $r = \alpha / L$; see equation 4.8.

Technical Note 4.3 Housing choice

The conditions for the optimal choice of the capital-land ratio k and the determination of economic equilibrium (price of housing per unit of land is equal to its costs) in the housing model of section 4.9 is given in equations 4.13 and 4.14 in the text and repeated here as equations (A4.10) and (A4.11). Remember that p and r are functions of d (which is not written out explicitly here).

$$\beta p k^{\beta-1} - i = 0 \tag{A4.10}$$

$$p k^\beta - ik - r = 0 \tag{A4.11}$$

Equation (A4.10) can be easily solved for the optimal choice of k as $k = \left(\beta p / i\right)^{1/(1-\beta)}$. We now solve equation (A4.11) for the rental rate r, then substitute for i from (A4.10), then simplify, and finally substitute for the optimal choice of k and simplify again to get $\left(\text{use } 1 + \dfrac{\beta}{1-\beta} = \dfrac{1}{1-\beta} \right)$:

$$r = pk^\beta - ik = pk^\beta - \left(\beta p k^{\beta-1}\right)k = (1-\beta)pk^\beta = (1-\beta)p\left(\left(\frac{\beta p}{i}\right)^{\frac{1}{1-\beta}}\right)^\beta = (1-\beta)\left(\frac{\beta}{i}\right)^{\frac{\beta}{1-\beta}} p^{\frac{1}{1-\beta}}$$

If we now define $A \equiv \left(\beta / i\right)^{1/(1-\beta)}$ and $B \equiv (1-\beta)\left(\beta / i\right)^{\beta/(1-\beta)}$, we can thus simplify notation to $k = Ap^{1/(1-\beta)}$ and $r = Bp^{1/(1-\beta)}$, as used in section 4.9.

To determine the rental rate in the city centre, recall that $p(d) = p(0)e^{-\tau d/\alpha}$ (see section 4.9) and (from above and by substituting for p): $\ln r(d) = \ln(B) + \dfrac{1}{1-\beta}\ln\left(p(d)\right)$

$= \ln(B) + \dfrac{1}{1-B}\ln\left(p(0)\right) - \dfrac{\tau d}{\alpha(1-\beta)}$. The term $\ln(B) + \dfrac{1}{1-B}\ln\left(p(0)\right)$ must

obviously be equal to $\ln(r(0))$. Let d_{max} be an indicator of the size of the city.

The rent at the city edge is equal to $\bar{r}$, such that $\ln(r(0)) - \dfrac{\tau d_{max}}{\alpha(1-\beta)} = \ln(\bar{r})$. This

allows us to solve for the rental rate at the city centre: $\ln(r(0)) = \ln(\bar{r}) + \dfrac{\tau d_{max}}{\alpha(1-\beta)}$

and subsequently for all other variables by direct substitution.

Technical Note 4.4 Heterogeneity

Individuals vary in income level y and maximize utility $U(C,L) = C + \alpha \ln(L(y))$. The function $L(y)$ is taken as given, with $L' > 0$. The amount available for consumption for an individual with income level y is: $C = y - \tau(y)d - r(d)L(y)$, where transport costs are linear with distance but the slope $\tau(y)$ depends on the income level with $\tau' > 0$. The first-order condition for the optimal choice of distance d is thus given by equation (A4.12). The second-order condition is given in equation (A4.13).

$$-\tau(y) - r'(d)L(y) = 0 \tag{A4.12}$$

$$-r''(d) < 0 \tag{A4.13}$$

The differential equation $r'(d) = -\tau(y)/L(y)$ now has a slope that varies with the income level at the relevant distance d. The spatial equilibrium is summarized by a matching function $y(d)$ which allocates individuals of a certain income level to a distance d from the city centre. Substituting this matching function in the slope of the rental rate derived from equation (A4.12) we get (A4.14). Differentiating with respect to distance d gives (A4.15).

$$r'(d) = -\frac{\tau(y(d))}{L(y(d))} \tag{A4.14}$$

$$r''(d) = -\frac{\tau'(y)y'(d)}{L(y)} + \frac{\tau(y(d))}{(L(y))^2}L'(y)y'(d) = \left(\frac{\tau(y)L'(y) - \tau'(y)L(y)}{(L(y))^2}\right)y'(d) > 0 \tag{A4.15}$$

The inequality follows from the second-order condition (A4.13). This implies that $y'(d) > 0$, such that richer people live further away from the city centre, if and only if $\tau(y)L'(y) > \tau'(y)L(y)$.

Exercises

Question 4.1 Alonso-Muth-Mills (AMM)

Consider the following version of the Alonso-Muth-Mills model. All agents have a utility function given in equation (Q4.1), where C is consumption, α is a parameter, and L is the consumption of land by the agent. An agent who travels a distance

d to the city centre to work and earns wage rate W incurs a cost of commuting equal to td. Such an agent also has to pay a rent $r(d)$, which is a function of the distance to the city centre, per unit of land used. Total rent costs are therefore $r(d)L$. Total consumption is therefore given in equation (Q4.2). The agent cannot influence the wage rate W, the rent cost function $r(d)$ or the per unit commuting costs t. She *can*, however, determine where to live (the distance d to the city centre) and how much land L to use.

$$U(C,L) = C + \alpha \cdot \ln(L) \tag{Q4.1}$$

$$C = W - td - r(d)L \tag{Q4.2}$$

Determine the first-order conditions for a utility maximum for the agent as a function of the distance d to the city centre and the amount of land L to use as follows:

- Substitute equation (Q4.2) into equation (Q4.1).
- Differentiate the resulting equation with respect to d and equate to zero.
- Differentiate the resulting equation with respect to L and equate to zero.

Question 4.2 AMM Continued

We continue from Question 4.1. In equilibrium all agents are indifferent regarding their location, which determines the rent curve. Recall that for a function $f(x)$ if we have the differential $f'(x) = af(x)$ for some constant a, then the function f must be $f(x) = be^{ax}$ for some constant b, since in that case $f'(x) = abe^{ax} = af(x)$. Note that $f(0) = b$. Now use this information to determine the rent gradient and density as follows:

- Substitute one first-order condition into the appropriate other to get a differential equation for the rent function.
- Solve the differential equation using the above information; this gives the rent function.
- One of the first-order conditions gives you the density $\dfrac{1}{L}$ as a function of the rent function and a parameter; substitute the rent function you found at the previous step and then take logs on both sides to determine the log of density as a function of, inter alia, distance d to the centre.
- Comment on the above steps taken, in particular regarding the usefulness in the final step (please phrase in words) for empirical verification and application.

Question 4.3 Transport Methods

The analysis in section 4.6 allows individuals to choose the optimum transport method before determining the optimum location to live. The analysis is illustrated for a two-transport-methods example in Figure 4.8, assuming that $d_{sw} < d_{max}$.

a. What is the value of the rent curve at the switching point d_{sw}?
b. What is the value of the rent curve at the city centre?
c. What is the value of the rent curve at the city centre if $d_{sw} > d_{max}$?

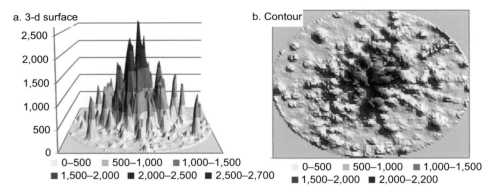

Figure Q4.1

Question 4.4 Indianapolis Spikes

Section 4.8 evaluates the relationship between population density and distance to the city centre for Indianapolis. Figure 4.13 provides detailed grid population density information based on census blocks within a 3 km radius from a grid point. The two panels in Figure Q4.1 provide the same information, but this time for a 2 km radius from the grid point.

What are the main differences between the panels shown in Figure Q4.1 and the panels shown in Figure 4.13? What is, in your opinion, the main reason for these differences? Explain why.

5 City Systems

LEARNING OBJECTIVES

- To know the main stylized facts about city-size distributions and be able to apply the concept of power laws to city-size distributions (including Zipf's Law).
- To know and understand the concept of a spatial equilibrium between cities.
- To be able to explain the main building blocks of the standard model of urban economics.
- To understand how the core model of urban economics can be extended by allowing for differentiation and heterogeneity.

5.1 Introduction

In Chapter 4 we skipped the question why cities exist to begin with, let alone why we observe many different sized cities next to each other (recall Chapter 1 for this stylized fact). Instead, we focused on the internal organization and structure of cities. But if we want to understand why there are cities or 'spikes' where people and economic activities are concentrated, we must answer the question what is the benefit for people and firms in clustering together? There may be obvious first nature geography (access to sea), historical (safety in numbers), sociological (family ties), political (locate near to rulers) or many other reasons for doing so, but we are interested in the economic reasons.

The short economic answer is: economic indivisibilities in combination with transport costs lead to advantageous clustering of economic activities in cities. If it is costly for people and firms to move themselves and/or goods across space, location becomes an important issue. And if economic activities are to some extent at least indivisible (workers and firms cannot split their activities into ever smaller units, it pays to concentrate your activities), the combination between transport costs and indivisibilities goes a long way towards rationalizing the existence of cities. But in the real world cities come in many shapes and sizes, so we do not only need to explain why cities exist to begin with but also why there are so many cities and why they differ in size. Chapter 5 takes up both questions in one go.

Even a casual look at a map reveals that cities vary in size. This chapter extends the analysis of Chapter 4 by looking at systems of cities. What is also striking if we compare an old map with a new map of the same country is the fact that these maps often look rather similar; in other words, city-size distributions are rather stable over time. Usually, the total population of a country increases over time and most cities grow, although some cities may become smaller. In most cases, however, initially small cities remain small, while initially big cities remain big. This raises the question of whether we are looking at an equilibrium of some sort. The answer is *yes*, and it is related to one of the core concepts of urban economics: the spatial equilibrium. In Chapter 4 we analysed the spatial equilibrium *within* cities, meaning that nobody has an incentive to move to another location within the city. In this chapter we analyse the spatial equilibrium *between* cities.

Definition – spatial equilibrium (between cities): In a spatial equilibrium between cities economic agents do not have an incentive to move to another city.[1]

We start in section 5.2 by simply looking at maps of city systems, first for the United States and next for the world in various years. We will point out that the importance of tropical cities in the world city system has been rising since 1950. Sections 5.3–5.5 help us to empirically characterize city systems using the urban power laws that we already encountered in the previous chapter (section 5.3), a specific case known as Zipf's Law (section 5.4), and information on estimating and testing power law exponents (section 5.5). These stylized facts call for a theoretical underpinning, in particular where it concerns the existence of multiple cities that vary in size and economic activity. This is done in the second part of Chapter 5 from section 5.5 onwards, where we focus on the theory of urban systems.

The literature of urban systems builds on Henderson (1974). The main model is explained in section 5.5 using a graphical representation of the Henderson model to discuss its core elements. We extend this framework in section 5.6 to analyse differentiated or heterogeneous cities using modern concepts and tools (such as super modularity). We illustrate this framework for Chinese cities to show that high-skilled people (and sectors) are relatively more abundant in large cities. Finally, section 5.7 concludes.

5.2   Cities on a Map

Even a casual inspection of a map indicates that countries contain many cities of unequal size. This is illustrated in Figure 5.1 (reproduced from Chapter 1, see Figure 1.6) for the USA as it shows the distribution and size of urban locations in 2010. We can make a few interesting observations just by eyeballing the

---

[1] Davis and Dingel (2017), see section 5.6, combine the two equilibrium concepts.

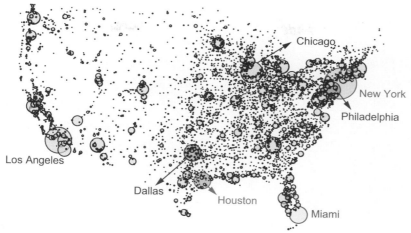

Figure 5.1 Distribution and size of urban locations in the USA, 2010
Source: created using data from US Census Bureau (www.census.gov); 3,535 locations included;
equilateral projection; bubbles proportional to population size; 48 contiguous states only.

map. Some large cities stand out: New York, Los Angeles, Chicago, and Miami are among the largest cities in the US. We also see many smaller cities, some of which are so small that they are difficult to see on the map. There also seem to be clusters of cities: around the biggest cities there appear to be smaller cities and together these groups form urban clusters with multiple cities.

Next, we have a closer look at the distribution of cities in the world and its evolution since 1950. The Population Division of the United Nations Department of Economic and Social Affairs (UN DESA) has issued estimates and projections of urban and rural populations of all countries in the world and their major urban agglomerations since 1988. We base our information on the 2018 Revision of World Urbanization Prospects using estimates on urban agglomerations, which are defined thus:[2]

> The term 'urban agglomeration' refers to the population contained within the contours of a contiguous territory inhabited at urban density levels without regard to administrative boundaries. It usually incorporates the population in a city or town plus that in the suburban areas lying outside of, but being adjacent to, the city boundaries.

Figure 5.2 depicts the distribution of urban agglomerations of at least 300,000 inhabitants for the world in 2015 using UN DESA data.[3] The bubbles are proportional

---

[2] See https://population.un.org/wup/; quoted, https://population.un.org/wup/Publications/Files/WUP2018-Methodology.pdf, p. 4.

[3] Where possible, data classified according to the concept of urban agglomeration are used. However, some countries do not produce data according to the concept of urban agglomeration but use instead that of metropolitan area or city proper. Where possible, such data are adjusted to conform to the concept of urban agglomeration. When sufficient information is not available to permit such an adjustment, data based on the concept of city proper or metropolitan area are used.

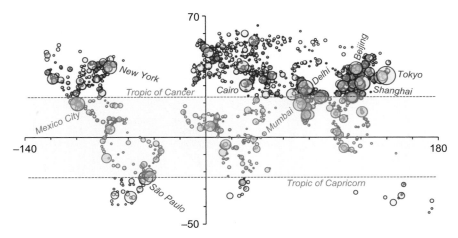

Figure 5.2 World urban agglomerations in 2015
Source: created using data from UN World Urbanization Prospects: The 2018 Revision; only 1,772 urban agglomerations of 300,000 or more people included; equilateral projection; bubbles proportional to population size.

to population size and the figure shows nine of the top ten largest urban agglomerations by name.[4] Tokyo in Japan is the world's largest urban agglomeration with more than 37 million inhabitants, followed by Delhi in India (25.9 million), Shanghai in China (23.5 million), and Mexico City in Mexico (21.3 million). Three countries have two urban agglomerations in the top ten, namely Tokyo and Osaka in Japan, Delhi and Mumbai in India, and Shanghai and Beijing in China. Regarding expected growth in the next two decades (up to 2035), three countries, namely India, China, and Nigeria, will account for about 35 per cent of the growth in urban population. Delhi in India is expected to become the largest urban agglomeration (taking over from Tokyo) in the second half of the 2020s. Delhi is also expected to become the first urban agglomeration to pass the 40 million inhabitants mark in the first half of the 2030s.

Figure 5.2 also shows the *tropical* zone (light-shaded) in between the Tropic of Capricorn in the south (about *minus* 23.44 degrees latitude) and the Tropic of Cancer in the north (about *plus* 23.44 degrees latitude), where the observations have a different colour. We refer to the remainder as the *temperate* zone for ease of reference. Clearly, most urban agglomerations in 2015, about two-thirds, are in the temperate zone. Most of the temperate observations are in the northern hemisphere, including North America, Europe, and large parts of Asia (including most of China and the north of India). About one-third of the urban agglomerations in 2015 are in the tropical zone, which includes mostly developing countries in

---

[4] Unlisted Osaka in Japan (partially hidden by Tokyo) is ranked 7th with 19.3 million inhabitants.
[5] We do not continue the count lines for the projection period as the data provided by UN DESA do not include agglomerations which will pass the 300,000 threshold in the period 2015–2035.

Middle America, South America, Sub-Saharan Africa, parts of India, and Southeast Asia. We provide this information because the importance of developing countries in the tropical zone for urban agglomerations has been rising fast. This is illustrated in Figure 5.3 for the number and size of tropical versus temperate observations in the period 1950–2035 and in Figure 5.4 using a map plot for 1950 (panel *a*) and 2035 (panel *b*). The number of urban agglomerations (above 300,000) in the temperate zone rose from 265 in 1950 to 1178 in 2015. The number of urban agglomerations in the tropical zone rose three times faster, from 40 in 1950 to 574 in 2015. The share of urban agglomerations in the developing tropics thus rose from 13.1 per cent in 1950 to 32.4 per cent in 2015.[5]

The average size of urban agglomeration above 300,000 rises by about 0.4 per cent per year from 0.98 million in 1950 to 1.29 million in 2015. As Figure 5.3 shows, the average size is similar for the tropical and temperate zones in this period. It is expected to rise substantially faster, however, in the tropics up to 2035, when the average size in the tropics is expected to be 2.05 million, compared to 1.63 million in the temperate zone.[6] The two panels of Figure 5.4 vividly illustrate the consequences of these developments for the distribution of the urban population in the world. In 1950 less than 14 per cent of the number of people living in urban agglomerations lived in the tropics. This is expected to rise to more than

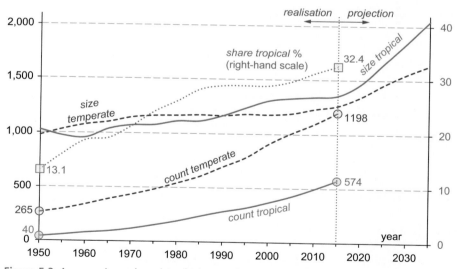

Figure 5.3 Average size and number of urban agglomerations in Tropical and Temperate regions
Source: created using data from UN World Urbanization Prospects: The 2018 Revision; size is the average size of urban agglomerations in the region (in thousands); count is the number of urban agglomerations in the region; share tropical is the share of tropical count in total count (in per cent).

---

[6] Note that these estimates are inflated because they exclude urban agglomerations which will pass the 300,000 threshold in this period; see preceding footnote.

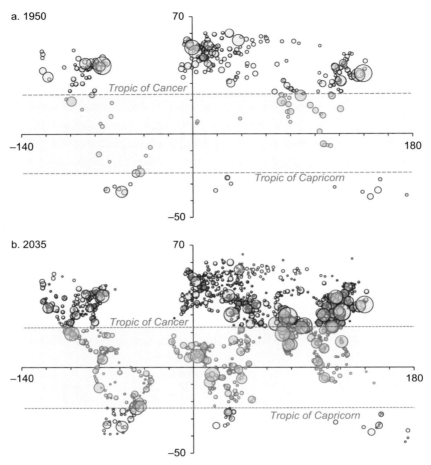

a. 1950

b. 2035

Figure 5.4 World urban agglomerations (above 300,000) in 1950 and (expected) 2035
Source: created using data from UN World Urbanization Prospects: The 2018 Revision; only cities
of 300,000 or more included; 305 cities in 1950 and 1,855 in 2035; equilateral projection; bubbles
proportional to population size.

38 per cent by 2035. By this time, the number of urban agglomerations above 10
million will have risen to 48 (from 29 in 2015). Most of this increase, namely 11
out of 19, will occur in the tropics.

5.3 Urban Power Laws

In Chapter 4 we argued that any convincing story about the creation and growth
of cities is ultimately based on the existence of (local) increasing returns to scale.
Other factors, like natural endowments, political factors (see also Box 5.2 on primate cities), or consumption externalities, are also thought to be relevant for determining the formation and growth of cities, but increasing returns is the dominant

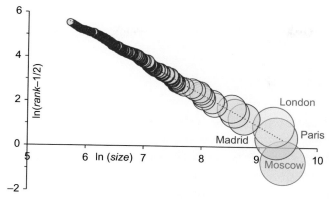

Figure 5.5 Urban power law in Europe, 2015
Source: estimates based on UN Population Division (2014) data using Gabaix-Ibragimov (2011) method and Kratz-Resnick (1996) standard errors; the dotted line is a regression line; 254 locations included; bubbles proportional to size of population; only cities above 300,000 inhabitants are included.

explanation. Regarding the scope of urban agglomeration economies (see Chapter 6), both static and dynamic externalities can be distinguished, but this literature is less useful for explaining urban systems and *stylized facts* about the size distribution of cities, because it focuses on the size and growth of individual cities and not on the interdependencies between cities. In contrast, geographical economics (Part III of the book) focuses on the spatial interaction between the centres of production (cities) and the rest of the economy; see Chapter 8 for a more detailed discussion. The contribution of urban economics will be evaluated at the end of this chapter.

What are the *stylized facts* mentioned above? This refers to a special case of Power Laws already briefly mentioned in Chapter 1 (Zipf's Law, see section 1.9.1); it is a means of organizing the maps of urban agglomerations discussed in section 5.2. Box 5.1 discusses some details of power laws.

BOX 5.1 **Power Laws**

Vilfredo Pareto (1896) 'discovered' the first power law in economics when studying the distribution of income. He has a distribution function named after him. The reasoning is as follows. He found that for large values of x (thus for large income levels), the number of people with an income level *larger* than x is proportional to $x^{-\gamma}$ for some value of γ, by using the notation $P(.)$ to denote probabilities, and $F(x) = P(X < x) = 1 - ax^{-\gamma}$ for the cumulative distribution; this is the standard definition of $F(x)$. The second equality sign applies this definition to the Pareto distribution.

BOX 5.1 (cont.)

It follows that the *counter-cumulative* distribution defined as $P(X > x) = 1 - F(x) = ax^{-\gamma}$ for sufficiently large x. The density function is then $a\gamma x^{-(1+\gamma)}$.

The lower the power law exponent γ, the fatter the tails of the distribution. For the distribution of income, this means that low γ implies more inequality between people in the top quantiles of income. If the power law exponent γ is close to one ($\gamma \approx 1$), as is the case for the distribution of city sizes in some countries, we say that *Zipf's Law* holds, named after the Harvard linguist George Kingsley Zipf (who analysed the frequency of words in books).[7] Functions of two variables that have a power law distribution are generally well-behaved in the sense that their sum, product, maximum, minimum, scalar multiplication, and a simple power function of either variable generate new variables that also have a power law distribution.

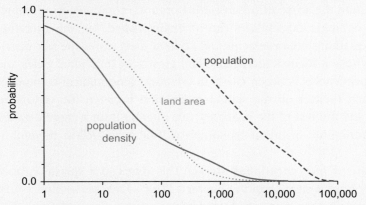

Figure 5.6 USA: ZCTA counter-cumulative distributions of population, land area, and density
Source: calculations based on US Census data 2000, downloaded from the Missouri Census Data Center website; population in number of people, land area in km², and population density in people per km²; see box text for details.

---

[7] Zipf (1949) attempted to capture a broad range of observed social and spatial regularities by means of simple equations. His book is part of a larger tradition, sometimes referred to as the literature on gravity models, which, inspired by Newtonian physics, typically stipulates that economic or social interaction between the objects of interest is a function of the mass (economic size) of these objects weighed by their distance. These equations are not meant to explain the social or spatial phenomenon at hand. Their objective is simply, analogous to the physical sciences, to come up with an equation that describes the phenomenon. This 'un-deductive' approach, called *social physics* by Krugman (1995), led not only to Zipf's Law, but also to the gravity model and the market potential function. George Zipf, a lecturer of linguistics at Harvard, argues that the rank–size distribution holds for many phenomena. A well-known example is in the use of language, where the expressions that are most frequently used are also the least complex. Zipf had a reputation for being eccentric. The story goes that he applauded the *Anschluss* of Austria to Nazi Germany in 1938 because the resulting city-size distribution was more in line with the rank–size rule!

BOX 5.1 (cont.)

An easy way to illustrate a power law distribution is by plotting the counter-cumulative distribution using a log scale for the horizontal axis. This is done in Figure 5.6 for the distribution of population, land area, and population density for the ZIP Census Tabulation Areas (ZCTA) discussed in section 4.2. If a variable has a power law distribution, the counter-cumulative distribution should be approximately a straight line in the right-hand tail of the distribution (above some minimum level). This clearly is not the case in Figure 5.6 for land area and population density, but approximately the case for population (the slope of the distribution above 1,000 is approximately –0.133, suggesting a power law exponent of $\gamma = 0.133$). We should not read too much into this information because the ZCTAs are defined in peculiar ways. Instead, just view it as a way to illustrate power laws in practice.

The question becomes: under what conditions can we expect that the counter-cumulative distribution will be a straight line? Gabaix (1999b) shows that if the growth of cities follows Gibrat's Law, that is, if all cities grow randomly independent of their original size, this growth process converges to a Pareto distribution. This holds if the size of cities cannot fall below a minimum size. The intuition is explained by Desmet and Henderson (2015, p. 1473). If cities cannot be smaller than a certain minimum size the density function peaks at that minimum size, and the lower bound pushes the distribution towards larger cities resulting in a fatter upper tail (for a primer on Gibrat's Law in relation to Zipf's Law, see Ioanides, 2013, ch. 8). There is a small literature that tries to derive Zipf's Law from economic principles or simulate city systems that are consistent with rank–size rules and Zipf's Law; Brakman et al. (1999), Hsu (2012), Lee and Li (2013), and Behrens, Duranton, and Robert-Nicoud (2014).

The step to a rank–size rule is now easy to make. The probability of finding a city larger than the largest city, with rank 1 (the biggest city), is very small, the probability of finding cities larger than the second largest city, with rank 2, is somewhat larger (because there is a bigger city), the probability of finding a city larger than the third largest city with rank 3 is larger than that. One can complete this reasoning for all cities up to the very smallest city; the probability of finding cities larger than the smallest city is very large. This reasoning implies that there is a correlation between the rank of cities and the probability of finding larger cities than the city in question: the smaller the city (and larger the rank), the larger the corresponding probability. The probabilities follow the Pareto distribution. So, the *Size Rank of city x*, correlates with $P(X > x) = ax^{-\gamma}$. Taking logs motivates an empirical specification like: *Log (City Rank)* $= \log(a) - \gamma \log(x)$, where *x* is city size and *City Rank* the associated rank of that city. This is why rules like these are called rank–size rules.

Ordering the cities from large to small (giving rank 1 to the largest city, rank 2 to the second-largest city, and so on) and plotting the rank of the cities versus the size of the cities (in logs) results in plots like Figure 5.7.[8] The figure includes all urban agglomerations of 300,000 people or more at the world level. Panel *a* provides the counter-cumulative distribution for a selection of years, while panel *b* illustrates the power law using a log-log graph of rank and size (as in Figure 5.5). Tokyo is the world's largest urban agglomeration (38 million people), and is thus given rank 1 in panel *b*, followed by Delhi (25.7 million) with rank 2, Shanghai (23.7 million) with rank 3, and so on. The panel *b* graph shows that cities are also remarkably well-organized according to a power law at the world level, except for the top ten cities or so (which start to deviate substantially from the regression line; remember that this is only a small fraction of all locations). This deviation is not unusual at the country level for the largest city, which translates to the top ten largest cities at the world level; see also Box 5.2 on primate cities. Panel *a* of Figure 5.7 shows the counter-cumulative distribution at the world level for a selection of years. All cities with 300,000 or more population in 2014 are included in the panel for each year. Since many cities were below 300,000 before 2014, the distribution shifts to the right over time, indicating rising population levels in most cities.[9] The (absolute value of the) slope of the counter-cumulative distribution (log scale) above a certain threshold is indicative of the power law exponent γ. The fit starts to deviate for the largest cities, as indicated by the less steep slope at the bottom-right corner.

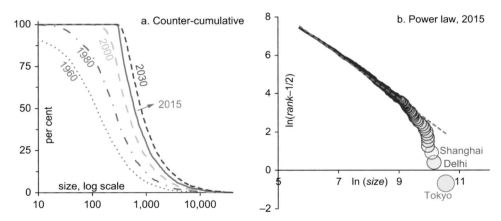

Figure 5.7 World urban counter-cumulative distributions and power law, selected years
Source: based on data from UN Population Division (2014) for 1,692 urban agglomerations of 300,000 people or more in 2014; see main text for details; dashed line in panel *b* is a regression line; size measured in thousands; bubbles in panel *b* proportional to size.

---

[8] Based on this graph, power laws are therefore also known as rank-size distributions.
[9] This gives selection bias in an empirical analysis over time, so Chapter 8 uses the 300,000 threshold for all years.

The question arises, of course, what economic forces may be responsible for this empirical regularity, whether it also occurs in other continents (or other locations), and whether it varies over time. We analyse this in Chapter 8.

5.4 Zipf's Law

Zipf's Law is a special case of a power law distribution with exponent $\gamma = 1$. This special case has received special attention in the literature on city-size distributions. If Zipf's Law holds (so if $\gamma = 1$), the slope of the regression line in Figure 5.5 and of panel b in Figure 5.7 should be -1. In fact, both estimated exponents deviate significantly from Zipf's Law; the exponent for the world as a whole in 2015 is 1.16 and for Europe is 1.42 (see Chapter 8). The visualization in the above figures is based on ordering the data from large to small, giving rank 1 to the largest observation, rank 2 to the second-largest, and so on. Only the observations above some threshold value are included. We will follow the UN Population Division (2014) and use 300,000 as the threshold value, but there is no consensus on how to pick the optimal threshold value (Beirlant et al., 2004). Given N included observations i with $rank_i$ (in ascending order) and associated $size_i$ (in descending order), the graphs in Figure 5.5 and panel b of Figure 5.7 are thus based on:

$$ln\left(rank_i - shift\right) = a - \gamma ln\left(size_i\right) + noise \qquad 5.1$$

The *shift* parameter in this equation is used to correct for small sample bias.[10] Empirical research thus estimates the power law exponent γ. A relevant research question may be whether the estimated exponent deviates significantly from Zipf's Law, or not. If Zipf's Law holds, the largest city is approximately k times as large as the k-th largest city. Note that a *lower* power law exponent γ is indicative of a more *uneven* distribution (with relatively larger big cities), while the reverse holds for a higher power law exponent.

Using mostly American data, some authors have stressed that (i) Zipf's Law holds ($\gamma = 1$) and (ii) the estimated exponent γ hardly changes over time; see Krugman (1996a, b), Gabaix (1999a,b), and Fujita, Krugman, and Venables (1999, ch. 12). Indeed, most estimates of the exponent in equation 5.1 are close to one

---

[10] Gabaix and Ibragimov (2011) provide an overview of the various estimators that have been developed to address this bias. More importantly, they provide an elegant and effective solution for the estimation problems: an unbiased estimate of the coefficient is obtained when OLS is used in equation 5.1 with a shift parameter equal to 0.5, hence the value 1/2 in Figure 5.5 and panel b of Figure 5.7. We refer to this estimate as $\hat{\gamma}_{GI}$. Moreover, the correct asymptotic standard errors are based on Kratz and Resnick (1996) and equal to $\hat{\gamma}_{GI}\sqrt{2/N}$, where γ is the estimated coefficient and N is the number of observations. See also, for example, Giesen and Südekum (2011), who use this correction.

when US data are used. Carroll (1982), however, provides an early survey of the empirical evidence on the rank–size distribution and already finds that Zipf's Law does not always hold for the USA. In another influential early paper on Zipf's Law, Rosen and Resnick (1980, p. 167) find that $\gamma = 1.19$ for the US, which implies a much more even city-size distribution than if Zipf's Law holds. Similarly, Black and Henderson (2003) find that the estimated exponent for the US not only differs from one, but also changes slowly during the twentieth century (see also Dobkins and Ioannides, 2000). For other countries also, a mixed picture emerges. Eaton and Eckstein (1997) find for Japan and France that Zipf's Law nearly holds, and that γ hardly changes over time. Rosen and Resnick (1980, p. 167), however, argue that γ is bigger than one for both countries. Soo (2005) and Nitsch (2005) survey the available evidence and conclude that for many countries and periods, γ is significantly different from one and not constant over time. Giesen and Südekum (2011) find, for a large sample of German cities, that for Germany as a whole and for the (West) German States that γ is most often larger than one (but not always significantly different from one). We will analyse these issues and the possible economic underpinning for Zipf's Law in Chapter 8. Here, in Chapter 5, we confine ourselves to actual estimations of urban power laws and Zipf's Law.

BOX 5.2 Primate Cities

As illustrated in Figure 5.8, empirical urban distributions may deviate from power law distributions especially for the largest cities. The deviation can be in either direction. The largest cities may be too small, as is the case in Figure 5.7*b*, or they may be too large, in which case they may be referred to as *primate cities*. One can

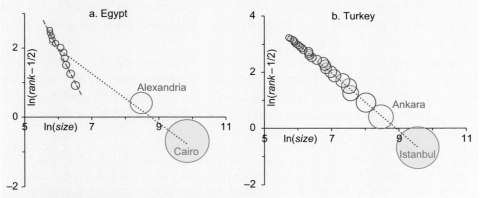

Figure 5.8 Urban power laws in Egypt and Turkey, 2015
Source: based on data from UN Population Division (2014); 13 observations for Egypt and 26 for Turkey; dashed lines are regression lines, see Box 5.1 text for details; size measured in thousands; bubbles proportional to size.

BOX 5.2 (cont.)

think of mega-cities in advanced countries, like Tokyo in Japan or Paris in France, or of mega-cities in developing countries, like Buenos Aires in Argentina or Manila in the Philippines. A vivid example of a primate city is provided for Egypt in panel *a* of Figure 5.8. Cairo is Egypt's largest city with 18.8 million people, followed by Alexandria with 4.8 million. Both cities are much larger than number 3, which is Bur Saïd with 670,000 people. There are only 13 urban agglomerations in Egypt with 300,000 people or more. As panel *a* shows, the distribution of cities 3 to 13 closely follow a power law distribution. The steep dashed line is a regression line based on only these cities and explains 96.8 per cent of the variance. Including the much larger cities Cairo and Alexandria give rise to the less steep dotted regression line, which explains 88.8 per cent of the variance. In that sense, primate cities may affect the power law fit and exponent.

Panel *b* of Figure 5.8 illustrates that the largest cities can also be perfectly in line with the power law distribution, using Istanbul and Ankara in Turkey as an example. Indeed, the estimated power law exponent remains 1.03 if Istanbul is excluded and becomes 1.02 if both Istanbul and Ankara are excluded, while more than 99 per cent of the variance is explained in all cases. Similar observations hold for the urban power law for Europe, as illustrated in Figure 5.5.

To illustrate the big city problem, we follow Rosen and Resnick (1980) by calculating the primacy ratio, which is defined as the size of the largest city relative to the sum of the size of the five largest cities (in per cent).[11] Based on UN Population Division (2014) data for urban agglomerations, we can only include

Table 5.1 Primacy ratio statistics: countries in world regions, 2015

Region	mean	median	# of countries
Africa	57	54	10
Asia	53	52	21
Europe & Offshoots	44	41	15
Latin America	59	59	7
World	51	50	53

Source: based on data from UN Population Division (2014); primacy ratio is size of largest agglomeration relative to size of five largest agglomerations combined (per cent).

[11] Other indicators of primacy are possible. The World Bank, for instance, gives the population in the largest city as a percentage of the *urban* population, which is equal to 100 per cent for city-countries like Hong Kong and Singapore.

BOX 5.2 (cont.)

countries with at least five cities above 300,000 inhabitants, which leads to 53 country observations grouped together in four main regions: Africa, Asia, Latin America, and Europe & Offshoots. The results are summarized in Table 5.1 and illustrated in Figure 5.9.

At the world level, the average primacy ratio is 51 and the median is 50. On average, the primacy ratio is much lower in Europe & Offshoots (44 per cent) and much higher in Africa (57 per cent) and Latin America (59 per cent), with Asia in between (53 per cent). There is, however, substantial variation within the global regions. In Asia it ranges from 29 per cent in China to 75 per cent in the Philippines, in Europe it ranges from 31 per cent in the Netherlands to 68 per cent in France, in Africa it ranges from 40 per cent in Morocco to 74 per cent in Egypt, and in Latin America it ranges from 32 per cent in Venezuela to more than 76 per cent in Argentina and Peru.

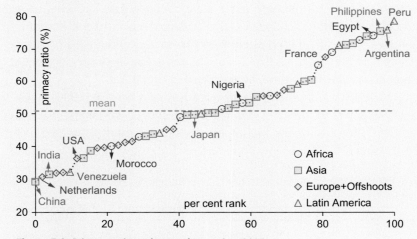

Figure 5.9 Primacy ratios: urban agglomeration, 2015
Source: based on data from UN Population Division (2014); primacy ratio is size of largest agglomeration relative to size of five largest agglomerations combined (per cent); 53 countries included.

5.5   Urban Economics Theory of City Systems

Modelling systems of cities requires us to answer many questions. Abdel-Rahman and Anas (2004) list 14 questions that need to be answered in models on systems of cities. Among these questions are issues that need to be resolved in the model, such as: are cities specialized or diversified?, is there perfect or imperfect competition?, how are cities linked to each other?, what type of transportation costs exists?, is the number of cities pre-determined or endogenous?, what is the geography (are cities, for example, located on a circle)?, do cities have an internal geographical structure (do they have a Central Business district)?, do market failures exist that might require a central planner? And so on.

In practice only some of these questions are addressed explicitly in models on city systems. An extensive overview of the current state of affairs is given by Behrens and Robert-Nicoud (2015). The standard reference of modelling systems of cities is the canonical Henderson (1974) model. Why pick this model? The main reason is that the discussion of the stylized facts on cities and city-size distributions in the first part of this chapter shows clearly that we need a model that can account for the co-existence of multiple cities where cities vary in size and the type of economic activity per city. This is what the Henderson model and its modern equivalents help to deliver. As we will see below, the model does *not* offer a convincing economic explanation for Zipf's Law or any other empirical regularity about city-size distributions. An economic explanation for Zipf's Law exists, but this has to wait until Chapter 8 where we will return to this topic.

We give a simplified version of this model and illustrate key elements with a graph introduced by Combes, Duranton, and Overman (2005) hereafter. The focus of the analysis is on the labour market. Combes et al. distinguish between four different curves, namely (i) the wage curve, (ii) the cost of living curve, (iii) the net wage curve, and (iv) the labour supply curve. Together, these curves for different sectors determine the spatial equilibrium between cities, as illustrated in Figure 5.10.

(i) The wage curve

This curve gives the wage rate w in a location $c = A, B$ as a function of the size of the total local labour force N. In this case c refers to a city. The wage curve $w(N)$ may be upward sloping, downward sloping, or bell-shaped depending on the precise nature of the scale economies involved. In a neo-classical model (with diminishing returns to labour) the wage curve has a negative slope. With increasing returns to scale, the curve has a positive slope. Note that in a competitive equilibrium – without increasing returns – transport costs can always be avoided. This relates to the so-called Spatial Impossibility theorem (see Box 5.3). The wage curve is the result of profit maximization of firms in the model. The micro-economic foundation of the direction of the slope can, for example, be explained by referring to the sharing, matching, and learning mechanisms that can relatively easily be given a micro-economic foundation; see Behrens and Robert-Nicoud (2015). The larger the scope of the externalities, the larger the (absolute) value of the slope.

$$Y_{ic} = D_{ic} E_{ic} K_{ic}^{1-\alpha} L_{ic}^{\alpha} \qquad 5.2$$

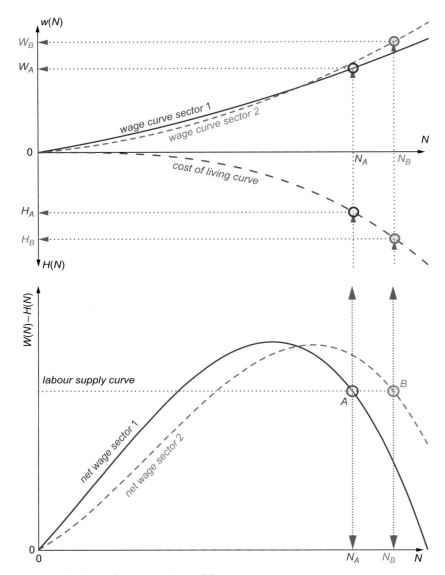

Figure 5.10 Core urban economics model
Note: the vertical scale of the bottom graph differs from the vertical scale of the top graph for clarity.

A specific example of a simple production function is provided in equation 5.2, where Y_{ic} is total output of sector $i = 1$, 2 in city c, D_{ic} is a productivity term (some sectors are more productive than others), E_{ic} is a city-specific agglomeration effect for sector i in city c that is external to the firm, K_{ic} is the input of capital and L_{ic} is the input of labour for sector i in city c. Assuming perfect factor mobility between sectors in a city results in identical wages across sectors, which is combined with profit maximization and free entry and exit of firms in a sector (zero profit condi-tion). The wage in a city equals: $W_c = D_c E_c$.

Note that wages can differ between cities because of productivity differences. Think, for example, of the greater San Francisco area where highly productive IT firms cluster together, which leads to high average local wages, possibly also because of external effects. A simple way of modelling these external effects could be $E_{ic}(N_c) = N_c^\varepsilon$, where N_c is the size of city c and ε is a mnemonic for the elas-ticity of external agglomeration economies. Larger cities increase wages because in large cities one can benefit from so-called matching, sharing, and learning externalities.

Duranton and Puga (2004) describe these externalities in detail. Sharing refers to indivisibilities. An opera house is only economically feasible in large cities because of sharing costs. Matching refers to the quality of a match between worker and employer in labour market models, where large cities offer a higher probabil-ity of a successful match. Learning refers to the need for face-to-face contact. In large cities with more contacts the quality of learning is higher. In a meta study on these economies Melo et al. (2009) estimate that the range of ε is between 0.02 and 0.1. Combes and Gobillon (2015) argue that the lower bound is the most plau-sible if proper care is taken of reverse causation, and unobserved heterogeneity (see Chapter 3 for a discussion of these topics). In Chapter 6 we will return to the empirics underlying the productivity (and wage) differences between cities in more detail.

(ii)   The cost of living curve

This curve depicts how the cost of living H in city c depends on the size of the total local labour force N. The costs are defined in expenditure terms, instead of a price index. Again, the model details need to inform us what the cost of living curve $H(N)$ looks like. One could, for example, use a simple congestion specification such as $H(N) = N^\beta$, where β is a congestion parameter associated with larger cities. In the Henderson (1974) model congestion or crowding costs are a strictly positive function of the overall size of city c measured by the size of the local labour force N_c, as drawn in Figure 5.10. There are many ways to model these congestion costs. One aspect could be that in large cities commuting becomes more expensive (see Fujita and Thisse, 2013, for the many ways this can be modelled). There are only a few estimates of β, which suggest that it is around 0.02 (Behrens and Robert-Nicoud, 2015).

(iii)   The net wage curve

Utility in these models is a function of real wages (see Chapter 7 for details on the relationship between utility and real wages). The net wage curve is given by the difference between the wage curve and the cost of living curve in a city

$W(N) - H(N)$, which is different for different city sizes and sectors. It gives the net disposable wage for every level of the local labour force N. The shape of this curve is, of course, determined by the underlying shapes of the wage curve and the cost of living curve.

(iv)   The labour supply curve

This curve, finally, is a function of the net wage rate. In this model, labour is fully mobile between locations and any net wage difference, however small, induces migration. This means the labour supply curve is perfectly elastic (flat).

Equilibrium in the model is determined by the intersection of the labour supply curve and the net wage curve, where the size of the local labour force N is on the horizontal axis and the net wage $W(N) - H(N)$ on the vertical axis. The intersection point gives the equilibrium city labour force and the equilibrium net wage for city c. This simple set-up includes the main elements of the Henderson (1974) urban systems model by using the above curves, as illustrated in Figure 5.10.

How does the model help to explain the existence of a system of cities? First, the assumption that the positive spillovers of location are sector-specific implies that each sector has its own optimum size. Second, the model provides a rationale as to why cities specialize in the production of those goods for which the economies of scale are relatively strong. It rationalizes an urban system in which cities of different sizes trade with each other. So, the notion that cities are like 'floating islands' (Fujita and Mori, 2005, p. 395) does not apply to the Henderson model, because specialization forces cities to trade with each other. However, despite the inter-city trade interdependency, economic geography is not part of the analysis yet as there are zero transport costs between cities.

Figure 5.10 illustrates the urban economics model by depicting the *wage curve* for two sectors (1 and 2). The slope of the two wage curves indicates that there are strictly positive returns to scale in both sectors: wages rise when the total city labour force increases. Note that initially (for low levels of N) sector 1 has stronger increasing returns – and thus higher wages – but this is reversed for higher levels of N. The figure also shows the *cost of living curve*, which rises when the total labour force N increases.

Equilibrium is determined by equating the net wage curve $W(N) - H(N)$ with the labour supply curve in the bottom panel of Figure 5.10. Note that the combination of sector-specific increasing returns and a cost of living that depends only on the overall city-size implies that for an equilibrium to be stable each city will be *fully specialized* in either sector 1 or 2. Diversification is only possible if by chance the wages in both sectors are the same (this is at the intersection of both curves in the top panel of the figure). In all other cases, the larger sector grows at the expense of the smaller sector, and will keep on growing until all workers are employed in that sector.

This process holds for all cities, such that there is a matching between cities and sectors. There is, however, a complication. Suppose we have two relatively large cities – the total workforce of each city is to the right of the intersection of the two curves in the top panel – will this result in two cities both specialized in sector 2? The answer is no. If both goods are indispensable (it is assumed they are), the larger city will specialize in sector 2 because economies of scale work in favour of the larger city. This forces the other city out of sector 2 production and into sector 1 production.[12] The result is that all cities are specialized. This also implies trade between consumers across cities. In this sense the model is not a 'floating island' model; cities are trading with each other and are not autarkic. It is, however, a floating island model in the sense that it does not matter where cities are located on the map.

The cost of living rises with total city population.[13] The combination of the two sector wage curves and the cost of living curve thus gives the net wage curves. The short-run equilibrium is now determined by the intersection of each net wage curve with the labour supply curve, assuming perfect labour mobility between cities. Labour will migrate towards cities with relatively high real wages, that is, wages corrected for the cost of living. This assumption results in a horizontal labour supply curve. As Figure 5.10 shows, the resulting equilibria are denoted by A and B where the net wage is the same across cities and the city specialized in sector 1 has population of size N_A, while the city specialized in sector 2 has population size N_B. In the *spatial equilibrium* the net wage (utility) is thus equalized in all cities.

Three aspects of the spatial equilibrium are worth mentioning. First, cities specialized in a sector must be of the same size, as we have assumed that the cost of living curves are the same in each city and economies of scale are sector-specific, not city-specific. Second, since economies of scale are stronger in sector 2 than in sector 1 this means that cities specialized in sector 2 are larger than cities specialized in sector 1. Third, since cities are fully specialized, inter-city trade will arise. Henderson (1974) thus rationalizes the existence of a system of (specialized) cities that trade with each other, driven by the tension between sector-specific returns to scale (the wage curve) and city-specific congestion (the cost of living curve).

The short-run equilibrium refers to the situation where the number of cities is fixed. In Henderson (1974) the number of cities is endogenous; in the model there

---

[12] Note that full specialization requires a full model that specifies demand relations; for given initial prices, it is unlikely that complete specialization automatically implies market clearing. So, prices will adjust to clear markets. Although this is possible in principle we do not discuss it here, as we only want to stress different mechanisms leading to systems of cities. It is important to note that the city specializing in sector 2 always has a higher wage rate than a city specializing in sector 1 (or a combination of sector 1 and 2).

[13] Note that the cost of living only depends on city-specific variables and not on expenditures on imported commodities that include transportation costs.

is a trade-off between moving to another existing city or starting a new one. If a new site offers higher (real) wages a new city will form. This requires the presence of a central planner as economies of scale are external to the firm and only a central planner knows that distributing the existing labour force over more cities could be welfare increasing. For an individual it is never beneficial to start a new city as one always starts somewhere in the left part of the bottom panel in Figure 5.10 . A long-run equilibrium is characterized by an optimal number of cities that maximizes utility for the cities in the model.[14]

This set-up is remarkably versatile and can easily be generalized, as analysed by Glaeser (2008). Firms in the model maximize profits and a wage curve results. It is straightforward to include additional factors of production such as land or differentiate between types of labour (such as high-skilled and low-skilled). Also, various types of externalities can be included by making E_{ic} a function of different externalities. Box 5.3 provides a reminder of why some type of increasing returns to scale is necessary to explain the existence of cities. The cost of living curve from the basic urban systems model can be extended to include the prices of additional factors that affect the cost of living, such as housing prices and various amenities or nuisances.

According to Glaeser (2008, p. 4), the *spatial equilibrium* is the 'single most important concept in urban or regional economics ... if identical people are choosing to live in two different places then those two different places must be offering an equivalent bundle of advantages, like wages, prices and amenities. Essentially, there must be no potential for arbitrage over space.'

In a qualitative sense, Figure 5.10 thus covers many extensions and illustrates the spatial equilibrium. If additional factors are location-specific then cities of different sizes result and the model can produce a system of cities. Given our discussion in sections 5.2–5.4 the question is: do these models produce a system of cities that can be described by an urban power law? This is a reality check on the usefulness of a model on a system of cities. As we have seen above, power laws and the special case of Zipf are a salient characteristic of actual city-size distributions. If a model of a system of cities can explain a power law it is preferred over a model that cannot.

In principle the Henderson (1974) model *can* produce such a system of cities in an *ad hoc* way, simply by manipulating D_{ic} in equation 5.2 in such a way that

---

[14] Economic agents do not include the external effects of congestion in their decisions. This implies that cities tend to become too large in the sense that points A and B in the lower panel of Figure 5.10 are to the right of the maximum of the net wage curves. From a welfare point of view, city sizes that correspond to the maximum of the net wage curves are ideal. This solution would require the hand of a city developer, that is, someone with the power to create new cities. The final situation where the net wages in all cities are the same and each city has its optimal size is the long-run equilibrium; see Combes, Duranton, and Overman (2005, pp. 322–3).

BOX 5.3 Starret's Spatial Impossibility Theorem

The *Spatial Impossibility theorem* states that in an economy with a finite number of locations and a finite number of consumers and firms, where space is homogeneous and transport is costly, no competitive equilibrium exists in which actual transport takes place. This is intuitively easy to understand as in such an economy transport cost can always be avoided because production and consumption can take place at an arbitrarily small level, without additional costs (this situation is referred to as backyard capitalism). In such a hypothetical world of perfect divisibility, it would be impossible to explain why clustering or agglomeration of activities occurs (as we observe in reality). Only if there are indivisibilities, or extra costs involved if production is split, does the location of economic activities become important (Starrett, 1978, p. 27): 'as long as there are some indivisibilities in the system (so that individual operations must take up space) then a sufficiently complicated set of interrelated activities will generate transport costs'. This principle is known as Starrett's Spatial Impossibility theorem; see Chapter 2 in Fujita and Thisse (2013) for a formal analysis and summary. It is interesting to note that Koopmans (1957) already pointed out that we can only begin to understand the importance of location or geography for economics if we recognize the fact that economic activities are not infinitely divisible. Or, in Koopmans' words, 'Without recognizing indivisibilities – in human person, in residences, plants, equipment, and in transportation – … location patterns, down to those of the smallest village, *cannot* be understood' (Koopmans, 1957, p. 154).

a power law results. Recent studies analyse this question in depth. Using Monte Carlo simulations, Lee and Li (2013) show, for example, for a single sector city, that if E_c in equation 5.2 is split into many separate underlying (abstract) elements e_{fc}, where f is an index of factors that are randomly distributed and not correlated, a size distribution follows that is consistent with Zipf's Law. These factors are abstract, statistical entities and do not correspond to something in the real world.

Behrens and Robert-Nicoud (2015) extend this analysis by using real-world factors instead of simulated ones to construct E_c. They use amenity variables collected by the US Department of Agriculture: mean January temperature, mean January hours of sunlight, the inverse of mean July temperature, the inverse of mean July humidity, the percentage of water surface, and the inverse of the topography index. The January variables are positive amenities, whereas the July variables indicate dis-amenities (therefore the inverse is taken). The topography index describes the terrain; the higher the index, the more difficult the terrain (the reason why the inverse is taken): it ranges from 1 (flat plains) to 21 (high mountains). The E_c is constructed on the county level and subsequently aggregated to the MSA level.

(MSAs are Metropolitan Statistical Areas, which are spatial units closely related to cities.) The findings, based on these real-world factors, indicate that constructing E_c variables from underlying factors does not support the idea that high values correlate with large cities as the correlation coefficient is just 0.147.

The conclusion is that we have a model that can explain a system of cities, but that has difficulties producing a system of cities corresponding to a power law. This is the reason that we will use another model from the literature on geographical economics, to be introduced in Chapter 8, to show how an economic model can give rise to Zipf's Law.

5.6   Differentiated Cities

A large part of the literature on (systems of) cities assumes a homogeneous city population and ignores for instance heterogeneity among workers (Abdel-Rahman and Anas, 2004). This is an assumption that is at odds with reality. Cities are often diverse and not fully specialized, while city labour markets vary: some cities attract many high-skilled people and other cities do not. Davis and Dingel (2017) and Behrens et al. (2014) develop models of a system of cities that allow for such labour market heterogeneity and thereby for specialization patterns of cities that are different from the model discussed in section 5.5: in contrast to the Henderson (1974) world of specialized cities, they develop models in which cities are incompletely specialized and house a large variety of people.

We illustrate this line of research with a theoretical model developed by Davis and Dingel (2017), who create a general framework in which L heterogeneous individuals with a continuum of skills s select a sector σ to work in and choose a location δ within a city c. The indices σ and s are defined such that higher values imply more skill-intensive sectors and higher levels of skills. In the discussion below we focus on the relationship of worker skills and city sizes, but the same line of reasoning can be applied to the skill-intensity of sectors.

Individuals maximize utility U, which is defined as the difference between the individual's *value* of productivity and the rental rate at a location within the city. The individual's value of productivity depends on many things: the city where you work, the sector in which you are employed, and the location within a city. Formally, we can describe this as: $q(c,\delta,\sigma;s)\,p(\sigma)$, where q is productivity and p is the price of the good you produce.

The cost of living is a rental rate which can be described by $r(c,\delta)$, and only depends on the city and the location within the city. Some cities are expensive in general and within cities there are expensive locations; think of Central Park in New York City. To make the model manageable we can specify the productivity function into separate elements. In the model it is assumed that an individual's productivity $q(.)$ depends on the city-level total factor productivity $A(c)$, which is given for all individual workers but depends on the city's size.[15] Furthermore, a location-specific term indicates that productivity also depends on where one lives in a city. If you must commute for a long period of time, your productivity could suffer from this. This is represented by $D(\delta)$. The index δ is defined in such a way that higher values of δ indicate locations in a city that are less attractive / productive, so $D'(\delta) < 0$. Finally, productivity depends on the skills of a worker and the sector of employment, represented by $H(s,\sigma)$. All these factors are assumed to work independently and enter the objective function separably, as given in equation 5.3. Note that this equation (again) forms the basis of the spatial equilibrium as discussed in the previous section; in the words of Glaeser (2008, p. 4): 'there must be no potential for arbitrage over space'.

$$U(s,c,\delta,\sigma) = q(.)p(.) - r(.) = A(c)D(\delta)H(s,\sigma)p(\sigma) - r(c,\delta) \qquad 5.3$$

The function H is assumed to have a special characteristic that is useful for empirical research. It is assumed to be strictly log-supermodular (in s and σ) and strictly rising in skills.[16] What do we mean by this in plain English? Log-supermodularity ensures that higher-skilled individuals are not only more productive in general, but also *relatively* more productive in skill-intensive sectors with higher σ. This characteristic of H is related to the more familiar concept of comparative advantage; more productive or high-skilled individuals thrive in skill-intensive sectors or occupations, and low-skilled workers are *relatively* more productive in low-skill intensive sectors.

Individuals supply one unit of labour inelastically and pay rent to absentee landlords. This concept makes the modelling of rents simple: an individual pays a rent to someone who is not there, so we do not have to deal with this group of persons in the model.

We order the system of cities in terms of total factor productivity such that $A(C) \geq A(C-1) \geq .. \geq A(1)$. Since the most skilled workers can afford to choose the most attractive locations, there will be a range of highly skilled people located in large cities (like New York) who cannot be found in smaller cities (like Buffalo in the state of New York), followed by a range of workers with similar skill levels found in both cities. Since skilled people work in skill-intensive sectors, larger cities contain relatively more skilled workers. If we let $f(s,c)$ be the distribution of skills over cities, this can be characterized by equation 5.4, which implies large cities accommodate relatively more high-skilled people and sectors. We do not go

---

[15] This is closely related to the D term in equation 5.2.

[16] That is: $s > s', \sigma > \sigma' \Rightarrow H(s,\sigma)H(s',\sigma') > H(s,\sigma')H(s',\sigma)$

into the details of deriving this distribution, but it is the result of an aggregation within cities over sectors and skills.[17]

$$f(s,c)f(s',c') \geq f(s,c')f(s',c), \ for \ c \geq c' \ and \ s \geq s' \qquad 5.4$$

We illustrate the model with the help of two graphs. Figure 5.11 focuses on the relationship between skill abundance and city size. Positive utility requires that the value of a worker's production $R(.) \equiv A(c)D(\delta)H(s,\sigma)p(\sigma)$ is at least as high as the rent costs $r(cost \ of \ living)$; see equation 5.3. The figure shows four lines: two curves that describe how the value of productivity varies with skill, one for city 1 and one for city 2, where city 2 is the larger city and the value of productivity is always larger than that for city 1; and two lines showing the level of rents (cost of living) in both cities. As drawn, the rents in the larger city are always higher than in the smaller city. A city is only viable for a worker of a certain skill level if for her $R(.) > r(.)$.

The model implies that for city 1 the skill level of workers must be at least s_1^*; see point E_1 in Figure 5.11. Workers with lower skill levels experience negative utility, $R(.) < r$, and will choose another location. The same line of reasoning implies that for the larger city 2 the skill cut-off value moves to s_2^* at point E_2. The cut-off value moves to the right. This is the result of the increased value of productivity in the larger city combined with a higher cost of living. This trade-off provides a sorting mechanism with respect to skills: only high-skilled people can afford to live in high-productivity places, as inhabitants of New York and San Francisco can

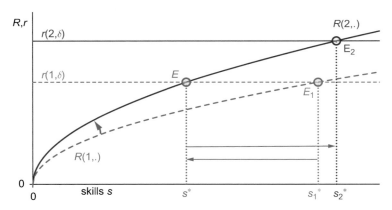

Figure 5.11 Skills and city size

---

[17] Under a regularity condition (namely that the supply of locations in a city is decreasing and log-concave), the distribution of skills over cities $f(s,c)$, which is derived from equation 5.3 by integrating over sectors and locations within the city, is log-supermodular, see equation 5.4. This inequality satisfies the so-called monotone likelihood ratio property, which says that the relative returns to increasing skills (s) *in*crease with city size (Costinot, 2009, Costinot and Vogel, 2015; Milgrom, 1981).

confirm. The figure also shows the outcome if the cost of living were independent of city size. If the cost of living is the same for both cities, say $r(1,\delta)$, then the more productive city 2 could house also relatively low-skilled people and the cut-off skill level would be s^*.

So far, city sizes are given. In reality (as well as in this model), this is not the case. Figure 5.12 illustrates the relationship between worker skills and city selection for two workers (a and b) with efficiency levels s_a and s_b, respectively. We want to find out how these two workers select a city, and when there is no longer an incentive to relocate to another city, which is the spatial equilibrium. We assume that worker b is more efficient than a, so: $s_b > s_a$. In the situation depicted in Figure 5.12, the more skilled worker b prefers to live in the large city 2 over living in smaller city 1 since $R_{2,b} - r_2(.)$ is larger than $R_{1,b} - r_1(.)$. Note that both options are viable for worker b; in both cases utility is positive. For the less skilled worker a the location choice is unambiguous. The high costs in the large city 2 make location in that city not viable for her: $R_{2,a} < r_2(.)$. The only option is to go to the smaller city 1: $R_{1,a} > r_1(.)$. In this example, the more skilled worker b selects a location in the large city and the less skilled worker a selects a location in the small city. This selection process affects, of course, the equilibrium variables in the model. For example, rents: the more people move to a city, the higher the rents and the lower utility. This process continues until spatial equilibrium is reached and nobody has an incentive to relocate to another city.

Based on the above model, we see that workers must (i) be skilled enough and (ii) select cities that offer sufficient agglomeration rents, to cover the location costs; it is the combination of these two elements that will make a city viable for a worker. Davis and Dingel (2017) do not study whether their model produces a system of cities that corresponds to a power law. Behrens et al. (2014) show, however, that a model which includes sorting of high-skilled workers into larger cities, where larger cities are more productive and larger cities are home to more

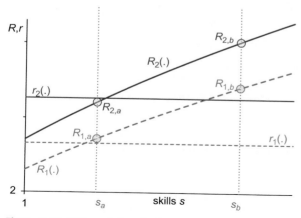

Figure 5.12 Skills and city selection

productive firms (tougher selection), can produce a system of cities corresponding to Zipf's Law.

Gaubert (2018) also develops a related and innovative model that allows for firm heterogeneity where firms from various sectors have to determine which city would be their best location choice. Two main mechanisms are at work: (i) more productive firms self-select or sort themselves into larger, more densely populated cities and (ii) larger, more densely populated cities cause firms that locate there to become more productive because of the existence of the kind of increasing returns emphasized in our urban systems model in this chapter. The second mechanism is thus the urban agglomeration effect on productivity. Testing the model for a large data set with French firms it turns out that both mechanisms are about equally important to explain why city productivity increases with city size for French cities. In the next chapter, we will return at length to the distinction between self-selection and agglomeration effects to explain why larger cities typically have a higher level of productivity (and hence wages). In her important paper, Gaubert (2018) uses the estimations for French cities also to investigate the possible policy implications. Policies that, for instance via subsidies, aim to boost the economic plight of smaller French cities lead on average to a welfare loss for the French economy as whole. This important policy implication will be the main topic in Chapter 11 of the book.

Returning to the Davis and Dingel (2017) model, an important advantage of the model is that it can be evaluated using two straightforward empirical tests: an *elasticity* test and a *pairwise comparison* test.

The elasticity test simply evaluates whether people with higher skill levels are relatively more abundant in larger cities. This is illustrated for Chinese cities in 2010 in Figure 5.13 using log scales and three skill levels: illiterate, middle school, and bachelor or more (based on Brakman, Hu, and van Marrewijk, 2014).[18] The figure also reports elasticities, which is the percentage increase in people with certain skill levels if the size of the city rises. The number of people with a low education level (illiterates) rises slower than the size of the city; the elasticity is 0.846 (less than one). The number of people with middle-school level rises about as fast as the size of the city; the elasticity is 0.971 (close to one). Finally, the number of people with a high education level (bachelor or more) rises faster than the size of the city; the elasticity is 1.300 (above one). This illustrates the sorting of higher-skilled workers into larger cities. Table 5.2 reports the population elasticities of six educational groups for cities in China in 2000 and 2010. In general, the estimated elasticities confirm that larger locations have relatively more skilled

---

[18] See Brakman, Hu, and van Marrewijk (2014) for details on the data that are used and definitions of spatial units. Our primary data sources are the population census of 2000 and the population census of 2010.

Table 5.2 Population elasticities in Chinese cities, 2000 and 2010

Educational attainment	City level year	
	2000	2010
Illiterate	0.930 (0.035)	0.846 (0.039)
Primary school	0.946 (0.023)	0.890 (0.022)
Middle school	1.012 (0.010)	0.986 (0.010)
High school	1.012 (0.028)	1.033 (0.016)
College	1.029 (0.038)	1.092 (0.026)
Bachelor or more	1.326 (0.054)	1.300 (0.041)
Observations	1,506	1,626
R^2	0.889	0.899
Education FE	Yes	Yes

Source: Brakman et al. (2014); standard errors in parentheses, clustered by spatial unit.

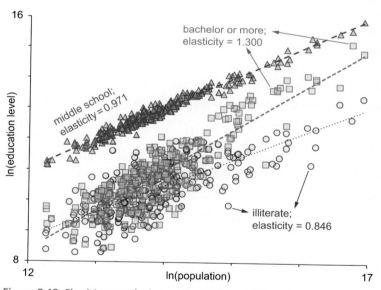

Figure 5.13 Elasticity test of urban sorting in China, 2010
Source: based on Brakman et al. (2014).

inhabitants: the elasticities are higher for higher-skilled educational groups in both years. Moreover, this trend is stronger in 2010 than in 2000.

The pairwise comparison test, which is based on equation 5.4, can best be explained using an example. Suppose we have empirical information on the distribution of four types of skills, ranked according to skill level, across 40 cities, ranked according to size. We can then directly compare any two arbitrary cities and the associated two skill types to see if inequality 5.4 holds. If so, we verify that the larger city in this pairwise comparison has relatively more workers of the higher skill type. We call the comparison a *success* if the condition holds (value = 1) and a *failure* if not (value = 0). We can compare 40 cities in (40 × 39)/2 = 780 different pairs, and each city pair has four skill types giving (4 × 3)/2 = 6 different skill combinations for each pair of cities. This gives a total of 780 × 6 = 4680 pairwise comparisons. For each comparison we find either a success or failure. The extent to which the average success rate exceeds the random distribution benchmark of 0.5 (comparing success or failure to the flip of a coin; Heads a success, and Tails a failure) can then be taken as an indication regarding the sorting-predictive power of the model. The comparison with flipping a coin also gives us the opportunity to calculate the significance of the results: are the results comparable with what you would expect of flipping a coin? So, the question we want to answer is whether the pairwise comparison is a random result or a significant result explained by the model (see also the discussion in Box 3.3 in Chapter 3).

In application to the Chinese cities, we expect that the comparison between a very large city (such as Shanghai with 23 million people) and a much smaller city (such as Wuhai in Inner Mongolia with 0.5 million people) is almost sure to be successful and is a more revealing test of the prediction of the model than a comparison between two similar-sized cities, such as Wuhai (532,902 persons) and Nujiang (534,337 persons). In the latter case the test outcome might be just a random result. We will therefore report *weighted* success rates, where we use the difference in log population for a city pair as weight: if the size difference between two cities is large, success or failure receives a larger weight. We consider the weighted success to be the most relevant.

Moreover, we do not have to restrict ourselves to comparing individual cities. We can also compare groups of cities that are allocated to *bins* of different size. Suppose we have two distinct groups of cities C and C' with the smallest city in C being bigger than the biggest city in C' and two skill types with $s > s'$. The inequality in equation 5.4 then also holds for the bin:

$$\sum_{c \in C} f(s,c) \sum_{c' \in C'} f(s',c') \geq \sum_{c \in C} f(s',c) \sum_{c' \in C'} f(s,c')$$

This inequality implies that if the cities are grouped into a series of bins ordered by city size, then in any pairwise comparison of two bins and two skills the bin containing the larger cities has relatively more of the high-skilled workers. When we create 2 bins we have just 1 comparison (the group containing the largest cities versus the group containing the smallest cities). When we create 4 bins we have 6 comparisons, and so on. In the analysis below, we divide the cities into 2, 4, 10, 30, 90, and individual bins.[19] If m is the number of bins and n is the number

---

[19] Individual bins consist of one city per bin.

of skills (sectors / occupations) the total number of pairwise comparisons is thus $[m(m-1)/2] \times [n(n-1)/2]$. We report both the unweighted and weighted success rate of the pairwise comparisons per bin.[20]

The bins are indicated on the horizontal axis in Figure 5.14, which summarizes the results for the unweighted and weighted success rate of the pairwise comparison tests. Simply eyeballing the outcomes, we see that the model is better than just flipping a coin. The prediction of success is outside the confidence intervals created by flipping a coin (the dashed lines indicate 95 per cent confidence intervals of tossing a fair coin: the random outcome). The success rates of these comparisons are significant and higher in 2010 than in 2000. It is also clear that the success rate of the pairwise comparison tests improves if we lump cities together in bigger groups (and thus a lower number of bins, that is, more to the left on the horizontal axis). The smallest groups of individual cities have a weighted success above 60 per cent in 2010. In contrast, the success rate when we have only two bins (containing half of the sample per bin) is 100 per cent. The weighted success rates are higher than the unweighted ones, indicating that the comparison test is more likely to hold if the difference in the size of the populations of the compared locations is large.

The findings above suggest that the theoretical model works quite well regarding the relationship between location size and skill abundance. In addition, the tests perform better in 2010 than in 2000. We could take this as an indication of China's move over time to a more market-oriented economy allowing for greater labour mobility and specialization. Box 5.4 provides an example of a pairwise comparison test for cross-border and national mergers and acquisitions in the USA.

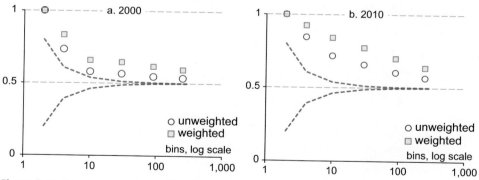

Figure 5.14 Pairwise comparison of six educational skill levels in Chinese cities
Source: Brakman et al. (2014); the bins are 2, 4, 10, 30, 90, individual; the associated numbers of pairs are 15, 90, 675, 6,525, 60,075, at least 548,775; the dashed lines indicate the upper and lower limits of a 95% confidence interval of tossing a fair coin; results within these bands are considered random outcomes.

---

[20] We use the difference of the log of the average population in a bin as weight.

BOX 5.4 Mergers and Acquisitions in the USA

The Davis and Dingel model discussed in section 5.6 can also be used to analyse the location of mergers and acquisitions (henceforth M&As), as shown by
Brakman et al. (2019). The authors analyse in detail the location of both national
and cross-border M&As in the USA for the period 1985–2012 using the 3,000
largest urban locations depicted in Figure 5.1. For various reasons they argue that
there is a relative sorting of cross-border M&As in larger locations, indicating that
larger locations tend to have relatively more cross-border M&As.

The authors support their claim using a variety of elasticity and pairwise comparison tests. An example of the latter is provided in Figure 5.15 using the number of M&As in an urban location. In this case, a success indicates that the larger
(bin of) location(s) has relatively more cross-border M&As. The success rate is high
(but a bit erratic) for low bin numbers (with only a few comparisons), relatively
small (but above the confidence interval) for medium bin numbers, and high
again for high bin numbers (with many, detailed comparisons). This suggests that
there is indeed relative sorting of cross-border M&As in larger locations.

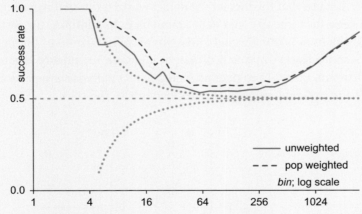

Figure 5.15 Pairwise comparison of cross-border and national mergers and acquisitions, USA
Source: based on Brakman et al. (2019); the figure is based on the number of M&As using
population size for Urban Location; the confidence lines indicate the limits of a 95% confidence
interval for tossing a fair coin; based on the central limit theorem for 8 bins (28 pairs) and higher
and exact below (not shown below 5 bins); each line is based on almost 7 million comparisons.

5.7 Conclusions

In this chapter we analysed systems of cities, both empirically and theoretically,
based on the concept of a spatial equilibrium between cities, which means that
economic agents do not have an incentive to move to another city. On the empirical side, we illustrated city systems using maps and characterized them using

urban power laws, of which Zipf's Law is an interesting special case. On the theoretical side, we graphically explained the structure of the Henderson model and similar models, as well as elaborating on modern extensions of differentiated cities where matching of workers and firms in different sectors plays an important role.

For the purposes of our book, the Henderson (1974) model and its graphical illustration, however, help us to understand why city systems exist. The next and final chapter on urban economics will try to back up the main insights from Chapter 5 by providing empirical evidence for a *between-city* spatial equilibrium as well as for agglomeration economies as the main drivers of differences in city sizes and city fortunes.

Exercises

Question 5.1 Empirical Power Law
Go to the website for this book. Compare the power law distributions for developing countries with those for advanced countries and give possible explanations for the relative difference in the importance of primate cities in these countries.

Question 5.2 Dynamic Power Law
One can compare the power law exponent for a country over time. Suppose a country moves from an agricultural economy to an industrial economy; what do you think happens to the power law exponent over time? Is the exponent in the industrial period larger or smaller than in the agricultural period? Why?

Question 5.3 Urbanization Economics
Use the diagrammatic representation of the core urban systems model of Henderson (1974) (see Figure 5.10) and discuss whether this representation of the model would have to be changed if urbanization economies were included.

Question 5.4 Labour Supply Elasticity
In Figure 5.10 it is assumed that the supply of labour is infinitely elastic (what does this mean and how do you see this?). How would the figure change if the supply of labour were not infinitely elastic, and what would be the consequence for the analysis?

Question 5.5 Gibrat's Law
It is by now well known that if the growth of city size is independent of city size – Gibrat's Law – the resulting city size can be described by Zipf's Law. Give an intuitive explanation for this result.

Question 5.6 Testing Gibrat's Law
How would you test whether city size growth is independent of city size?

6 The Empirics of Agglomeration

LEARNING OBJECTIVES

- To understand the empirics of urban agglomeration economies and be able to apply the spatial equilibrium concept.
- To understand the sources and mechanisms of agglomeration economies.
- To understand the main econometric problems for estimating agglomeration economies.
- To have a basic understanding of the latest theoretical developments in urban economics and know how to approach its main econometric problems.

6.1 Introduction

As explained in Chapter 1 on the spiky world, the starting point for our book is that economic activity is spatially clustered. We are interested in the economic reasons for this. Within countries, people and firms alike cluster together in cities. In fact, as we saw in Chapter 1 nowadays most of the world population lives in cities or urban agglomerations. Cities come in all kinds of sizes and shapes. For all countries with multiple cities, the distribution of cities allows large, medium-sized, and small cities to co-exist in a rather stable city-size distribution; see Chapter 5. In Chapter 6 we will analyse the economic reasons that make individual workers or households as well as individual firms choose a city as their preferred location in more detail. The main question to be addressed is thus: what determines the location choice when mobile workers and firms choose a location? In doing so, we will discuss a number of important recent empirical insights and studies in urban economics. From the worker's perspective, the benefits of a city are related to its economic prospects in terms of wages or employment opportunities, while the cost of living and the amenities a city has to offer also come into play. From the firm's perspective, the availability of a market for its goods, productive workers, and other inputs must be weighed against issues like local factor prices, land prices, and congestion costs.

To put our discussion in a proper perspective, Figure 6.1 shows the relationship between *city wages* (measured as mean annual earnings for male workers) and *city size* (measured as the number of people within 10 km of the average worker) for 76 Spanish cities. There is a clear positive relationship between wages and city size. The figure thus *suggests* that people might prefer larger cities like Madrid and Barcelona as their preferred location, since wages are higher. But if only wages mattered, everybody would end up living in one large city (Madrid), where wages are highest. Apparently, people's location choice does not only depend on wages. The fact that larger cities are also more expensive immediately comes to mind. Nevertheless, the wage differentials are substantial, as De la Roca and Puga (2017, p. 106) point out: 'workers in Madrid earn 31,000 euros annually on average, which is 21% more than workers in Valencia (the country's third largest city), 46% more than workers in Santiago de Compostela (the median sized city), and 55% more than workers in rural areas'.

From the firms' perspective, Figure 6.1 raises the question why firms want to locate in large cities if wages, and hence labour costs, are higher there? Somehow, it must be beneficial to choose Madrid or Barcelona as a firm's location despite higher wages. Armed with our knowledge of Chapter 5 on city systems (and see specifically the discussion of the wage curve based on equation 5.3), the main reason must be that larger cities offer agglomeration rents, which explains why firms do not necessarily opt for locations with the lowest wages. Whether it is true that cities somehow makes firms and workers more productive is a key question analysed in urban economics. As we will learn in this chapter, the answer depends on the strength of agglomeration economies at the city level. Figure 6.1 also hints at the possibility that larger cities display stronger agglomeration economies and therefore are places where wages (and thus productivity) are higher. But as we will see, it is far from obvious why causality should run from city size to city wages,

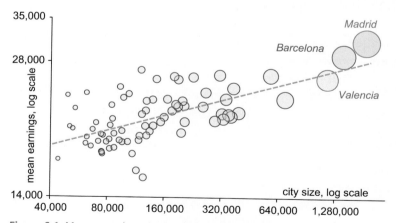

Figure 6.1 Mean annual earnings and city size in Spain, 2004–9
Source: created using data kindly provided by Diego Puga; city size = people within 10 km of average worker, 2006; mean earnings = mean annual earnings 2004–9 average in 2009 euro; bubbles proportional to city size.

or why there should be a direct causal relationship at all between these two variables. At this point it suffices to note that both wages and city size are endogenous variables and from Chapter 3 we know that the endogeneity problem is thus really a big issue in urban economics.

The set-up of Chapter 6 is as follows. In section 6.2 we briefly discuss the main ingredients of a workhorse model in urban economics for the location choice of people across cities. The model is the spatial equilibrium model that we already encountered in Chapter 4 and Chapter 5. In section 6.3 we analyse the empirical relevance of amenities in people's location choice. In section 6.4 we turn our attention to the city location choice from the perspective of firms. In doing so, our central concept will be that of agglomeration economies. We will show how research on agglomeration economies in urban economics draws its inspiration from the model on urban systems analysed in Chapter 5. After clarifying some terminology in section 6.5, we discuss some initial empirical evidence in sections 6.6 and 6.7 that sets the stage for section 6.8, where we evaluate more recent research on agglomeration economies in urban economics. Here we will see how empirical methods introduced in Chapter 3 (like instrumental variables and fixed effects) are used in modern research on agglomeration economies. Section 6.9 concludes, noting that in the models discussed in Part II of our book on urban economics there is not really a role for spatial interdependencies between locations. In other words, there is not yet a proper role for economic geography in terms of spatial linkages. Incorporating this role by adding such linkages is the main task of the geographical economics literature analysed in Part III.

6.2   The Spatial Equilibrium Revisited

In Chapter 4, we focused on the location choice of individuals *within* a single city.[1] Using a monocentric framework, we introduced the concept of *spatial equilibrium* to show how the basic trade-off between transport costs and housing costs determines location choice, given that all firms are in the central business district of the city. Living close to work saves on transport or commuting costs, but is also more expensive in terms of housing costs. The addition of other transport methods, or heterogeneity across individuals or urban amenities, did not alter this basic trade-off as modelled in equations 4.1 to 4.3. The framework outlined in Chapter 4 is known in urban economics as the Alonso-Muth-Mills model (Glaeser, 2008). This model came about in the 1960s and is still a workhorse model in modern urban economics. As such, the model is a straightforward extension of the first urban

---

[1] Part of this section is based on Garretsen and Marlet (2017).

economics model (von Thuenen, 1826), where farmers must pick a location around the monocentric city as to where to grow their crops which they then must sell at the market in the city centre. In doing so, farmers face a similar bid–rent curve as commuters do in the Alonso-Muth-Mills model; see Chapter 4.

Individuals do not only face a decision about where to locate in a city, but also which city to pick in the first place. Allowing for labour mobility across cities, we are then confronted with the question of what determines an individual's location choice. In terms of Figure 6.1, why might Barcelona be preferred over Sevilla? This question is certainly relevant for cities within a country assuming that people are free to move and pick their preferred location choice. In principle it is also relevant in an international setting, but since international labour mobility is far more limited than intranational labour mobility, we restrict our analysis to the case of picking a location within a single country.

In urban economics, the concept of spatial equilibrium is also used to analyse the individual's location choice across cities (Roback, 1982). Indeed, this has been the main focus of our discussion of the urban systems model in Chapter 5. Individuals now try to maximize their utility across cities, where an individual city or location is literally just a single one-dimensional point on the map. In this version of the spatial equilibrium framework, cities can differ from each other in three respects, namely nominal wages, housing rents, and amenities. In the basic model of Chapter 4 nominal wages and amenities do not enter the analysis since the focus is on intra-city housing rents and transport costs only.[2]

Since nominal wages are only one of the three determinants of the individual's location choice across cities, the simple fact that nominal wages are higher in Madrid than in Salamanca does not necessarily imply that people prefer Madrid as their location compared to Salamanca. Firms remain in the background in this spatial equilibrium framework. The fact that wages are higher in Madrid must somehow be linked to firms in Madrid being more productive because of agglomeration economies offered by Madrid (see Chapter 5) but we will leave this part of the discussion for the next section, where we discuss agglomeration economies.

To be more specific, in choosing their optimal location, individual households maximize their utility. If the utility of location j is higher than that at their present location, i, individuals migrate from i to j. Migration stops when utility between locations is equalized; a spatial equilibrium is reached. Glaeser, Kolko, and Saiz (2001, p. 30) stipulate that three elements enter the individual's utility function, namely the urban productivity premium, the urban rent premium, and the urban amenity premium.

---

[2] But see already section 4.10.2 as to how amenities can be added to the basic monocentric model of Chapter 4.

The *urban productivity premium* is positive and captures the idea that productivity increases with city size (more on this below; here we merely take these productivity differences between cities as given; again see also the urban systems model of Chapter 5). A positive productivity premium simply means that (nominal) *wages* increase with city size, which is often observed (see e.g. Kemeny and Storper, 2010). Diseconomies of scale are given by the negative *urban rent premium*, meaning that housing rents are higher in larger (or denser) cities. The *urban amenity premium* can be either negative or positive since amenities can be negative (such as a high urban crime rate and bad climate) or positive (such as a low crime rate and nice weather).

The location or migration decisions of all individuals are such that in a spatial equilibrium for everyone the balance between a city's wages, housing rents, and amenities is the same across locations, which means that no individual has an incentive to relocate to another city. In the distribution of Figure 6.1, larger Spanish cities do indeed pay higher nominal wages, but the fact that people also opt to live in smaller cities indicates that housing rents are lower there and/or these smaller cities offer better amenities. The spatial equilibrium thereby allows for cities to differ in population size and the process towards such an equilibrium means that cities differ in population *growth* rates, which is why population growth is the dependent variable in many empirical studies that try to assess the empirical relevance of urban amenities. To do so, one can measure amenities directly or indirectly by taking the difference between a city's wages and housing rents; see Glaeser (2008, ch. 3).

This modelling of the location choice as the tension across cities between productivity (or efficiency), diseconomies of scale (housing rents), and urban amenities is quite general and can even be given a general equilibrium interpretation that does not only yield an equilibrium city size but also predictions about the welfare implications of the overall city size distribution (Desmet and Rossi-Hansberg, 2013). In the full-blown spatial equilibrium model that focuses on the inter-city spatial equilibrium (see Glaeser and Gottlieb, 2009 for a good introduction), with households (as well as firms) making their location choices, there are three main endogenous variables at the city level, namely wages, population size, and the price of non-traded goods (such as housing rents).

6.3   Measuring the Relevance of Amenities

When it comes to the empirical relevance of a spatial equilibrium for inter-city location choice, most research has focused on American cities (Glaeser, 2011). Overall, there is indeed evidence that location choices across American cities can be understood as the interplay between a city's wages, housing rents, and amenities. San Francisco offers higher wages and better amenities (climate, scenery, and cultural offerings) than, for example, Detroit, but housing rents are also much higher. Having said this, there is still a debate in the literature as to the robustness of the empirical evidence. This is to large extent due to the measurement of amenities. Good urban and regional data on wages and housing rents are relatively easy to come by, but this is by no means the case for urban amenities.

The notion that cities with superior natural amenities (like a mild climate) and/or a high quality of man-made amenities (such as a wide range of consumer goods and local public services) are attractive seems undisputed (Glaeser and Gottlieb, 2009; Partridge, 2010). But the availability of data on amenities is limited. The emphasis is often on a narrow set of (physical) amenities like the weather, coastal location, or the general scenery (Cheshire and Magrini, 2006; Rappaport, 2006). But, as Box 6.1 shows, the value of amenities has to set be against the two other elements in the spatial equilibrium condition: urban wages (and hence productivity) and urban housing costs.

BOX 6.1 Amenities Versus Attractiveness of Cities

In a survey about the most attractive city in the USA, respondents in 2016 picked Honolulu on Hawaii as the winner.[3] In the annual America's Favorite Places Survey, respondents can score cities (places with more than 100,000 inhabitants) across an impressive 65 categories. Some of these categories are exogenous, like those pertaining to the weather or nearness to sea or mountains and the like, but many are clearly endogenous, like the attractive features that relate to the quality of all kinds of public and private services on offer, such as the quality of restaurants, cultural offerings, friendliness of people, and so on. In the research on amenities in urban economics, the value of a city's amenities is typically not derived from surveys like this. Instead, researchers use a revealed preference approach where the value of a city's amenities is reflected by the difference between urban wages and housing costs. Asking people about attractive features has as a major drawback that it may be subject to all kinds of biases. A good example of state-of-the-art research on amenities for US cities is the work of David Albouy (2016, 2018). Here the amenity value per US city follows from a meticulous application of our spatial equilibrium framework to US city data. To drive home the point that attractiveness ≠ amenity value, Table 6.2 lists the top 15 US cities from the attractiveness survey against the amenity value derivation in Albouy (2016). Even though the city definition is not identical between 2016 vs 2000, it is clear that the two lists differ. In terms of the amenity value measurement, larger and coastal cities rule, whereas this is less so for Attractiveness in the top 15 list.

---

[3] https://www.travelandleisure.com/americas-favorite-places/most-attractive-cities#salt-lake-city-utah (accessed on 16 September 2018).

BOX 6.1 (cont.)

Table 6.2 Top 15 US cities: attractiveness versus amenity value

Attractiveness survey	Amenity value (Albouy, 2016)
Honolulu, TX	San Francisco, CA
Boulder, CO	Santa Barbara, CA
Scottsdale, AZ	Honolulu, HI
Salt Lake City, AZ	Monterey, CA
San Diego, CA	San Diego, CA
Nashville, TN	Los Angeles, CA
Charleston, SC	San Luis Obispo
Denver, CO	New York, NY
Houston, TX	Boston, MA
Madison, WI	Cape Cod, MA
Alexandria, VA	Seattle,
Las Vegas, NV	Naples
Savannah, GA	Santa Fe
Norfolk, VA	Denver
San Antonio, TX	Chicago,

Source: left panel, see footnote 3; right panel, Albouy (2016), Table 2.

The availability of amenity data matters even more if local wages and housing rents are imperfect signals for locational choices across cities. In the case of the USA with its relatively flexible labour and housing markets, wage differentials (for similar jobs) and regional housing prices respond to market forces. In continental Europe, however, often wages are determined via centralized wage setting and the housing market is heavily regulated, resulting in a low regional housing supply elasticity. With little or no wage variation across cities and a quasi-fixed housing supply, the important question becomes whether and how the concept of spatial equilibrium can be used to analyse an individual's location choice.

The urban system of the Netherlands, one of the oldest urban systems in the world, is a case in point. In the Netherlands, inter-city wage variation is limited and the housing supply is mostly determined by large-scale government planning (and not by market forces).[4] Given the small size of the country and the dense network of transport linkages, many workers live in one city and work in another city (in

---

[4] Parts of the text of this section are adapted from Garretsen and Marlet (2017).

contrast to the USA). By making use of a rich data set of 23 city-specific amenities for Dutch cities, Garretsen and Marlet (2017) show how the spatial equilibrium condition can still be used. With little or no wage variation across cities and with inelastic urban housing supply, inter-city or inter-regional differences in the attractiveness of cities should show up in differences in housing prices for Dutch cities.

In this case, the spatial equilibrium condition boils down to two variables: the differences in urban amenities should be mirrored by differences in housing prices. Table 6.1 shows the estimation results for the case of Dutch cities with all data

Table 6.1 Basic estimation results (ZIP code level): housing prices (euro per m²), 2006

	(1)	(2)	(3)	(4)
Job opportunities				
Job potential	0.563***	0.459***	0.539***	0.507***
Proximity of train station	0.072***	0.037***	0.025	0.032**
Natural amenities				
Proximity to nature	0.254***	0.162***	0.125***	0.104***
Proximity to the sea	0.183***	0.170***	0.174***	0.177***
Constructed amenities				
Distance to city centre	−0.094***	−0.095***	−0.089***	−0.112***
Proximity to live performances	0.082***	0.114***	0.187***	
Proximity to musical venues	−0.062***	−0.037**	−0.037**	
Proximity to art museums	0.030**	0.021**	0.015	
Proximity to history museums	0.043**	0.042***	0.044**	
Proximity to recreational grounds	−0.474***	−0.313***		
Proximity to shops for fun shopping	0.447***	0.306***		
Professional soccer team	0.031	0.003	−0.007	
Quality restaurants	0.059***	0.067***	0.066***	
Diversity in restaurants	−0.019	0.033		
University in town	0.136***	0.046*		0.045***
Share monumental buildings	0.086***	0.080***	0.086***	0.096***
Share canals (length per building)	−0.022	−0.025*	−0.022	−0.012
Share kindergarten in town	0.126***	0.082***	0.071***	
Number of bars in the neighbourhood	0.039**	0.033**	0.027**	
Parks in town	−0.026	−0.037*	−0.051***	
Public water in the neighbourhood	0.073***	0.061***	0.069***	
Sport facilities in town	0.065**	0.090***	0.071***	
Distance to shops for daily shopping	−0.015	0.004	0.003	

Table 6.1 (cont.)	(1)	(2)	(3)	(4)
Dis-amenities				
Nuisances	−0.180***	−0.156***	−0.155***	−0.143***
Crime rate	−0.184***	−0.115***	−0.068**	−0.052**
Housing characteristics				
Share social housing	−0.118***	−0.104***	−0.095***	−0.118***
Share pre-war houses	0.026***	0.037***	0.048***	0.095***
Share single detached houses	0.216***	0.271***	0.269***	0.261***
Share semi-detached houses	0.035	0.088***	0.085***	0.082***
Share terraced houses	−0.117***	−0.114***	−0.116***	−0.112***
Share apartments	−0.098**	−0.057*	−0.066*	−0.010
Method	OLS	ML	ML	ML
Lambda (spatial error coefficient)		2.95***	3.33***	2.68***
Number of observations	2328	2328	2328	2328
Adjusted R^2	0.64			
Log likelihood		−16,036.5	−16,057.7	−16,151.3

Standardized coefficients; ***>99%; **>95–99%; *>90%; weight matrix based on inverse distances; for data set and definitions: see Garretsen and Marlet (2017).

measured at the zip-code level and with housing prices as dependent variable. Given the fact that many Dutch workers commute, the two job potential variables assess the availability of jobs for each zip code area, where job potential measures the number of jobs that can be reached within a certain travel time. The empirical specification also includes a number of housing characteristics as control varia-bles. The focus is on three sets of amenities: (i) natural or exogenous amenities, (ii) constructed or man-made amenities and (iii) dis-amenities.

An important difference between natural and constructed amenities is that whereas the former are given and hence exogenous, the latter are (potentially) endogenous in the sense that they are the result of the attractiveness of cities, however determined, as reflected in Dutch housing prices. In this respect, the main aim of Table 6.1 is to show that urban housing prices and amenities are at least to some degree positively correlated as the spatial equilibrium condition states, even in institutional settings that differ markedly from American cities.

Two of the amenity variables (proximity to nature and sea) are natural amen-ities and can clearly be considered as exogenous. Also, the two dis-amenities (nuisances and crime rate) are significant with the expected (negative) sign. With the man-made or constructed urban amenities and the two dis-amenities, there is clearly an issue of causality in the sense that fast growing cities may simply attract these amenities as a by-product. Although it was found that the most attractive cities in the Netherlands are not the fastest growing cities, one could argue that, for instance, the quality of restaurants (a consumer good amenity) merely reflects that sought-after lively cities or municipalities, as exemplified by high housing prices, attract high-quality restaurants.

So, some amenity indicators might suffer from the endogeneity problem highlighted in Chapter 3. As pointed out there, finding a good instrument could be a solution. Reverse causality, by definition, is not a problem for historical variables, such as the share of monumental (mainly seventeenth-century) buildings and possibly not for the presence of a university, since most Dutch universities were founded many decades or even centuries ago. For the other constructed amenities, like theatres, museums, and restaurants, endogeneity remains a problem.[5] Often historical data are not available. That is why column (4) has been added in Table 6.1. In this specification indicators that clearly suffer from endogeneity problems, such as quality restaurants and proximity to cultural events, are dropped. Restricting the model to amenity indicators that are exogenous does not affect the main conclusion: the attractiveness of Dutch cities in terms of its amenities is reflected in housing prices.

6.4   Agglomeration: Introduction and Key Concepts

At the start of Part II of our book, in section 4.1, we referred to one of the leading urban economists Edward Glaeser (2008), who stated that there are three main actors in urban economics: utility-maximizing individuals, profit-maximizing firms, and builders or developers. The third set of actors is not the focus of this book (but see section 4.8), while Chapter 4 and the previous section of the current chapter discuss the main ingredients of the spatial equilibrium condition, where the individual household/worker's location choice *within* and *between* cities is analysed respectively. The location choice of (profit-maximizing) *firms* has been less the focus of the spatial equilibrium concept until now.

But firms are obviously a main actor in urban economics as well. Again, consider Figure 6.1: in large Spanish cities workers earn higher nominal wages. But why would firms located in larger cities be willing to pay higher wages to begin with? The main reason must be that for *whatever reason* firms and their workers located in larger cities are relatively more productive than in smaller cities. A main

---

[5] A solution, if data allow, is to re-estimate the model with lagged amenity variables; this does not change the basic results shown in Table 6.1.

reason that immediately comes to mind after reading Chapter 5 on city systems (check again equation 5.3) is that the firms located in larger cities, which employ relatively more skilled and expensive workers, can afford to do so because firm productivity increases with city size.

As explained in Chapter 5, the main concept that links firm productivity and hence wages to city size is *agglomeration economies*. Indeed, next to the spatial equilibrium condition, agglomeration economies are the second main building block of modern urban economics. Agglomeration economies refer to the fact that firms operate under increasing returns at the location level, be it a city, region, or country. By moving to a larger location, a firm and its workers become more productive, because they benefit from location-specific increasing returns to scale.

Note, as we stressed again and again, especially in Chapter 3, that firms and workers located in larger cities could also be more productive for reasons *unrelated* to city size. A positive relationship between local wages and local productivity might be caused by a third omitted variable or by sorting of high-productivity firms and workers into larger cities. We turn to this topic below.

6.5   Terminology, Sources, and Mechanisms

From now on, we focus on agglomeration economies, that is, increasing returns at the location level. Since we are dealing with urban economics in this part of our book, locations must mainly be thought of as cities. We first briefly discuss terminology and the main mechanisms or sources of agglomeration economies in this section before turning to the empirical evidence in section 6.6.

6.5.1   Terminology

Agglomeration economies are an example of increasing returns to scale. At the most general level, increasing returns to scale means that an increase in the level of output produced decreases the average costs per unit of output for the firm: size matters. When the reasons for such a downward-sloping cost curve are firm-specific and thus unrelated to its (city-) location, we have a case of *internal* increasing returns to scale. If, however, the reasons for increasing returns to scale are not at the firm level but outside the individual firm at the sector-level or city-level, we have a case of *external* increasing returns to scale. Agglomeration economies are a prime example of external increasing returns to scale. As such, agglomeration economies can be either positive or negative with respect to city size; see Chapter 5. Larger and more densely populated cities make it easier for firms located there to share and find relevant information. These information spillovers or externalities at the city level are an example of positive agglomeration economies. Similarly, congestion costs that increase with city size are an example of negative agglomeration economies.

Before we turn to the mechanisms and sources that are used in the literature to rationalize (and measure) agglomeration economies, a few remarks on terminology are in order. With *pure* (or *technological*) agglomeration economies an increase in industry-wide output in a city alters the technological relationship between inputs and output for each individual firm in that city. It therefore has an impact on the firm's production function. In much of urban economics, pure agglomeration economies are the focus of the analysis. The market structure can then be perfect competition since the size of the *individual* firm does not matter. *Pecuniary* external or agglomeration economies are transmitted by the market through price effects for the individual firm, which may alter its output decision. Two examples, dating back to Marshall (1920[1891]), are the existence of a large local market for specialized inputs and labour market pooling. A large industry can support a market for specialized intermediate inputs and a pool of industry-specific skilled workers, which benefits the individual firm. Contrary to pure external economies, these (pecuniary) spillovers do not affect the technological relationship between inputs and output (the production function). Pecuniary externalities exist in the geographical economics literature through a love-of-variety effect in a large local market (more on this in Chapter 7 and Chapter 8 in Part III of our book). In the model in section 6.6.1 we will illustrate how agglomeration economies are estimated in urban economics.

Finally, agglomeration economies can be *static*, as in the cases referred to above, but the urban economics literature also considers *dynamic* agglomeration economies. In that case the average costs per unit of output per firm are a negative function of the *cumulative* output of the industry in a city or of the overall size of the city. When we discuss the empirical evidence for agglomeration economies we will make use of the distinction between static and dynamic agglomeration economies.

The take-away message from this short discussion on agglomeration economies for urban economics is that agglomeration economies refer to increasing returns to scale that originate at the urban level and that make a firm more productive. This raises two important sets of follow-up questions. First, what are the reasons in terms of underlying sources or mechanisms for these localized agglomeration economies to exist to begin with (see section 6.5.2)? Second, how can we measure or approximate these agglomeration economies and what does the empirical evidence tell us (see section 6.6)?

6.5.2   Sources and Mechanisms

The main categorization of the *sources* for agglomeration economies dates back to Alfred Marshall (1920[1891]), particularly in empirical research (see also Box 6.2). In (t)his view, there are three main sources of localized agglomeration economies:

BOX 6.2 Marshall and Agglomeration Economies

The British economist Alfred Marshall (1842–1924) was the first (political) economy professor at the University of Cambridge and cannot only be seen as the founder of what became the Cambridge school of economics (via his students and successors like John Maynard Keynes, Joan Robinson, or Nicholas Kaldor), but also of modern mainstream economics via his major work the *Principles of Economics*, first published in 1890. The contributions of Marshall to the modern analysis of economics are manifold, but here the focus is on his thinking about industrial districts. In his view successful industrial districts are characterized by many small and highly specialized firms. The benefits of agglomeration or clustering within such a district for a single firm are basically to be found in the sharing of information and inputs. The increasing returns or agglomeration economies are thus not related to the size of the industrial districts or city but very much tied to the specialization structure of the city where the exchange and shared access to information and (labour) inputs provide a strong incentive for these firms to cluster within that district and location thereby saving on transaction and transport costs. It is fair to say that Marshall's thinking on the rationale of industrial districts has now for more than a century provided a main backbone for the theoretical and above all empirical work on agglomeration economies in urban economies. The increasing returns 'mantle' in Cambridge was passed on from Marshall to Nicholas Kaldor (1908–86), who broadened the scope of the increasing returns analysis, and in contrast to Marshall, by turning to models of imperfect competition (where agglomeration economies reside with the firm and not the sector) and economic growth. This approach of increasing returns is more at home in Parts III and IV of the book where we will deal with firm-specific agglomeration economies (Part III), and economic growth (Part IV).

(i) *information or knowledge sharing*, (ii) *labour market pooling*, and (iii) *the sharing of (specialized) inputs.* In addition to this well-known Marshallian trilogy, the following sources of agglomeration economies are also used to explain the existence of cities and their variation in size (Rosenthal and Strange, 2004, Table 2; see also Combes and Gobillon, 2015):

Natural advantages: differences in factor endowments (first nature geography) also matter at the city level; see also Chapter 1 and the discussion on urban amenities in section 6.3;

Home market effects at the industry level: this is the idea that a larger market size at a certain location will provide a source of pecuniary agglomeration economies; more on this in Chapter 9;

Consumption externalities: various city-specific amenities explain why consumers prefer to live (and work) in cities and why some cities are preferred over others; see again section 6.3 on urban amenities;

Rent seeking: the empirical literature (see Ades and Glaeser, 1995, Henderson, 2003, and Baldwin and Robert-Nicoud, 2007) points out that rent-seeking behaviour may lead to cities that are too large (see for instance our discussion on power laws in Chapter 8). This contrasts with the Marshallian trilogy and the additional sources mentioned above, which focus on the efficiency- and growth-enhancing effects of agglomeration economies of cities.

In a seminal and influential paper, Duranton and Puga (2004) focus on *mechanisms*, rather than sources, as the mechanisms are a more precise description what affects agglomeration economies. We have already made use of their division of agglomeration economies into three distinct mechanisms in Chapter 5 when we discussed the possible underpinnings for the wage curve in the Henderson (1974) urban systems model. Duranton and Puga (2004, p. 2066) note: 'consider, for instance, a model in which agglomeration facilitates the matching between firms and inputs. These inputs may be labelled workers, intermediates, or ideas. Depending on the label chosen, a matching model of urban agglomeration economies could be presented as a formalization of either one of Marshall's three basic *sources* of agglomeration economies even though it captures a single *mechanism*.'

Duranton and Puga identify three basic mechanisms: *sharing, matching,* and *learning*. Sharing refers to indivisibilities: an opera-house, for example, is only economically feasible in large cities. Matching refers to the quality of a match between worker and employer in labour market models, where large cities offer a higher probability of a successful match. Learning refers to the need for face-to-face contact, where large cities with more contacts lead to higher quality of learning. In empirical research, the distinction between the older Marshallian trilogy and the modern mechanisms introduced by Duranton and Puga (2004) is not always clear cut, but in modern empirical research on urban agglomeration economies the Marshallian typology of sources has been mostly replaced by the three mechanisms identified by Duranton and Puga; see the extensive survey on modelling, measuring, and estimating agglomeration economies by Combes and Gobillon (2015).[6]

Since agglomeration economies cannot be directly observed, they must be approximated to assess their empirical relevance. This means that one cannot test directly for the presence of a specific source or mechanism that underlies localized agglomeration economies. As we will see next, the main *catch-all* concept that has been used in empirical research related to city size is the density of a

---

[6] Another distinction that is sometimes made concerns the scope of urban agglomeration economies, where scope refers not the source or mechanism but to the extent or strength of agglomeration economies. Rosenthal and Strange (2004, Table 1) distinguish agglomeration economies according to their industrial, temporal, geographic, and organizational scope.

location. In their survey of the empirics of agglomeration economies Combes and Gobillon (2015, p. 2) define agglomeration economies as the 'effect that increases firms' and workers' income when the size of the local economy grows'. They also make the important observation that despite the theoretical identification of various sources and mechanisms for agglomeration economies, as discussed above, empirical research still relies on composite and indirect measures of agglomeration economies that make it impossible to directly test for a specific source or channel. In the next section, we will discuss two of these composite measures or proxies for agglomeration economies: *local size* or *density* and *local economic specialization*.[7]

A second important observation made by Combes and Gobillon (2015) after reviewing the empirical literature on agglomeration economies, is that despite the lack of progress in identifying the exact sources or mechanisms of agglomeration economies, there has been real progress in the empirical methods or strategies employed in dealing with the endogeneity problem that plagues empirical research in urban economics; see Chapter 3. In section 6.8 we return to this second observation and discuss how modern estimation techniques are used to tackle the endogeneity issue when testing for agglomeration economies.

6.6   Empirical Research on Agglomeration Economies

It is beyond the goal of this chapter to give a complete survey of the (vast) empirical literature on urban agglomeration economies; see for a comprehensive survey Combes and Gobillon (2015).[8] We highlight two aspects of the literature. The first is to show what a stripped-down model, which underlies modern empirical research in urban economics on agglomeration economies, looks like. The second aspect is to point out the advantages of the use of micro-data to estimate agglomeration economies.

6.6.1   A Stripped-down Model to Test for Agglomeration Economies

In a simple model on agglomeration economies it is assumed that larger and more densely populated cities offer stronger versions of the sources and mechanisms underlying agglomeration economies than less dense cities.

---

[7] Besides a city's density or specialization structure, a city's human capital is also used as a composite measure of agglomeration economies, the basic idea being that cities with higher levels of human capital will also have higher (growth) levels of productivity (and wages); see Moretti (2012) or Glaeser (2008). Florida (2002, 2006) introduced the notion of a city's creative class, which is closely related to the idea of human capital, to show that creative class is a key carrier of urban agglomeration economies (Brakman, Garretsen, and van Marrewijk, 2009a, ch. 7).

[8] Part of this section is based on Brakman, Garretsen, and van Marrewijk (2009b).

An example of such a model that already provides a remarkably rich variety of forces is summarized by Combes, Mayer, and Thisse (2008, ch. 11). Assume that a firm with a Cobb-Douglas production function that uses labour and (a composite of) other inputs sells to all destination markets and maximizes profits. It can pay the following wage (see Technical Note 6.1 for a derivation):

$$w_i = \frac{\mu(1-\mu)^{(1-\mu)/\mu}}{N_i} \sum_{j \in i} s_j \left(\frac{p_j A_j}{r_j^{1-\mu}} \right)^{1/\mu} \qquad 6.1$$

In this equation, w_i is the wage rate in location i, μ is the share of labour in the production process, N_i is the number of firms in location i, s_j is a labour productivity variable, p_j is the price of good j, A_j is a Hicks-neutral technology parameter, and r_j is the (composite) price of other inputs.

Equation 6.1 shows that wages in location i can be high because labour productivity s_j is high or the level of technology A_j is high. Both terms might reflect location-specific Marshallian externalities, for example knowledge spillovers between firms or labour pooling, in that location. Similarly, labour productivity and/or technology might be high in a location because of the sharing, matching, or learning mechanisms as emphasized by Duranton and Puga (2004). An increased supply of intermediate inputs, that results in lower intermediate product prices r_j, also allows for higher wages. Furthermore, a higher number of firms N_i in the location i results in lower wages, reflecting the idea that a large city in terms of the number of firms also has its downside via lower wages because of more competition and/or congestion and cost of living effects.

So, despite being simple, equation 6.1 already captures a rich menu of potential agglomeration economies. For our present purposes, it is important to note that all variables in equation 6.1 reflect characteristics of the location only and not those of surrounding locations. Any evidence on agglomeration economies must therefore be due to the characteristics of the location only. Recall that agglomeration economies can be positive or negative, which is precisely what the urban systems model of Chapter 5 brings across. The wage curve in that chapter indicates the presence of positive agglomeration economies as exemplified in equation 6.1 by for instance the role of labour productivity s_j, whereas the cost of living curve illustrates the presence of negative agglomeration economies, which shows up in equation 6.1 because an increase in the number of firms N_i in the location lowers the wage rate. In a nutshell, wage equation 6.1 represents the *net wage curve* from the model in Chapter 5.

6.6.2 Empirical Specification

For empirical research, the next question is how to estimate equation 6.1. A straightforward procedure is as follows. Taking logs of equation 6.1 gives:

$$\ln(w_i) = \alpha_1 + \alpha_2 \ln(dens_i) + \varepsilon_i \qquad 6.2$$

In this equation $ln\left(dens_{i}\right)=\dfrac{1}{N_{i}}\sum_{j\in i}s_{j}\left(\dfrac{p_{j}A_{j}}{r_{j}^{1-\mu}}\right)^{1/\mu}$ is the employment or population density in region i. As a catch-all term for agglomeration economies, density thus indirectly captures (i) various possible sources or mechanisms for agglomeration economies and (ii) potentially not only positive but also negative agglomeration economies.

Apart from the potential impact of density, there are other variables that are important. The economic specialization, for example, of a location potentially matters as agglomeration economies can be sector-specific; this implies that labour productivity is not only location-specific but also sector-specific.

In a panel setting, the inclusion of location fixed effects and time fixed effects captures the possible relevance of respectively cross-section and time-specific variation in locational wages; recall the discussion on fixed effects in Chapter 3. Fixed effects capture other determinants of wages that vary in the cross-section or time dimension (like a location's human capital).[9]

The idea that agglomeration economies could be determined by a location's overall size or density (see equation 6.2) as well as by the specialization structure of that location is known in the literature in urban economics as the distinction between *urbanization* economies and *localization* economies. When applied to cities, the former imply that larger, more densely populated, and more diverse cities will have stronger agglomeration economies and hence higher nominal wages and income. The latter form of agglomeration economies implies that it is not only overall city size or density that matters, but also whether the city's economic structure is characterized by a high degree of specialization and firm concentration in sectors with strong agglomeration economies.[10]

The verdict in the recent empirical literature is that both types of agglomeration economies matter. Duranton (2011, p. 38) observes that 'the current consensus is that, in term of elasticities, urbanization effects are about as large as localization effects', although he also notes that 'even though the elasticities are about the same, a larger size seems to be more desirable than increased specialization'. The two most extensive surveys on the empirics of agglomeration economies, Rosenthal and Strange (2004) and the follow-up by Combes and Gobillon (2015), confirm this conclusion. The review of the latest empirical work on agglomeration economies by Combes and Gobillon (2015) also makes clear that the older empirical literature (by relying on aggregate data and simple estimation techniques) is not ideal for making a clear-cut distinction between various agglomeration economies. This is

---

[9] Ideally, one would like to have micro-data to estimate equation 6.2; see Combes, Duranton, and Gobillon (2008); see also section 6.8.

[10] In a setting of urban growth models, following Glaeser et al. (1992), urbanization economies are called Marshall-Arrow-Romer (MAR) externalities or sector-specific spillovers, whereas localization economies are dubbed Jacobs externalities or city-specific spillovers.

the starting point for section 6.8, where we return to Figure 6.1 and the underlying paper by De La Roca and Puga (2017). They show how the empirical literature on agglomeration economies has made progress by using micro-data.

6.7   Regional Agglomeration Economies

Agglomeration economies are not only important for cities. Brakman, Garretsen, and van Marrewijk (2009b) estimate equation 6.2 for a large sample of European regions and countries spanning a long time-period. In doing so, we not only looked at the relevance of our proxy for agglomeration economies (density), but also included a so-called market potential variable to allow for the fact that a region's income is not only determined by its own features, here summarized by its population density, but also by economic geography, indicating where the region or country is positioned relative to other regions or countries on the map. The market potential of a location r consists of the income of all other locations corrected for the distance between location r and these other locations. Including such a simple market potential function acknowledges that wage equations 6.1 and 6.2 do not include variables that capture the spatial interdependencies between locations in the sense that somehow other locations also have an impact on the wages in location r. As will become clear, this is the key difference between urban economics (Part II of our book) and geographical economics (Part III of our book). In fact, the models of geographical economics in Part III provide a theoretical foundation for market potential, thereby allowing spatial interdependencies to affect a location's wages or income as well.

   As a first pass to assess the relevance of economic geography we not only estimated wage equation 6.2, but also a wage equation with a simple market potential function term as independent variable (alongside location and time fixed effects):

$$ln\left(w_i\right) = \beta_1 + \beta_2 ln\left(MP_i\right) + \varepsilon_i \qquad\qquad 6.3$$

   In this equation MP_i is the market potential of location i measured as $MP_i = \sum_s \dfrac{\delta_s Y_s}{d_{is}}$, where Y_s is income for location s, δ a parameter, and d_{is} the distance between locations i and s. It is implicitly assumed that prices do not vary

across locations. Note that MP can include the location's own income. We can also distinguish between *domestic* and *foreign MP*, where foreign MP excludes the income of the location itself and as such provides the clearest contrast with wage equation 6.2. The equations were estimated for 213 European regions and 14 European countries in the period 1975–2006. Due to limited data availability, GDP per capita was used as a proxy for wages as the dependent variable.

   The first two columns in Table 6.3 show the separate results for European regions of foreign market potential and density on income per capita. Both are

Table 6.3 Income per capita, market potential, and density for European regions

Dependent variable is *ln(income per capita)*, panel estimates (t-statistics), 1975–2006			
ln(foreign market potential)	0.321		0.255
	(36.7)		(23.4)
ln(population density)		0.090	0.081
		(37.9)	(34.7)
Time fixed effects	yes	yes	yes
Region fixed effects	yes	yes	yes
Adjusted R^2	0.782	0.800	0.815
F-statistic	521	580	625
Observations	6,816	6,816	6,816

Source: Brakman, Garretsen, and van Marrewijk (2009b); see the paper for exact data definitions.

positive and highly significant. The third column provides the combined effects of foreign market potential and density. The estimated coefficients are slightly lower, but still positive and highly significant. The main conclusion from Table 6.3 is that both market potential and density are significant and have a positive impact on regional income per capita.

A number of important caveats are in order.

First, both density and foreign market potential are potentially endogenous variables. To correct for this, we also performed instrumental variables (IV, see Chapter 3) estimations with a region's *area* and *distance to Brussels* as instruments. In general, the IV estimates lead to similar conclusions.

Second, we may overestimate the role of market potential or density because limited data availability did not include other possible time as well as cross-section *varying* independent variables (like a region's human capital or trade between regions) that are not covered by the inclusion of fixed effects. These variables are not readily available for our sample period for the European regions (see also Breinlich, 2006).

Third, the estimation results for the 14 European countries as well as the estimation results for these countries for a much longer period (1870–2006) indicate that the impact of market potential is not constant, neither across spatial scales nor across time. Foreign market potential (and hence economic geography) seems to be more relevant at the country level, whereas the opposite holds at the regional level for (population) density (and hence for urban economics).

Fourth, estimation results such as those shown in Table 6.3 are of a reduced form type where the main dependent and independent variables are not derived from a single underlying model. Density can be given a theoretical foundation (see equation 6.1), but this not yet true for the market potential function. This observation motivates Part III of our book on geographical economics.

Fifth, the fact that we use aggregate (regional or country) data for income per capita (our proxy for wages), density, and market potential makes it hard to conclude whether Table 6.3 contains proof of agglomeration economies, either of the urban economics or economic geography type. It could be that workers or people with more skills and/or a higher income prefer to live in larger, more densely populated regions (recall section 6.2 on location choice across cities), thereby potentially boosting a region's population density and market potential. Both explanatory variables are then endogenous. As we discuss in the next section, the way to disentangle cause and effect requires detailed data and better methods. More specifically, we turn to the use of micro-economic or individual firm and worker data in combination with better estimation methods (like instrumental variables or difference-in-differences), as introduced in Chapter 3.

Finally, agglomeration economies is a rather elusive concept in the sense that it can only be approximated empirically. Direct measures of sharing, learning, or matching (Duranton and Puga, 2004) or, more in the Marshallian terminology, of knowledge sharing within cities or other agglomerations are not available. Also, as we discussed above, there is more generally a host of sources or mechanisms invoked to rationalize and then quantify agglomeration economies. The empirical study summarized by Table 6.3 offers only one example, where population density is our proxy for agglomeration economies. So, can we somehow generalize the findings in the empirical literature on agglomeration economies? Box 6.3 gives the answer (spoiler alert: not really, more research is needed).

BOX 6.3 Meta-findings on Agglomeration Economies

In a comprehensive meta-analysis of the studies that try to operationalize and measure the impact of urban agglomeration economies, Melo, Graham, and Noland (2009) look at an impressive 727 elasticities, that is coefficients that give the impact of the agglomeration proxy of choice on some urban outcome variable, like urban wages or productivity. These 727 elasticities are taken from a total of 34 studies. It turns out that the elasticities found are sensitive to a host of features of the studies involved. To name the most relevant ones: country effects, sector effects, the agglomeration proxy used, and also the type of control variables all matter; the elasticities are rather sensitive to their inclusion. In addition, the elasticities seem to be time-specific. In other words, the relevance of urban agglomeration economies is context-dependent and the findings are not easy to generalize. So, as emphasized by Combes and Gobillon (2015), there has indeed been real progress in the empirics of agglomeration economies where it concerns the study design and the tools available to correct for reverse causality or other issues that stand in the way of causal inference or identification of the effect of agglomeration economies, but progress on methods used is not the same thing as consensus regarding the relevance of agglomeration economies. The (re)search continues …

6.8   Agglomeration: The Way Forward

Rosenthal and Strange (2004) conclude in their much-cited survey on agglomeration economies that there is a lot we do *not* know about the empirical relevance of (urban) agglomeration economies. The follow-up survey by Combes and Gobillon (2015) by and large confirms this conclusion. This is, perhaps, not surprising since (i) the spillovers/externalities cannot be observed directly and (ii) the model-based testable hypotheses in this literature are subject to observational equivalence (it is often difficult or impossible to distinguish between the different sources of agglomeration economies), which also leads to problems of endogeneity as mentioned before.

Two options to deal with these problems immediately present themselves, namely (a) the use of detailed case studies, or (b) the use of better data and testing techniques. Option (a) is preferred by most geographers, but findings are difficult to generalize.[11] Option (b) has become possible by the increased availability of micro-data.

The use of micro-economic data in combination with instrumental variables (IV), fixed effects, difference-in-differences (DID), or a (spatial) regression discontinuity design (RDD) can go a long way towards addressing and eliminating endogeneity and reverse causality concerns. We discuss two examples of well-known studies that illustrate how micro-data are used in combination with state-of-the-art estimation strategies to link agglomeration economies with city wages or productivity.

6.8.1   Spanish Wages and City Size, Once Again

Figure 6.1 shows a clear positive relationship between *mean annual earnings* (average earnings 2004–9 for male Spanish workers) and *city-size* for Spanish urban areas (where city size is measured as the number of people within 10 km of the average worker). To assess whether and how this relationship represents urban agglomeration economies driving individual wages, De la Roca and Puga (2017) make use of (1) micro-data (a detailed panel data set with employment, location, and other individual characteristics for male workers) and (2) fixed effects and IV.

More specifically, De la Roca and Puga postulate that there are three main reasons why mean wages (and productivity) could be higher in larger cities. First, because of mechanisms like superior sharing of information and better matching of inputs. These are the standard, static agglomeration economies associated with large cities. Second, workers who are more productive might self-select into larger cities. This is the sorting argument. Third, workers may learn more by working in

---

[11] See Combes and Gobillon (2015, section 7.3) for recent attempts at using case studies to identify the sources underlying agglomeration economies.

large cities which makes them over time more productive. This is a dynamic argument linked to the learning mechanism identified by Duranton and Puga (2004).

To disentangle the relevance of each of these three candidates for a positive relationship between mean city-wages and city size, De la Roca and Puga first regress *individual* earnings on a host of individual worker characteristics and a city fixed effect. They thus show (while controlling for individual worker features like skill level, job tenure, work experience, and education) how individual earnings differentials can be attributed to the city where the workers are located. They then show, for the 76 Spanish cities in their sample, how strongly these estimated city fixed effects (capturing the static agglomeration economies) are correlated with city size. This is illustrated in Figure 6.2. As shown in the graph, there is a clear positive relationship between the earnings premium and city fixed effects; the estimated elasticity is 0.0455. De la Roca and Puga continue with adding worker fixed effects to this estimation procedure to control for the possibility of sorting. This reduces the elasticity of the earnings premium to 0.0241, which is in line with other studies using micro-data to disentangle agglomeration economies and sorting (see Chapter 9).

The combination of individual data with city and worker fixed effects allows us to arrive at a better estimate of the size of agglomeration economies and to differentiate between agglomeration economies and sorting. The longitudinal nature of the data set in De La Roca and Puga also allows us to trace out the relevance of *dynamic* agglomeration economies associated with the learning mechanism. This is possible because the data include the employment history of workers,

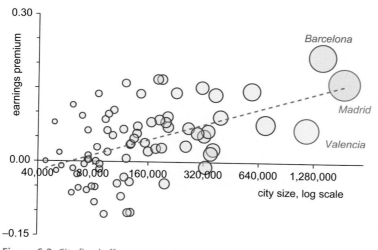

Figure 6.2 City fixed effects versus city size
Source: created using data kindly provided by Diego Puga; city size = people within 10 km of average worker, 2006; earnings premium in per cent (static estimation, pooled OLS); bubbles proportional to city size.

so we observe if (and when) workers switched jobs but also if (and when) they moved between cities. It turns out that working experience gained while living (and working) in larger cities results in a significantly larger earnings premium than experience gained in smaller cities. More importantly, the earnings (and thus productivity) bonus of experience gained in larger cities is (partially) maintained when workers move to a smaller Spanish city.

This suggests that gaining working experience in Madrid or Barcelona permanently boosts a worker's human capital even if one later moves to smaller cities. Note, however, that there is some depreciation of this learning experience. This is illustrated in Figure 6.3 where a comparison is made over a ten-year window of the earnings premium relative to Santiago de Compostela (a median-sized city in the sample). The horizontal axis thus coincides with working for ten years in Santiago. The lower solid line depicts the rising earnings premium for workers who continue to work in Sevilla for ten years. The higher solid line depicts the same for workers who work in Madrid for ten years. The premium is thus higher for Madrid (the largest city) than for Sevilla. The two dashed lines indicate what happens to the earnings premium for workers who first work in Madrid or Sevilla for five years and then move to Santiago for the next five years. At the year of the move to Santiago there is a sharp drop in earnings premium, but the premium is still substantially higher than for workers remaining in Santiago all the time. This

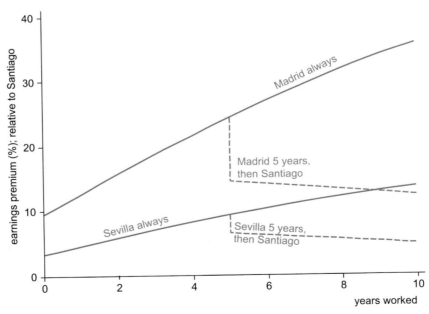

Figure 6.3 Earnings premium and experience
Source: based on De la Roca and Puga (2017); earnings premium in per cent relative to Santiago de Compostela, a median-sized city.

advantage gradually erodes over time, as indicated by negative slopes of the two dashed lines.

6.8.2　The Endogeneity of City Size

The availability of micro or individual worker or firm data, combined with fixed effects, is useful for differentiating between agglomeration and sorting effects and thereby helps to reduce or solve endogeneity issues that arise if one is not able to discriminate between aggregate effects on the one hand and individual effects on the other hand. Still, endogeneity remains a concern also in the above discussion of De la Roca and Puga (2017) to the extent that city size is endogenous because of an omitted variable problem. Such a variable that simultaneously stimulates earnings in a city and induces workers to move there (thus increasing the size of the city) could make the positive relationship depicted by Figure 6.1 spurious. In addition, and as another source of potential endogeneity, we can have a problem of reverse causality if higher earnings lead to an increase of city size.

The standard remedy to tackle endogeneity problems is to use instrumental variables (IV). In this case, a valid instrument would be a variable that has significant predictive power for city size but not for city wages (other than through city size). Similar requirements hold when we use density as a proxy for agglomeration economies, as in the previous section.

In the modern empirical literature on agglomeration economies historical and geological variables are typically used as instruments; see Combes and Gobillon (2015, pp. 39–41). Two types of historical variables are often used: lagged dependent variables (in this case lagged dependent variables of city size) or a historical variable, such as early settlements by the Romans (see Bosker, Buringh, and van Zanden, 2013), which affects current city size but not earnings.

The idea of using these kinds of historical data and lagged city size (or density) in empirical studies of urban agglomeration economies goes back to Ciccone and Hall (1996). De la Roca and Puga use the city size in 1900 as an instrument. The use of geological data as an instrument was inspired by Combes et al. (2010), who use land fertility data in France to this end (see also Chapter 3). The idea is that historically city density was partially determined by the geology of the land, in agriculture-oriented societies, more fertile places being better city locations. They then show that these (exogenous) fertility data do indeed still have explanatory power for present-day (employment) density for their sample of 306 French regions, but not for the wages and productivity in those regions.[12] By instrumenting city size or density, one tries to ensure that endogeneity is not a problem and

---

[12] The use of land fertility as an instrument is a good example of how so-called first nature geography (see Chapter 2) is employed to infer causality. Part III of our book is instead about second nature or man-made economic geography.

causality runs from the agglomeration economies variable of choice (size, density) to the local outcome variable (wages, productivity).

In their paper on French regions, Combes et al. (2010) do not only use land or soil fertility data as an instrument, but also historical data. Their main explanatory variable of interest is regional employment density as a source of agglomeration economies. They use regional employment density in 1831 also as an instrument. Moreover, and in contrast to De la Roca and Puga (2017), they also include spatial interdependencies between the French regions by including a measure of market potential. As in our discussion in section 6.7 (see Table 6.3), both the density variable and market potential have a significant positive impact on local wages. Both density and market potential are instrumented and the estimates are based on micro-data. As can be seen from Table 6.4 (which extends our discussion of Combes et al. (2010) from Chapter 3), the elasticity of wages with respect to agglomeration economies (in this case: local employment density) is about 0.002, which is in line with the elasticities found in De la Roca and Puga (2017); see also Chapter 9.

6.8.3 Alternative Approaches and Strategies

The use of micro-data in combination with modern empirical strategies offers innovative new ways to come up with more conclusive empirical evidence on the relevance of agglomeration economies. However, even these studies do not offer

Table 6.4 Wages in France as a function of density and market potential using instruments

Estimated equation: $ln\left(w_{it}\right) = \gamma ln\left(dens_{it}\right) + b\left(market\ potential_{it}\right) + \varepsilon_{it}$

Variable	Instruments			
	Historical IV only	Historical density IV only	Historical density + soil IV	Historical density + soil IV
ln(density)	0.033[***]	0.018[***]	0.020[***]	0.020[***]
ln (market potential)	0.034[***]	0.048[***]	0.036[***]	0.033[***]
Historical instruments				
pop density (1831)	Yes	Yes	Yes	Yes
pop market pot. (1831)	Yes	No	No	No
Soil instruments				
Ruggedness	No	No	Yes	No
Depth to rock	No	No	No	Yes

Source: Combes et al. (2010), Table 1.10; [***] indicates significance at 1 per cent level; the authors use various ways to define wages (we select results for W[3]; these are wages after controlling for sector effects, observable time-varying individual characteristics, and all fixed individual characteristics).

conclusive evidence regarding the sources or mechanisms underlying agglomeration economies. For this reason, there is a growing strand of research in economics that no longer opts for estimating structural or reduced-form wage equations (like equations 6.1 to 6.3) but instead opts for an alternative research design by using (quasi-) natural experiments to infer cause and effect (see Chapter 3). In urban economics, studies under this heading try to exploit historical, policy-induced, or truly experimental shocks and the exogenous variation across space to which these shocks give rise to tease out causal effects (see for a survey Baum-Snow and Ferreira, 2015, and Chapter 9).

An example of this approach is Redding and Sturm (2016), who model and test for the impact of World War II bombing destruction on the neighbourhoods and its people in London. Their approach combines agglomeration economies and sorting with the notion of spatial equilibrium (see Gaubert, 2018 for a related paper for French cities). Similarly, when analysing agglomeration economies there is an asymmetry since most research focuses on the benefits and not the costs. It might be useful to analyse the costs of agglomeration in more detail by looking at housing and land prices to learn more about the determinants of agglomeration effects; see Combes, Duranton, and Gobillon (2012) and Albouy and Ehrlich (2013).

The second way forward is to look for inspiration beyond (urban) economics from other social sciences, like geography, sociology, or psychology. We provide an example of combining economics, geography, and psychology in Box 6.4 on the impact of psychology on the Brexit vote in the UK.[13] It builds on the new *geographical psychology* literature (Rentfrow, Gosling, and Potter, 2008; Rentfrow, Jokela, and Lamb, 2015) which shows that people's personality traits are spatially clustered, such that the psychological make-up of people living in London is rather different from those living in Newcastle or Cambridge. New evidence is emerging that these spatially clustered personality traits matter for urban economic growth. Garretsen et al. (2019) show for UK cities that urban growth is also significantly affected by a city's personality traits. Cities that score high, for example, on Neuroticism display a significantly lower employment and output growth over the sample period 1981–2011 across 63 large UK cities.

As before, endogeneity problems arise. Are spatially clustered personality traits the cause or consequence of urban growth? Do people with a high score for Neuroticism move to low-growth cities? If so, causality would be from urban growth to regional personality traits. To analyse this, Garretsen et al. (2018) use a traumatic youth experience as an instrument. Other recent studies, like Lee (2017) or Stuetzer et al. (2016, 2018), also show how local outcomes can be better understood by also looking at personality traits.

---

[13] For the full paper on the regional Brexit vote and regional personality traits see Garretsen et al. (2018).

BOX 6.4 Brexit Versus Remain Vote and Psychological Openness

On 23 June 2016 a small majority (52 per cent) of the UK electorate voted in a referendum for the UK to leave the European Union (EU) soon, known as *Brexit*. In view of the predicted negative economic consequences of Brexit (Dhingra et al., 2016; HM Treasury, 2016), the outcome of the referendum came as a shock to most academic and policy experts; see Los et al. (2017), Brakman, Garretsen, and Kohl (2017), or Baldwin (2016). There is a prominent geographical divide for the 380 local authority districts (LAD), where many districts near London and in the north (Scotland) and the west of Northern Ireland voted to *Remain* and the rest to Brexit.

Remarkably, many UK districts strongly intertwined with the EU voted for Brexit. To explain the paradoxical result where regions seem to vote against their (own) economic interests, Garretsen et al. (2019) argue that what is lacking is a psychological perspective; see also Kaufmann (2016) or Krueger (2016). Based on recent research on *geographical psychology* (Rentfrow, Gosling, and Potter, 2008; Rentfrow, Jokela, and Lamb, 2015), they investigate the relevance of regional personality traits for the Brexit vote.

Research shows that an individual's personality traits are a strong predictor of individual political preferences. In the psychological literature, these traits are referred to as the *Big Five*: Openness, Conscientiousness, Extraversion, Agreeableness, and Neuroticism (John and Srivastava, 1999; John, Naumann, and Soto, 2008). When it comes to voting outcomes, there is clear evidence indicating that individual personality traits matter for individual political attitudes and outcomes (Gerber et al., 2011), particularly for the trait Openness. Crucially, personality traits not only explain individual voting behaviour, but these traits are also regionally clustered. This offers a potential explanation for the above-mentioned regional differences in the Brexit referendum.

For each of the districts we have data on the Big Five personality traits (Rentfrow, Jokela, and Lamb, 2015). The relationship between the trait Openness, which measures how conventional and traditional people are in their outlook, and the Remain vote is illustrated in Figure 6.4. Note that low scores on Openness indicate a more inward-looking attitude and a preference for familiar routines instead of new experiences, and vice versa for high scores on Openness. The psychological trait Openness alone can explain 45.3 per cent of the variance of the percentage of the Remain vote (R^2). We take this goodness of fit indicator as a simple reflection of explanatory power, as summarized in Figure 6.5. Openness is, of course, not the only determinant of the Remain vote. The Scottish districts, for example, score relatively low on Openness but relatively high on the Remain vote.

BOX 6.4 (cont.)

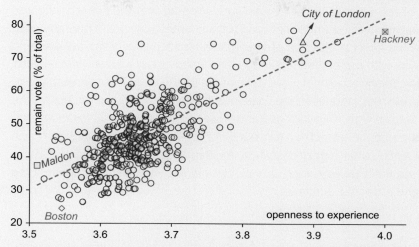

Figure 6.4 The Remain vote share and psychological openness for 380 districts
Source: created using data from Garretsen et al. (2018); dashed line is a regression line which explains 45.5 per cent of the variance in the remain vote.

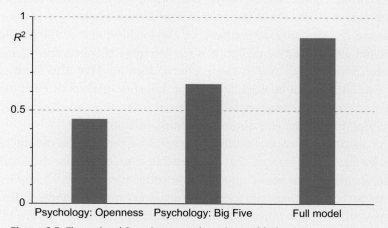

Figure 6.5 The regional Remain vote and goodness of fit for three models

A purely psychological regional explanation of the Remain vote includes all Big Five psychological traits at the regional level. It can explain 64.3 per cent of the Remain vote. We can and should, of course, also include other relevant control variables, like proportion of employment in manufacturing, the unemployment rate, average age of the adult population, population size, level of higher-educated people, number of educational qualifications, immigration, and a dummy for Scotland. We refer to this as the Full model. It can explain 89.1

per cent of the variance in the Remain vote. We find that the Remain vote was significantly higher in districts that are Scottish, larger, younger, better educated and/or with a lower proportion of immigrants. In economic terms, we also find that districts with more manufacturing employment show a lower Remain vote. From a psychological point of view, three of the Big Five variables (Agreeableness, Conscientiousness, and Openness) continue to have a significant impact on the regional Remain vote. If we look at standardized coefficients for all the independent variables at the district level in our full model, Openness is ranked fourth most influential, after higher education, median age, and the Scotland dummy. In short, we find that psychological variables are also important for determining political and economic outcomes.

6.9   Conclusions

We used spatial equilibrium and agglomeration economies, the two main building blocks of modern urban economics, to better understand the location choices of people and firms across cities. From the spatial equilibrium concept, it became clear that wages are not the only determinant of the location choice for people as housing rents and amenities also matter. It is the interplay between these three variables that determines which city is the preferred location. We also showed how the spatial equilibrium can be used if labour or housing markets or even the whole economic geography of a country looks different from the concept typically assumed, by applying the spatial equilibrium condition to Dutch cities.

The concept of agglomeration economies is central to the understanding of location choices by firms. We learned that the possible sources and mechanisms underlying agglomeration economies cannot (yet) be tested directly, which implies that empirical research uses approximations for agglomeration economies, like city size, density, economic specialization, or human capital. Since these are all endogenous variables, any effect on local outcomes, like wages and productivity, cannot be taken as direct evidence of the relevance of agglomeration economies. To be on firmer ground, we discussed studies using individual worker or firm data in combination with instrumental variables or fixed effects.

In the end, and here we have come full circle, the positive relationship between Spanish wages and city size shown in Figure 6.1 in the introduction to this chapter is indeed to some degree evidence that agglomeration economies matter. Apart from the use of micro-data and clever empirical estimation strategies, we also discussed several alternative strategies for urban economics to further increase our knowledge of the location choices made by people as well as firms. Among these alternative strategies are the quasi-experimental research design, the integration of the two building blocks (spatial equilibrium and agglomeration economies), a shift of attention from agglomeration benefits to costs, and looking for inspiration outside economics, as illustrated by our example with regionally clustered personality traits.

We have now come to the end of both Chapter 6 and Part II of our book, that is the part on urban economics. We will use the analytical insights on spatial equilibrium, agglomeration economies, and empirical methods to add another layer to the overarching question for the whole book: why do economic agents cluster in space? To continue our search for answers to this fundamental question, we will add the role of spatial interdependencies or economic geography. The notion that spatial linkages matter (see Chapter 2) or that locations are not *freely floating islands* is the starting point of the geographical economics approach introduced and discussed in Part III of this book. The idea that it matters where you are literally located as a worker or firm on the map will thus be given a theoretical and empirical foundation in the next three chapters.

Technical Note

Technical Note 6.1 Derivation of the wage equation

In this note we briefly derive equation 6.1. The set-up is straightforward. Consider a firm in region j that uses labour l and a (composite) input k in its production process to produce output y using Cobb-Douglas technology: $y_j = A_j \left(s_j l_j \right)^{\mu} k_j^{1-\mu}$, where A_j is a Hicks-neutral technology parameter, μ is the share of labour in the production process, and s_j is a labour-productivity variable. The profits π_j of this firm, which exports to all regions s, are:

$$\pi_j = \Sigma_s \, p_{js} y_{js} - w_j l_j - r_j k_j = p_j y_j - w_j l_j - r_j k_j \,, \text{ where } p_j = \Sigma_s \, p_{js} \frac{y_{js}}{y_j}.$$

In this equation w_j is the wage in region j, p_j is the price of good j, and r_j is the (composite) price of other inputs. The first-order conditions for profit maximization are:

$$w_j = \mu p_j A_j s_j^{\mu} \left(\frac{k_j}{l_j} \right)^{1-\mu} \text{ and } r_j = (1-\mu) p_j A_j s_j^{\mu} \left(\frac{k_j}{l_j} \right)^{-\mu}.$$

Substituting the second condition into the first one gives the (individual) firm wage equation:

$$w_j = \mu (1-\mu)^{(1-\mu)/\mu} \, s_j \left(\frac{p_j A_j}{r_j^{1-\mu}} \right)^{1-\mu}.$$

Summing over all firms N_i in region i gives equation 6.1 in the main text.

Exercises

Question 6.1 Amenities

Cities that are larger or grow faster also seem to be home to a larger and more varied set of urban amenities. Explain the causality issue that plagues the investigation of the alleged positive relationship between urban size or growth on the one hand and urban amenities on the other hand.

Question 6.2 Marshall, Duranton, and Puga

Discuss in your own words how the Marshallian terminology of agglomeration economies relates to the terminology or typology of agglomeration economies as introduced by Duranton and Puga (2004).

Question 6.3 Madrid and Valencia

Look again at Figure 6.1. Mean earnings in Madrid are thus higher than in Valencia. Armed with the analysis of this chapter list what you consider to be all the relevant arguments that help to decide whether these higher earnings are indeed (to some extent) the result of agglomeration economies in Madrid being stronger than in Valencia.

Question 6.4 Instrumental Variables (IV)

Table 6.3 presents evidence on regional agglomeration economies for a sample of European regions. Try to come up with an *economic* (and hence not a statistical) rationale why a region's area or a region's distance to Brussels could have been used as instrumental variables.

Question 6.5 IV Continued

In Table 6.4 the physical geography of the French soil and also historical French market potential as well as historical French population density are used as instrumental variables (IV). In the main text we briefly explain the economic reasoning behind the use of these two sets of IVs. But what are the statistical or econometric reasons that need to be met for these variables to be valid IVs? [Hint: check out https://en.wikipedia.org/wiki/Instrumental_variables_estimation]

Question 6.6 London Metropolis

Agglomeration economies (recall Chapter 4 of the book) not only determine the size and growth differences between cities (and regions) but also how economic activity is 'spiky' within cities. A good and innovative recent research example is given by the work of Heblich, Redding, and Sturm (2018) on the rise of London as a modern metropolis; see https://voxeu.org/article/making-modern-metropolis-evidence-london for a short introduction to their research and also Steve Redding's home page for a link to the underlying paper: www.princeton.edu/~reddings/

redwps.htm. Discuss how agglomeration economies are part of their analysis and also discuss for the case of London the interaction between transport costs and agglomeration economies in Heblich, Redding, and Sturm (2018).

Question 6.7 Geographical Psychology

One promising alternative or new research avenue for urban economics seems to be coming from the so-called *geographical psychology* literature. In this literature a central concept is the idea that people with certain personality traits are spatially clustered. Think of reasons or mechanisms why this might be the case. [Hint: check out the following paper: https://journals.plos.org/plosone/article?id=10.1371/journal.pone.0122245.]

Question 6.8 Geography

In Part II of the book on urban economics, geography did and did not (yet) play a role. Now that we are about to start our discussion of geographical economics in Part III of the book discuss the various ways through which geography entered the analysis and in doing so also pay attention to aspects of geography that were not covered. [Hint: look again at the stylized facts covered in Chapter 1 and Chapter 2.]

PART III
Geographical Economics

The main aim of our book is to explain the spikiness of human and economic activity as observed at all levels of aggregation, between and within countries but also between regions and cities. As outlined before, we have two basic explanations at our disposal for the uneven distribution of activity across space: first nature and second nature explanations. First nature explanations deal with the role of physical geography, like climate or access to sea and rivers. We covered this in the first part of Chapter 2. Second nature explanations centre around human interactions as the main driver of our spiky world. These human interactions can be analysed through various analytical lenses and approaches. Some of them focus on the role of history, psychology, or politics. These kinds of human interactions were covered in the second part of Chapter 2. The bulk of our book is concerned with the second nature explanations that arise from economic interactions. And here the field of economics has basically two flavours to offer: urban economics and geographical economics, respectively Part II and Part III of the book.

In Part II on urban economics we learned that the two concepts of spatial equilibrium and agglomeration economies are key to understanding how cities are internally shaped and organized, why a system of heterogeneous cities can exist, and also what the main agglomeration economies are that determine where footloose firms and households prefer to locate. It seems therefore that urban economics might be able to explain the main economic reasons behind the spiky world. So, why do we need Part III on geographical economics? The fundamental reason is that in urban economics it does not matter where cities (or regions or countries) are on the map. Literally speaking, in an attempt to understand the urban system of for instance the UK, it is immaterial where cities are placed vis-à-vis each other. London could swap places with Glasgow and the outcome for both cities would be the same. Or for the economic fortunes of Oxford or Cambridge it is not relevant that both are relatively close to London. Relocating both cities to Wales would yield the same results in terms of their city size, economic structure, and so on. In urban economics, spatial interdependencies between locations are largely ignored. *Or, to be blunter, in urban economics there is no real role for economic geography.*

This is where geographical economics comes in because the main aim of this approach is to come up with an explanation for the observed spikiness that is based on the idea that spatial interdependencies and economic geography are crucial. In Part III of the book we first develop the core model of geographical economics (Chapter 7) via an extensive discussion of its main nuts and bolts. Second, we introduce and discuss model extensions (Chapter 8). Third, armed with the knowledge about the basic models of geographical economics, we discuss and summarize its main empirical explanations in Chapter 9. As we go along, we will see that geographical economics is not that different from urban economics in many respects. In geographical economics too, the concepts of spatial equilibrium and agglomeration economies play a key role. In geographical economics a spatial equilibrium is reached if all footloose firms and/or workers can see no net benefit in relocating to another location. Similarly, various agglomeration economies will be again invoked to understand why certain locations are preferred over others and why locations may be of different shapes and sizes, hence contributing to our knowledge of the spiky world in which we live. The main and fundamental difference with urban economics is that the agglomeration economies do not only concern the features of the location itself (as in urban economics), but also the proximity of the location to other economically (un)attractive locations.

7 The Core Model

LEARNING OBJECTIVES

- To be able to understand the main demand and supply building blocks of the core model of geographical economics.
- To understand the crucial role of transport costs in the core model and the way these costs are modelled.
- To understand the difference between the short-run and long-run equilibria in the core model of geographical economics.
- To get a grasp of the dynamics of the core model, summarized in the so-called Tomahawk diagram.
- To understand the main differences between the core model of geographical economics and the standard model of urban economics.

7.1 Introduction

Urban and geographical economics both start from the idea that space or physical geography does not a priori make it more or less likely that one location is preferred over another. The task is to come up with economic reasons that shape the economic interaction between firms and/or households in such a way that we can understand and explain the uneven spatial distribution observed in the real world. In Part II of the book we dealt with urban economics and in Part III we introduce and discuss geographical economics. As we stated in our introduction to Part III, the main difference between urban and geographical economics is that spatial interdependencies or economic geography does play a key role in the latter, but is largely ignored in the former.

Geographical economics can be seen as a marriage between two strands of literature in the field of mainstream economics. On the one hand, there is international trade theory that sets out to explain international trade between countries and firms. In international trade theory, traditionally, it is assumed that countries are dimensionless points in space. Trade theorists are mostly interested in how market structure, production techniques, firm and consumer behaviour interact (Feenstra, 2016). The resulting factor and commodity prices determine the pattern of international trade flows. Location is at best an exogenous factor and often does not play a role of any significance.[1] On the other hand, as we saw in Part II of the book, urban economics typically takes the market structure and prices as given and tries to find out which economic allocation of space is most efficient. The underlying behaviour of consumers and producers, central in trade theory, is often less important (see also Fujita and Thisse, 2013 for an in-depth discussion). Although both strands of literature produce valuable insights in their own right, they are combined in geographical economics.

This chapter discusses and explains the core model of geographical economics at length. The model is a small general-equilibrium model as developed by Paul Krugman (1991). As we will see, the equilibrium equations of this model are non-linear and although the model is small in terms of the number of (equilibrium) equations, its implications are far from straightforward. This is why we will take a full chapter to go through the complete set-up of the model. We are not only dealing with a non-linear world, but also a world where the location of both supply and demand is not pre-determined. That is to say, both firms and households have to decide about their location, whereas in urban economics location is given. Furthermore, and in contrast to urban economics, all locations will be connected since the model has spatial interdependencies as a defining feature. In this sense geography is more important in geographical economics than in urban economics; it matters where on the map a location is.

In Chapter 9 we discuss how the models of Chapters 7 and 8 can be estimated. In Chapter 10 and Chapter 11 we specify how these models can be used in policy applications. Note that the core model of geographical economics as developed by Krugman (1991), together with its two forerunners (Krugman 1979, 1980), earned him the Nobel prize in economics in 2008. So, in terms of motivation, we are about to enter Nobel prize territory here (see also Box 7.7).

We explain the core model in three steps. First, we explain the basic structure of the core model of geographical economics from scratch. Second, we focus on characteristic solutions: a spreading equilibrium (characterized by an equal distribution of economic activity) and complete agglomeration (where mobile economic activity is concentrated in one location). Third, we provide some analytical results that illustrate important characteristics of the equilibria that will motivate our discussions and applications of geographical economics in subsequent chapters.

---

[1] Gravity models are the exception to the rule; see Chapter 1. These models are easily extended to include all kinds of transport costs. See for a discussion of the gravity model Head and Mayer (2014) and Technical Note 10.1 in Chapter 10.

7.2   Origin of the Core Model

The nuts and bolts of the core model are laid out in Dixit and Stiglitz (1977) and Krugman (1979, 1980). This work stimulated a large body of work on monopolistic competition and international trade theory (see Neary, 2004). Krugman (1991) extended the latter by allowing cross-border factor mobility, and this has become the core model of geographical economics.[2]

The structure of the model is simple. We have demand, supply, and an equilibrium. We introduce the model details for one region in order to get familiar with key concepts of the monopolistic competition model. Next we introduce a second region, introduce the possibility of relocation of workers and firms, and highlight the importance of transportation costs. Once we introduce a second region we can analyse possible core–periphery patterns. We place more technical derivations in Technical Notes. We advise the reader to *skip all Technical Notes on first reading* in order to more easily follow the flow of arguments. The mathematically inclined reader can then return to the technical details in the notes at a later stage

7.3   Demand in the Core Model

We assume that the economy has two goods sectors, manufactures M and food F, where 'manufactures' consist of many different varieties. Sometimes we can represent them as a group and define a group price index, sometimes we look at the individual varieties.

The basic problem is similar to standard models of consumer behaviour. If a consumer earns an income Y (from working either in the food sector or the manufacturing sector) she has to decide how much of this income is spent on food and how much on manufactures. The solution to this problem depends on the preferences of the consumer, assumed to be of the Cobb-Douglas specification given in equation 7.1 for all consumers, where F represents food consumption and M represents consumption of manufactures, which is an aggregate of all possible varieties which we will specify in the next section. Obviously, any income spent on food cannot simultaneously be spent on manufactures, that is, the consumer must satisfy the budget constraint in equation 7.2.

$$U = F^{1-\delta}M^{\delta} \; ; \; 0 < \delta < 1 \qquad 7.1$$

$$F + I \cdot M = Y \qquad 7.2$$

---

[2] Readers who wish to have an intuitive understanding of the model before reading this chapter can first consult the website for a simple example that illustrates key elements of the model.

BOX 7.1 **Terminology**

The terminology used in economic analysis can be confusing to the reader for various reasons. Sometimes the same term has different meanings in different fields of economics. Sometimes a term can be interpreted in various ways. Sometimes the same area of research is known under a range of names. Although the terminology used in our book will, inevitably, occasionally also puzzle the reader, we would like to limit this puzzlement to a minimum. This box therefore briefly explains our main terminology.

Agglomeration and spreading. We are interested in explaining, and will describe, various forms of clustering of (economic) activity, which we refer to as 'agglomeration'. We use the term 'spreading' to refer to the opposite of 'agglomeration'. Other terms used in the literature, such as 'centripetal', 'centrifugal', 'convergent', and 'divergent', will not be used in this book because they can be confusing. For example, 'converging' may either indicate that all industry 'converges', that is tends to locate in one region, or that all regions 'converge', that is all industries are spread across regions.

Numéraire. The economic agents in the general equilibrium models of geographical economics do not suffer from money illusion, that is, their decisions are based on relative prices and do not depend on the absolute price level. This allows us to set the price of one of the goods in the model equal to one, and express all other prices in the model relative to the price of the numéraire good. The remainder of the book chooses food as the numéraire good, such that the price of food is always equal to one.

Wages and real wages. The core general-equilibrium modelling approach used in this book chooses a numéraire good to pin down relative prices. Wages in different regions expressed in the numéraire should be referred to as 'numéraire wages'. Although better than the frequently used term 'nominal wages' (since the monetary sector is not explicitly modelled) it is a cumbersome term. We therefore use the shorter term 'wages' whenever we refer to 'numéraire wages' and explicitly use the term 'real wages' when the numéraire wages are corrected for the price level to determine purchasing power.

Note the absence of the price of food in equation 7.2. This is a result of choosing food as the numéraire (see Box 7.1), which implies that income Y is measured in terms of food. Thus, only the price index of manufactures I occurs in equation 7.2. To decide on the optimal allocation of income over the purchase of food and manufactures the consumer now has to solve a simple optimization problem, namely maximize utility given in equation 7.1, subject to the budget constraint of equation 7.2. The solution to this problem is given in equation 7.3, and derived in Technical Note 7.1.

$$F = (1 - \delta)Y \ ; \ I \cdot M = \delta Y \qquad 7.3$$

As equation 7.3 shows, it is optimal for the consumer to spend a fraction $(1 - \delta)$ of income on food, and a fraction δ of income on manufactures. We will refer to the parameter δ given in equation 7.1 as the fraction of income spent on manufactures.

7.3.1 Spending on Manufacturing Varieties

Now that we have determined that the share δ of income is spent on manufactured goods, we still have to decide how this spending is allocated among the different varieties of manufactures. In essence, this is a similar problem as in section 7.3, that is, we have to optimally allocate spending over the consumption of a number of goods which can be consumed. This problem can only be solved if we specify how the preferences for the aggregate consumption of manufactures M depends on the consumption of particular varieties of manufactures. In this respect the core model of geographical economics fruitfully applies a model of monopolistic competition developed in the industrial organization literature by Dixit and Stiglitz; see Box 7.2. Let c_i be the level of consumption of a particular variety i of manufactures, and let N be the total number of available varieties. The Dixit-Stiglitz approach uses a Constant-Elasticity-of-Substitution (CES) function to construct the aggregate consumption of manufactures M as a function of the consumption c_i of the N varieties:[3]

$$M = \left(\sum_{i=1}^{N} c_i^{\rho} \right)^{1/\rho} ; 0 < \rho < 1 \qquad 7.4$$

Note that the consumption of all varieties enters equation 7.4 symmetrically. This greatly simplifies the analysis in the sequel. The parameter ρ is discussed further below. We assume $\rho < 1$ to ensure that the product varieties are imperfect substitutes (if $\rho = 1$ all varieties are identical). In addition, we need $\rho > 0$ to ensure that the individual varieties are substitutes (and not complements) for each other, which enables price-setting behaviour based on monopoly power; see section 7.4.[4]

It is worthwhile to dwell a little longer on the implication of equation 7.4. Suppose all c_i are consumed in equal quantities, that is $c_i = c$ for all i. We can then rewrite equation 7.4 as:

---

[3] Many textbooks discuss the properties of the CES function. See also Brakman and van Marrewijk (1998), who compare it with other utility functions.

[4] One might wonder what happens if $\rho > 1$. Reducing the number of varieties increases utility in this case: 100 units of one variety is clearly better than 1 unit of 100 varieties (see also equation 7.5).

BOX 7.2 Dixit-Stiglitz Monopolistic Competition

It has often been said that there is only one way for competition to be perfect, but many ways to be imperfect. Consequently, many competing models exist to describe imperfect competition, investigating many different cases and assumptions with respect to market behaviour, the type of good, the strategic interaction between firms, preferences of consumers, and so on. That was also the case with monopolistic competition (see, for example, Tirole, 1988), until Avinash Dixit and Joseph Stiglitz published an article in 1977, entitled 'Monopolistic competition and optimum product diversity', in the *American Economic Review* that would revolutionize model building in at least four fields of economics: trade theory, industrial organization, growth theory, and geographical economics.[5]

The big step forward was to make some heroic assumptions concerning the symmetry of new varieties and the structural form, which allowed for an elegant and consistent way to model production at the firm level benefiting from internal economies of scale in conjunction with a market structure of monopolistic competition, without getting bogged down in a taxonomy of oligopoly models. These factors are responsible for the present popularity of the Dixit-Stiglitz model. In all fields that now use the Dixit-Stiglitz formulation intensely, researchers were aware that imperfect competition was relevant as an essential feature of many empirically observed phenomena. This meant that the model was immediately accepted as the new standard for modelling monopolistic competition; its development was certainly very timely. In international trade theory, the introduction of the monopolistic competition model enabled international economists to explain and understand intra-industry trade, which until then was empirically observed but never satisfactorily explained (Krugman, 1979, 1980). In industrial organization it helped to get rid of many ad hoc assumptions, which hampered the development of many industrial organization models (Tirole, 1988). The Dixit-Stiglitz model was also used to explore the role of intermediate differentiated goods in international trade models and provided the theoretical backbone of the heterogeneous firms model of Melitz (2003). The Melitz (2003) model turns out to be useful for explaining the export versus FDI decision if firms are heterogeneous (see Feenstra, 2016 for a survey). Finally, the model is the backbone of many models in geographical economics, and very much so of its core model which is the topic of the current chapter.

---

[5] Brakman and Heijdra (2004) give a historical account of the influence of the Dixit–Stiglitz approach in economics; and in that book Dixit and Stiglitz themselves reflect on the pros and cons of their 1977 contribution (the volume also contains working paper versions of the 1977 model, inter alia showing that referees are not always correct when suggesting that sections of working papers are dropped in order to become publishable in journals ☺).

$$M = \left(\sum_{i=1}^{N} c^{\rho} \right)^{1/\rho} = \left(N c^{\rho} \right)^{1/\rho} = N^{1/\rho} c = N^{\left(\frac{1}{\rho} \right)-1} (Nc) \qquad 7.5$$

Since $0 < \rho < 1$, the term $(1/\rho)-1$ is larger than zero. So, from equation 7.5 it is immediately clear that 100 units of $N=1$ variety gives a consumer less utility than one unit of $N = 100$ varieties. The term $Nc = 100$ in both cases while the term $N^{(1/\rho)-1}$ represents a bonus for large markets. The latter is called the *love-of-variety* effect. In this sense an increase in the extent of the market, which increases the number of varieties N the consumer can choose from, more than proportionally increases utility.

Now that we have briefly digressed on the love-of-variety effect it is time to go back to the problem at hand: how does the consumer allocate spending on manufactures over the various varieties? Let p_i be the price of variety i for $i = 1,.., N$. Naturally, funds $p_i c_i$ spent on variety i cannot be spent simultaneously on variety j, as given in the budget constraint for manufactures in equation 7.6. In order to derive consumer demand, we must now solve a somewhat more complicated optimization problem, namely maximizing utility derived from the consumption of manufactures given in equation 7.4, subject to the budget constraint of equation 7.6. The solution to this problem is given in equations 7.7 (total demand for each variety) and 7.8 (total utility). Both are derived in Technical Note 7.2.

$$\sum_{i=1}^{N} p_i c_i = \delta Y \qquad 7.6$$

$$c_j = p_j^{-\varepsilon} \left(I^{\varepsilon-1} \delta Y \right); I \equiv \left(\sum_{i=1}^{N} p_i^{1-\varepsilon} \right)^{1/(1-\varepsilon)}, j = 1,.., N \qquad 7.7$$

$$M = \frac{\delta Y}{I}; \varepsilon \equiv \frac{1}{1-\rho} \qquad 7.8$$

7.3.2 Demand Effects: Income, Price, Elasticity ε, and Price Index I

A discussion and explanation of the meaning of equations 7.7 and 7.8 is warranted. The demand for variety 1, for example, is given by $c_1 = p_1^{-\varepsilon} \left(I^{\varepsilon-1} \delta Y \right)$; see equation 7.7. The demand is influenced by four elements, namely (i) the income level δY, (ii) the price p_1 of good 1, (iii) some parameter ε, and (iv) the price index I.

Point (i) is straightforward. The more the consumer spends on manufactures in general, the more she spends on variety 1. In fact, this relationship is equiproportional: other things being equal a 10 per cent rise in spending on manufactures results in a 10 per cent increase in the demand for all varieties of manufactures.

Point (ii) is also straightforward. Obviously one expects that the demand for variety 1 is a function of the price charged by the firm producing variety 1. It is important in view of *how* demand for variety 1 depends on the price p_1. Note that the last part of equation 7.7 is written in brackets. It depends on the price index for manufactures I and the income δY spent by the consumers on manufactures in general. Both are economy-wide entities which each firm takes as given, that is, it assumes that it has no control over these variables (see below for a further discussion). In that case, we can simplify the demand for variety 1, by defining the constant B as $B \equiv I^{\varepsilon-1}\delta Y$. So, $c_1 = Bp_1^{-\varepsilon}$. This in turn implies that the price elasticity of demand for variety 1 is constant and equal to the parameter $\varepsilon > 1$ (implying that $-(\partial c_1 / \partial p_1)(p_1 / c_1) = \varepsilon$). This simple price elasticity of demand is a main advantage of the Dixit-Stiglitz approach (see Box 7.2) as it greatly simplifies the price-setting behaviour of monopolistically competitive firms. Note, that the larger ε, the larger the drop in demand for a variety as a result of a small price increase.

Point (iii) becomes clear after the discussion in point (ii). We have defined the parameter ε not only to simplify the notation of equation 7.7 as much as possible, but also because it is an important economic parameter as it measures the price elasticity of demand for a variety of manufactured goods. In addition, this parameter measures the elasticity of substitution between two different varieties, that is, how difficult it is to substitute one variety of manufactures for another variety of manufactures (see Technical Note 7.2). Evidently, the price elasticity of demand and the elasticity of substitution are identical in the Dixit-Stiglitz approach, a point which has been criticized in the literature. Be that as it may, our intuitive explanations of some phenomena in the remainder of this book will sometimes be based on the price elasticity of demand interpretation of ε, and sometimes on the elasticity of substitution interpretation, using what we feel is easiest for the problem at hand. A final remark on the parameter ε. It was defined using the parameter ρ in the preference for manufacturing varieties equation 7.4 as: $\varepsilon \equiv 1/(1-\rho)$. Does this mean we will not use the parameter ρ anymore in the rest of the book? No. The reason is that we want to keep the notation as simple as possible, which sometimes requires the use of ε and sometimes requires the use of ρ. These are the only two parameters for which we will do this, referring to ε as the 'elasticity of substitution', and to ρ as the 'substitution parameter'.

Point (iv), finally, indicates that the demand for variety 1 depends on the price index I. If the price index I increases, implying that 'on average' the prices of the manufacturing varieties competing with variety 1 are rising, then the demand for variety 1 is increasing (recall that $\varepsilon > 1$).

Note that the definition of the price index I implies that $M = \delta Y / I$; see equation 7.8. So, utility derived from M increases if, and only if, spending on manufactures δY increases faster than the price index I. It is obvious that an increase in the number of varieties decreases I, as is apparent from equation 7.7. Furthermore, the term I enables us to write the demand equations more efficiently as $c_j = p_j^{-\varepsilon}\left(I^{\varepsilon-1}\delta Y\right)$.

To finish our discussion of the demand structure of the core model we make two comments.

First, we discussed the price index I for manufactured goods. However, consumption also consists of Food. An obvious question is, what is the consumer price index of the consumption basket that includes both manufacturing goods and food? This is simple. We know that a share δ is spent on manufactured goods, and $(1-\delta)$ on Food. So, the consumer price index is $1^{1-\delta}I^{\delta} = I^{\delta}$, where the '1' on the left-hand side represents the price of food, which is set equal to one because food is the numéraire. Thus, the consumer's total utility increases if and only if Y/I^{δ} rises, that is if the income level rises faster than the consumer price index I^{δ}. Or put differently, if *real income* increases. Similarly, if the wage rate is W we can also define the *real wage w*. So:

$$\text{real income} = y = Y/I^{\delta}; \text{real wage} = w = W/I^{\delta} \qquad 7.9$$

The second remark concerns point (ii) above, where we argued that the (own) price elasticity of demand for the producer of variety 1 is equal to ε. Recall the demand function $c_1 = p_1^{-\varepsilon}\left(I^{\varepsilon-1}\delta Y\right)$. We argued that the term in brackets is treated as a constant by the producer because these are macro-economic entities. Although this is true it overlooks a tiny detail: one of the terms in the specification of the price index of manufactures I is the price p_1. Thus, a truly rational producer would also take this minuscule effect on the aggregate price index into consideration.[6] For that reason it is often assumed that the number of varieties N produced is 'large', that is, if our producer is one of 200 firms we can already safely ignore this effect, but the smaller the number of varieties, the larger the error.

7.4 Supply in the Core Model

We start the analysis of the supply side of the core model with a description of the production structure for food and manufactures. Food production is characterized by constant returns to scale and is produced under conditions of perfect competition. Workers in this industry are assumed to be immobile. Given the total labour force L, a fraction $(1-\gamma)$ is assumed to work in the food sector. The labour force in the manufacturing industry is therefore γL. Production F in the food sector equals, by choice of units, food employment; see equation 7.10. Since farm workers are paid the value of marginal product this choice of units implies that the wage for the farm workers is one, because food is the numéraire.

$$F = (1-\gamma)L; 0 < \gamma < 1 \qquad 7.10$$

$$l_i = \alpha + \beta x_i \qquad 7.11$$

---

[6] Using equation 7.7 the exact price elasticity of demand for a specific variety can be derived. Illuminating is the analysis in the neighbourhood of p if $p_i = p$ for all other varieties, in which case $-(\partial c_1/\partial p_1)(p_1/c_1) = \varepsilon(1-1/N)$. The term between brackets on the right-hand side rapidly approaches 1 if N becomes large.

Production in the manufacturing sector is characterized by internal economies of scale, which means that there is imperfect competition in this sector. The varieties in the manufacturing industry are symmetric and are produced with the same technology. Note that at this point we already introduce an element of location. Internal economies of scale means that each variety is produced by a single firm; the firm with the largest sales can always outbid a potential competitor. Once we introduce more locations each firm has to decide where to produce. The economies of scale are modelled in the simplest way possible as given in equation 7.11, where l_i labour units are needed to produce x_i units of variety i. The coefficients α and β are the fixed and marginal labour input requirements, respectively. The fixed labour input α ensures that as production expands less average labour is needed to produce a unit of x_i, which means that there are internal economies of scale. This is illustrated in Figure 7.1, which shows the rising total labour required to produce a certain amount of output, as well as the constant marginal labour required and the falling average labour required to produce that amount of output. Because we have only one factor of production, labour, the cost of producing a variety can easily be calculated by multiplying equation 7.11 by wages W.[7]

7.4.1 Price Setting and Zero Profits

Each manufacturing firm produces a unique variety under internal returns to scale. If two firms were to start producing the same variety, the one with the larger initial market share would drive out its competitor: it has lower average cost of production and by charging a lower price it can force its competitor out of the market. This can be illustrated in Figure 7.1: a firm with an output of, say, three has lower average costs than a firm with an output of one. This implies that the firm has

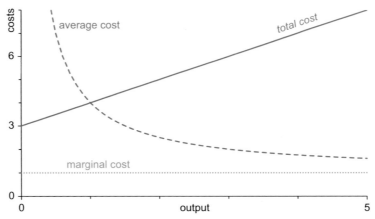

Figure 7.1 Production costs (labour units) for a variety of manufactures
Parameters: $\alpha = 3$; $\beta = 1$

[7] To get production costs in terms of the numéraire in Figure 7.1, simply multiply by W.

some monopoly power, which it will use to maximize its profits. We therefore have to determine the price-setting behaviour of each firm. The Dixit-Stiglitz monopolistic competition model makes two assumptions in this respect. First, it is assumed that each firm takes the price-setting behaviour of other firms as given, that is if firm 1 changes its price it assumes that the prices of the other $N-1$ varieties remain the same. Second, it is assumed that the firm ignores the effect of changing its own price on the price index I of manufactures. Both assumptions seem reasonable if the number of varieties N is large, as also discussed in section 7.3.2. For ease of notation we drop the sub-index for the firm in this section. Note that a firm which produces x units of output using the production function in equation 7.11 will earn profits π given in equation 7.12 if the wage rate it has to pay is W.

$$\pi = px - W(\alpha + \beta x) \qquad 7.12$$

Naturally, the firm will have to sell the units of output x it is producing, that is these sales must be consistent with the demand for a variety of manufactures derived in section 7.3. Although this demand was derived for an arbitrary consumer, the most important feature of the demand for a variety, namely the constant price elasticity of demand ε, also holds when we combine the demand from many consumers with the same preference structure (see also the exercises). If the demand x for a variety has a constant price elasticity of demand ε, maximization of the profits given in equation 7.12 leads to a simple optimal pricing rule, known as mark-up pricing, as given in equation 7.13 and derived in Technical Note 7.3.

$$p\left(1 - \frac{1}{\varepsilon}\right) = \beta W; \text{ or } p = \frac{\beta W}{\rho} \qquad 7.13$$

The meaning of the term 'mark-up pricing' is evident from equation 7.13. The marginal cost of producing an extra unit of output is equal to βW, while the price p the firm charges is higher than this marginal cost. How much higher depends on the price elasticity of demand. If demand is inelastic, say $\varepsilon = 2$, the mark-up is high (in this case 100 per cent). If demand is more elastic, say $\varepsilon = 5$, the mark-up is lower (in this case 20 per cent). This is illustrated in Figure 7.2 where the iso-elastic demand function leads to an inward-shifted marginal revenue function by the amount $(1 - 1/\varepsilon)$. Firms equate marginal revenue with the constant marginal costs at point C, which leads to the mark-up price p determined from the demand curve at point A and operating profits (op) equal to the area $\beta WCAp$. Note that the firm must charge a higher price than marginal cost in order to recuperate the fixed labour costs αW. Since the price elasticity of demand ε is constant, the mark-up of price over marginal cost is also constant, and therefore invariant to the scale of production.

Now that we have determined the optimal price a firm will charge to maximize profits, we can actually calculate those profits (if we know the constant B

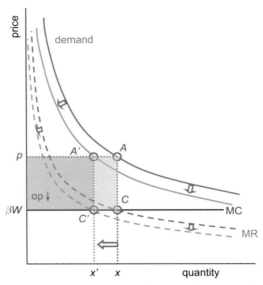

Figure 7.2 Optimal pricing and entry in the Dixit-Stiglitz model

in Technical Note 7.3). This is where another important feature of monopolistic competition comes in. If profits are positive (sometimes referred to as excess profits) it is apparently attractive to set up shop in the manufacturing sector. One would then expect that new firms enter the market and start to produce a different variety. This implies, of course, that the consumer will allocate her spending over more varieties of manufactures. Since all varieties are imperfect substitutes for one another, the demand curve for a particular variety shifts inward, as shown by the arrows in Figure 7.2. As a consequence, the marginal revenue shifts inward as well and production declines from x to x'. As a result of constant mark-up pricing, the price p remains the same, but the entry of new firms in the manufacturing sector implies that profits for the existing firms will fall. This process of entry of new firms will continue until profits in the manufacturing sector are driven to zero. A reverse process, with firms leaving the manufacturing sector, operates if profits are negative. Monopolistic competition in the manufacturing sector therefore imposes as an equilibrium condition that profits are zero. If we do that in equation 7.12 we can calculate the scale at which a firm producing a variety in the manufacturing sector will operate (equation 7.14) how much labour is needed to produce this amount of output (equation 7.15) and how many varieties N are produced in the economy as a function of the available labour in the manufacturing sector (equation 7.16); see Technical Note 7.4.

$$x = \frac{\alpha(\varepsilon - 1)}{\beta} \qquad\qquad 7.14$$

$$l_i = \alpha\varepsilon \qquad\qquad 7.15$$

$$N = \frac{\gamma L}{l_i} = \frac{\gamma L}{\alpha \varepsilon} \qquad\qquad 7.16$$

Equation 7.14, which gives the scale of output for an individual firm, may seem strange at first sight. No matter what happens, the output per firm is fixed in equilibrium. It implies that the manufacturing sector as a whole only expands and contracts by producing more or fewer varieties, as the output level per variety does not change. From equation 7.16 we see that a larger market resulting, for example, from immigration, only affects the number of varieties. As a result of economies of scale it is not profitable to have the same variety produced by more than one firm; each firm will produce only one variety.

Now that we have calculated demand for each variety and supply of each variety we can calculate the equilibrium price by setting demand equal to supply, or equation 7.7 is equal to equation 7.14 (see Chapter 7 exercises). Once we know the equilibrium price, equilibrium wages follow from the mark-up price equation 7.13. The reason that we want to have an equilibrium equation in terms of wages rather than prices is because in the end we are interested in migration between locations, which is determined by wage differentials.

7.5   Transport Costs: Icebergs in Geography

The aim of the core model of geographical economics is to introduce spatial interdependencies or economic geography in a non-trivial way. The model must thus show how geography affects the decisions of individual consumers and producers and how these decisions in turn shape the spatial distribution of economic activity. To be able to do so, transport costs have to be introduced. Only if it is costly to move products and people over space does geography makes sense in the core model.

The transport costs we introduce are special. In principle one could model a transport sector and add this to the model, but this is cumbersome, because transport costs are income for the transport sector so one must deal with spending from this sector: where do transport workers live and where do they spend their money? Also the location decision of the transport sector might be different from the location decisions of the other sectors. It is for these reasons that Samuelson (1952) has introduced the concept of *iceberg* transport costs. In the context of the core model of Geographical Economics, iceberg transport costs imply that a fraction of the manufactured goods does not arrive at the destination when goods are shipped between regions. The fraction that does not arrive represents the cost of transportation. The core model uses T as a parameter to represent these costs, where T is defined as the number of goods that need to be shipped to ensure that one unit arrives per unit of distance. Suppose, for example, that the unit of distance is equal

BOX 7.3 The Relevance of Transport Costs

Transport costs are essential in geographical economics. Without transport costs there is no geography, and the whole exercise of transforming economic models into geographical economics models becomes pointless or academic. Adam Smith already noted the importance of locations near the coast, which reduces transport costs, 'so, it is upon the sea-coast, and along the banks of navigable rivers, that industry of every kind naturally begins to subdivide and improve itself, and it is frequently not till a long time after that those improvements extend themselves to the inland part of the country' (Adam Smith cited in Radelet and Sachs, 1998). Redding and Turner (2015) observe that over a long period of time transportation costs have declined in general, but that these costs remain substantial, especially the costs of moving people around, such that transport costs still affect the location of economic activity.

Anderson and van Wincoop (2004, pp. 691–2) note that transport costs involve more than just transportation: policy barriers (tariffs and non-tariff barriers), information costs, contract enforcement costs, costs associated with the use of different currencies, legal and regulatory costs, and local distribution costs (wholesale and retail). Their rough 'representative' estimate for industrialized countries is that total trade costs are about 170 per cent of their ad valorem tax equivalent. This number breaks down as follows: 21 per cent transportation, 44 per cent border-related trade barriers, and 55 per cent retail and wholesale distribution costs ($1 + 1.7 = 1.21 \times 1.44 \times 1.55$).

Now that we have seen that transport costs between and within countries are substantial, one might ask whether or not they matter. The answer is, they do. McCallum (1995) finds that Canadian provinces trade more than 20 times the volume of trade with each other than they trade with similar counterparts in the USA. This number is not undisputed; consistent estimates reduce the value of 20 to about 10, which is still high. In general, borders have a large impact on trade costs (see for a discussion on border effects Feenstra, 2016, and Head and Mayer, 2014). A meta-study that looks at all other studies estimating the effects of trade costs concludes that the 'estimated negative impact of distance on trade rose around the middle of the [twentieth] century and has remained persistently high since then. This result holds even after controlling for many important differences in samples and methods' (Disdier and Head, 2008, p. 37).

to the distance from Naaldwijk, in the centre of the Dutch horticultural agglomeration, to Paris, and that 107 flowers are sent from Holland to France, while only 100 arrive unharmed in Paris and can be sold. Then $T = 1.07$. It is as if some goods have melted away in transit, hence the name iceberg costs. This way of modelling the transport costs without introducing a transport sector is attractive because we do not have to model a separate transport sector. Box 7.3 discusses the relevance of transports costs.

Throughout the rest of the book the parameter T denotes the number of goods that need to be shipped to ensure that one unit of a variety of manufactures arrives per unit of distance, while T_{rs} is defined as the number of goods that need to be shipped from region r to ensure that one unit arrives in region s. We will assume that this is proportional to the distance between regions r and s and that the distance of a region to itself is zero. If D_{rs} denotes the distance between region r and region s (which is 0 if $r = s$), we have:

$$T_{rs} = T^{D_{rs}};$$ 7.17

with $T_{rs} = T_{sr}$ and $T_{rr} = T^{0} = 1$

These definitions ease notation in the equations below and allow us to distinguish between changes in the parameter T, which represents a general change in (transport) technology applying to all regions, and changes in the 'distance' D_{rs} between regions, which may result from a policy change, such as tariff changes, a cultural treaty, new infrastructure, and so on. For the two-region core model discussed here we always assume that the distance between the two regions is one. Equation 7.17 and the equations below do not yet use this fact in order to develop a general model of multiple regions at the same time.

7.5.1 Introducing Different Locations

With multiple regions it becomes important to know where the economic agents are located. We have to (i) specify a notation to keep track of how labour is distributed over the two regions, and (ii) investigate what the consequences are for the model discussed in sections 7.3 and 7.4. Our aim is to determine whether workers and firms have an incentive to relocate. We assume that workers relocate if real wages are higher in the other region. To determine whether this is the case we have to calculate real wages in each region and need information on W and I (see equation 7.9).

To start with (i), we have already introduced the parameter γ to denote the fraction of the labour force in the manufacturing sector (see section 7.4), such that $(1 - \gamma)$ is the fraction of labour in the food sector. We now assume that of the laborers in the food sector a fraction ϕ_i is located in region i and of the laborers in the manufacturing sector a fraction λ_i is located in region i. Figure 7.3 graphically illustrates the division of labour. The arrows below the boxes of the manufacturing sector indicate that the size of the working population can increase or decrease, depending on the mobility of the manufacturing workforce.

Point (ii) involves a bit more work. We will concentrate on region 1. Similar remarks hold for region 2. It is easiest to start with the producers. Since there are

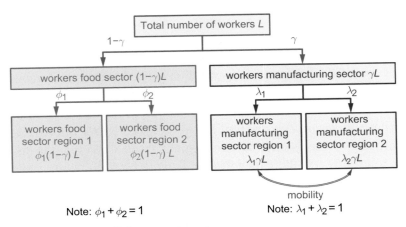

Note: $\phi_1 + \phi_2 = 1$ Note: $\lambda_1 + \lambda_2 = 1$

Figure 7.3 Division of labour over the regions

$\phi_1 (1 - \gamma) L$ farm workers in region 1 and production is proportional to the labour input (see equation 7.10) food production in region 1 equals $\phi_1 (1 - \gamma) L$, which is equal to the income generated by the food sector in region 1 and the wage income paid to farm workers there. Since we introduced transport costs in the model, the wage paid to manufacturing workers in region 1 will in general differ from the wage paid to manufacturing workers in region 2. We identify these with a sub-index, so W_1 is the manufacturing wage in region 1. From now on, and throughout the remainder of the book, whenever we speak of 'the wage rate' we refer to the manufacturing wage rate. If we know the wage rate W_1 in region 1, we can see from equation 7.13 that the price charged in region 1 by a firm located in region 1 is equal to $\beta W_1 / \rho$. The price this firm charges in region 2 will be T_{12} times higher than in region 1 (in this case: $T_{12} = T^{D_{12}} = T$) as a result of the transportation costs. Note that this holds for all N_1 firms located in region 1. Finally, since there are $\lambda_1 \gamma L$ manufacturing workers in region 1, we can deduce from equation 7.16 the number of firms N_1 located in region 1, namely $N_1 = \lambda_1 \gamma L / \alpha \varepsilon$. Note in particular that the number of firms located in region 1 is directly proportional to the number of manufacturing workers located in region 1.

We now turn to the demand side of the economy. As discussed above, the price a firm charges depends both on the location of the firm (which determines the wage rate) and on the location of the consumer (which determines whether or not the consumer will have to pay transport costs). As a result, the price index of manufactures will differ between the two regions. So I_1 is the price index in region 1. We can now find an expression for the price index. All we have to do is substitute the price information in the definition of I in equation 7.7 (see Technical Note 7.5):

$$I_1 = \left(\frac{\beta}{\rho}\right)\left(\frac{\gamma L}{\alpha \varepsilon}\right)^{\frac{1}{1-\varepsilon}} \left(\lambda_1 W_1^{1-\varepsilon} + \lambda_2 T^{1-\varepsilon} W_2^{1-\varepsilon}\right)^{\frac{1}{1-\varepsilon}} \qquad 7.18$$

The impact of location on the consumption decisions of consumers in different locations on the basis of equation 7.7 requires us to know the income level of region 1. This brings us to the determination of equilibrium in the next section.

7.6 Equilibrium in the Core Model

The next step is to derive an equilibrium in the multi-region setting. In particular, we have to determine the way in which the equilibrium relationships determine the spatial distribution of economic activity, as indicated by the arrows in Figure 7.3 which reflect the mobility of manufacturing workers and firms between the two regions.

We proceed in three steps. First, we focus on the *short-run* equilibrium analysis in section 7.6.1. Short run refers to an *exogenously given* spatial distribution of the manufacturing labour force. The spatial distribution of the manufacturing workers and firms is not yet determined by the model itself, but simply imposed upon the model. Second, we characterize the *long-run* equilibrium, by moving through a sequence of short-run equilibria (exogenously assuming different spatial distributions of workers) in sections 7.6.2 and 7.7. Third, we investigate the dynamics of the model, starting in section 7.7 by explaining the economic forces at work and some illustrations based on simulations, and continued in section 7.8 with some analytical results based on the (so-called) sustain point and break point.

7.6.1 Short-run Equilibrium

What are the short-run equilibrium relationships? We have already assumed that the labour markets clear, such that all workers have a job, either in the Food sector or in the Manufacturing sector. Furthermore, (utility-maximizing) demand equals (profit-maximizing) supply. There are no profits for firms in the manufacturing sector (because of entry and exit), nor for the farmers (because of constant returns to scale and perfect competition). This implies that all income earned in the economy for consumers to spend derives from the wages they earn in their respective sectors. This brings us to the next equilibrium relationship: the determination of income in each region. In view of the above, this is simple. There are $\phi_1(1-\gamma)L$ farm workers in region 1, each earning a farm wage rate of 1 (food is the numéraire), and there are $\lambda_1\gamma L$ manufacturing workers in region 1, each earning a wage rate W_1. As there are no profits in either sector, this is the only income generated in region 1. If we let Y_i denote total income generated in region i the income level for region 1 is thus given by equation 7.19, where the first term on the right-hand side represents income for the manufacturing workers and the second term reflects income for the farm workers.

$$Y_1 = \lambda_1\gamma LW_1 + \phi_1(1-\gamma)L \qquad 7.19$$

As discussed in section 7.5, the actual amount of transport costs between regions for the manufacturing sector is given by $T-1$ (this is the additional amount that has to be shipped in order to let one unit arrive at the destination). Since all firms in a region face identical marginal production costs and the same constant elasticity of demand (see also below), they all charge the same price to local producers, say P_1 for region 1 producers and P_2 for region 2 producers (see exercise 7.5). This mill price, or free on board (f.o.b.) price, of a variety produced in region 1 charged to consumers in region 1, is related to the marginal production costs in region 1 through the optimal pricing condition 7.13, so $P_1 = \beta W_1 / \rho$. This indicates that the f.o.b. price is directly proportional to the wage rate. The price of a variety produced in region 1 after being delivered in region 2 is TP_1, which is the cost insurance and freight (c.i.f.) price of this variety. Also recall from section 7.5.1 that since there are $\lambda_1 \gamma L$ manufacturing workers in region 1, it follows from equation 7.16 that the number of firms N_1 located in region 1 equals $N_1 = \lambda_1 \gamma L / \alpha \varepsilon$. That is, the number of firms located in region 1 is directly proportional to λ_1, the share of manufacturing workers located in region 1. All three aspects discussed above, namely (i) prices of locally produced goods are directly proportional to the local wage rate, (ii) prices charged in the other region are higher by the transport costs between regions, and (iii) the number of varieties produced in a region is directly proportional to the number of manufacturing workers in that region, are important for understanding why the price index I can have a different value in both regions. For region 1 the price index I_1 is (see again Technical Note 7.5):

$$I_1 = \left(\frac{\beta}{\rho}\right)\left(\frac{\gamma L}{\alpha \varepsilon}\right)^{\frac{1}{1-\varepsilon}} \left(\lambda_1 W_1^{1-\varepsilon} + \lambda_2 T^{1-\varepsilon} W_2^{1-\varepsilon}\right)^{\frac{1}{1-\varepsilon}} \qquad 7.20$$

The price index in region 1 is thus essentially a weighted average of the price of locally produced goods and imported goods from region 2. At this stage we notice that the only variables that are unknown in equations 7.19 and 7.20 are the wages in both regions. These wages can be derived from the equilibrium equation in the goods market: demand equals supply. How to proceed?

First we look at total demand, which is the demand from both regions. Demand in region 1 for products from region 1 is based on individual demand derived in equation 7.7 by summing the demand for all consumers in region 1. It is thus dependent on the aggregate income Y_1 in region 1, as given in equation 7.19, the price index I_1 in region 1, as given in equation 7.20, and the price $\beta W_1 / \rho$ charged by a producer from region 1 for a locally sold variety in region 1. We simply have to substitute these three terms for individual income, price index, and charged price in equation 7.7 to get $\left(\delta \beta^{-\varepsilon} \rho^{\varepsilon}\right) Y_1 W_1^{-\varepsilon} I_1^{\varepsilon-1}$, which is total demand in region 1 for a variety produced in region 1. However, region 1 also exports to region 2.

We can derive demand in region 2 for products from region 1 in a similar manner, by substituting aggregate income Y_2, price index I_2, and the price $T\beta W_1 / \rho$

charged by a producer from region 1 for a good sold in region 2 in equation 7.7 to get $\left(\delta\beta^{-\varepsilon}\rho^{\varepsilon}\right)Y_2 W_1^{-\varepsilon}T^{-\varepsilon}I_1^{\varepsilon-1}$ as total demand in region 2 for a variety produced in region 1. If there are positive transport costs, that is $T > 1$, demand in region 2 for products from region 1 is lower than without transport costs, because transport costs makes them more expensive. Total demand x_1 for a producer in region 1 is the sum of the demand from region 1 and demand from region 2 as given in equation 7.21. This equation states that total demand for a particular variety depends on income in *both* regions, transportation costs, and the price (proportional to the wage rate) relative to the price index.

$$x_1 = \left(\delta\beta^{-\varepsilon}\rho^{\varepsilon}\right)\left(Y_1 W_1^{-\varepsilon}I_1^{\varepsilon-1} + Y_2 W_1^{-\varepsilon}T^{-\varepsilon}I_1^{\varepsilon-1}\right) \qquad 7.21$$

Next we turn to supply. The break-even level of production was given by equation 7.14 as $x = \alpha(\varepsilon-1)/\beta$. Equating this to the total demand derived in equation 7.21 allows us to determine what the equilibrium price of a variety should be, in order to sell exactly this amount. For a producer in region 1 this implies $\alpha(\varepsilon-1)/\beta = \left(\delta\beta^{-\varepsilon}\rho^{\varepsilon}\right)\left(Y_1 W_1^{-\varepsilon}I_1^{\varepsilon-1} + Y_2 W_1^{-\varepsilon}T^{1-\varepsilon}I_1^{\varepsilon-1}\right)$. Note the important difference with equation 7.21 for the term T on the right-hand side, namely to the power $1-\varepsilon$ instead of $-\varepsilon$. This follows from the fact that the producer includes the amount which melts away *en route* from region 1 to region 2; in order to supply one unit of a variety in region 2, T units have to be shipped *and* produced. Solving the above equation for the wage rate in region 1 gives (see Technical Note 7.6):

$$W_1 = \left(\rho\beta^{-\rho}\right)\left(\frac{\delta}{(\varepsilon-1)\alpha}\right)^{1/\varepsilon}\left(Y_1 I_1^{\varepsilon-1} + Y_2 T^{1-\varepsilon}I_2^{\varepsilon-1}\right)^{1/\varepsilon} \qquad 7.22$$

Intuitively the equation makes perfect sense: wages in region 1 can be higher if it is located close to large markets (Y_1 for region 1 with $T = 1$ and Y_2 for region 2 with $T > 1$) and the less competition a firm in region 1 faces (recall point (iv) in section 7.3.2). As we will see in Chapter 9 this important consequence of the core model is used in empirical research.

Note that there is a close resemblance between this equation and the market potential approach, or the gravity approach discussed in Chapter 1. Similar to those approaches, the attractiveness of a region is related to the purchasing power of all surrounding regions, weighted by distance or transport costs, and of the region itself.

Given the distribution of the manufacturing workforce λ_i, we have now derived the short-run equilibrium equations for region 1. These are equation 7.19 to determine income level Y_1, equation 7.20 to determine the price index I_1, and equation 7.22 to determine the wage rate W_1. Similar equations hold for region 2, which gives a total of six non-linear equations. These equations describe the short-run equilibrium.

7.6.2   Long-run Equilibrium

To determine the long-run equilibrium in the core model, we analyse the implications of the short-run equilibrium developed in section 7.6.1 together with its dynamic implication based on the associated real wage rate as given in equation 7.9. This equation distinguishes long-run equilibria from short-run equilibria. A long-run equilibrium is reached if the *real* wages (equation 7.26) are equal ($w_1 = w_2$), which implies that there is no incentive for manufacturing workers to relocate. In the short-run equilibrium, real wages are not necessarily the same between regions, thus creating an incentive to migrate until real wages are equalized. Note that for both short-run equilibria and long-run equilibria supply equals demand (commodity markets clear).

Although not strictly necessary, it is convenient to simplify the equations by using some normalizations. This enables us to ignore combinations of parameters that make the expressions look more complicated than they actually are. It is convenient to use the normalizations given in Table 7.1; see the discussion in Box 7.4. In addition, we assume that space is inherently neutral. To do so, we distribute the farm workers equally over the two regions, such that $\phi_1 = \phi_2 = 1/2$ and the demand from immobile activities is the same in the two regions. As a consequence, any differences between the two regions in the long-run equilibrium can only arise from differences in the manufacturing sector. First, note that as a result of the

---

BOX 7.4 Normalizations

The units in which we measure variables may simplify the analysis without affecting the solution of the model (in our case: the relative position of one region versus another). The essence of *normalizations* is that whether you measure a football field in feet or inches, it does not change the size of the field. Table 7.1 lists the normalizations we use in this book. First, we normalize the total labour supply to unity, so $L = 1$. Suppose that your country has 300 million inhabitants, then this is the unit of measurement we use (hence $L = 2$ would imply 600 million inhabitants). Second, we can choose the units in which we measure labour. Usually this is labour hours. However, we use a unit of measurement such that the fixed labour requirement α is equal to $\gamma L / \varepsilon$. This choice of units also affects the marginal labour requirement units. Third, we can choose a unit of measurement for output. Usually this is in kilograms, tons, or units. We choose a rather special unit such that the marginal labour requirement – in terms of the newly defined labour unit – of an additional unit of output implies $\beta = \rho$. Fourth, and finally, we assume that $\gamma = \delta$. This 'normalization', however, affects, so to say, the size of the football field. The good news is it does so only very marginally. You are stimulated to think about these issues in the exercises.

Table 7.1 Parameter normalization

$\gamma = \delta$	$\beta = \rho$	$L = 1$	$\alpha = \gamma L/\varepsilon$

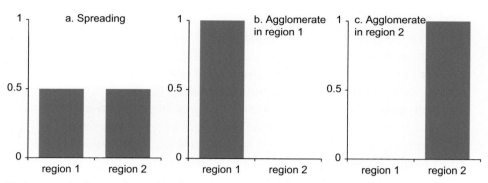

Figure 7.4 Distribution of manufacturing labour force: three examples

normalizations the awkward constants in equations 7.20 and 7.22 are equal to one, which greatly simplifies notation. Second, note that the normalizations in combination with neutral space allow us to reduce the number of parameters to three only, namely δ (the share of income spent on manufactures), ε (the price elasticity of demand), and T (the transport costs). This is shown in equations 7.23 to 7.26, which provide the short-run equilibrium equations for both region 1 and region 2 using the normalizations and neutral space; they are the income equations, price index equations, wage equations, and real wage equations, respectively.

$$Y_1 = \lambda_1\delta W_1 + (1-\delta)/2 ; Y_2 = \lambda_2\delta W_2 + (1-\delta)/2 \qquad 7.23$$

$$I_1 = \left(\lambda_1 W_1^{1-\varepsilon} + \lambda_2 T^{1-\varepsilon}W_2^{1-\varepsilon}\right)^{\frac{1}{1-\varepsilon}} ; I_2 = \left(\lambda_1 T^{1-\varepsilon}W_1^{1-\varepsilon} + \lambda_2 W_2^{1-\varepsilon}\right)^{\frac{1}{1-\varepsilon}} \qquad 7.24$$

$$W_1 = \left(Y_1 I_1^{\varepsilon-1} + Y_2 T^{1-\varepsilon}I_2^{\varepsilon-1}\right)^{1/\varepsilon} ; W_2 = \left(Y_1 T^{1-\varepsilon}I_1^{\varepsilon-1} + Y_2 I_2^{\varepsilon-1}\right)^{1/\varepsilon} \qquad 7.25$$

$$w_1 = W_1 I_1^{-\delta} ; w_2 = W_2 I_2^{-\delta} \qquad 7.26$$

Although we have stripped the core model of geographical economics now down to its bare essentials (two regions, identical in all respects except for the manufacturing labour force, and with a suitable choice of parameters), the non-linear aspects of the model make it not easy to analyse, except for three special cases illustrated in the three panels of Figure 7.4. Each is discussed in turn below.

- *Spreading* of economic activity (panel *a*). Suppose the two regions are identical in *all* respects, that is the manufacturing workforce is also evenly distributed $\lambda_1 = \lambda_2 = 1/2$. Naturally, we then expect the wage rates of the short-run equilibrium to be the same for the two regions. Can we explicitly calculate this wage rate? Yes, if you're clever enough. One way to proceed is to guess an equilibrium wage rate, and then verify if you guessed right (a procedure we will also use for simulations). So, let's guess (for no particular reason, except that we turn out to be right in the end) that the equilibrium wage rates are $W_1 = W_2 = 1$. It then follows from equation 7.24 that $I_1 = 0.5^{1/(1-\varepsilon)}\left(1+T^{1-\varepsilon}\right)^{\frac{1}{1-\varepsilon}}$ (and similarly for I_2), while from equation 7.23 it follows that $Y_1 = 0.5$ (and $Y_2 = 0.5$). Using these results in equation 7.25 shows indeed that $W_1 = W_2 = 1$, so we guessed right. Note, that in the spreading equilibrium all variables are the same for the two regions; therefore the real wages must be the same as well, which can be confirmed by substituting the values for the nominal wages and the price indices in equation 7.26. So, the spreading equilibrium is *always* a long-run equilibrium, independent of the values of the parameters.

- *Agglomeration in region 1* (panel b). Suppose now that all manufacturing activity is agglomerated in region 1 (such that $\lambda_1 = 1$) and there are no manufacturing workers in region 2 (such that $\lambda_2 = 0$). Can we determine the short-run equilibrium? Yes. Let's guess again that $W_1 = 1$. Then, it follows from equation 7.24 that $I_1 = 1$ (and $I_2 = T$), while from equation 7.23 it follows that $Y_1 = (1+\delta)/2$ (and $Y_2 = (1-\delta)/2$). Using these results in equation 7.25 confirms that $W_1 = 1$, so we guessed right. We can thus analytically derive the solutions for the short-run equilibrium in this case. Note that the wage rate W_2 is not mentioned in the above discussion. Since there are no manufacturing workers in region 2 we cannot say what their wage rate is. It is instructive to see what the implied wage rate is if a firm decides to move to region 2. From equation 7.25 it follows that this is equal to:

$$W_2 = \left(\left((1+\delta)/2\right)T^{1-\varepsilon} + \left((1-\delta)/2\right)T^{\varepsilon-1}\right)^{1/\varepsilon}$$

The implied real wage in region 2 can now be derived from equation 7.26 and is equal to:

$$w_2 = \left((1+\delta)/2\right)T^{1-\varepsilon-\varepsilon\delta} + \left((1-\delta)/2\right)T^{\varepsilon-1-\varepsilon\delta}$$

It is easily verified that for $T = 1$, the real wages in region 1 and 2 are both equal to one, while for sufficiently small values of T the real wage in region 2 is smaller than one. Agglomeration in region 1 is therefore sustainable and a long-run equilibrium.

- *Agglomeration in region 2* (panel c). This is the mirror image of the second situation described above.

Note that each equilibrium also has consequences for trade flows. Complete agglomeration results in manufactured goods – from the agglomerated region – traded for food from the food region. In this case, the farmers have to import all manufacturing varieties from the region that produces all manufactured goods. It has to export food in exchange for manufacturing varieties, an example of pure inter-industry trade (trade between regions of different types of goods). In contrast, suppose that manufacturing production is evenly spread over the two regions, as is food production (the symmetric equilibrium). From the analysis of the spreading equilibrium (see above) we know that $Y_1 = Y_2 = 0.5$, which implies that the demand for food in either region is equal to $(1-\delta)/2$, which is exactly equal to the production of food in either region. In the spreading equilibrium, there is thus no trade of food between the two regions. Since all consumers will spend money on all manufacturing varieties, also those produced in the other region, there will be trade in manufacturing varieties between the two regions. This is thus an example of pure intra-industry trade (importing manufacturing varieties in exchange for other manufacturing varieties).

We are able to derive the short- and long-run equilibrium analytically for three special cases. Unfortunately, these are only three cases. Recall that λ_1 can vary all the way from 0 to 1, so there are infinitely many other possibilities. We don't know, for example, if the three equilibria we have identified are the only long-run equilibria, or if the number of long-run equilibria depends on the value of certain parameters. We would like to draw a complete picture of all possible equilibria, long-run as well as short-run, instead of just the three possibilities depicted in Figure 7.4. In order to do so we have to introduce dynamics into the model: how do we move from one equilibrium to the next one, and what economic forces determine such relocations? What we already know at this stage is that the model is characterized by multiple equilibria.

7.7   A First Look at Dynamics

We have argued repeatedly throughout this chapter that the introduction of a general-equilibrium model, which incorporates location, increasing returns to scale, imperfect competition, and crucially transport costs, in conjunction with mobility of factors of production makes up for the defining characteristics of the geographical economics approach. It implies that the manufacturing sector in Figure 7.3 which illustrates the structure of the core model can change in size over time as a result of factor mobility, which in turn implies that the short-run equilibrium changes. Since labour is the only factor of production in the core model we must therefore address labour mobility. At this point it suffices to note that one would expect the mobile workers to react to differences in the real wage w (see equation 7.26), which adequately measures the utility level achieved, rather than the wage rate W (see equation 7.25), which does not take the price index into consideration. Adjustment of the short-run equilibrium over time is now simple. If the real wage for manufacturing workers is higher in region 1 than in region 2, we expect that manufacturing workers will leave region 2 and move to region 1. If the real wage

242 7 The Core Model

is higher in region 2 than in region 1, we expect the reverse to hold. We let the parameter η denote the speed with which manufacturing workers react to differences in the real wage, and use the simple dynamic system given in equation 7.27, where $\bar{w}$ gives the average real wage in the economy.

$$\frac{d\lambda_1}{\lambda_1} = \eta\left(w_1 - \bar{w}\right); \quad \bar{w} \equiv \lambda_1 w_1 + \lambda_2 w_2 \qquad 7.27$$

Now that we have specified how the manufacturing workforce responds to differences in the real wage between regions, we can also note when a long-run equilibrium is reached. This occurs when one of three possibilities arises, namely (i) the distribution of the manufacturing workforce between regions 1 and 2 is such that the real wage is equal in the two regions, (ii) all manufacturing workers are located in region 1, or (iii) all manufacturing workers are located in region 2.

What are the main economic forces at work for determining whether a worker relocates to another region? The model we have analysed in this chapter is non-linear, and therefore complicated. However, at the symmetric equilibrium we can illustrate the three main economic forces that are at work in the model. Two of these forces stimulate agglomeration: *the price index effect* and *the home market effect*. The third force stimulates spreading: *the extent-of-competition effect*. The balance between these forces determines if it is beneficial to relocate to the other region. The analysis around the symmetric equilibrium allows for important simplifications. Define the index of trade costs $Z \equiv \left(1 - T^{1-\varepsilon}\right)/\left(1 + T^{1-\varepsilon}\right)$, which varies from zero to one as transport costs rise. We denote variables at the spreading equilibrium without a sub-index and let a tilde denote relative changes ($\tilde{x} \equiv dx / x$) in order to discuss the three forces at work.

- *The price index effect.* Technical Note 7.7 shows that differentiation of the price index equation 7.24 around the spreading equilibrium leads to: $\tilde{I} = Z\tilde{p} - \left(Z/(\varepsilon-1)\right)\tilde{N}$. Assume for the moment that the supply of labour is perfectly elastic, such that from equation 7.13 we have: $\tilde{W} = \tilde{p} = 0$. In that case $\tilde{I} = -\left(Z/(\varepsilon-1)\right)\tilde{N}$, which shows that the price index falls if a location becomes larger because more workers and firms move there and is able to offer more varieties. This so-called price index effect makes the larger region more attractive because a smaller share of the varieties have to be imported at (large) transportation costs.

$$\tilde{Y} = Z\tilde{N} + \left(\frac{\varepsilon}{Z} + (1-\varepsilon)Z\right)\tilde{W} \qquad 7.28$$

- *The home market effect.* Applying a similar procedure as used in Technical Note 7.7 to the wage equation 7.25 leads to (see exercise 7.7): $\varepsilon\tilde{W} = Z\tilde{Y} + (\varepsilon-1)Z\tilde{I}$. Substitute the total price index effect $\tilde{I} = Z\tilde{p} - \left(Z/(\varepsilon-1)\right)\tilde{N}$ into this result, use $\tilde{W} = \tilde{p}$, and solve for the change in income to get equation 7.28. Recall from equation 7.16 that changes in the number of varieties are proportional to

BOX 7.5 The Burden of History and the Role of Expectations

History can be decisive. The term 'history' is used here in a broad sense and can imply differences in tastes, technology, factor endowments, and so on. Past circumstances can influence future outcomes. In his famous, but not undisputed QWERTY keyboard example, David (1985) argues that relatively small, and at first sight unimportant, factors can cause certain technologies to become 'locked-in', that is, the initial advantage of a certain technology is almost impossible to overcome by new technologies. His example involves the QWERTY keyboard layout of typewriters which, once established, became impossible to substitute for other (perhaps more efficient) keyboard layouts.[8]

Expectations may be the most important force determining which specific long-run equilibrium gets established. Expectations become particularly important if one takes future earnings into consideration when making decisions. In the examples given above, the initial conditions determine the fate of an equilibrium; new entrants only look at the present situation, and then decide what to do. In expectation-driven equilibria, the importance of future earnings is decisive. This holds, for example, for the role of ICT technologies, where network externalities are most important. The optimal choice for adoption of a new technology depends crucially on what you expect other people will decide to use. The more widely a specific technology is adopted, the easier it is to exchange information with other people, and the more attractive this technology becomes. Facebook and Twitter are good examples. The attractiveness increases if more people use it.

To this date, little empirical research is available to determine if expectations dominate history, or vice versa. Harris and Ioannides (2000) is an attempt in this direction. History is in principle a strong force but by no means precludes a strong role for expectations. Harris and Ioannides extend the core model by introducing housing and land explicitly. Furthermore, they assume that labour is forward looking and workers are able to calculate the present value of wages in a specific city. The migration decision of workers influences the price of land and housing, and thus influences the calculation of the present values. Conclusions can only be drawn with caution, but Harris and Ioannides (2000, p. 11) argue that 'history rules and expectations at best helps history along'. Baldwin (1999) shows that the standard (ad hoc) migration behaviour in geographical economics is consistent with optimal behaviour, subject to quadratic migration costs and static expectations. The often criticized migration equation in the core model is therefore not as primitive as sometimes stated. The relative importance of history versus expectations depends on adjustment costs. As Redding and Turner (2015) show, these adjustment costs are substantial.

---

[8] For an entertaining collection of examples in which historical accident, initial conditions, and the successive arrival of newcomers in the market determine the final equilibrium, see Schelling (1978).

changes in the labour force, such that $\tilde{N}$ can also be interpreted as such. If we again assume perfectly elastic labour supply $\tilde{W}$ and equation 7.28 simplifies to $\tilde{Y} = Z\tilde{N}$. Since $0 \leq Z \leq 1$, this implies that the larger market has a *more* than proportional gain in the number of varieties. This so-called home market effect makes the larger region more attractive. Empirical research (see Chapter 9) frequently does not assume perfectly elastic labour supply, and therefore uses equation 7.28 in many applications.

- *The extent-of-competition effect.* This final effect is immediately clear by studying the demand for variety i (equation 7.7), which equals: $c_i = p_i^{-\varepsilon}\left(\delta Y_1 I_1^{\varepsilon-1} + \delta Y_2 T^{1-\varepsilon} I_2^{\varepsilon-1}\right)$. We have already established that the price index in the larger market becomes smaller. For an individual firm, given p_i, this reduces the demand as its competitive position declines.

It is the balance between these three forces that determines whether, once a firm relocates, others will follow. If so, the equilibrium is *unstable*. This process is sometimes referred to as *cumulative causation*. If others do not follow, the equilibrium is *stable*. Box 7.6 illustrates these forces graphically.

BOX 7.6 Agglomeration and Spreading Forces: A Simple Diagram

It is instructive to take a closer look at the economic forces of agglomeration and spreading in the core model by using a simple diagram (based on Neary, 2001), as depicted in Figure 7.5, which is an extended version of Figure 7.2. The volume of sales x is depicted along the horizontal axis, and the price p along the vertical axis. The D, AC, MC, and MR lines are the demand curve, the average cost curve, the marginal cost curve, and the marginal revenue curve, respectively. As always, the intersection of marginal revenue and marginal cost at point A gives the profit-maximizing volume of sales $x = (\varepsilon-1)\alpha/\beta$ and the corresponding price $\varepsilon\beta W/(\varepsilon-1)$ at point B. Note that at point B the demand curve and average cost curve are tangent because of the zero profit condition.

In this partial equilibrium setting it is simple to see what happens, starting from the spreading equilibrium, if one firm decides to move from region 1 to region 2. If this raises profits in region 1 the initial equilibrium was *unstable* and more firms will follow; if it lowers profits the initial equilibrium was *stable* and the firm has an incentive to return. We can distinguish two immediate effects. The first is the extent-of-competition effect, which shifts the demand curve (indicated by arrow 1 in Figure 7.5) and the corresponding marginal revenue curve down. It follows immediately from equation 7.7, and given that an increase in the number of firms (varieties) lowers the price index, that this price index effect reduces the demand for each individual firm. This effect is a spreading force. The second effect is that the new firm (and the corresponding labour force) raises income. This can be

BOX 7.6 (cont.)

due to more workers or an increase in the demand for labour, leading to wage increases. The subsequent income increase shifts the demand curve upward; the combination of equations 7.23 and 7.25 makes this clear (indicated by arrow 2 in Figure 7.5). This effect is related to the home market effect, and is an agglomeration force.

A third (agglomeration) force (indicated by arrow 3 in Figure 7.5) is related to what we called the price index effect. Starting from the symmetric equilibrium, if one firm decides to move to region 1, this reduces the cost of living in the larger region, because the number of varieties increases. This makes the region attractive for further migration. Migration stops when real wages are equalized between regions. As β is constant this implies that in Figure 7.5 the marginal cost and average cost curves shift downward, raising profitability and thus providing an extra agglomerating force.

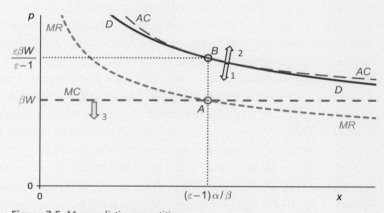

Figure 7.5 Monopolistic competition
Notes: D = demand; MR = marginal revenue; MC = marginal cost; AC = average cost; see Box text for details.

7.7.1   Simulations

Now that we have analysed three special cases in section 7.6.2 and discussed the dynamic forces in section 7.7, we will use computer simulations to learn more about the structure of the model:[9] in this case, by investigating how the short-run equilibrium changes if the distribution of manufacturing workers changes. Varying λ_1 between 0 and 1 gives a description of all possible distributions of the

---

[9] See Brakman, Garretsen, and van Marrewijk (2009, ch. 4) for a discussion of computer simulations.

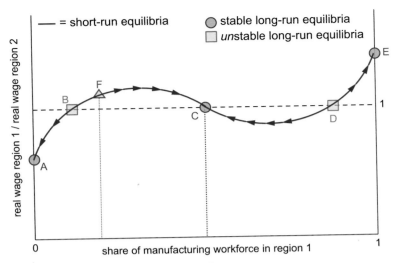

Figure 7.6 Relative real wage: base scenario

mobile workforce. We focus attention on the real wage in region 1 relative to the real wage in region 2, as this determines the dynamic forces operating in the model through migration flows. Once we find a short-run equilibrium for a distribution of the mobile labour force, it is easy to calculate the relative real wage w_1 / w_2.

Figure 7.6 illustrates how the relative real wage in region 1 varies as the share of the mobile workforce in region 1 varies for some base scenario choice of the parameters ε, δ, and T (with $T = 1.7$). It is the result of a range of simulations in which the value of λ_1 is gradually increased from 0 to 1. The implied relative real wage is then plotted in the figure. What can we learn from this exercise?

First, we can identify the location of long-run equilibria. Mobile workers move to regions with a higher real wage, such that a short-run equilibrium is also a long-run equilibrium if the real wage for the mobile workforce is the same in the two regions. A long-run equilibrium therefore requires that the relative real wage is 1 if there are mobile workers in both regions, such as at points B, C, and D in Figure 7.6. When a long-run equilibrium implies complete agglomeration (one region ends up with all mobile workers) the relative real wage is not equal to one (see points A and E).[10]

Second, there are three types of long-run equilibria: (i) equal spreading of manufacturing production over the 2 regions (point C), (ii) complete agglomeration of manufacturing production in either region (points A and E), or (iii) partial agglomeration in one of the two regions (points B and D). This leads to a total of five long-run equilibria. We can only find equilibria B and D as a result of our simulations.

---

[10] If there is complete agglomeration the relative real wage cannot actually be calculated since there are no manufacturing workers in one of the regions. Points A and E in the figure are therefore limit values.

Third, we can determine adjustment over time and the stability of long-run equilibria. Suppose, for example, that $\lambda_1 = F$ in Figure 7.6. The mobile work-force is then smaller in region 1 than in region 2. As illustrated, the associated short-run equilibrium implies $w_1 / w_2 > 1$. The higher real wage in region 1 gives mobile workers an incentive to move from region 2 to region 1. This migration process represents an increase of λ_1 in the figure. Migration continues until the spreading equilibrium at point C is reached, where the real wages are equalized. Similar reasoning leading to point C holds for any arbitrary initial distribution of the mobile labour force in between points B and D. The spreading equilibrium is a *stable* equilibrium in the sense that a small deviation of the mobile labour force away from point C activates economic forces to bring us back to point C. Similar reasoning holds for the two agglomeration equilibria (points A and E). In contrast, the partial agglomeration long-run equilibria (points B and D) are *un*stable. If, for whatever reason, we are initially at point B or D, a long-run equilibrium is reached in the sense that the real wage is equal for the two regions. However, any small perturbation of this equilibrium will set in motion a process of adjustment leading to a *different* long-run equilibrium. For example, a small negative disturbance of λ_1 at point B leads to complete agglomeration of manufacturing activity in region 2 (point A), while a positive disturbance leads to equal spreading (point C).

7.7.2   Transport Costs and Stability

The most important parameter in geographical economics models is transport cost, assumed to be zero within a region and positive between different regions. The term 'transport costs' is a shorthand notation for many different types of obstacles to trade between locations, such as tariffs, language and culture barriers, and indeed the costs of actually getting goods or services at another location. An important question is thus what the impact is of a change in transport costs. To answer this question we repeat the simulation procedure of Figure 7.6 for both higher ($T = 2.1$) and lower ($T = 1.3$) transport costs: see Figure 7.7.

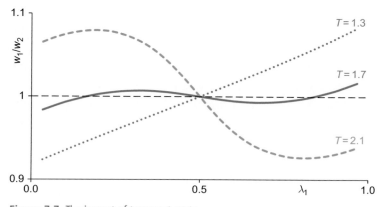

Figure 7.7 The impact of transport costs

Note that:

- If transport costs are large, the spreading equilibrium is the only stable equilibrium. It makes intuitive sense that if manufactures are difficult to transport from one region to another the dynamics of the model lead to spreading of manufacturing activity; distant provision of manufactures is too costly, such that they need to be provided locally.

- If transport costs are small, the spreading equilibrium is unstable while the two agglomerating equilibria are stable. An initial share of the mobile workforce λ_1 in between 0 and ½ serves as the basin of attraction for complete agglomeration in region 2, while an initial λ_1 in between ½ and 1 serves as the basin of attraction for complete agglomeration in region 1. Again this makes sense intuitively. With very low transport costs, the immobile market can be provided effectively from a distance, which therefore does not pose a strong enough force to counter the advantages of agglomeration.

- For a range of intermediate values of transport costs (here for example if $T = 1.7$) there are five long-run equilibria. Three of those five, namely spreading and the two agglomeration equilibria, are stable. The other two equilibria are unstable. In this situation, the transport costs are high enough to allow for the local provision of manufactures (spreading). At the same time transport costs are low enough to allow for the provision of the immobile market from a distance (agglomeration).

The suggestions about the impact of a change in transport costs on the stability of agglomeration and spreading in the geographical economics model, as discussed on the basis of Figure 7.7, hold in fact quite generally (Fujita, Krugman, and Venables, 1999; Neary, 2001), as we analyse in the next section.

7.8   Analytical Results: The Tomahawk Diagram

The non-linear character of the model makes it difficult to solve it analytically. Sometimes we can rely on simulations, sometimes analytical analysis is possible. The agglomeration and spreading equilibria can be analysed in more detail. We can ask for what parameter values complete agglomeration can be 'sustained' and when spreading is 'broken'. We will do this for different values of T. This is the *sustain and break* analysis. Although the analysis in this section is somewhat more advanced, it also gives a clear understanding of the forces at work in the model. Apart from the sustain and break points, this section also introduces two other important concepts, the *no-black-hole condition* and *path dependency*.

7.8.1   Sustain Point

Suppose that all manufacturing activity is located in region 1. In section 7.6.2 we show that, for $\lambda_1 = 1$, the long-run equilibrium is given by $W_1 = 1$, $Y_1 = (1+\delta)/2$, $Y_2 = (1-\delta)/2$, $I_1 = 1$, and $I_2 = T$. There are no manufacturing workers in region 2, so it is not really appropriate to talk of their wage W_s, but we can calculate what this wage would have been by using equation 7.25. Similarly, we can calculate the implied real wage w_2 by using equation 7.26. Noting that the real wage in region 1 is equal to one, we see that it will be attractive for mobile workers located in region 1 to move to region 2 if the implied real wage in region 2 is larger than one. If this is the case, complete agglomeration of manufacturing activity in region 1 is not 'sustainable'. The analysis is simplified by focusing on the implied value of w_2^ε as given in equation 7.29 (see Technical Note 7.8) rather than the implied real wage itself.[11]

The value of $T > 1$ for which equation 7.29 is equal to one is called the *sustain* point. For convenience we use the short-hand notation $f(T)$ for the right-hand side of equation 7.29. The function $f(T)$ is illustrated in Figure 7.8 (ignore $g(T)$ for the moment), provided $\rho > \delta$ (see below). It shows the real wage in region 2 as a function of T. Note that $f(1) = 1$ which says that complete agglomeration is a long-run equilibrium in the *absence* of trade costs: real wages are identical in both regions and there is no incentive to relocate. Technical Note 7.8 shows that this also holds for small transport costs, since $f'(1) = -\varepsilon\delta(1+\rho) < 0$. Thus, for small transport costs (T close to one) the function $f(T)$ will be smaller than one (and $w_2 < 1$). This implies that complete agglomeration of manufacturing in one region is always a sustainable equilibrium for sufficiently small transport costs, since the real wage in the periphery will be smaller than in the centre.

$$w_2^\varepsilon \equiv f(T) \equiv \frac{1+\delta}{2} T^{-(\rho+\delta)\varepsilon} + \frac{1-\delta}{2} T^{(\rho-\delta)\varepsilon} \qquad 7.29$$

As transport costs increase, however, the first term in equation 7.29 becomes arbitrarily small, while the second term becomes arbitrarily large if, and only if, $\rho > \delta$ (ensuring that the exponent in the second term is positive). We can conclude therefore that complete agglomeration of manufacturing in one region is not sustainable for sufficiently large transport costs if $\rho > \delta$. Fujita, Krugman, and Venables (1999, p. 58) label this the *'no-black-hole' condition* because if this condition is not fulfilled 'the forces working toward agglomeration would always prevail, and the economy would tend to collapse into a point'. Stated differently, if the no-black-hole condition is not met, full agglomeration occurs irrespective of the level of transport costs. In Chapter 9, we discuss some empirical evidence regarding the no-black-hole condition.

---

[11] Sustainability of agglomeration requires $w_2 < 1$, which is equivalent to $w_2^\varepsilon < 1$.

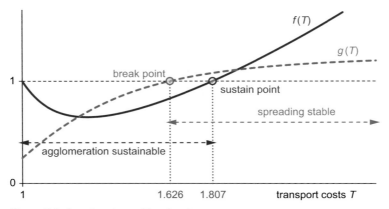

Figure 7.8 Sustain point and break point
Parameters: $\delta = 0.4$; $\varepsilon = 5$; other parameters: see Table 7.1.

Figure 7.8 illustrates the above discussion if the no-black-hole condition is met. For sufficiently small transport costs the function $f(T) < 1$ and complete agglomeration in one region is sustainable. If the transport costs exceed a critical level, labelled the 'sustain point' in the figure, the function $f(T) > 1$ and complete agglomeration is not sustainable.

7.8.2   Break Point

We now turn to the spreading equilibrium. Suppose manufacturing activity is evenly spread over the two regions. We already showed in section 7.6.2 that $\lambda_1 = \lambda_2 = 1/2$ implies that $W_1 = W_2 = 1$, $Y_1 = Y_2 = 0.5$, and $I_1 = I_2 = 0.5^{1/(1-\varepsilon)}\left(1 + T^{1-\varepsilon}\right)^{\frac{1}{1-\varepsilon}}$. So, real wages are identical.[12] We want to investigate changes in this spreading equilibrium if a small (infinitesimal) number of workers are relocating from region 1 to region 2. In particular, we want to establish whether this small movement results in a higher real wage for the moving workers, thus setting in motion further relocation of labour and a process of agglomeration. If so, the spreading equilibrium is unstable, if not it is stable. The point where the spreading equilibrium switches from stable to unstable is labelled the 'break-point' by Fujita, Krugman, and Venables (1999) and Puga (1999). The technical details of this analysis are a bit cumbersome and given in Technical Note 7.9. At this point it suffices to note that the spreading equilibrium is *un*stable if the inequality in equation 7.30 holds.[13]

$$g(T) \equiv \frac{1 - T^{1-\varepsilon}}{1 + T^{1-\varepsilon}} + \left(1 - \frac{\delta(1+\rho)}{\delta^2 + \rho}\right) < 1 \qquad\qquad 7.30$$

---

[12] Note that the ratio of regional real wages is *always* equal to one in the symmetric equilibrium, irrespective of T. We are interested in whether the symmetric equilibrium is stable or unstable.

[13] Note that sub-indices indicating regions are absent in the expression. We did not forget these; close to the symmetric equilibrium we can ignore all second-order effects of induced changes for the other regions. We can thus write $dY \equiv dY_1 = -dY_2$ and similarly for other variables. This facilitates the notation considerably.

Note that the first term on the left-hand side of equation 7.30 is the Z term that was already defined in section 7.7, which is monotonically rising (from 0 to 1) as transport costs T rise (from 1 to ∞). The second term is a constant fraction strictly in between 0 and 1 if, and only if, $\rho > \delta$, that is, if the no-black-hole condition is fulfilled. In that case, therefore, the function $g(T)$ is smaller than one (which means the spreading equilibrium is unstable) for sufficiently small transport costs (T close to one). Once transport costs exceed a certain threshold level, labelled the 'break point' in Figure 7.8, the function $g(T) > 1$ and the spreading equilibrium is stable. If the no-black-hole condition is not fulfilled the spreading equilibrium is unstable for *all* transport costs. The break-point can be derived explicitly using equation 7.30; see the exercises.

Proposition 7.1 (Fujita, Krugman, and Venables, 1999) Suppose the 'no-black-hole' condition $(\rho > \delta)$ holds in a symmetric 2-region setting of the Geographical Economics model, then (i) complete agglomeration of manufacturing activity is not sustainable for sufficiently large transport costs T, and (ii) spreading is a stable equilibrium for sufficiently large transport costs T.

Note that the transport cost level chosen in Figure 7.6 ($T = 1.7$) lies in between the break point and the sustain point, such that (i) the spreading equilibrium is stable and (ii) the agglomeration equilibria are sustainable. It turns out that the sustain point is always to the right of the break point, such that there is always a range of transport costs as illustrated in Figure 7.8. We can make a graph to summarize our findings in terms of the share of mobile workers in each region. It is given in Figure 7.9 and is known as the *Tomahawk diagram* because of its shape.

In Figure 7.9 we have transport costs T on the horizontal axis and λ_1, the share of the mobile workforce in region 1, on the vertical axis. From left to right transport costs increase. Higher values of T indicate a lower degree of economic integration. Complete agglomeration in region 1 is indicated by $\lambda_1 = 1$ and complete agglomeration in region 2 by $\lambda_1 = 0$. The spreading equilibrium is given by $\lambda_1 = 1/2$. The points indicated by S_0 and S_1 are the sustain points, while B is the break point.

First, assume that T is relatively small, such as $T = 1.3$ in Figure 7.7. We then see that the symmetric equilibrium is unstable, while simultaneously complete agglomeration in region 1 or 2 is stable. Starting in the symmetric equilibrium, a small disturbance – for example a relocation of one of the firms to the other region – will lead to complete agglomeration. The area for which this holds is indicated by the two arrows that point away from the symmetric equilibrium in Figure 7.9. We can distinguish two basins of attraction, one for region 1 and one for region 2. For values of T that are small enough, these basins indicate that the larger region will attract *all* footloose labour from the other region. That is, if one worker relocates all others will follow. This is called *cumulative causation*. The dashed lines in Figure 7.9 indicate that the long-run equilibrium is an *un*stable equilibrium.

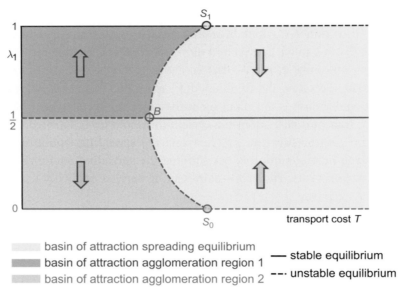

Figure 7.9 The Tomahawk diagram

Second, assume that T is relatively high, say $T = 2.1$ in Figure 7.7. We see that things change dramatically. Now complete agglomeration is unstable, but the symmetric equilibrium is stable, which is indicated by a solid line in Figure 7.9. This holds for values of T that are larger than S_0 or S_1. The arrows in the associated two basins of attraction now point towards the (stable) symmetric equilibrium.

Third, assume that T is larger than B, but smaller than S_0 or S_1, say $= 1.7$ in Figure 7.7. We see that – besides the symmetric equilibrium and complete agglomeration – an additional long-run equilibrium arises in between complete agglomeration and the symmetric equilibrium. This is because between two stable equilibria one always finds an unstable equilibrium (see exercises). This equilibrium moves closer to the symmetric equilibrium if T becomes smaller in the area between B and S_0 or S_1, and moves closer to complete agglomeration if T becomes larger. These unstable equilibria are indicated by the curved-dashed lines that connect B to S_0 and B to S_1.

The Tomahawk diagram shows the interplay between transport costs T and the share of the mobile work-force in region 1, λ_1. Stepping back from the technical details of the core model that we introduced and explained in this chapter, the essence of the core model in economic terms comes down to the combination of three model parameters. Alongside T and λ_1, the presence of the fixed costs α in the production of manufactured goods (recall equation 7.11) goes a long way towards explaining the main message of the core model, as Box 7.7 illustrates.

To conclude this subsection, it is useful to point out the *hysteresis* or path-dependency aspect of the model. This means history matters. Look again at the

BOX 7.7 **How α, T, and λ Sum Up the Core Model (and got Paul Krugman the Nobel Prize)**

In 2008 Paul Krugman was awarded the Nobel prize in economics for his work on geography and trade. The jury report makes it clear that Krugman got the prize for essentially three of his papers: Krugman (1979, 1980, and 1991).[14] With the benefit of hindsight, it is easy to see how each of the three papers introduced and added an essential part of what finally became the core model of geographical economics in this chapter. In Krugman (1979), the main aim was to come up with a model that could explain intra-industry trade, that is countries trading similar goods with each other and not (as conventional trade theory would have it) countries specializing in and hence trading different types of goods (inter-industry trade). At that time, the data already showed that the bulk of international trade was of the intra-industry trade type, but a convincing theoretical model was still lacking. It was clear that such a model would have to be built on a market structure of imperfect competition. Using the Dixit and Stiglitz (1977) model of imperfect competition as introduced earlier in this chapter (Box 7.2), where fixed costs (the α parameter) imply increasing returns to scale at the firm level, combined with a CES demand with a love-of-variety effect as also introduced in section 7.3.1, Krugman was able to come up with a convincing model for intra-industry trade.

   With fixed costs of producing a manufacturing variety, firms have an incentive to concentrate their production, but in the absence of transport costs they do not really care yet where they locate. Consumers and hence demand might be highest in say the EU for a particular variety but the firm could throw up a coin where to locate. This changed in Krugman (1980) where essentially iceberg transport costs T as we know from our model in section 7.5 were added to the 1979 trade model. Suddenly, manufacturing firms start to care where they locate because a location that is remote in the sense of being distant from the main customer market could now be a bad location choice. This leads to the home market effect in Krugman (1980) that we also discussed in this chapter.

   The combination of α and T gives us a rudimentary model of economic geography. But all the action in terms of deciding where to locate is still only with the firms, that is on the supply side of the economy. The spatial or geographical allocation of demand, that is the location of consumers, is still taken as given. The main innovation of the Krugman (1991) model is to add inter-regional labour mobility such that the location choices of workers/consumers also becomes

---

[14] https://www.nobelprize.org/prizes/economics/2008/press-release/ and the academic background report there.

BOX 7.7 (cont.)

endogenous. This is of course what the introduction of λ in the model (see Figure 7.3) is all about.

Hence, the parameters α, T, and λ do not only characterize the three papers that got Paul Krugman the Nobel prize in 2008; when combined they also capture the essence of the core model of geographical economics. As we will see in Chapter 8, the Krugman (1991) model resulted in a flurry of theoretical extensions and refinements in subsequent years, but the main ingredients of the core model to this day continue to produce key and innovative new models in international and geographical economics, like the by now vast literature on firm heterogeneity and trade with FDI following Melitz (2003), or the work on so-called quantitative spatial economics (Redding and Rossi-Hansberg, 2017) of which the ground-breaking new empirical work on structural (transport) changes and their locational impact is an example; see Donaldson (2018). More on the latter in Chapter 9.

Tomahawk diagram of Figure 7.9 and assume that the break point B and the sustain points S correspond with the values depicted in Figure 7.8. Suppose that transport costs are initially high, say $T = 2.5$ in Figure 7.9. Then spreading of manufacturing activity is the only stable long-run equilibrium. Now suppose that transport costs start to fall, given that the spreading equilibrium is established, say to $T = 1.7$. This will have no impact on the equilibrium allocation of manufacturing production since spreading remains a stable equilibrium. Only after the transport costs have fallen even further, below the break point in Figure 7.9, will the spreading equilibrium become unstable. Any small disturbance will then result in complete agglomeration of manufacturing production in one region. It is not possible to predict beforehand which region this will be, but suppose that agglomeration takes place in region 1. Given that region 1 contains all manufacturing activity assume now that the transport costs start to rise again, perhaps because of the imposition of trade barriers, say back to $T = 1.7$. What will happen? The answer is: nothing! Agglomeration of manufacturing activity remains a stable equilibrium. So for the same level of transport costs ($T = 1.7$) the equilibrium that becomes established depends on the way this level of transport costs is reached, on history. This phenomenon is called *hysteresis* or *path-dependency*. Obviously, predictions of what will happen if certain parameters change are considerably harder in models characterized by path-dependency.[15]

---

[15] It is possible to show this mathematically, but this is not trivial (see Neary, 2001, pp. 559–60).

7.9   Conclusions

The core model of geographical economics due to Krugman (1991) that we introduced and developed in this chapter has five important characteristics.

Cumulative causation. If, for some reason, one region attracts a manufacturing firm, a new firm has an incentive to follow if real wages become higher in that region (see section 7.7).

Multiple equilibria. In the discussion of the core model in section 7.6.2 three short-run equilibria were discussed, namely agglomeration in region 1, agglomeration in region 2, and spreading of manufacturing activity over the two regions. We guessed that all three of these short-run equilibria are also long-run equilibria (see the next point).

Stable and unstable equilibria. Equilibria can be stable or unstable, as is indicated in Figure 7.6.

Interaction of agglomeration and trade flows. In section 7.6.2, we noted that the distribution of economic activity also has consequences for trade flows. Suppose, for example, that manufacturing production is agglomerated in region 1, then we have inter-industry trade: manufactured goods exchanged for food (and vice versa for complete agglomeration in region 2). In the spreading equilibrium we have intra-industry trade: the exchange of manufactured products produced in each of the regions.

Endogenous determination of spatial equilibria. Most importantly, spatial equilibria are determined endogenously for both the supply side of the economy (footloose manufacturing firms) and the demand side of the economy (footloose manufacturing workers that are also the consumers of manufacturing goods varieties produced).

Taken together, these five model features make for a model that is clearly different from the models of urban economics that were the focus of Part II of our book. At the time of its conception in 1991, it was also different from models of international trade out of which Krugman's (1991) core model of geographical economics arose. In a nutshell (see also Box 7.7 above) the model centres around the interplay of increasing returns to scale, transports costs, and inter-regional labour mobility, or in parameter terms, α, T, and λ. The interaction of increasing returns to scale with transport costs already suffices for a simple model of economic geography since for firms it then matters where they locate. Krugman came up with this insight in Krugman (1980). It took him another 11 years to figure out how this model could be expanded by endogenizing the location choice of workers/consumers in Krugman (1991): see Box 7.8.

How to proceed?

Since this chapter is about the set-up of one single highly stylized model of geographical economics only, we will proceed along two lines. The first line concerns extensions of the core model so as to incorporate different aspects and make it

BOX 7.8 The $100 Bill on the Sidewalk Between 1980 and 1991

The core model of geographical economics by Krugman (1991) is similar to the international trade model of Krugman (1980), except for one crucial difference: the *endogenization of regional market size* that is the direct result of inter-regional labour mobility in Krugman (1991). In the core model, the mobility of manufacturing workers implies that each region's market size, as well as the regional distribution of manufacturing firms and labour, is no longer given. On the continuity of the Krugman (1980) and the Krugman (1991) approach, it is illuminating to quote Krugman himself (1999, p. 6):

> It is obvious – in retrospect – that something special happens when factor mobility interacts with increasing returns … This observation is, as I suggested, obvious in retrospect; but it certainly took me a while to see it. Why exactly I spent a decade between showing how the interaction of transport costs and increasing returns at the level of the plant could lead to the 'home market effect' (Krugman, 1980) and realizing that the techniques developed there led naturally to simple models of regional divergence (Krugman, 1991) remains a mystery to me. The only good news was that nobody else picked up that $100 bill lying on the sidewalk in the interim.

With the benefit of hindsight, it seems that the decision to add labour mobility to the Krugman (1980) model really paid off in academic terms. At the time of writing this chapter, Krugman's most cited paper is Krugman (1991), which is cited far more often than Krugman (1980): according to Google's Scholar search engine, Krugman (1991) was cited 14,605 times relative to 6,359 citations for Krugman (1980).[16]

When asked by us, Paul Krugman wrote the following about the origins of the core geographical economics model of Krugman (1991):

> Michael Porter had given me a manuscript copy of his book on *Competitive Advantage of Nations*, probably late 1989. I was much taken by the stuff on clusters, and started trying to make a model – I was on a lecture tour, I recall, and worked on it evenings, I started out with complicated models with intermediate goods and all that, but after a few days I realized that these weren't necessary ingredients, that my home market stuff basically provide the necessary. I got stumped for a while by the analytics, and tried numerical examples on a spreadsheet to figure them out. It all came together in a hotel in Honolulu …

---

[16] https://scholar.google.nl/scholar?hl=nl&as_sdt=0%2C5&q=paul+krugman&btnG (accessed on 5 September 2018).

more realistic. This is the main motivation for Chapter 8, where we will see how the model can be adapted to include intermediate goods production, different assumptions on inter-regional labour mobility, and more generally how the core model can be changed so as to allow for more 'possible states of the world' besides full agglomeration or perfect spreading. The second line along which we will proceed is to turn to empirics. This will mainly be done in Chapter 9, but also in Chapter 10 and Chapter 11. What are the main empirical implications (if any) to which the core model (and its extensions in Chapter 8) give rise? To pre-empt our discussion in Chapter 9 somewhat and with the main ingredients of the core model that we have just discussed still fresh in mind, these issues are relevant from an empirical point of view:

- The equilibrium wage equation 7.25 suggests that wages will be higher if a region is close to regions with a higher real income.
- Equation 7.28 on the home market effect indicates that larger regions have a more-than-proportional share of the varieties produced and associated number of manufacturing firms.
- The Tomahawk diagram (Figure 7.9) suggests that changes in transport costs could have a quite dramatic impact on the degree of agglomeration.
- The model displays multiple equilibria; see Figure 7.6 where we encountered five equilibria. Can we test which equilibrium applies when and how? Or can we apply the core model and its feature of multiple equilibria to see when a real-world economy might move from one equilibrium to another?
- More generally (and finally) given the 'trouble' of including spatial interdependencies (via iceberg transport costs) that makes for a more complicated model to understand 'spikiness' compared to the cities as 'freely floating islands' in urban economics, how important are these spatial interdependencies empirically? And if they matter, at which level of economic geography (cities, regions, or countries) do they matter most?

Before we can turn to the empirical applications and evidence in Chapter 9, we will first extend the core model in Chapter 8 with the aim of incorporating several other, empirically relevant features to make it better suited to confront the real world.

Technical Notes

Technical Note 7.1 Derivation of equation 7.3

To maximize equation 7.1 subject to the budget constraint 7.2 we define the Lagrangian Γ, using the multiplier κ:

$$\Gamma = F^{1-\delta}M^{\delta} + \kappa\left(Y - (F + IM)\right)$$

Differentiating Γ with respect to F and M gives the first-order conditions:

$$(1-\delta)F^{-\delta}M^{\delta} = \kappa \; ; \; \delta F^{1-\delta}M^{\delta-1} = \kappa I$$

Taking the ratio of the first-order conditions gives:

$$\frac{\delta F^{1-\delta}M^{\delta-1}}{(1-\delta)F^{-\delta}M^{\delta}} = \frac{\kappa I}{\kappa} \text{ or } IM = \frac{\delta}{1-\delta}F$$

Substituting the latter in budget equation 7.2 gives:

$$Y = F + IM = F + \frac{\delta}{1-\delta}F \text{ or } F = (1-\delta)Y$$

Which indicates that the share $(1-\delta)$ of income is spend on food, and thus the share δ on manufactures, as given in equation 7.3.

Technical Note 7.2 Derivation of equations 7.7 and 7.8

We proceed as in Technical Note 7.1. To maximize equation 7.4 subject to the budget constraint 7.6 we define the Lagrangian Γ, using the multiplier κ:

$$\Gamma = \left(\sum_{i=1}^{N} c_i^{\rho}\right)^{1/\rho} + \kappa\left(\delta Y - \sum_{i=1}^{N} p_i c_i\right)$$

Differentiating Γ with respect to c_j and equating to 0 gives the first-order conditions:

$$\left(\sum_{i=1}^{N} c_i^{\rho}\right)^{\frac{1}{\rho}-1} c_j^{\rho-1} = \kappa p_j, \; j = 1,..,N.$$

The next step is to take the ratio of the first-order conditions of a variety j with respect to another, say variety 1. Note that the first term on the left-hand side cancels (as does the term κ on the right-hand side), and define $\varepsilon \equiv 1/(1-\rho)$ as discussed in the main text, then:

$$\frac{c_j^{\rho-1}}{c_1^{\rho-1}} = \frac{p_j}{p_1} \text{ or } c_j = p_j^{-\varepsilon}p_1^{\varepsilon}c_1$$

Substituting these relations in the budget equation 7.6 gives:

$$\sum_{j=1}^{N} p_j c_j = \sum_{j=1}^{N} p_j\left(p_j^{-\varepsilon}p_1^{\varepsilon}c_1\right) = p_1^{\varepsilon}c_1 \sum_{j=1}^{N} p_j^{1-\varepsilon} = p_1^{\varepsilon}c_1 I^{1-\varepsilon} = \delta Y \text{ or } c_1 = p_1^{-\varepsilon}I^{\varepsilon-1}\delta Y$$

Where use has been made of the definition of I in equation 7.7 of the main text. This explains the demand for variety 1 as given in equation 7.7. The demand for the other varieties is derived analogously. The question remains why the price index I was defined as given in equation 7.7. To answer this question we have to substitute the derived demand for all varieties in equation 7.4 and note along the way that $-\varepsilon\rho = 1-\varepsilon$ and $1/\rho = -\varepsilon/(1-\varepsilon)$:

$$M = \left(\sum_{i=1}^{N} c_i^{\rho}\right)^{1/\rho} = \left(\sum_{i=1}^{N} \left(p_i^{-\varepsilon} I^{\varepsilon-1} \delta Y\right)^{\rho}\right)^{1/\rho} = I^{\varepsilon-1} \delta Y \left(\sum_{i=1}^{N} p_i^{-\varepsilon\rho}\right)^{1/\rho} = I^{\varepsilon-1} \delta Y \left(\sum_{i=1}^{N} p_i^{1-\varepsilon}\right)^{-\varepsilon/(1-\varepsilon)}$$

Using the definition of the price index I from equation 7.7 simplifies this expression to:

$$M = I^{\varepsilon-1} \delta Y \left(\sum_{i=1}^{N} p_i^{1-\varepsilon}\right)^{-\varepsilon/(1-\varepsilon)} = I^{\varepsilon-1} \delta Y I^{-\varepsilon} = \frac{\delta Y}{I}$$

This is discussed further in the main text.

Technical Note 7.3 Derivation of equation 7.13

The demand x for a variety can be written as $x = Bp^{-\varepsilon}$, where B is some constant (see the discussion in section 7.3.1 where we explained that firms take I and Y as given). Substitute in the profit function to get:

$$\pi = Bp^{1-\varepsilon} - W\left(\alpha + \beta Bp^{-\varepsilon}\right)$$

Profits are now a function of the firm's price only. Differentiating with respect to the price p and equating to 0 gives the first-order condition:

$$(1-\varepsilon) Bp^{-\varepsilon} + \varepsilon W \beta Bp^{-\varepsilon-1} = 0$$

Cancelling the term $Bp^{-\varepsilon}$ and rearranging gives equation 7.13.

Technical Note 7.4 Derivation of equations 7.14 to 7.16

Put profits in equation 7.12 equal to zero and use the pricing rule $p\left(1 - \dfrac{1}{\varepsilon}\right) = \beta W$ from equation 7.13 to get the following successive steps: $px - W(\alpha + \beta x) = 0$;
$px = \alpha W + \beta Wx$;

$$\left(\frac{\varepsilon}{\varepsilon-1} \beta W\right) x = \alpha W + \beta Wx ; \quad \left(\frac{\varepsilon}{\varepsilon-1} - 1\right) \beta Wx = \alpha W ; \quad x = \frac{\alpha(\varepsilon-1)}{\beta}$$

This explains equation 7.14. Now use the production function 7.11 to calculate the amount of labour required to produce this much output: $l_i = \alpha + \beta x$

$$= \alpha + \beta \frac{\alpha(\varepsilon-1)}{\beta} = \alpha + \alpha(\varepsilon-1) = \alpha\varepsilon .$$

This explains equation 7.15. Equation 7.16, finally, which determines the number of varieties N produced, simply follows by dividing the total number of manufacturing workers by the number of workers needed to produce one variety.

Technical Note 7.5 Derivation of equation 7.18

The number of firms in region s equals $\dfrac{\lambda_s \gamma L}{\alpha\varepsilon}$. The price these firms from region s charge in region r equals $\dfrac{\beta W_s T_{rs}}{\rho}$. Substituting these two results in the price index for manufactures (equation 7.8, defined in equation 7.7), assuming that there are $R \geq 2$ regions, gives the price index for region r as:

$$I_r = \left(\sum_{s=1}^{R} \left(\frac{\lambda_s \gamma L}{\alpha \varepsilon} \right) \left(\frac{\beta W_s T_{rs}}{\rho} \right)^{1-\varepsilon} \right)^{\frac{1}{1-\varepsilon}} = \left(\frac{\beta}{\rho} \right) \left(\frac{\gamma L}{\alpha \varepsilon} \right)^{\frac{1}{1-\varepsilon}} \left(\sum_{s=1}^{R} \lambda_s W_s^{1-\varepsilon} T_{rs}^{1-\varepsilon} \right)^{\frac{1}{1-\varepsilon}}$$

Equation 7.18 in the text is a special case for $R = 2$ and $r = 1$.

Technical Note 7.6 Derivation of equation 7.22

Equation 7.7 gives the demand for an individual consumer in a region. If we replace in that equation the income level Y with the income level Y_r of region r, the price index I with the price index I_r of region r, and the price p_j of the manufactured good with the price $\beta W_s T_{rs} / \rho$ which a producer from region s will charge in region r, we get the demand in region r for a product from region s:

$$\delta Y_r \left(\frac{\beta W_s T_{rs}}{\rho} \right)^{-\varepsilon} I_r^{\varepsilon-1} = \delta (\beta / \rho)^{-\varepsilon} Y_r W_s^{-\varepsilon} T_{rs}^{-\varepsilon} I_r^{\varepsilon-1}$$

To fulfil this consumption demand in region r note that T_{rs} units have to be shipped and produced. To derive the total demand in all $R \geq 2$ regions for a manufactured good produced in region s, we must sum production demand over all regions (that is, sum over the index r in the above equation and multiply each entry by T_{rs}):

$$\delta (\beta / \rho)^{-\varepsilon} \sum_{r=1}^{R} Y_r W_s^{-\varepsilon} T_{rs}^{1-\varepsilon} I_r^{\varepsilon-1} = \delta (\beta / \rho)^{-\varepsilon} W_s^{-\varepsilon} \sum_{r=1}^{R} Y_r T_{rs}^{1-\varepsilon} I_r^{\varepsilon-1}$$

In equilibrium this total demand for a manufactured good from region s must be equal to its supply $(\varepsilon - 1)\alpha / \beta$; see equation 7.14. Equalizing these two expressions gives:

$$\frac{(\varepsilon - 1)\alpha}{\beta} = \delta (\beta / \rho)^{-\varepsilon} W_s^{-\varepsilon} \sum_{r=1}^{R} Y_r T_{rs}^{1-\varepsilon} I_r^{\varepsilon-1}$$

Which can be solved for the wage rate W_s in region s:

$$W_s = \rho \beta^{-\rho} \left(\frac{\delta}{(\varepsilon - 1)\alpha} \right)^{1/\varepsilon} \left(\sum_{r=1}^{R} Y_r T_{rs}^{1-\varepsilon} I_r^{\varepsilon-1} \right)^{1/\varepsilon}$$

Equation 7.22 in the text is a special case for $R = 2$ and $r = 1$.

Technical Note 7.7 Deriving the price index effect around the spreading equilibrium

To derive the price index effect for small changes around the symmetric equilibrium, write equation 7.24 as $I_1^{1-\varepsilon} = \lambda_1 W_1^{1-\varepsilon} + \lambda_2 T^{1-\varepsilon} W_2^{1-\varepsilon}$ and totally differentiate:

$$(1-\varepsilon) I_1^{-\varepsilon} dI_1 = \overbrace{W_1^{1-\varepsilon} d\lambda_1}^{a} + \overbrace{(1-\varepsilon)\lambda_1 W_1^{-\varepsilon} dW_1}^{b} +$$

$$+ \underbrace{T^{1-\varepsilon} W_2^{1-\varepsilon} d\lambda_2}_{c} + \underbrace{(1-\varepsilon)\lambda_2 T^{1-\varepsilon} W_2^{-\varepsilon} dW_2}_{d} + \underbrace{(1-\varepsilon)\lambda_2 T^{-\varepsilon} W_2^{1-\varepsilon} dT}_{e}$$

Around the spreading equilibrium, the changes are identical but of opposite sign, so defining $dI \equiv dI_1 = -dI_2$, $dW \equiv dW_1 = -dW_2$, and $d\lambda \equiv d\lambda_1 = -d\lambda_2$ allows us to combine terms a and c and terms b and d. We ignore changes in transport cost, so term e is zero. In the steps below, we first collect terms, then evaluate at the symmetric equilibrium with $\lambda \equiv \lambda_1 = \lambda_2 = 0.5$, $W \equiv W_1 = W_2 = 1$, and $I^{1-\varepsilon} \equiv I_1^{1-\varepsilon} = I_2^{1-\varepsilon} = \lambda(1+T^{1-\varepsilon})$, and finally divide by the term $(1-\varepsilon)\lambda(1+T^{1-\varepsilon})$ to simplify as follows:

$$(1-\varepsilon)I^{1-\varepsilon}\frac{dI}{I} = (1-T^{1-\varepsilon})\lambda W^{1-\varepsilon}\frac{d\lambda}{\lambda} + (1-\varepsilon)(1-T^{1-\varepsilon})\lambda W^{1-\varepsilon}\frac{dW}{W}$$

$$(1-\varepsilon)\lambda(1+T^{1-\varepsilon})\frac{dI}{I} = (1-T^{1-\varepsilon})\lambda W^{1-\varepsilon}\frac{d\lambda}{\lambda} + (1-\varepsilon)(1-T^{1-\varepsilon})\lambda W^{1-\varepsilon}\frac{dW}{W}$$

$$\frac{dI}{I} = -\frac{1}{(\varepsilon-1)}\frac{(1-T^{1-\varepsilon})}{(1+T^{1-\varepsilon})}\frac{d\lambda}{\lambda} + \frac{(1-T^{1-\varepsilon})}{(1+T^{1-\varepsilon})}\frac{dW}{W}$$

Let $Z \equiv \dfrac{(1-T^{1-\varepsilon})}{(1+T^{1-\varepsilon})}$. This definition of Z can be interpreted as an index of trade costs; in the absence of transport costs (for $T=1$) the term Z is equal to zero, while Z approaches one if transport costs become arbitrarily high (as $T \to \infty$). If we denote relative changes by a tilde (as in $\tilde{x} \equiv dx/x$), use the index of trade costs Z, and note from the optimal price equation 7.13 that wage changes are proportional to price changes ($\tilde{p} = \tilde{W}$) and from equation 7.16 that labour force changes are proportional to changes in the number of varieties ($\tilde{\lambda} = \tilde{N}$), we can write the last expression also as: $\tilde{I} = Z\tilde{p} - (Z/(\varepsilon-1))\tilde{N}$.

Technical Note 7.8 Sustain point
Following the procedure as described in section 7.8.1 the implied wage in region 2, given complete agglomeration of manufacturing in region 1, is given by:

$$W_2 = \left(\frac{1+\delta}{2}T^{1-\varepsilon} + \frac{1-\delta}{2}T^{\varepsilon-1}\right)^{1/\varepsilon}$$

Using that to determine the implied real wage in region 2, it is convenient to note that:

$$w_2^\varepsilon = \frac{1+\delta}{2}T^{1-\varepsilon-\varepsilon\delta} + \frac{1-\delta}{2}T^{\varepsilon-1-\varepsilon\delta} = \frac{1+\delta}{2}T^{-(\rho+\delta)\varepsilon} + \frac{1-\delta}{2}T^{(\rho-\delta)\varepsilon} \equiv f(T)$$

$$f'(T) = \varepsilon\left(-\frac{1+\delta}{2}(\rho+\delta)T^{-(\rho+\delta)\varepsilon-1} + \frac{1-\delta}{2}(\rho-\delta)T^{(\rho-\delta)\varepsilon-1}\right)$$

$$f(1) = 1; \quad f'(1) = -\varepsilon\delta(1+\rho) < 0; \quad \lim_{T\to\infty} f(T) = \infty \Leftrightarrow \rho > \delta$$

The starting value of f at $T=1$ is thus one, with f continuously declining towards zero if $\rho < \delta$ and f initially declining, reaching a minimum, and then approaching infinity if $\rho > \delta$. In the latter case, which is analysed in section 7.8.1, f is thus equal to one for some value $T > 1$.

Technical Note 7.9 Stability of the spreading equilibrium

To analyse the break point we want to know what happens to the real wage if labour relocates to another region, making that region a little larger than the region from which labour originates. We have to analyse the change of real wages around the symmetric equilibrium. From equation 7.26 we know that we need two pieces of information: the change in the nominal wage, and the change in the price index. If we have these we can calculate the change in the real wage. If the real wage rises in the larger region, all footloose labour will follow, so the symmetric equilibrium is unstable. If the real wage falls the defecting worker will return to the original location, so the symmetric equilibrium is stable.

The spreading equilibrium is given by $\lambda \equiv \lambda_1 = \lambda_1 = 1/2$, $W \equiv W_1 = W_2 = 1$, $Y \equiv Y_1 = Y_2 = 1/2$, and $I^{1-\varepsilon} \equiv I_1^{1-\varepsilon} = I_1^{1-\varepsilon} = I_2^{1-\varepsilon} = \lambda(1+T^{1-\varepsilon})$. We want to investigate changes in the equilibrium if an infinitesimal number of workers are relocating from region 1 to region 2, where we will ignore all second-order effects of induced changes for the other regions. Thus we can write $dI \equiv dI_1 = -dI_2$, $dW \equiv dW_1 = -dW_2$, and $d\lambda \equiv d\lambda_1 = -d\lambda_2$, differentiate equation 7.23 and evaluate at the spreading equilibrium to get:[17]

$$dY = \delta d\lambda + \frac{\delta}{2} dW \tag{*1}$$

Doing the same with equation 7.24 gives:

$$(1-\varepsilon)\frac{dI}{I} = I^{\varepsilon-1}(1-T^{1-\varepsilon})\left(\frac{1-\varepsilon}{2}dW + d\lambda\right)$$

Define the index of transport barriers $Z \equiv (1-T^{1-\varepsilon})/(1+T^{1-\varepsilon})$, as in section 7.7 and Technical Note 7.7, and remember that Z ranges from zero when there are no transport costs $(T = 1)$ to one when transport costs are prohibitive $(T \to \infty)$. This notation allows us to rewrite the above equation as:

$$\frac{dI}{I} = \frac{2Z}{1-\varepsilon}d\lambda + ZdW \tag{*2}$$

Differentiating equations 7.25 and 7.26 and evaluating at the spreading equilibrium gives:

$$\varepsilon dW = 2ZdY + (\varepsilon-1)Z\frac{dI}{I} \tag{*3}$$

$$I^\delta dw = dW - \delta\frac{dI}{I} \tag{*4}$$

The four (*) equations above can be solved to determine the effect of a small disturbance on the real wage. Substitute (*1) in (*3) and combining with (*2) gives:

$$
\begin{bmatrix} 1 & -Z \\ Z & (\varepsilon - \delta Z)/(1-\varepsilon) \end{bmatrix} \begin{bmatrix} dI/I \\ dW \end{bmatrix} = \begin{bmatrix} 2Z/(1-\varepsilon)d\lambda \\ 2Z\delta/(1-\varepsilon)d\lambda \end{bmatrix}
$$

Solving this system of linear equations gives:

$$
\begin{bmatrix} dI/I \\ dW \end{bmatrix} = \frac{1}{\Delta} \begin{bmatrix} (\varepsilon - \delta Z)/(1-\varepsilon) & Z \\ -Z & 1 \end{bmatrix} \begin{bmatrix} 2Z/(1-\varepsilon)d\lambda \\ 2Z\delta/(1-\varepsilon)d\lambda \end{bmatrix},
$$

Where $\Delta \equiv \left((1-\varepsilon)Z^2 - \delta Z + \varepsilon\right)/(1-\varepsilon)$. This implies:

$$
\frac{dI}{I} = \frac{d\lambda}{\Delta}\frac{2Z\varepsilon}{(1-\varepsilon)^2}(1-\delta Z) \text{ and } dW = \frac{d\lambda}{\Delta}\frac{2Z\varepsilon}{(1-\varepsilon)^2}(\delta - Z).
$$

These are the two pieces of information we need. Substituting these results in equation (*4) gives the change in the real wage:

$$
\frac{dw}{d\lambda} = \frac{2ZI^{-\delta}}{(\varepsilon-1)}\left(\frac{\delta(2\varepsilon-1) - Z\left(\varepsilon(1+\delta^2)-1\right)}{\varepsilon - \delta Z - (\varepsilon-1)Z^2}\right) = \frac{2ZI^{-\delta}(1-\rho)}{\rho}\left(\frac{\delta(1+\rho) - Z(\delta^2+\rho)}{1 - \delta Z(1-\rho) - \rho Z^2}\right)
$$

The spreading equilibrium is unstable if $dw/d\lambda$ is positive. The sign depends on the numerator of the expression since the denominator is always positive. Therefore $dw/d\lambda = 0$ if, and only if, the transport cost index $Z = \delta(1+\rho)/(\delta^2+\rho)$. The equilibrium is thus unstable if $Z < \delta(1+\rho)/(\delta^2+\rho)$, while it is stable if the opposite holds. Note that in equation 7.30 in the main text we add one to both sides of the equation to facilitate the comparison of the sustain point and break point in Figure 7.8.

Exercises

Question 7.1 Geo Econ Example

Go to the website of the book and study the example. Start again from the example developed on the website, but now assume that each firm has the possibility to open a second plant in the other region. Each firm minimizes the combined costs of setting up a second plant and transportation costs. Suppose setting up a firm costs 2 units. Decide where to locate given the location of the other firms.

a. If all other firms have a single firm in South, what is optimal for our firm?
b. Suppose all firms have two plants, one in each location; what is optimal for our firm?

Question 7.2 Prices and Wages

Derive the equilibrium price for each variety in the manufacturing sector in the monopolistic competition model developed in section 7.2 by using equations 7.6 and 7.13. Once you have found the equilibrium price for each variety, calculate the associated equilibrium wage. The important lesson from this exercise is that once you have calculated the equilibrium price, the equilibrium wage rate follows.

Question 7.3 Perfect and Imperfect Competition

From introductory micro-economics we know that the condition for profit maximization for a firm is $MC = MR$, that is marginal costs equals marginal revenue. Under perfect competition this condition implies that $MC = p$, that is marginal cost is equal to the price of a good (marginal cost pricing). Now use Figure 7.1 to show that with the average cost curve in the core model (use equation 7.10), marginal cost pricing always results in a loss for the firm, implying that imperfect competition is the dominant market form.

Question 7.4* Equilibrium

Suppose we start with a situation of complete agglomeration of manufacturing production in region 1, that is $\lambda_1 = 1$. Without calculating the equilibrium values explicitly one might suspect that $W_1 = 1$ is the equilibrium value in this case. Substituting this in the income and price equations we find:

$$Y_1 = \frac{1+\delta}{2} \;;$$

$$Y_2 = \frac{1-\delta}{2};$$

$$I_1 = 1\;;\; I_2 = T$$

Using these values, $W_1 = 1$ is indeed an equilibrium value for wages in region 1, as can be verified. Real wages also equal one in region 1. Calculate under which condition this is always a long-run equilibrium no matter how large transportation costs become.

[Hint: use the expression for real wages in region 2 for this case and let T become arbitrarily large.] Show that this only happens if $(\varepsilon - 1) - \varepsilon\delta < 0$.

Question 7.5* Optimal Price

Suppose a monopolistic producer located in region 1 can either sell in region 1 or in region 2. Let p_{11} be the price charged in region 1, p_{12} the price charged in region 2, x_{11} the demand in region 1, and x_{12} the demand in region 2. Obviously, the demand functions depend on the price charged in either region. Production requires only labour as an input, which is paid wage rate W_1 and benefits from internal returns to scale, using α fixed labour and β variable labour. Finally, there are (iceberg) transport costs: the firm must produce Tx_{12} units to ensure x_{12} can be sold in region 2, with $T > 1$. The firm's profit π and demand functions x_{11} and x_{12} (with $\varepsilon > 1$ and Y_1 and Y_2 treated as constants) are given below:

$$\pi = p_{11}x_{11} + p_{12}x_{12} - W_1\left(\alpha + \beta x_{11} + \beta Tx_{12}\right);\; x_{11} = p_{11}^{-\varepsilon}Y_1\;;\; x_{12} = p_{12}^{-\varepsilon}Y_2$$

First, give some comments on the profit function above. Second, substitute the demand functions in the profit function. Third, determine what the optimal prices

p_{11} and p_{12} are; that is, solve the profit maximization problem. Fourth, show that $p_{12} = Tp_{11}$; that is, the optimal price charged in region 2 is exactly T times higher than charged in region 1.

Question 7.6 *Welfare

In the example developed on the website we showed that some equilibria are better from a welfare perspective than other equilibria. Can you show this using equations 7.23 to 7.26? Assume that the farmers are not symmetrically distributed over both regions. Suppose region 1 has $1/3$ of all farmers and region 2 has $2/3$ of all farmers. Can you show that from a welfare point of view, agglomeration in region 2 is better than agglomeration in region 1, as might be expected because region 2 potentially has the largest market?

[Hint: make sure that complete agglomeration in region 1 and complete agglomeration in region 2 are both equilibria.] Use the resulting equations to show that (U indicates utility)

For $\lambda_1 = 1$ we have: $U_{\lambda_1=1} = 1 + \frac{1}{3}(1-\delta) + \frac{2}{3}(1-\delta)T^{-\delta}$

And for $\lambda_1 = 0$ we have: $U_{\lambda_1=0} = 1 + \frac{2}{3}(1-\delta) + \frac{1}{3}(1-\delta)T^{-\delta}$

Question 7.7 *Home Market Effect

Technical Note 7.7 derives the price index effect around the spreading equilibrium. Following a similar procedure, do the same for the home market effect by first rewriting equation 7.25, then totally differentiating this equation, and subsequently collecting terms and evaluating at the spreading equilibrium to show that: $\varepsilon\tilde{W} = Z\tilde{Y} + (\varepsilon-1)Z\tilde{I}$.

Question 7.8 Break Point Versus Sustain Point

The text in this chapter has not proved that the break point arises for a lower value of transport costs T than the sustain point. Convince yourself that it does, by calculating these values for a grid of admissible (ρ,δ)-parameter combinations, as in Figure 7.8.

Question 7.9 Break Point

Explicitly calculate the break point as a function of the transport costs T; your answer should be:

$$T = \left(\frac{(\rho-\delta)(1-\delta)}{(\rho+\delta)(1+\delta)}\right)^{1/(1-\varepsilon)}$$

Question 7.10 Transport Costs

Go to the website of the book where you will find Excel files containing the data and some of the figures used in this book. Look up the file for Figure 7.7, where you will find additional information on the relationship between the relative real wage and transport costs. Make xy-scatter plots (using smoothed lines) for the transport cost ranges $T = 1.50;1.55;1.60;1.65;170$ and $T = 1.75;1.80;1.85;1.90$. Comment on your findings (in terms of stability).

8 Extensions of the Core Model

LEARNING OBJECTIVES

- To understand the structure and location implications of the intermediate goods model (with output of final goods also as an input for the production process).
- To know the generalized model (with the core model and intermediate goods model as special cases) and its main implications (Tomahawk diagram versus bell-shaped curve).
- To understand how an additional factor of production (human capital) gives rise to the solvable model and how to apply all models in a many-location setting.
- To know the empirics of urban power laws and understand how geographical economics models can help to explain these laws by adding a spreading force (congestion) to the core model of geographical economics.

8.1 Introduction

Chapter 7 developed and analysed the main features of the core model of geographical economics. The model provides a coherent framework: it is a miniature world in which the demand in one region for the manufactures of another region is not exogenously imposed, but derived from the income generated in the region through production and exports. We used simulations to better understand the dynamic characteristics of the core model, as summarized in the Tomahawk diagram. Building on this knowledge, we now provide three main steps in this chapter to further enhance our knowledge of geographical economics. The model extensions are also welcome because for most parameter configurations the core model of Chapter 7 gives only two stable long-run equilibria (recall the Tomahawk diagram), either full agglomeration or perfect spreading. This is too stark to be true. In the real world it is not true that either all footloose activity ends up in one location or in multiple locations that are all of equal size. So when we want to apply geographical economics to empirical or policy matters, we need a more diversified arsenal of models. This is what we will deliver in Chapter 8, which proceeds in three steps.

First, we discuss three alternative geographical economics models in sections 8.2–8.4. Each of these models could be labelled an alternative 'core' model, but to avoid confusion we will only use the term core to refer to the model developed in Chapter 7. In Part IV we will see how these models can be and have been used for empirical and policy applications. The three alternative models are:

- The *intermediate goods model.* In the absence of inter-locational labour mobility, the main agglomeration mechanism is the connection to suppliers of intermediate goods.
- The *generalized model.* Incorporating both the core model of Chapter 7 and the intermediate goods model in one framework allows for a richer menu of long-run equilibria.
- The *solvable model.* Identifying different factors of production in the manufacturing sector (one mobile and one not) allows for explicit analytical solutions.

Second, we extend the geographical economics model to a more general, multiple-location setting in section 8.5 and introduce congestion as an additional spreading force in section 8.6. The reason for analysing congestion is not only based on the empirical relevance of congestion itself, but also on the empirical observation of the co-existence of many cities of different size at any given time period. The latter aspect is hard to explain by the core model of geographical economics as we show that the agglomerating forces tend to be too strong, leading to only a few large locations. Adding congestion to the core model allows for the economic viability of locations of different sizes. This model of geographical economics will also pop up again in the empirical and policy discussion of Chapters 9–11.

Third, we connect geographical economics with urban economics in sections 8.7 and 8.8 when we return to the analysis of urban systems (see Chapter 5), in particular regarding the city-size distribution that can be characterized by a power law, with Zipf's Law as a special case. In Chapter 5 we used Zipf's Law and the power laws characterizing most city-size distributions to motivate the discussion on models of city systems but we ended the chapter without a convincing (economic!) explanation for the documented stylized facts on city-size distributions and in particular Zipf's Law. We will return to the empirical relevance of urban power laws in sections 8.7 and 8.8 and show how the core model with congestion can be used to better understand changes in power law exponents related to changes in economic conditions. We conclude in section 8.9 with a brief summary of what we have learned.

8.2   Intermediate Inputs Without Inter-Regional Labour Mobility

In this section we develop a model where intermediate inputs in the manufacturing production process open up an alternative channel for agglomeration.[1] The presence of intermediate inputs creates upstream and downstream linkages: where upstream sectors deliver intermediate goods used as inputs for downstream final products. The crucial simplifying assumption is that the products demanded by consumers as final goods are also used in the production process as intermediate inputs. As every consumer demands every variety (love-of-variety), we also assume that each manufacturing firm uses every good as an intermediate input in its production process. Moreover, we assume (as is customary in international trade theory) that labour is mobile *between sectors* within a location, but *not between locations*. There are thus two main differences with the core model of Chapter 7, namely (i) there are intermediate goods in the production process and (ii) labour is not mobile between locations. Otherwise, the model is quite similar; see Figure 8.1. Workers can be employed in both sectors and receive wage income in exchange for labour. This income is spent on both food and manufactures. As we will see in Chapter 10, this specification of a geographical economics model has for instance been used as a foundation for a discussion of the consequences of globalization on the spatial allocation of economic activity across the globe.

We now turn to the model in more detail.

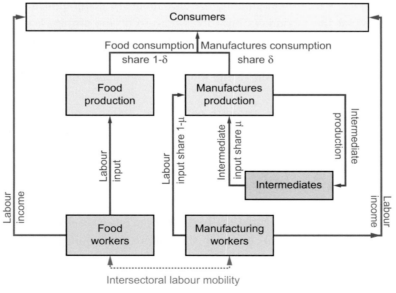

Figure 8.1 Intermediate goods model

---

[1] The model is based on Krugman and Venables (1995) and Venables (1996). Our discussion follows the exposition in Fujita, Krugman, and Venables (1999, ch. 14).

8.2.1   Demand

The demand side of the model is familiar. There are two sectors, a food sector F which is used as numéraire and a manufacturing sector M. Every consumer has Cobb-Douglas preferences for determining spending on food and manufactures (shares δ and $1-\delta$, respectively; equation 8.1) and a CES sub-utility function to determine spending on manufacturing varieties (equation 8.2). Maximizing this sub-utility function subject to the relevant income constraint (the part δY spent on manufactures) gives consumer demand for each variety j as given in equation 8.3, where I is the price index for manufactures, $\varepsilon \equiv 1/(1-\rho)$ is the elasticity of substitution, and Y is consumer income.

$$U = M^{\delta}F^{1-\delta} \tag{8.1}$$

$$M = \left(\sum_{i=1}^{N} c_i^{\rho}\right)^{1/\rho} \tag{8.2}$$

$$\bar{c}_j = p_j^{-\varepsilon}I^{\varepsilon-1}\delta Y \ ; \ I \equiv \left(\sum_{i=1}^{N} p_i^{1-\varepsilon}\right)^{1/(1-\varepsilon)} \tag{8.3}$$

So far the model is almost the same as the core model of Chapter 7. The major difference on the demand side is that firms also use varieties from the M sector as intermediate inputs. Assuming that all varieties are necessary in the production process and that the elasticity of substitution is the same for firms as for consumers, we can use the same CES-aggregator function for producers as for consumers, with the same corresponding price index I. Given that we now also have to take spending on intermediate goods into account, we can derive total demand for a variety depending on *total* spending $E = \delta Y + \mu npx^*$, where the first term represents the share of consumer income spent on manufactures and the second term represents intermediate input demand (equal to the value of all varieties produced in a region npx^* multiplied by the share μ of intermediates in the production process; see below) as in equation 8.4.

$$c_j = p_j^{-\varepsilon}I^{\varepsilon-1}E \tag{8.4}$$

8.2.2   Manufacturing Supply

Each firm producing variety i uses both labour and all varieties as intermediate inputs. The production process is a Cobb-Douglas composite of labour (with price W for the wage rate) and intermediates (with price index I). Total costs $C(x_i)$ are given in equation 8.5, where the coefficients α and β are the fixed cost and marginal input requirement for the production of varieties. Maximizing profits gives the familiar mark-up pricing rule (note that marginal costs now consists of *two* elements: labour and intermediates) as given in equation 8.6, which simplifies to $p_i = I^{\mu}W^{1-\mu}$ using our normalization $\beta = 1-1/\varepsilon$. Note that the price index I in equation 8.4 is now a function of I itself, because of the presence of intermediate goods. Note also that the equations reduce to those in Chapter 7 if $\mu = 0$ (no intermediate inputs). Use the zero profit condition $p_i x_i = I^\mu W^{1-\mu} (\alpha + \beta x_i)$ and the mark-up pricing rule 8.6 to determine the break-even supply of a variety i (each produced by a single firm) in equation 8.7. Substituting this in the labour demand function $l = \alpha + \beta x$ gives $l = \alpha \varepsilon$ and thus $N = \lambda L / \alpha \varepsilon = \lambda / \alpha \varepsilon$ for our normalizations.[2] We can use this in the expression for total expenditures E. To determine the income Y of workers, we take a closer look at the agricultural sector.

$$C(x_i) = I^\mu W_i^{1-\mu} (\alpha + \beta x_i) \qquad 8.5$$

$$p_i (1 - 1/\varepsilon) = \beta I^\mu W^{1-\mu} \qquad 8.6$$

$$x_i = \frac{\alpha}{1-\beta} = \alpha \varepsilon \equiv x^* \qquad 8.7$$

As in Chapter 7, the term x^* denotes the equilibrium supply of a manufacturing variety by a single firm (equation 8.7).

8.2.3 Supply of Food

The income of consumers comes from two sources, namely the wages earned in the manufacturing sector analysed above and the income earned in the agricultural sector. As in Chapter 7, we use food as numéraire and assume that it is freely tradable between locations. Food production F depends on the amount of labour available in the agricultural sector L_F such that $F = F(L_F)$. We will focus on two possibilities:

Constant returns to scale: $F = 1 - \lambda$. This option is analysed in this section. A proper choice of units ensures $W = 1$. Consequently, in the long-run equilibrium nominal wages will not only be equal in the manufacturing and food sectors, but also between locations.
Decreasing returns to scale: $F'(1 - \lambda) > 0$ and $F''(1 - \lambda) < 0$. This option leads to rather different outcomes, because in the long-run equilibrium wages will be equal for the two sectors within a location, but may differ between locations. Section 8.3 analyses this case with inter-regional wage differences as an additional spreading force.[3]

Consumer income equals the sum of wage income and the output in the food sector (the numéraire), so for two regions we have:

$$Y_1 = W_1 \lambda_1 + F(1 - \lambda_1); \ Y_2 = W_2 \lambda_2 + F(1 - \lambda_2) \qquad 8.8$$

---

[2] Note that the distribution of labour between the two regions is given. For two identical countries we can still use $L = 1$. Because labour is mobile between sectors we only have one parameter (λ) to describe the distribution of labour between manufactures and food.
[3] See also Puga (1999, pp. 306–307). One reason for assuming diminishing returns is to think of a second production factor in food production (such as land) that is in fixed supply and only used in food production.

Labour mobility between locations (migration) is not possible by assumption, and thus only takes place between sectors within a location. Workers in either sector living in the same location face the same price index, implying that the difference between *nominal* wages determines if a worker moves from one sector to the other:

$$\frac{d\lambda}{\lambda} = \eta\left(W - F'(1-\lambda)\right)$$ 8.9

We thus assume that the wage rate in the agricultural sector is equal to the marginal product of labour and that workers move to the sector with the higher wage rate (with speed of adjustment parameter η). If both sectors produce positive amounts, equilibrium wages are the same. If $\lambda = 1$, wages in the manufacturing sector are higher than in the food sector. If $\lambda = 0$ wages in the manufacturing sector are lower than in the food sector.

8.2.4 Equilibrium with Transport Costs

Transportation of food is costless but for manufactures it is costly, consisting of iceberg transport costs $T > 1$ between the two locations. Total demand for a variety is the sum of the demand from the two locations, where consumers and firms in the other location have to pay transportation costs on their imports:

$$x_1 = E_1 p_1^{-\varepsilon} I_1^{\varepsilon-1} + E_2 p_2^{-\varepsilon} T^{-\varepsilon} I_2^{\varepsilon-1} \; ; \; x_2 = E_2 p_2^{-\varepsilon} I_2^{\varepsilon-1} + E_1 p_1^{-\varepsilon} T^{-\varepsilon} I_1^{\varepsilon-1}$$ 8.10

We already know that the break-even supply is equal to $x^* = \alpha / (1 - \beta)$. Equating this to total demand gives:[4]

$$\frac{\alpha}{1-\beta} = E_1 p_1^{-\varepsilon} I_1^{\varepsilon-1} + E_2 p_2^{-\varepsilon} T^{-\varepsilon} I_2^{\varepsilon-1} \; ; \; \frac{\alpha}{1-\beta} = E_2 p_2^{-\varepsilon} I_2^{\varepsilon-1} + E_1 p_1^{-\varepsilon} T^{-\varepsilon} I_1^{\varepsilon-1}$$ 8.11

Inserting the mark-up pricing rule in equation 8.11 and solving for the wage rate gives the two-region wage equation in the presence of intermediate demand for varieties:[5]

$$W_1 = \left(\frac{1-\beta}{\alpha}\right)^{\frac{1}{\varepsilon(1-\mu)}} I_1^{-\frac{\mu}{1-\mu}} \left(E_1 I_1^{\varepsilon-1} + E_2 T^{1-\varepsilon} I_2^{\varepsilon-1}\right)^{\frac{1}{\varepsilon(1-\mu)}} \; ;$$

$$W_2 = \left(\frac{1-\beta}{\alpha}\right)^{\frac{1}{\varepsilon(1-\mu)}} I_2^{-\frac{\mu}{1-\mu}} \left(E_2 I_2^{\varepsilon-1} + E_1 T^{1-\varepsilon} I_1^{\varepsilon-1}\right)^{\frac{1}{\varepsilon(1-\mu)}}$$ 8.12

These equations closely resemble the wage equations that we already derived for the core model of Chapter 7 (in fact, with $\mu = 0$ the wage equation is the

---

[4] Note that the demand from the other region is multiplied by T in order to compensate for the part that melts away during transportation.

[5] The motivation to derive a wage equation instead of a traditional equilibrium price equation is twofold. First, labour migration between regions is a function of (real) wages; second, in empirical applications this is useful because data on regional wages are easier to obtain than regional manufacturing price data.

same). There are also important differences. First, equation 8.12 does not use consumer income Y but total expenditures E. This indicates that demand for a variety comes not only from consumers but also from firms, who need varieties as intermediate inputs. Second, the terms $I_1^{-\mu/(1-\mu)}$ and $I_2^{-\mu/(1-\mu)}$ on the right-hand side of the equations show that the *lower* the price index, the higher the break-even wage rate can be. Thus, the closer a firm is to its suppliers of intermediate products, the lower its costs, and the higher the wage rate it can pay. We now have a second channel whereby the location of firms matters. Redding and Venables (2004) have dubbed it the *supplier access* effect. In Chapters 9 and 10 we will encounter both supplier and market access from an empirical point of view. This geographical economics model is also known as the *vertical linkages* model, as it introduces an extra agglomeration force through linkages between firms affecting production costs.

8.2.5   Intermediate Good Simulations

As in Chapter 7 for the core model, we can get a grip on the workings of the model by using simulations. Keep in mind that for the remainder of this section we assume that the production of food is characterized by constant returns to scale: $F = 1 - \lambda$. Repeating the exercise leading to the Tomahawk diagram of Chapter 7 for this model results in Figure 8.2. Note that we assume that δ (the share of income spent on manufactures) is smaller than one half.[6] This ensures that even if *all* manufactures are produced in a single country, both countries still produce

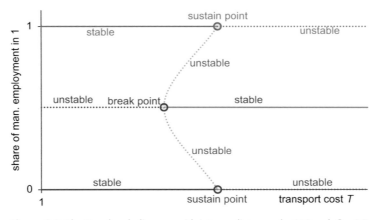

Figure 8.2 The Tomahawk diagram with intermediate goods: CRS and $\delta < 0.5$

---

[6] Compare sections 14.2 and 14.3 in Fujita, Krugman, and Venables (1999) on this matter.

food.[7] That, in turn, implies that the equilibrium wage rate in both countries is equal to 1. If δ is larger than one half and, say, all workers in region 1 produce manufactures, the remaining part of manufactures would have to be produced in region 2. In this situation, manufacturing wages in region 1 will differ from those in region 2 because inter-regional arbitrage through the food sector is no longer possible.

Figure 8.2 (with constant returns in food production and with $\delta < 0.5$) is qualitatively the same as the Tomahawk diagram of the core model of Chapter 7: the relation between transportation costs and long-run equilibria still looks like a tomahawk. The mechanisms behind agglomeration and spreading are, however, different. Potentially, there are *four* forces at work in this model, two of which are familiar (see Chapter 7 for a detailed explanation) and two of which are new.[8] The familiar forces are (i) the extent-of-competition effect (a higher λ results in more varieties, and thus more competition and a lower price index) and (ii) the market size effect (a higher λ increases the market for manufactures). The competition effect is a spreading force, the market size effect is an agglomerating force. The two new forces are (iii) the marginal productivity effect in the food sector (a reduction of employment in the food sector increases [for a concave production function] marginal productivity), and (iv) backward linkages (higher λ implies that firms have easy access to intermediate production of manufactures). The marginal productivity effect (not operative in this section) is a spreading force: if workers move from the food to the manufacturing sector because firms start to agglomerate in region 1, the existence of diminishing returns to food implies that wages will have to increase in region 1 compared to region 2 (thus creating inter-regional wage differences). The only new force in this section (backward linkages) is an agglomerating force. It is therefore, as Figure 8.2 shows, not surprising that the combination of these three forces again leads to the Tomahawk diagram, where low transport costs result in full agglomeration.

The analysis of the sustain and break points can be done in a similar fashion as with the core model. In fact the break condition for the Krugman and Venables (1995) model is the *same* as for the core model, with δ (the share of income spent on manufactures) being replaced by μ (the share of intermediate goods in the production process; Puga, 1999, p. 326; note that in our notation the last exponent is equal to -1):

---

[7] We often use the general term 'locations', of which cities, regions, and countries are special cases; to show how the approach can be applied to different situations we give examples for cities, regions, and countries.

[8] One force disappears: the cost of living effect. Migration between regions, by assumption, is not possible. So real wage effects on migration are not relevant in this model (but they remain important for welfare).

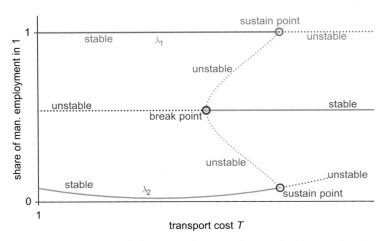

Figure 8.3 The Tomahawk diagram with intermediate goods: CRS and $\delta > 0.5$
Parameters: $\varepsilon = 5$; $\delta = 55$; $\mu = 0.4$

$$\varphi_{break} = T_{break}^{1-\varepsilon} = \left(\left(\frac{1+\mu}{1-\mu} \right) \left(\frac{\varepsilon(1+\mu)-1}{\varepsilon(1-\mu)-1} \right) \right)^{\frac{1-\varepsilon}{\varepsilon-1}}$$

To round up the discussion of the Krugman and Venables (1995) model we ask ourselves (see section 14.3 in Fujita, Krugman, and Venables, 1999) what happens under constant returns to scale if $\delta > 0.5$. The answer to this (seemingly innocuous) change is given in Figure 8.3.

Figure 8.3 looks rather similar to Figure 8.2, but it is not exactly the same upon closer inspection. The most visible change is the extent of specialization in manufactures in region 2. If we read along the horizontal axis from right to left in Figure 8.3, we know that there is a level of transport costs for which the symmetric equilibrium is no longer stable (the break point).[9] Now moving further to the left, region 1 becomes completely specialized in the production of manufactures, while some manufacturing production still takes place in region 2 (obviously, it could be *vice versa*: we could have swapped country labels). From the set-up of the model we already have some information about the nominal wages. In region 2 the (nominal) wages in both sectors are equal and identical to 1 (labour can freely move between sectors and wages in the food sector are equal to 1). In region 1, wages in the manufacturing sector are larger than or equal to 1 (if wages were smaller than 1, workers would be better off by starting to produce food).

A further reduction in transportation costs (moving further to the left) lowers the price index in region 1, and thus raises real wages. This decline in production

---

[9] Note that the sustain point is to the right of the breakpoint. So, agglomeration is already a stable equilibrium before symmetry becomes unstable.

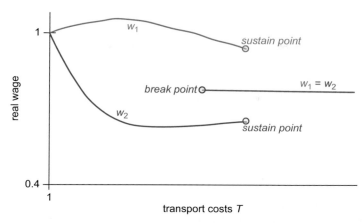

Figure 8.4 Real wages in both regions with intermediate goods: CRS and $\delta > 0.5$
Source: based on Krugman and Venables (1995); parameters: $\varepsilon = 5$; $\delta = 0.55$; $\mu = 0.4$.

costs drives up demand for labour, but labour supply is fixed by assumption. So market clearing on the labour market in region 1 results in higher wages. If transportation costs decline further, the advantage of being near consumers and producers of intermediate products becomes less important, and differences in wages become more important for production costs. This implies that the peripheral region becomes more attractive for manufacturing production as transport costs decline, which explains the curvature of λ_2 in Figure 8.3. This process stimulates manufacturing production in the peripheral region and drives up real wages until they become identical in both countries. Figure 8.4 illustrates this process by drawing the *real* wages for both regions.

Based on Figure 8.4, Krugman and Venables (1995) argue that the process depicted by the gradual lowering of transport costs T can be used to understand the globalization process from the late nineteenth century until the end of the twentieth century (they call it 'history of the world, part I'). In the two-region model with the regions *North* (let's say the OECD countries) and *South* (the developing countries), high transport costs (low levels of economic integration) go along with real wage equalization. When economic integration really takes off, one region (North) becomes the core region and real wages start to differ between North and South. This is what happened during a large part of the twentieth century. With ongoing integration (think of post-1990 globalization), real wages start to converge; see also Crafts and Venables (2003) and Baldwin (2006). In Chapter 10 we will discuss modern-day globalization and address the convergence of real income between 'North and South' building on Baldwin (2016) who has dubbed the period post-1990, with the fall of the Berlin Wall in 1989, the entry of China (and India) into the world economy, and the ICT revolution that enabled the international fragmentation of manufacturing production, as the period of The Great Convergence.

8.3   The Bell-Shaped Curve and a Generalized Model

As noted in the previous section, the intermediate goods model without inter-regional labour mobility may work quite differently once we replace the assumption of constant returns to scale in food production by diminishing returns to scale: $F = F(1 - \lambda)$, with $F'(1 - \lambda) > 0$ and $F''(1 - \lambda) < 0$. Once manufacturing firms start to agglomerate in a region, say region 1, the additional demand for manufacturing labour must pull workers out of the food sector in region 1. With diminishing returns for food production, fewer workers means higher productivity and thus higher nominal wages. This creates a wage difference between the two regions (wages remain equal between sectors within a region). In terms of the four agglomeration and spreading forces discussed in section 8.2.5, the third force (marginal productivity effect) now becomes operative. Dropping the assumption of a perfectly elastic supply of labour adds an additional spreading force to the model.

8.3.1   Decreasing Returns

Let's denote the elasticity of a region's labour supply by η. If $\eta = 0$, no inter-sectoral labour mobility is possible. If $\eta = \infty$ there is perfect labour mobility between sectors (infinite elasticity). In the latter case, wages in the manufacturing sector and the food sector are identical until a region becomes specialized in manufactures. If $0 < \eta < \infty$ migration from the food sector to the manufacturing sector can be consistent with a wage increase in *both* sectors. The inclusion of an upward-sloping labour supply function thus generalizes the Krugman (1991a) model of Chapter 7 (where $\eta = 0$) and the Krugman and Venables (1995) model of the previous section (where $\eta = \infty$). Most importantly, Puga (1999) shows that for $0 < \eta < \infty$ the bang-bang long-run character of the core model disappears.[10] With an upward-sloping labour supply function, agglomeration drives up wages in the core region, which reduces the incentive for firms to agglomerate (particularly for low transport costs). Without inter-regional labour mobility the long-run relationship between the transport costs (economic integration) and agglomeration *might* look like Figure 8.6, which has aptly been called the *bell-shaped curve* by Head and Mayer (2004) and Ottaviano and Thisse (2004).[11]

---

[10] This version (Puga, 1999) is also provided in section 14.4 of Fujita, Krugman, and Venables (1999).

[11] The exact shape of the curve depends on the parameter configuration; see Puga (1999) or Robert-Nicoud (2005). The important distinction is whether or not low transport costs lead to agglomeration or spreading. This is depicted 'smoothly' in Figure 8.6, but can also come from a double tomahawk or Pitchfork (Robert-Nicoud, 2005).

Before we discuss the Bell-shaped curve, we illustrate the workings of this model (maintaining $\delta < 0.5$) by drawing the relative wage rates of the two regions for three specific values of transport costs. Panel *a* of Figure 8.5 shows that for high transport costs ($T = 1.5$) the spreading equilibrium is stable, while panel *b* shows that for intermediate transport costs ($T = 1.3$), the spreading equilibrium is *un*stable. Both the results are the same as what we have seen before. The surprise lies in panel *c* of Figure 8.5 which shows that for *low* transport costs ($T = 1.1$) the spreading equilibrium is again *stable*. Apparently, for low enough transport costs the intermediate-linkage advantages created by agglomeration no longer dominate the cost disadvantage (high wages) as the other region can now always be supplied at relatively low cost.

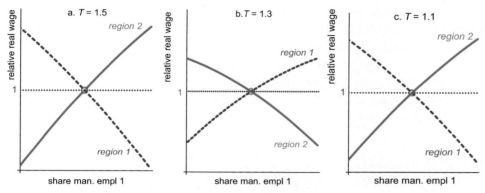

Figure 8.5 Relative wage rates: diminishing returns in food production

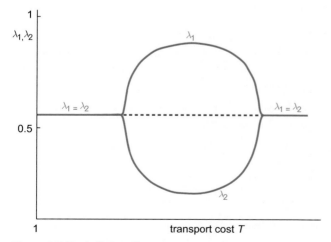

Figure 8.6 The bell-shaped curve

This discussion of Figure 8.5 explains the shape of the long-run equilibrium distribution curves given in Figure 8.6: spreading–agglomeration–spreading. This bell-shaped curve has become popular among empirical researchers (and policy makers) because (in contrast to the Tomahawk diagram) it does not predict catastrophic changes in agglomeration patterns as transportation costs fall. In addition, for low enough levels of transport costs, spreading forces start to dominate agglomeration forces, which is good news for peripheral regions or countries that can now benefit from ever increasing economic integration. As before, the empirical analysis will have to determine the position of the country or region within the diagram. Now, however, we also have to determine whether either the bell-shaped curve or the Tomahawk diagram is relevant in a given situation. We address these issues in Chapter 9 and Chapter 11. For a (largely non-technical) application of Tomahawks and Bell-shaped curves to EU regions see already Puga (2002). Before we move to solvable models (our third and final class of alternative models) in section 8.4, we discuss if other models can give rise to the bell-shape in Box 8.1 and analyse break and sustain points in section 8.3.2. The bell curve and the model upon which it is based (following Puga, 1999) will be used when we discuss how the degree of agglomeration changes when transport costs change.

BOX 8.1 Bell-shape or Tomahawk?

Is the intermediate goods model with decreasing returns in the food sector and without inter-regional labour mobility the only model giving rise to a Bell-shaped curve? To answer this question, Head and Mayer (2004, p. 2652) argue that the core model of Chapter 7

> continues to predict full agglomeration even as transport costs become tiny. This is because the 'centrifugal' forces that would promote dispersion decline with trade costs at an even more rapid rate than the 'centripetal' forces that promote agglomeration. With any other congestion [=spreading] force unrelated to trade costs, the equilibrium pattern of location will return to dispersion for some (low) trade costs threshold where all trade-related forces become so weak that they must dominate the congestion force

So, when one wants to get rid of the Tomahawk summarizing the core model, we need a spreading force that does not weaken when T falls. One way to do this, as we just learned, is to drop the assumption of inter-regional labour mobility and to replace it by inter-sectoral labour mobility with a positive wage elasticity. As Puga (1999, p. 322) notes:

BOX 8.1 (cont.)

This is because as trade costs continue to fall, the cost saving from being able to buy intermediates locally instead of having to import them falls with trade costs, but the wage gap between regions remains.

Other mechanisms may do the trick as well. Helpman (1998) replaces the agricultural sector with a housing sector, which can give rise to a bell-shaped curve despite the fact that this model assumes inter-regional labour mobility. In fact, the model is the same as the core model in all other respects. Housing acts as a non-traded consumption good. With a fixed supply of housing, agglomeration goes along with rising housing prices in the larger region. The increase in housing prices acts as a spreading force, the strength of which does *not* get weaker as transports costs fall.[12] In Chapter 9 we use the Helpman model in our discussion of attempts to estimate the equilibrium wage equation.[13]

8.3.2 Generalized Model

To analyse break and sustain points for the bell-shaped model we turn to Puga (1999), who develops a general model of geographical economics that includes all models discussed so far (including the core model itself) as a special case. In addition to the key model parameters of the core model δ, ε, and T (or $\varphi \equiv T^{1-\varepsilon}$, the so-called *free-ness of trade* parameter), the generalized model allows for an upward-sloping inter-sectoral labour supply curve (parameter $\eta > 0$) as well as for intermediate inputs (parameter μ). With these five model parameters, the generalized model is essentially a marriage between the core model of Chapter 7 and the intermediate input model outlined in section 8.2. It is analysed for two cases, namely (i) inter-regional labour mobility and (ii) inter-regional labour *im*mobility. This distinction is crucial, as it turns out that the model with inter-regional labour mobility yields a Tomahawk diagram (thus showing that the core model is just one model to do so) and the model *without* inter-regional labour mobility gives rise to the bell-shaped curve.

The conditions for the break points in these two general models, with and without inter-regional labour mobility, are given below.[14] The first break condition (for the general model with inter-regional labour mobility) looks familiar because with $\mu = 0$ (no intermediate inputs) and $\eta = 0$ (no inter-sectoral labour mobility between food and manufactures) it reduces to that of the core model; see Chapter 7.

---

[12] See also Ottaviano, Tabuschi, and Thisse (2002).

[13] For other models yielding a bell-shaped curve see Head and Mayer (2004a, pp. 2652–3).

[14] Similar relatively 'easy' expressions are again not available for the sustain points.

$$\varphi_{bream,mobile} = \left(1 + \frac{2(2\varepsilon - 1)(\delta + \mu(1-\delta))}{(1-\mu)((1-\delta)(\varepsilon(1-\delta)(1-\mu)-1))-\delta^2\eta}\right)^{\frac{1-\varepsilon}{\varepsilon-1}}$$

The break condition for the bell-shaped curve of the general model without inter-regional labour mobility is given by the quadratic expression in the free-ness of trade φ in in the equation below at the end of this section. Note from Figure 8.6 that we are looking for two roots or solutions of the equation, since the bell-shaped curve has two break points: one where full spreading turns into (partial) agglomeration and one where (partial) agglomeration turns into full spreading. The reader can again use the *break* excel file on the website to experiment with these two break conditions. Please keep in mind that these conditions have only been derived for the case of two regions.[15]

$$a\varphi^2_{break,immobile} + b\varphi_{break,immobile} + c = 0 \text{ , } where$$

$$a \equiv (\varepsilon(1+\mu)-1)((1+\mu)(1+\eta)+(1-\mu)\gamma)$$

$$b \equiv -2((\varepsilon(1+\mu^2)-1)(1+\eta)-\varepsilon(1-\mu)(2(\varepsilon-1)-\gamma\mu))$$

$$c \equiv (1-\mu)(\varepsilon(1-\mu)-1)(\eta+1-\gamma)$$

8.4 The Solvable Model: Two Factors of Production for Manufactures

The models discussed so far have one factor of production in the manufacturing sector. An extension of the model allowing for different production factors (such as skilled- and unskilled labour) makes the model suitable for analysing the effects of modern-day globalization (which tends to focus on this distinction). As a rather surprising bonus, it turns out that this extension simplifies matters in some respects as it allows us to derive an explicit analytical solution for equilibrium wages. This section briefly introduces the analytically solvable model developed independently by Rikard Forslid and Gianmarco Ottaviano and combined in Forslid and Ottaviano (2003).[16] The idea of using two factors of production in the

---

[15] Similar break conditions for N regions (with $N > 2$) only exist if one assumes that these regions are all at equal distance (see Puga, 1999, p. 306, footnote 6). This is a problem if we take bell curves or Tomahawks to the real world as discussed in Chapter 9.

[16] See also section 8.2.3 in Fujita and Thisse (2013) for an exposition of this solvable model. In general, these types of models lend themselves for policy analysis precisely because they are solvable and can be used for welfare analysis. Baldwin et al. (2003) is an excellent source for a discussion on solvable models in geographical economics, as are Combes, Mayer, and Thisse (2008) and Fujita and Thisse (2013).

manufacturing sector in the solvable model will be used in other chapters as well. In particular, our discussion on geography, growth, and development in Chapter 10 will centre around a further discussion and application of this very model (following Baldwin, 2016).

The general structure of the model is illustrated in Figure 8.7. Regarding the set-up of the model, we refer to the two production factors as labour and human capital. We assume that labour is *im*mobile but that human capital is mobile between regions (there is no inter-sectoral factor mobility). In practice, it is frequently argued that labour is less mobile than human capital. It is the ability to distinguish between mobile and immobile production factors in the manufacturing sector that explains why this model has become popular for policy analysis in the context of geographical economics (see Baldwin et al., 2003).

There are two regions ($j = 1,2$). Each region has L_j workers and K_j human capital.[17] Each agent is either a worker or a capital owner, where capital can be

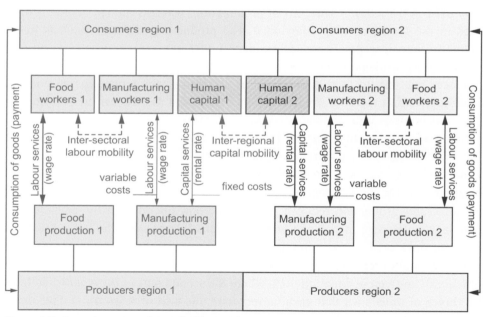

Figure 8.7 General structure of the solvable model

---

[17] The main point here is to include a mobile and an immobile factor of production. The labelling of these two factors (unskilled versus skilled labour or labour versus capital) is not material as long as the mobile factor (be it skilled labour or capital) spends its income in the region where it is used for production. This class of solvable models (where the mobile factor spends its income in the region where it is earned) is known as 'footloose entrepreneur' models (Baldwin et al., 2003, ch. 4). Solvable models where the mobile factor repatriates its income to the region of origin are known as 'footloose capital' models (Baldwin et al., 2003, ch. 3).

thought of as human or knowledge capital. Workers are thus geographically immobile whereas human capital is mobile. Workers earn the wage rate W and human
capital owners get a return r for their efforts. We assume that the two regions
are identical with respect to the immobile factor of production: $L_1 = L_2 = 0.5$. All
agents have the same preferences, depending on the consumption of food F and
manufactures M (see equation 8.13), where M is a composite of N different varieties c_i (see equation 8.14), δ is the share of income spent on manufactures, and ε
is the elasticity of substitution between different varieties of manufactures. Utility
maximization leads to the same expressions for the demand functions as derived
in Chapter 7.

$$U = M^\delta F^{1-\delta}$$
8.13

$$M = \left(\sum_{i=1}^{N} c_i^{\frac{\varepsilon-1}{\varepsilon}} \right)^{\frac{\varepsilon}{\varepsilon-1}}$$
8.14

The next step is crucial. In the manufacturing sector we assume that labour is
only used in the *variable cost* part of production β whereas human capital is only
used in the *fixed part* of production α. The production of food, which is freely
traded at zero transport costs, takes place under constant returns to scale and
requires only workers. A suitable choice of units ensures that one unit of labour
produces one unit of food. Using food as numéraire and assuming free trade in
food implies that the food price, and hence the wage rate W, can be set equal to
one. This holds as long as food is produced in both countries.

Standard profit maximization in the manufacturing sector leads to
$p_i(1 - 1/\varepsilon) = \beta W$. Using our normalization $\beta = 1 - 1/\varepsilon$, this implies $p_i = 1$. If the
variety is exported, the price in the foreign market thus becomes $Tp = T$. As will
be shown below, the assumption that labour is also used in the variable part of
manufactures production removes most of the non-linearity on the demand side
that makes the core model of Chapter 7 impossible to solve analytically. With
$W = 1$ we only have to determine the return to human capital r. Market clearing for
human capital in region j allows us to determine the number of varieties produced
in region j as given in equation 8.15, where the second part of the equality follows
by choice of units such that each variety uses one unit of K (so $\alpha = 1$). Free entry
and exit in the manufacturing sector ensures that total profits are zero, which –
using mark-up pricing – determines the equilibrium output per firm (see equation
8.16).[18] Using our normalization of wages, the income in region j is given in
equation 8.17. Using the 'free-ness of trade' parameter $\varphi \equiv T^{1-\varepsilon}$, we can write the
market clearing conditions for manufactures as given in equations 8.18 and 8.19,

---

[18] Rearrange the zero profit condition $px - (r + \beta x) = 0$ and use the mark-up pricing rule to get
equation 8.16.

where $I_1 \equiv \left(N_1 p_1^{1-\varepsilon} + \varphi N_2 p_2^{1-\varepsilon} \right)^{1/(1-\varepsilon)} = \left(N_1 + \varphi N_2 \right)^{1/(1-\varepsilon)}$ is the price index for manufactures in region 1 (similarly for region 2 by interchanging sub-indices 1 and 2).

$$N_j = \frac{K_j}{\alpha} = K_j \qquad 8.15$$

$$x_j = \varepsilon r_j \qquad 8.16$$

$$Y_j = r_j K_j + L_j \qquad 8.17$$

$$\varepsilon r_1 = \frac{p_1^{1-\varepsilon} \delta Y_1}{I_1^{1-\varepsilon}} + \frac{\varphi p_2^{1-\varepsilon} \delta Y_2}{I_2^{1-\varepsilon}} = \frac{\delta Y_1}{N_1 + \varphi N_2} + \frac{\varphi \delta Y_2}{\varphi N_1 + N_2} \qquad 8.18$$

$$\varepsilon r_2 = \frac{p_2^{1-\varepsilon} \delta Y_2}{I_2^{1-\varepsilon}} + \frac{\varphi p_1^{1-\varepsilon} \delta Y_1}{I_1^{1-\varepsilon}} = \frac{\delta Y_2}{N_2 + \varphi N_1} + \frac{\varphi \delta Y_1}{\varphi N_2 + N_1} \qquad 8.19$$

The left-hand sides of equations 8.18 and 8.19 give the equilibrium (value of) output per firm and the right-hand sides give the associated demand. Inspection of the two equations reveals that we have a linear system of two equations and two unknowns, which can readily be solved. Substituting equations 8.15 and 8.17 into equations 8.18 and 8.19 and defining λ as the share of human capital in region 1 (so $N_1 = \lambda$ and $N_2 = 1 - \lambda$) finally gives:

$$\frac{r_1}{r_2} = \frac{\varepsilon \left(2\varphi\lambda + (1-\lambda)(1+\varphi^2) \right) + (\varphi^2 - 1)(1-\lambda)\delta}{\varepsilon \left(2\varphi(1-\lambda) + \lambda(1+\varphi^2) \right) + (\varphi^2 - 1)\lambda\delta} \qquad 8.20$$

To round up the discussion of our model, we note that the location decision of human capital involves not only the factor rewards r_1 and r_2 but also the respective price levels. As in the core model of Chapter 7, differences in real rewards determine migration flows. The incentive for human capital to relocate is therefore determined by the ratio v:

$$v = \frac{r_1}{r_2} \left(\frac{I_2}{I_1} \right)^{\delta} = \frac{\varepsilon \left(2\varphi\lambda + (1-\lambda)(1+\varphi^2) \right) + (\varphi^2 - 1)(1-\lambda)\delta}{\varepsilon \left(2\varphi(1-\lambda) + \lambda(1+\varphi^2) \right) + (\varphi^2 - 1)\lambda\delta} \left(\frac{(1-\lambda) + \varphi\lambda}{\lambda + \varphi(1-\lambda)} \right)^{\frac{\delta}{1-\varepsilon}} \qquad 8.21$$

Apart from the case of complete agglomeration, human capital has no incentive to relocate if welfare is the same in the two regions ($v = 1$), while human capital moves from region 2 to region 1 if welfare is higher in region 1 ($v > 1$) and from region 1 to region 2 if welfare is lower in region 1 ($v < 1$). This completes our discussion of the set-up of the solvable model.

We can calculate the two most important 'points' of this model, the break point and the sustain point, as given below in (#b) and (#s). The break point can be derived by calculating the derivative of equation 8.21 with respect to λ and evaluating at $\lambda = 0.5$. For values of transport costs that are smaller than the break value, the symmetric equilibrium is no longer stable, and exogenous changes in the distribution of human capital will lead to agglomeration. The core–periphery outcome cannot be sustained for transportation costs higher than the smallest root of (#s), which can be derived from equation 8.21 by starting from complete agglomeration and calculating the value of transportation costs for which the real reward of human capital in the periphery becomes larger than in the core (the equation calculates the point where the owners of human capital are indifferent and the periphery is on the brink of becoming more attractive).

$$\varphi_{break} = \frac{(\varepsilon - \delta)(\varepsilon - 1 - \delta)}{(\varepsilon + \delta)(\varepsilon - 1 + \delta)} \tag{#b}$$

$$1 = \frac{1}{2}\varphi_{sus}^{\delta/(\varepsilon-1)}\left((1 + \delta/\varepsilon)\varphi_{sus} + (1 - \delta/\varepsilon)/\varphi_{sus}\right) \tag{#s}$$

Combining the information we have derived so far, we can again draw a Tomahawk figure for this model that is qualitatively the same as the one derived in Chapter 7. We thus conclude that the implications of the core model also hold for this model (although the exact values of the sustain and break points are not the same; see Baldwin et al., 2003). Note, however, that we can now derive explicit solutions for the rewards of the mobile factor of production. Moreover, we have multiple production factors, rather than one. These two differences are useful for subsequent analysis. Other extensions are discussed in Box 8.2.

BOX 8.2 More Extensions

We discuss the most important extensions of the core model of geographical economics in sections 8.2 to 8.4. There is, of course, more that can be said about these extensions. In addition, there are some other extensions that we did not yet discuss. The purpose of this box is to provide some more information on various other types of extensions, and thus gain more insight into the core model itself.

- *Learn more.* To improve your understanding of the core model and the three extensions discussed in this chapter, see the books by Baldwin et al. (2003), Fujita and Thisse (2002), Combes, Mayer, and Thisse (2008), or Fujita, Krugman, and Venables (1999). The most complete analysis is provided by Robert-Nicoud (2005), in particular regarding the similarities (in terms of the underlying structure) of models based on inter-regional labour mobility and models based on intermediate input linkages.
- *Two flavours.* Solvable models come in two basic flavours. The first flavour follows the core model and includes inter-regional factor mobility. The footloose entrepreneur model of Forslid and Ottaviano (2003) and

BOX 8.2 (cont.)

the footloose capital model of Baldwin et al. (2003) belong to this group. The footloose capital model assumes (in contrast to the core model and the footloose entrepreneur model) that the income of the mobile factor is repatriated to the region of origin of the mobile factor, which greatly simplifies the analysis as it avoids most of the demand and cost linkages that normally characterize geographical economics models. The second flavour of models is based on the intermediate goods model of section 8.2. Ottaviano and Robert-Nicoud (2006) provide a synthesis; see also Ottaviano (2007).

- *Forward looking.* An extension that is certainly worth mentioning is on including forward-looking expectations. Take for instance the migration equation of the core model of Chapter 7. In making the decision whether or not to migrate, manufacturing workers display what can be called my-opic behaviour. They look only at present real wages (and they ignore the migration decision made by other workers). But what about the prospect of future wages? Following Krugman (1991b), models have been devel-oped that take the role of expectations into account and that also ad-dress the theoretical foundation of the simple migration model. In section 8.2.3.2 of Fujita and Thisse (2013) this topic is discussed in depth.

- *Quasi-linear preferences.* Another type of extension is based on quasi-linear preferences rather than Dixit-Stiglitz utility: see Ottaviano, Tabuchi, and Thisse (2002) and Fujita and Thisse (2002). It turns out that this greatly simplifies the model and leads to a more straightforward demand struc-ture. On our website we discuss the use of quasi-linear utility functions in relation to the solvable model of Pflüger (2004), who uses a quadratic version of quasi-linear preferences (instead of a log version; see also Pflüger and Südekum, 2008). Both models assume inter-regional labour mobility and give rise to a different dynamic diagram. The main difference is that in the Ottaviano, Tabuchi, and Thisse (2002) model the break and sustain points occur for the same value of T (or φ), which eliminates the feature of path-dependency, but otherwise looks like the tomahawk diagram. In Pflüger (2004) there is a break point but no catastrophic agglomeration once spreading becomes unstable as T falls. Instead, there is a smooth, continuous increase of agglomeration until full agglomeration is reached. The resulting figure thus looks more like a *pitchfork* than a tomahawk.

- *Tomahawk.* More generally, the tomahawk shape of the dynamic diagram is not robust. We already saw this for the bell shape in section 8.3 and

> **BOX 8.2 (cont.)**
>
> quasi-linear preferences. It also holds if we combine inter-regional labour
> mobility with decreasing returns to labour in agriculture (Puga, 1999),
> introduce a housing sector (Helpman, 1998), analyse heterogeneous tastes
> (Tabuchi and Thisse, 2002), or use a CES instead of Cobb-Douglas upper
> tier utility function in the footloose entrepreneur model (Pflüger and Süde-
> kum, 2007)

8.5   Many Regions

The bulk of the analysis and most examples have dealt with a *two-region* model
up to now. Nonetheless, the short-run equilibrium equations hold generally if we
identify an arbitrary number R of locations, as long as we specify the distances
D_{rs} between all locations r and s, such that we can calculate $T_{rs} = T^{D_{rs}}$, and know
the production level ϕ_r of the immobile activity food in each location r. In general
(see our discussion of the bell-shaped curve at the end of section 8.3) it is virtually
impossible to derive analytical results for a setting with an arbitrary number of
locations. So, how does the core model of geographical economics behave if we
apply it to R regions instead of just two regions? This is analysed in this section
in the so-called *racetrack economy*. In section 8.6 we will discuss a more detailed
specification.

8.5.1   Many Locations in Neutral Space

The main advantage of the two-region core model is that space is inherently (and
deliberately) neutral. Neither location is preferred by construction over the other
location, because the distance between the two locations is the same, and hence so
is the transport cost. Any endogenous location results (agglomeration or spreading) that arise in the two-region core model are therefore a consequence of the
structure of the economic interactions between agents within the model, and do
not arise from some pre-imposed geographic structure favouring economic activity in a particular location.

   To preserve the neutrality of space in a multiple-location setting, it is useful
to analyse a simple geometry, in which the locations are evenly distributed in
a circle with transportation only possible along the rim of that circle. This setting has been used before, for example in economic geography or in industrial
organization. In Brakman et al. (1996) we refer to this setting as the *equidistant
circle*, but Fujita, Krugman, and Venables (1999, pp. 82–5) more aptly call it
the *racetrack economy*. The structure of the racetrack economy is quite simple,

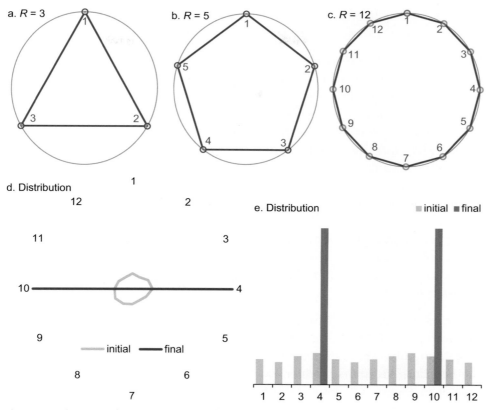

Figure 8.8 The racetrack economy; number of locations is *R*

as illustrated in Figure 8.8. The *R* locations are equally and sequentially spaced around the circumference of a circle, with location *R* next to location 1, as in a clock. The distance between any two adjacent locations is 1, thus the transport costs between adjacent locations is *T*. The distance between any two arbitrary locations is the length of the shortest route along the circumference of the circle. We assume the production of the immobile food activity is evenly distributed among all locations.

Panel *a* of Figure 8.8 illustrates the racetrack economy if there are three locations. The distance between all locations is 1, since they are all adjacent to one another. Panel *b* of Figure 8.8 illustrates the racetrack economy if there are 5 locations. The distance from location 1 to locations 2 and 5 is 1, because these are adjacent locations, and the distance from location 1 to locations 3 and 4 is 2, because it requires 2 steps from location 1 to reach either location. Similarly, panel *c* of Figure 8.8 illustrates the racetrack economy if there are 12 locations, where, for example, the distance from location 1 to locations 5 and 9 is 4, as both locations require 4 steps to be reached from location 1.

Panels *d* and *e* of Figure 8.8 show a typical simulation run for the racetrack economy with 12 locations.[19] The simulation procedure is as follows.

1. As in the core model we start with an initial distribution of the manufacturing labour force across the 12 locations. This distribution is chosen randomly.
2. We determine the short-run equilibrium, given this initial distribution, using the iterative procedure described in Chapter 7.
3. We calculate the real wage in the short-run equilibrium for all 12 locations.
4. We redistribute the manufacturing workforce across the locations, moving workers towards locations with high real wages and away from locations with low real wages; it is possible at this stage that a location stops producing manufacturing goods because there are no manufacturing workers anymore.
5. We repeat steps 2–4 until a long-run equilibrium is reached in step 3; that is until the real wage is equal in all locations with a positive manufacturing labour force, or until all manufacturing labour is agglomerated in a few symmetric locations.

Panel *d* in Figure 8.8 illustrates the simulation run using the same graphical approach as panels *a–c*. Apparently, all manufacturing production eventually ends up in only two cities, namely locations 4 and 10, exactly opposite to one another. Both locations produce exactly half of the manufacturing varieties. Panel *e* in Figure 8.8 shows the same simulation run using a column chart of the initial and final distribution of manufacturing production. The cities 4 and 10, which eventually emerge from the simulation as the only locations with manufacturing production, were already large initially, which allowed them to grow. Initial size is, however, not the only determining force for the long-run equilibrium. This is demonstrated by location 9, which at first is slightly larger than location 10, but eventually disappears as it is too close to location 4.

If we repeat the simulation with the 12-location racetrack economy for a different randomly chosen initial distribution of the manufacturing workforce (and for different parameter values), it turns out that the outcome depicted in Figure 8.8 panels *d* and *e* is quite typical. Usually, all manufacturing production is eventually agglomerated in only one or two cities. If there are two cities, they are equal in size and opposite one another (but these are, of course, not always in locations 4 and 10). All other locations eventually do not produce any manufacturing goods. The next subsection briefly discusses this phenomenon and two problems associated with it.

---

[19] The parameters for Figure 8.8 panels *d* and *e* are: $\delta = 0.4$; $\varepsilon = 5$; $T = 1.25$.

8.5.2   Preferred Frequency

Using an ingenious analysis, that is beyond the scope of this book, Fujita, Krugman, and Venables (1999, pp. 85–94) assume that there are infinitely many locations on the racetrack economy to show that there tends to be a *preferred frequency* number of long-run equilibrium locations, depending on the structural parameters. For a large range of parameter values the preferred frequency is one, indicating that eventually all manufacturing production is produced in only one city: the mono-centric equilibrium. For other parameter values the preferred frequency is two: half the manufacturing production is eventually produced in one city, the other half in another city at the opposite side of the racetrack economy. Similarly, if the preferred frequency is three, one-third of the manufacturing varieties are eventually produced in each of three cities, evenly spread across the racetrack economy. And so on.

The preferred frequency tends to increase if (i) the transport costs increase, (ii) the share of income spent on manufactures decreases, and (iii) the elasticity of substitution increases. All three results are intuitively plausible:

(i)   If transport costs increase one would expect production to locate close to the market, increasing the number of long-run equilibrium locations.
(ii) If the share of income spent on manufactures decreases the immobile food sector becomes economically more important, thus increasing the spreading force in the model, such that manufacturing firms locate more closely to their consumers and the number of long-run equilibrium locations increases.
(iii) If the elasticity of substitution decreases the market power of firms increases as it becomes harder to substitute one variety for another, such that the firms can get away with producing manufacturing varieties only at a few locations.

The preferred frequency analysis convincingly shows two fundamental *shortcomings* of the core model as generalized by the racetrack economy. First, the powers of agglomeration tend to be too strong, a feature that we have discussed in this chapter. For a large range of parameter settings only one city emerges, particularly if the share of income spent on manufactures, the mobile activity, is not too small. In this respect we are already glad when we find two cities in the long-run equilibrium of our simulations (with 12 locations), and delighted to find three cities in the final equilibrium. Most locations end up with no manufacturing activity whatsoever. The second problem is the monotone size of cities in the long-run equilibrium. This, of course, vacuously holds if we have only one city, but even if we have more than one city in the long-run equilibrium, those cities are exactly equal in size and evenly distributed across the racetrack economy. This poses, of course, a problem for empirical applications, say if we want to explain the rank-size distribution of India as described in Chapter 1, which requires the existence of many cities of unequal size.

8.6   Congestion as an Additional Spreading Force

The idea that agglomeration, driven by positive external economies of scale, may itself give rise to external *dis*economies of scale is, of course, not new.[20] When for instance cities get larger they start to suffer from increasing commuting costs and higher land or housing rents (see Chapter 4). External diseconomies of scale also arise from environmental pollution or limited storage facilities. We will refer to all these diseconomies of scale as examples of congestion. We do not discriminate between the various forms of congestion, because our aim is to analyse the consequences of congestion, rather than its origin. The direct consequence of congestion is straightforward since it provides an incentive for firms and mobile workers to relocate from the congested centres to the relatively uncluttered periphery. This may be helpful in analysing systems of cities, as we now explain based on an extension of the core model. The model to be introduced in this section turns out to be rather versatile when it comes to possible empirical applications. We will show this in the final sections of Chapter 8 for actual city-size distributions and Zipf's Law, but the model can also be used as a base model for instance to discuss the implications of increased inter-regional labour mobility in China, as Chapter 10 will make clear.

8.6.1   The Modelling of Congestion

In the core model of Chapter 7, the manufacturing production function is characterized by internal increasing returns to scale. This production structure can be easily adapted to introduce congestion costs. The main idea is that the congestion costs depend on the *overall size* of the location of production. In this sense it resembles the Henderson (1974) model for urban systems from our Chapter 5. The size of city r is measured by the total number of manufacturing firms N_r in that city. Congestion costs are thus not industry- or firm-specific, but solely a function of the size of the city as a whole:[21]

$$l_{ir} = N_r^{\frac{\tau}{1-\tau}}\left(\alpha + \beta x_i\right) ; \quad -1 < \tau < 1 \qquad 8.22$$

where l_{ir} is the amount of labour required in city r to produce x_i units of a variety, and the parameter τ represents external economies of scale. There are no location-specific external economies of scale if $\tau = 0$. Equation 8.22 then reduces to

---

[20] This section is based on Brakman et al. (1996); see also Gabaix and Ioannides (2004) for a discussion.
[21] This specification simplifies the equations below considerably. Other specifications, such as dependence of costs on the total production level in a city, are also possible. This does not alter the analysis in any essential way.

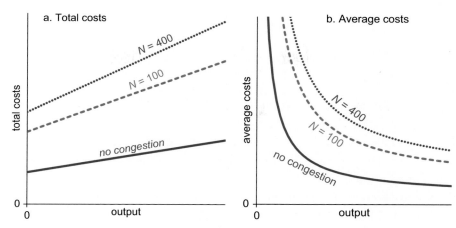

Figure 8.9 Total and average labour costs with and without congestion
Parameter values: $\alpha = 1$; $\beta = 0.2$; $\tau = 0.15$; for 'no congestion' $\tau = 0$.

the production function of the core model: see Chapter 7. There are positive location-specific external economies if $-1 < \tau < 0$. Such a specification could be used to model, for example, learning-by-doing spillovers. For our present purposes, the case of negative location-specific external economies arising from congestion is relevant, in which case $0 < \tau < 1$. This is illustrated for total labour costs (panel *a*) and average labour costs (panel *b*) in Figure 8.9.

If the parameter τ lies between zero and one, each manufacturing firm i in city r is confronted with a cost increase if other firms also decide to locate in this city. As Figure 8.9 shows, a rise in the number of firms located in the city raises the fixed and marginal costs of producing there, and thus also the average costs of production. This can be compared in Figure 8.9 with the 'no congestion' lines for $\tau = 0$. As with any other external effect, we assume that each individual firm does not take into account that its location decision has an impact on the production functions (and thus indirectly on the decision processes) of all the other manufacturing firms.

To keep the analysis tractable, this is the only modification we make to the core model. We must now retrace our steps taken in Chapter 7 when deriving the short-run equilibrium of the core model to see how the introduction of congestion costs affects each step. Details of this process can be found on the website, which also reproduces the normalization analysis for the core model with congestion. Equations 8.23 to 8.25 give the short-run equilibrium, incorporating the congestion modification of equation 8.22.

$$Y_r = \delta\lambda_r W_r + (1-\delta)\phi_r \qquad\qquad 8.23$$

$$I_r = \left(\sum_{s=1}^{R} \lambda_s^{1-\tau\varepsilon}\lambda_s^{1-\tau\varepsilon}T_{rs}^{1-\varepsilon}W_s^{1-\varepsilon}\right)^{\frac{1}{1-\varepsilon}} \qquad\qquad 8.24$$

$$W_r = \lambda_r^{-\tau} \left(\sum_{s=1}^{R} Y_s T_{sr}^{1-\varepsilon} I_s^{\varepsilon-1} \right)^{\frac{1}{\varepsilon}}$$

8.25

When comparing this short-run equilibrium with the normalized short-run equilibrium of Chapter 7, it is immediately obvious that the equations are the same if $\tau = 0$. Note that the income equation 8.23 is not affected by the congestion parameter τ.[22] From the wage equation 8.25 it is clear that an increase of congestion in city s (resulting from an increase in the share of manufacturing workers λ_s in that city) tends to reduce the wage rate in city s and (through equation 8.24) simultaneously tends to reduce the price index in other regions. Both forces make other cities more attractive.

Given the distribution of the manufacturing labour force across cities, which determines the number of varieties produced and hence the number of manufacturing firms in each city, equations 8.23 to 8.25 determine the short-run equilibrium. We will not analyse the short-run equilibrium for the congestion model. To assess the relevance of congestion for the long-run equilibrium allocation of economic activity, when the distribution of the mobile labour force is not fixed, we rely on simulations and proceed in two steps. In the first step, we illustrate the relevance of congestion in the two-city model. This allows us to compare with the simulations of Chapter 7. Since it is one of the objectives of this chapter to apply the core model with congestion to actual city-size distributions, a two-city model will not do. In the second step, we therefore introduce many cities and congestion in the racetrack economy of the core model. Remember that in the racetrack economy space is neutral, which implies that by construction no location is preferred over any other location. Any results derived in such a setting can be attributed to the workings of the model, rather than the geometric construction of space.

8.6.2 The Two-City Model and Congestion

In the simulations of the core model with congestion, where food production is again evenly divided over the two cities, we focus on the relative real wage of city 1 compared to city 2 to determine the direction of change of the distribution of the manufacturing labour force, and thus the stability of long-run equilibria. This is similar to our approach in Chapter 7. For each value of λ_1 (the share of the manufacturing labour force in city 1) we first determine the short-run equilibrium by solving equations 8.23 to 8.25, then we calculate the relative real wage of city 1, which we then plot as a function of the share of manufacturing labour in city 1: see Figure 8.10.

A long-run equilibrium is reached either when the real wages in the two cities are equal, that is when the relative real wage in Figure 8.10 is equal to one, or when the entire manufacturing labour force is agglomerated in one city. The long-run

---

[22] This obviously also holds for the real wage equation, not shown here.

equilibrium is stable if, going from left to right, the relative real wage cuts the '1' line from above. To illustrate how the introduction of congestion alters the long-run equilibrium and its stability, we vary the transport costs T in Figure 8.10, which is arranged in panels $a–i$ for *de*creasing transport costs. Recall that we concluded in Chapter 7 that the spreading equilibrium is stable for high transport costs, whereas full agglomeration in either city is stable for low transport costs. This 'bang-bang' tendency of the stable long-run equilibrium without congestion (either spreading or complete agglomeration) is not a satisfactory outcome from an empirical point of view. As demonstrated in Figure 8.10, even if we add only a little bit of congestion ($\tau = 0.01$) the possibilities for long-run equilibria change drastically.

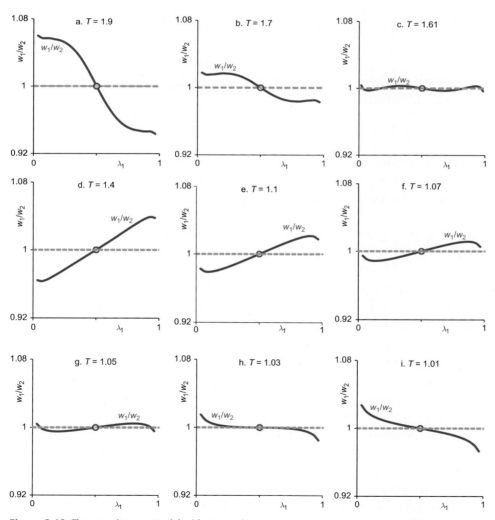

Figure 8.10 The two-city core model with congestion parameters: $\varepsilon = 5$; $\delta = 0.4$; $\tau = 0.01$

Discussing the panels of Figure 8.10 sequentially, that is for gradually decreasing transport costs, five different stages can be identified.

1. For very high transport costs, spreading is the only stable equilibrium; see panels *a* and *b*.
2. As transport costs decrease, spreading is still a stable equilibrium, but there are now also two other stable equilibria with *partial* agglomeration, see panel *c*. Apparently, the introduction of congestion costs enriches the possible long-run equilibrium outcomes considerably, in particular by allowing partial rather than complete agglomeration as a stable equilibrium. Also note that there are seven long-run equilibria in panel *c* (including complete agglomeration); going from left to right these are alternately unstable and stable.
3. Complete agglomeration in either city is a stable equilibrium as transport costs continue to fall: see panels *d–f*. The range of transport costs for which this holds is fairly large.
4. As transport costs become very small, their impact relative to congestion costs is limited. Initially this implies that *partial* agglomeration in either city is a stable equilibrium: see panel *g*.
5. For very low transport costs, finally, spreading is again the only stable equilibrium: see panels *h* and *i*.

Two conclusions emerge from this analysis. First, the range of possible long-run equilibrium outcomes with congestion is considerably wider than without congestion. Second, the phenomenon of partial agglomeration establishes the possibility of the simultaneous existence of small and large centres of economic activity as a stable long-run equilibrium outcome in a model with neutral space.

8.6.3   Many Locations and Congestion

After analysing the two-city version of the core model with congestion, it is time to extend the analysis to the neutral-space racetrack economy with congestion. As analysed in section 8.5, without congestion the racetrack economy usually ends up with only one city with manufacturing production (or possibly with two cities of equal size) in the long-run equilibrium. Now that we have seen in the previous subsection that the two-city model with congestion allows for the viability of small economic centres of manufacturing production, we extend this analysis to a structure with many cities.

Figure 8.11 shows two simulation results of a 24-city racetrack economy with congestion. One simulation has transport costs $T = 1.2$, the other has transport costs $T = 1.3$. The initial distribution of the manufacturing labour force was chosen randomly, but is the same in the two simulations. Panels *a* and *b* of Figure 8.11 show both the initial and the final (long-run equilibrium) distribution of the manufacturing labour force. The larger the distance from the centre of the circle, the larger the manufacturing labour force in that city is. So, for example, cities

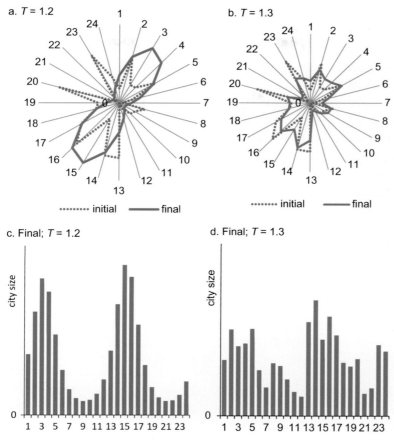

Figure 8.11 The racetrack economy with congestion
Parameters: $\varepsilon=5$; $\delta=0.7$; $\tau=0.1$

1 and 21 are initially very small, while cities 20 and 23 are initially very large. Panels c and d of Figure 8.11 just show a column chart of the final distribution of the manufacturing labour force.

Panels a and c, depicting the simulation results for transport costs $T = 1.2$, lead to the following observations. First, with congestion many cities, not just one or two, still have manufacturing production in the long-run equilibrium. Second, these cities vary considerably in economic size, which is promising from an empirical point of view. Third, the final distribution of manufacturing production is well-structured around two centres of economic activity in cities 3 and 15; see in particular panel c. Fourth, whether an individual city increases or decreases in economic size during the adjustment process towards the long-run equilibrium largely depends on its relative place in the initial distribution of city sizes, that is on the size of cities in its neighbourhood. Cities 20 and 23, for example, are initially very large, but isolated. Consequently, they both shrink considerably during the adjustment process. City 15, on the other hand, is initially quite small, but surrounded on both sides by large cities, namely cities 13, 14, 16, and 17. This allows city 15 to eventually become the largest city of all, even larger than cities 20 and 23 were initially. The cluster of cities 2, 3, and 4 thrives in particular because they are exactly opposite the 'agglomeration shadow' imposed by the cluster surrounding city 15.

Relative to the above discussion, panels b and d for $T = 1.3$ show two additional results, namely that, depending on the parameter values, the final distribution may be much more determined by the initial distribution (see panel b) and thus be less structured: see panel d. In this sense the importance of the initial conditions or in other words 'history' may vary.

Before we turn to the empirical evidence for Zipf's Law, it must be emphasized that we do not pretend to offer a full-fledged analysis of the economics of congestion. However, the core model with congestion does illustrate that the inclusion of an additional spreading force may give rise to many centres of economic activity which vary considerably in size, even in a setting of neutral space. This is a necessary condition for applying such a model to explain urban systems and city-size distributions.

BOX 8.3 Primate Cities and Geographical Economics

In Chapter 5 we briefly discussed the role of primate cities in Box 5.2. Primate cities dominate the economic landscape in some countries, like London in the UK, Mexico City in Mexico, or Cairo in Egypt. Primate cities are related to estimated power law exponents as noted in section 8.7. Here we briefly evaluate primate cities in the geographical economics literature.

Krugman and Livas Elizondo (1996) offer a theoretical explanation for primate cities from a geographical economics perspective based on the Mexico experience. Why do firms want to locate in Mexico City despite the relatively high wages? According to the core model of Chapter 7 it is because of the high demand for their products. In the extensions discussed in this chapter it is also because their main suppliers are located there. Similarly, workers and hence demand are located in Mexico City because the suppliers (firms) are there. Krugman and Livas Elizondo (1996) argue that this line of reasoning depends on the assumption that Mexico is a *closed* economy. Suppose, however, that Mexican firms produce largely for the world market, buy their inputs on these markets, and that Mexican demand for goods is also directed at the world market. Suppose also that agglomeration is accompanied by high land rents in the centre, which then acts as a spreading force. In that case, it no longer makes sense for Mexico City to be the centre of production and thus for Mexico to have a large primate city. One

BOX 8.3 (cont.)

would expect a more even distribution of economic activity, with agglomeration in regions with good access to foreign markets (near the Mexican–US border or in sea harbours). Krugman and Livas Elizondo show that as the economy in their model moves from a closed to an open economy, the initial stable equilibrium of agglomeration at one location is replaced by a spreading equilibrium.

This suggests that increased openness of the economy goes along with a relatively smaller size of the primate city; see Ades and Glaeser (1995). There are two caveats. First, the direction of causality remains unclear as it may also run from size to trade: 'concentration of population in a single city might give local firms a transport cost advantage over foreign suppliers and thus lower the amount of foreign trade' (Ades and Glaeser, 1995, p. 213). Second, the empirical results point to the relevance of political (non-economic) factors in explaining the existence of large primate cities. In particular, countries with a totalitarian regime have large primate cities, which is also the political centre of the country and puts firms and workers outside the primate city at a disadvantage (for rent-seeking reasons).

Finally, Diego Puga (1998) develops an alternative geographical economics model that can account for the relatively large size of primate cities in many developing countries. His model is similar to the core model of Chapter 7, but also allows labour to move between the manufacturing and agricultural sectors depending on the elasticity of labour supply. Puga shows that when transport costs are becoming low and increasing returns to scale are relatively strong, an urban system with a large primate city develops. With relatively high transport costs and weaker economies of scale a more balanced urban system takes shape. According to Puga the latter applies to nineteenth-century European urbanization, whereas the former applies to late twentieth-century urbanization in developing countries.

8.7 Empirics of Urban Power Laws

The evidence on power law exponents and the relevance of Zipf's Law in Chapter 5 is to some extent caused by differences in sample size and city definitions. We now return to this topic because we want to show how a geographical economics model with congestion as an additional spreading force from section 8.6 can be used to analyse city-size distribution and may even yield an economic explanation for Zipf's Law, something that our discussion on city-size systems from urban economics in Chapter 5 did not deliver. Before we do that, in section 8.8, this section provides the empirical regularities on power laws that we need to explain.

Regarding sample size, power laws hold for the upper part of the distribution, so small cities below some threshold level should be excluded. There is no consensus regarding the appropriate threshold level, but we will follow the United Nations Population Division (2014) procedure by focusing on cities with 300,000 or more inhabitants, which seems a quite reasonable threshold value. In our analysis below we also exclude estimated power law exponents based on fewer than 15 observations as the variance of these estimates is simply too large. This second threshold is again arbitrary but, we think, quite reasonable.

The United Nations Population Division (2016, p. 1) identifies three type of city definitions:

> One type of definition, sometimes referred to as the 'city proper', describes a city according to an administrative boundary. A second approach, termed the 'urban agglomeration', considers the extent of the contiguous urban area, or built-up area, to delineate the city's boundaries. A third concept of the city, the 'metropolitan area', defines its boundaries according to the degree of economic and social interconnectedness of nearby areas, identified by interlinked commerce or commuting patterns, for example.

These different definitions have, of course, implications for the population size of cities. The UN Population Division (2014) strove to use the 'urban agglomeration' definition whenever possible. The majority of the data we use in this section is thus based on the urban agglomeration definition. For consistent estimates over time, however, a fairly large fraction is based on city proper (35 per cent) or metropolitan area (10 per cent). Our analysis is in two steps. Section 8.7.1 analyses power law exponents for the world and continents over time, while section 8.7.2 focuses on country estimates in 2015.

8.7.1   The World and Continents

The UN Population Division data are available in five-year intervals from 1950 to 2030, where the last three observations are based on predicted values for 2020–2030. We analyse the time dimension of estimated power law exponents for the world as a whole and for individual continents. The Australian continent is excluded as it does not meet the minimum threshold of 15 observations. Similarly for Africa in 1950 and 1955. Detailed estimates and associated standard errors for a selection of years are given in Table 8.1. The estimates are illustrated for all years in Figure 8.12, namely for the world in panel *a* and for the continents in panel *b*.

At the world level, the estimated power law exponent is 1.359 in 1950 and gradually declines to 1.161 in 2015, with a further predicted small decline to 1.147 in 2030. This is indicative of a relative increase in the size of large cities, as probably expected, and illustrated in panel *a* of Figure 8.12, together with the 90 per cent confidence intervals based on the estimated standard errors. Since the number of

Table 8.1 Estimated urban power law exponents: continents and world, 1950–2030

Year	Africa	Asia	Europe	Latin America	North America	World
1950		1.3053	1.4763	1.1287	1.1920	1.3590
		(0.1946)	(0.1867)	(0.3258)	(0.2384)	(0.1099)
1960	1.3780	1.2021	1.4695	1.1629	1.1856	1.3014
	(0.4726)	(0.1463)	(0.1703)	(0.2600)	(0.2064)	(0.0906)
1970	1.4263	1.1797	1.4649	1.1213	1.1548	1.2673
	(0.3410)	(0.1204)	(0.1536)	(0.2064)	(0.1861)	(0.0764)
1980	1.4071	1.1638	1.4626	1.1221	1.1460	1.2459
	(0.2468)	(0.1000)	(0.1445)	(0.1711)	(0.1728)	(0.0656)
1990	1.3395	1.1661	1.4749	1.1589	1.1154	1.2326
	(0.1954)	(0.0818)	(0.1378)	(0.1466)	(0.1585)	(0.0562)
2000	1.2445	1.1677	1.4652	1.1207	1.0834	1.2013
	(0.1613)	(0.0674)	(0.1349)	(0.1298)	(0.1393)	(0.0483)
2010	1.1783	1.1494	1.4382	1.0908	1.0833	1.1725
	(0.1322)	(0.0574)	(0.1289)	(0.1116)	(0.1299)	(0.0421)
2015	1.1510	1.1407	1.4240	1.0929	1.0830	1.1614
	(0.1190)	(0.0543)	(0.1264)	(0.1077)	(0.1246)	(0.0399)
UN Population Division prediction						
2020	1.1467	1.1385	1.4169	1.0989	1.0913	1.1554
	(0.1186)	(0.0542)	(0.1260)	(0.1083)	(0.1256)	(0.0397)
2030	1.1354	1.1464	1.4248	1.1083	1.1081	1.1468
	(0.1174)	(0.0546)	(0.1279)	(0.1092)	(0.1275)	(0.0395)

Source: estimates based on UN Population Division (2014) data using Gabaix-Ibragimov (2011) method; Kratz-Resnick (1996) standard errors in parentheses; Africa in 1950 has less than 15 observations.

observations rises over time, from 306 in 1950 to 1,692 in 2015, as more and more cities pass the threshold level of 300,000 inhabitants, the bandwidth of the confidence interval also falls over time. The Zipf hypothesis of a power law exponent equal to one is also shown in panel *a*. It is immediately clear that at the world level the Zipf hypothesis is rejected for the entire period 1950–2030. Moreover, the world estimated power law exponents are outside the confidence interval of the 2015 estimate for the entire period 1950–1985, suggesting that the power law exponent may change over time; see also Box 8.4.

Panel *b* of Figure 8.12 shows the estimated power law exponents at the continent level. The confidence intervals are not shown as they would clutter the diagram. The special role of Europe is immediately clear: its power law exponent

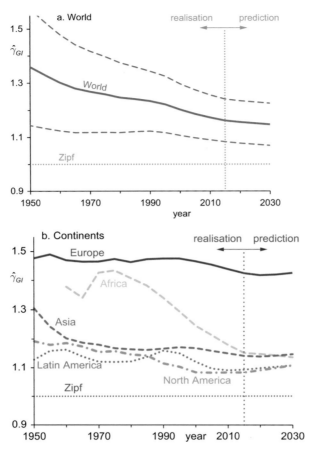

Figure 8.12 Urban power law exponents: world and continent level, 1950–2030
Source: estimates based on UN Population Division (2014) data using Gabaix-Ibragimov (2011) method and Kratz-Resnick (1996) standard errors; dashed lines in panel *a* show 90 per cent confidence interval; vertical axis starts at 0.9.

is fairly constant over time and much higher than for the other continents, indicating a relatively less important role for large cities in Europe than in the rest of the world. The large decline in the estimated power law exponent in Africa, particularly in the period 1980–2015, is also clear. It indicates the rapidly rising relative importance of large cities in Africa in this period. A similar rapid decline of the estimated power law exponent took place earlier in Asia, namely in the period 1950–1970. A modest decline took place in North America (USA and Canada) in the period 1950–2000, after which the estimated exponent stabilized and is now predicted to rise. The Latin American estimated power law exponent fluctuates around 1.12 throughout the whole period.

Panel *b* of Figure 8.12 also shows the Zipf hypothesis of a power law equal to one. As suggested by the much higher estimated exponent for Europe, the Zipf hypothesis is rejected for Europe for the whole period. Remember that the width of the confidence interval is related to the number of observations available. This number rises over time for all continents, but it rises particularly fast for Asia, from 90 in 1950 to 881 in 2015. As a consequence, the confidence interval narrows faster for Asia and the Zipf hypothesis is rejected for Asia from 1990 onwards. For all other continents and all other years the Zipf hypothesis is not rejected. We return to the power of the Zipf hypothesis at the end of section 8.7.2.

8.7.2 Country Estimates in 2015

We now turn to country estimates of power law exponents in 2015. Our combination of thresholds (a minimum of 300,000 inhabitants and 15 observations) means that only 25 countries are included in the analysis. We report summary statistics for the world as a whole and for Africa, Asia, Latin America, and Europe & Offshoots separately in Table 8.2, which also lists all included countries. We illustrate the distribution of the country-level exponents in Figure 8.13 using the same regional classification. For the world as a whole, the estimated power law exponent ranges from 0.605 for Japan to 1.497 for Germany. The mean value is 1.14, which is almost the same as the median value of 1.13. All estimated power law exponents are significantly different from zero (see also below) and the goodness of fit is high. On average 96.6 per cent of the variance is explained by the power law regression, ranging from a low of 91.4 per cent for the Philippines to a high of 99.7 per cent for Turkey. In this sense, the performance of the power law for urban systems is strong.

For the country estimates grouped at the regional levels in Table 8.2, we note that the mean estimate is much higher in Europe & Offshoots than in Africa, Asia, or Latin America. As illustrated in Figure 8.13, this is related to the high estimates

Table 8.2 Statistics for estimated urban power law exponents: country level, 2015

Statistic	World	Africa	Asia	Europe & Offshoots	Latin America
Minimum	0.605	0.991	0.605	1.026	0.945
Maximum	1.497	1.257	1.220	1.497	1.271
Mean	1.14	1.12	1.06	1.28	1.08
Median	1.13	1.12	1.11	1.30	0.99
Number of countries	25	2	10	8	5

Source: based on data from UN Population Division (2014); only countries with 15 or more observations included; Africa: DR Congo and Nigeria; Asia: China, India, Indonesia, Iran, Iraq, Japan, Pakistan, Philippines, S. Korea, and Turkey; Europe & Offshoots: Canada, France, Germany, Italy, Russia, UK, Ukraine, and USA; Latin America: Argentina, Brazil, Colombia, Mexico, and Venezuela; average R^2 is 0.996 (min 0.914, max 0.997).

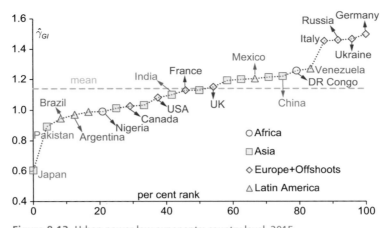

Figure 8.13 Urban power law exponents: country level, 2015
Source: estimates based on UN Population Division (2014) data using Gabaix-Ibragimov (2011) method and Kratz-Resnick (1996) standard errors; see Table 8.2 for details.

in Germany, Ukraine, Russia, and Italy (with a more even city-size distribution) compared to the lower estimates in Canada, USA, France, and UK (with a more uneven city-size distribution). China has the highest estimated exponent in Asia (1.220) and thus a relatively even city-size distribution, while Japan has the lowest (0.605) and thus a relatively uneven distribution. Latin America tends to have low estimated exponents, particularly in Brazil, Argentina, and Colombia, and thus a relatively uneven city-size distribution. There are only two African countries included, with a fairly low estimate for Nigeria and a fairly high estimate for DR Congo. The estimated power law exponent is higher than one for 19 countries (76 per cent of all countries), which is in line with the meta-analysis of 29 studies performed by Nitsch (2005).

The question now arises whether the Zipf hypothesis of a power law exponent equal to one is accepted or rejected at the country level. The answer is simple: the Zipf hypothesis is rejected only for Japan and China (at the 10 per cent level) and accepted for all other countries. Although at first sight this suggests strong support for the Zipf hypothesis, we have to take the (lack of) power of the Zipf hypothesis into consideration. Remember that the estimated standard errors are equal to $\hat{\gamma}_{GI}\sqrt{2/N}$ (see Chapter 5), where $\hat{\gamma}_{GI}$ is the estimated power law exponent. The confidence interval around the estimated exponent is thus strongly dependent on the number of observations available. This number is small at the country level for almost all countries. In our case, it is equal to the minimum of 15 for DR Congo and Ukraine. The median number of observations is only 25. It is only larger than 63 (Russia's value) for three countries, namely USA (135), India (166), and China (400). This implies that the confidence level is wide for almost all countries.

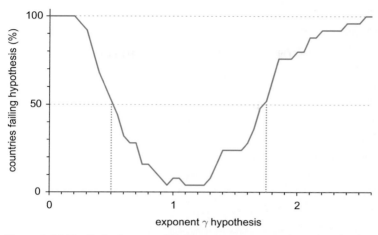

Figure 8.14 The (lack of) power of Zipf for urban systems at the country level, 2015
Source: see Figure 8.13; graph shows the percentage of countries (vertical axis) failing a hypothetical power law exponent (horizontal axis) in the range from 0 to 2.6 (in steps of 0.05).

Figure 8.14 illustrates the lack of power of the Zipf hypothesis for urban systems at the country level. On the horizontal axis we show a hypothetical value of the power law exponent, ranging from zero to 2.6 in steps of 0.05. On the vertical axis we show the percentage of countries that fail that specific power law exponent hypothesis. All estimated exponents are significant, so all countries fail a hypothetical value of zero. This also holds for any hypothetical value below 0.2. Once we reach a hypothetical value of 0.25, Japan is the first country for which we accept the hypothesis that its estimated exponent of 0.605 could actually be equal to 0.25. Similarly, once we reach the hypothetical value of 2.50, Ukraine is the last country for which we accept the hypothesis that its estimated exponent of 1.465 could actually be equal to 2.50. A hypothetical value of 2.55 or higher is therefore rejected for all countries.

For the Zipf hypothesis of a power law exponent equal to one, Figure 8.14 shows that 8 per cent of the countries fail the hypothesis, namely two countries (Japan and China) out of 25 countries. Suppose our selection criterion for an 'optimal' hypothesis is to choose a hypothetical power law exponent that minimizes the number (or percentage) of countries that fail the hypothesis. Then we should not choose Zipf's Law (a value of one), but either a value close to 0.95 (which is only failed by China) or any value in the range from 1.10 to 1.30 (which is only failed by Japan). Suppose, instead, that we are less strict and argue that a 'reasonable' hypothetical power law exponent should not be failed by more than a certain 'acceptable' percentage of countries. Figure 8.14 shows the range of reasonable hypotheses if the acceptable percentage is 50, namely all hypothetical power law exponents from 0.50 all the way to 1.75. If the acceptable percentage is 25 the range reduces from 0.70 to 1.60, while if the acceptable percentage is 10 the range reduces from 0.85 to 1.35. In all cases, the reasonable range of power law exponents is wide simply because most countries have a low number of observations and the associated confidence interval is wide.

To summarize, all of our estimated power law exponents are larger than one at the world and continent levels and about three-quarters are larger than one at the country level. Moreover, all of the estimated exponents are significant and the goodness of fit is high. The estimated exponents may vary over time and usually declined in the period 1950–2015, indicating a move towards a more uneven city-size distribution. The hypothesis of Zipf's Law is rejected at the world level and for the European and Asian continents, but usually accepted at the country level. This is related to the low number of observations for most countries. As a result, the 'optimal' hypothesis is a power law exponent of either 0.95 or anywhere in the range from 1.10 to 1.30, while a 'reasonable' hypothesis could basically be anywhere between 0.50 and 1.75.

8.8   Explaining Urban Power Laws

Our analysis in the previous section points to two requirements that an economic explanation of urban power laws must meet. First, the implied power law exponent should be able to account for deviations from Zipf's Law. This is in marked contrast with Gabaix (1999a, b), Krugman (1996b), and Fujita, Krugman, and Mori (1999, pp. 216–17), who take a value of one as their starting point. Second, the implied power law exponent should be able to change over time in response to changing circumstances, such as the rapid urbanization and agglomeration processes taking place in many Asian and African countries since the second half of the twentieth century. This is again in contrast with some authors, such as Krugman (1996b), Eaton and Eckstein (1997), and Gabaix (1999a, b). Box 8.4 analyses changing power law exponents from a European historical perspective.

In section 8.8.2 we briefly discuss a geographical economics approach to explain urban power laws, where the exponent can be different from one and can change over time in response to changing circumstances. Our approach is based on the core model with congestion as explained in section 8.6. In this approach the balance between agglomerating and spreading forces is crucial for determining the spatial equilibrium and thus the power law exponent. There is, however, another route that can be taken regarding urban power laws with a focus on explaining Zipf's Law (an exponent of one). This alternative route takes as its starting point that the relative size of cities does not matter. Two main examples are provided by Simon (1955) and Gabaix (1999a, b).[23] The next section first discusses these two examples.

---

[23] See also Krugman (1996a), Eeckhout (2004), Bosker et al. (2006), Córdoba (2008), and Rossi-Hansberg and Wright (2007).

8.8.1 Non-economic Explanations

The basic idea of Simon (1955) is simple, the mathematics underlying the model is not.[24] Imagine a population characterized by random growth. The 'newly born', who for some unexplained reason arrive in cohorts, and not one by one, may begin a new city (with probability π), or they can cling to an existing city (with probability $1-\pi$). If they cling to an existing city, the probability that they choose any particular city is proportional to the size of the population of that city. It can then be shown (provided the cohorts of newly born are neither too large nor too small) that the random growth of the population will eventually result in Zipf's Law ($\gamma = 1$). The point to emphasize is the lack of economic content in this explanation for Zipf's Law. The size of the city, and hence the aforementioned tension between agglomerating and spreading forces, is not an issue. This also implies that changes in the city-size distribution are thought to be random. There are other difficulties; see also Fujita, Krugman, and Venables (1999, pp. 222–3) or Gabaix (1999a, p. 129), who points out that 'the ratio of the growth rate of the number of cities to the growth rate of the population of existing cities (...) is in reality significantly less than 1' (this ratio is assumed to be 1 by Simon).

Gabaix (1999a, b) provides a different explanation for Zipf's Law, where the relative size of cities does not matter and where the economics of city formation are not part of the explanation. He calls upon Gibrat's Law which, when applied to cities, states that the growth process of a city is independent of its size. He proves that if every city, large or small, shares the same common mean growth rate, and if the variance of this growth rate is also the same for every city, then Zipf's Law must result. Again, the point to notice is that this explanation is not based on an economic model. Nonetheless, it is an interesting question, which type of city-growth model gives rise to a steady-state growth rate leading to Gibrat's Law. Gabaix shows that Gibrat's Law (and hence Zipf's Law) results if cities are either characterized by constant returns to scale, or by external economies of scale with positive and negative externalities cancelling out. The latter would mean that a geographical economics model can give rise to Zipf's Law only if for each city the agglomeration forces are exactly as strong as the spreading forces.[25]

---

[24] Our discussion of Simon (1955) is based on Krugman (1996a).

[25] The idea of using Gibrat's Law to explain the power law distribution may be relatively new to economists, but it is not to geographers; see the well-known introductory textbook on economic geography by Dicken and Lloyd (1990), or the survey paper by Carroll (1982, section 2). The assumption that the variance of the growth rate is the same for every city has been criticized by Fujita, Krugman, and Venables (1999, p. 224), who argue that this variance must be larger for smaller, less-diversified cities. Gabaix (1999b) agrees with this point, but says that this is precisely why the power law distribution does not hold in the lower tail. Dobkins and Ioannides (2001) do not find empirical support for the 'uniform variance' assumption.

BOX 8.4 Historical Urban Power Laws in Europe

Although large cities arose earliest in Africa (Memphis, Egypt) and Asia (Akkad, Lagash, and Ur in Babylonia), Europe was the earliest intensively urbanized continent. Kooij (1988) distinguishes three stylized periods of urbanization in Europe.

1. *Pre-industrialization: around 1600–1850*, characterized by high transport costs and production dominated by immobile farmers. In this period there was not really an integrated urban system. The industrialization process had yet to begin and the relatively high transport cost between cities is thought to be the main cause for the lack of an urban system.
2. *Industrialization: around 1850–1900*, characterized by declining transport costs and increasing importance of 'footloose' industrial production with increasing returns to scale. In the second half of the nineteenth century an integrated urban system was formed. Two interdependent economic changes were mainly responsible for this formation. First, the development of canals, a railroad network, and, to a lesser extent, roads significantly lowered transport costs between cities, which enhanced trade between cities. Second, due to lower transport costs, the industrialization process really took off (starting in England) and cities often became more specialized, which stimulated trade between cities.
3. *Post-industrialization: around 1900–present*, characterized by declining importance of industrial production, and increased importance of negative externalities, like congestion. Structural changes in the rank-size distribution take decades to materialize, so it was only well into the twentieth century that the industrialized countries gradually entered the post-industrialization era. The share of the services sector in total employment becomes ever more important, at the expense of the footloose industrial sector.

Figure 8.15 illustrates urban power laws in Europe for the period 1500–1800, identifying the three largest cities and the ranking of Amsterdam in particular. The city-size distribution was relatively even in 1500, with $\hat{\gamma} = 1.594$ and Amsterdam as a small city. Although Amsterdam becomes rapidly more important in the next 100 years, there is little change in the distribution in 1600, with $\hat{\gamma} = 1.555$. More substantial change occurs in the periods up to 1700 and 1800, the era leading up to the industrial revolution, with $\hat{\gamma} = 1.207$ in 1700 and $\hat{\gamma} = 1.059$ (close to Zipf's Law) in 1800. London becomes the most important city, while Amsterdam's relative peak is reached around 1700. The city-size distribution becomes more uneven. This process continues up to around 1900, after which the city-size distribution becomes more even and the estimated power law exponent rises again; see Chapter 5 and Figure 8.12.

BOX 8.4 (cont.)

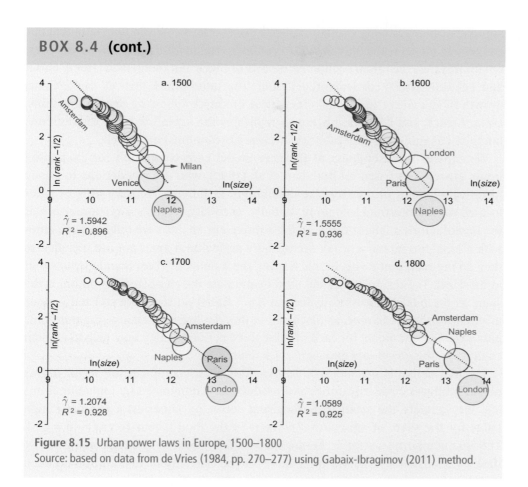

Figure 8.15 Urban power laws in Europe, 1500–1800
Source: based on data from de Vries (1984, pp. 270–277) using Gabaix-Ibragimov (2011) method.

There are two main problems with these explanations from our point of view. First, they are not founded on a coherent framework of economic principles. Second, they do not meet the requirements for an explanation of the empirical city-size distribution as formulated at the beginning of section 8.8, namely that the explanation must take account of the fact that the power law exponent can deviate from one and change over time. Both Simon's model and the approach of Gabaix using Gibrat's Law predict $\gamma = 1$.

8.8.2 Urban Power Laws in the Core Model with Congestion

The explanation we want to offer for urban power laws is based on the congestion model of section 8.6. In a nutshell, this explanation combines the geographical economics approach with modern urban economics, where the spreading force arises from the congestion costs associated with urban agglomeration. This additional spreading force is important to ensure that the geographical economics approach can reasonably explain city-size distributions.[26] We do not claim that our congestion model is the only possible economic explanation for urban power laws; see for instance the urban economics models of Black and Henderson (1999), Eaton and Eckstein (1997), or Duranton (2006). The latter study uses an endogenous growth model where individual cities grow or shrink following new innovations. Using French and US data, his model replicates the actual city-size distributions (and the changing position of cities in these distributions) quite well.

We explain the usefulness of the core model with congestion for explaining urban power laws based on Brakman et al. (1999), who use simulations to mimic historical changes in the city-size distribution in Europe. We start with 24 cities located on the racetrack economy. Initially, each city receives a random share of the manufacturing labour force. In the subsequent analysis we only include cities with a long-run manufacturing sector; pure agricultural areas are not included as they do not represent a city. In this respect, the number of cities is endogenous (but at most 24). The rest of the model used to simulate the city-size distribution is the same as the model discussed in section 8.6.[27] Based on the three stylized periods of urbanization for Europe, as discussed in Box 8.4, we now change the economic parameters in our model for each of these three periods, which may help to explain changes in the power law exponent over time.

The first period is *pre-industrialization*. The small manufacturing sector in this period produces close substitutes and production is dominated by immobile farmers. We simulate the small manufacturing sector by choosing a relatively high value for the share of agricultural workers in the total labour force $(1 - \delta = 0.5)$. The manufacturing sector is homogeneous (does not yet produce many varieties), by choosing a relatively high value for the elasticity of substitution between varieties $(\varepsilon = 6$; this simultaneously implies that increasing returns to scale are relatively unimportant – see Chapter 7). The low level of regional integration (high transport costs) is described by choosing high transport costs $T = 2$. Negative

---

[26] Fujita, Krugman, and Venables (1999, ch.11) develop an intricate urban hierarchy (central-place) model based on Fujita, Krugman, and Mori (1999) which does not match the empirical facts, as also acknowledged by Fujita, Krugman, and Venables (1999, p. 217); see in particular their figure 12.2. The basic idea can be understood as follows. Suppose that in the core model of Chapter 7 instead of one manufacturing good (which is produced in many varieties, one variety per firm) we now have two of these manufacturing goods. Suppose also that the first manufacturing good consists of many highly differentiated varieties with a low elasticity of substitution and the second good consists of varieties that are close substitutes, i.e. have a high substitution elasticity. It can be shown that the first good will be produced at a single location (the largest or central city) whereas the second good will be produced at both locations. Extending this idea to a large number of locations and a large number of manufactured goods (with a different substitution elasticity) leads to a hierarchy of locations as in Christaller's central place theory.

[27] The specification for the production function in the simulations is $l_{ir} = \alpha N_r^{\tau/(1-\tau)} + \beta x_i$.

economies of scale are not very important in this period, but also not absent (think of the disease-ridden large cities in the middle ages), which is simulated by choosing a moderate value of $\tau = 0.2$. It turns out that under these circumstances the simulations give rise to a fairly even city-size distribution with a high estimated power law exponent, close to the empirical estimate of 1.6 for Europe around 1500–1600; see panel *a* of Figure 8.15.

The second period is referred to as the period of *industrialization*. The basic characteristic in this period is the spectacular decrease in transport costs and the increasing importance of 'footloose' manufacturing production with increasing returns to scale. At the same time negative externalities are not absent, but also not very important, in the sense that they prevent large cities to become even larger. In the model we simulate these factors by lowering transport costs to $T = 1.25$, and increasing the share of the manufacturing labour force in total employment, $\delta = 0.6$. The increased importance of economies of scale and differentiated manufacturing products are represented by choosing $\varepsilon = 4$. Under these circumstances the simulations give rise to a fairly uneven city-size distribution with an estimated power law exponent close to one (close to Zipf's Law), which is the empirical estimate of Europe around 1800–1900; see panel *d* of Figure 8.15.

The last period is called *post-industrialization*. In this period transport costs remain low and, as before, the manufacturing sector is characterized by differentiated products and increasing returns to scale. The notable difference with earlier periods is congestion, such as the growing traffic jams, air pollution, rising land rents in larger cities, and so on. Smaller cities are less troubled by such effects and therefore have a tendency to grow faster. In the model we simulate this by increasing the congestion parameter to $\tau = 1/3$. Under these circumstances the simulations give rise to a more even city-size distribution, with an estimated power law exponent close to 1.4, which is the current empirical estimate for Europe; see Chapter 5, panel *b* of Figure 8.12, and Table 8.1.

The core model with congestion is thus able to explain changes in estimated power law exponents over time, in particular the U-shaped pattern already identified by Parr (1985), through changes in the economic circumstances as given by the parameter adjustments in the discussion above. According to this pattern, the power law exponent γ starts well above one. As economic development gathers pace, γ decreases and may become smaller than one. As the economy matures, γ starts to rise again. The first two phases of this process are illustrated for Asia and Africa in panel *b* of Figure 8.12 and for Europe in Figure 8.15. The last phase is illustrated for Europe in panel *b* of Figure 8.12. Actual power law distributions can thus in principle be reproduced by varying those model-parameters that have been identified in the literature to be relevant for understanding changes in the city-size distribution. This basic approach is more or less the first attempt to explicitly use a geographical economics model to study empirically testable aspects of the urban system (see Gabaix and Ioannides, 2004, pp. 2363–4 for this assessment).[28]

8.9 Conclusions

We introduce three alternative models that build on and extend the core model of Chapter 7: the intermediate goods model, the generalized model, and the solvable model.

The *intermediate goods model* includes intermediate production and inter-sectoral labour mobility, instead of inter-regional labour mobility. Especially in empirical applications, where the comparison between countries is important, this model is attractive as trade in intermediate products is important and labour is more mobile within countries than between countries. In addition, this model has the nice feature that decreasing returns in food production can lead to a bell-shaped curve: as trade costs fall, we see that a country goes through a spreading phase, then through an agglomeration phase, and finally towards spreading again. This is qualitatively different from the Tomahawk diagram summarizing the core model (which is biased towards agglomeration).

The *generalized model* incorporates both the core model of Chapter 7 and the intermediate goods model in one framework, which allows for a richer menu of long-run equilibria.

The *solvable model* introduces a second production factor in the manufacturing sector. For some applications such a model is more appealing than the core model of Chapter 7, for example when analysing the consequences of globalization for different types of workers. As a surprising bonus the model leads to explicit solutions for factor rewards. Analytically, solvable models seem to be preferable to the core model of geographical economics of Chapter 7, which requires numerical simulations. This potential advantage only comes to the fore when we focus on the case of two regions. Once we turn to a multi-region setting and no longer get away with the assumption of neutral space, we have to rely on simulations anyway (see Fuijta and Mori, 2005, and Behrens and Thisse, 2007).

In a continuation of our discussion of the urban economics literature on urban systems, in which congestion plays a key role (recall Chapter 5), we also extend the core model of Chapter 7 to a multi-region setting with congestion affecting the production structure of the model. We introduce congestion as an additional spreading force for two main reasons. First, to clarify the impact of congestion on the nature of the long-run equilibria. With congestion, the model typically results

---

[28] Brakman et al. (1999) also analyse non-neutral space and how structural the link is between parameter values and estimated power law exponents.

in a more even equilibrium allocation of the manufacturing labour force. Complete agglomeration is now the exception and not, as in the core model, the rule. Second, to apply the geographical economics model with congestion to an important topic in urban economics that we encountered (but left 'unsolved') in Chapter 5: the empirical city-size distribution as characterized by urban power laws. We briefly empirically evaluate urban power laws at the world, continent, and country level and discuss the lack of power of power laws at the country level. On this basis, we show that the core model with congestion is able to explain changes in estimated power law exponents over time through changes in the economic circumstances as given by parameter adjustments.

The discussion of the model extensions of the core model of geographical economics introduced in Chapter 8 serves a dual purpose. On the one hand, these extensions are important in their own right. They show how changes in the set-up and assumptions of the core model can lead to new and different conclusions regarding the spatial equilibrium allocation of economic activity. On the other hand, the model extensions turn out to be useful when we start to discuss the empirical and policy implications of urban and geographical economics. This is the topic to which we turn next.

Exercises

Question 8.1 Human Capital
Derive equation 8.21. Also calculate the break and the sustain points of the solvable model.

Question 8.2 Three Structural Models
What are the three alternative structural models of geographical economics and what is their main characteristic? (Note: the *generalized* model is excluded from the answers.)

Which model would you prefer to analyse the consequences of building a new railway line across the strait of Gibraltar (from Spain to Morocco)? Explain.

Question 8.3 China Migration and Tomahawk
The World Development Report 2009 by the World Bank discusses, among other things, the migration flows of Chinese workers in the context of geographical economics.

Where in the Tomahawk diagram (Figure 7.9, Figure 8.2, and Figure 8.3) would you argue that the Chinese economy is operating according to the World Bank discussion? What are the consequences for (what type of) international trade? Explain.

9 Empirics of Economic Geography

LEARNING OBJECTIVES

- To know the basic empirical hypotheses associated with geographical economics.
- To understand how to test for the home market effect and the spatial wage structure (and how these are related).
- To understand why it is difficult to test the full model of geographical economics and how shocks can be used to assess the relevance of geographical economics.
- To be able to see how the use of better (micro-)data and estimation techniques yield new insights into the empirical relevance of geographical economics.

9.1   Introduction

Chapter 1 of this book presents a number of stylized facts about the clustering of economic activity to justify an inquiry into our 'spiky world'. In Part II we analysed the clustering of economic activity from the perspective of urban economics. In these models and their empirical applications (see Chapter 5 and Chapter 6) spatial interdependencies between cities typically play no role. Locations are analysed as if they were 'freely floating islands' which are not really connected to each other. The starting point of geographical economics is that these spatial interdependencies are key to understand the clustering of economic activity across space. In Chapter 7 and Chapter 8 we introduced the main models of geographical economics. The present chapter focuses on the *empirics* of geographical economics, in order to assess whether the major spatial stylized facts can be explained by geographical economics models.

In the first part of this chapter (sections 9.2–9.5), we discuss two implications of the geographical economics models, namely (i) the existence of the home market effect and (ii) a spatial wage structure. The home market effect implies that if a region displays a relatively large demand for a certain good, this increased demand will lead to a more-than-proportional increase in the region's production of that good. The spatial wage structure (see already the two-region equilibrium wage equation 7.25) implies that wages will be higher in or near economic centres. These investigations are the first steps towards a full-fledged empirical assessment.

Given the observed core–periphery patterns in real life, if both of these predictions were refuted by the data, further empirical research would be rather futile.[1] In section 9.3 we look at empirical research into the home market effect. In section 9.4 we will do the same for the existence of a spatial wage structure.

We will conclude that the empirical studies on the home market effect and the spatial wage structure in general confirm their relevance, but that they do not offer a complete or convincing test of the geographical economics model as such. The main reason, as will be discussed in section 9.5, is that both implications take the spatial distribution of economic activity as given, and in doing so are primarily concerned with what we dubbed in Chapter 7 and Chapter 8 the *short-run* equilibrium version of geographical economics. A real test of geographical economics should also look at the empirical validity of this approach when the spatial distribution of economic activity is no longer fixed but subject to change. This is the starting point and motivation for the second part of this chapter (sections 9.6–9.9), where we will test for the impact of shocks on the spatial allocation of economic activity (section 9.6) and for the relationship between transport costs and agglomeration (section 9.7). In section 9.8 we will see why and how modern empirical research in geographical economics has gradually submerged into and thereby became part of the broader empirical research agenda in spatial economics. Section 9.9 concludes.

9.2 Empirical Hypotheses Based on Geographical Economics

Most stylized facts on the spatial concentration, specialization, or agglomeration of economic activity can be accounted for by various economic theories. If we look for instance at the stylized facts on agglomeration and specialization for cities and the empirical research on urban economics in Chapter 3, various theories can be used to explain the basic urban facts. In a seminal paper that has aged quite well, Glaeser et al. (1992) try to establish which types of externalities or agglomeration economies are more relevant in explaining the growth of US cities. In the end, however, they rightly conclude (p. 1151) that the 'evidence on externalities is indirect, and many of our findings can be explained by a neo-classical model in which industries grow where labour is cheap and demand is high'. As for the finding as summarized and explained in Chapter 3 that industries are geographically concentrated, Ellison and Glaeser (1997) show that their empirical results can be substantiated by a model in which the concentration of sectors is the result of either natural advantages of a location (first nature or physical geography) or

---

[1] The reader may note that this statement does not hold at the spreading equilibrium where all regions are of equal size.

location spillovers (second nature or man-made geography). In fact, it turns out that the relationship between the levels of concentration and the sector characteristics is the same for concentration being the result of first nature or second nature causes. Ellison and Glaeser (1997, p. 891) therefore conclude that 'geographic concentration by itself does not imply the existence of spillovers; natural advantages have similar effects and may be important empirically'.[2] Despite a vast array of empirical studies and new empirical tools since Edward Glaeser and his co-authors reached these conclusions some 20-odd years ago in the 1990s, the fact remains that the main findings about spatial agglomeration can be reconciled with multiple and quite different theories.

For the assessment of the empirical relevance of geographical economics there are two specific analytical problems that must be mentioned upfront. First, key model variables, notably market size or market potential, are endogenous variables which are in the long run determined by the location decisions of workers and firms in the geographical economics approach. To see what's at stake, take the wage equation 7.25 from the core model. Wages in any location j are higher if the region faces a larger market potential, as illustrated by equation 7.25 for region 1:

$W_1 = \left(Y_1 I_1^{\varepsilon-1} + Y_2 T^{1-\varepsilon} I_2^{\varepsilon-1}\right)^{1/\varepsilon}$. The right-hand side of this equation illustrates that

wages depend not only on the size of the domestic market but also on the market size of (neighbouring) regions (in this case only region 2). But the main elements of the market potential, income Y and the price index I, are endogenous. Second, geographical economics models are characterized by multiple equilibria (recall Figure 7.6). Which equilibrium gets established depends on initial conditions, as explained in Chapter 7. Without knowledge of the initial conditions it is difficult to test the model. Moreover, the relationship between the key model parameters (the level of transport costs and the degree of agglomeration) is non-linear, making it difficult to use simple linear reduced-form specifications to test for the relevance of geographical economics.

Against this background, can we devise empirical hypotheses that (1) potentially differentiate between geographical economics models and other approaches (not least, urban economics); and (2) can deal with the two analytical problems mentioned above? The following five key features of geographical economics have been singled out for empirical research (Head and Mayer, 2004, p. 2616):

* *The home market effect.* Regions with a large demand for increasing-returns sectors have a more than proportional share of production and are net exporters of these goods (see equation 7.28 for the home market effect in the core model).

---

[2] Ellison and Glaeser (1999) show that natural advantages can explain a considerable part of the geographical concentration of sectors in the USA.

- *A large market potential raises local factor prices.* A large market will increase demand for local factors of production and this raises factor rewards. From the equilibrium wage equation 7.25 we know that regions that are surrounded by or close to regions with high real income (indicating strong spatial demand linkages) will have relatively higher wages.

- *A large market potential induces factor inflows.* Footloose factors of production will be attracted to those markets where firms pay relatively high factor rewards. In our core model from Chapter 7, footloose workers move to the region with highest real wages and similarly firms prefer locations with good market access.

- *Shock sensitivity.* Changes in the economic environment can (but need not!) trigger a change in the equilibrium spatial distribution of economic activity. This hypothesis goes to the heart of the idea that geographical economics models are characterized by multiple equilibria.

- *Reduction in transportation or trade costs induces agglomeration*, at least beyond a critical level of transport or trade costs. Figure 7.9, for example, shows that for a large range of transport costs a change in these costs does not lead to a change in the equilibrium degree of agglomeration, but if a shock moves the economy beyond its break or sustain point the economy goes from spreading to agglomeration or vice versa, respectively. This also implies that more economic integration (interpreted as a lowering of transport costs) should at some point lead to (more) agglomeration of the footloose activities and factors of production.

With the exception of the third of these five hypotheses, we will discuss empirical work carried out for each hypothesis in the remainder of this chapter. In doing so, we will stick to the order of the above list.[3] The fourth and fifth hypotheses differ in a rather substantial way from the other hypotheses. In a nutshell, the home market and spatial wage studies that are the subject of the remainder of this chapter are thus based on the *short-run* equilibrium of geographical economics, where the spatial differences in agglomeration are still taken as given. In the *long run*, as we know from Chapter 7, it is the aim of geographical economics to explain these spatial differences as well. The last two hypotheses precisely fall into this category: what happens to the spatial distribution of economic activity itself?

---

[3] The reason for not discussing the 'factor inflow hypothesis' here is that not much work has been done on testing this hypothesis – see Crozet (2004) or Head and Mayer (2004) for notable exceptions – and there is also not really a conceptual difference with the 'higher factor prices' hypothesis. The idea that mobile workers migrate to regions with a large manufacturing production sector is tested in a model where labour flows are (mainly) a function of (real) market potential just like, as we will see in section 9.4, in the case of the second hypothesis dealing with a spatial wage structure where wages will be a function of (real) market potential.

9.3   In Search of the Home Market Effect

In a series of important papers some time ago, Davis and Weinstein (1996, 1997, 1999, 2001, 2003) developed an empirical methodology that enabled them 'to distinguish a world in which trade arises due to increasing returns as opposed to comparative advantage' (Davis and Weinstein, 2003). Following Krugman (1980) – and see equation 7.28 for a precise definition – the home market effect implies that if a country or a region has a relatively high demand for a good, like cars, it will lead to a *more than proportional* increase in that country's production of cars and thus to exports. Note, and again check equation 7.28, that the home market effect assumes a perfectly elastic labour supply. If this is not the case, a change in demand will translate into a change in wages, which is precisely the motivation for the spatial wage structure hypothesis, the second hypothesis on our list above.

The central empirical equation used by Davis and Weinstein is derived from a theoretical model where it is assumed that comparative advantage determines trade and production at the sector level, whereas increasing returns drive within-sector specialization. In fact, they thus acknowledge that in practice more than one theory explains the structure of trade flows. The geographical unit of analysis is either a country or, as in Davis and Weinstein (1999), a region within a country. The following equation is estimated:[4]

$$X_{gnr} = \kappa_{gnr} + \kappa_1 share_{gnr} + \kappa_2 idiodem_{gnr} + end + err_{gnr} \qquad 9.1$$

where:

X_{gnr}	= output of good g in sector n in country r
$share_{gnr}$	= share of output of good g in sector n in country r in the total output of good g in sector
$idiodem_{gnr}$	= difference between the demand for good g of sector n in country r and the demand for good g of sector in other countries
end	= (factor endowments for country r) × (input coefficients for good g in sector n)
err_{gnr}	= error term
κ_{gnr}	= constant

The crucial variable is $idiodem_{gnr}$, a mnemonic for *idio*syncratic *dem*and. This variable represents the home market effect. If every country demanded the same share of good g in sector n it would be zero. A coefficient for $idiodem_{gnr}$ exceeding one implies that an increase in demand for good g of sector n in country r leads to a more than proportional increase in output X_{gnr}. The inclusion of the variable $share_{gnr}$ captures the tendency that, absent idiosyncratic demand, each country r

---

[4] In the following r is referred to as a country, but it could denote a region.

produces good g in sector n in the same proportion as other countries do. The fact that endowments can also determine the output X_{gnr} is the reason for the inclusion of *end*, ensuring that the role of neo-classical trade theory is not neglected. *The home market effect is therefore verified if $\kappa_2 > 1$.*[5]

9.3.1 Evidence to Support the Home Market Effect

Equation 9.1 is estimated for a sample of OECD countries in Davis and Weinstein (1996, 1997). In the construction of the variables, the aim is to stick as closely as possible to the theoretical model of Krugman (1980). As far as *idiodem* is concerned, this means that the variable lacks some real geographical content, since it is assumed that the relative location of countries does not matter, implying that demand linkages between two neighbouring countries are, *a priori*, not stronger than the linkages between two countries on opposite sides of our planet. This is not very realistic, and it is partly for this neglect of geography that the evidence in Davis and Weinstein (1996, 1997) with respect to the home market effect is rather mixed. For example, in Davis and Weinstein (1997) the parameter κ_2 exceeds one for only nine sectors in their sample of 22 OECD countries and 26 sectors.

In subsequent work on the home market effect, Davis and Weinstein (2003) used the same data set of OECD countries, but *idiodem* is measured differently by introducing different transport costs for each sector. This modification of *idiodem* is important because the support for the home market effect is now much more conclusive. The second strategy that is followed, see Davis and Weinstein (1999), is to stick to the initial measurement of *idiodem* (without transport costs), but to apply equation 9.1 to *regions within a single country*, rather than between countries. A sample consisting of 40 regions r, 19 goods g, and 6 sector aggregates n, is analysed for Japan. The main results are given in Table 9.1, where the second column shows the results of the pooled regression if factor endowments (*end*) are not included. In this case κ_2 is not only significant but also larger than one, thus supporting the home market effect. Davis and Weinstein (1999, p. 396) interpret this result as 'clearly in the range of economic geography'. Things change, however, when factor endowments *end* are included: see the last column of Table 9.1. The coefficient for *idiodem* is still significant, but now smaller than one. The second specification, therefore, does not provide support for the home market effect in the aggregate. A breakdown of the data to the goods level shows that for 8 of the 19 goods κ_2 is larger than one (at a 5 per cent level of significance).

---

[5] If only factor endowments mattered for the determination of output, given the technology matrix, equation 9.1 would reduce to $X_{gnr} = end$. If $\kappa_2 < 1$ this is taken as evidence that neo-classical trade theory or new trade models are more relevant.

Table 9.1 Home market effect for Japanese regions

idiodem	1.416	0.888
	(0.025)	(0.070)
share	1.033	– 1.7441
	(0.007)	(0.211)
end included?	No	Yes
# Observations	760	760

Source: Davis and Weinstein (1999); standard errors between brackets; seemingly unrelated regressions.

9.3.2 The Home Market Effect and Geographical Economics: An Assessment

The empirical work of Davis and Weinstein on the home market effect is obviously important from the perspective of geographical economics since the home market effect is a crucial element of the core geographical economics model. The main problem that limits the usefulness of the home market effect as a test of the empirical relevance of the geographical economics model is that the home market effect is not only at home in geographical economics but also in other trade models with positive transportation costs. Davis and Weinstein do not consider this to be a problem because they refer to Krugman (1980) as their economic geography model, but Krugman (1980), although close, is not a geographical economics model because regional market size and thus demand is still exogenous. In geographical economics market size and demand are endogenous. This endogenization of market size and demand arises because manufacturing labour (and firms) can move between regions (Krugman, 1991) and / or because firms require the output of other firms as intermediate input (Venables, 1996) as we discussed at length in Chapter 7 and Chapter 8. So, in the long-run equilibrium version of the geographical economics models the distribution of mobile firms and/or workers is not fixed, but determined by the spreading and agglomerating forces that are the hallmark of this approach.[6] The home market effect studies therefore do not offer a convincing or complete test for the relevance of the geographical economics literature.

   The spurt of empirical research on the home market effect as initiated by the work of Davis and Weinstein some 20-odd years ago has, however, undergone a revival on two fronts in more recent years. On the one hand, see for instance

---

[6] More specifically, in their estimation of the determinants of the production of Japanese manufacturing sectors, Davis and Weinstein (1999, pp. 396–7) include factor endowments along with the region's demand for manufactured goods. In terms of the long-run version of the geographical economics model this is not without problems since both the regional demand for manufactured goods and the region's share of factor endowments are determined simultaneously.

Matsuyama (2015), progress has been made to give the home market effect a firmer theoretical foundation. On the other hand, the availability of novel and richer data sets now allow for a more rigorous testing of the home market effect: Costinot et al. (2016) do for instance find strong confirmation for the existence of the home market effect when analysing detailed drug sales data from the global pharmaceutical industry in the sense that countries tend to be net sellers of the drugs that they demand the most. This new research on the home market effect is very important as such, but for our present purposes it remains the case, as has been argued above, that the home market effect studies rely on the short-run version of the core geographical economics model at best.

Notwithstanding the rather special nature of the home market effect, it does point to another possible way to test for the empirical relevance of geographical economics (again, recall equation 7.28). If, unlike the models of the home market effect, labour supply is not perfectly elastic, the increased demand will not only lead to increased production but also to higher nominal wages in that region. Hence, given the (reasonable) assumption that labour supply is not perfectly elastic, it is expected that regions with a relatively high demand for manufactures also pay relatively higher wages. This topic is addressed in the next section, where we discuss the second empirical hypothesis: a large market potential leads to relatively higher factor prices for a region.

9.4   The Spatial Wage Structure and Real Market Potential

In neo-classical trade theory, there is no foundation for a spatial wage structure. The existence of economic centres can be rationalized by location-specific endowments, but this does not imply a spatial wage structure. Even with (endowment-driven) agglomeration, the main prediction of neo-classical trade theory is that trade will lead to factor price equalization. In the new trade models – without transport costs – it is true that in autarky wages are higher for the country with the larger labour force, but when trade opens up wages are equalized. This follows from the specialization in production of varieties of the manufactured good, such that some varieties are produced in one country and other varieties in the other country. This rules out a spatial wage structure in new trade models because there is no endogenous agglomeration of manufacturing production across space, and thus no possibility of a centre of manufacturing production.

Of course, when we allow for *productivity* differences between countries, regions, or cities it is perfectly possible to arrive at the conclusion that wages are higher in economic centres. In fact, and as we discussed in Chapter 6, much of the empirical work in modern urban economics argues that we expect wages to be higher in economic centres because of the existence of local human capital or (pure) technological externalities that lead to productivity and wage differences across locations. Typically, however, these spillovers or externalities are confined to the location as such and spatial interdependencies, the key ingredient of geographical economics, has no role to play.

9.4.1 Wages and the Market Potential Function

The market potential function dates back to Harris (1954) and has a long tradition in economic geography. It basically states the market potential of region j is large when the firms from this region face a large demand for its goods from nearby regions k. So, a region's market potential depends positively on the demand coming from other regions and negatively on the distance between a region and the other regions. This basic idea also shows up via the wage equation from the geographical economics model. To see this, take the normalized version of the equilibrium wage equation 7.25 for the case of k regions instead of just two regions:

$$W_j = \left(\sum_k Y_k I_k^{\varepsilon-1} T^{D_{jk}(1-\varepsilon)} \right)^{1/\varepsilon}$$

9.2

Recall that W is the wage rate, Y is income, I is the price index, ε is the elasticity of substitution, T is the transport cost parameter, and $T_{jk} = T^{D_{jk}}$, where D_{jk} is the distance between locations j and k. The parameter T is defined as the number of goods that have to be shipped in order to ensure that one unit arrives over one unit of distance. Given the elasticity of substitution ε, equation 9.2 immediately shows that a region's wages are higher when demand in surrounding markets (Y_k) is higher, access to those markets is better (lower transport costs T), and when there is less competition (competition effect, measured by the price index I_k). With the notable exception of the competition effect – measured by the price index (see below) – the wage equation is very close to the simple market potential function alluded to above.

To get from equation 9.2 to a market potential function for wages that can be tested, the equation can be simplified by assuming that wages in region j depend only on a constant and income Y_k, with the impact of the latter on wages in j increasing, the shorter the distance between the regions. Distance is measured relative to the economic centre of a region. The resulting specification is:

$$log\left(W_j\right) = \kappa_0 + \kappa_1 log\left(\sum_k Y_k e^{-\kappa_2 D_{jk}} \right) + err_j$$

9.3

where κ_0, κ_1, and κ_2 are parameters to be estimated. This specification is an example of a market potential function for wages with one big difference compared to a standard market potential function: W is the explanatory variable. The advantage is that it is easy to estimate and shows if there is a spatial wage structure or not. The disadvantage of this market potential function for wages is that there is not a one-to-one correspondence between the theoretical model and its structural parameters: wage equations 9.2 and 9.3 are not the same! As the reader might have noticed, equation 9.2 includes the price index I_k, which is absent in equation 9.3 . This is why in the literature the terms *nominal* and *real* market potential are used; in equation 9.3 the *nominal* market potential (NMP) matters whereas in the wage equation from our core model the *real* market potential (*RMP*) is central. The difference between the two concepts is the price index effect $I_k^{\varepsilon-1}$. If a firm faces more competitors in region j this will be reflected in a lower price index and a lower market share for this firm. This competition effect tells us that being close to a large market also has a drawback. In recent years, wage equations like 9.3 have been estimated for various (groups of) countries and regions. By and large, they confirm that a spatial wage structure exists but it is also concluded that the distance decay is quite strong. The latter implies that the spatial reach of demand linkages is limited, as measured by the κ_2 coefficient in equation 9.3.

9.4.2   Spatial Wages and Real Market Potential: the Hanson (2005) Model

In this sub-section, we will discuss an attempt based on the seminal work by Hanson (2005) to estimate the equilibrium wage equation 9.2, that is by trying to estimate the impact of *real* market potential on wages. In doing so, we are able to estimate the key model parameters of geographical economics. Before we turn to the estimation strategy and results, it is useful to remind ourselves that the equilibrium wage equation 9.2 is part of our core model from Chapter 7. We also know from Chapter 8 that this model is a special case of a more general geographical economics model (Puga, 1999). The same is true for the model and the corresponding wage equation used by Hanson (2005) in his empirical work discussed below. Head and Mayer (2004, pp. 2621–7) clearly show that an equilibrium wage equation like 9.2, where regional wages are a function of real market potential (*RMP*), only follows if one assumes that labour is the only primary factor in the production process and that there are no intermediate inputs.[7]

   When the aim is to estimate wage equation 9.2, the literature offers two estimation strategies. The first option was pioneered by Redding and Venables (2004) and it is to estimate a wage equation like 9.2 in two steps; see also Bosker and

---

[7] In a geographical economics model with intermediate inputs (hence not the Krugman, 1991 nor the Hanson, 2005 model) supplier potential enters the wage equation next to market potential; see our discussion of the Krugman and Venables (1995) model in Chapter 8. Supplier access means that when the price index is low, intermediate input-supplying firms are relatively close to your location of production, which strengthens agglomeration (and vice versa if the price index is high). A better supplier access (a lower value of I) lowers wage costs. This effect is stronger the larger the share of intermediate products in production; without intermediate inputs only the real market potential term is left in the wage equation.

Garretsen (2012). In the first step a proxy for *RMP* is estimated using bilateral trade data and a gravity trade equation. In the second step, the estimated *RMP* is inserted into the wage equation, which is subsequently estimated. In an influential application of this strategy Head and Mayer (2006) analyse 13 sectors and 57 EU regions for the period 1985–2000 and find clear confirmation that wages respond positively to market potential; on average a 10 per cent increase in *RMP* raises wages by 1.2 per cent. In Chapter 10 (Technical Note 10.1), we will return to this first estimation strategy and explain its workings and its relationship to the main empirical workhorse model in international trade, the gravity model.

The second option is to estimate wage equation 9.2 directly. An advantage of this strategy is that estimates are derived for the structural model parameters from the underlying geographical economics model. This is the route taken by Hanson (2005). Before we turn to the empirical results, we briefly discuss the theoretical approach in Hanson (2005). Following Helpman (1998) and Thomas (1996), the agricultural sector of the core model of Chapter 7 is replaced by a housing sector which reflects demand for a non-tradable service in a specific region (note that Food is a tradable good in the core model). The motivation for this assumption is that the core model of Chapter 7 displays a bias towards monocentric equilibria: for low enough transport costs all manufactures end up being produced at one location (recall the Tomahawk diagram of Figure 7.9). This is clearly not in accordance with the facts about the spatial distribution of manufacturing activity for the USA or any other (economically) advanced country. A local non-tradable service provides an alternative spreading force, because if demand for this service increases due to agglomeration, prices of these services increase too, which stimulates spreading. Moreover, for the advanced countries agriculture provides only a weak spreading force in contrast to the effects of prices of non-tradables, like housing. The perfectly competitive housing sector serves as the spreading force, because housing is relatively expensive in large agglomerations where demand for housing is high. The geographical economics model with a housing sector typically results in a more even distribution of manufacturing activity than the core model of Chapter 7 (recall our discussion of the bell-shaped curve in Chapter 8, to which inter alia the Helpman (1998) model may give rise!). Fortunately, the equilibrium conditions are still very similar to the core model; in particular the wage equation, which is central to the empirical analysis, is identical to wage equation 9.2.

Lack of reliable data on regional manufacturing price indices I_k and on the regional prices of housing P_k make an adaption of the wage equation necessary. In order to arrive at a testable equation, the following strategy is followed by research following Hanson (2005). Besides the equilibrium wage equation, the equilibrium price index equation, and the well-known condition that regional income Y_j equals income derived from labour ($Y_j = \lambda_j L W_j$) there are two additional equilibrium conditions (Hanson, 2005, p. 5; Bosker et al., 2012):

(i) the equilibrium condition for the housing market: $P_j H_j = (1-\delta)Y_j$;

(ii) real wage equalization between regions: $W_j / \left(P_j^{1-\delta} I_j^{\delta}\right) = W_k / \left(P_k^{1-\delta} I_k^{\delta}\right)$

Condition (i) states that payments for housing in j equal the share of expenditures allocated to housing in j and condition (ii) states real wage equality, implying that the economy is by definition in its long-run equilibrium. This last condition is far from innocent and we will return to it below.

To get from equation 9.2 to equation 9.4, first substitute (i) into (ii) to get rid of the housing price variable P_j and use (ii) in 9.2 to get rid of the price index I_j. We then arrive at (in logs):

$$log\left(W_j\right) = \kappa_0 + \varepsilon^{-1} log\left(\sum_k Y_k^{\varepsilon+(1-\varepsilon)/\delta} H_k^{(1-\delta)(\varepsilon-1)/\delta} W_k^{(\varepsilon-1)/\delta} T^{(1-\varepsilon)D_{jk}}\right) + err_j \qquad 9.4$$

where κ_0 is a parameter and H_k is the housing stock in region k. Note that equation 9.4 includes the three structural parameters of the core model, namely δ, ε, and T. Given the availability of US data on wages, income, the housing stock, and a proxy for distance, equation 9.4 can be estimated. The dependent variable is the wage rate measured at the US county level.[8] The results of estimating 9.4, and using various controls not shown here, are summarized in Table 9.2 for the full

Table 9.2 Estimation of the structural wage equation

	1970–1980	1980–1990
δ	0.961 (0.015)	0.956 (0.013)
ε	7.597 (1.250)	6.562 (0.838)
$log(T)$	1.970 (0.328)	3.219 (0.416)
Adjusted R^2	0.256	0.347
# Observations	3075	3075
$\varepsilon/(\varepsilon-1)$	1.152	1.180
ρ	0.868	0.847

Source: Hanson (2005), Table 3; standard errors between brackets; ε = substitution elasticity, δ = share of income spend on manufactures, T = transport costs; $\varepsilon/(\varepsilon-1)$ = mark-up; $\varepsilon = 1/(1-\rho)$.

[8] An alternative version uses US county employment as the dependent variable. To control for correlation of the error term with the regression function, Hanson uses various checks (i.a. measuring independent variables at the state level, using time differences, and excluding the high-population counties).

sample of 3,075 US counties in the periods 1970–1980 and 1980–1990. Note that all three structural parameters are significant in both estimation periods.

Looking at the estimation results in Table 9.2, a first (surprising) conclusion is that transportation costs seem to have increased over time, which would imply that the benefits of spatial agglomeration have increased over time. Similarly, the elasticity of substitution ε has decreased somewhat, implying that imperfect competition has become more important and mark-ups over marginal costs have increased during the period 1970–1990. The estimate for δ, the share of income spent on manufactures, is fairly high and constant over time (above 0.9). It implies that less than 10 per cent of US personal income is spent on housing (or non-tradable goods in general), which is too low compared to actual spending on housing. Alternative specifications lead to lower estimates of δ but these results are not statistically superior to those shown in Table 9.2 (Hanson, 2005, p. 19).

It can also be shown, based on the parameter values for δ and ε in Table 9.2, that the degree of agglomeration of US manufacturing production depends on the level of transport costs. To understand this, we must return to the no-black-hole condition, discussed in section 7.8.2 for the core model, where the condition was stated as $\rho > \delta$.[9] It was argued in Chapter 7 that if the condition $\rho > \delta$ is fulfilled, the equilibrium regional distribution of economic activity depends on the level of transportation costs, whereas if this condition is not fulfilled full agglomeration (a monocentric equilibrium) is the only feasible equilibrium in the long run, such that the equilibrium spatial distribution of manufacturing activity would not depend at all on transport costs.

Based on the estimated value of δ and the implied value of ρ, it *appears* that the no-black-hole condition is violated, suggesting that the location of US manufacturing activity does not depend on the level of transportation costs. This conclusion is *not* correct because the interpretation of the condition is reversed in the housing model of geographical economics that underlies Table 9.2. Why does this switching of the interpretation of the no-black-hole condition take place? The reason is that Hanson builds on the model developed by Helpman (1998), where the agricultural sector of the core model is replaced by a housing sector. Since the agricultural good is freely traded between regions, whereas housing is a non-tradable good, the interpretation of the no-black-hole condition is reversed; see Helpman (1998, pp. 50–51).

To verify the strength of demand linkages across space, Hanson analyses the spatial decay of the predicted wage changes of the estimation results reported in Table 9.2. For the estimation results shown in the table there is a very strong distance decay; the value for the transportation costs coefficient T is such that

---

[9] The no-black-hole condition, without the label attached to it, can already be found in Krugman (1991, p. 496).

'changes in the market potential index affect wages only within 200 km' (Hanson, 2005, p. 20), which would mean that the spatial reach of demand linkages as exemplified by the *RMP* variable seems rather limited.[10]

9.4.3 An Extension: Spatial Wages Without Real Wage Equalization

The fact that we discuss Hanson (2005) in some detail reflects our view that this study and related real market potential studies to date still constitute the most important attempt to arrive at an empirical validation of the geographical economics approach regarding the hypothesis that a larger market potential raises a region's factor prices. Still, there are a number of objections that can be raised (see also Hanson, 2005, pp. 20–21). In this sub-section we focus on a particular issue, the use of the rather strong assumptions of inter-regional real wage equalization which may be of limited use in other cases than the USA (such as Europe). More generally, and just like with the empirical attempt to test for the home market effect, one can ask if the studies that estimate the impact of market potential or market access on wages constitute a defining test of the geographical economics model to begin with. This is the topic of section 9.5.

The assumption of real wage equalization is needed in equation 9.4 in order to get rid of the price index I. Assuming that we do not have data on regional manufacturing prices, can we estimate equation 9.2 without invoking real wage equalization? Brakman, Garretsen, and Schramm (2004a) try to do so for their sample of German regions by simplifying the price index while also allowing for labour productivity differences between regions. As a benchmark, when real wage equalization is assumed to hold and the estimation strategy of Hanson (2005) discussed in the previous sub-section is applied to their sample of 151 western and eastern German districts for the period 1994–1995, the estimated coefficients for the three key model parameters are not plausible to begin with. They end up with the following wage equation (see Brakman, Garretsen, and Schramm, 2004a, for full details):

$$log\left(W_j\right) = \kappa_0 + \varepsilon^{-1}log\left(\sum_k Y_k T^{(1-\varepsilon)D_{jk}} I_k^{\varepsilon-1}\right) + \kappa_1 EG \qquad 9.5$$

With: $I_j^{1-\varepsilon} = \left(\lambda_j \left(W_j(1+\gamma_j)\right)^{1-\varepsilon} + \left(1-\lambda_j\right)\left(\overline{W}T^{D_{j-center}}\right)^{1-\varepsilon}\right)$, where γ_r represents the productivity gap between West Germany and district j, which is $(MPL_{west} / MPL_r) - 1$; EG is a dummy variable equal to 1 if j is in East Germany; $\overline{W}_r$ is the average wage outside district j; $D_{r-center}$ is the distance from district j to the economic centre (the district *Giessen* near Frankfurt); and λ_r is the district's share of manufacturing employment.

---

[10] The specification of the distance effect is also relevant for this conclusion; see Bosker and Garretsen (2010).

Table 9.3 No real wage equalization

ε	3.652	(23.4)
$\log(T)$	0.003	(13.7)
District Specific Control Variables		
EG dummy	−0.633	(−16.2)
$D_{country}$	−.056	(−1.4)
Industry	1.052	(5.8)
Other services	1.983	(5.4)
High-skilled	5.456	(11.7)
Adjusted R^2	0.99	

Estimation method for equation 9.5: WLS; number of observations 151; district-specific control variables that are not statistically significant are omitted; result for the dummy for the city of Erlangen is not reported, t-statistic between brackets.

Table 9.3 shows the estimation results for the two remaining model parameters, the substitution elasticity ε and the transport cost parameter T, as well as for the various control variables that were used. As to the results for the controls: the regional wage is higher when a region is not in East Germany (EG dummy), is not a country but a city district, its sectoral employment shows more industry or services employment, and when its workers are high-skilled.

The results in Table 9.3 show that the transport cost parameter T is significant and has the right sign. The same holds for the substitution elasticity ε. The results support the notion that nominal wages in district r are higher if this region has a better access (in terms of distance) to larger markets. That is, our alternative estimation strategy yields a spatial wage structure for Germany. To some extent this is a surprising result. Certainly compared to the case of the USA as reported by Hanson (2005), the German labour market is considered to be rigid, which could imply in terms of our model that, for whatever institutional reason, inter-regional wages are set at the same level. For a country like Germany one might thus very well expect that the spatial distribution of real market potential is *not* only reflected in spatial wage differences but (also) in the spatial distribution of quantity variables like regional (un)employment (see also Puga, 2002, pp. 389–390, for this assertion for Germany).[11]

We can illustrate the strength of the inter-regional demand linkages that give rise to the spatial wage structure, using the following thought experiment. Based on the estimated coefficients in Table 9.3 we derived the impact on regional wages

---

[11] Inter-regional wage differences are for instance not feasible if a union ensures centralized wage setting, that is, irrespective of regional economic conditions, $W_r = W_s$. Centralized wage setting (at the sector level) is a tenet of the German labour market.

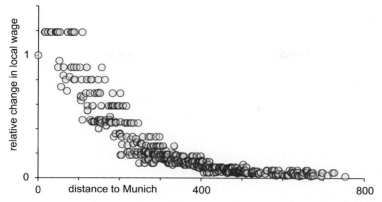

Figure 9.1 Wage growth (%) and distance, following a 10% increase in Munich GDP
Note: relative change in local wage is normalized to one for Munich; distance in km.

from a 10 per cent GDP increase in the city-district of Munich. The localization of demand linkages turns out to be quite strong. The positive GDP shock leads to an increase of wages in Munich itself by 0.8 per cent and the impact on wages in other regions strongly decays with distance. In Berlin, for instance, the impact is a mere 0.08 per cent. This is in line with the findings of Hanson (2005) for the USA in the previous sub-section. Figure 9.1 shows the results of our 'Munich-experiment' for each of the German districts. It clearly shows that the impact of the GDP shock on wages rapidly declines the further one moves away from Munich: the empirical relevance of the spatial interdependencies seems rather limited in the sense that the shocks of local RMP to regional wages are rather small and rather quickly fade away with increased distance.

This concludes our discussion of the second testable hypothesis to which geographical economics gives rise: a larger market potential, be it nominal or real market potential, implies higher wages. All in all, there is evidence in favour of a spatial wage structure but the strength or spatial reach of spatial interdependencies seems limited.

9.5 Taking Stock

How can we relate the findings in the previous section about spatial wages and the role of real market potential to the other hypotheses that are on our list of testable geographical economics implications introduced at the beginning of this chapter (home market effect; factor inflows; shock sensitivity; trade costs-induced agglomeration)?

To start with the home market effect, stating that an increase in a region's demand for a good will lead to a more than proportional increase of this region's production of the good. As with any shock that hits an economy, a standard question in economics is: what is adjusting, prices or quantities? In home market effect studies (see Head and Mayer, 2006), factor price equalization is always and everywhere assumed to hold, so the answer is straightforward: employment and production are doing the adjustment to the effect that real market potentials (RMP) are equalized across regions. In real market potential studies like Hanson (2005), but also Redding and Venables (2004) discussed, in the previous section it is precisely the other way around: the location of firms and workers is fixed and so is the RMP for each region and hence factor prices (here, wages) do all the adjusting. But we know from the discussion in Chapter 7 on the core model of geographical economics that in the long run demand or income, prices, wages, production, and employment are all *endogenous*! To understand what any shock might do to the equilibrium spatial allocation of footloose economic activity (the *holy grail* in geographical economics) requires us to allow for the possibility of all these variables changing. In this respect, *both the empirical work on the home market effect and the market potential hypothesis do not deal with the key question in geographical economics*: what do shocks to demand or transport costs imply for the equilibrium spatial allocation of economic activity?[12] We look again at Figure 7.6, repeated here as Figure 9.2 for ease of reference, to see that these questions go to the heart of what geographical economics is about. Two sets of empirical questions that are not addressed by either home market or market potential studies are:

- When hit by a shock does a location (city, region, country) return to the initial stable equilibrium like point C in Figure 9.2? If not, can we establish how large the shock must be (see the unstable equilibria or thresholds B and D) for the location to switch to a new stable equilibrium (A or E)?
- Given the key role of transportation or trade costs in geographical economics, can one come up with an empirical yard stick for transportation costs in order to determine whether changes in trade costs give rise to a change in agglomeration pattern?

In the remainder of this chapter we discuss two strands of empirical research that try to answer these two sets of questions. We will first discuss the empirical research on the shock sensitivity hypothesis and then continue with research on trade cost-induced agglomeration. In doing so, we want to establish the empirical validity of the fourth and fifth hypotheses (shock sensitivity and trade costs-induced agglomeration) from the list of testable hypotheses for geographical economics.

---

[12] The same applies to the 'factor inflow hypothesis', where the spatial allocation of economic activity is also considered to be given (notably a fixed market potential) when it is investigated whether it makes sense for a firm or worker to migrate to another region (see Crozet, 2004).

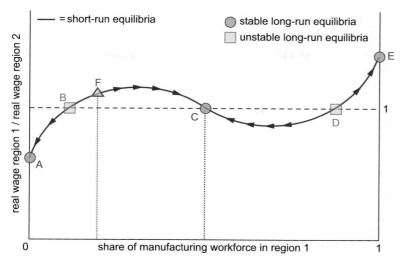

Figure 9.2 Relative real wage: base scenario

In section 9.6, and drawing on pioneering studies by Davis and Weinstein (2002, 2008) on Japan, we analyse whether a large, exogenous, and temporary shock, like the destruction of Japanese and German cities during World War II, provides a test for the shock sensitivity hypothesis of the geographical economics model. We start by asking whether war-struck cities return to their initial, pre-shock equilibrium. We then proceed by asking whether these WW II shocks also constitute evidence of multiple equilibria. In section 9.7 we will deal with the fifth testable hypothesis (trade costs-induced agglomeration) of geographical economics. In this case, there are also clear linkages with our theoretical models of Chapter 7 and Chapter 8. When does a change in trade costs or (in the terminology of this chapter) in the *free-ness of trade* lead to changes in agglomeration in the real world? We will see that it is rather difficult to answer this question in a satisfying manner using the two-region versions of the models of geographical economics of Chapter 7 and Chapter 8.

9.6 The Impact of Shocks on Equilibria

9.6.1 City Growth, the WW II Shock, and the Return to the Initial Equilibrium

The core model of geographical economics is characterized by multiple equilibria, some of which are stable, and some of which are unstable; see Figure 9.2.[13] To answer the question whether a shock can move the economy out of the initial,

---

[13] This section is based on Brakman, Garretsen, and Schramm (2004b) and Bosker et al. (2007).

'pre-shock' equilibrium, one ideally would like to conduct a quasi-natural experiment in which the economy under consideration is hit by a large, temporary, and exogenous shock. The shock needs to be *large* in size and scope in order to be possibly felt at all locations and to be potentially able to move the economy from one equilibrium to the next, even if it is initially in a stable equilibrium; the shock needs to be *temporary* to be able to isolate the impact of the shock in question from other changes; and the shock is *exogenous* to ensure that causality runs from 'shock to location'. Regarding the size of the shock: as Figure 9.2 illustrates, with an initially stable equilibrium the economy may also move back to the pre-shock equilibrium. Suppose the economy finds itself in C before the shock. A shock only moves the economy to a new stable equilibrium, *in casu* point A, if the fall in λ_1 is such that the resulting level of λ_1 is lower than that associated with point B, otherwise the economy returns to C. The unstable equilibrium B acts as a *threshold*.

Research into the impact of shocks on locations is not only confined to geographical economics. In urban economics, one can distinguish between two basic and long-established views about the possible impact of large temporary shocks on city growth. The first view is based on the pioneering models of urban growth in the Alonso-Muth-Mills tradition that all go back to the first 'model' of urban economics by Von Thünen (1826); see Chapter 4. In these models each city has its own optimal or natural city size. Following a large shock (like a war or large-scale natural disaster), the expectation is that after some time each city has returned to its natural city size. The key to this approach is that there is a city-specific level of productivity not influenced by the shock. As a result, the shock will *not* have a permanent impact. In the second view, city productivity is a (positive) function of the city size and possibly also of the interactions (spillovers) with other (nearby) cities. Changes in the level of population will change city productivity and city growth. In this case, the prediction would be that a large shock might have a lasting impact. Geographical economics is in line with this second view and so is, admittedly, urban economics to the extent that the latter (recall Chapter 5 and the urban systems model introduced there) posits a positive relationship between city size and city productivity (recall also Figure 6.1).

The key issue is whether one can come up with real-world examples of a large, temporary, and exogenous shock that can act as a testing ground for the shock sensitivity hypothesis. In a seminal paper, Donald Davis and David Weinstein (2002) use the case of the allied bombing of Japanese cities during World War II as an example of such a shock. As to the impact this WW II shock might have had on Japanese cities, Davis and Weinstein (2002) distinguish between three basic theoretical approaches, in their terminology *fundamental geography, increasing returns*, and *random growth*. In the case of fundamental geography, exogenous and fixed characteristics like access to waterways, climate, mountains, and other fixed endowments determine city growth. This approach is in line with the first view in urban economics mentioned above. The increasing returns approach is in line with the second view, which is consistent with the geographical economics approach. The WW II shock can have a permanent effect if the shock is large enough. Finally, they introduce the random growth approach, which predicts that the evolution of city sizes by definition follows a random path and a large, temporary shock like the WW II shock must have a permanent effect (see also Chapter 8 on random city growth in our discussion of Zipf's Law).

Brakman, Garretsen, and Schramm (2004b) apply the Davis and Weinstein (2002) approach to the case of the allied bombing of German cities during WW II. In both studies the question is the same: did individual cities return to their initial, pre-war growth path after WW II? In terms of Figure 9.2 and assuming that the initial equilibrium is at point C, the question is whether there was a return to C after WW II. If not, this would be evidence for the geographical economics approach. In subsequent work (see the next sub-section) Davis and Weinstein (2008) and Bosker et al. (2007) use these WW II shocks to answer a related but different question: is there evidence that city-growth is characterized by multiple equilibria? In terms of Figure 9.2, is there evidence, besides C, of equilibria described by points A and E (stable equilibria besides C, with B and D as unstable 'thresholds'). This would be additional evidence in favour of geographical economics.

The underlying model of city growth in the above studies is as follows. The approach is basically to test whether the growth of city size (measured as a share of total population) follows a random path. The relative city size s for each city i at time t can be represented by (in logs):

$$s_{i,t} = \Omega_i + \epsilon_{i,t} \qquad\qquad 9.6$$

where Ω_i is the initial size of city i and ϵ_{it} represents a city-specific change in size at time t. This change consists of two parts, past changes and current shocks (subscript t for time):

$$\epsilon_{i,t+1} = \zeta \epsilon_{i,t} + v_{i,t+1} \qquad\qquad 9.7$$

where $v_{i,t+1}$ is a shock that takes place in period $t + 1$. 'History' (or the persistence of past shocks) is taken care of by the parameter $\zeta \in [0,1]$. If $\zeta = 1$ all shocks are permanent and history is always important. If $\zeta = 0$ the shock has no persistence at all and history does not play any role. For other values $(0 < \zeta < 1)$ there is some degree of persistence, but ultimately the relative city size is stationary and hence any shock will dissipate over time. For some intuition with respect to the role of ζ, it is instructive to rewrite equation 9.6 as $s_{i,t+1} = \Omega_i + \epsilon_{i,t+1}$. Now using equation 9.7 in this expression gives $s_{i,t+1} = \Omega_i + \zeta \epsilon_{i,t} + v_{i,t+1}$. With $\zeta = 1$ the relative city size $s_{i,t+1}$ increases with the full amount of the shock in period t such that the past will have a maximum impact on the future city size. With $\zeta = 0$ a shock in period t has no impact on city size in period $t + 1$. This is also known as a mean reverting process because city size returns to its long-run expected value. With $0 < \zeta < 1$ there is some degree of persistence of the shock and only a partial return to the pre-shock city size in $t+1$.

To test this model we now proceed as follows. By first-differencing equation 9.6 and making use of equation 9.7, we arrive at equation 9.8, which is used in the empirical application.

$$s_{i,t+1} - s_{i,t} = (\zeta - 1)v_{i,t} + \left(v_{i,t+1} + \zeta(\zeta - 1)\epsilon_{i,t-1}\right) \qquad 9.8$$

Note that the left-hand side of equation 9.8 is the growth of relative city size. What makes the case of Japan and Germany interesting is that we can identify the WW II shock: take $\left(s_{i,1946} - s_{i,1939}\right)$ as a proxy for $v_{i,t}$ in the estimates;[14] the change in relative city size between these two dates – just before and just after the war – is thought to be caused by the war. The test version of equation 9.8 becomes (in logs):[15]

$$s_{i,1946+t} - s_{i,1946} = \alpha\left(s_{i,1946} - s_{i,1939}\right) + \beta_0 + err_i \qquad 9.9$$

where $\alpha \equiv \zeta - 1$. If $\alpha = 0$ the war shock has a permanent effect. If $\alpha = -1$ there is evidence that the war shock had no effect at all, while there is a temporary effect if $-1 < \alpha < 0$.

Before presenting the estimation results of equation 9.9 for Japan and Germany, we have to decide on the relevant period $1946 + t$ for the dependent variable. It should neither be too short a period (since that prevents cities from adjusting to the WW II shock) nor too long a period (because then other, more recent shocks could influence city-growth). Davis and Weinstein (2002) and Brakman et al. (2004b) set the cut-off for t at 18 years. Thus in both cases we test whether the impact of WW II on city growth had vanished by the mid 1960s. Using the housing stock destruction and/or related WW II shock indicators as instruments, the estimate of equation 9.9 is given in Table 9.4.

For Japan the estimates strongly indicate that 18 years after WW II Japanese cities had fully recovered from the WW II shock and returned to their pre-war growth path (the α-coefficient does not differ significantly from –1). In terms of the model above, this suggests that WW II had no permanent effect and Japanese cities returned to their initial equilibrium. According to Davis and Weinstein (2002) this finding supports the first nature geography view of the impact of shocks on city growth. The results for West German cities also indicate a tendency for the

---

[14] For the case of Japan, the city growth rate during WW II is the growth rate between 1940 and 1947 in Davis and Weinstein (2002).

[15] It follows from equation 9.8 that the shock, as proxied by a city's growth rate between 1939 and 1946, is correlated with the error term in the estimating equation. This indicates that we have to use instruments. The instruments used are city-specific variables like the destruction of the housing stock, the number of casualties, or the amount of rubble. For an explanation of the reason for using instrumental variables (IV) see Chapter 3.

Table 9.4 Do shocks matter?

	Dependent variable: $s_{i,1946+t} - s_{i,1946}$	
Japan; $n = 303$	$\alpha = -1.03$	(0.163)
West Germany; $n = 79$	$\alpha = -0.52$	(5.47)
East Germany; $n = 21$	$\alpha = -0.003$	(0.02)

Source: Davis and Weinstein (2002) and Brakman et al. (2004b); n = # of observations; shock is 1939 to 1946; for Japan and East Germany $t = 18$, for West Germany $t = 17$; standard error in parentheses.

effects of the shock to be reversed but here, as opposed to Japan, the return is only partial, which indicates that on average west German cities had not fully recovered from the WW II shock. This suggests that some cities might actually have moved to a new equilibrium growth path. Finally, the results for East German cities might lead to the conclusion that there is a permanent effect ($\alpha = 0$). However, East German cities were part of the socialist German Democratic Republic (GDR) and in the communist planning regime that ruled the GDR, people were not free to choose their location, suggesting that the GDR case is ill-suited for testing models where economic agents are 'free to choose'. Box 9.1 and Box 9.2 discuss the implications of various other types of shocks (the September 2011 attack, hurricane Katrina, the medieval plague, the bombing of Vietnam, and the German division).

BOX 9.1 The 9/11 Attack, Hurricane Katrina, and the Medieval Plague

Writing only a few weeks after the 9/11 terrorist attack hit New York city and destroyed the Twin Towers, Paul Krugman (2001) in a column in the *NY Times* pointed out that the findings of Davis and Weinstein (2002) would imply that 'if the Japanese parallel is at all relevant, the attack on New York, for all its horror, will have no effect worth mentioning on the city's long-run economic prospects'. Even more recently, in the wake of the destruction of the city of New Orleans by hurricane Katrina (August 2005), commentators have explicitly used the two studies discussed in the main text to ask what they imply for the future of New Orleans (Bernasek, 2005). The crucial issue here is whether these and other historical cases can be compared with recent shocks. One difference between the WW II studies and the cases of 9/11 and Katrina is that the WW II studies concern a shock to an entire urban system, instead of a shock to a single city. Another concern is that the initial conditions (why did a particular city come into existence?) and government (rebuilding) policies may be hard to compare. Thirdly,

BOX 9.1 (cont.)

even if a city returns to its pre-shock size or if government policies try to achieve this, one could ask whether this is really welfare-enhancing. Edward Glaeser has argued *against* rebuilding New Orleans because the former inhabitants and the US economy might be better off without rebuilding.[16] Fourthly, by just looking at the two studies discussed in the main text and the incidence of WW II on Japanese and German cities, it is easy to forget that there also examples of more ancient shocks that clearly had a huge and long-lasting impact on city growth.

A good example of this last point is the fourteenth-century plague (black death) that hit large parts of Europe, in particular Italy, with Europe's most developed urban system in those days. Figure 9.3 shows the death toll for various (Northern) Italian cities as a percentage of the population. Faced with the magnitude of this 'shock', it took most Italian cities centuries to recover and some cities – like

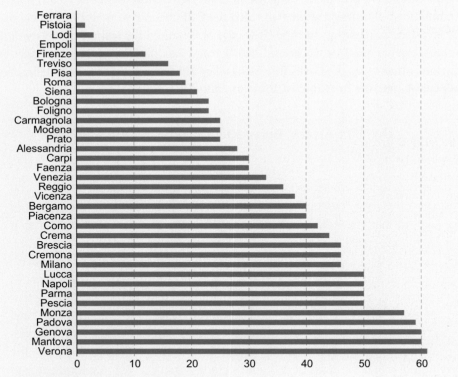

Figure 9.3 The plague and death in Italian cities
Source: based on Bosker et al. (2008b); death as a percentage of population.

---

[16] For Glaeser's view on the impact of (war)shocks on cities see also Glaeser and Shapiro (2002).

BOX 9.1 (cont.)

Siena – never did. The Black Death that ravaged Italy between 1346 and 1353 wiped away about 40 per cent of the population. Calculations by Malanima (1998) indicate that the population in central and northern Italy declined from an estimated 7.75 million to 4.72 million between 1300 and 1400. The urbanization rate for Italy as a whole fell in this period from 15 per cent to 9 per cent. By 1500 the overall population had increased again to 5.31 million and the urbanization rate had regained its 1300 level. Between 1600 and 1700 population growth stagnated again. A new wave of plague epidemics swept across Italy, killing more than one million people. Particularly the plagues of 1629–31 and of 1656–7 had detrimental effects on the population level, with an average death rate of at least 20 per cent and even more in the large cities. Urban recovery from these disasters was slow. In 1700 the urbanization rate had further declined to 14 per cent, well below that of 1600. Many cities would not regain their earlier position. 'There is no doubt that in Italy the consequences of the plagues were always heavier for the urban than for the rural populations' (Malanima, 1998, p. 99).

BOX 9.2 More Evidence on Shock Sensitivity: Vietnam and the German Division

Miguel and Roland (2011) investigate the long-run impact of US bombing on Vietnam. Using a sample of 584 Vietnamese districts and a detailed data set on the bombing intensity, they analyse the effects of US bombing on the Vietnamese post-war development of consumption, poverty, and population density. They conclude that the long-run effects of the US bombing are limited in the sense that most districts have recovered rather quickly from the war destruction. Whether this conclusion is bad news for geographical economics is an open question (see Miguel and Roland, 2011, p. 6) to the extent that agglomeration effects were probably less relevant for a, certainly at that time, still relatively poor country like Vietnam (compared to Japan and Germany). Moreover, the US bombing in the Vietnam war was not targeted specifically at cities but at rural districts, which probably limited the war damage done to the economic infrastructure of Vietnam. Another feature of this shock is that in the post-war period (from 1976 onwards) the government of the centrally planned economy of Vietnam undertook major reconstruction efforts, with districts that were more heavily bombed receiving more government investment, which helped the recovery process.

The break-up of Germany in 1949 into the Federal Republic of Germany FRG (West Germany) and the German Democratic Republic GDR (East Germany)

BOX 9.2 (cont.)

and the subsequent re-unification of the two Germanies in 1990 after the fall of the Berlin Wall is another example of a large, temporary (40-year) shock. Redding, Sturm, and Wolf (2011) use this example and the shift in the location of Germany's main airport hub from Berlin to Frankfurt am Main as a test case for multiple equilibria. The airline sector and the location of hubs fits well with the geographical economics model in the sense that it is a sector in which transport costs are (obviously) relevant, where the activity is footloose, and where scale economies are important. Before 1949, Berlin was the main hub and after the division of Germany Frankfurt took over from Berlin. After the re-unification in 1990, Frankfurt remained the largest airport hub in Germany. While controlling for various other factors, Redding, Sturm, and Wolf (2011) conclude that the switch of the main airline location in Germany constitutes evidence supporting the existence of multiple equilibria. In a related paper, Redding and Sturm (2008) use the same shock to test whether *West* German border cities (close to the former East–West border) experienced a substantial decline compared to non-border cities in West Germany after 1949. Their answer is affirmative. Border cities within a 75 km range of the intra-German border suffered a significant decline. The authors note that there is some evidence that these cities made a recovery after re-unification (when they ceased to be border cities). According to the authors, the main reason the West German border cities fell behind after 1949 is their loss of real market potential (RMP) as a result of the loss of markets in nearby GDR. From a sample of 119 West German cities, 20 are classified as border cities. The basic empirical specification is as follows (sub-index c indicates city and sub-index t indicates time) and uses a difference-in-differences (DID) estimation procedure (see Chapter 3 for an introduction to this often used estimation strategy in modern urban and geographical economics):

$$popgrowth_{c,t} = \beta border_c + \gamma border_c \times division_t + d_t + err_{c,t} \qquad 9.10$$

The border dummy ($border_c$) captures differences in city population growth between the two groups of West German cities before the division. The main coefficient of interest is γ for the interaction term $border_c \times division_t$ between the border and the division dummy, which 'captures any systematic change in the relative growth performance of treatment and control groups of cities following German division' (Redding and Sturm, 2008, p. 1777) where the 'treatment group' are the border cities and the control group the other western German cities. The hypothesis is that γ is negative because that implies that the population growth of the border cities was lower than that of non-border cities. As Redding and Sturm show, this is indeed the case. One question that comes to

BOX 9.2 (cont.)

mind is which of the two shocks is the most important: WW II or the German division. Bosker et al. (2008a) use a long time series on individual (West) German city growth, annual data for the period 1925–1999, and let the data determine where a break can be detected. It turns out that (almost) without exception the data indicate that the WW II shock dominated other shocks (see the website of the book for more information). See Ahlfeldt et al. (2015) for a detailed attempt to investigate the impact of WW II and the German division for the case of Germany by looking at the city of Berlin and the Berlin Wall. Finally, all the studies discussed in section 9.6 are examples of modern empirical studies where the idea of (historical) quasi-natural experiments (see section 3.5.3) is used to enable a better identification of cause and effect as compared to the estimation of for instance the wage equation from geographical economics where the independent variables are typically also endogenous. In section 9.8 we will return to this important topic.

9.6.2 Shocks and Multiple Equilibria

The two shock sensitivity studies discussed in section 9.6.1 suggest that urban systems are rather stable. Head and Mayer (2004, p. 2662) therefore conclude, on the basis of this and related results, that the shock sensitivity in models of geographical economics should be considered a fascinating theoretical 'exotica', rather than a relevant element of actual economic geography. This verdict on the empirical relevance of geographical economics may be somewhat premature. First, it is one thing to test for the stability of an initial equilibrium and something quite different to test for the presence of multiple equilibria (some stable and some unstable). Second, given the crucial role of spatial interdependencies between locations in geographical economics models, the omission of such interdependencies in the two studies in the previous sub-section is important. Third, a number of other studies on shocks suggest that these can have permanent effects (see Box 9.2).

Again using the WW II shock for Japan, Davis and Weinstein (2008) develop an analytical framework to test for multiple equilibria. In doing so, they look not only at city population but also at the economic structure of Japanese cities. Bosker et al. (2007) use this framework for the WW II shock and Germany, also taking spatial interdependencies into account. The basic framework developed by Davis and Weinstein (2008) is summarized in Figure 9.4 (translating Figure 9.2 of the core model into a dynamic framework), where Δs_t indicates the change in size – or shock – in period t. The points A–E in Figure 9.2 play a similar role as Δ_1, b_1, Ω, b_2, and Δ_3 in Figure 9.4.

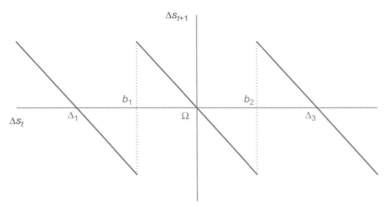

Figure 9.4 Two-period growth representation of a model with three stable equilibria

Figure 9.4 depicts three stable equilibria (Δ_1, Ω, and Δ_3) and two unstable equilibria (b_1 and b_2, which act as a threshold between stable equilibria).[17] Given that the economy is initially in a stable equilibrium (like C in Figure 9.2 or Ω in Figure 9.4), a shock can in theory have two implications depending on the size of the shock. A (small) shock around the initial stable equilibrium Ω in period t is completely undone in the next period $t+1$. This implies that the slope of the solid line that passes through the origin in Figure 9.4 is *exactly* equal to -1, with the solid line depicted as $\Delta s_t = -\Delta s_{t+1}$. If the shock is, however, large enough to pass one of the thresholds (b_1 or b_2), the economy moves towards another stable equilibrium with a new corresponding solid line $\Delta s_t = -\Delta s_{t+1} + constant$.[18] It is an empirical matter whether $t+1$ is long enough such that we really observe $\Delta s_t = -\Delta s_{t+1}$, but from a theoretical point of view we know that at some point cities must again return to a stable equilibrium (be it the initial or a new stable equilibrium) after a shock (the previous sub-section used an 18-year period). So, in practice, even if the initial equilibrium is stable, the slope could be less than one (in absolute terms) if $t+1$ is too small. To facilitate comparison with the model of section 9.6.1, we use the symbols introduced above. Our main variable of interest is the (log-) share of city i in total population (denoted s_i; we suppress the subscript i since all cities are assumed to be alike in terms of their reaction to a particular city-specific shock of

---

[17] Note that the origin has no special meaning other than indicating the initial situation.

[18] A complication discussed in Chapter 8 is that in the real world partial agglomeration seems to be the rule. Applied to cities, this means that the underlying model should allow for multiple stable equilibria where cities (agglomerations) exist that differ in size. Our core model is not equipped to deal with this observation, since it typically only allows for either a mono-city (full agglomeration) or equally sized cities (spreading). As we saw in Chapter 8 it is straightforward to extend the core model to include partial agglomeration as a stable equilibrium outcome: by adding an additional spreading force (congestion) to an otherwise unchanged core model of geographical economics one can indeed end up with alternating stable and unstable equilibria.

a given size; this is an important assumption as it means that the model underlying Figure 9.4 is based on the notion of a representative city).[19]

If the shock is large enough to move the city's population share outside the range $b_1 - b_2$ a new stable equilibrium will be established and the economy will move to either Δ_1 or Δ_3, depending on the shock. For either new stable equilibrium $\Delta s_t = -\Delta s_{t+1}$ must hold in a two-period setting. For the three stable equilibria shown in Figure 9.4, these possibilities are indicated by the two solid lines through Δ_1 and Δ_3, both with a slope of minus one. To sum up, with multiple equilibria in the two-period growth setting of Figure 9.4, we have a sequence of lines with slope -1, each corresponding to a different stable equilibrium. As Davis and Weinstein (2008) note:

> the two-period growth space thus provides a very simple contrast between a model of unique equilibrium versus one of multiple equilibria. In the case of a unique equilibrium, an observation should simply lie on a line with slope minus unity through the origin. In the case of multiple equilibria, we get a sequence of lines, all with slopes minus unity, but with different intercepts. Because in this latter case these lines have slope minus unity, the intercepts are ordered and correspond to the displacement in log-share space from the initial to the new equilibrium. These elements will be central when we turn to empirical analysis.

Imagine a scatter plot of data on city growth during WW II (s_t) and post-WW II city growth (s_{t+1}) for Japanese or German cities. Estimating equation 9.9 then simply tests whether the data points lie on a slope with minus one through the origin, in fact only taking a single equilibrium like Ω into account and ignoring the possibility of multiple equilibria. Using the same scatter plot in terms of Figure 9.4, the question now becomes whether the data are indeed best described by allowing for one or more equilibria (where thresholds b_i provide a better fit). The question arises how many parallel lines with slope -1 must we use to describe the scatter plot best.

A drawback of the framework depicted by Figure 9.4 is that spatial interdependencies are not taken into account. What happens to a particular city following a shock can also be determined by the impact on other cities. Think, for example, of a lucky city not hit by war destruction surrounded by cities that are. We expect that the destruction of these other cities also affects the lucky city. For that reason, Bosker et al. (2007) use $\Delta s_{t+1,i} = f\left(\Delta s_{t,i}, \Delta s_{t,j\neq i}\right)$ incorporating time subscript t and city subscripts i and j. Empirically, we look at the change in the size of a city i *and* changes in the size of surrounding cities j, corrected for inter-city distances between i and j.

Our starting point is again equation 9.9, with some adjustments. First, assuming (for the moment) that there are indeed three stable equilibria, we have to look

---

[19] Note that the use of log-shares reformulates the model in growth rates.

at three versions of this equation (one for each equilibrium). Second, we now *assume* that $\alpha = -1$ (or $\zeta = 0$). Recall that in section 9.6.1 our focus was on the question whether or not α was different from -1. So why do we now *assume* this to be the case? Because the need for the $\alpha = -1$ assumption already follows from the theoretical model summarized in Figure 9.4. Under the assumption that period $t + 1$ in this figure is long enough for the period t shock to have dissipated, a solid line in Figure 9.4 represents a stable equilibrium with slope minus one because that is what a *stable* equilibrium implies: $\Delta s_t = -\Delta s_{t+1}$. Any other assumption is difficult to reconcile with the underlying model of city growth. A third difference with the estimate of equation 9.9 is that we have to take into consideration that the model places restrictions on the coefficients to be estimated. Basically, we want to arrive at the empirical equivalents of Δ_1, b_1, Ω, b_2, and Δ_3 as illustrated in Figure 9.4. The figure itself already suggests a specific ordering for the coefficients to be estimated (labelled δ_i [where i denotes the i-th equilibrium] and b_i [where i denotes the i-th threshold]). If there are three equilibria, we must have the following intercept and threshold ordering condition: $\delta_1 < b_1 < 0 < b_2 < \delta_3$. Finally, since neither the number of equilibria nor the positioning of the thresholds are known beforehand (any number of equilibria is possible), the multiple equilibria version of equation 9.9 needs to determine the appropriate number of equilibria (see the website for more details).

Table 9.5 provides the estimation results for Japan and Germany. The data sets are the same as in section 9.6.1. The German results use *spatial interdependencies* (geography) because the war shock is not only a function of a city's own

Table 9.5 Testing for multiple equilibria in city population growth

Country	Japan		Germany	
# of equilibria	2 equilibria	3 equilibria	2 equilibria	3 equilibria
δ_1	0.0978	−0.0720	−0.193	−0.341
δ_2 (constant)	0.196	0.315	0.284	0.458
δ_3		−0.127		−0.220
b_1	−0.001	−0.056	−0.004	−0.004
b_2		0		0.017
Intercept ordering criteria 2 equilibria: $\delta_1 < b_1 < 0$ 3 equilibria: $\delta_1 < b_1 < 0 < b_2 < \delta_3$	fail	fail	accept	fail
# of observations	303	303	81	81

Source: Japan – Davis and Weinstein (2008); Germany – Bosker et al. (2007). Only West German cities are present in the German city sample; dependent variable is city growth.

destruction but also of the sum of the distance-weighted destruction of all other cities (measured as changes in the housing stock). This captures the idea that the 'geography' of bombing matters. Geography also enters the post-WW II period in a simple way as (in line with a market potential function) the distance from economic centres (here, Munich) is allowed to affect a city's post-WW II growth rate.

For the case of *Japan,* and restricting ourselves to either two or three equilibria, the evidence does not support the hypothesis of multiple equilibria: in both estimates the intercept ordering condition is violated. Keeping in mind the results for Japan in Table 9.4 from section 9.6.1, this outcome is not surprising since we concluded that Japanese cities returned to the initial equilibrium after WW II (α was not significantly different from -1) and the effects of the WW II-shock have completely dissipated after 18 years. For the *German* case we only found a partial return, so there is *a priori* more scope for multiple equilibria. Table 9.5 confirms this, as we find evidence for the presence of two equilibria. There is, however, one caveat: estimates for Germany without taking geography into account do *not* confirm the existence of multiple equilibria.

The evidence presented here on the impact of WW II on Japanese and German cities is mixed regarding the sensitivity of equilibria with respect to shocks. To round up our discussion on shock sensitivity, Box 9.2 reviews a number of studies for different shocks and time periods. The general conclusion is that shocks can have permanent effects, thereby vindicating the relevance of a key building-block of geographical economics. In addition, we find that local history, institutions, and policies are also important. Sensitivity to shocks and the underlying notion of multiple equilibria are thus not theoretical curiosa, even though it is clear that the stability or resilience of locations to shocks is greater than Figure 9.2 seems to suggest.

9.7 Trade Costs and Agglomeration

9.7.1 Where on the Tomahawk Diagram or Bell-Shaped Curve Are We?

The fifth and last item on our list of testable hypotheses from geographical economics models concerns the relationship between transport or trade costs on the one hand and the degree of agglomeration on the other hand. From Chapter 7 and Chapter 8 we learned that geographical economics models can be summarized in two figures. The *Tomahawk diagram* (Figure 7.9) captures the core model of geographical economics, where trade costs are sufficiently low at the break point to induce (complete) agglomeration from then on. The *bell-shaped curve* (Figure 8.6) summarizes the basic geographical economics model *without* inter-regional labour mobility.

Again, if trade costs fall below the break point the spreading of economic activity will turn into agglomeration. In this case, however, a further drop in trade costs will reverse the agglomeration equilibrium again to the spreading equilibrium. The main difference between the two classes of models is thus caused by allowing (or not) for inter-regional labour mobility. In the core model of Chapter 7 – leading to the Tomahawk diagram – manufacturing labour can move between regions. If labour is not inter-regionally mobile the bell-shaped curve appears (since higher wages act as an additional spreading force). Notwithstanding these differences, *both* classes of models convey the same message: in a full-fledged general equilibrium framework agglomeration is determined by history and changes in variables and parameters (of which trade costs are the most important). In a more general setting, this very basic idea and thereby the relevance of history or initial conditions is for instance confirmed by Allen and Donaldson (2018).

Testing the fifth hypothesis would thus imply answering the question: *where* on the Tomahawk diagram or Bell-shaped curve are we? Knowing the answer to this question informs us about the inter-connections between trade costs and agglomeration. In the remainder of this section we discuss why it is inherently difficult to answer this question empirically by discussing various possible approaches to doing so.

9.7.2   The Free-ness of Trade and the Limitations of the Two-Region Models

To facilitate the discussion and to ease comparison with other studies, we focus on the free-ness of trade parameter $\varphi \equiv T^{1-\varepsilon}$ as introduced in Chapter 8. Baldwin et al. (2003b): $\varphi = 0$ denotes autarky and the absence of economic integration, whereas $\varphi = 1$ denotes free trade and full economic integration. Note, however, that in the two-region models of Chapter 7 and Chapter 8 (where the distance D_{rs} between regions r and s equals one), the transport costs T and the free-ness of trade φ do not have sub-indices (are not region-specific). In a case with more than two regions where regions are not all equidistant to each other, as in any real-world application with multiple regions, we use $\varphi_{rs} = T_{rs}^{1-\varepsilon} = T^{(1-\varepsilon)D_{rs}}$. This is just another way of saying that in the real world the theoretical assumption made in Chapter 7 and Chapter 8 that $D_{rs} = 1$ is problematic.

It is problematic because analytical solutions for the geographical economics models that should help us to determine where we are on the Tomahawk or bell curve, and hence what in the real world the relationship between trade costs and agglomeration looks like, only exist for the case of two regions or for the case of multiple regions where one assumes $D_{rs} = 1$ between all pairs of regions! This assumption effectively means that the *actual geography* (where regions are located on a map) does not play a role, and thus that space is neutral in that sense. Any real-world application clearly violates this assumption. What to do?

Given that the models discussed in Chapter 7 and Chapter 8 do not offer much analytical guidance, we have to come up with different empirical strategies and/or uses of these models regarding the relationship between trade costs and agglomeration. Here we want to highlight three issues that matter when empirically addressing the relationship between trade costs and agglomeration.

The first issue concerns the *actual measurement of trade costs*. If the notion of $T^{(1-\varepsilon)D_{rs}}$ with $D_{rs} = 1$ will not do, one somehow has to come up with an alternative specification of trade costs that can actually be taken to the data. In our discussion of the spatial wage structure and the relevance of real market potential for wages (recall equation 9.4) we simply assumed trade costs between any two locations to be an exponential function of the distance between those two locations. This is, however, just one example as to how trade costs can be specified and research shows that the specification might matter quite a bit for the results, as Box 9.3 illustrates.

BOX 9.3 Does the Empirical Specification of Trade Costs Matter?

As Anderson and van Wincoop (2004, p. 706) already noted: 'A variety of ad hoc trade cost functions have been used to relate the unobservable cost to observable variables' and (ibid, p. 710) 'theory has used arbitrary assumptions regarding functional form of the trade cost function, the list of variables, and regularity conditions'. The (implicit) assumptions underlying the use of a trade cost function concern in particular: (i) functional form, (ii) variables included, (iii) regularity conditions, (iv) modelling trade costs involved with internal trade, (v) the unobservable component of trade costs, and (vi) estimating the trade cost function's parameters (see Anderson and van Wincoop, 2004). We do not deal with all of these issues here (see Bosker and Garretsen, 2010, for a survey of various trade costs specifications used in geographical economics), but merely wonder to what extent the conclusions on the relevance of market potential (for wages or GDP per capita) depend on the trade cost specification. Hanson (2005), for example, uses an *exponential distance decay function* (recall equation 9.5), whereas the seminal market potential study by Redding and Venables (2004) uses a *power function*: $T_{rs} = D_{rs}^{\delta}$.

Bosker and Garretsen (2010) estimate the equivalent of wage equation 9.5 for a sample of 80 countries in the year 1996 (using GDP per capita) for both the Hanson (2005) and the Redding and Venables (2004) trade costs specifications. In both cases market potential was positive and significant. The differences between the two approaches come to the fore when the estimation results were used to conduct the following experiment.

Suppose that Belgium, a country in the heart of Europe, experiences a positive 5 per cent income shock. To what extent will this shock, given the estimation results, lead to spillovers to other countries through the market potential variable? The magnitude of this increase for a specific country depends, of course, on the strength of the spatial linkages. The lower the trade costs with Belgium, the larger the impact on a country's income per capita. Figure 9.5 illustrates the

BOX 9.3 (cont.)

spatial reach of the Belgian income shock by plotting the percentage change in income per capita against the log of distance for the two approaches.

Using the Hanson exponential approach (panel *b*), the distance decay is strong and the size of the income per capita changes are relatively small. In the Redding and Venables power function approach (panel *a*), the income per capita change is much larger (about *seven* times as large for the Netherlands, for example).[20] The effect of the income shock in the Hanson exponential distance approach also quickly peters out; there is no discernible effect any more in countries lying

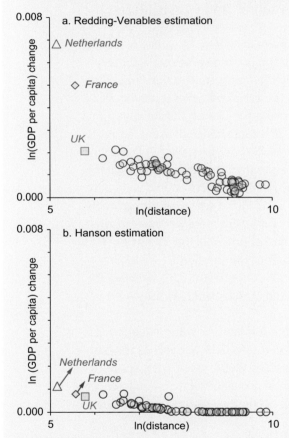

Figure 9.5 Income per capita changes: 5% GDP shock in Belgium
Source: based on Bosker and Garretsen (2010); correlation shock and distance is −0.77 for panel *a* and −0.84 for *b*.

---

[20] Head and Mayer (2004, p. 2626) already noted that the strong distance decay in Hanson (2005) 'may be a consequence of the functional form of the distance decay function'.

BOX 9.3 (cont.)

farther from Belgium than Egypt. In the power function approach, in contrast, Egypt still experiences a 0.1 per cent increase in income per capita (about equal to the size of the income increase in the most heavily affected country, the Netherlands, when using the Hanson specification!). Consequently, the effect of the Belgian income shock is less correlated with distance and has a larger effect on its contiguous neighbours. The shock has a larger effect, for example, on Germany than on the UK (while the latter is closer to Belgium as measured by distance between capital cities). The income shock also peters out much slower when using a power law to specify trade costs and affects all countries in the sample in some way (Japan, with only a 0.02 per cent increase in income per capita, is affected the least). To conclude: trade costs are a crucial element of geographical economics (without trade costs there is no role for geography). This example shows that the trade cost specification can determine the conclusions on the empirical relevance of market potential and the geographical reach of spatial interdependencies to a large extent.

The second issue is that it is still possible to come up with useful *estimates of the impact of (changes in) trade costs on agglomeration* once one drops the idea of pinpointing where we are in the real world on the Tomahawk or bell-shaped curve. Recall that trade costs make up a key component of what we dubbed real market potential in section 9.4. Estimating the impact of large-scale changes in a country's infrastructure on changes in the spatial income distribution in that country can thus be looked upon as estimating the impact of changes in market potential on income (see Redding and Rossi-Hansberg, 2017 for an overview). This is exactly what the detailed recent studies by Donaldson and Hornbeck (2016) and Donaldson (2018) do for the impact of changes in the (rail) infrastructure network for the historical cases of US infrastructure development and infrastructure investments by the UK in the 'Raj' (nowadays, India and Pakistan), respectively.

The strength of these recent studies (see also Duranton and Turner, 2012) is inter alia that they use a rich data set that allows them to tackle the endogeneity issue (see Chapter 3). This problem potentially plagues any investigation into the impact of changes in trade or transport costs on spatial income or land values or any other regional performance variable since causality could be reversed (high-performing regions attract more infrastructure anyway?) or the relationship could be driven by a third (omitted) variable (political forces favour infrastructure investment within or between larger regions?). Despite their considerable and innovative empirical strengths and also despite the fact that these studies have a firm footing in the geographical economics model that are the topic of Part III of our book, these recent studies do not aim to test a specific model.[21] The aim is to do theoretically well-grounded empirical research, where the underlying model is typically not only a mix of the main mechanisms from the second nature geography models of urban and geographical economics but where first nature geography is also allowed to matter. See Rossi-Hansberg (2019) for a recent survey of this approach, with a focus on quantifying actual agglomeration patterns. Its aim is not, in the terminology of this section, to come up with an empirical verdict as to where we are on the Tomahawk or bell curve. This leads us to our third issue.

The third issue is that the empirical relationship between trade costs and agglomeration and in particular the impact of changes in trade costs and agglomeration can be addressed by *using full model simulations* based on real-world data. Since analytical solutions for the multi-region versions of geographical economics models with non-neutral space do not exist, we will use multi-region model simulations in the remainder of this section in order to get an idea of what the relationship between trade costs and agglomeration might look like in the real world. In doing so, the real value added of geographical economics comes to the fore (Krugman, 2011) in the sense that it is well-suited to answer so-called *what if* questions: what happens in the real world with non-neutral space to the equilibrium degree of agglomeration, as measured by spatial wages or income, if a certain key variable or parameter (here, trade costs) changes? The real-world simulations shown below for the core (Krugman, 1991) model (section 9.7.3) and a more general geographical economics model (section 9.7.4) will turn out be most useful when we discuss economic development and policy making in *what if* terms in Chapter 10 and Chapter 11 of our book.

9.7.3   Free-ness of Trade, Agglomeration, and Multi-Region Simulations: An Example

There is no easy fix to the thorny issue of the exact relationship between free-ness of trade and agglomeration in a geographical economics setting. We agree with Fujita and Mori (2005, p. 394) when they state that 'in order to investigate the spatial pattern of agglomeration, the asymmetry rather than the symmetry of location

---

[21] Donaldson and Hornbeck (2016, p. 803, fn 4) clearly place their study also in the geographical economics tradition of the market potential studies, like Hanson (2005) or Head and Mayer (2006) – see our section 9.4 – as well as the 'shock' studies like Redding and Sturm (2008) or Davis and Weinstein (2002, 2008); see our section 9.6. The same holds for Donaldson (2018) or Allen and Donaldson (2018). The underlying model, following Eaton and Kortum (2002), encapsulates the core geographical economics model. In fact, recent theoretical advances in the general equilibrium modelling of the spatial economy still have a firm footing in Krugman (1991) – see for instance Allen and Arkolakis (2014), and Redding and Rossi-Hansberg (2017) for an overview. Dave Donaldson (MIT) is one of the rising stars in modern research on economics, trade, and geography and together with his co-author Arnaud Costinot (MIT), another young but already prominent researcher in this field, has compiled a set of lectures that are useful for readers of our book as well: see for the slides https://dave-donaldson.com/teaching/#tab-id-1.

space is necessary where not all other regions are neighbours of each region'. This sub-section[22] illustrates what changes in the free-ness of trade imply for the degree of agglomeration across the EU regions. In doing so, we use a multi-region model of geographical economics for 157 (EU NUTS II) regions. We run simulations for a set of model parameters to determine the equilibrium allocation of economic activity, measured as gross value added (the Y variable in our core model). The model is based on Krugman (1991), the core model of geographical economics in our book and extensively summarized in Chapter 7, extended to *non-neutral* space by taking the actual physical geography of Europe into account, based on the Stelder (2005) approach; see Box 9.4.

BOX 9.4 An Experiment with Non-neutral Space: The Stelder Approach

Stelder (2005) has implemented the basic model of Krugman (1991), that is to say our core model of geographical economics from Chapter 7, on non-neutral spaces. This is defined as a grid of n locations on a two-dimensional surface. The distance between two locations is calculated as the shortest path between them, assuming that each location on the grid is connected to its direct (horizontal or vertical) neighbours with a distance of one and to its diagonal neighbours with distance $\sqrt{2}$. Non-neutral space is then introduced by making 'holes' in the grid: see Figure 9.6. Assuming no transport takes place across the sea or along the coast, transportation from A to F in the figure would follow C, D, and E with a total distance of $2 + 2\sqrt{2}$. The geographical shape of a country or a region is approximated by using a grid resolution as high as possible. The model allows for specific costs for transport across land, sea, and in hubs where (un)shipping

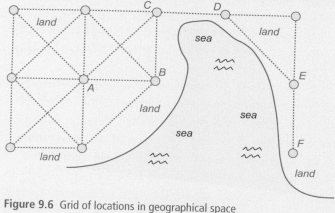

Figure 9.6 Grid of locations in geographical space

---

[22] This sub-section is taken from Brakman, Garretsen, and Schramm (2006).

BOX 9.4 (cont.)

takes place. In addition, with an extra altitude layer the grid is extended to a third dimension (height), such that the model can handle mountains too.

The model by Stelder starts with a flat initial distribution in which all locations on the grid are of equal size, an assumption that could be paraphrased as 'in the beginning there were only small villages'. The task of the model is then to calculate the equilibrium distribution of economic activity, given the assumed parameter values for the division of labour between farmers and workers δ, the elasticity of substitution ε, and the distance between grid points. Different parameter configurations result in long-run equilibria with highly asymmetric hierarchies of cities depending on the specific geographical shape of the economy. Stelder (2005) uses a large geographical grid of Western Europe with over 2,800 locations (see Figure 9.7) in order to determine if the model can simulate Europe's actual city distribution. The inlay in Figure 9.7 shows how sea transportation is made possible by extending the grid with some additional points in the sea, which are part of the network but do not act as potential locations for cities.

Figure 9.8 shows a model run (with $\delta = 0.5$, $\varepsilon = 5$, and $T = 1.57$) producing an equilibrium of 94 cities. The red dots are the simulated outcomes and the blue dots the 94 largest actual cities in 1996. As was to be expected with a flat initial distribution, the model produces an optimal city distribution that is more evenly spread than in reality. Large agglomerations like Paris, London, Madrid, and Rome are not correctly simulated, because population density is for historical reasons higher in the North than in the South. The model predicts too many large cities in Spain and too few cities in the UK, the Netherlands, and Belgium. The results are nevertheless relatively good for Germany: the Rurhgebiet, Bremen, Berlin, Frankfurt, Stuttgart, and Munich (also Vienna) are not far from the right place. In the periphery of various countries some cities also appear correctly, like Lille, Rouen, Nantes, Bordeaux, and Nice in France, Lisbon and Porto in Portugal, and Sevilla and Malaga in Spain.

Stelder points out that these kinds of model results of course *should be* wrong. A good fit would mean 'total victory of economics over all other social sciences because then the whole historical process of city formation would be explained with the three parameters δ, ε and T'.[23] One of his goals with the model is to clarify to what extent pure economic factors have contributed to the city formation process. The main conclusion is that even the core model can produce differentiated city hierarchies without any theoretical extensions once it is applied to space more closely resembling geographic reality. Stelder concludes

---

[23] We adjusted the parameters in the quote to our notation.

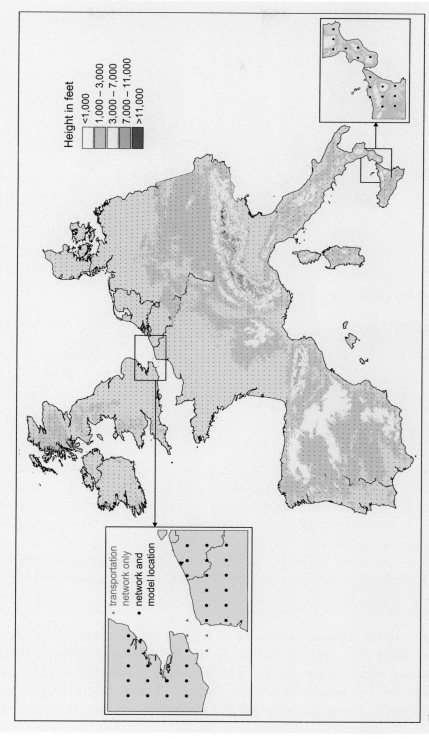

Figure 9.7 A grid model of Western Europe

Height in feet

<1,000
1,000 – 3,000
3,000 – 7,000
7,000 – 11,000
>11,000

transportation
network only

network and
model location

BOX 9.4 (cont.)

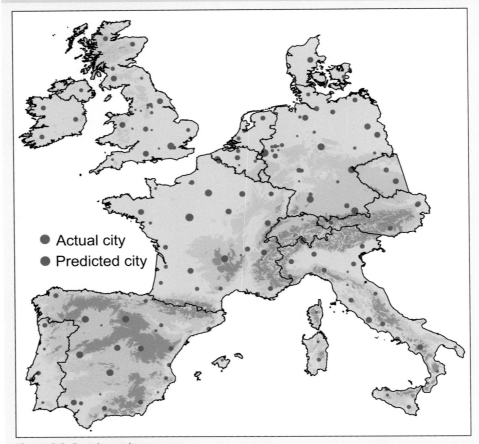

Actual city
Predicted city

Figure 9.8 Experimental outcome

that the 'geography' via the depiction and modelling of the actual, non-neutral space deserves more attention in geographical economics. Two good recent examples of the grid approach combined with an underlying model of geographical economics are Bosker, Buringh, and Van Zanden (2013) and Bosker and Buringh (2017) that both trace and map the urban development in Europe through time.[24]

Apart from the depiction of non-neutral space, the model is exactly the same as the core model of Chapter 7, which means that the simulation of the equilibrium allocation of economic activity hinges on three model parameters only: the share of income spent on manufactures δ, the elasticity of substitution ε, and transport cost function T_{rs}. Recall that these last two parameters constitute the free-ness of

---

[24] See https://sites.google.com/site/maartenbosker2/ for a visualization of their approach.

trade parameter $\varphi_{rs} = T_{rs}^{1-\varepsilon}$. The use of the actual geographical information also means that our simulations are more 'realistic' than, for instance, the *racetrack* simulations (where locations are not equidistant but space is neutral; locations

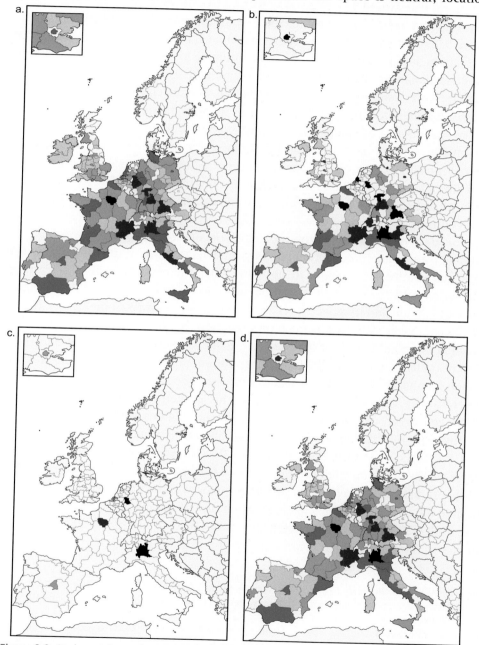

Figure 9.9 Agglomeration and multi-region simulations

Notes: *a* = initial (1992) distribution; *b* = equilibrium simulation; *c* = equilibrium simulation with lower transport costs; *d* = equilibrium simulation with higher substitution elasticity; shades are quintiles, except for panel *c*.

are situated on a circle; see Chapter 8). The sample for the simulation experiment includes most EU regions.[25]

Starting with the initial distribution of regional gross value added (the Y variable) and given estimates of T and ε, one can simulate the long-run equilibrium situation in Europe (derive an outcome where real wages across regions are equalized). Figure 9.9 shows the outcome of some simulations. Panel a gives the initial (1992) distribution and panels b–d show the equilibrium distribution for three multi-region simulations, namely the equilibrium distribution with estimates for the free-ness of trade, for lower transport costs, and for higher substitution elasticity, respectively.[26] Of course, the addition of non-neutral space does not alter the simulation procedure. For a given distribution of mobile workers, the equilibrium wage equation together with the equilibrium price index equation and the income equation determine solutions for the endogenous variables Y_r, W_r, and I_r for every region r. With inter-regional labour mobility, a long-run equilibrium is reached if real wages $w_r = W_r I_r^{-\delta}$ are equalized.

Panel a depicts the initial (1992) distribution. Ranging from black to white, darker areas denote regions that have a relatively larger share of gross value added. Agglomerations are found roughly along the lines of the so-called *European banana*, ranging from London to Belgium and the southwestern part of the Netherlands via west and southwest Germany to northern Italy; the central position of Paris is also noteworthy (to highlight the special position of London, each figure gives the share of London and its adjacent regions in the upper-left part of the figure). Based on the parameter estimates, panel b uses the multi-region simulation to determine the long run equilibrium for the European regions based on our estimates of free-ness of trade. Compared to the initial distribution, the region around Paris and the region around Milan are able to attract more economic activity. The same holds for other initially large regions like London or the southern part of western Germany. In general, when comparing panels a and b, core regions gain at the expense of nearby regions. Also, our equilibrium simulation predicts more agglomeration than was actually observed in 1992. Even with this tendency towards agglomeration, however, the long-run equilibrium in panel b has not collapsed into a strong core–periphery pattern (where one or just a few regions attract all economic activity). Despite the above mentioned agglomeration bias of the model, panel b still yields a considerable degree of dispersion that is qualitatively (but not quantitatively) similar to the actual spatial distribution shown in panel a.

[25] To be specific in the multi-region simulations we use real GDP data for 157 regions in 10 EU countries (Austria, Belgium, France, Germany, Ireland, Italy, Netherlands, Portugal, Spain, UK) and Switzerland.

[26] In these three simulations the share of income spent on manufactured goods δ is set at 0.3. For the regions included in our multi-region experiment, the maps show the share of the region in total gross valued added. A darker (lighter) colour signals a larger (lower) share. Since we are interested in relative changes, we want to find out if a region changes 'colour' when we compare panels a–d.

To investigate what happens to the degree of agglomeration when the free-ness of trade changes (compared to panel *b*), one can also simulate long-run equilibria for larger values of the free-ness of trade. This is illustrated in panel *c*, which reinforces the above conclusions. An increase in the free-ness of trade (decrease in transport costs or the elasticity of substitution) further raises the importance of core regions at the expense of smaller regions in the vicinity. For a high level of free-ness of trade, panel *c* shows that only five regions 'survive' and attract all economic activity. These regions are London, Paris, Madrid, the Ruhr-area in Germany, and Lombardia in Italy. This result is in line with the underlying model, since a high free-ness of trade leads to complete agglomeration in a two-region setting. Similarly, when the free-ness of trade falls, spreading of economic activity occurs. Panel *d* illustrates this by increasing the elasticity of substitution (weaker economies of scale). Compared to panels *b* and *c*, peripheral regions now have a larger share of economic activity. In fact, the resulting equilibrium is rather similar to the initial (1992) distribution depicted in panel *a*.

9.7.4 Where on the Curves Are We? A Multi-Region Simulation Answer

The last item on the list of five testable hypotheses of geographical economics thus asks: do changes in the free-ness of trade lead to agglomeration? By giving up the analytical tractability of the two-region model and its associated break points, we can use multi-region simulations to determine what changes in trade costs imply for the equilibrium allocation of economic activity. So far, we have used the core model of geographical economics from Chapter 7 as an example of non-neutral space to simulate the impact of changes in free-ness of trade on the equilibrium degree of agglomeration. The answer provided by Figure 9.9 is, however, still incomplete (and maybe incorrect!) to the extent that we know from Chapter 8 that the core model of geographical economics is just a special case of a more general economics model (Puga, 1999; see the model discussed in section 8.3) which forms the basis for our discussion of the Tomahawk diagram and bell-shaped curve. By adding non-neutral space to a multi-region version of the *general* model of geographical economics (which allows for intermediate inputs and inter-sectoral labour mobility) one may find a more systematic answer to the following question: *where are we in the 'real world' on the multi-region equivalents of the Tomahawk and bell-shaped curves?*

To answer this question, we proceed as follows (Bosker et al., 2010). We eliminate the equidistant assumption and define the free-ness of trade between region r and region s as: $\varphi_{rs} = \varphi_{sr} = T_{rs}^{1-\varepsilon} = \left(TD_{rs}^{\gamma}\left(1+bB_{rs}\right)\right)^{1-\varepsilon}$ if $r \neq s$ and $\varphi_{rs} = 1$ if $r = s$ where D_{rs} is the great-circle distance between the capital city of regions r and s, γ is the distance coefficient, T is the transport cost parameter, B_{rs} is an indicator function taking the value zero if two regions belong to the same country and one if not, and $b \geq 0$ is a parameter measuring the strength of this border effect. Specifying transport costs this way is fairly common in empirical studies (see

Bosker and Garretsen, 2010, for a survey). It captures the notion that transportation costs increase with the distance over which goods have to be shipped as well
as the fact that inter-country trade is more costly than trade within a country
(through tariffs or through differences in language, culture, and so on).

This non-neutral space version of φ_{rs} is added to the Puga (1999) model as discussed and summarized in section 8.3 using 194 NUTS II regions. By simulating
the long-run equilibrium for this more general multi-region, non-neutral space
model, we can answer our question 'Where are we on these curves?'. Although
we can analyse any parameter change, we focus our discussion on changes in
transport cots T.[27] Because we are dealing with more than two regions we use the
Herfindahl index (defined as $HI = \sum_i \lambda_i^2$) as a measure of the degree of agglomeration measure (λ_i denotes a region's share in the total number of firms or workers).
If there are N regions included, this index varies between $1/N$ and one. The closer
it is to one, the more uneven the distribution of economic activity, and thus the
higher the degree of agglomeration.

To answer the question, 'Where are we on these curves?', we first note that not
only distance matters but also the interaction between the economic mass of a
region and the distance to other regions. So, we simulate the long-run equilibrium
for the 194-region model not only using the aforementioned trade cost function
but also based on the actual distribution of labour and land across the 194 EU
regions as initial conditions. The resulting long-run equilibria are shown in panels
a (labour mobility) and b (labour immobility) of Figure 9.10. Panel a represents the
world of the model underlying the Tomahawk diagram and panel b that of the bell-
shaped curve. The simulations indeed show a resemblance with our Tomahawk
diagram and the bell-shaped curve from Chapter 7 and Chapter 8, respectively.

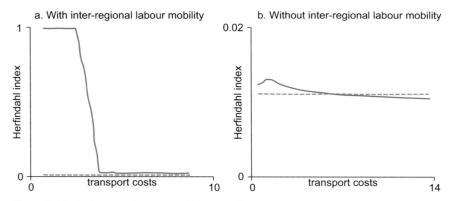

Figure 9.10 Trade costs, distance, and initial conditions
Source: based on Bosker et al. (2010); the dashed line is the Herfindahl index associated with the initial
distribution.

---

[27] For other parameters see Bosker et al. (2010) and the website of the book.

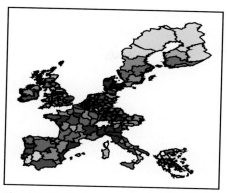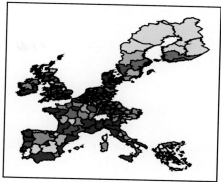

Figure 9.11 Similarity between actual distribution and simulated distribution

Suppose there is inter-regional labour mobility (panel *b* of Figure 9.10). We can now give a potential answer to the million dollar question: where on the bell-shaped curve are we? Plotting the actual value of the Herfindahl index for the 194 EU regions in the figure we see that at a certain value of transport costs ($T = 6.183$) the Herfindahl index of the simulated long-run equilibrium is the same as the Herfindahl index of the actual distribution of manufacturing employment (the dashed line). Recall that different spatial distributions can give rise to the same Herfindahl index. With this in mind it is even more striking to note the resemblance between the simulated long-run equilibrium distribution for this 'critical' level of transport costs and the actual distribution of manufacturing labour; see panels *b* and *a* of Figure 9.11, respectively.[28]

This finding for the first time suggests a satisfactory answer to the central question of section 9.7 in our query about the relationship between trade costs and agglomeration: 'Where on the curve are we?' Taking our pin-pointed T (= 6.183) seriously, and looking at panel *b* of Figure 9.10 we conclude that increased economic integration is likely to result in *rising* agglomeration. Only in the very distant future, when we have passed the peak of the curve in this figure will a further increase in economic integration result in a *fall* in agglomeration.

9.8 Geographical Economics in Modern Empirical Research

Now that we have dealt with the testable hypotheses that arise from the geographical economics models from Chapter 7 and Chapter 8, it is time to see how this empirical research relates to the state-of-the-art empirical research in spatial economics more generally. Modern empirical research in spatial economics, much like empirical research in economics overall, is concerned with the identification of cause and effect. When discussing modern research methods in Chapter 3 as well as empirical insights

---

[28] The correlation coefficient is 0.809.

from urban economics in Chapter 6, we already touched upon this issue. To see how this also affects the empirical testing of *geographical* economics have another look at the equilibrium wage equation 9.2, repeated here for ease of reference:

$$W_j = \left(\sum_k Y_k I_k^{\varepsilon-1} T^{D_{jk}(1-\varepsilon)} \right)^{1/\varepsilon} \qquad\qquad 9.11$$

When testing for a spatial wage structure like we did in section 9.4, one would like the right-hand side of the wage equation (the real market potential term) to be exogenous and ideally wages should only be driven by market potential. From the long-run version of the geographical economics models, we know, however, that real market potential contains two endogenous variables (income Y and the price index I), and we also know that a region's income is the summation of the wages of the workers residing in that region. This shows why it is far from straightforward to claim that real market potential 'causes' wages. In addition, wages and real market potential might be positively correlated but this might be because workers who earn a high(er) wage like to live and work in large(r) agglomerations but for reasons that are unrelated to the market potential of these agglomerations, for example because, as we saw in Chapter 6, they like the amenities of larger urban centres or because they simply like to live next to other (like-minded) high income earners. In that case high-earning workers (or more productive firms) self-select into agglomerations but this is *not* the result of agglomeration externalities. To address these kinds of identification problems, empirical research in geographical economics (in line with modern empirical research in spatial economics) has built on the findings discussed in this chapter by taking two approaches that characterize the research design of modern empirical research (Baum-Snow and Ferreira, 2015; Donaldson and Hornbeck, 2016; Holmes and Sieg, 2015):

- Use *micro-data* to estimate equations like our wage equation 9.2 so as to be better able to infer causality.
- Abandon the estimation of equations like 9.2 altogether and try to set up *quasi-natural experiments* to arrive at exogenous variation and to infer causality

In the remainder of this section we will briefly illustrate both approaches. A third (and highly topical) approach, quantitative spatial economics, falls outside the scope of our book; see Rossi-Hansberg (2019) for a recent survey. The example on micro-data (section 9.8.1) can be seen as a direct extension of the empirical research discussed in section 9.4 on the wage equation and also as an extension of the discussion of (Spanish) wages and city-size in Chapter 6. The discussion of the use of quasi-natural experiments (section 9.8.2) can be seen as encompassing the empirical research on shocks as discussed in section 9.6. The prevalence in modern empirical research of micro-data and/or quasi-natural experiments has led to a situation where empirical research in geographical economics has submerged into a more general empirical testing of spatial phenomena that incorporates elements from both urban and geographical economics. In that sense, modern empirical research in spatial economics, like in economics more generally, focuses rather strongly on the research design and less on testing a specific theory or model, be it urban or geographical economics (for a very good state-of-the-art survey on these matters see Baum-Snow and Ferreira, 2015).

9.8.1 How to Use Micro-data to Test for Agglomeration (vs Selection) Effects

The models of geographical economics that have been discussed in our book have as a key message that agglomerations are characterized by higher wages; see wage equation 9.2. In geographical economics, but also in urban economics (Chapter 6), the explanation for this *agglomeration bonus* is the existence of various positive localized externalities. So it is the spatial concentration of firms and workers that creates the agglomeration benefits and *causes* higher productivity and hence wages. But, as we already discussed in Chapter 3 and Chapter 6, the modern literature on firm or worker heterogeneity shows that the observed agglomeration bonus may simply be the result of a *selection or sorting effect*. Firms are on average more productive in larger markets merely because only the more productive firms survive in larger markets. If this is the case, the higher productivity of firms in larger or more centrally located regions is *not* caused by the alleged positive agglomeration economies but is instead the result of a selection process. Similarly, more productive workers may simply like to live in larger cities which gives these places a larger market potential to begin with.

To test the 'agglomeration bonus' explanation against the competing selection explanation, the models and empirical work discussed in Chapter 7 and Chapter 8 will not do for two reasons. First, the core models do not include the possibility of firms' or workers' *heterogeneity* to begin with. The way forward here would be to build theoretical models that allow for both agglomeration and selection effects; see Behrens and Robert-Nicoud (2015) for a survey. Baldwin and Okubo (2006), for instance, show how the geographical economics model can be extended to include selection effects. Second, to test these competing explanations requires the use of *micro-data*, but the empirical work in geographical economics discussed in this chapter so far is based on data that are typically not firm- or worker-specific. Ideally, one would like to tackle the agglomeration versus selection issue by developing a theoretical model that allows for both explanations and then test such a model. This is precisely what Combes et al. (2012) do in a paper that became a leading example of modern empirical research on agglomeration effects. For a survey of the measurement and estimation of agglomeration effects using micro-data see again Combes and Gobillon (2015).

We focus here on the empirical contribution by Combes et al. (2012). They use a detailed panel data set of French firms (1.15 million firms for 1994–2002) that covers (almost) all French firms. The main empirical prediction from their underlying model is that even though both the agglomeration and selection effect predict that average productivity will be higher in large markets, the (log) productivity distribution will be different in both cases when comparing larger and smaller markets. In particular, 'stronger selection effects in larger markets should lead to an increased left truncation of the distribution of firm log productivities whereas stronger agglomeration effects should lead to a rightwards shift of the distribution of firm log productivities' (Combes et al., 2012). The empirical work then basically exploits this difference in the predicted firm productivity distribution across large and small French locations between the agglomeration and selection effect. Total factor productivity is computed at the establishment level for each firm at the two-digit sector level for every large and small location (metropolitan areas with more and less than 200,000 people, respectively). The econometric specification is such that instead of specifying the underlying productivity distribution, Combes et al. (2012) directly estimate the 'left-truncation' effect associated with the selection effect as well as the 'rightward shift' effect associated with the agglomeration effect. More specifically, with i and j denoting large and small locations, the parameters to be estimated are S and A; see Table 9.6, where S captures the selection effect and A captures the agglomeration effect as follows:

$$S \equiv \frac{S_i - S_j}{1 - S_j} \text{ and } A \equiv A_i - A_j \qquad\qquad 9.12$$

This, in turn, gives rise to the following predictions:

- The strength of the selection effect is invariant to location size: $S = 0$
- Stronger selection effect in large locations: $S > 0$
- The strength of the agglomeration effect is invariant to location size: $A = 0$
- Stronger selection effect in large locations: $A > 0$

Given the theoretical predictions regarding the A and S coefficients, it is clear that the estimation results suggest that typically $A > 0$ and that $S \approx 0$. This implies that productivity differences across French metropolitan areas are primarily the result of the agglomeration effect. This does not mean that selection effects are not important, but only that the strength of this effect does not depend on the location size. Regarding the quantitative importance of the A-effect, Combes et al. (2012, p. 2566) note:

> In our model, the extent to which there are common productivity advantages from larger cities is closely related to the extent to which interactions are local or global (national in this case). Our results are consistent with a situation where interactions are quite local. This matches the existing empirical literature (see Rosenthal and Strange (2004)).

This last observation on the limited spatial reach of agglomeration economies is in line with our conclusions about the empirical evidence on geographical economics when estimating for a spatial wage structure (recall Figure 9.1 in section 9.4 on spatial wages in Germany). The main conclusion to take away from the above example is that the use of micro-data enables one to differentiate between

Table 9.6 Agglomeration versus selection in France

Sector	Agglomeration effect A	Specialization effect S	R^2	# observations
Food, beverages and tobacco	-0.11	0.02	0.50	25,853
Clothing and leather	0.39	-0.10	0.87	5,964
Publishing and printing	0.27	-0.01	0.97	10,493
Pharmaceuticals products	0.35	-0.01	0.91	1,831
Domestic equipment	0.20	-0.01	0.99	6,880
Motor vehicles	0.31	-0.09	0.80	1,816
Ships, locomotives and rolling stock	0.34	0.03	0.97	1,143
Machinery and equipment	0.40	-0.02	0.90	16,332
Electric and electronic equipment	0.22	-0.00	0.98	7,735
Textiles	0.16	0.00	0.96	3,718
Wood, pulp and paper	0.18	0.00	0.99	5,985
Chemicals	0.26	-0.01	0.98	6,987
Basic metals and fabr. metal products	0.12	0.01	0.97	15,161
Electric and electronic components	0.10	0.02	0.96	3,337
Construction	0.28	-0.01	0.91	78,511
Vehicle sale and maintenance	0.22	-0.00	0.96	32,052
Wholesale and commission trade	0.30	-0.02	0.98	70,242
Transportation	0.26	-0.01	0.86	39,948
Consultancy and assistance activities	0.36	-0.01	0.99	56,129
Average	0.26	-0.01	0.92	

Source: Combes et al. (2012).

agglomeration and selection effects and that by doing this agglomeration effects are still relevant even if the spatial decay is quite strong. This finding has been corroborated by other empirical studies that use micro data to test for agglomeration effect on wages; see Combes, Duranton, and Gobillon (2008), Hering and Poncet (2010), Combes et al. (2010), or De la Roca and Puga (2017). The last two studies were discussed at length in Chapter 6. These studies do not only rely on micro (panel) data to infer a causal effect of the agglomeration variable of interest but also use other modern econometric methods, like instrumental variables.

The shift in empirical research to using micro-data to test agglomeration effects versus other competing explanations (such as sorting) has led to a situation where the exact source of the agglomeration effect is of less interest, which means that many studies use variables from both urban and geographical economics models but do not (any longer) aim to test a specific model (Combes and Gobillon, 2015). In Combes et al. (2010), for instance, agglomeration effects stemming from only the location itself (like in urban economics models) 'co-exist' with a market potential variable derived from geographical economics that is meant to measure the relevance of spatial interdependencies.

9.8.2   The Use of Quasi-Natural Experiments

At the beginning of this section, we stated that there are basically two dominant approaches in modern empirical research in urban and geographical economics to inferring causality. The first approach is to rely on micro-data and the second approach is to focus on a research design where one makes use of (quasi-)natural experiments to identify cause and effect. Both approaches can be used to test the relevance of geographical economics but, as we already concluded at the end of the previous sub-section for micro-data research, they do not focus on testing a specific model. The micro-data can be used to arrive at better-founded estimations of the wage equation from geographical economics that was the topic of section 9.4. At the same time, as we saw in Chapter 6, micro-data can also be used to be on firmer 'causality' ground when it comes to the possible impact of city size or city density on urban wages and productivity, which is a main topic in urban economics.

The use of quasi-natural experiments can be looked upon as an extension of the research on shocks that we discussed in section 9.6, but here too this research is not restricted to a particular model or theory and is used in urban as well as geographical economics. The shocks that we discussed in section 9.6 were deemed relevant because they were large (affected a substantial sample of cities to a varying degree), temporary (enabled study of the impact of the shock), and, most importantly, exogenous (allowing causality to be inferred).

In economics more generally, there has been a revolution in the way economists conduct empirical research. Instead of estimating equations that have been derived from a specific model, like our wage equation 9.2, it basically discards estimating (structural) models and instead tries to set up a research design where an experiment either was deliberately conducted or arose by historical accident. The main idea is to distinguish, much like in the random trials in the testing for a new drug in the medical sciences, between a treatment group and a control group where (ideally) the two groups are the same except for one effect, the treatment itself. This research design is now common practice in fields such as development economics, labour economics, or international economics and it is associated with estimation methods like a regression discontinuity design (RDD) or the difference-in-differences approach (DID) that we already introduced in Chapter 3.

For our present purposes it is relevant that this new research design has also caught on in spatial economics where space or geography is used to simulate the treatment. A good example is the research by Dachis, Duranton, and Turner (2012), also mentioned in Chapter 3, which analyses the (unexpected) introduction of a land transfer tax by the city of Toronto in 2008, and the impact the tax had on housing prices. Instead of estimating a structural housing model that includes as many possible drivers of the local housing prices alongside the tax itself, they opt for a different research design. They compare the development of housing prices before and after the introduction of the tax by comparing houses that are really close to each other with the difference being that one group of houses fall just inside the jurisdiction of the city of Toronto where the tax applies whereas the other houses, in the same neighbourhood or even the same street, technically fall just outside the city of Toronto and were hence not affected by the tax. When it comes to amenities, distance to downtown Toronto, housing quality, and so on the two groups do not differ. The set-up is that the two groups are thought to differ only when it comes to the introduction and impact of the land transfer tax. Assuming that the research design is such that the two sub-samples of houses indeed differ only in this one crucial aspect (whether or not the land transfer tax applies), a simple before and after test of the average housing prices between the two sub-samples suffices to assess the impact of the 'shock'. It turns out that the introduction of the land transfer tax had a significant *negative* impact on the housing prices for the sub-sample of houses to which the tax applied compared to the group of houses in the control group that were not subject to the tax.

In Box 9.5 we provide an additional example of the use of (quasi-)natural experiments to infer causality in spatial economics. The basic idea is always to distinguish between a treatment group and a control group where the two groups differ ideally only in the treatment or shock, which may arise exogenously or can be allocated randomly. The exact econometric details need not concern us here, but see section 3.5.3 and again the survey by Baum-Snow and Ferreira (2015). What matters in the context of our quest to test hypotheses of models of geographical economics, which is after all the topic of the present chapter, is that the research on the 'shock sensitivity' hypothesis as summarized in section 9.6 can be seen as now belonging to a much broader research agenda in spatial economics where shocks or experiments are used to establish causal effects of certain exogenous or man-made events on spatial outcomes. Like with the research on agglomeration effects and the use of micro-data in the previous sub-section, the submergence of the 'shock sensitivity' studies into a broader empirical literature implies that these studies are not only or even not at all to be seen as attempts to test the specifics of the geographical economics models. This trend in urban and geographical

BOX 9.5 The Impact of Flooding on Dutch Housing Prices

The Netherlands is one of the most flood-prone countries in the world. It is the 12th most exposed country to natural disasters in the world (World Risk Report, 2014). The Dutch have a long history of dealing with the flood risk posed by the sea and rivers that surround them. As the map in Figure 9.12 shows, a larger part of the country is below sea level (blue part < 0 metres). Today, the country is protected by arguably the best flood defences in the world. The Dutch government spends over €1.1 billion per year on the 3,767 km of dikes and (artificial) dunes and 1,458 other primary waterworks (dams, weirs, locks, etc.) that protect the country. In the best-protected parts of the country they should reduce the likelihood of a flood to once every 10,000 years. Without these defences 36 per cent of the Netherlands would be at risk of floods, home to approximately 2.7 million houses/households. Note that the flooding risk does not only or even primarily come from the sea but also from the rivers like the Rhine and the Meuse that enter the Dutch delta via Germany and Belgium respectively. In line with the idea of using space or geography itself for a research design where a treatment and control group can be distinguished, as is done by for example Dachis, Duranton, and Turner (2012), the impact of flooding risk (or other natural disasters) on housing prices can analysed in a similar way.

Bosker et al. (2019) exploit a unique data set on Dutch house prices and predicted flood water levels in the event that the country's flood defences fail. It covers all 459,279 Dutch six-digit postal code (6PPC) areas over the period 1999–2011. The median 6PPC area is only 60 by 60 metres, containing 20 houses. The quality and spatial detail of this data set allow one to rely on a *border discontinuity design* in the vein of Dachis, Duranton, and Turner (2012) that overcomes many of the difficulties in identifying people's willingness to pay to avoid flood risk using hedonic valuation methods. Such a research design is an example of the regression discontinuity design introduced in Chapter 3, but here space demarcates the difference between the treatment group (houses with flooding risk) and control group (houses without flooding risk). We restrict ourselves to considering flooding risk from the sea, i.e. applying only to areas below sea level. To be more precise, the border discontinuity design used implies that one only looks at those border-line areas that are home to houses (just) above and below sea level or in other words houses with (marginally) flooding and no flooding risk from the sea, the idea being that within those border-line areas one can indeed compare houses and hence housing prices for houses that are similar in all respects (house quality, access to amenities, local job prospects, etc.) bar one: the flooding risk.

To be more specific, Bosker et al. (2019) infer people's willingness to pay to (not) live in an area with flooding risk from housing prices in three ways.

BOX 9.5 (cont.)

First, and inspired by Black (1999), Bayer, Ferreira, and McMillan (2007), and Gibbons, Machin, and Silva (2013), they use a border discontinuity design. Second, they restrict attention to areas containing only terraced houses: two randomly selected terraced houses have much more comparable housing characteristics than e.g. two detached houses. Third, they base their inference on the variation in house prices and flood risk within the same year and same five-digit postal code (5PPC) area, which have a median size of only 294 by 294 metres. This substantially reduces the risk of unobserved, possibly time-varying, neighbour(hood) characteristics confounding our estimated willingness to pay to avoid flood risk. In the estimations this is covered by using (5PPC) *fixed effects*, and as we discussed in Chapter 3, location fixed effects are a way to tackle unobserved, time-invarying determinants of, in this case, local housing prices.

Using all three of the above-described strategies, Bosker et al. (2019) find an average *1 per cent price discount* on houses facing flood risk, in money terms; given the average housing prices this implies a discount of 3,500 euros. In assessing this effect, one should keep in mind that the actual flooding risk is very low. Still, Dutch houses in areas at flooding risk sell at a discount compared to similar (terraced) houses in the same area. For the overall sample, see right-hand panel of Figure 9.12, a general comparison of the distribution of housing prices for houses with and without flooding risk which suggests that houses with flooding risk sell at a discount (a larger part of the distribution is to the left of the median housing price compared to housing prices without flooding risk).

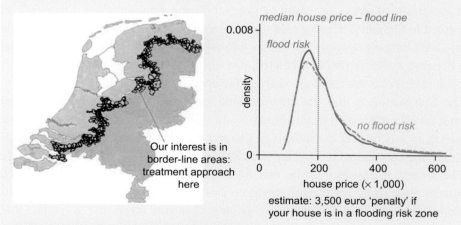

Figure 9.12 Flooding risk figures in the Netherlands
Source: based on Bosker et al. (2019).

economics in which modern empirical research and the associated methods are not linked to a specific theory or model is also evident in recent studies that use shocks or events to study the *resilience* of cities or regions. This analyses whether and how local areas return to their pre-shock path in terms of output or employment following a shock; see Fingleton, Garretsen, and Martin (2012, 2015) for the resilience of UK regions and European regions following the onset of UK recessions and the entry into the Economic and Monetary Union (EMU). Brakman, Garretsen, and van Marrewijk (2015) investigate the resilience of European regions in the wake of the Great Recession following the financial crisis of 2008.

9.9 Conclusion: the 'What If' Question of Geographical Economics

All in all, the empirical evidence presented in this chapter on the hypotheses that come out of the geographical economics models of Chapter 7 and Chapter 8 provides some empirical support for the geographical economics approach. As outlined at the beginning of the chapter, two basic problems for empirical verification of the geographical economics models are (i) many empirical studies are not only consistent with geographical economics models but also with other theories of trade and location and (ii) attempts, like the testing of the hypotheses discussed throughout this chapter, to focus on the relevance of geographical economics as such provide considerable empirical support but the multi-region, non-neutral, multiple-equilibria nature of the geographical economics approach make conclusive testing rather difficult. So, how to proceed from here?

Two ways to go forward for empirical research are using better data and research design, as discussed at length in section 9.8. A third avenue is the improvement and extension of the core model of geographical economics from Chapter 7 as discussed in Chapter 8. Having said that, it is undeniable that after the initial surge in research on geographical economics following Krugman (1991), the core model has become, as Neary (2001) predicted, just one of the general equilibrium models one can use. What are the main reasons for this?

The first reason is that the theories have not resulted in an overall empirical testing specification such as, for example, the gravity model in international trade research. In this respect the models in Chapter 8 are only marginally more tractable than the core model as developed in Krugman (1991).

The second reason is that the two fields adjacent to geographical economics, economic geography proper and urban economics, have been reluctant to take its main insights on board. For economic geography proper this is due to the fact that the depiction of geography and indeed of the way in which economic agents spatially interact in geographical economics is deemed too simplistic (Garretsen and Martin, 2010). According to economic geographers the modelling of geography is more complicated than merely introducing a transport cost parameter T. Compared to modern urban economics (see Part II of our book), the key difference with geographical economics is the fact that spatial interdependencies are not part of the former whereas they are arguably the hallmark of the latter. Many urban economists see no real need to adapt their modelling ways as long as it is not clear whether the neglect of spatial interdependencies substantially reduces the explanatory power of their own models, certainly if the spatial reach of the interdependencies is quite limited (as discussed in this chapter).

The third reason is that, as we have argued in section 9.8, the empirical research on aspects of geographical economics has become part of a broader empirical literature in spatial economics, where the distinction between urban and geographical economics is of secondary importance and where a sound empirical research design matters more than the testing of a specific theory or model.

When looking back on the development of geographical economics that won him the Nobel prize in economics, Krugman (2011) did, however, point out that the main selling point that really differentiates geographical economics from related (or competing) approaches is to be found in the possibility that geographical economics can provide answers to the *what if* questions. This is related to the general-equilibrium nature of the underlying models. Questions like 'What will happen to the spatial allocation of economic activity if transport costs change?' (the last item on the list of testable hypotheses analysed in section 9.7) can in principle be addressed by geographical economics.[29] In our present day and age, where all kinds of exogenous, technological, or policy-induced shocks, like changes in trade and transports costs, potentially impact on the spatial allocation of economic activity within and between countries, geographical economics has a distinctive value added.

In the next chapter we will therefore discuss examples where the geographical economics approach has been used to address important 'what if' questions when it comes to the relationship between geography and economic development both within and between countries.

Exercises

Question 9.1 Spatial Wage Structure

Take the idea of a spatial wage structure as introduced in this chapter. Do you think it is possible to arrive at such a wage structure using either the concepts of spatial equilibrium or agglomeration economies as introduced and developed in Part II of our book on urban economics, in particular in Chapter 5 and Chapter 6?

---

[29] Which is precisely what the so-called quantitative spatial economics approach aims to do (Redding and Rossi-Hansberg, 2016, 2017; Rossi-Hansberg, 2019).

Question 9.2 Experiment

Take the estimation results for the wages in German city-districts based on equation 9.5. Now assume that the income in the city of Essen (one of the German city districts) is increased by 10 per cent and calculate the impact of this income shock for city-district wages. Explain the findings you would expect of this experiment in terms of the geographical economics model.

Question 9.3 Wage Equation

Take the short-run equilibrium wage equation 9.2. This equation states that low transportation costs (low T) are good for regional wages. Why does this equation, however, not tell us what happens with regional wages when transportation costs are changed, for instance when T is lowered?

Question 9.4 Trade Costs and Home Market Effect

In practice almost all goods are costly to trade. The study by Davis (1998) suggests that in that case the home market effect might cease to exist. Can you find evidence that this is indeed the case? [Hint: are large countries net exporters of commodities produced under firm-specific scale economies (use intra-sector trade figures as an indication)?]

Question 9.5 Wage Equation and Market Potential

As explained in Chapter 7, the equilibrium wage equation of the core model is given by

$$W_j = \left(\sum_k Y_k I_k^{\varepsilon-1} T^{D_{jk}(1-\varepsilon)} \right)^{1/\varepsilon}$$

where W is the wage rate, Y is income, I is the price index, ε is the elasticity of substitution, T is the transport cost parameter, and $T_{jk} = T^{D_{jk}}$, where D_{jk} is the distance between locations j and k.

a) Discuss the main differences between this wage equation and a simple market potential function for wages.
b) Explain whether or not the estimation of this wage equation can be looked upon as a test of the underlying geographical economics model.

Question 9.6 Germany and World War II

Suppose that in the research on the impact of WW II bombing on German city growth the conclusion would have been that 16–17 years after WW II had ended German cities had returned to their initial, that is pre-WW II, relative population size. Discuss why such a finding would not necessarily be at odds with the core model of geographical economics.

Question 9.7 Storm in the Netherlands

Apart from the impact of WW II on German and Japanese cities, this chapter also includes brief discussions of other 'shock' examples. Suppose a huge storm leads to the flooding of the urban agglomeration of Rotterdam in the Netherlands (Rotterdam is partly located below sea level). How would you apply the insights from the models of this chapter to this case? Answer the same question if all cities in the Dutch lowlands (Netherlands means lowlands) were affected. [Hint: also keep Box 9.5 in mind.]

Question 9.8 Symmetric Trade Costs with Many Regions

In Chapter 7 and Chapter 8 in the discussion of the core model of geographical economics it was assumed that $D_{rs} = 1$. Explain why this is an innocent assumption when one is dealing with a two-region economy but not when one is dealing with an N-region economy where N is a large number.

Question 9.9 Geography and Geographical Economics

Many geographers are rather critical of geographical economics. In their view, one major problem is that geographical economics, also known as new economic geography, contains too little geography. Discuss whether the arguments presented in the current chapter back up the claim that geographical economics contains too little or even no geography at all in your view.

Question 9.10 Testable Hypotheses

The central theme underlying Chapter 9 was the list of testable hypotheses that came out of geographical economics. All in all, there is some evidence supporting these hypotheses but the evidence is mixed. Two ways to make progress and to arrive at more definite conclusions are better testing and better data; see section 9.8. Discuss in your own words for both options how one may go about this and why this would help the empirical research in geographical economics forward.

PART IV
Development and Policy

· ·

When it comes to explaining the spiky distribution of human economic activity (see Chapter 1), we have now come full circle. Chapter 1 stated that there are two types of explanations for this uneven distribution, *first nature* and *second nature* explanations. The focus of our book is on second nature explanations and in particular on explanations that emphasize economic interactions between firms, workers, and/ or households as well as on the consequences of these interactions for their location choices and hence for the economies of these locations, be they cities, regions, or countries. Urban and geographical economics are the two main building blocks available in mainstream economics to model and test these economic interactions and their locational consequences, as analysed in Parts II and III of our book.

Part IV addresses two topics that we have largely ignored so far: growth and policy. In Chapter 10 we use insights from urban and geographical economics to understand the growth and development of economies. We will not only make use of the models from Parts II and III of our book but also turn to the deep or ultimate determinants of economic development. We argue, in line with Chapter 2, that first nature geography as well as second nature geography is linked to the role of history as well as institutions. A main goal of Chapter 10 will also be to give further examples of empirical applications of geographical economics that points towards its strength (see the conclusions of Chapter 9) in analysing *and* answering so-called *what if* questions.

In Chapter 11 we analyse whether and how policy issues can be dealt with by using the insights from urban and geographical economics of the previous chapters. In addition to addressing and illustrating policy implications, the final chapter of our book puts urban and geographical economics into a broader perspective by briefly discussing its relationship with other approaches to explaining the spiky world.

10 Geography and Development

LEARNING OBJECTIVES

- To know the stylized facts about economic growth.
- To understand how a dynamic geographical economics model could explain these facts.
- To learn about the interplay between economic geography and institutions for economic development.
- To understand how the 'what if' approach of geographical economics can be applied.

10.1 Introduction

The take-away message from Chapter 1 was that the world is *spiky*, meaning that both human and economic activity are not distributed evenly across space but instead cluster at certain locations as any satellite picture of the 'earth by night' already indicates: clusters of lights that signal concentration of economic activity amidst large swaths of darkness. This spikiness does not only hold for countries, but also within countries or even within regions and cities. The theories and empirics of urban economics and geographical economics, as introduced in Parts II and III of our book respectively, each try to offer explanations for the stylized facts of this spiky world. In doing so, these theories tend to focus on the allocation or distribution of people and economic activity across space. For a *given* overall population size or amount of economic activity the theories offer (testable) explanations for how cities are structured internally (Chapter 4), why cities exist and differ in size (Chapter 5 and Chapter 6), or how spatial interdependencies may explain the co-existence of core and peripheral regions (Chapter 7 to Chapter 9).

Both urban and geographical economics are, however, less concerned with the important question of why local or national economies grow over time both in terms of population size and economic activity. To the extent that the models discussed so far do deal with economic *growth*, they typically do so by neglecting the role of geography or space, thereby assuming that the economic development of individual *spikes* can be studied in isolation. In this chapter we take up the challenge to better explain how the spiky world may grow and hence develop over time. We are thus interested in the relationship between economic growth and geography and how this relationship may impact on the economic development within and between countries. Since urban economics, as introduced in Part II of the book, typically only offers urban growth models where economic geography has no or only a limited role to play, we will mainly try to understand the relevance of *growth and geography* for spatial economic development from the perspective of geographical economics (Part III of the book). In addition, the subfield of economic development is primarily focused on a comparison of growth between countries whereas urban economics typically emphasizes (urban) growth differences within a single country. Nonetheless, the phenomenon of urbanization is widely thought to be important for economic development; see Box 10.1.

BOX 10.1 Economic Development and Urbanization

The idea that urbanization matters for economic development follows directly from the models of urban economics in Part II of the book. There we learned that, other things being equal, density pays off. There are net agglomeration benefits associated for both firms and people to locate in or to cluster in cities. In addition, there is strong empirical evidence that the economic make-up of cities matters: successful fast-growing cities can often be linked to a certain specialization structure or set of amenities. Against this background, it is no surprise that some degree of urbanization is viewed as a prerequisite for economic development. Figure 10.1 (see also Chapter 1) shows that there is indeed a clear positive relationship between the level of economic development, as measured by income per capita, and the degree of urbanization at the country level. Every bubble in Figure 10.1 represents a country (proportional to population size). Keep the largest bubble for China in mind since we return to it at the end of this chapter. Indeed both leading scholars in urban economics and the main policy institutions for economic development agree that the evidence clearly favours the view that urbanization plays an important role in the process of economic development; see Glaeser and Henderson (2017), Henderson et al. (2018) for the academic view and the World Bank for the policy view (World Bank, 2009).

The reasons why and mechanisms through which urbanization is favourable for economic development are the same as discussed in the context of national urban growth and national urban systems in Part II. Having said that, the evidence also shows that urbanization has drawbacks and in fact that the relationship between urbanization and economic growth is perhaps hill-shaped, implying

BOX 10.1 (cont.)

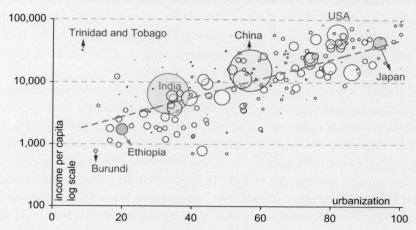

Figure 10.1 Income per capita and urbanization, 2016
Source: created using World Bank Development Indicators online; income per capita: GNI PPP
(current int. dollar); urbanization: urban population (% of total); bubbles proportional to size of
population; 180 countries included.

that beyond a certain threshold the degree of urbanization starts to become
detrimental for growth (see Henderson, 2003, for early evidence). In addition,
urbanization (which is the share of the national population living in cities) has
to be distinguished from the size of individual cities. The argument that the net
agglomeration benefits of cities for growth and development increase when cities get larger cannot stand close scrutiny. Again, the evidence points to a hill-
shaped relationship; see Spence, Clarke Annez, and Buckley (2009) and Frick
and Rodríguez-Pose (2018). A final point on the measurement of urbanization
(see also Chapter 3): scholars increasingly use other measures than the traditional ones that rely on official administrative demarcations for cities, regions, or
even countries. Urbanization and hence the clustering of people and firms often
transcend those demarcations. A good alternative is the use of light intensity to
measure urbanization. Henderson et al. (2018), for instance, examine the determinants of the global spatial distribution of economic activity as proxied by lights
at night, observed across 240,000 grid cells.

Chapter 10 is organized as follows. First, we give a short introduction on the
stylized facts of economic growth in sections 10.2 and 10.3 to set the agenda for
the remainder of the chapter, in particular in terms of the preferred type of model
of economic development that includes both growth and geography, which could
account for these stylized facts. Section 10.4 introduces two basic approaches to

incorporating these stylized facts. We synthesize these approaches in section 10.5 based on a dynamic model by Baldwin and Forslid (2000) and Baldwin (2016).

Our *growth with geography* model is open to two lines of criticism. The first is that it only deals with the proximate and not the deep determinants of economic development. These deep determinants are first nature determinants of the spiky world like physical geography, which we already encountered in Chapter 2; this is the topic of section 10.6.

A second line of criticism is that the growth model ignores the interplay between economic geography and economic development *within* a country. Taking China as an example, we return to the geographical economics model by Puga (1999), as introduced in Chapter 8, to answer the question of how increased labour mobility might impact on the economic geography of China. By doing so in section 10.7, we deliver on the promise made at the end of Chapter 9, that geographical economics is well-suited to deal with *what if* questions, in this case: What are the structural consequences for economic development in China if intra-regional labour mobility rises? Section 10.8 concludes.

10.2   Income, Economic Growth and Stylized Facts 1 & 2

The field of economic growth deals with two questions: 'Why do countries grow over time?' and 'Why do some countries grow faster than others?'. In a standard growth model, diminishing returns to capital ensure that 'poor', capital-scarce countries grow faster than 'rich', capital-abundant countries since the return on investment in capital is higher in poor countries. As a result, there will be a catching-up process where initially poor countries grow faster than initially rich countries.

In the standard growth model, countries end up having the same level of income per capita in the long run. In the absence of technological progress, which is exogenous in the standard growth model, income per capita eventually does not grow at all. This leads to two predictions: (1) convergence of income per capita across countries and (2) no growth of income per capita in the long run (if technological progress is absent). Both predictions are not borne out by the evidence. This is not only the case for the growth experience of countries but also for the growth experience of regions or cities. This implies that the standard neo-classical growth model is less useful for our present purposes and that we should look for alternative models to explain the stylized facts of economic growth.

Figure 10.2 presents the distribution of income per capita in real terms using a log scale (in constant 2011 US $) at the country level in 1950 and 2016 based on information from the Maddison Project Database 2018. The graph uses kernel density estimates (see Chapter 3, Box 3.2). In 1950 the simple average income per capita was $2,118, ranging from a low of $398 in Lesotho to a high of $15,241 in the USA. In 2016 the average income per capita was $10,448, ranging from a low of $619 in Central African Republic to a high of almost $140,000 in Qatar. The shift of the density to the right over time indicates *rising* income per capita levels for most countries. Note that the average income level in 2016 is 4.9 times higher than in 1950, the lowest income level is only 1.6 times higher, and the highest income level is 9.2 times higher. This suggests that the relative range of income levels is widening rather than declining, indicative of an increase in income dispersion; see Brakman and van Marrewijk (2008) for a discussion. For reference (see section 10.7) Figure 10.2 also depicts the position of China, the world's most populous country, in the income distributions. In 1950 China's income was $757, or 64 per cent below the world average in that year. In 2016 China's income per capita is more than 16 times higher at $12,320, or 18 per cent above the world average in that year. This illustrates the dramatic relative improvement of China in this period.

We are also interested in the connection between the initial income level and the long-run growth rate. This is a question of *convergence*: where poor countries *on average* have *higher* long-run growth rates than initially rich countries, they will catch up and income inequality at the country level will not exacerbate over time. The reverse holds if this is not the case. Figure 10.3 illustrates the connection between initial income level (on the horizontal axis, using a log scale) and the long-run growth rate (on the vertical axis, in per cent) using a bubble diagram, where the size of the bubbles is proportional to the size of the population in 2000. Our conclusions on convergence are summarized in the two regression lines in the figure.

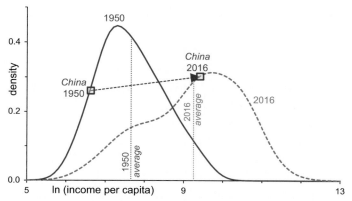

Figure 10.2 Distribution of income per capita at country level: kernel densities, 1950 and 2016
Created using Maddison Project Database 2018 (cgdppc); real GDP per capita in 2011 USD; based on normal distribution with bandwidth $(4/3)^{1/5}\, \hat{\sigma} n^{-1/5}$, where $\hat{\sigma}$ is standard deviation and n is the number of observations (144 in 1950 and 166 in 2016); see also Box 3.2.

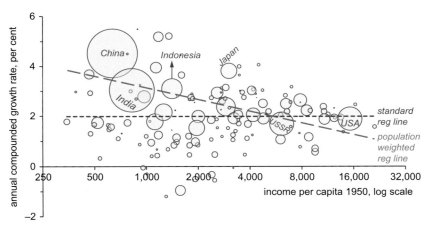

Figure 10.3 Initial income per capita and long-run growth rates, 1950–2016
Source: calculations based on Maddison Project Database 2018; 140 countries included; for Cuba, N. Korea, and Palestine data for 2015 instead of 2016 are used; real income is based on GDP per capita in 2011 USD with benchmark 2011 (rgdpnapc variable); bubble size proportional to population in 2000; reg line = regression line.

The first regression line is a standard regression line: it is horizontal. Try to look at Figure 10.3 while making all countries equally important by imagining all bubbles to be of equal size. If you draw a regression line through this imaginary figure, the standard regression line results. Its slope (coefficient is 0.0004) is not statistically different from zero and the regression explains 0.00 per cent of the variance in growth rates. On the basis of this information, therefore, we would conclude that there is *no* relationship between the initial income level and the long-run growth rate. Initially poor countries do not *on average* grow faster than initially rich countries and there is no long-run convergence of income.

If you now look again at Figure 10.3, you will notice that some of the biggest bubbles, such as China and India which are countries with a large population, are in the upper-left corner. These countries are thus initially poor (hence in the left part of the figure), but clearly have above-average growth rates (hence in the upper part of the figure). An alternative to the standard regression line, therefore, is to determine a *population-weighted* regression, where the importance of an observation is weighted by the size of the population. This line is also depicted in Figure 10.3. Its slope is clearly negative (equal to –0.673) and highly significant; this line explains about 29.7 per cent of the weighted variance in long-run growth. We thus conclude that there is evidence of convergence of income in the period 1950–2016 at the country level when we take the size of the population into consideration.

10.3   Income Inequality and Stylized Facts 3 & 4

At the country level analysed in section 10.2, most countries do not stay in the same place over time as far as absolute income per capita is concerned and there is across-the-board *growth* of income levels. More importantly, income dispersion seems to have increased from 1950 to 2016. Given these facts, growth models must thus be able to explain (i) continued growth in income per capita and (ii) convergence in income per capita alongside persistent differences in income levels across countries.

To further substantiate fact (ii) on convergence and persistence of income levels across countries, Figure 10.4 shows much more detailed information of changes in income levels for groups of people in different countries relative to the world as a whole for a shorter period from 1988 to 2008. This requires, of course, information on within-country or regional income inequality, which is not trivial as not all countries have household surveys to provide the necessary data, and if so do not use the same definitions of income (see Milanovic, 2006a,b). Figure 10.4 is the result of compiling and combining such detailed information for almost all countries in the world. As a result, the world population is ranked in 1988 on the horizontal axis from initially poorest to initially richest. This is much more detailed information than provided at the country level. For example, using the data of section 10.2 Mozambique is the poorest country in 1988 and Qatar is the richest country. Yet some people in Mozambique are fairly rich and thus not at the extreme left end of the graph, while some people in Qatar are fairly poor and thus not at the extreme right end of the graph. The vertical axis depicts the change in income per capita (in per cent) of the global population percentile depicted on

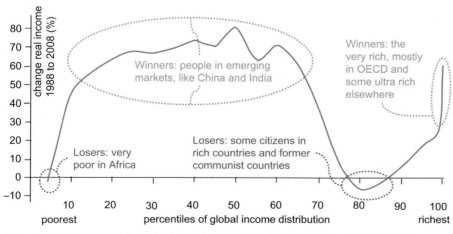

Figure 10.4 Winners and losers in global income distribution change from 1988 to 2008
Source: based on Lakner and Milanovic (2016); real income is PPP based in 2011 USD.

the horizontal axis from 1988 to 2008. The figure as a whole thus depicts which income groups fared relatively well in this period. Because of the shape of the graph, this is known as the *elephant curve* (Milanovic, 2016). Note, however, that this shape is time-specific and does not hold in general. It is used here for illustration purposes only.

The largest increase in real income in the period 1988–2008 (the *winners* in this period) are observed between the 20th and 70th percentiles of the global income distribution (that is for people in emerging markets like China and India) and at the extreme right of the distribution (the rich in OECD countries and the ultra-rich elsewhere), which creates the trunk of the elephant. A relatively small increase in real income (the *losers* in this period) is found for the poorest people in the world (mostly in Sub-Saharan Africa) and between 75th and 95th percentile (typically the middle classes in the Western world). Taken together, the information suggests both income convergence (as the bulk of income growth occurs for the relatively poor population) and rising dispersion (as growth is low for the poorest and high for the richest population percentiles). The growth model in section 10.5 suggests that the interplay between falling international transport costs and increasing knowledge spillovers (modern-day globalization) has made the convergence of emerging markets possible (Baldwin, 2016).

Figure 10.5 illustrates the evolution of global income inequality in the period 1988–2008 using the Gini index and the Generalized Entropy 0 index (*GenEnt* (0) or mean log deviation); see Chapter 3 for details. For both measures global inequality declines in this period, as suggested by Figure 10.4. The Gini index falls by 2.4 points (or 3.5 per cent) from 69.4 to 67.0. The *GenEnt* (0) index falls more substantially by 11.5 points (or 11.5 per cent). Since Generalized Entropy measures can also be decomposed into changes in *between*-country and *within*-country contributions, Figure 10.5 also shows the share of the between-country contribution (in per cent) in the various years for the *GenEnt* (0) index. The between share declines by 7.9 points (or 9.8 per cent) from 80.8 per cent in 1988 to 72.9 per cent in 2008. Although the between contribution depends, of course, on the parameter α chosen for the Generalized Entropy index, the following picture emerges. There is consensus that the between-country inequality has decreased in recent years and also that the between-country differences account for the bulk of global inequality (Sala-i-Martin, 2006, and Milanovic, 2016). The associated implication is, of course, that the *within*-country component has become *more important* over time. See Box 10.2 on expected changes in inequality in the near future (up to 2050).

As a further illustration of what growth of income per capita shows at various levels of aggregation, we add an *urban* growth example to the global evidence. Figure 10.6 shows output per capita (in gross valued-added [GVA] terms) for 12 UK cities in the period 1971–2015. For clarity, the figure focuses on the range between minimum (various cities) and maximum (London) while showing the evolution

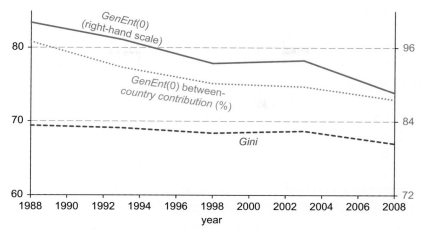

Figure 10.5 Global income inequality, 1988–2008
Source: created using Lakner and Milanovic (2016, Table A3); GenEnt = Generalized Entropy; in 2011 PPP USD; note: left scale starts at 60 and right scale is 1.2 times left scale.

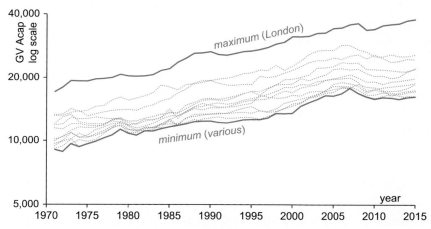

Figure 10.6 Economic divergence across 12 UK cities, 1971–2015
Source: based on data kindly provided by Emil Evenhuis; GVAcap is gross value added per capita; minimum is for (alphabetically): Cardiff (1974–1982, 2008, 2010, and 2014), Liverpool (1983–1985, and 1989–1997), and Sheffield (1971–1973, 1986–1988, 1998–2007, 2009, 2011–2013, and 2015); included cities: Birmingham, Bristol, Cardiff, Edinburgh, Glasgow, Leeds, Liverpool, London, Manchester, Newcastle, Nottingham, and Sheffield; thin, dotted lines track individual cities.

of individual cities as thin, dotted lines. Moreover, we use a log scale, such that the slope of a line indicates its growth rate. Again, we observe growth for all 12 cities (fact (i)), but with considerable persistent (and even increasing) differences in growth rates and thus GVA per capita levels (fact (ii)). The range from minimum to maximum tends to rise over time. In the period from 1971 to 2015 the minimum (Sheffield in both years) rises by 79 per cent while the maximum (London) rises by 120 per cent. We also see that the growth process is far from smooth and that episodes of faster growth can be followed by more sluggish or even negative growth. In addition, the ranking of cities is not constant and UK cities can overtake each other in terms of GVA per capita. Below we will see that these two additional stylized facts (erratic growth, change in ranking) also hold at the country level, which thereby gives us indeed additional stylized facts that a growth model should be able to explain at various levels of aggregation.

To see whether leading positions of *countries* in the world economy are stable over time, it is instructive to take a somewhat longer historical look. We can express the extent of a country's lead or lag in terms of a country's level of income per capita as a percentage of the world average income per capita in the year under consideration. As a bonus, this provides us with additional information on economic growth and the degree of income convergence or divergence.

For 28 individual (current) countries from all continents we have fairly reliable population and income data for the last 2,000 years (Maddison, 2007), namely two countries in Africa, three in the Americas, six in Asia, fifteen in Europe, Australia, and New Zealand. Together, these 28 countries represent about 82 per cent of the world population in the year 1, gradually declining to about 56 per cent of the world total in 2003. Although detailed information for the remaining 197 countries in the world is not available for the entire period, it is possible to construct 7 different regions – groups of countries for which fairly reliable aggregate population and income data are available for the last 2,000 years; see Table 10.1 for an overview. Taken together, this provides us with 35 observations (28 countries plus 7 regions) on the distribution of population and income across the world in the last two millennia.

Figure 10.7 depicts the respective leaders and laggards over time in terms of income per capita. In the year 1 Italy (Rome) was the leader, with an income level about 73 per cent higher than the world average. The leading position was taken over by Iran and Iraq (44 per cent above the average) in the year 1000, before it was regained by Italy (Venice, Florence) in 1500 (94 per cent above the average). The Dutch trading power gained prominence from 1600 to about 1820, with a relative income peak in 1700 (246 per cent above average). Since then, the lead has switched frequently, going first to the UK, then to Australia, followed by the USA, Switzerland, and again the USA. The highest relative peak (374 per cent above average) is reached in 1999. It is not only clear that the leadership changes from one country to another over time, but also that (despite prolonged periods of decline) the relative income position of the leader tends to increase over time.

Many countries qualified for the top 'lagging' position in the year 1, including all of the Americas, Australia, Japan, and what is now the former USSR; their income level lagged about 14 per cent behind the world average. Most of these countries (with the exception of Japan) are still lagging behind in the year 1000 (11 per cent

Table 10.1 Individual countries and country groups

28 individual countries

Australia	Greece	Norway
Austria	India	Portugal
Belgium	Iran	Spain
Canada	Iraq	Sweden
China	Italy	Switzerland
Denmark	Japan	Turkey
Egypt	Mexico	United Kingdom
Finland	Morocco	United States
France	Netherlands	
Germany	New Zealand	

7 groups of countries (# of countries)*

Eastern Europe (12)	Other East Asia (42)	Other West Asia (12)
Former USSR (15)	Other Latin America (46)	Other West Europe (15)
Other Africa (55)		

*See Brakman and van Marrewijk (2008) for details.

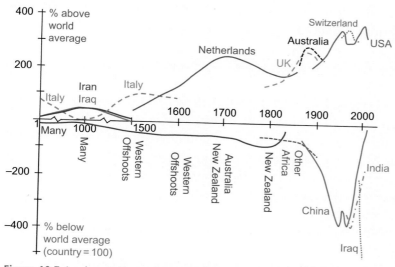

Figure 10.7 Leaders and laggards in income per capita: A widening perspective
Source: van Marrewijk (2017, ch. 2) based on Maddison Historical Statistics 1–2008 AD; deviation relative to world average; world index = 100 for positive deviations; country index = 100 for negative deviations; Western Offshoots = Canada, USA, Australia, and New Zealand.

below the average). In 1500 and 1600 only what Maddison labels the 'Western Offshoots' (Canada, USA, Australia, and New Zealand) still qualify for the top lagging positions, from which the USA and Canada escape after 1600, Australia after 1700, and New Zealand only after 1820. Note the remarkable increase in prosperity for these countries as both Australia and the USA become the world leader relatively shortly afterwards. Africa (excluding Egypt and Morocco) becomes the laggard in 1870, a position to which it returned in 1990. For most of the rest of the twentieth century, India and China (the currently 'feared' top globalization countries from an OECD perspective) took turns in being the world's laggard. It is again clear that there is leap-frogging (the top laggard position changes regularly) and that the relative income position of the laggard tends to decrease over time. Furthermore, Figure 10.7 suggests that long periods of stagnation can be followed by periods of rapid growth.

Based on our discussion in this and the previous section, we can now *summarize our four stylized facts on economic growth* as follows, where these facts hold at various levels of aggregation:

1. Over time, there is an ever *increasing* level of income per capita.
2. *Differences* in economic growth rates may persist for a long time and both income convergence and divergence is observed.
3. Growth is *erratic:* periods of stagnation are followed by periods of rapid growth.
4. There are changes in income ranking over time, a phenomenon known as *leap-frogging.*

It is now time to see how some of these observations can be explained. This provides the main motivation for the next part of this chapter.

BOX 10.2 Global Income Inequality: Past and Near Future

Rougoor and van Marrewijk (2015) analyse developments in global income inequality using detailed information on income levels, within-country income distributions, and demographic information on (projected) population age and structure. Around 200,000 years ago, when Homo sapiens first walked on the earth, global income inequality must have been small as most people were simply trying to stay alive. The Gini coefficient (see Chapter 3) is then close to zero. Since then global income inequality has been rising, particularly in the past two centuries, driven by the strong and continuous growth of a small number of (OECD) countries after the industrial revolution. This resulted in a twin-peaks world income distribution, characterized by a large number of people (countries) with a low income level and a smaller group of people (countries) with a high income level, and not much in between.

BOX 10.2 (cont.)

From the 1970s onwards 'equalizing' factors proved stronger than 'disequalizing' factors and a trend towards lower global inequality started (see Figure 10.5), largely because of a decline in between-country income inequality. Major equalizing factors were the faster-than-world-average income growth in China and South Asia combined with a slower-than-world-average population growth in Europe and the Western offshoots. Major disequalizing factors were slower-than-world-average income growth in Sub-Saharan Africa (combined with faster-than-world-average population growth in that region) and faster-than-world-average income growth in the Western offshoots.

Figure 10.8 illustrates the decline in global income inequality since the 1970s using data on income per capita for 176 countries as well as information on the distribution of income within each country. The decline is slow at first and not monotonic; the Gini coefficient falls by about 2.4 per cent from 1970 to 1983 and then rises again by 1.5 per cent from 1983 to 1991. In the new millennium the decline in global income inequality is more rapid; the Gini coefficient falls by about 7.9 per cent from 2000 to 2009.

Rougoor and van Marrewijk (2015) develop several global growth scenarios up to 2050 in order to project global income inequality in the next 40 years. Figure 10.8 also provides the projection of global income inequality up to 2050 for a 'base scenario'. Economic growth, driven by productivity increases, naturally plays a large part in this process, but given the long time horizon, demographic developments do so as well. For example, the population of Africa is projected

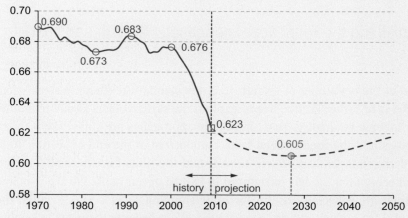

Figure 10.8 Global Gini coefficient: 1970–2050, base scenario
Source: based on Rougoor and van Marrewijk (2015).

BOX 10.2 (cont.)

to double in the coming four decades. At the same time Asian countries profit from a beneficial age structure, as many advanced countries have over the past decades. These countries are now starting to struggle with aging populations and fertility rates below replacement levels. All these developments directly (through economic growth) or indirectly (through the share of working age population) affect global income inequality.

Up to 2050 Asia's income share is expected to rise by about 15 percentage points and that of Africa and Oceania by less than 1 percentage point. The income shares of Latin America and North America decline by about 4 percentage points and that of Europe by about 9 percentage points. These changes are, of course, the result of changes in the total population, the working population, and production per worker. Total population more than doubles in Africa, compared to about 30 per cent for most of the rest of the world, except for Europe, which has a stagnant population. Africa is the only continent where the share of the working population increases, by 6.6 percentage points. In the other continents it declines, ranging from 1.5 percentage points for Latin America to 11.2 percentage points for Europe.

The base scenario projects a reversal of the current trend towards lower global income inequality.[1] The turning point is expected to be reached around 2027. Rising income levels in many Asian economies and continuing high population growth rates in Sub-Saharan Africa are the most important drivers behind this reversal. By 2050 global income inequality is expected to have returned to levels similar to that of 2010.

10.4   Explaining the Four Facts: Endogenous Growth and Spatial Economics

As we stated at the beginning of section 10.2, the standard textbook neo-classical growth model is of rather limited use to explain the stylized facts about economic growth and income inequality. Two alternative approaches are called upon to try to better understand the four stylized facts summarized at the end of section 10.3, namely modern (endogenous) growth models and the (thus far essentially static!) geographical economics models introduced in Part III of our book. We argue below that the former are especially useful for understanding facts 1 and 2, while the latter are useful for understanding facts 3 and 4. We subsequently argue in section

---

[1] Several alternative scenarios and measures of income inequality lead to similar conclusions.

10.5 that a marriage between modern growth theory and geographical economics is useful in order to come to terms with the four stylized facts above.

10.4.1   Endogenous Growth and Dealing with Facts 1 & 2

Our discussion on the usefulness of the endogenous growth models for explaining fact 1 is brief. Good surveys and introductions are given in Barro and Sala-i-Martin (2004, ch. 11), Helpman (2004), and van Marrewijk (2012, 2017). The essence of this literature is quite simple (but nevertheless also quite important: it got one of the main instigators of the endogenous growth models, Paul Romer, the Nobel prize in economics in 2018!). The aim is to construct models capable of explaining facts 1 and 2, that is persistent increases in income per capita and the possibility of persistent differences in economic growth rates. Essentially, this is done as follows. Take the standard neo-classical production function $Y = Af(K, L)$, in which production (income) Y rises if the variable A (total factor productivity) rises, or if the available inputs capital K or labour L rise. In the endogenous growth models the variable A is some function of other economic factors, for example capital K with technological spillovers, or research and development expenditures, or some kind of Schumpeterian innovation process (see also section 10.5 for a modelling example). This a crucial difference with the standard neo-classical growth model where A and hence ultimately the growth of Y is exogenous and thereby left unexplained. Consequently, instead of decreasing returns to capital like in the standard neo-classical growth model, we now assume increasing returns to scale, which enables the economy to grow forever. *This can explain fact 1: ever increasing income levels per capita.*

Most endogenous growth models analyse a closed economy. If the structural influence on the variable A is different in one country from another country this can vacuously explain fact 2: long-lasting differences in economic growth rates. The analysis is more interesting, and more challenging, in an open economy setting, as pioneered by Grossman and Helpman (1991). Their aim is to analyse along which channels international trade affects long-run innovation and growth. This depends fundamentally on what is assumed with respect to knowledge spillovers and the extent to which countries differ in factor endowments. The opening of trade might stimulate or reduce growth. If knowledge spillovers are geographically localized in specific countries, the smaller country might find that fierce competition from abroad can reduce the returns on investment in knowledge, which in turn might reduce the growth rate. Alternatively, if a country is relatively well endowed with unskilled labour, it might specialize in traditional sectors rather than the R&D sector, which also reduces the growth rate. To the extent that the structural influences on the variable A are localized in an international setting fact 2 may still hold, that is there may be long-lasting differences in economic growth, if international knowledge spillovers are imperfect. Fact 3 (alternating periods of stagnation and rapid growth) and fact 4 (leap-frogging) cannot be explained in endogenous growth models since these models focus on, and are even constructed to lead to, balanced growth equilibria, where erratic growth patterns and/or countries overtaking each other in GDP per capita terms have no place.

10.4.2 Geographical Economics and Dealing with Facts 3 & 4

The geographical economics approach that we developed in Part III of the book cannot contribute (yet) in explaining facts 1 (rising income levels) and 2 (persistent growth differences), simply because there is no mechanism in the models discussed so far leading to an increase in production levels or investment in R&D leading to the invention and development of new manufacturing varieties. This has to wait until the next section. The models discussed so far are essentially static and deal with the (re-)allocation across space of a given overall amount of economic activity. Fortunately, however, facts 3 and 4 can naturally arise even within this kind of static geographical economics framework, as indicated below.

In section 8.2 we provided a discussion of the Krugman and Venables (1995) model: a two-country model in which there is no labour mobility between countries and where the use of *intermediate inputs* acts as an additional agglomeration force. Labour combined with intermediate inputs produces the final product, which can be used for consumption and the intermediate product. The central questions in this particular set-up are: what determines the allocation of manufacturing industry over the two countries and what determines the allocation of the labour force over potential activities? If, for some reason, one country has a larger market for intermediate products this is an attractive place for other firms because all varieties are available without transport cost, which also lowers the cost of producing a final product.

Recall and check again your understanding of Figure 8.4: starting from an initially high level of transport costs, Krugman and Venables (1995) discuss what happens in this model if transport costs start to fall, taking this description as representative of actual developments in the world economy (the paper was initially and rather ambitiously titled 'the history of the world, part I'). Essentially, they interpret the workings of the model as if it describes *what happens if* an exogenous parameter, here transport costs, falls over time.[2] Initially, manufacturing production is evenly spread over the two countries. As transport costs start to fall, the world spontaneously divides itself into a core–periphery pattern. If the manufacturing sector is large enough this also results in different real wages in the two countries (different income per capita levels). Eventually, as transport costs continue to fall, the core–periphery pattern disappears again. Both the appearance and the disappearance of the core–periphery pattern is in accordance with fact 3 (periods of stagnation and

---

[2] This is an example of the kind of *what if* questions alluded to in the concluding section of Chapter 9, which sets geographical economics models apart from other approaches.

rapid economic growth). When applied to the actual world economy, Baldwin (2016) uses this geographical economics model to explain the actual impact of globalization on the North–South income divide as it occurred for much of the twentieth century. Globalization, proxied here by the fall in transport costs, makes the North (the OECD countries) the core region and the South (the developing world) the peripheral region with ever widening real wage differences between the two blocs. Once transport or trade costs get low enough, however, real wage convergence takes place.

Puga and Venables (1996) extend the Krugman and Venables (1995) model, not only by assuming three instead of two countries, but also by analysing how industrialization spreads from country to country. They assume that some exogenous force increases the size of the industrial sector in one of the countries relative to agriculture. Since it is assumed that the income elasticity of consumer demand for manufactures exceeds one, this increases demand for manufactures relative to agriculture, which leads to wage increases. Starting with the situation in which industrial activity is agglomerated in country 1, this implies that wages become higher but it is still profitable for firms to agglomerate because they benefit from inter-firm relationships. As wages increase further, at some point it becomes beneficial to relocate to a low-wage country. The process then repeats itself and might finally result in waves of industrialization. This phenomenon of a sequence of industrialization and the descriptions given in Puga and Venables (1996) are in accordance with fact 4 (leap-frogging). In section 10.5 when developing an actual growth model that could account for all four stylized facts of economic growth, we will use the Krugman and Venables (1995) model as summarized in Figure 8.4 as a main building block.

The seminal paper by Redding and Venables (2004; see also Chapter 9) gives some *empirical* evidence as to the relevance of this use of the geographical economics approach to 'explain' (changes in) economic development across countries. They essentially estimate the equilibrium wage equation 9.2 where the real market potential is approximated by estimating a gravity trade model and where, instead of wages, GDP per capita is the dependent variable (see Technical Note 10.1 for an explanation). The empirical implications are that the distance of countries to the markets in which they sell and the distance to countries which supply intermediates are crucial determinants for explaining cross-country income differentials. The further away final markets and suppliers of the intermediate products, the lower the income levels in the countries concerned.

Redding and Venables (2004) give a simple example to illustrate the potential impact of transport costs in such a model. They try to answer the *what if* question: what happens to economic development, and income per capita, when transport costs change? If the prices of all goods are set on the world market and transport costs are borne by the producing country, and if intermediates account for 50% of the total value, the effects of small changes in transport costs turn out to be large. Transport cost of 10% on both final products and intermediate products reduce the value added by 30%. Transport costs of 20% reduce value added by 60%. This example makes intuitively clear why Redding and Venables (2004) are able to explain more than 70% of cross-country variation in income per capita.

So far, this section has briefly described how the modern endogenous growth literature is useful for understanding stylized facts 1 and 2 as identified at the end of section 10.3, while the geographical economics models are potentially useful for understanding facts 3 and 4. A 'best of both worlds' model merging the endogenous growth approach and the geographical economics approach is presented in section 10.5. See Box 10.3 for an example in Africa to illustrate the potential of the Krugman and Venables (1995) model and the empirical what-if analysis of Redding and Venables (2004).

BOX 10.3 What If Example: Economic Development and Market Access in Africa

Using the empirical methodology as pioneered by Redding and Venables (2004) and explained in more detail in Technical Note 10.1, Bosker and Garretsen (2012) estimate the relevance of market access or market potential for GDP per worker for countries in Sub-Saharan Africa (SSA). Instead of (as discussed in Chapter 9) coming up with a direct measure of market access (like in Hanson, 2005) and estimating its impact on a country's wage rates (or GDP per worker for SSA countries), the Redding and Venables (2004) approach derives an *in*direct measure for market access by using a gravity trade model to first estimate market access itself. Technical Note 10.1 outlines the Redding and Venables (2004) method in more detail.

What matters for our present purposes is that first arriving at the determinants of market access and then estimating the impact of market access on a country's wages or income per worker indeed allows us to answer *what if* questions like: what if an SSA country improved its infrastructure, were no longer landlocked, signed up to trade agreements, and/or ended its regional conflicts? The answer to these what-if questions for the case of SSA involves two steps: (1) establish the impact of these changes on market access and (2) assess the relevance of the change in market access for income per worker and hence for economic development. The second step is relatively easy once a good measure for market access is found, as is indeed the case.

Table 10.2 shows the results of doing both steps for five different SSA countries by simulating the impact of six *policy experiments* on the change in income per worker (in %) via the impact these experiments have on market access. Halving distances to all trade partners (a rough proxy for improving the countries' connectivity through cross-border infrastructure projects or more effective border procedures) results in the largest improvements in income per worker, raising it by about 6 per cent. Next comes alleviating a landlocked country's burden of having

BOX 10.3 (cont.)

Table 10.2 Policy experiments and income per worker for five African countries

Change in income per worker (per cent) as a result of policy experiment

Experiment	1	2	3	4	5	6
Country	no longer landlocked	no longer island	infrastructure +1 s.d.	all distances halved	RFTA with S. Africa	SSA free trade zone
Cape Verde	–	2.76	4.14	6.05	0.16	1.14
Botswana	4.88	–	4.14	6.05	–	0.08
Cen. Afr. Rep.	4.88	–	4.14	6.05	0.04	0.21
Ethiopia	4.88	–	4.14	6.05	–	0.10
Sudan	–	–	4.14	6.05	–	0.16

no direct access to the coast (raising incomes by almost 5 per cent), followed by a 4 per cent increase in income per worker as a result of a one standard deviation improvement in a country's infrastructure (which corresponds, for example, to upgrading Ethiopia's infrastructure to resemble that in Botswana). With a resulting increase of 2.8 per cent on income, alleviating the remoteness of an island country has a small effect.

The effect on income per worker is calculated by multiplying the change in the market access per SSA country by the coefficient on SSA market access as reported in column (8) of Table 3 in Bosker and Garretsen (2012).

Finally, columns 5 and 6 in Table 10.2 show the effects of a newly established regional free trade agreement (RFTA). These are also positive but much smaller compared to the other policy experiments. Not surprisingly, this effect is larger, the larger the number of new partner countries in the RFTA[3] (compare column 5 to column 6, or the impact of the SSA-wide free trade zone for Cape Verde to that for Botswana; a SSA-free trade zone would more than triple the number of RFTA partners for Cape Verde whereas 'only' doubling it for Botswana). This much smaller effect of the establishment of an SSA-wide free trade zone compared to those of our other policy experiments should be taken with a pinch of salt. Due to the plethora of RFTAs officially in existence in SSA in 2008, the average SSA country already shared official RFTA membership with 46 per cent of its SSA trade partners. However, the effectiveness of SSA RFTAs in actually implementing policies favourable to intra-SSA trade varies widely.

---

[3] Moreover, the impact also depends on the relative importance of a country's newly added RFTA partners for its market access compared to that of the countries with which it already shares an RFTA.

10.5   Geography, Growth, and the Four Facts: A Synthesis Model

Set against the four stylized facts on economic growth and income equality as summarized at the end of section 10.3, the main conclusion of section 10.4 is that a combination or integration of endogenous growth and geographical economics might offer a good way forward. The model is based on Baldwin and Forslid (2000). It can be seen as a straightforward extension of the core model of geographical economics from Chapter 7. In a widely acclaimed analysis of (old and modern) globalization Richard Baldwin (2016) in his book *The Great Convergence* uses this model to show how modern-day globalization differs from the previous wave of globalization. Quantitative spatial economics provides a richer (but less tractable) modern alternative to this approach, based on a wider menu of (geographical) characteristics; see Rossi-Hansberg (2019).

10.5.1   Main Ingredients of the Synthesis Model

The early literature on agglomeration and growth already combines the insights of the endogenous growth literature with those of geographical economics (see Baldwin, Martin, and Ottaviano, 2001; Baldwin and Martin, 2004; Breinlich, Ottaviano, and Temple, 2013). All elements of the core model of Chapter 7 are present, but the main difference is the focus on the growth of capital. This focus on capital is crucial because growth – in essence – is caused by the accumulation of (a form of) capital. In addition, if (knowledge) spillovers are localized and hence not perfect between countries, agglomeration of firms can stimulate growth in the core, but not or to a lesser extent in the periphery. The process of cumulative causation can be enhanced in such a growth model. Interestingly, Baldwin, Martin, and Ottaviano (2001) already showed that an adapted version of this model can explain four well-known stages in economic development following the industrial revolution: (i) industrialization of the core, (ii) the subsequent growth take-off, (iii) the global income divergence, and (iv) the rapid trade expansion.

Baldwin and Martin (2004, p. 2673) start their survey of the agglomeration and growth literature by observing that agglomeration and growth are inextricably linked since 'agglomeration can be thought of as the territorial counterpart of economic growth'. Models incorporating both agglomeration and growth are characterized by (1) the introduction of capital as a production factor and (2) the assumptions made about inter-regional mobility of capital and the degree of knowledge spillovers. Assumptions regarding international capital mobility are now crucial. In the absence of capital mobility the resulting model is (still) rather similar in its main conclusions to, for instance, the core model of Chapter 7; catastrophic agglomeration (recall the Tomahawk diagram, Figure 7.9) is still an outcome of a growth model without capital mobility.

In a two-region setting, the production of capital K can take place in both regions and if K production is allowed to differ between regions, the assumptions made with respect to capital mobility are important. With *global* knowledge spillovers and perfect knowledge dispersion, the location or geography of K production does not matter. With *localized* knowledge spillovers, it matters where the K production takes place. Depending on the assumptions made with respect to capital mobility and knowledge spillovers, Baldwin and Martin (2004) show whether and how the findings about agglomeration and growth can differ from the standard models. In the next sub-section we give an example of such a model.

10.5.2 Agglomeration and Growth in the Baldwin-Forslid Model

Baldwin and Forslid (2000) provide an endogenous economic growth version of the core model of geographical economics. The model incorporates the fact that economic growth affects location and location in turn affects economic growth because of knowledge spillovers between locations. These are the driving force behind endogenous growth theories and related to the distribution of manufacturing activity across space. The seminal empirical study of Eaton and Kortum (1996), for example, already showed that knowledge creation at a distance gives rise to lower knowledge spillovers than locally produced knowledge.

Trade in *ideas* is equally as important as trade in goods, if not more important. Sharing knowledge internationally, about businesses, cultures, technology, and so on, through personal and business travel, cross-border mergers and acquisitions, and the like, has reduced the localization of commercially relevant knowledge, such as product and process innovation. Many governments stimulate knowledge flows to peripheral regions, setting up universities or high-technology industrial parks. These changes, in turn, have an impact on the interaction between economic growth and localization, as we will see below. We first present the basic structure of the Baldwin-Forslid model and then discuss its main findings and its relevance for understanding modern globalization and economic development.

The Baldwin-Forslid model is almost identical to the two-region core geographical economics model of Chapter 7; we note that there is an even distribution of immobile food production in two regions, on which $1 - \delta$ of income is spent, as well as production of many different varieties of manufactures, with an elasticity of substitution ε. Manufacturing production may relocate if workers decide to move to a region with a higher real wage.

To allow for economic growth in the model, we must explicitly model the time structure and explain the driving force behind economic growth. To start with the latter, producing a manufacturing variety requires a one-time fixed cost of one unit of capital K, as well as the traditional variable costs in terms of labour. Capital K can be viewed as human capital (see Baldwin and Martin, 2004, and van Marrewijk, 1999, for more discussion) and indicates knowledge embedded in a manufacturing facility that is immobile across regions. The cost function is therefore given by $R + W \beta x_i$, where R is the rental rate of capital, W is the wage rate, β is the unit labour requirement, and x_i is the output of variety i.

BOX 10.4 Discounting the Future

Consumers care not only about current consumption levels, but also about future consumption levels. This is important to determine their savings decisions, that is the supply of funds which can be used by firms to finance their investment decisions. To reflect the preference for current consumption by consumers, and take uncertainty about future developments into account, economic growth models assume that consumers discount future consumption using the discount rate $\theta > 0$. Consumption t periods from now is then *discounted* by the factor $(1/(1+\theta))^t$.

Suppose we take into consideration only three periods in which contemporaneous utility derived from consumption is ten in each period. Total utility derived from this consumption pattern if the discount rate $\theta = 0.1$ is then:

$$\left(\frac{1}{1.1}\right)^0 10 + \left(\frac{1}{1.1}\right)^1 10 + \left(\frac{1}{1.1}\right)^2 10 = 10 + 9.09 + 8.26 = 27.35$$

The weight given today for the utility derived from consumption two periods from today is therefore only 8.26, rather than 10. This effect is stronger if the discount rate rises. For example, if $\theta = 0.2$:

$$\left(\frac{1}{1.2}\right)^0 10 + \left(\frac{1}{1.2}\right)^1 10 + \left(\frac{1}{1.2}\right)^2 10 = 10 + 8.33 + 6.94 = 25.27$$

Which shows that consumption two periods from now is given a weight of only 6.94, rather than 10. These examples show that savings today, which is equivalent to foregone consumption today, require a higher return to make up for this foregone consumption in the future if the discount rate is high.

The capital needed for the production of manufactures must be manufactured in the investment good (or innovation) sector I, which produces under perfect competition using only labour as an input. One unit of capital is made using α_I units of labour. Individual firms in the investment goods sector view α_I as a parameter. However, and this is crucial, the investment goods sector benefits from technological externalities (knowledge spillovers): as output rises, the unit labour requirement for the investment goods sector *falls*; see Lucas (1988), Romer (1990), or Grossman and Helpman (1991). This fall in the unit labour requirement is necessary within the model for long-run economic growth to occur; without it output per capita would ultimately reach an upper limit, just like in the standard textbook neo-classical growth model, and economic growth would cease to exist. As suggested by the empirical work of Eaton and Kortum (1996), the distribution of manufacturing activity affects the degree of knowledge spillovers. In particular, firms benefit more from locally accumulated knowledge than from knowledge accumulated in the other region. The production function for the investment good or capital producing sector now becomes:

$$Q_K = \frac{L_I}{\alpha_I}; \quad \alpha_I = \frac{1}{K_{-1} + \kappa K_{-1}^*}; \quad 0 \le \kappa \le 1 \qquad 10.1$$

where Q_K is the flow of new capital, L_I is employment in the investment sector, K is the stock of knowledge, κ is a parameter, an asterisk denotes the other region, and the subscript -1 indicates a one-period time lag. Note that this specification implies knowledge spillovers with a one-period lag, leading to a gradual fall in the unit labour requirement α_I. The term κ measures the degree of knowledge spillovers, that is the extent to which knowledge accumulated in the other region contributes to this region's stock of knowledge. If $\kappa = 0$ knowledge is only locally generated: any knowledge generated in the other region does not contribute at all to this region's stock of knowledge. Similarly, if $\kappa = 1$ knowledge is a global phenomenon: any knowledge generated in the other region leads to an identical increase in this region's stock of knowledge. Baldwin and Forslid (2000) assume, for analytic convenience, that capital depreciates in one period (suggesting that one period stands for roughly ten years).

Analysing economic growth also requires intertemporal preferences. Consumers care not only about current consumption levels of food and manufactures, but also about future consumption levels. To reflect their preference for current consumption and their uncertainty about future developments consumers discount future consumption using the discount rate $\theta > 0$ (see Box 10.4). Preferences U are given by

$$U = \sum_{t=0}^{\infty} \left(\frac{1}{1+\theta}\right)^t \left(\ln\left(F_t^{1-\delta} M_t^\delta\right)\right); \quad M_t = \left(\sum_{i=1}^{N_t} c_{it}^\rho\right)^{1/\rho} \qquad 10.2$$

where the subscript t is a time index and all other variables are as defined in Chapter 7. The specification of utility derived from contemporaneous consumption is therefore identical to Chapter 7. This is crucial for the demand functions, implying that the price elasticity of demand for a variety of manufactures is again $\varepsilon \equiv 1/(1-\rho)$. Consequently, the producer of a particular manufacturing variety applies the same optimal pricing rule as in the core model.

Labour migration between the two regions arises from differences in real wages. To allow for forward-looking behaviour in this economic growth model, rather than the static expectations of the core model, the wage pressure is related to the log difference between the present values of the real wages in regions 1 and 2. Manufacturing workers therefore take (expected) future developments in real wages into account in the migration decision.

10.5.3   Discussion of the Main Implications of the Baldwin-Forslid Model

A complete analysis and derivation of the main results of the Baldwin-Forslid (2000) model is beyond the scope of our book as it requires knowledge of intertemporal optimization techniques. Fortunately, the three main results or implications of their approach, as discussed below, can be readily understood without going into the technical details.

First implication: similarity with core geographical economics model

---

Baldwin and Forslid (2000) show that there are only three possible stable long-run equilibria in which the distribution of the manufacturing workforce remains stable over time: (i) complete agglomeration in region 1, (ii) complete agglomeration in region 2, or (iii) even spreading of manufacturing activity across the two regions.[4] These three long-run equilibria are identical to those of the core model of geographical economics from Chapter 7. The main difference is, of course, that in this economic growth version of the model, firms indefinitely keep investing in knowledge and keep inventing new varieties of manufactures. The ceaseless increase in the number of varieties raises contemporaneous utility without bound through the love-of-variety effect.

Second implication: interaction between free-ness of trade and knowledge spillovers

---

Baldwin and Forslid (2000) analyse the stability properties of the steady-state equilibria using the free-ness of trade index $\phi = T^{1-\varepsilon}$ (see Chapter 7). Recall that this index ranges from 0 to 1 and rises as transport costs T fall or the elasticity of substitution ε falls. In the static geographical economics models, not just the core model in Chapter 7 but also the model extensions in Chapter 8, the key model parameter is the transport costs T or in other words the frees-ness of trade ϕ. Changes in the free-ness of trade crucially determine whether the economy ends up in a (partially) agglomerating or spreading equilibrium (recall the Tomahawk and bell-shaped curve figures from Chapter 7 and Chapter 8, respectively).

   The stability properties of the steady-state equilibria in our growth model now crucially hinge upon the size of not one but *two* parameters: the free-ness of trade parameter as defined above, and the degree of knowledge spillover parameter κ as used in equation 10.1. Both parameters may vary from 0 to 1, such that we can summarize the stability properties in a compact space as given in Figure 10.9. The plane in this figure is subdivided into three different areas: (i) an area in which spreading is a stable equilibrium and agglomeration is not, (ii) an area in which

---

[4] There may be other interior long-run equilibria, but they are unstable.

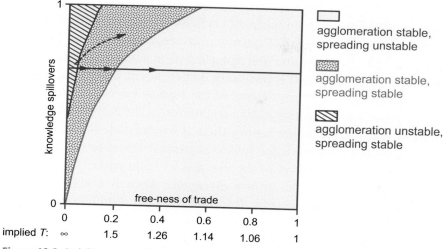

Figure 10.9 Stability in the Baldwin-Forslid economic growth model

agglomeration is a stable equilibrium and spreading is not, and (iii) an area in which both agglomeration and spreading are stable equilibria.

If we, for example, keep the degree of knowledge spillovers constant by analysing the horizontal solid line in Figure 10.9, we see a perfect correspondence between the stability properties of the Baldwin-Forslid model and the core model of Chapter 7. As transport costs fall over time (following the arrows on the horizontal line) initially spreading is the only stable equilibrium, then agglomeration and spreading are both stable equilibria, and finally only agglomeration is a stable equilibrium. This is the *Tomahawk diagram* all over again. It is most reassuring that the simple dynamics of the core model can be reproduced in this more sophisticated dynamic framework of the model.

In addition, and more importantly, Figure 10.9 shows that Baldwin and Forslid (2000) enrich our insights into the dynamic interaction between location and economic growth by incorporating the degree of inter-location knowledge spillovers. Notwithstanding the outcome of the Brexit referendum, the European Union, for example, is more closely integrated economically now than it was 50 years ago. This arises not only from a reduction in trade costs as measured by the transport costs parameter T, but also from improved information transmission across borders, an increase in κ. Think of increased travelling possibilities, watching foreign television channels, increased foreign direct investment, improved communication possibilities, the rise in intra-European mergers and acquisitions, and the funds spend on fostering intra-European knowledge exchanges. Arguably, then, the degree of knowledge spillovers between locations κ has indeed increased across time. Rather than the horizontal movement over time illustrated by the solid line in Figure 10.9, which brings us quite rapidly into the area where only agglomeration is a stable equilibrium, we have been witnessing a simultaneous rise in knowledge spillovers and a reduction in transport costs. Such a movement is illustrated by the dashed line in Figure 10.9. Evidently, this keeps the economy longer in the area where both agglomeration and spreading of manufacturing activity are stable equilibria, implying that it is less likely that economic integration leads to complete agglomeration. This may be one of the reasons we did not find much evidence in Chapter 5 on increasing agglomeration within the European Union. As emphasized by Baldwin (2016; see below), there is a clear trade-off between the free-ness of trade and the knowledge spillovers when it comes to the locational and growth effects. A higher level of the free-ness of trade pushes the economy towards more agglomeration and growth divergence whereas a higher level of knowledge spillovers does the opposite. This leads us to our third implication:

Third implication: the Great Divergence then and the Great Convergence now between countries

---

In his highly-recommended book 'The Great Convergence', Richard Baldwin (2016) sets himself the task of explaining how the process of globalization changed fundamentally around 1990 and how this had and continues to have far-reaching consequences for workers, firms, consumers, and policy makers in both the Western industrialized world (the *North* for short) and emerging market economies (the *South* for short). To illustrate why approximately 1990 can be considered as a watershed, Baldwin shows the development over time of the share of income of the G7 countries (Canada, Britain, France, Germany, Italy, Japan, and the USA) in world income. Figure 10.10 illustrates this share using the Maddison Project Database (based on PPP) for the period 1500–2016. The G7 share in world income peaked in the 1950s but started to decline rapidly around 1990. At the same time a limited number of emerging market economies, notably China, India, South Korea, Indonesia, Poland, and Thailand, saw their collective share in world income increase by roughly the same amount. Baldwin (2016) dubs this post-1990 period of globalization the period of the *second unbundling*, where the production process became internationally fragmented or unbundled and the associated rise in the international trade in intermediate inputs was largely responsible for the unprecedented increase in international trade from 1990 onwards.

According to Baldwin, this period of globalization has to be sharply distinguished from the globalization process that characterized the world economy for most of the twentieth century and the late nineteenth century. This *pre*-1990 process of globalization is dubbed the period of the *first unbundling* because it was primarily characterized by a world-wide international geographical decoupling (or unbundling) of production and consumption that facilitated the rise of modern international trade. It is visible in Figure 10.10 as the sharp increase of the

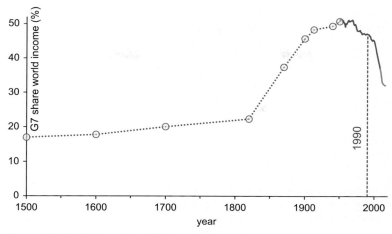

Figure 10.10 G7 share of world income: 1500–2016, per cent
Source: based on Baldwin (2016), created using data from Maddison Data Project; G7 = Britain, Canada, France, Germany, Italy, Japan, and USA; main info based on MPD2010; annual data from 1950 onwards (solid line), irregular intervals before (dotted line with observation circles); data for 2009–2016 uses MPD2018 changes from 2008 onwards.

share of G7 income since 1820. Whereas with the first unbundling consumption and production could be geographically separated across countries, the second unbundling concerns the unbundling of various stages of the production process whereby firms in G7 countries off-shored their assembly production to China or Korea, while retaining their headquarters and research and development (R&D) facilities. These are the days of spatially *slicing up the value chain* of production processes, where production of (mainly) manufactured goods but increasingly also services is fragmented across many locations and countries.

What is relevant for our present purposes is that Baldwin (2016) shows how the period of the first unbundling led to a substantial growth and income *divergence* between the North and South while using the Baldwin-Forslid model! To be more precise, in this period the free-ness of international trade increased markedly whereas the knowledge spillovers between the North and South were still limited as these spillovers are localized in the North. As Figure 10.11 shows this led to (most of) the industrial production and knowledge being located in the North with a self-reinforcing growth cycle that favoured further knowledge capital growth, just as in the Baldwin-Forslid model, with income divergence between North and South as a result.

The game changer in the globalization process that occurred around the mid-1990s is that, stimulated by the ICT revolution and further lowering of transports costs the degree of knowledge spillovers from the North to the South increased dramatically. Quite suddenly, innovation of knowledge capital that originated in the North could spill over to the South to be combined with relatively cheap local labour. In terms of

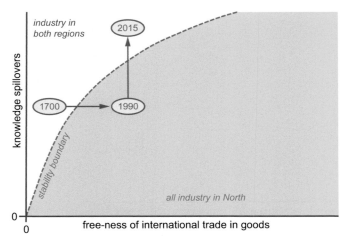

Figure 10.11 Baldwin-Forslid model and the great divergence/convergence
Source: based on Baldwin (2016, Figure 52).

the Baldwin-Forslid model (see again Figure 10.11 but also the production function for the capital good, equation 10.2) this increase in knowledge spillover meant that growth in the South (and in particular in those six emerging economies) accelerated and that the income differences between the North and the South rapidly narrowed. This income convergence was already shown in Figure 10.3.

The Baldwin-Forslid model is essentially an endogenous growth model that incorporates the main building blocks from geographical economics (Baldwin, 2016, p. 193) and models like this can indeed be used to explain the basic stylized facts of economic growth, development, and inequality. To recap our four facts: models like the Baldwin-Forslid (2000) model (i) allow for continued economic growth via the creation of knowledge capital, (ii) can account for persistent growth (and income) differences as well as growth (and income) convergence across countries via changes in key parameters like the transport costs and/or the degree of knowledge spillovers, (iii) via the same mechanism can also explain a spurt or slowdown in growth and development, and (iv) potentially allow countries (or regions or cities depending on the level of aggregation) to change position, that is to overtake each other in terms of income per capita.

This *growth with geography* approach is open to two important lines of criticism.

First, it still only deals with the proximate and not the deep determinants of economic development. These deep determinants are typical for the *first nature* or physical geography kind that we dealt with at length in Chapter 2. The deep determinants also refer to the relevance of the *second nature* explanations for the spiky world that are linked to the role of history, politics, and institutions as summarized in the second part of Chapter 2. These deep determinants are analysed in section 10.6.

Second, the synthesis growth-with-geography model focuses on differences in economic development between countries and ignores economic development *within* a country. Taking the case of China as an example in section 10.7, we use the geographical economics model developed by Puga (1999), as introduced in Chapter 8, to answer the question of how increased labour mobility might affect China's economic geography.[5]

10.6 Deep Determinants of Development: The Geography of Institutions

10.6.1 Institutions Trump Geography?

In principle, the class of 'growth with geography' models as illustrated by our discussion of the Baldwin-Forslid (2000) model can explain our four stylized facts of economic growth. According to some authors, however, the problem with such explanations is that it only reveals the *proximate* causes of economic growth. If income per capita differs between countries because of differences in localized knowledge creation and thus spillovers, human capital formation or, more generally, in total factor productivity, this begs the question why countries differ with respect to these determinants of growth to begin with. To explain growth and hence income differences, we wish to understand the *ultimate* or fundamental determinants of economic growth and income differences between countries. Three *deep* determinants have been emphasized in the literature: (i) institutions, (ii) first nature geography, and (iii) economic integration or openness.

As we already discussed at length in Chapter 2, the main conclusion in the literature is that institutions have a strong and direct impact on a country's income per capita and that first nature or physical geography is also of (indirect) importance to explain income differences via its impact on institutions. Moreover, economic

---

[5] Another recent example that addresses the relevance of agglomeration effects within a country in a dynamic spatial model is Giannone (2018). For US cities, it is shown how the combination of skill-biased technological change (biased in favour of high-skilled workers) and city agglomeration effects can account for the so-called 'Great Divergence' (Moretti, 2012) in US wages across cities, the fact that post-1980 the wage gap between richer and poorer US cities increased sharply, as opposed to the period 1940–1980 when these wages converged. This is a reminder that even though we have seen real income convergence between countries, within countries – and not just in the USA – there has been at the same time real income divergence in the modern era of globalization. A divergence that has not only occurred between high- and low-skilled but also in terms of widening the gap between agglomerations and more peripheral regions. Rodríguez-Pose (2018) argues that the growing real income divergence between regions within many countries has partly motivated the discontent against globalization and helps to explain the marked regional differences in recent populist voting (e.g. pro-Brexit in the UK, pro-Trump in the USA, or anti-Macron in France and pro-AfD in Germany), or in his words 'the revenge of the places that don't matter'.

integration, when set against institutions and geography, does not have a significant impact on income (see our discussion based on Spolaore and Wacziarg, 2013, and Acemoglu, Johnson, and Robinson, 2001, in Chapter 2).

The idea that institutions are more important is still best exemplified by the seminal paper by Rodrik, Subramanian, and Trebbi (2004), who boldly conclude that *institutions rule*. They find a strong positive relationship between institutional quality and income per capita. For similar conclusions, see Easterly and Levine (2003) and Acemoglu, Johnson, and Robinson (2001, 2002). In the bestselling book *Why Nations Fail*, Daron Acemoglu and James Robinson (2012) argue that institutions are key to economic development and geography only matters in so far as it can historically leave an imprint on present-day institutions and thereby on economic development. For the contrary view that geography trumps institutions, see for instance Sachs (2003). In the remainder of this section we will not argue which deep determinant of economic growth is most relevant (we think both are relevant; see Chapter 2) but instead offer a different perspective by showing how institutions and geography are inextricably linked.

The motivation for this alternative perspective is that literature on the deep determinants of growth only looks at the role of first nature or absolute geography (such as looking at the impact of variables like distance to the equator, climate, or disease environment) in explaining cross-country income differences. Second nature or economic geography, the key concept of Part III of our book, does not play a part at all. As a result, the relative geography of a country, that is the location of a country vis-à-vis other countries (in our view also a deep determinant) is no issue. This neglect, in fact, not only holds for economic interdependencies but also for other variables like political and institutional interdependencies that most likely are similarly affected by neighbouring countries.

10.6.2   The Geography of Institutions

Does the *geography of institutions* matter? Several authors have discussed channels through which the institutional set-up in neighbouring countries may be of importance. Easterly and Levine (1998) show that the poor economic performance of one country (as a result of, for instance, bad policy) negatively affects income levels in its neighbouring countries. Ades and Chua (1997) provide evidence that instability in neighbouring countries (measured by the number of revolutions and coups) has a negative effect on the economic performance of a country itself. Regional instability disrupts trade, especially for landlocked countries that depend on trade routes (access to the sea) through neighbouring territory. It also results in increased military expenditures to prevent spreading of conflict and/or to deter potential future military aggression from unstable neighbours (thereby crowding out productive investment by the government). In a similar vein, Murdoch and Sandler (2002) argue that civil war in neighbouring countries disrupts economic

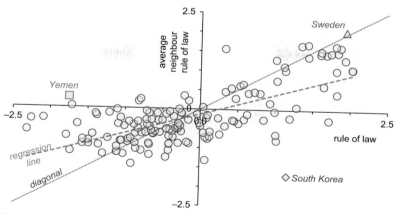

Figure 10.12 Rule of law: own versus neighbour countries, 2017
Source: World Bank governance data; rule of law ranges from −2.50 (worst) to +2.50 (best); neighbour rule of law based on average for contiguous neighbours using cepii data (cepii.fr); 149 countries included.

activity at home. Finally, Simmons and Elkins (2004) show that countries copy (avoid) policies from other (neighbouring) countries that were proven (un)successful or that countries are forced to adopt similar policies to stay economically competitive in order to comply with regional or global pressures.

For a sample of 149 countries, with institutions measured by the *rule of law* and using contiguity to define a country's neighbours, Figure 10.12 shows the correlation between a country's own institutions and that of its neighbours, as indicated by the regression line. Countries below the diagonal line (such as South Korea) have better own institutions than their neighbours (North Korea). Countries above the diagonal (such as Yemen) have worse institutions than their neighbours (Oman and Saudi Arabia). Countries close to the diagonal (like Sweden) have similar institutions as their neighbours (Finland and Norway).

When estimating the impact of own and neighbouring institutions on income per capita (with percentage of population speaking a European language as instrument for institutions; Hall and Jones, 1999), it turns out that neighbouring institutions do matter. This result is robust to various checks (sample size, various controls, definition of neighbour, and so on). Both better own and neighbouring institutions increase a country's income per capita; first nature geography does not matter. From the perspective of our book, however, it might be argued that the real importance in terms of including second nature geography is not so much spatial institutions but spatial income. That's at least what the core model of geographical economics shows. As a first pass, Table 10.3 therefore includes nominal market potential or nominal market access MA among the set of explanatory variables which is measured as $MA_j = \sum_i Y_i / D_{ij}$, where Y_i is country i's income level and D_{ij} is the great circle distance between the capital cities of countries i and j. This measure of market access is a simple market potential function. Using far

Table 10.3 Market access (MA) and the geography of institutions

	I Baseline	II Market Access	III MA + neighbour institutions
Geography (distance equator)	−2.45 (−2.13)		−0.62 (−0.60)
Institutions (rule of law)	0.92 (2.75)		0.90 (4.55)
Neighbouring institutions (rule of law)	0.75 (2.69)		0.54 (2.87)
Market Access (MA)		0.84 (5.38)	−0.41 (−1.97)
# of observations	147	147	147

Source: Bosker and Garretsen (2009); the estimates are 2SLS with at the first stage as instruments % speaking European language, geography, and distances to New York, Brussels, and Tokyo. Similar conclusions hold if regional dummies (Africa, Latin America, and Southeast Asia) and other geography measures (landlocked, island, and area) are included. Dependent variable = log GDP per capita, 1995; (t-value).

more sophisticated market access measures, the study by Redding and Venables (2004; see section 10.4.2 and Technical Note 10.1) invariably finds that market access is important for explaining cross-country differences in income per capita: better market access implies higher income levels. This finding also holds when they control for the role of institutions.

Column I in Table 10.3 shows the baseline results, with only own and neighbouring institutions and first nature geography as explanatory variables. Column II illustrates that, when looked upon in isolation, market access *MA* has the expected significant positive effect on income per capita. Following Redding and Venables (2004), *MA* is instrumented by using the log of the distance to three economic centres (New York, Brussels, and Tokyo). When we subsequently add own-country institutions and neighbouring institutions *MA* has the wrong sign. More importantly, the addition of the market access variable does not alter our main finding that institutions matter and that neighbouring institutions play a role. After controlling for regional and other fixed geography effects, where the landlocked dummy is significant, (spatial) institutions remain significant and market access becomes insignificant (not shown). As to the question why these findings differ from those of Redding and Venables (2004), a number of possibilities arise. They do not instrument institutions, only look at own country institutions, and their country sample is somewhat smaller (101 countries, excluding a number of mainly African countries with bad institutions). Moreover, the focus of their analysis is different. Even though they report estimation results for the specification with our simple market access variable and institutions, the bulk of their paper and estimation results deals with market access measures that are more sophisticated and better grounded in geographical economics; see section 10.4.2. An interesting question for future research is to investigate which kinds of spatial interdependencies matter most in explaining income differences between countries.

The main conclusion for now is that existing models of economic growth, including dynamic geographical models like the Baldwin-Forslid model, can be criticized for not dealing with the deep determinants of growth. At the same time, recent attempts to include these deep determinants and the role of institutions by and large ignore the possible relevance of spatial interdependencies. The way forward is to come up with models and estimations that allow for spatial interdependencies at all levels. This implies use of economic history to better understand the relationship between growth on the one hand and first and second nature geography on the other hand; see Box 10.5. The reason to turn to economic history is that the literature on the deep determinants of economic development (and this is in line with geographical economics at large) suggests that economic development is strongly history- or path-dependent.

BOX 10.5 A Historical Example: Bad and Old Geography?

A closer historical look at the importance of geography for the growth of countries and cities reveals that geography is important, but not always in the way one expects. Nunn and Puga (2012), for instance, argue that *bad* (first nature) geography can also have a favourable effect on income per capita. For Africa they show that the ruggedness of the terrain has an indirect positive effect, whereas the direct effect is negative. A more rugged terrain makes the agricultural use of land more difficult, makes building more expensive, and in general increases the costs of doing economic transactions. Indeed for all countries an increase in ruggedness or *bad geography* has this direct negative effect on income levels. The main conclusion of their analysis is that 'in Africa, additional to this negative direct effect, ruggedness may also have had a positive indirect effect on economic outcomes, by allowing areas to escape from the slave trades and their negative consequences' (Nunn and Puga, 2012).

The basic idea is that ruggedness of terrain offered protection to those areas in Africa that were raided by slave traders in the era of the slave trade (1400–1900). It turns out that for African countries (and only for African countries) ruggedness has the predicted positive effect. This paper is important for two reasons. First, and keeping the discussion in the main text in mind, it helps to differentiate between the direct and indirect impact of (first nature) geography on income

BOX 10.5 (cont.)

Table 10.4 Estimates for Italian city growth, 1300–1861

	Dependent variable = log of city size, 1995; [p-value]			
	Combined		Separate	
Geography				
Seaport	0.316	[0.016]	0.250	[0.046]
Roman road	0.070	[0.287]	0.036	[0.571]
Hub	0.339	[0.063]	0.277	[0.047]
Navigable waterway	0.388	[0.008]	0.433	[0.033]
Mountains	−0.087	[0.116]	−0.091	[0.098]
Urban potential	0.015	[0.815]	−0.042	[0.566]
Institutions				
Capital	0.702	[0.000]		
North			0.535	[0.000]
South			1.575	[0.001]
R^2	0.50		0.57	
# of observations	623		623	

Source: Bosker et al. (2008); cut-off city size is 10,000 inhabitants; time-fixed effects and north–south controls not reported.

per capita, which is indeed important given the unsettled debate between the researchers (like Jeffrey Sachs) who argue that the impact must be a significant direct one and the researchers (like Dani Rodrik) who argue that the impact of geography is at best an indirect one. Second, Nunn and Puga (2012) remind us that bad geography is not always and everywhere bad for economic outcomes.[6]

Reliable historical data on growth at the country or regional level are hard to come by, certainly if one takes a really long-term view. One reason is that in the Middle Ages, or even before that period, our present-day countries were often still non-existent. Data on cities are more useful since they go back many centuries. So for a historical look at the role of geography and other 'deep' determinants on economic prosperity, a number of recent papers have turned to the analysis of city growth. The papers that include measures of first nature as well as second nature

---

[6] For those interested in similar research, please check out the personal webpage of Nathan Nunn and in particular the data sets available for research like the unique data on ancestral characteristics of modern populations at https://scholar.harvard.edu/nunn/pages/data-0 (accessed on 14 January 2019).

BOX 10.5 (cont.)

geography are particularly interesting. One finding seems to be that the results on the importance of geography are more robust for first nature geography.

As we already briefly mentioned at the end of Chapter 9 and based on a data set from Malanima (1998, 2005), Bosker et al. (2008) analyse urban growth in Italy (one of the earliest urbanized countries in the world) for the period 1300–1861. First nature geography variables (like whether the city was a seaport, located near or at a Roman road, or had access to a navigable waterway) are significant in explaining urban growth; see Table 10.4. The geographical divide between the North and South of Italy is also an important determinant of city growth. Second nature geography (here measured by a simple *urban potential function*, that is essentially a market potential with population size replacing income) is, however, never significant. One reason might be that in the days before our modern economy (let's say before the nineteenth century) an integrated urban system where locations (Italian cities) were economically connected did not yet exist. Table 10.4 also shows that institutions (here, whether a city was a capital city) are important. More research, as to the relative importance of 'old' first versus second nature geography for urban growth is warranted, as the results in Bosker, Buringh, and van Zanden (2013) illustrate. Using a data set that covers (almost) all cities in Western Europe and, rather uniquely, (the Muslim world of) North Africa and the Middle East for the period 800–1800, they find that second nature geography (again measured by an urban potential variable) is significant.

10.7 *What* Happens to China *If* Its Internal Labour Mobility Rises?

In this chapter on geography, growth, and development, the emphasis has been on the international comparison, that is the models and empirical examples discussed focus on a cross-country comparison. However, economic growth and development and the role of geography can also be analysed from a *within-country* perspective. In section 10.1 and Box 10.1, we already mentioned that the within-country spatial allocation of people and economic activity, as for instance proxied by the degree of urbanization, matters for economic growth and development. More fundamentally, in the literature on economic development the structural changes that are associated with the transformation from a rural, pre-industrialized economy towards a modern, industrialized economy are crucially about changing the internal economic geography too. A prime example of such a structural change is the process of rural–urban migration whereby labour moves from the countryside to the city, thereby contributing to urbanization and the industrialization process.

Ever since Harris and Todaro (1970), understanding rural–urban migration has been a key topic in the economic development literature. In modern times, the rural–urban migration that has occurred in China since the start of the policy of economic liberalization by then party leader Deng Xiaoping in the late 1970s is probably the prime example in recent times. of how migration has not only transformed a country's economic geography but also has been of massive importance to the ensuing economic growth process. The labour migration from rural to urban areas also has clear drawbacks, however, since jobs may be in short supply in the cities, which may become over-crowded and thus congested and people may end up in living conditions that are actually a setback compared to their previous rural life (see World Bank, 2009). In addition, some governments also try to discourage massive urbanization because they fear it might erode their political power. Keeping the pros and cons of rapid urbanization in mind, the Chinese government has ever since the 1950s put policies in place that try to limit rural–urban migration and also inter-urban migration. This set of policies goes under the name of the *Hukou* system

The *Hukou* system can be best seen as an internal visa arrangement that is meant to regulate migration (Au and Henderson, 2006a,b; Chan and Buckingham, 2008; Henderson, 2009; Poncet, 2006; Zhang and Zhao, 2011). Without a visa for a particular location, a Chinese citizen has no or only limited rights to housing, to sell property, to education, food, or social security in that location. Those rights are tied to one's official place of residence and a change in residency (if a citizen for instance tries to move from a rural area to a city) is only matched with a transfer of these rights if the (local) authorities hand out a visa or permit for the new place of residence. Despite the rapid rise in the number and size of Chinese cities, it has been argued (Au and Henderson, 2006a,b) that Chinese cities are still undersized due to the severe restrictions on labour mobility that are imposed through this *Hukou* system. The under-urbanization claim is then illustrated by earlier versions of Figure 10.1 where China is below the regression line and thus 'under-urbanized' given its level of economic development. This is analysed by Brakman, Garretsen, and van Marrewijk (2016), who show that the peak of under-urbanization in China was in 1995 and has since then virtually disappeared.

Leaving aside the precise workings of the *Hukou* system and the nature of the under-urbanization of China, the question that naturally arises is *what* would happen to China's economic geography *if* its internal or inter-regional labour mobility were increased. The *what if* italics illustrate that this matter plays to the strength of the geographical economics models where labour mobility is also a key variable (Krugman, 2011). In Chapter 8 (section 8.3), we introduced the main ingredients of a general geographical economics model that allows for both inter-regional labour mobility and immobility. The model is general since it includes the core geographical economics model of Chapter 7 and the Krugman and Venables (1995) intermediate inputs model (section 8.2) that was used in section 10.4. This model and its extensions display a rich menu of agglomerating and spreading forces that (in contrast to the core model of Chapter 7) not only allows for stable full-agglomeration and spreading equilibria but also for stable *partial*-agglomeration equilibria where multiple cities of unequal size co-exist in equilibrium.

Bosker et al. (2012) apply the Puga (1999) model summarized in section 8.3 to 264 Chinese so-called prefecture cities that make up the bulk of China. They estimate the equilibrium wage equation from the underlying model (similar to equation 9.2) for this sample of Chinese cities. The equilibrium wage equation is used to answer the underlying *what if* question with respect to changing China's internal labour mobility.[7] In doing so, they analyse various labour mobility regimes. The benchmark is the distribution of people and economic activity in 2000 across the prefecture cities (where economic activity is approximated by secondary industry employment); see Figure 10.13. In 2000 the distribution under the Hukou system reflects restricted labour mobility. Details need not concern us here but looking at the population shares (left panel), the data show that the largest concentration of population can be found in the eastern part of China. This area includes some of China's largest coastal cities (such as Beijing, Shanghai, and Guangzhou) but also *non-coastal* provinces like Honan, Hupeh, Anhwei, Kiangsu, and Sjantung. Taken together these five provinces alone are home to 29 per cent of the Chinese population and to 34 per cent of the total population in our 264 prefecture cities.

The presence of quite a few, relatively populous prefecture cities in China's (non-coastal) heartland in Figure 10.13 under the actual *Hukou* system turns out

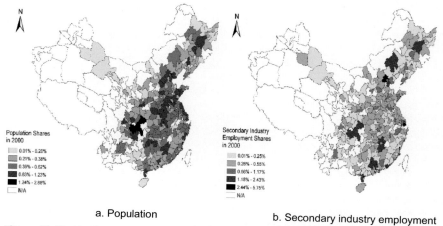

a. Population   b. Secondary industry employment

Figure 10.13 Distribution of people and firms across prefecture cities in 2000
Source: Bosker et al. (2012); N/A = not available and/or not a prefecture city.

---

[7] For details we refer to Bosker et al. (2012).

to depend on the degree of labour mobility. Simulations show that a relaxation of the *Hukou* system leads to much stronger core–periphery patterns. Figure 10.14 shows the resulting spatial equilibrium in the no-*Hukou*-scenario.[8] Compared to the baseline 2000 *Hukou* case shown in Figure 10.13, population and industry are both much more concentrated. Only 52 prefecture cities still have a positive share of firm and worker population. Within this group, three types of cities can be distinguished.

First, there are the four largest cities: Beijing, Shanghai, Guangzhou, and Chongqing. We refer to these as the Big Four. These cities are already China's largest cities today. Loosening the restrictions on labour mobility only reinforces their dominant position: in equilibrium these four cities house a third of total population. Market and supplier access are high in these four, initially already large agglomerations.

A second group of cities is located *within* the area demarcated by the Big Four: roughly speaking the area indicated by the dotted lines in Figure 10.14. This area comprises some of China's most populated provinces, such as Sjantung, Fujian, Kwantung, Anhwei, Honan, and Hunan. These 31 cities (together they comprise 41 per cent of total population in equilibrium) are all part of the populous heartland

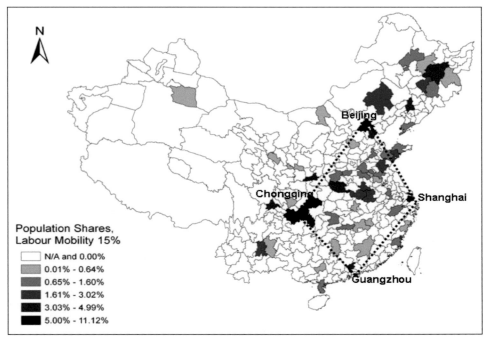

Figure 10.14 China's economic geography: relaxing *Hukou*
Source: Bosker et al. (2012).

---

[8] To allow for the fact that migration is costly, the threshold wage difference level that induces migration is set at 15% in Figure 10.14.

of China. They benefit from increased labour mobility because of their prime location in the centre of China's economic geography. Compared to the Big Four, it is not their (initial) size that is decisive, but the easy access to nearby markets and cities. They do face competition for people and firms from the attractive agglomeration economies offered by the Big Four, yet 'survive' in equilibrium because of the lower cost of housing, which at some point stops people from being willing to incur the migration costs needed to move to Shanghai or Beijing. Also, compared to the more peripheral cities, they can more cheaply import goods produced in one of the four main cities.

The third group of cities are initially (in terms of 2000 population) large but peripheral cities (outside the dotted line area shown in Figure 10.14) such as Harbin in the Heilunkiang province in northern China, or Kunming in the western province Yunnan. In equilibrium these 17 cities contain around 25 per cent of total population. Despite being peripheral, these cities 'survive' the relaxation of the *Hukou* restrictions and are able to resist the attraction of the more central cities.

The simulation results shown in Figure 10.14 are certainly not meant as an actual pinpoint prediction as to what will happen to China's economic geography and hence to its economic development once the Chinese authorities do allow more labour mobility. They do, however, show how in a qualitative sense the model we developed in Part III of our book can be used to answer important *what if*-type questions that relate to structural changes that can be mimicked by changes in the structural parameters of these models. It also shows once more that the abstract models of Chapter 7 and Chapter 8 can be put to use for actual development issues. The founder of geographical economics Paul Krugman was therefore spot-on when he argued that these models seem of particular use for countries like China that are undergoing a structural transformation (Krugman, 2011). To illustrate this, the case of China has been proven to lend itself well to address structural *what if* questions. Besides Bosker et al. (2012) for the above discussion, there are a number of papers that use a complete long-run version of a geographical economics model to estimate and simulate the impact of structural changes (especially through large-scale investments in China's infrastructure) for China's economic geography and development (see Baum-Snow et al., 2017; Bosker, Deichmann, and Roberts, 2018; Faber, 2014; Roberts et al., 2010; and Whalley and Zhang, 2007).

10.8 Conclusions

We started with a brief look at empirical evidence on economic growth and development as summarized in four stylized facts: (i) rising income levels, (ii) lasting differences in growth rates, (iii) periods of stagnation followed by rapid growth, and (iv) leap-frogging. We argued that the (endogenous) growth literature can help us understand the first two facts, while geographical economics can help us understand the last two facts, in particular by using simulations. To this end, we discussed the *agglomeration and growth* class of models within geographical economics and in particular the Baldwin-Forslid (2000) model, a merger of the core model of geographical economics with an endogenous growth model. The main conclusions derived in this framework are consistent with the findings in the core model, in particular with respect to the stability analysis. It justifies the shortcuts we have been taking in other chapters of this book. At the same time, for readers who want to move beyond the core models of this book to analyse the interplay between geography and development, we refer to Desmet, Nagy, and Rossi-Hansberg (2018), who develop a model with geography and global interactions. Given certain frictions on migration, the model, which belongs to the class of 'quantitative spatial economics' models (see for a survey Rossi-Hansberg, 2019), yields a variety of spiky worlds.

The Baldwin-Forslid model also gives us some new insights, for example on the importance of inter-regional knowledge spillovers and on the distinction between static and dynamic welfare effects. But, as is to be expected from any model, however elaborate it may be, this model also has its shortcomings. We zoomed in on the argument that this model, like all modern growth models, has been criticized for focusing only on the proximate causes of growth at the neglect of the so-called deep determinants of economic development: institutions and geography. Finally, using the case of China's economic geography as an example, we showed how the class of models we developed and summarized in Part III of our book can be used to answer *what if* questions pertaining to the possible impact of structural changes on a country's economic growth and development. It is time for our final chapter on policy implications of urban and geographical economics.

Technical Note

Technical Note 10.1 The gravity model in geographical economics

The basic version of the gravity model for explaining bilateral international trade flows relates the size of these flows to the economic size of the two countries and their distance is given in equation 10.3, where Tr_{ij} is the international trade flow from country i to country j, C is a constant, Y_i is the income level of the origin country, Y_j is the income level of the destination country, D_{ij} is the distance between the two countries, e_{ij} is an error term and the parameters θ_1, θ_2, and θ_3 have to be estimated.

$$Tr_{ij} = CY_i^{\theta_1} Y_j^{\theta_2} D_{ij}^{\theta_3} e_{ij} \qquad 10.3$$

Until fairly recently, the most popular approach to estimating the gravity model using panel data was by linearizing it; that is, by taking logarithms and then estimating the log-linear model through fixed effects ordinary least squares (OLS). A main problem with this approach is that the log-linearized model is not defined for observations with zero trade flows (as is frequently the case for bilateral trade flows involving developing countries). Two common methods of handling the presence of zeros are (*i*) simply discarding the zeros from the sample and (*ii*) add a constant factor to each observation on the dependent variable. The first approach is correct as long as the zeros are randomly distributed, which is, of course, rarely the case. The second approach leads to biased and inconsistent estimates. Better strategies are developed by Helpman et al. (2008), who propose a theoretical model rationalizing the zero flows and suggest estimating the gravity equation with a correction for the probability of countries to trade, and by Santos Silva and Tenreyro (2006), who suggest directly estimating the level equations using a Poisson estimate.

$$W_s = \left(\sum_{r=1}^{R} Y_r T_{sr}^{1-\varepsilon} I_r^{\varepsilon-1}\right)^{1/\varepsilon} \qquad 10.4$$

The equilibrium wage equation 9.2, reproduced here as equation 10.4, lies at the heart of the core model of geographical economics from Chapter 7. As we explained in Chapter 9 (section 9.4.2), there are basically two strategies for estimating the equilibrium wage equation. The first one is based on the seminal paper of Hanson (2005), has been discussed at length in Chapter 9, and involves an attempt to *directly* estimate the wage equation. The second strategy has been pioneered by Redding and Venables (2004) and here a wage equation like 10.4 is estimated in two steps. In the *first step* a proxy for real market potential is estimated using bilateral trade data and a gravity equation like 10.3. In a *second step*, the estimated real market potential is then plugged into the wage equation which is then estimated. Two questions that deserve our attention are:

1. Why go through the trouble of this indirect or two-step estimation strategy?
2. How does the indirect strategy work?

Starting with the first question, the indirect approach advocated by Redding and Venables (2004, p. 56) has the advantage that 'the use of trade data reveals both observed and unobserved characteristics of market access' (where market access is just a different term for market potential). If trade data can be used to construct market potential, then the analysis of (changes in) the determinants of trade can be used to infer what (changes in) these determinants imply for market potential. With the direct Hanson (2005) strategy discussed in Chapter 9, we just plug in market potential as an explanatory variable in the wage equation, but we do not know how changes in other variables in turn affect the market potential which was taken as *given* in our estimations in Chapter 9.

Turning to the second question, and to learn how the *gravity model* for bilateral trade can be used to construct market access or market potential, it is useful to recall the equilibrium wage equation 10.4. This equation is at the heart of the empirical studies trying to establish if, as indicated by equation 10.4, there is indeed a spatial wage structure. More precisely, equation 10.4 says that the wage level a region s is able to pay its manufacturing workers is a function of that region's real market potential, the sum of trade cost weighted market capacities.[9] Note the presence of trade costs T_{sr} in equation 10.4.

The connection between bilateral trade flows and market access, and hence the connection with the gravity model, now follows directly from the core model of geographical economics. To see this, we proceed in two stages. The *first stage* is to connect bilateral trade with market access. Go back to the manufacturing demand equations from the core model, which give the total demand for a manufacturing variety. Aggregating the demand of consumers in region r for all manufacturing varieties produced in region s over all firms producing in region N_s gives aggregate trade equation 10.5, indicating that trade flows Tr_{sr} from country s to country r depend on the 'supply capacity' of the exporting country $N_s p_s^{1-\varepsilon}$, that is the number of firms and their price competitiveness, and the 'market capacity' of the importing country , that is its income level Y_r multiplied by its price index I_r (its real spending power), and the bilateral trade costs between the two countries T_{sr}.

$$Tr_{sr} = N_s p_s^{1-\varepsilon} Y_r I_r^{\varepsilon-1} T_{sr}^{1-\varepsilon} \qquad\qquad 10.5$$

Comparing equations 10.4 and 10.5, we note that wage rates and market potential use the *same* market capacities, weighted by bilateral trade flows. One can thus construct a measure of each country's market access using the coefficients of an empirical trade model that estimates Tr_{sr}. This is where the *second stage* (the gravity model) comes in, which is used to approximate real market access and subsequently used in the estimation of the wage equation 10.4. A gravity model consists of two sets of variables, namely (i) country-specific variables (such as the income levels of the importing and exporting country) and (ii) bilateral variables (such as the distance between the countries). Redding and Venables (2004, pp. 60–61) estimate a gravity equation where the country-specific characteristics are not specified as such but captured by importer and exporter fixed effects through the use of importer and exporter dummies (recall our brief discussion on the use of fixed effects in gravity models in Chapter 3). The bilateral trade costs Tr_{sr} are a function of the bilateral distance and a common border dummy. This trade cost specification differs from the one used by Hanson (2005; where trade costs are an

---

[9] The actual wage equation estimated may differ slightly from the one presented here in each particular empirical study, but the basic idea behind it is always the same, i.e. with wage depending on real market access and, in a model with intermediate inputs, the price index of manufactures. Following Breinlich (2006), we discuss the Redding and Venables (2004) strategy for the case of no intermediate inputs, which implies that we only deal with market (not supplier) access.

exponential function of distance). In the modern gravity literature (see Anderson and Van Wincoop, 2004), the exact specification of trade costs is subject to close scrutiny. The reason for this attention is based on the sensitivity of the outcome regarding this specification. See Chapter 9, Box 9.3 for a further discussion on the empirical specification of trade costs.

Exercises

Question 10.1 Stylized Facts

At the end of section 10.3 'stylized facts' about economic growth were formulated. Discuss whether and how these facts can in principle be explained by the Baldwin-Forslid (2000) model of economic growth and location.

Question 10.2 Leap-frogging

Figure 10.6 and Figure 10.7 show some examples of 'leap-frogging' for respectively UK cities and individual countries. How can this phenomenon be explained in a geographical economics model?

Question 10.3 Reverse Globalization

These days there is much talk of globalization 'going into reverse'. Assuming a backlash against globalization really gained momentum, how would you analyse the consequences in terms of agglomeration using Figure 10.9 or Figure 10.11?

Question 10.4 Brexit

Assume an economic policy maker asks you to make an assessment of *what* would happen *if* the UK were no longer a member of the European Union. Use the approach based on Redding and Venables (2004) as discussed in section 10.4 to discuss how you would go about making such an assessment.

Question 10.5 Economic Growth and City Size

The size of cities or more generally the degree of urbanization matters for economic growth; see Box 10.1. In urban economics there is considerable debate about what the relationship between urbanization and city size on the one hand and economic growth on the other hand looks like. There seems to be a consensus that this relationship is hill-shaped: cities that get too small or too big hurt economic growth. Think of reasons why this relationship might be hill-shaped.

Question 10.6 Geography, Institutions, and Development

In Chapter 2 we discussed and illustrated the relevance of geography as well as institutions for economic development. With the basic ideas of geographical economics in mind what are the key differences between the discussion on this topic in Chapter 2 and in section 10.6 in the present chapter in your view?

Question 10.7 Geography is Destiny?

When it comes to economic growth and development it is sometimes argued that 'geography is destiny', meaning that a country's or region's geography for better or worse determines its economic development. With the discussion surrounding Figure 10.9 or Table 10.4 on the geography of institutions in mind do you agree with this view? Explain your answer.

Question 10.8 'What if' in China

The 'what if' question that we dealt with for China at the end of this chapter concerned the impact on agglomeration of an increase in inter-regional labour mobility. Using a similar geographical economics approach a number of recent papers try to answer the question 'What happens to agglomeration in China if there are considerable investments in the Chinese infrastructure?'. How would you go about answering this question and what would be your answer? [Hint: check out the papers mentioned right at the end of section 10.7 for clues.]

Question 10.9 New Silk Roads

See Question 10.8, but now think of the Chinese Belt Road Initiative (also known as the New Silk Roads).

11 Policy Implications

LEARNING OBJECTIVES

- To understand why cluster policies are popular, but might not work in practice.
- To know and understand the criteria by which to evaluate the welfare effects of cluster policies.
- To understand why it is sometimes better to have modest policy objectives for regional economic policies.
- To understand the main policy consequences of the core geographical economics models of Chapters 7 and 8.

11.1   Introduction

So far, we have only touched upon the policy implications of urban and geographical economics. In this chapter we do so more structurally. What insights gained from the urban and geographical economics literature can be used for policy analysis? The question is relevant as there is ample evidence that the agglomeration of economic activity goes along with higher productivity and wages. Returning once more to the theme of the spiky world that runs through our book, can policy makers increase the economic *spikiness* of their location? If so, this seems to give governments an attractive option: stimulate local agglomeration to increase the local spike and the local economy will be better off.

As it turns out, the analysis of government policy in a spiky world makes clear that policy making is much more complicated than merely pushing an agglomeration button! By using the insights from urban and geographical economics, we will address the fundamental question of whether governments could and/or should use policies to interfere with the agglomeration of economic activity across space in the final chapter of this book.

The discussion of the policy implications of urban and geographical economics will focus on two key concepts: *agglomeration economies* and *spatial interdependencies*. As will be clear by now, agglomeration economies play a central role in both urban and geographical economics. In urban economics (see

Part II), the agglomeration economies are crucial to understanding the location of economic activity and hence of firms and households within and between cities. Together with the concept of spatial equilibrium, they provide a direct handle for policy questions: can policies change agglomeration economies or other elements of the spatial equilibrium condition (like local transport costs, housing rents, or urban amenities) in such a way that a city or region will be better off after the policy intervention? In geographical economics (see Part III), agglomeration economies and the idea of spatial equilibrium are also present but the focus (and thereby the difference with urban economics) is on the spatial linkages or interdependencies between locations. From a policy perspective this opens up the additional question of whether and how policies can change the spatial interdependencies in such a manner that not only does the spiky world look different after the policy intervention but the system as a whole has benefited from the intervention.

We zoom in on regional policy, that is on policies that aim to change the economic plight of specific regions. The term *region* can apply to a city but also to more peripheral or rural areas. Similarly, a region can be as large as a whole country and the analysis of regional policy does not only refer to within-country analysis (can policies create more of an economic balance between, say, the northern regions in the UK versus the London region?), but also to between-country analysis (can EU regional policies improve the economic outlook for more backward regions across the EU?). The use of regional policy as an overarching term will be useful to capture the policy discussions that pertain to urban as well as geographical economics. It is also useful because alternative approaches inside and outside economics (like human geography, innovation and business studies, political sciences, or public administration) also routinely use the term regional policy when discussing how policies could shape local economic outcomes.

Central in all the discussions among policy makers is the concept of clusters. In this chapter we will translate the cluster concept to our models of the agglomeration of economic activity.

The literature on cluster policies can be subdivided into two broad groups: the academic side and the policy maker's or practitioner's side. As we will see, and with some exceptions, the opinions of these two groups differ strikingly. On the one hand, there are sceptical reflections on the usefulness of regional policies in the guise of cluster policies from economists and geographers alike (see Duranton, 2011, or Martin and Sunley, 2003, respectively) with illustrative headings like *the feeble case for cluster policies* or *deconstructing clusters*. On the other hand, one can find optimistic policy reports that take the usefulness of clusters and thus regional policies largely for granted, and in which the only problem left is the proper identification of promising or *winning* locations and sectors.

In this chapter we analyse the rationale of regional policies, discuss the evidence, and highlight some methodological problems. In doing so, we also take a closer look at policy consequences that follow from or can be linked to the models as discussed in this book. In some of our thought experiments, we take the models of the book literally: that is, suppose we assume that the world is exactly described by our models, what would be the lessons for policy makers? When we discuss actual cluster and regional policy thinking, there are always three main elements to take into account. First, whether it is a *people-* or *place*-based policy (or a mix of these two). Second, to go beyond the observation that a policy can change spatial economic outcomes by showing that a policy is somehow welfare-improving. Third, to take into consideration the important macro/micro distinction in terms of regional policy effectiveness: a 'good' regional policy at the city or regional level does not necessarily imply that it is also beneficial for the economy as whole.

The main message of Chapter 11 is that regional policies should be handled with care.

In an explicit and elaborate analysis by the World Bank (2009) on the relationship between growth and development on the one hand and economic geography on the other hand, the World Development Report 2009 (entitled *Reshaping Economic Geography*) has as its main policy conclusion that countries that succeed in increasing their *D*ensity, lowering their *D*istance to and decreasing their *D*ivisions with other countries will foster their growth and development. This 3*D* advice has a clear meaning in terms of economic geography. *D*ensity refers to urbanization and to allowing people (and firms) to move to their preferred location or city; see our China example (and of course also the urban economics models in Part II of the book). The roles of *D*istance and *D*ivision, where the latter refers to the impact of borders and conflicts, both relate to the geographical economics models from Part III.

The role of density and how it is used as an all-encompassing term for various agglomeration economies will be central in the first part of this chapter (sections 11.2 to 11.4) where the role of clusters and regional policy is discussed with this very concept in mind. The role of division and distance relates to spatial interdependencies and how these could (or should) matter for economic policy making in a spiky world. This is covered by the second part of this chapter (sections 11.5 to 11.7). In section 11.8, we focus on the discipline of *economic geography* (rather than urban and geographical economics) regarding the same policy questions and we briefly discuss how our approach (and thus the whole book) relates to what has been dubbed 'proper' economic geography (Martin, 2008). Section 11.9 has some closing remarks on this chapter and the whole book.

11.2   The Temptation of Regional Policy: A Closer Look at Clusters

Regional policy is popular, not least among policy makers themselves.[1] The *European Cluster Policy Group* (ECPG, 2010) as well as the cluster-mapping project in the United States point out the allegedly clear benefits of cluster formation.[2] Kline and Moretti (2014a,b) estimate that every year $40–50 billion is spent on disadvantaged regions in the US and note that this is more than the amount spent on unemployment insurance in a typical year. Criscuolo et al. (2012) document similar policies for the EU and they analyse in detail the composition of regional policies in the UK. The term 'cluster' is a catch-all term and describes all sorts of activities that come under such names as Special Economic Zones, Enterprise Zones, Zona Franca, Science Parks, Business Parks, Smart Specialization, and all kinds of 'Valleys', with or without 'Silicon' added to it (Prager and Thisse, 2012).[3]

Central to all these cluster initiatives and ideas is that the formation of economic clusters at the regional level will allow regions to benefit from the productivity-enhancing effects of density, be it the density of (certain types of) people/workers or of firms. The evidence that increased density goes along with increased productivity or wages is pervasive as we have seen many times in earlier chapters of this book. We have also seen that 'goes along' is certainly not the same thing as 'does cause'. In addition, agglomeration effects have to be distinguished from sorting or self-selection effects. But the key issue is that if clusters or, in our parlance, regional policies could be shown to have a productivity- and income-enhancing effect via increased density this would provide a clear rationale for such policies.

As we concluded at the end of both Chapter 6 and Chapter 9, the density or agglomeration elasticity of wages (productivity) is usually estimated in the range between 0.02 and 0.05, which implies that an average increase of density of 1 per cent raises productivity by 0.02 to 0.05 per cent (see Combes and Gobillon, 2015, and Ahlfeldt and Pietrostefani, 2017, for extensive surveys).[4]

---

[1] Sections 11.2 to 11.4 are partially based on Brakman and van Marrewijk (2013).

[2] For material on the ECPG: http://www.clusterobservatory.eu/; see also European Commission (2003). For the US cluster mapping Project: http://clustermapping.us/index.html. The World Economic Forum routinely assumes that clusters benefit the competitiveness of countries or regions (see https://www.weforum.org/agenda/2018/09/how-cities-are-saving-china, for example, for a discussion on Chinese clusters).

[3] The term 'smart specialization' has rapidly become the new buzz word in EU policies; it is a concept in which the existence of the benefits of clusters are taken for granted (see EU Cohesion Policy 2014-2020: Research and Innovation Strategies for Smart Specialization: http://ec.europa.eu/regional_policy/sources/docgener/informat/2014/smart_specialisation_en.pdf).

[4] The implication is that a doubling of density (employment) increases labour productivity by between 1.4 and 3.5 per cent (since $100 \times (2^{0.02} - 1) = 1.4\%$ and $100 \times (2^{0.05} - 1) = 3.5\%$), which is substantial.

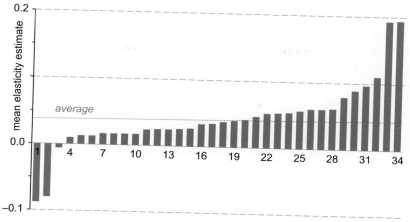

Figure 11.1 Mean estimates of urban agglomeration economies, 34 studies
Source: based on data from Melo et al. (2009, Table 1).

Although some consensus thus exists about the range of the outcomes, a meta-study based on 729 estimates from 34 studies reveals that there is large variation in the estimates, as illustrated in Figure 11.1 (this meta-study is also covered in Box 6.1). According to Melo, Graham, and Noland (2009, p. 341), there is 'no a priori reason to expect similar estimates of comparable magnitude between sectors, urban areas, or countries'.[5] The typical specification on which the estimates are based, recall equation 6.2, is given in equation 11.1, where w is a measure of wages (or productivity), *dens* is a measure of density, Z are control variables, ϵ is the error term, and r indicates spatial units.

$$ln\left(w_r\right) = \alpha ln\left(dens_r\right) + \beta ln\left(Z_r\right) + \epsilon_r \qquad 11.1$$

Estimates like these suggest a strong correlation between agglomeration or density and productivity or wages. As we have shown in Chapter 6 (recall equation 6.3 and Table 6.3), density might stand for the agglomeration economies associated with urban economics, but the same equation can be used to capture the agglomeration effect of market potential, a key variable in geographical economics. Linking cluster or regional policies to equations like 11.1 and thereby indirectly to our models of urban and geographical economics is one thing; whether clusters or more generally regional policies do actually have the alleged positive agglomeration effects is quite another matter.

Note that cluster policy is similar but not necessarily the same as regional policy; clusters can in principle cross regional borders and connect distant places, so

---

[5] The causes of variation in the results can to some extent be attributed to differences in methods, but Melo, Graham, and Noland (2009) also find some evidence of publication bias to publish results confirming positive agglomeration economies.

in geographical terms it is not always clear where a cluster begins and ends 'on the map'. For policy makers this might imply that in practice it is a problem to define a policy target area. We will return to this issue in section 11.4.

The empirical evidence regarding cluster policies is rather mixed. Despite empirical evidence that cluster policies might not always work, these policies continue to be popular. The most well-known exponent of cluster policies remains the management scholar Michael Porter (1990, 1998, 2000a,b). We use Porter's cluster concept as a heuristic device for the discussion on cluster policies and to critically evaluate cluster policy and hence regional policy with the rest of our book in mind. The basic idea goes back to Alfred Marshall (1890; recall Box 6.2 in Chapter 6), who points out that industry tends to agglomerate in order to benefit from forward and backward linkages, thick labour markets, and spillovers of all sorts.

Porter wrote extensively and famously on the cluster concept and despite the fact that over time his interpretation changed somewhat, the essence is still best explained by the so-called Porter Diamond in Figure 11.2. We discuss this at some length because many practitioners and policy makers on cluster/regional policy take their cues not from the models of our book but straight from Porter's writings. The fact that the founding father of geographical economics, Paul Krugman, states that Porter's Diamond was a main inspiration for what is now the core model of geographical economics is in this respect rather ironic (see Box 7.8).

The diamond illustrates that the business environment in a specific location determines its competitiveness. Competitiveness is defined as productivity of a firm (Porter, 2000a). Anything that increases productivity also increases

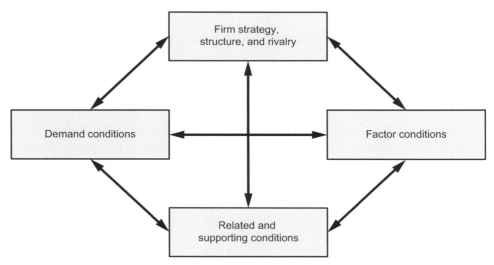

Figure 11.2 Porter's Diamond
Source: based on Porter (2000a, p. 20).

competitiveness; the four factors mentioned in the boxes in Figure 11.2 all contribute to competitiveness. A local cluster feeds into the four boxes: firm rivalry, factor inputs, related industries, and demand conditions. The influences among the four boxes are interrelated, indicated by the two-way arrows. The diamond is used as a visualization of Porter's cluster concept, and its attractive looks and catchy name have, no doubt, contributed to its popularity.

Porter (2000a,b) defines a cluster as 'a geographically proximate group of interconnected companies and associated institutions in a particular field, linked by commonalities and complementarities'. Originally, Porter stated that clusters contain only one element of the diamond – related and supporting industries – but he later added that (Porter 2000b, p. 258) 'clusters are best seen as a manifestation of the interaction among all four facets'. The interactions between the four boxes strengthen each other and result in a highly competitive cluster. According to Porter (2000b) a firm can best be located (pp. 268–9) 'where the home base environment provides the greatest benefits. New business development should concentrate in these areas.' The archetypical cluster used for illustration purposes is Silicon Valley. According to Porter, the most successful clusters are not only competitive regionally, but also globally. Once a cluster is regionally established, global competitiveness follows as a consequence.

Porter's cluster analysis gives direction to regional policy makers. Each element in the diamond has been associated in actual policy making with a cluster or regional policy that is directly aimed at that particular part of the diamond. Local tax reductions can attract firms that together form a business park, which then might turn into a cluster. Policies like these seem successful as they attract suppliers from other locations in order to stimulate sourcing from cluster participants (see for instance Barba-Navaretti and Venables, 2004, for a case study of Ireland). This stimulates forward and backward linkages which feed into local economies of scale. Governments can thus help to facilitate location decisions of new firms. The access to clusters should be efficient, suggesting investments in supporting infrastructure. Knowledge development should also be stimulated, which can be supported by creating interrelated and specialized vocational, technical, and university curricula. It is easy to lengthen the list, but all policy initiatives are aimed at facilitating growth and productivity of a particular cluster.

Armed with our knowledge of models and urban and geographical economics, the question, after this short excursion on Porter's Diamond and cluster policies, is how to evaluate all of this. We know (see the discussion of equation 11.1 above) that *if* cluster policies indeed raise density in a way that also increases regional wages and productivity then we would have a case for cluster and regional policies. Let's therefore take a closer look at these types of policies.

11.3   The Rationale for Regional Policy: Motivation and Measurement

Regional cluster policy is often a combination of what is called people-based policy and place-based policy. Strict people-based policies are aimed at 'disadvantaged' persons in general. These policies do not have a regional dimension. Examples are tax credits or financial support for unemployed workers who need temporary help. Similarly, policies aimed at increasing the human capital of workers in 'backward' regions and facilitating them to move to their preferred location is also an example of a people-based policy. In fact, the policies that the World Bank (2009; see the introduction to the chapter) labels under *density* are typically people-based policies. Here, it is important to note that the design of these policies does not incorporate a regional dimension.

In contrast to the space-neutral people-based policies, place-based regional policies are all policies aimed to increase the economic performance of a region which have a clear spatial component. These policies are also designed to fit a specific region. Examples are policies to revive downtown business districts, or infrastructure projects in peripheral places that are in decline. These policies can also be aimed directly at economic agents in specific regions, such as education programmes that help unemployed workers in specific places. These are place-based people policies (Neumark and Simpson, 2015). The distinction between the two policies is thus not always clear-cut. Creating an enterprise zone near areas with unemployed people has elements of both people-based and place-based policies.[6]

Place-based policies have direct benefits, such as travel-time saved after infrastructure improvements. But they also have indirect effects, which relate to how people and firms respond to the policies. They can, for example, reconsider their location decision after a new bridge is built. The geographical economics model discussed in Chapter 7 is a clear example of these elements; a reduction in transport costs saves 'time' and workers and firms respond to this change and reconsider the optimality of their location and possibly move (which establishes the long-run equilibrium).

Regional policy is a more general concept than cluster policy but for both types of policies it is worthwhile to think about the theoretical justifications for these policies. The bottom-line for all these justifications is that there must be some form of market failure: if we let market forces do their work the result in terms of economic spikiness is not optimal and welfare can be increased if the government steps in. So what are the specific reasons mentioned in the literature to justify

---

[6] Table 18.1 in Neumark and Simpson (2015, p. 1204) gives an overview of possible policies, subdivided under the following headings: examples, policy goals, targeting, incentives, and recipients of support. It shows that these policies come in many shapes and forms.

regional policies and how valid are these reasons upon closer inspection? Here, we single out two main reasons, namely (1) *agglomeration economies* being sub-optimal, (2) *equity considerations*.

1. Agglomeration economies. This reason focuses on the level of regional agglomeration economies being too 'low' without policy interventions. In line with our discussion of Duranton and Puga (2004) in Chapter 5 and Chapter 6, the matching, sharing, and learning across firms and workers could be improved upon. An agglomeration or cluster might enhance matching between firms and workers and business-to-business relations. It could for instance divide the costs of large infrastructure projects over more people and can stimulate learning. These agglomeration economies are strengthened by nearby and frequent interactions. If firms and people move to a specific location this has positive effects on the welfare and productivity of other people and firms. The problem is that these effects are externalities and thus not part of the decision process of those who relocate. These positive externalities constitute a market failure and in theory make a case for government intervention. Note that there could also be negative externalities: stimulating people and firms to migrate to a large(r) location could increase commuting costs, increase housing prices, pollution and other costs that are related to density or congestion.

The 'learning' factor or knowledge spillovers that are mentioned above have a long history in urban economics. As we know from Chapter 10, Baldwin (2016) has documented two waves of 'unbundling' with respect to globalization. He notes forcefully that face-to-face contact is still important and is responsible for the fact that people and firms agglomerate.[7] Dense agglomerations enable the spread of new ideas and innovation. This can, for instance, take place through spatially concentrated networks (Hellerstein, Kutzbach, and Neumark, 2014). In general, spillovers are more likely to occur between high-skilled people, because problem solving and discussing the solutions is part of their job. This makes agglomerations especially attractive for high-skilled people and, as we have seen in Chapter 5 and Chapter 6, high-skilled people can afford to live in expensive and large locations. This linkage between knowledge spillovers and high-skilled people is attractive for policy makers. It gives them a rationale for building knowledge clusters, and it stimulates the creation of all sorts of 'valleys' in the hope of copying the success of the ICT cluster of Silicon Valley near San Francisco in the USA.[8]

---

[7] The first unbundling, due to the transport revolution in the nineteenth century, separated production from consumption. The second unbundling started with the ICT revolution in the mid-1990s and fragmented the production process.

[8] For the inflation of the use of 'valley' cluster ideas see https://en.wikipedia.org/wiki/List_of_technology_centers

2. Equity considerations. This reason can motivate place-based policies. Peripheral regions often lag behind compared to more central locations in terms of growth, productivity, wages, and employment. The equity motive can stimulate governments to redistribute economic activity to peripheral locations. Economic efficiency considerations might then be less important for policy makers; more equity can be at the expense of less efficiency. Whether this trade-off actually exists 'always and everywhere' when it comes to economic agglomerations is open to debate; see Gardiner, Martin, and Tyler (2010). Here, we take the view of Kline and Moretti (2014a) that equity–efficiency trade-offs can be quite pervasive when it comes to cluster policies or (place-based) regional policies.

Next to the above two main theoretical motivations for regional policy, there is the empirical issue of how to actually *measure the impact* of a regional or cluster policy. One would like to compare the development of the treatment region/cluster with the hypothetical situation that this region had not received policy treatment. This counterfactual situation does, by definition, not exist. The solution is, as we know from Chapter 3 on project evaluation, to find a control group that is identical to the treatment group, except for the treatment itself. Comparing the control group to the treatment group gives information on the success of a treatment.

Finding a control group is often a challenge and the method assumes that regions receive a single treatment whereas in practice multiple treatments might take place. Extensive reviews can be found in Glaeser and Gottlieb (2008) and Moretti (2010). In the next section, we will discuss possible analytical problems with cluster and regional policies, but the first step is to see whether at least the targeted region is affected by the policies (which is thus not the same thing as the policy being effective, in the sense that (all) regions are clearly better off with than without the policies).

In an influential study, Greenstone, Hornbeck, and Moretti (2010) find that a subsidy to attract large plants to a region has important spillover effects. Regions compete with each other in order to attract important new firms; comparing the region that wins the competition to the runner-up region shows that after five years the productivity of the incumbent firms in the winning region is 12 per cent higher than in the runner-up region. This indicates important spillover effects and a rationale for a place-based policy targeted at the firm level. Neumark and Kolko (2010) look at the effects of the California Enterprise zone programme. This programme comprised various tax incentives to firms in the designated areas. The aim was to start new firms and to employ the disadvantaged in and around these areas. One tax incentive was a large state tax credit incentive equal to 50 per cent of the relevant wages. Applying the use of control groups they find no evidence that this programme stimulated employment. This is confirmed by the survey table in Neumark and Simson (2015, Table 18.2, p. 1233); results are small, and positive effects are as frequent as negative effects. Similar conclusions can be drawn with respect to stimulating clusters or agglomerations, or large infrastructure projects: the effects seem mixed. Much depends on the empirical strategy involved. Often it is unclear which way causality runs, from the (cluster) policy to some target outcome variable, or vice versa. In a recent paper, Criscuolo et al. (2019) employ an instrumental variable approach to infer that local (industrial) policies can indeed have (significantly positive) effects on local outcome variables.

The seminal study by Kline and Moretti (2014b) also shows mixed results. We already encountered this study in Chapter 3 when discussing natural (policy) experiments as a modern research method to differentiate between cause and effects of (policy) changes. They looked at the activities of the Tennessee Valley Authority (TVA) that started a development programme in the Tennessee Valley in the 1930s in the USA, where the TVA area consists of Tennessee and some areas in Kentucky, Alabama, and Mississippi. It was an extensive and long-running regional development plan that involved investment in infrastructure, transport, and schools. It is a classic study, using a (variant of) difference-in-differences (DID) approach, and, crucially, a careful discussion of all sorts of possible control groups. Some areas were also initially targeted to receive government support for the same reasons as the Tennessee Valley area, but for political reasons did not receive aid. These areas are therefore suited as control groups.

Following the treatment (= TVA area) and control areas for a long period (1934–2000) and presenting outcomes for the period 1940–2000 and two sub-periods (1940–1960 and 1960–2000; after 1960 the programme essentially was ended), Kline and Moretti find that initially agricultural employment was stimulated during the programme but that this effect disappeared once the programme stopped. Manufacturing employment increased during the programme and this effect remained visible after the programme ended. This would have been a positive outcome for place-based policies if not for the fact that they also find that these positive effects in the Tennessee Valley are offset by losses elsewhere.

This last conclusion is important: one cannot only look at the target region in isolation; other regions have to be taken into account too. What might have been good for the TVA area was at the cost of other areas and hence there is also the question whether the TVA programme was beneficial for the US economy as a whole. This observation brings us to a discussion of some fundamental difficulties with respect to the rationale of regional policies. Such policies are not only subsidies for the receiving regions: there is also a cost side, and regions might start to compete for government funds, which leads to the question whether this kind of policy competition is welfare improving. In Box 11.1 in section 11.6 we will discuss land taxes and regional tax competition and return to these issues.

11.4   Regional Policy: Think Twice!

As we already indicated in the introduction to this chapter, the academic litera-ture is critical of regional policies that try to stimulate agglomerations or clusters. This discussion is more than just an academic debate, because the criticism could explain why cluster policies often do not work and explain why governments should think twice before engaging in regional policies that might be potentially wasteful: see Duranton (2011) for a survey or Leslie and Kargon (1996) on a failed attempt to replicate the success of Silicon Valley elsewhere.

What are the main criticisms? There are quite a few, as we will see in this section, but the main concern is the fact that the use and operationalization of the cluster concept is too fuzzy to justify a policy intervention. To see this, it is instructive to take a closer look at the famous diamond developed by Porter in Figure 11.2. Some problems now become evident.

First. Cluster policies are aimed at stimulating successful agglomeration. But how to define these clusters and thus agglomerations from a spatial point of view? Martin and Sunley (2003, Table 1) give no less than 10 definitions that stress different elements of Porter's original definition: from 'similar firms located close together' (Crouch and Farrell, 2001) to 'related and supporting institutions that are more competitive by virtue of their relationship' (Feser, 1998) or 'strongly interde-pendent firms ... linked to each other in a value-added production chain' (Roelandt and Den Hertog, 1999). Recent contributions also stress networks of 'actors' that cross regional borders (Lorenzen and Mudambi, 2013). These definitions either extend or limit Porter's definition. They extend it to include institutions (with-out necessarily specifying the spatial dimension) or limit it by referring to inter-dependencies through the supply chain (which is only one element of Porter's Diamond). Note that supply chains are potentially long and cross borders, even national borders. For a definition of Silicon Valley this would imply that some parts of Asia could be included in the spatial definition of Silicon Valley, as the supply chain for some electronic parts extends to Asia. Menzel and Fornahl (2009, p. 222), for example, note that Silicon Valley 'went on to integrate distant places like Hsinchu/Taiwan ... into its development'.

Second. Some assumptions regarding the production structure surrounding clus-ter policies are questionable. Production takes place in a limited area, and this is done for a reason. Locating in a particular area must bring about some agglom-eration benefits. This implies that within clusters some production factors, inter-mediate goods, and (knowledge) spillovers have to be immobile in order to create agglomeration economies. If all elements are immobile except the final com-modity that is produced this could indicate the presence of a cluster. In practice, all elements are mobile to some extent, except factors like land or housing. The more mobile intermediate steps are in the production process, the more difficult it becomes to define a cluster in the sense of Figure 11.2. Clusters themselves can also be mobile as activities are increasingly footloose (Duranton, 2007). Glaeser (2005) points out, for example, that Boston was and continues to be a productive city not because it held on to certain industries, but because it was able to reinvent itself, by changing the character of the 'cluster' over time.

Third. Porter's analysis is rather partial. The four elements in his diamond strengthen each other without negative feedback mechanisms. A growing cluster, for example, has consequences for local prices of non-tradable services (housing) or increases congestion and pollution. Adding these elements reduces the benefits of clusters.

Fourth. As emphasized at the end of section 10.3, the growth of one cluster may have consequences for other clusters. Kline and Moretti (2014a,b) stress that a rationale for cluster-type place-based policies only exists if these place-based policies are (highly) non-linear, that is, the productivity gains in one area outweigh the productivity losses in another area. The empirical evidence suggests that this is often not the case. Even if these non-linearities do exist, regional policy can easily result in regional policy competition if policy makers are only concerned with their own region and do not consider the 'bigger picture'. The consequence could be wasteful policy competition, where local policy makers are competing with each other by investing in local amenities or business parks in order to attract firms and workers to their region. This may result in an over-supply of amenities or business parks in regions that lose the policy battle.

Also, as is well known from the international trade literature, rent-seeking is an issue to consider for policy makers (Bhagwati, 1982). Like other policies, regional policies are shaped by lobbying activities for special treatment. This lobbying is unproductive but requires the input of resources that could have been put to more productive use. In the international trade literature evidence of these activities is well documented (see Baldwin and Robert-Nicoud, 2007, for references). In the context of regional policies, similar activities might be expected. If lobbying industries or regions are successful they benefit from a special treatment at the expense of other regions (tax money can only be spent once). These rent-seeking activities could explain why especially weak regions or industries are lobbying: because these regions or industries gain the most from rent-seeking behaviour (successful industries or regions have less to gain). The consequence could be that resources end up in those industries or regions that are relatively less productive. The fact that most cluster initiatives are found in backward regions could point towards rent-seeking (again, see Baldwin and Robert-Nicoud, 2007).

Suppose we are able to solve the four issues mentioned above and are able to define a cluster or agglomeration consistently and unambiguously. What would be the correct action for a government in that case? Unfortunately, the problems for policy makers are not over. The fact that cluster or agglomeration economies exist does not necessarily point towards the need for government policies to stimulate a regional cluster and hence local agglomeration economies. The central question that first has to be answered before any policy is implemented is what market failure exists that needs to be repaired by the government? Duranton and Puga (2004) discuss the mechanisms behind localized agglomeration economies: sharing, matching, and learning. Government intervention requires a diagnosis of the exact source of the problem, which is difficult to establish in practice. Duranton (2011), for example, illustrates that market failures with respect to matching (labour market) require a different policy than market failures with respect to learning (knowledge spillovers). Matching could be improved by making the labour market more efficient, whereas problematic knowledge spillovers might point towards an inadequate schooling system.

Without detailed, location-specific knowledge of the exact nature of market failures, a corrective policy is destined to be ineffective as well as inefficient. The informational requirements for cluster policies are particularly large as it requires knowledge on the specific nature of externalities and the associated market failures. Furthermore, clusters should also not be evaluated in isolation. Stimulating a cluster in one location might thus be at the expense of another location as it might simply persuade existing firms and workers to move from one location to another with no net gain from a national or macro-economic point of view. Stronger still, it might result in the overall economy being worse off if the policies incentivize firms and workers to stick to the 'wrong' place for too long, This is what Glaeser (2011a, p. 2) calls 'leaning against the trend', that is keeping people from moving to more productive areas. Glaeser and Gottlieb (2008, p. 197), for instance, note: 'it is not clear why the federal government spent over $100 billion after Hurricane Katrina to bring people back to New Orleans, a city that was hardly a beacon of economic opportunity before the storm'.

The critical discussion of cluster policies so far is rather general in its coverage. Case studies might, potentially, reveal more positive effects. Well-known and well-studied examples are Silicon valley, Route 128 (Boston area), and Hollywood in the USA or Bollywood in India (see Glaeser, 2005, Saxenian, 1994, or Lorenzen and Mudambi, 2013). Descriptions of cases like these reveal, however, that the success or lack thereof of a cluster is highly specific and idiosyncratic. For the success of Bollywood (a film industry cluster in Mumbai), it turns out that Indian emigration to the US from the 1950s onwards was particularly important by creating a large and profitable (export) market. During the 1970s and 1980s imports of Bollywood VHS videos and later DVDs and the use of satellite TV increased the visibility of Bollywood films in the US and stimulated contacts between the US film industry and Bollywood, enabling Bollywood to catch up with Hollywood (Lorenzen and Mudambi, 2013). The success of Silicon Valley relative to Route 128 can be attributed to institutional differences. The industries along Route

128 were organized in hierarchy and rigid, whereas the organizations of industries in Silicon Valley were more flexible and facilitated transitions in response to changing demands in the computer industry (Saxenian, 1994). This illustrates that specific circumstances can dominate other explanations. For policy makers these circumstances only add to the informational requirements before engaging in regional policies.

Finally, and quite crucially, there is a lesson for regional policy makers that stems directly from the main models of urban and geographical economics. To see this, take the urban systems model of Chapter 5 and in particular Figure 5.9 on the basic urban economics model. In terms of this model, cluster policies and also typically regional policies more generally focus on shifting the wage curve upwards. Such an upward shift can be rationalized (see equation 5.3) by an increase of the agglomeration effect E via cluster or regional policies. In fact, cluster policies are largely an attempt to exactly achieve this! But what the model of Chapter 5 shows is that for the attractiveness or size of the city it is not so much the wage curve that is decisive. Instead, it is the *net* wage curve, the difference between the wage curve and the cost of living curve. In principle, the same effect that cluster policies aim for by shifting the wage curve could also be achieved by lowering the cost of living, that is by shifting the cost of living curve inwards! Policies that would reduce housing costs, commuting costs (see also the within-city model of Chapter 4), or provide for a better amenity mix at the city level could be as effective as trying to boost agglomeration economies via cluster or regional policies. This should not come as a surprise since the spatial equilibrium conditions that determine both within and between cities where footloose firms and workers prefer to locate do indeed show that agglomeration economies are only one of several factors in determining location choices and hence the spiky world.

What overall conclusion can be drawn from the brief and rather critical discussion of the rationale behind cluster policies in this section and of regional policies in general in the previous section? The main conclusion is that it is difficult for policy makers to pinpoint what such policies should or could address, as the exact nature of market failures is often not clear. In addition, the (long-run) mobility of factors of production implies that clusters compete with each other for resources; the growth of one region might be at the expense of another region. Negative feedbacks of clusters (such as congestion, high prices, and pollution) are also often ignored in the debates on cluster and regional policies.

Given (a) the difficulties surrounding cluster and much of regional policies aimed at increasing agglomeration economies and (b) the availability of other options, Duranton (2011, p. 36) gives policy makers the advice to re-focus their policies: do not aim to create the next Silicon Valley, but try instead to improve land-use planning, urban transport, provision of local public goods, and so on. These policies may not be as 'sexy' as setting up the next bio-tech cluster, but they might be far more effective. The recommendation for local governments is to improve their traditional areas of intervention rather than try to do 'new things' that will become the next 'big thing'. Given the right local circumstances, maybe, just maybe, the next Silicon Valley might follow.

11.5   Policy Making in Urban and Geographical Economics Models

So far, our discussion of cluster and regional policies leads to rather humble conclusions as to what policies might actually achieve. But what if all the knowledge and information problems that have been highlighted so far are solved? In other words, what if the world is perfectly described by the urban and geographical economics models of the book? What would or could policy making then look like? To answer this question, we now turn to the idealized world of formal models and take a look at the policy conclusions that can be derived from these models. We do so by turning to the policy analysis within the hypothetical world of the core geographical economics models. Why? As stated in section 11.1, the use of the concept of agglomeration economies unifies urban and geographical economics (even though the sources and mechanisms behind these economies differ in the two approaches). This means that our discussion on cluster and regional policy was based on arguments that pertain to both approaches. There is, however, one crucial difference between Part II and Part III of the book. In the latter the spatial interdependencies are the heart of the analysis whereas they are basically ignored in the former. In sections 11.5 to 11.7 we will therefore return to the core model of geographical economics and by taking it at face value investigate what kind of policy implications may follow by letting the spatial interdependencies take centre stage. In doing so, and keeping the *3D* split of the World Bank (2009) analysis on economic geography and policy in mind, we are now leaving *density* behind and turn to the world of *division* and *distance* between regions.

11.5.1   Policy and Spatial Equilibrium for Both Urban and Geographical Economics

The spatial equilibrium concept that we developed in Chapter 5 and Chapter 6 for urban economics and in Chapter 7 and Chapter 8 for geographical economics can be summarized by a simple equation, an indirect utility function for a specific location (we drop the location sub-index to avoid too much notation): $V(W, P, N)$, where V is indirect utility, W is income or wages, P is price index, and N is an indicator of the size of the local market, which may lead to spillovers or more amenities, but can also imply more congestion. The impact of a change in N on V is thus not straightforward.

In Glaeser (2008), the indirect utility function is central to his treatment of urban economics. But in geographical economics models, the long-run equilibrium is essentially based on the same concept (see below in section 11.7 how real wages can be translated into utility). If locations offer the same utility, the system is characterized by a spatial equilibrium. It implies, for example, that if in two similar sized locations one location offers an annual wage of $100,000 and the other location an annual wage of $80,000 the difference in spatial equilibrium is compensated by prices (of local amenities), say $40,000 in the high-paying location and $20,000 in the low paying location, assuring that net income is the same between the two locations ($60,000 in our example). In general, any variable that changes W has a compensating effect on P, given a fixed N.

This line of reasoning explains why it may be difficult in practice to use policies to get people from peripheral locations to more central higher-paying locations: net income effects are small and higher wages are possibly compensated by higher prices of local services (and perhaps more congestion). Also, the benefits of relocating activity to peripheral locations could be offset by higher housing prices, and so on. The relationship between high incomes in certain areas and the accompanying high local (housing) prices have been documented extensively (see Glaeser and Gottlieb, 2008). Another policy handle that the spatial equilibrium concept offers relates to tackling P. In some locations P is high, for example due to high housing prices. The cause of these high housing prices could be 'market regulation'. Some cities are reluctant to offer building permits for housing projects, such as the city of Amsterdam in the Netherlands. Amsterdam could benefit more from agglomeration economies with a less regulated housing market.

The geographical economics approach extends the concept of the spatial equilibrium by stressing that locations are interconnected by transportation costs and this is where the role of spatial interdependencies enters, to which we will turn next. With some exaggeration, in urban economics locations are floating islands but within geographical economics it matters above all how well connected locations are. Policy initiatives can take this on board. In the example of Amsterdam: policy makers can, for example, deregulate the housing market in the nearby town of Almere in order to affect the housing market in Amsterdam. Almere is one of the fastest-growing cities in the Netherlands, in no small part because it is near to Amsterdam and whereas in Amsterdam housing demand far outstrips (new) housing supply, Almere is the prime location in the country in terms of adding housing capacity (Garretsen and Marlet, 2017). This is largely done to affect policy choices. Whether this is efficient is another question. Glaeser (2011b) has been arguing for a long time that large cities like Amsterdam could and should become much larger if only building capacity and building densities were allowed to increase.

11.5.2   Stylized Policy Implications in the World of the Tomahawk

We now use the core geographical economics model to illustrate some policy implications by taking the core model at face value. Following Ottaviano (2003, pp. 669–672) and more fundamentally Baldwin et al. (2003), we can illustrate the basic policy implications of the core model of geographical economics by using the Tomahawk diagram; see Figure 7.9 as a benchmark. For convenience, we replicate the Tomahawk diagram with the free-ness of trade $\varphi = T^{1-\varepsilon}$ along the horizontal axis (thus reversing the shape of the diagram) in Figure 11.3. Ottaviano (2003) argues that the core model gives rise to the following six general policy implications:

- Regional side-effects
- Trade interaction effects
- Lock-in effects
- Selection effects
- Coordination effects
- Threshold effects

We will briefly discuss these six effects. Note that these policy implications do not refer to a specific policy instrument nor to the impact of policies, but instead emphasize how policy analysis differs once we enter the non-linear, multiple-equilibria world of geographical economics.

Regional side-effects. The policy implication here is merely that all kinds of allegedly *non-regional* policies can have consequences for the regional

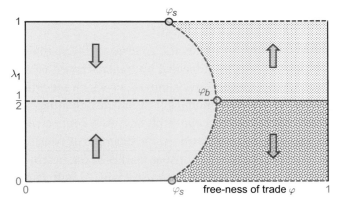

basin of attraction spreading equilibrium
basin of attraction agglomeration region 1
basin of attraction agglomeration region 2

— stable equilibrium
--- unstable equilibrium

Figure 11.3 The Tomahawk diagram (with free-ness of trade)

or spatial allocation of economic activity. For instance, trade liberalization, competition policy, or (inter-regional) income redistribution are typically not placed-based but all of them can, in principle, affect core–periphery patterns. We know from the core models of geographical economics that any policy-induced change in the key model parameters *potentially* may affect the equilibrium spatial allocation of economic activity. Potentially, as Figure 11.3 illustrates, because whether the equilibrium will be affected depends crucially on if and how the policy measure changes the balance between agglomerating and spreading forces.

Trade interaction effects. These focus on the fact that any policy intervention on the spatial allocation of economic activity depends on the (initial) level of trade or economic integration (transport costs). Any policy intervention that brings an economy beyond the sustain or break points could have a large impact.

Lock-in effects. These can be illustrated using the Tomahawk diagram; see Figure 11.3. The central idea is that temporary policies can have permanent effects on the equilibrium spatial allocation of the footloose economic activity. Suppose that we start to the right of both the sustain point φ_s and the break point φ_b in Figure 11.3 and that all footloose economic activity happens to be agglomerated in region 1 ($\lambda_1 = 1$). Now suppose that the peripheral region, region 2, introduces a subsidy to footloose firms and workers that succeeds in convincing all footloose agents to migrate from region 1 to region 2. The lock-in (or hysteresis) effect indicates that once the footloose agents have all moved to region 2, this region may withdraw or stop its subsidy because for the same (unchanged) level of the free-ness of trade, complete agglomeration in region 2 is also a stable long-run equilibrium and without the subsidy no footloose agent has an incentive to move back to region 1; temporary policies (the subsidy) can have lasting effects.

Selection effects. To illustrate this policy implication Figure 11.3 is useful again. Suppose initially that the spreading equilibrium is stable and that the actual free-ness of trade is lower than φ_b. If the actual free-ness of trade increases such that $\varphi > \varphi_b$, we see in Figure 11.3 that all footloose agents will either end up in region 1 or region 2. As long as the two regions are identical the outcome is undetermined. In this situation any policy intervention, however small, that gives one of the two regions an advantage will be enough to ensure that all footloose agents end up in that region. Policy acts as a selection device between spatial equilibria.

Coordination effects. This policy implication refers to the way policy makers can influence the expectations of individuals as to where all other agents will locate. This is important if multiple equilibria are possible. In terms of Figure 11.3, if the actual free-ness of trade is such that $\varphi_s < \varphi < \varphi_b$, both spreading and agglomeration are stable equilibria. Policy makers can determine which equilibrium gets established (like full agglomeration in region 1) if they succeed in convincing (some of) the footloose agents to locate in that region (by offering a subsidy if they move to region 1). This policy will lead to self-enforcing agglomeration (as long as agents expect the government to pay the subsidy and act accordingly). Ironically, the policy might work without the government actually handing out any subsidy as long as expectations of economic agents are influenced by the government.

Threshold effects. This last policy implication is arguably the most important. Policy measures will only have an effect on the equilibrium spatial distribution of footloose economic activity if these measures have a certain critical mass. An increase in the degree of economic integration or, in modelling terms, an increase in the free-ness of trade can have either no or a huge impact. What will happen crucially depends on the initial level of the free-ness of trade and on the gap between the initial level of the free-ness of trade and the break or sustain point. The possibility of a non-linear impact of policy measures means that it can be misleading to use the standard approach to policy analysis, which analyses the impact of *marginal* policy changes under the assumption that the impact of policies on the economy is continuous. In terms of Figure 11.3, with $\varphi < \varphi_b$ policy interventions, however large, that will not succeed in ensuring $\varphi > \varphi_b$ will not have an effect on agglomeration. At the same time, if φ is initially smaller but close to φ_b, the threshold effect implies that a small policy intervention that raises φ just beyond φ_b may do the job. The reason for the threshold effect is that, even though initially there exists a high degree of flexibility of location, once these choices have been made, the spatial pattern turns out to be rigid. This threshold or non-linear property visualized by the Tomahawk diagram implies that 'marginal policy changes are completely ineffective until the cumulated change remains a certain threshold. After the threshold is crossed, the impact is catastrophic' (Ottaviano, 2003, p. 670).

To end this sub-section, it is worthwhile to recapitulate some of the general problems with regional policies that we highlighted in section 11.4 and indicate that these are not necessarily a problem if the policy maker knows perfectly how the world works. Locations are clearly defined in the model and market failures can be identified as it is possible to calculate the welfare gains of increasing a home market and concentrate activity in one of the two locations or spread activity over two locations. Overall welfare changes can also be calculated (assuming utility for each person can be added) if it is clearly defined which commodities and production factors are mobile such that given model parameters the consequences of different policies can be calculated. As always, the proof of the pudding is in the eating. So, we now turn to an example where we will use a main model of geographical economics (the congestion model as discussed in section 8.6) to conduct a hypothetical policy experiment.

11.6   Building a Bridge in Geographical Economics

Time and again throughout Part III on geographical economics, we have analysed what will happen to the spatial distribution of economic activity when transport costs change. We know that the conclusion depends on a number of factors, like (i) the initial level of transport costs; (ii) the underlying model; (iii) the specification of the transport cost function and the modelling of the infrastructure; and (iv) the definition of transport costs, in particular whether or not these costs include tariffs and other trade restrictions as well. Transport costs do not only change when the transport technology changes but also when trade policy induces a change in trade restrictions.

So when it comes to a discussion of the policy implications of geographical economics, it is also important to deal with the question of how policy interventions that somehow alter the transport costs and thereby the spatial interdependencies between locations might change the spatial allocation of economic activity. In this section we conduct our own simple experiment to address this issue. The example is highly stylized but at the end of this section we will see how it relates to similar real-world policy experiments that have already been discussed in our book.

BOX 11.1   On Taxes, Tax Competition, Rents, and the Race to the Bottom

It is well known in the public economics literature that by taxing land, society could recapture some of the (speculative) land rents that would otherwise flow to landowners. These taxes could be used to finance local expenditures and could prevent land speculation when sites lie vacant. Stiglitz (1977) showed that under certain conditions a land tax is efficient and also the only tax necessary to finance public expenditures (see for a survey Brülhart, Bucovetsky, and Schmidheiny, 2015). This proposition is called the *Henri George Theorem*, after the nineteenth-century political economist Henri George. The idea is straightforward. If landowners are taxed according to the value of their land, a land tax would recapture part of the windfall gains to landowners if they happen to own land in a prosperous agglomeration. Because the amount of land is fixed – in contrast to anything built on top of it – a land tax does not interfere with supply of land and would create

BOX 11.1 (cont.)

an incentive to develop the land. One of the consequences is to relax planning restrictions in order to allow land development. In many cities, however, strict – building and housing – regulations exist that prevent land development, which is sub-optimal from the perspective of economic development. This theorem is behind much of the policy advice in urban economics (see Glaeser, 2008). For one, it reduces the incentive for NIMBY-ism (NIMBY = Not-In-My-Back-Yard) in attractive places as it does not pay to leave valuable land undeveloped because the (high) land taxes have to be paid, irrespective of whether or not the land is developed. If land or the transfer of land is taxed one would like to know whether and how land prices (and as a consequence housing prices) are affected. This is a question that is plagued with causality and endogeneity issues. In Chapter 3 we introduced the regression discontinuity design (RDD). Using this methodology and applying it to the land transfer tax in Toronto (recall Figure 3.15), Dachis, Duranton, and Turner (2012) show how the land transfer tax indeed had an impact on the housing market when comparing sales transaction and housing prices between house owners that were and were not affected by this tax.

The Henri George Theorem is most often used to analyse tax consequences in a single location. What happens if we introduce more locations and thus more local governments that can raise taxes in a world where firms and/or households are mobile? In a neo-classical world, capital or labour mobility could then easily lead to tax competition between local or national governments and a race to the bottom with ever lower tax rates; a government with high tax rates runs the risk of capital or labour flight. The presence of agglomeration rents changes this outcome. With a positive agglomeration rent and perfect factor mobility, the core country – the country where (most) capital or labour is located – can have higher tax rates than the peripheral country, as long as the agglomeration rent exceeds the tax differ-ential. Attempts by the peripheral country to lure the factors of production away from the core country by decreasing its tax rate will not lead to a relocation of productions factors as long as the tax gap falls short of the agglomeration rent.

Starting from complete agglomeration and applied to the case where capital is the mobile production factor, Baldwin and Krugman (2004) show in a two-country geographical economics model that even with full capital mobility a race to the bottom need not materialize. The assumption of agglomeration is impor-tant because it ensures that the agglomeration rent is positive. The model used in Baldwin and Krugman (2004) is a two-region (North and South) model with two factors of production, labour L and human capital K. The model is basically the solvable model that was introduced in Chapter 8. Both factors of production are

BOX 11.1 (cont.)

necessary to produce a variety of the manufacturing good, which requires one unit of K and a_x units of labour per unit produced. The cost function for a manufacturing firm i is then $r + Wa_xx_i$, where r is the wage for human capital and W is the wage for labour. Apart from this production structure, the model is essentially the same as the core model with one more exception: labour is assumed to be immobile between countries, only capital can freely move between North and South. Capital moves to the region with the highest *after tax* real wage. With agglomeration rents present the after tax real wage does not have to be smaller than in the region with lower tax rates or no tax rates at all. A race to the bottom is not an inevitable outcome of the model. This insight has important consequences in our present day and age of globalization where it is often feared that a (tax) race to the bottom is inevitable. The existence of agglomeration rents or in other words the bonus of being located in a larger agglomeration explains why larger, richer, and more centrally located regions and countries can allow themselves to impose (somewhat) higher tax rates even with full capital or labour mobility.

Although the Baldwin and Krugman (2004) model provides a relevant policy insight, it ignores the fact that governments usually tend to levy taxes in order to provide useful public services (such as infrastructure, rule of law, and public safety) which may lower the production costs in a location, thereby allowing for the possibility that a higher tax rate as a means to finance public goods could make a location *more* attractive for mobile factors of production. In contrast, Brakman, Garretsen, and van Marrewijk (2008) focus on such a classic cost–benefit analysis of taxes for the 'solvable geographical economics model' of section 8.4. They focus on the differences in the model with government spending as compared to the Baldwin-Krugman model without government spending.

Under the assumption that the two regions have a constant and given level of public goods and the influence of government spending on the cost of production in the two regions is the same, Brakman, Garretsen, and van Marrewijk (2008) show that the introduction of public goods into the model usually leads to a fall in the free-ness of trade break point and thus tends to reduce the stability of the spreading equilibrium. For Europe, for example, this suggests that continued economic integration, which raises the free-ness of trade parameter, is more likely to lead to instability of the spreading equilibrium, or equivalently more likely to result in core–periphery outcomes. For empirical proof as to how sensitive (Swiss) firms are to tax differences when deciding upon their location when agglomeration effects are also allowed to play a role see Brülhart, Jametti, and Schmidheiny (2012).

11.6.1   The Pancake Economy

The model to be used in this section is the core model with congestion as analysed in section 8.6. The example used not only serves to illustrate some of the policy implications, it also provides an example of non-neutral space. Other examples of policy experiments exist, such as income subsidies or local tax exemptions. Box 11.1 discusses some of these policy examples and the way they have been analysed from a geographical economics perspective.

Suppose that we take the congestion model of Chapter 8 and illustrate what happens in a 12-city version. The simple geography we use is the racetrack economy where cities are located along a circle and we flatten this circle to the *pancake* shape illustrated in Figure 11.4.[9] Assume, moreover, that the manufacturing workforce and the farm workers are initially uniformly distributed over the 12 cities, such that each city produces one-twelfth of the economy total.

As we know from our discussion of the congestion model in Chapter 8, such a symmetric racetrack economy structure (see panel *a* of Figure 11.4) implies that

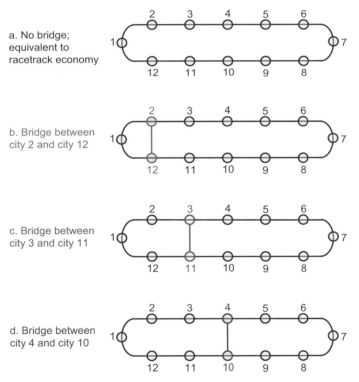

Figure 11.4 Building bridges in the pancake economy

---

[9] One might argue that the pancake economy actually looks more like a racetrack than the racetrack economy.

this initial distribution represents a long-run equilibrium, which Fujita, Krugman, and Venables (1999) dubbed the *flat earth* equilibrium. We will analyse the consequences of disturbing this long-run flat earth equilibrium as a result of an active policy intervention involving two of the twelve cities. In our discussion below we refer to it as a bridge-building infrastructure project (but it could have been a road or a tunnel) which directly connects the two cities and thus reduces the distance between them. The policy project can, however, also be interpreted as a reduction in distance between the two cities as a result of closer cooperation, say resulting from economic integration or monetary unification. Building a bridge between two cities in the pancake economy implies that space is no longer neutral, in contrast to the racetrack economy. We analyse three possible infrastructure policy projects, namely:

- building a bridge between cities 2 and 12 (see panel *b* of Figure 11.4)
- building a bridge between cities 3 and 11 (see panel *c* of Figure 11.4)
- building a bridge between cities 4 and 10 (see panel *d* of Figure 11.4)

In all cases, we assume that the bridge between the two cities reduces the distance between them to one unit. In principle, there could be five 'vertical' bridges (in addition to the three mentioned above, one could also envisage a bridge between cities 6 and 8 or between cities 5 and 9, but this is analytically equivalent to a bridge between cities 2 and 12 or cities 3 and 11, respectively).

The cities that are not directly linked by the vertical bridge may or may not benefit from the bridge in terms of reducing the distance to other cities. In particular, cities 1 and 7 never benefit in this sense from any of the possible bridges. The other cities do benefit, either directly or indirectly. For example, the bridge between cities 3 and 11 not only reduces the distance between those two cities (which falls from 4 to 1), but also reduces the distance between some of the other cities. For example, the distance between cities 3 and 10 falls from 5 to 2, and the distance between cities 4 and 12 falls from 4 to 3. Table 11.1 gives an overview of the impact, in

Table 11.1 Average distance in the pancake economy

City	No bridge	Bridge 2–12	Bridge 3–11	Bridge 4–10
1	3	3.00	3.00	3.00
2	3	2.58	2.67	2.75
3	3	2.67	2.08	2.33
4	3	2.75	2.33	1.92
5	3	2.83	2.58	2.33
6	3	2.92	2.83	2.75
Average	3	2.79	2.58	2.51

terms of the average distance to other cities (including the city itself) for the cities when there are no bridges and for the three different bridges mentioned above. In our set-up it suffices to analyse only these six cities.[10] As is intuitively obvious, the bridge between cities 4 and 10 leads to a larger reduction in average distance than the bridge between cities 3 and 11, or 2 and 12. Similarly, the greatest reduction in average distance arises of course for the linked cities themselves.

11.6.2   Bridges and the Equilibrium Spatial Distribution

To analyse the general impact of the infrastructure projects on the distribution of manufacturing activity in our pancake economy, we calculate the long-run equilibrium for each of the three bridges, starting from a uniform initial distribution. For our base scenario we chose the following parameter values: the share of income spent on manufacturing δ is equal to 0.6, the elasticity of substitution ε is 5, the transport costs parameter T is 1.2, and the congestion parameter τ is equal to 0.1. It is important to note that in the absence of a bridge the flat earth equilibrium is a stable equilibrium for the base scenario parameter setting. We have thus essentially stacked the deck *against* economic agglomeration.[11] Nonetheless, as is clear from Table 11.2 and illustrated in Figure 11.5 (with the share of manufacturing activity λ_i on the vertical axis), building bridges in the pancake economy has a large impact on the distribution of manufacturing production, and leads to considerable agglomeration of economic activity (see especially the bold entries in Table 11.2).

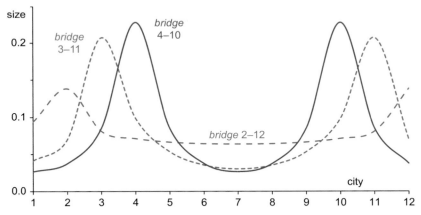

Figure 11.5 Impact of building a bridge on spatial distribution
Note: size is share of manufacturing workforce.

---

[10] By construction, the impact on average distance for cities 2 and 12; 3 and 11; 4 and 10; 5 and 9; and 6 and 8 are identical, while there is no impact for cities 1 and 7. It therefore suffices to list just the first six cities.

[11] In fact, we have stacked the deck rather strongly. Even the simulations with an initial distribution far away from the uniform distribution lead to the flat earth equilibrium in the absence of bridges.

Table 11.2 Distribution of manufacturing workers (% of total) with different bridges

City	Bridge 2–12	Bridge 3–11	Bridge 4–10
1	8.2	4.1	2.7
2	16.4	7.0	3.8
3	10.3	20.7	8.5
4	7.1	9.8	22.8
5	5.4	5.3	8.5
6	4.6	3.5	3.8
7	4.3	3.0	2.7

Note: the impact on cities 8, 9, 10, 11, and 12 is identical to the impact on cities 6, 5, 4, 3, and 2, respectively.

The reduction of transport costs that is the result of building a bridge benefits the cities that undertake such a project by enabling them to attract a large share of manufacturing production. The rationale behind this phenomenon is straightforward. If manufacturing activity is evenly distributed, the workers in the two cities at each end of the bridge have the highest real wage as they have to pay lower transport costs. This attracts other manufacturing workers into the linked cities, which on the one hand reinforces the process and on the other hand leads to more congestion and makes demand in the more remote markets more attractive. These forces are balanced in the long-run equilibrium. In general, the impact of building the bridge, an obvious example of non-neutral space, is remarkably high. Even the link on the edge between cities 2 and 12 leads to a doubling of manufacturing activity in cities 2 and 12.

11.6.3 The Hypothetical Bridge Versus Real Bridges

The bridge policy experiment in our pancake economy yields useful insights as to how a (policy-induced) change in the spatial economy can have an impact on the (re)location of footloose firms and workers. The underlying model of geographical economics and our depiction of geography as a pancake are of course much too simplistic to be applied to an actual real-world policy question. Having said that, and returning to some of the research discussed in earlier chapters, the main idea is to be able to frame a policy question in *what if* terms: what happens to the allocation of economic activity (across the 12 cities) if we build a bridge between two cities that changes the (pancake) geography? This *what if* quality is a hallmark of the models discussed throughout our book and especially of geographical economics models (Krugman, 2011).

Modern research takes this *what if* quality to the data by using models that explicitly build on and are a mix of the main mechanisms underlying the urban and geographical economics models. They are essentially fleshed-out models of the pancake economy. By this we mean that they are general equilibrium models that are specified and quantified in such a way that basically all relevant first and second nature geography mechanisms for agglomeration and hence for the existence of *spikes* that have been discussed could be included in these models. Right at the start of our book (see even before section 1.1) we already referred to this approach as 'quantitative spatial economics' (Redding and Rossi-Hansberg, 2016, 2017).

The use of these and related models can certainly enrich the actual policy analysis of changes in the degree of agglomeration. To give just a few examples which have already popped up before:

- Donaldson and Hornbeck (2016) on the impact of the creation of the US railroad system on the economic geography of the USA. Or similarly, Donaldson (2018) on the long-run impact of the construction of the railway network in India by the British rulers at the time;
- Gaubert (2018) on the agglomeration of economic activity within France and crucially, given the purpose of this chapter, how policy interventions (such as subsidies to lagging French regions) might (not) change the agglomeration patterns;
- Desmet, Nagy, and Rossi-Hansberg (2018) on global economic development and the role of geography, where the *what if* question refers to different scenarios for global migration;
- Redding and Sturm (2016) on the impact of WWII bombing on London neighbourhoods;
- Bosker and Garretsen (2012), who discuss the *what if* implications for economic development and market access of policy (infrastructure) interventions in Sub-Saharan Africa;
- Bosker et al. (2012) on how changes in inter-regional labour mobility via policy changes in the *Hukou* system could change the economic geography of China. When it comes to China, the *what if* approach using the models of urban and geographical economics is also applied to analyse the impact of the massive investment in railways and highways: see Baum-Snow et al. (2017) or Faber (2014).

Arguably, one of the best examples to date of this new approach to analysing the spatial impact of policy-induced changes on the spatial growth and distribution of spikes is Heblich, Redding, and Sturm (2018). They analyse how changes in London's infrastructure brought radical changes to the internal urban agglomeration of Greater London. The authors do not only show how the enlargement and improvement of the railway network from the mid nineteenth century onwards enabled millions of people to split their work and living location across the Greater London space, but also how, thanks to the changes in the infrastructure, the population of London was 30 per cent larger than it otherwise (=counterfactually) would have been.[12] For our present purposes, we want to single out that the Heblich et al. (2018) paper succeeds in encompassing virtually all drivers of agglomeration that have been introduced throughout our book and they not only show how policy changes can be analysed in a meaningful manner when it comes to the effect of these changes on economic spikiness (here, the internal agglomeration structure of London), but they crucially also develop a rich analytical model that encapsulates our discussion of the bridge in the hypothetical pancake economy.

To illustrate their findings, Figure 11.6 shows from the mid nineteenth century until the early twentieth century how changes in the London railway network enabled the unbundling (or decoupling) of work place and living place for many Londoners by plotting the divergence that occurred over time between the day-time and the night-time population in the City of London in terms of employment. The figure also shows the accuracy of the model in explaining this trend (= line for 'model day population'). The analysis underlying Figure 11.6 is far more advanced than the bridge in our pancake economy, but the analysis is still based on the fundamental *what if* question, as argued above.

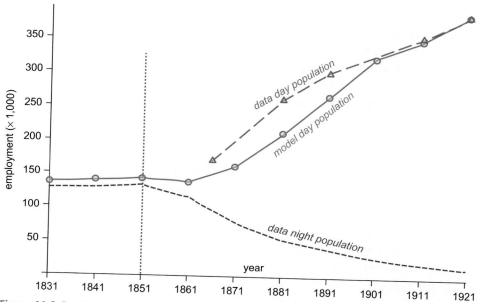

Figure 11.6 Day-time and night-time population in the city of London
Source: based on Heblich et al. (2018).

---

[12] For a summary of the main ideas and findings of the paper: https://voxeu.org/article/making-modern-metropolis-evidence-london.

11.7   Welfare Implications

11.7.1   Introducing Welfare Analysis

So far, little attention has been paid to the welfare implications of policy changes or other changes that affect the equilibrium spatial distribution of economic activity. A main reason for this reluctance to deal with welfare implications is that the models of geographical economics are thought to be too simplistic and/or to be too much biased towards agglomeration as the preferred equilibrium to warrant an attempt to address the welfare implications. Nevertheless, and without neglecting these reservations, we think that a chapter on policy implications should deal with welfare implications. In doing so, we will first explain how a welfare analysis can be introduced and then apply the insights to our bridge experiment in the pancake economy of the previous section. In this way we give the reader an idea of how the normative implications might be addressed.

Taking the core model of Chapter 7 as our benchmark for the moment, it is clear that different allocations of manufacturing activity will have different welfare implications for different sets of people. Given transport costs T it is, for example, clear that the mobile workforce tends to generate a higher welfare level in the complete agglomeration equilibrium than in the spreading equilibrium, since in the latter they have to import part of their consumption of manufactures from the other region. It is also obvious that the immobile workforce in region 2, given complete agglomeration in region 1, is worse off compared to the spreading equilibrium as they will have to import all their manufactures from the other region. It is impossible to argue *ex ante* which effect is more important, so we will somehow have to *weigh* the importance of various groups, using their size as weight.

Recall that in the core model there are two types of agents within each region in the core model, namely the share λ_i of all manufacturing workers and the share ϕ_i of all farm workers. Since there are γL manufacturing workers in total and $(1-\gamma)L$ farm workers, we concluded in equation 7.19 that total income in region i is equal to $Y_i = \lambda_i W_i \gamma L + \phi_i (1-\gamma) L$, because manufacturing workers in region i earn wage W_i and farm workers earn wage 1. To determine the welfare level for both types of workers we will have to correct for the price level I_i in region i. In this chapter, we will focus attention on total welfare. To determine this, let $y_i \equiv Y_i I_i^{-\delta}$ be the real income in region i and note that total welfare is simply given by adding over the locations, see equation 11.2.

$$total\ welfare = \Sigma_i\, y_i \qquad\qquad 11.2$$

Also for different groups in the economy we can easily calculate welfare consequences by simply analysing real wages for that particular group. With this welfare measurement instrument we can now return to our pancake economy of the previous section.

11.7.2 Welfare Implications of a Bridge in the Pancake Economy

To round off our bridge experiment, we now get to the reasons for building a bridge in terms of the welfare implications using the welfare criteria discussed above. After all, building a bridge is costly, such that the authorities must have a good reason to start and complete such a project. Although one can think of various reasons for building a bridge, we will concentrate in this subsection on the welfare implications of building a bridge, where a city's welfare is given by its real income and total welfare is the summation of real income over 12 cities.

The basic effect of building a bridge is, of course, the reduction of the distance between cities, either directly or indirectly. Here we are more interested in the long-run welfare implications of building a bridge, that is to say in the welfare implications *once we allow for manufacturing workers to migrate* in reaction to the building of the bridge. As is clear from the above description and the uneven distribution of the reduction in average distance over the cities, inhabitants in different cities enjoy different welfare effects from the completion of the bridge. The inhabitants of the linked cities initially enjoy the largest welfare gain. This sets in motion a process of migration which, as we have seen in section 11.6.2, leads to substantial economic agglomeration in the linked cities. This second effect – the migration process – thus also influences the distribution of welfare gains. In general, inhabitants of the cities that grow in size enjoy a positive welfare effect in the second stage as they can purchase a larger number of manufacturing varieties locally. As we will see below, the second effect can dominate the first effect.

There are essentially 13 (=12+1) different economic agents in the long-run equilibrium, namely the farm workers in the 12 cities *and* the manufacturing workers as a whole. Since the manufacturing workers will migrate to other cities until their real wage is equalized, the long-run welfare impact of building a bridge is the same for all manufacturing workers. Table 11.3 summarizes the average long-run welfare effects of building a bridge, namely for the economy as a whole, for the average farm worker, and for the manufacturing workers. For the economy as a whole the average welfare effect (in our example) is always positive, although the economy will obviously benefit more from a more centrally placed bridge, linking cities 4 and 10, than from a more peripherally placed bridge, linking cities 2 and 12. This reasoning holds more strongly for the manufacturing workers, that is they benefit more than the economy on average, and the extent of their welfare increase is larger the more centrally the bridge is located. Box 11.2 illustrates this by means of a real-world example.

Table 11.3 Overview of welfare effects (%): long-run equilibrium

	Bridge 2–12	Bridge 3–11	Bridge 4–10
Average change in real income	0.9	1.9	2.2
Average change in real farm income	−0.3	0.2	0.2
Average change in real manufacturing income	1.6	2.8	3.5

BOX 11.2 Building a Tunnel

In this box we describe the economic effects of the construction of a tunnel in the Netherlands. This quasi-experiment highlights what can happen when a 'bridge' (in this case a tunnel) is built to connect two areas of land that were previously only connected by ferries or other boat transport.

The decision to construct the Westerschelde tunnel in the Netherlands was made in September 1995, and the tunnel was opened in 2003. Essentially, this is a real-world example of our building-a-bridge experiment. For our purposes, there are no differences between a bridge and a tunnel; both connect formerly unconnected places. The main reason for the Dutch government to construct the tunnel was that in the long run a tunnel would be less expensive to operate than maintaining the two ferry services. Before the tunnel was opened, ferry services connected *Zeeuws-Vlaanderen* and *Midden-Zeeland* (see Figure 11.7). The ferry services stopped operating on the day the tunnel was opened.

The study of Hoogendoorn et al. (2019) estimates how the tunnel affected housing prices at both ends of the tunnel. Housing prices can be viewed as a proxy for the attractiveness of locations and as such signal whether the tunnel has made more concentration of economic activity feasible near the tunnel and

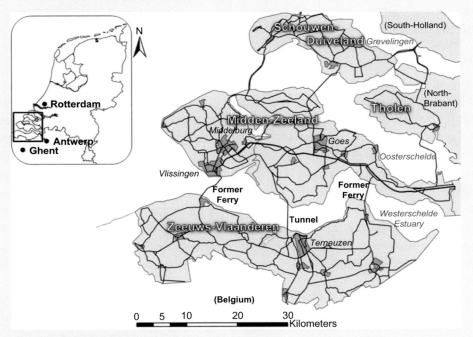

Figure 11.7 The Westerschelde tunnel in the Netherlands
Source: Hoogendoorn et al. (2019).

BOX 11.2 (cont.)

whether these locations have thus become more attractive because of a new connection, the tunnel. The findings suggest that on average a 1 per cent increase in accessibility (see Figure 11.8) results in a 0.8 per cent increase in housing prices. In the regions that experienced a decline in accessibility (former ferry locations) this finding implies a decline of housing prices in those areas.

The analysis of the quasi-experiment of the building of the Westerschelde tunnel in the province of Zeeland in the Netherlands shows that:

- A new connection indeed increases the accessibility of the locations at both ends of the new connection and confirms what we showed in Figure 11.5.
- The increase of the attractiveness of the locations at the end of a new connection is at the expense of locations that have, suddenly, become relatively more peripheral. Once again, this is a serious warning for policy makers who promote a project for their own region; do other regions possibly suffer from such a project?

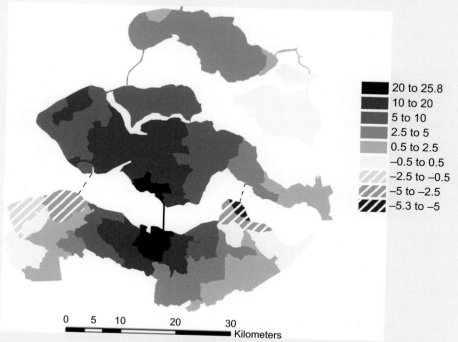

Figure 11.8 Percentage change in accessibility due to the Westerschelde tunnel
Source: Hoogendoorn et al. (2019); accessibility is defined as the number of jobs that are accessible, weighted by a distance decay function.

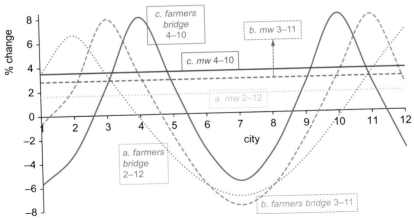

Figure 11.9 Real income changes with different bridges
Note: *mw* 2–12 is manufacturing workers with bridge 2–12; similarly for *mw* 3–11 and *mw* 4–10.

The welfare picture is not so positive for the average farm worker. In particular, if the bridge is peripherally placed, linking cities 2 and 12, the average farm worker 'enjoys' a reduction in real income of 0.3 per cent as a large share of manufacturing activity is moved to peripherally placed cities, requiring the average farm worker to pay large transport costs. Even if the bridge is more centrally placed, linking cities 3 and 11, or cities 4 and 10, the average farm worker enjoys only a small gain (0.2 per cent) in real income. The calculation of averages can be deceptive, however, which is clearly the case here.

As illustrated in Figure 11.9, the information in Table 11.3 on the welfare of the average farm worker is a poor indicator for what happens to a particular individual farm worker. The welfare increase for the farm workers in the linked cities is always positive, and much larger than the average increase for the manufacturing workers (up to an 8.1 per cent improvement for the farm workers in cities 4 and 10 when there is a bridge between these cities). In contrast, the welfare impact for the farm workers in the cities far away from the linked cities is always negative, and substantially so (up to −7.7 per cent for the farm workers in city 7 if there is a bridge between cities 3 and 11).

What are the main lessons of this policy-simulation example? First, it shows that policy experiments, however simple, can be performed with straightforward applications of the core model. Second, that even a simple policy experiment with a simple model can have quite complex implications.

For real-world analyses one should, again, be careful. As mentioned before, the knowledge requirements of regional policies might be beyond what is possible in practice, as pointed out already by Neary (2001) when discussing the use of models of geographical economics for policy purposes. This statement remains relevant today. The models suggest that policy makers can pick the equilibrium they prefer.

The presence of multiple equilibria indeed suggests that policy makers can try to pick a 'better' equilibrium. This supposes that equilibria can be ranked from a welfare perspective and that policy makers know how to move the economy from one equilibrium to another. In practice this is not possible; see also our discussion of cluster and regional policies in section 11.4. Or, as Neary (2001, p. 27) puts it:

> it is tempting to suggest a role for government in 'picking equilibria'. This in turn may encourage a new sub-field of 'strategic location policy', which (...) has produced much interesting theory but no simple robust rules to guide policy making. All these are temptations to be resisted, since they take too literally the neat structure of the [geographical economics] model, and ignore the econometric difficulties in estimating the non-linear, non-monotonic relation it predicts.[13]

11.8 Places, People, Policies, and *Proper* Economic Geography

We began this chapter on policy implications by pointing out that the literature on clusters and regional policy more generally can be subdivided into two broad groups: economists and geographers represent the academic side of the debate, and policy makers represent the practitioner's side. However, geographers and economists do not always agree on what is the most important policy target. Stronger still, they also do not agree (usually) on the analytical framework for studying our spiky world. Now that we have almost come to the end of our book, it is important to point out that the models discussed in the book can lay no claim on the analysis of the spatial distribution of economic activity. *Proper* economic geography, as Martin (2008) puts it, helps to put the approach of our book into a broader perspective. To do so seems fitting at the end of our book in which the spiky world has thus been analysed almost exclusively through the lenses of urban and geographical economics.

The main point of departure between the theories discussed in this book (urban economics and geographical economics) and the approach under the heading of 'proper' economic geography is that proponents of the latter think that the general equilibrium framework and the deductive theorizing upon which urban and geo-graphical economics is based are ill suited to deal with the analysis of real-world economic geography (for an early and influential statement on this as a reaction to Krugman, 1991, see Martin, 1999). The framework is thought to be *unable* to deal with the role of institutions, uncertainty, and the resulting non-optimizing behav-iour of agents, all of which are argued to be decisive for the location of economic

---

[13] This is probably also the reason why Fujita, Krugman, and Venables (1999), the authors of the seminal book on geographical economics, are reluctant to discuss policy implications.

activity in the real world according to modern economic geographers. To put it more bluntly, the complaint is that modern urban and geographical economics is neither new (but merely a restatement of outdated earlier insights of economic geographers and regional scientists) nor is it economic geography (since there is no place for real-world geography).

Given this position, it is hardly a surprise that most economic geographers think that urban and geographical economics cannot be applied to intricate policy issues because in their view spatial policy making is too complicated for the too stylized and abstract models of urban and geographical economics. This is why leading economic geographer Michael Storper (2003, p. 81) referred to economists as *the kings and queens of generality* whereas economic geographers are *the kings and queens of specificity and particularity*. Economic geographers do not only point to the limitations of the analytical framework, but also to the alleged over-simplification in urban and geographical economics by, for instance, not discriminating between various levels of spatial aggregation. Indeed, in the previous chapters the location or index r interchangeably represented a city, a region, or a country.

The field of economic geography is itself far from unified and there is much internal debate and disagreement. For a fruitful debate between urban and geographical economists on the one hand and economic geographers on the other hand some minimum requirements have to be fulfilled (see also Box 11.3). First, both camps have to have at least a basic understanding of each other's work and to show a willingness to study what the other side has to say (so one at least knows what to disagree with). While this requirement (in our experience) is not met by most economic geographers, it is certainly not met by almost all urban and geographical economists, who simply neglect what's going on in the field of economic geography. Second, there has to be some middle-ground or overlap that might enable a useful exchange of opinions or that even allows for mutual research or new research initiatives. Regarding the dangers of the status quo on the non-debate between urban and geographical economists and economic geographers, it is useful to quote a grand old man of economic geography, Allen Scott (2006, pp. 106–7) at some length.[14]

> In any case, the ill-considered advice put forth recently by some geographers to the effect that all attempts at intellectual exchange with economics confraternity should now be more or less brought to an end, strikes me as being only a recipe for self-marginalization. In spite of the important ideological, political, and scientific differences between the two camps, geographers will profit significantly from continued critical engagement with the often insightful and original research of economists. There may even be some possibility – dare I say it? – of using any such engagement as an opportunity for recovering some of the discipline's lost quantitative and analytical skills. If economists, for their part,

[14] The quote is from his review of the *Handbook of Regional and Urban Economics*, volume 4, a book which according to Scott (2006, p. 104) 'geographers will neglect at their peril'.

continue to proceed as though geographers do not exist, then that presumably is their problem, though in view of their own peculiar form of self-marginalization in the contemporary social sciences, it is probably one they will not recognize.

The inclusion of the above quotation in the present book signals that its three authors, all born and bred mainstream economists, think that Scott's call for more engagement has to be taken seriously by economists and geographers alike. To back up this last claim and also to show that 'there is much work to be done', we tried to quantify how much urban and geographical economists and economic geographers do actually take notice of each other by looking at cross-references and citations (Brakman, Garretsen, and van Marrewijk, 2011). The bottom line of this inquiry is that both camps hardly cite each other's work, the number of cross-references is very limited, and (with only a few notable exceptions) research on the same phenomenon, the spiky world, is done in two almost parallel universes.

BOX 11.3 Are *Homo Economicus* and *Homo Geographicus* Two Different Species?

In an interesting take on the (non-)debate between economists and geographers from an anthropological angle, Gilles Duranton and Andrés Rodríguez-Pose (2005) ask the question whether *homo economicus* and *homo geographicus* are really that different. Their conclusion is that there are considerable differences in terms of both style and content but that nevertheless a (renewed) debate between geographical economists and economic geographers might be beneficial for all parties concerned. Duranton (an urban economist) and Rodríguez-Pose (an economic geographer) note the following barriers to a more fruitful communication:

- (Geographical) Economists and (economic) geographers ignore each other's publications. This is evident from the lack of citations of work done by economic geographers in leading geographical economics journals and vice versa (for evidence, see Brakman et al., 2011).
- Economists and geographers do not go to the same conferences and when they do there is a culture shock with respect to presentation and discussion style.
- The research methods often differ so markedly that communication becomes rather difficult.
- There is in many cases an unwillingness to take each other's work seriously.

These are not small obstacles, to say the least. Duranton and Rodríguez-Pose (2005), however, see a number of ways for a debate to be (re-)launched. In

BOX 11.3 (cont.)

their view a key word here is *compromise*. Only if both parties are willing to compromise (more) on what constitutes acceptable research and on the use of concepts (more or less fixed in economics and changeable and rather fluid in geography) will such a debate be feasible. Duranton and Rodríguez-Pose (2005, pp. 1704–5) conclude their analysis by stating that 'despite their differences in methods, terminology, and organization, geographical economists and economic geographers … share a common genetic code that makes them more similar to one another than each species is willing to admit. They can try to grow apart, but their instinct always brings them back to their original shared set of research questions and interests.'

This co-existence of two largely separate fields mainly refers to the underlying theories and analytical framework used. The differences are much smaller (and narrowing it seems) when it comes to empirical research. Stronger still, as far as policy making is concerned, many of the issues like those pertaining to the choice between place- or people-based policies are the same between economists and geographers. So despite large analytical or theoretical (and some might say insurmountable) differences, these differences are much smaller in applied work on empirics or policies. For an example of the latter, Barca, McCann, and Rodríguez-Pose (2012) offer a discussion of place- and people-based regional policies that could have been written by any contemporary urban and geographical economist that shows up in the list of references in Part II and Part III of our book. To give another example: the economic geographers Iammarino, Rodríguez-Pose, and Storper (2017) discuss for EU regions how policy that tries to change the economic conditions for the people in a certain region by targeting only the local economic structure and not the people, or vice versa, misses the complex interdependencies between the two. This idea of a mix between place- and people-based regional policies is echoed in an important paper by the economists Austin, Glaeser, and Summers (2018) in their discussion as to how regional policies in the USA might be put to better use to improve the plight of the lagging regions.

11.9   Closing Remarks

In the second part of this chapter we have analysed a policy experiment in non-neutral space (sections 11.6 and 11.7): the building of a *bridge* in the pancake economy. In this sense we have given in to the temptation mentioned by Neary

(2001) because the bridge example shows in a simple and general manner how the introduction of non-neutral space, created by policy intervention, affects the equilibrium outcome and welfare. We have also discussed other more general and also more specific policy implications of urban and geographical economics, but the conclusions with respect to the bridge experiment apply to these other discussions as well. It is one thing to criticize policy makers for adhering too much to policy concepts like clusters that lack a solid underpinning. It is quite another thing to come up with alternative models and empirical strategies that lend themselves to actual policy analysis. Two final observations come to mind.

First, do these kinds of simulation experiments and the models discussed in our book have any relevance for 'real world' policy issues? When it comes to policy applications, simulations with such a highly stylized model are only of limited practical day-to-day relevance. There is clearly not enough flesh on the bone of the core model to tackle the costs and benefits of a particular plan to build a bridge. Obviously, when deciding on the costs and benefits of a specific issue, one first has to construct a model taking the most important aspects of this issue into consideration, possibly using elements from urban and geographical economics models. In a qualitative sense, we do, however, think that simulation examples, such as building bridges or tunnels in the pancake economy, are useful thought experiments for policy makers. It at least forces them to think in non-partial terms about policy proposals and their geographical (non-linear or lumpy) implications. Having said that, the rise of quantitative spatial economics (Redding and Rossi-Hansberg, 2016, 2017) and the examples we have given in section 11.6.3 show how nowadays, close to 30 years after Krugman (1991) published what became the core model of geographical economics, new models filled with real-world data that combine the main mechanisms of geographical and urban economics and that use the modern empirical toolkit can address the implication of large-scale and also smaller (policy-induced) changes for the spiky world. In our view, this bodes rather well not only for future research but also for future policy applications.

This brings us to our final point. Policy makers might be tempted by the well-documented positive association between productivity and agglomeration to try to build the next Silicon Valley so as to create their own economic spike. Policy intervention, however, assumes the existence of some kind of market failure. The two concepts that played a central role in this chapter (agglomeration economies and spatial linkages) are real, multi-faceted concepts and have many dimensions. This poses a fundamental question: is the knowledge of policy makers sufficient to know which market failures are present and what kind of policy interventions are required, if any? The models of urban and geographical economics suggest that both researchers and policy makers should be modest in this respect. The available knowledge is in general insufficient. As a consequence, policy interventions should be rather general (improving infrastructure, reducing congestion, and so on), but should refrain from building the next top sector or cluster (recall the shifting the wage curve *versus* shifting the cost-of-living curve halfway through this chapter). We simply cannot predict the future and do not know what the next top firm or top sector will be a decade from now and which policy intervention could or should then be called for. However, what we can predict is that research in urban and geographical economics will continue to flourish and that, if time permits, we hope to report on these developments in the next edition of our book.

Exercises

Question 11.1 Porter Clusters

On the Harvard Business School website (www.isc.hbs.edu/competitiveness-economic-development/frameworks-and-key-concepts/Pages/clusters.aspx)   a wealth of information can be found on Porter's cluster concept and on the man himself. The website also gives links to other cluster initiative websites and to specific examples of (successful) cluster initiatives.

One such example is: www.isc.hbs.edu/Documents/pdf/NJ_lifescience.pdf. This is the 'New Jersey Life Science Super-Cluster Initiative'.

a. Can this initiative be described in terms of Porter's Diamond? If your answer is Yes, complete the diamond in terms of the Life-Science Super-Cluster.
b. What is the role of the government in this cluster initiative?
c. Is the cluster well-defined in terms of geography and firms that are included in the cluster?
d. Is the initiative an example of a place- or people-based policy?
e. In the final assessment of the cluster, are the following elements taken into account:

Is the production structure clear (what is (im-)mobile)?
Are possible negative externalities documented and taken into account?
Is it a partial analysis or are the effects on other (nearby) regions taken into account?
Is there evidence of lobbying/rent-seeking activity?
What market failures were corrected by this initiative?
Is the initiative aimed at raising productivity or at reducing the cost of living (see Figure 5.9)?

Question 11.2 Policy Statements

In section 11.2 six basic policy implications of geographical economics were briefly discussed. Consider the following two statements about these implications:

1. The threshold effect refers to the possibility of a sudden or catastrophic change in the equilibrium allocation of economic activity across space.
2. The lock-in effect does not occur in the case of a bell curve (as shown by Figure 8.6).

Are these statements true or false and why?

Question 11.3 Geographers

Some economists are rather reluctant to use geographical economics for policy analysis, but why do you think geographers object to the use of geographical economics for policy purposes?

Question 11.4 Corporate Income Tax

Use the analysis of agglomeration rents to discuss the prospects for a future race to the bottom in the European Union in terms of corporate income taxation when economic integration continues to increase.

Question 11.5 Pancake Economy

Why is space non-neutral in the pancake economy (in contrast to the racetrack economy)?

Question 11.6 Welfare

Let $y_i \equiv Y_i I_i^{-\delta}$ be the real income in region i and define: *total welfare* $= \Sigma_i \, y_i$.

a. Why is this definition of welfare too simple from the perspective of section 11.3?
b. 'According to this definition of welfare, the welfare for mobile workers must always be the same in geographical economics.' Discuss the validity of this statement.

References

Chapter 1 References

Brakman, S., H. Garretsen, and C. van Marrewijk (2001), *An Introduction to Geographical Economics: Trade, Location and Growth*, Cambridge University Press, Cambridge, UK.

Brakman, S., H. Garretsen, and C. van Marrewijk (2009), *The New Introduction to Geographical Economics*, Cambridge University Press, Cambridge, UK.

Brakman, S., H. Garretsen, and C. van Marrewijk (2016), Urban Development in China, *Cambridge Journal of Regions, Economy, and Society*, 9: 467–77.

Chandler, T. (1987), *Four Thousand Years of Urban Growth: An Historical Census*, Edwin Mellen Press, Lewiston, NY.

Compton, N. (2015), What is the Oldest City in the World?, *The Guardian*, 16 February.

Gabaix, X., and R. Ibragimov (2011), Rank–1/2: A Simple Way to Improve the OLS Estimation of Tail Exponents, *Journal of Business & Economic Statistics*, 29(1): 24–39.

Head, K., and T. Mayer (2014), Gravity Equations: Workhorse, Toolkit, and Cookbook, in: G. Gopinath, E. Helpman, and K. Rogoff (eds.), *Handbook of International Economics*, Vol. 4, Elsevier (North Holland), Amsterdam.

Head, K., T. Mayer, and G. Ottaviano (2017), A Review of Volume 5 of the Handbook of Regional and Urban Economics, *Journal of Regional Science*. See https://doi.org/10.1111/jors.12356.

Jaubert, J., S. Verheyden, D. Genty, M. Soulier, H. Cheng, D. Blamart, C. Burlet, H. Camus, S. Delaby, D. Deldicque, R. L. Edwards, C. Ferrier, F. Lacrampe-Cuyaubère, F. Lévêque, F. Maksud, P. Mora, X. Muth, É. Régnier, J.-N. Rouzaud, and F. Santos (2016), Early Neanderthal Constructions Deep in Bruniquel Cave in Southwestern France, *Nature*, 435: 111–15.

Krugman, P.R. (1991), Increasing Returns and Economic Geography, *Journal of Political Economy*, 99: 483–99.

Marrewijk, C. van (2017), *International Trade*, Oxford University Press, Oxford.

Proost, S., and J-F. Thisse (forthcoming), What Can Be Learned From Spatial Economics?, *Journal of Economic Literature*. See https://www.aeaweb.org/articles?id=10.1257/jel.20181414&&from=f.

Redding, S., and E. Rossi-Hansberg (2016), Quantitative Spatial Economics: A Framework for Evaluating Regional Policy and Shock in the Real World, *VOX EU*, 27 October. See https://voxeu.org/article/evaluating-regional-policy-and-shocks-real-world.

Redding, S., and E. Rossi-Hansberg (2017), Quantitative Spatial Economics, *Annual Review of Economics*, 9(1): 21–58.

Tinbergen, J. (1962), *Shaping the World Economy*, The Twentieth Century Fund, New York.

United Nations Population Division (2017), *World Population Prospects: the 2017 Revision*, regularly updated information. See https://esa.un.org/unpd/wpp/.

Zipf, G. K. (1949), *Human Behaviour and the Principle of Least Effort*, Addison Wesley, New York.

Chapter 2 References

Acemoglu, D., S. Johnson, and J. Robinson (2001), The Colonial Origins of Comparative Development: An Empirical Investigation, *American Economic Review*, 91(5): 1369–1401.

Acemoglu, D., S. Johnson, and J. Robinson (2002), Reversal of Fortune: Geography and Institutions in the Making of the Modern World Income Distribution, *Quarterly Journal of Economics*, 117(4): 1231–94.

Acemoglu, D., and J. Robinson (2010), The Role of Institutions in Growth and Development, *Review of Economics and Institutions*, 1(2): 1–33.

Ashraf, Q., and O. Galor (2011), Dynamics and Stagnation in the Malthusian Epoch, *American Economic Review*, 101(5): 2003–41.

Brakman, S., H. Garretsen, and C. van Marrewijk (2009), *The New Introduction to Geographical Economics*, Cambridge University Press, Cambridge, UK.

Chen, D., and H. Chen (2013), Using the Koppen Classification to Quantify Climate Variation and Change: An Example for 1901–2010, *Environmental Development*, 6: 69–79.

Diamond, J. (1997), *Guns, Germs, and Steel*, 2005 rev. ed., Vintage, London.

Glaeser, E. L., R. La Porta, F. Lopez-de-Silanes, and A. Shleifer (2004), Do Institutions Cause Growth?, *Journal of Economic Growth*, 9(3): 271–303.

Krugman, P. R. (1993), First Nature, Second Nature and Metropolitan Location, *Journal of Regional Science*, 33: 129–44.

La Porta, R., F. Lopez-de-Silanes, A. Shleifer, and R. Vishny (1998), Law and Finance, *Journal of Political Economy*, 106(6): 1113–55.

Marrewijk, C. van, S. Brakman, and J. Swart (2018), *The Economics of Developing and Emerging Markets*, mimeo, Utrecht University.

North, D. (1990), *Institutional Change and Economic Performance*, Cambridge University Press, New York.

Olsson, O., and D. A. J. Hibbs (2005), Biogeography and Long-Run Economic Development, *European Economic Review*, 49: 909–38.

Putterman, L., and D. Weil (2010), Post-1500 Population Flows and the Long-Run Determinants of Economic Growth and Inequality, *Quarterly Journal of Economics*, 125(4): 1627–82.

Sachs, J., A. Mellinger, and J. Gallup (2001), The Geography of Poverty and Wealth, *Scientific American*, March: 70–75.

Smith, A. (1776), *An Inquiry into the Nature and Causes of the Wealth of Nations*, 1937 Modern Library edition, Random House.

Smith, B. (1998), *The Emergence of Agriculture*, Scientific American Library, New York.

Spolaore, E., and R. Wacziarg (2013), How Deep Are the Roots of Economic Development?, *Journal of Economic Literature*, 51(2): 325–69.

The Economist (2014a), An Astonishing Record, *The Economist*, 22 March.

The Economist (2014b), Commander of his Stage, *The Economist*, 22 March.

Wolchover, N. (2012), Why It Took So Long to Invent the Wheel, *Scientific American*, March 6.

World Health Organization (2014), *World Malaria Report 2014*, WHO Press, Geneva.

Chapter 3 References

Anselin, L. (1988), *Spatial Econometric Methods and Models*, Kluwer Academic, Boston.

Atkinson, A. (1970), On the Measurement of Inequality, *Journal of Economic Theory*, 2: 244–63.

Brakman, S., H. Garretsen, and C. van Marrewijk (2009), *The New Introduction to Geographical Economics*, Cambridge University Press, Cambridge, UK.

Brakman, S., H. Garretsen, C. van Marrewijk, and A. Oumer (2012), The Border Population Effect of EU Integration, *Journal of Regional Science*, 52: 40–59.

Brakman, S., H. Garretsen, and Z. Zhao (2017), Spatial Concentration of Manufacturing Firms in China, *Papers in Regional Science*, 96: 179–205.

Brülhart, M., and R. Traeger (2005), An Account of Geographical Concentration patterns in Europe, *Regional Science and Urban Economics*, 35: 597–624.

Combes, P.-P., and H. G. Overman (2004), The Spatial Distribution of Economic Activities in the EU, in: J. V. Henderson and J.-F. Thisse (eds.), *Handbook of Regional and Urban Economics*, Vol. 4, Elsevier (North Holland), Amsterdam.

Combes, P.-P., G. Duranton, L. Gobillon, and S. Roux (2010), Estimating Agglomeration Economies with History, Geology, and Worker Effects, in: E. L. Glaeser (ed.), *Agglomeration Economics*, NBER, University of Chicago Press, Chicago.

Cowell, F. (2011), *Measuring Inequality*, 3rd edition, Oxford University Press, Oxford.

Dachis, B., G. Duranton, and M. A. Turner (2012), The Effects of Land Transfer Taxes on Real Estate Markets: Evidence from a Natural Experiment in Toronto, *Journal of Economic Geography*, 12(2): 327–54.

De La Roca, J., and D. Puga (2017), Learning by Working in Big Cities, *Review Of Economic Studies*, 84: 106–42.

DiNardo, J., and J. L. Tobias (2001), Nonparametric Density and Regression Estimation, *The Journal of Economic Perspectives*, 15 (4): 11–28.

DuPont, W., and I. Noy (2015), What Happened to Kobe? A Reassessment of the Impact of the 1995 Earthquake in Japan, *Economic Development and Cultural Change*, 63: 777–812.

Duranton, G., and H. Overman (2005), Testing for Location Using Micro-Geographic Data, *Review of Economic Studies*, 72: 1077–1106.

Duranton, G., and H. Overman (2008), Exploring the Detailed Location Patterns of U.K. Manufacturing Industries using Microgeographic Data, *Journal of Regional Science*, 48(1): 213–43.

Duranton, G., J. V. Henderson, and W. Strange (eds.) (2015), *Regional and Urban Economics*, Vol. 5, Elsevier (North Holland), Amsterdam.

Elhorst, J. P. (2014), *Spatial Econometrics: From Cross-Sectional Data to Spatial Panels*, Springer, New York.

Ellison, G., and E. L. Glaeser (1997), Geographic Concentration in U.S. Manufacturing Industries: A Dartboard Approach, *Journal of Political Economy*, 105(5): 889–927.

Foster, J., S. Seth, M. Lokshin, and Z. Sajaia (2013), *A Unified Approach to Measuring Poverty and Inequality; Theory and Practice*, The World Bank, Washington.

Gibbons, S., and H. G. Overman (2012), Mostly Pointless Spatial Econometrics?, *Journal of Regional Science*, 52(2): 172–91.

Gibbons, S., H. G. Overman, and E. Patacchini (2015), Spatial Methods, in: G. Duranton, J. V. Henderson, and W. Strange (eds.), *Regional and Urban Economics*, Vol. 5, Elsevier (North Holland), Amsterdam.

Gini, C. (1912), *Variabilità e Mutuabilità: Contributo allo Studio delle Distribuzioni e delle Relazioni Statistiche*. C. Cuppini, Bologna.

Kline, P., and E. Moretti (2014), Local Economic Development, Agglomeration Economies, and the Big Push: 100 Years of Evidence from the Tennessee Valley Authority, *The Quarterly Journal of Economics*, 129: 275–331

Lee, D. S., and T. Lemieux (2010), Regression Discontinuity Designs in Ecnomics, *Journal of Economic Literature*, 48: 281–355.

Lee, D. S., and T. Lemieux (2014), Regression Discontinuity Designs in Social Sciences, in: H. Best and C. Wolf (eds.), *The SAGE Handbook of Regression Analysis and Causal Inference*, SAGE Publications Ltd, London.

Marrewijk, C. van (2019), Global Income Inequality, in: G. Ritzer and C. Rojek (eds.), *The Wiley-Blackwell Encyclopedia of Sociology*, 2nd edition, Blackwell-Wiley, Oxford.

Maurel, F., and B. Sedillot (1999), A Measure of Geographical Concentration of French Manufacturing Industry, *Regional Science and Urban Economics*, 29: 575–604.

Meyer, K. E., A. van Witteloostuijn, and S. Beugelsdijk (2017), What's in a p? Reassessing Best Practices for Conducting and Reporting Hypothesis Testing Research, *Journal of International Business Studies*, 48: 535–61.

Redding, S., and D. M. Sturm (2008), Costs of Remoteness: Evidence from German Division and Reunification, *American Economic Review*, 98(5): 1766–97.

Vega, S. H., and J. P. Elhorst (2015), The SLX Model, *Journal of Regional Science*, 55(3): 339–63.

Wooldridge, J. M. (2016), *Introductory Econometrics: A Modern Approach*, Cengage Publishers, USA.

Chapter 4 References

Alonso, W. (1964), *Location and Land Use*, Harvard University Press, Cambridge, MA.

Anas, A., R. Arnott, and K. A. Small (1998), Urban Spatial Structure, *Journal of Economic Literature*, 36: 1426–64.

Autor, D. (2019), Work of the Past, Work of the Future, Richard T. Ely Lecture, American Economic Association Annual Meeting, Atlanta.

Becker, G. S. (1965), A Theory of the Allocation of Time, *Economic Journal* 75(299): 493–517.

Black, S.E. (1999), Do Better Schools Matter? Parental Evaluation of Elementary Education, *Quarterly Journal of Economics*, 114: 577–99.

Brueckner, J. (1987), The Structure of Urban Equilibria: A Unified Treatment of the Muth-Mills Model, in: E. W. Mills (ed.), *Handbook of Regional and Urban Economics*, Vol. 2, Elsevier (North Holland), Amsterdam.

Duranton, G. (2006), Some Foundations for Zipf's Law: Product Proliferation and Local Spillovers, *Regional Science and Urban Economics*, 36: 543–63.

Fujita, M. (1989), *Urban Economic Theory: Land Use and City Size*, Cambridge University Press, Cambridge, UK.

Fujita, M., and H. Ogawa (1982), Multiple Equilibria and Structural Transition of Non-Monocentric Urban Configurations, *Regional Science and Urban Economics*, 12(2): 161–96.

Henderson, J. V. (1985), The Tiebout Model: Bring Back the Entrepreneurs, *Journal of Political Economy*, 93(2): 248–64.

Henderson, J. V., and A. Mitra (1996), The New Urban Economic Landscape Developers and Edge Cities, *Regional Science and Urban Economics*, 26(6): 613–43.

Glaeser, E. L. (2007), *The Economic Approach to Cities*, mimeo, Department of Economics, Harvard University, Cambridge, MA.

Glaeser, E. L. (2008), *Cities, Agglomeration, and Spatial Equilibrium*, Oxford University Press, Oxford.

Glaeser, E. L., M. Kahn, and J. Rappaport (2008), Why Do the Poor Live in Cities? The Role of Public Transportation, *Journal of Urban Economics*, 63(1): 1–24.

Lucas, R., and E. Rossi-Hansberg (2002), On the Internal Structure of Cities, *Econometrica*, 70(4): 1445–76.

Mills, E. S. (1967), An Aggregative Model of Resource Allocation in a Metropolitan Area, *American Economic Review Papers and Proceedings*, 57(2): 197–210.

Mills, E. S. (1972), *Studies in the Structure of the Urban Economy*, Johns Hopkins Press, Baltimore.

Muth, R. (1969), *Cities and Housing*, University of Chicago Press, Chicago.

Von Thünen, J. H. (1826), *Der Isolierte Staat in Beziehung auf Landwirtschaft und Nationalökonomie*, Perthes, Hamburg.

Wheaton, W. (1977), Income and Urban Residence: An Analysis of Consumer Demand for Location, *American Economic Review*, 67(4): 620–31.

Chapter 5 References

Abdel-Rahman, H. M., and A. Anas (2004), Theories of Systems of Cities, in: J. V. Henderson and J.-F. Thisse (eds.), *Handbook of Regional and Urban Economics*, Vol. 4, Elsevier (North Holland), Amsterdam.

Behrens, K., G. Duranton, and F. Robert-Nicoud (2014), Productive Cities, Sorting, Selection, and Agglomeration, *Journal of Political Economy*, 122: 507–53.

Behrens, K., and F. Robert-Nicoud (2015), Agglomeration Theory with Heterogeneous Agents, in: G. Duranton, J. V. Henderson, and W. Strange (eds.), *Handbook of Regional and Urban Economics*, Vol. 5, Elsevier (North Holland), Amsterdam.

Beirlant, J., Y. Goegebeur, J. Segers, and J. Teugels (2004), *Statistics of Extremes: Theory and Applications*, Wiley,Chichester, England.

Black, D., and V. Henderson (2003), Urban Evolution in the USA, *Journal of Economic Geography*, 3: 343–72.

Brakman, S., H. Garretsen, C. van Marrewijk, and M. Van Den Berg (1999), The Return of Zipf: Towards a Further Understanding of the Rank–Size Curve, *Journal of Regional Science*, 39: 183–215.

Brakman, S., H. Garretsen, C. van Marrewijk, and van Witteloostuijn (2019), The Location of Cross-Border Mergers & Acquisitions in the USA, *CESifo Working Pap*er No. 5331.

Brakman, S., S. Hu, and C. van Marrewijk (2014), Smart Cities are Big Cities – Comparative Advantage in Chinese Cities, *CESifo Working Paper* No. 5028, http://www.cesifo-group.de/DocDL/cesifo1_wp5028.pdf.

Carroll, G. (1982), National City-Size Distributions: What Do We Know After 67 Years of Research?, *Progress in Human Geography*, 6: 1–43.

Combes, P-P., G. Duranton, and H. Overman (2005), Agglomeration and the Adjustment of the Spatial Economy. *Papers in Regional Science*, 84(3), p. 311–349.

Combes, P.-P., and L. Gobillon (2015), The Empirics of Agglomeration Economies, in G. Duranton, J. V. Henderson, and W. Strange (eds.), *Handbook of Regional and Urban Economics*, Vol. 5, Elsevier (North Holland), Amsterdam.

Costinot, A. (2009), On the Origins of Comparative Advantage, *Journal of International Economics*, 77(2): 255–64.

Costinot, A., and J. Vogel (2015), Beyond Ricardo: Assignment Models in International Trade, *Annual Review of Economics*, 7: 31–62.

Davis, D. R., and J. I. Dingel (2017), The Comparative Advantage of Cities, updated version of 2014 NBER Working Paper No. 20602. See http://faculty.chicagobooth.edu/jonathan.dingel/.

Desmet, C., and J. V. Henderson (2015), The Geography of Development Within Countries, in: G. Duranton, J. V. Henderson, and W. Strange (eds.), *Handbook of Regional and Urban Economics*, Vol. 5, Elsevier (North Holland), Amsterdam.

Dobkins, L. H., and Y. M. Ioannides (2000), Dynamic Evolution of U.S. City Size Distributions, in: J.-M. Huriot and J.-F. Thisse (eds.), *The Economics of Cities*, Cambridge University Press, Cambridge, UK.

Duranton, G., and D. Puga (2004), Micro-foundations of Urban Agglomeration Economies, in: J. V. Henderson and J.-F. Thisse (eds)., *Handbook of Regional and Urban Economics*, Vol .4, Elsevier (North Holland), Amsterdam.

Eaton, J., and Eckstein, Z. (1997), Cities and Growth: Theory and Evidence from France and Japan, *Regional Science and Urban Economics*, 27: 443–74.

Fujita, M., P. R. Krugman, and A. J. Venables (1999), *The Spatial Economy: Cities, Regions, and International Trade*, MIT Press, Cambridge, MA.

Fujita, M., and T. Mori (2005), Frontiers of the New Economic Geography, *Papers in Regional Science*, 84(3): 377–407.

Fujita, M., and J.-F. Thisse (2013), *Economics of Agglomeration: Cities, Industrial Location, and Globalization*, Cambridge University Press, Cambridge, UK.

Gabaix, X. (1999a), Zipf's Law and the Growth of Cities, *American Economic Review, Papers and Proceedings*, 89: 129–32.

Gabaix, X. (1999b), Zipf's Law for Cities: an Explanation, *Quarterly Journal of Economics*, 114: 739–66.

Gabaix, X., and R. Ibragimov (2011), Rank–1/2: A Simple Way to Improve the OLS Estimation of Tail Exponents, *Journal of Business & Economic Statistics*, 29(1): 24–39.

Gaubert, C. (2018), Firm Sorting and Agglomeration, *American Economic Review*, 108 (11): 3117–53.

Giesen, K., and J. Südekum (2011), Zipf's Law for Cities in the Regions and the Country, *Journal of Economic Geography*, 11: 667–86.

Glaeser, E. L. (2008), *Cities, Agglomeration, and Spatial Equilibrium*, Oxford University Press, Oxford.

Henderson, J. V. (1974), The Sizes and Types of Cities, *American Economic Review*, 64: 640–56.

Hsu, W.-T. (2012), Central Place Theory and City Size Distribution, *Economic Journal*, 122: 903–22.

Ioannides, Y. (2013), *From Neigborhoods to Nations: The Economics of Social Interactions*, Princeton University Press, Princeton.

Koopmans, T. C. (1957), *Three Essays on the State of Economic Science*, McGraw-Hill, New York.

Kratz, M., and S. I. Resnick (1996), The QQ-Estimator and Heavy Tails, *Communications in Statistics. Stochastic Models*, 12: 699–724.

Krugman, P. R. (1995), *Development, Geography and Economic Theory*, MIT, Cambridge, MA.

Krugman, P. R. (1996a), *The Self-organizing Economy*, Blackwell, Oxford.

Krugman, P. R. (1996b), Confronting the Mystery of Urban Hierarchy, *Journal of the Japanese and International Economies*, 10: 399–418.

Lee, S., and Q. Li (2013), Uneven Landscapes and the City Size Distribution, *Journal of Urban Economics*, 78: 19–29.

Melo, P., D. Graham, and R. Noland (2009), A Meta-Analysis of Estimates of Urban Agglomeration Economies, *Regional Science and Urban Economics*, 39(3): 332–42.

Milgrom, P. (1981), Good News and Bad News: Representation Theorems and Applications, *The Bell Journal of Economics*, 12: 380–91.

Nitsch, V. (2005), Zipf Zipped, *Journal of Urban Economics*, 57: 86–100.

Pareto, V. (1896), *Cours d'Economie Politique*, Droz, Geneva.

Rosen, K.T., and M. Resnick (1980), The Size Distribution of Cities: An Examination of the Pareto Law and Privacy, *Journal of Urban Economics*, 8: 165–86.

Soo, K.T. (2005), Zipf's Law for Cities: A Cross-Country Investigation, *Journal of Urban Economics*, 35: 239–63.

Starrett, D. (1978), Market Allocations of Location Choice in a Model with Free Mobility, *Journal of Economic Theory*, 17: 21–37.

UN Population Division (2014), *World Urbanization Prospects: The 2014 Revision*, United Nations, New York.

Zipf, G.K. (1949), *Human Behaviour and the Principle of Least Effort*, Addison Wesley, New York.

Chapter 6 References

Ades, A., and E. L. Glaeser (1995), Trade and Circuses: Explaining Urban Giants, *Quarterly Journal of Economics*, 110: 195–228.

Albouy, D. (2016), What are Cities Worth? Land Rents, Local Productivity, and the Total Value of Amenities, *Review of Economics and Statistics*, 98 (3): 477–87.

Albouy, D. (2018), *Are Big Cities Bad Places to Live? Estimating Quality of Life across Metropolitan Areas*, mimeo, accessed via http://davidalbouy.net/.

Albouy, D., and G. Ehrlich (2013), *The Distribution of Urban Land Values: Evidence from Market Transactions*, mimeo, University of Illinois.

Baldwin, R. E. (ed.) (2016), *Brexit Beckons: Thinking Ahead by Leading Economists*, CEPR Press, London.

Baldwin, R.E., and F. Robert-Nicoud (2007), Entry and Asymmetric Lobbying: Why Governments Pick Losers, *Journal of the European Economic Association*, 5(5): 1064–93.

Baum-Snow, N., and F. Ferreira (2015), *Causal Inference in Urban and Regional Economics*, in: G. Duranton, J. V. Henderson, and W. Strange (eds.), *Regional and Urban Economics*, Vol. 5, Elsevier (North Holland), Amsterdam.

Bosker, M. Buringh, E., and J. L. van Zanden (2013), From Baghdad to London: Unravelling Urban Development in Europe and the Arab World 800–1800, *Review of Economics and Statistics*, 95 (4): 1418–37.

Brakman, S., H. Garretsen, and C. van Marrewijk (2009a), *The New Introduction to Geographical Economics*, Cambridge University Press, Cambridge, UK.

Brakman, S., H. Garretsen, and C. van Marrewijk (2009b), Economic Geography Within and Between European Nations: The Role of Market Potential and Density Across Space and Time, *Journal of Regional Science*, 49: 777–800.

Brakman, S., H. Garretsen, and T. Kohl (2017), Consequences of Brexit and Options for a 'Global Britain', *Papers in Regional Science*, 97 (1); see also VoxEU: http://voxeu.org/article/options-global-britain-after-brexit.

Breinlich, H. (2006), The Spatial Income Structure in the European Union – What Role for Economic Geography?, *Journal of Economic Geography*, 6: 593–617.

Cheshire, P., and S. Magrini (2006), Population Growth in European Cities: Weather Matters – But only Nationally, *Regional Studies*, 40 (1): 23–37.

Ciccone, A., and R. E. Hall (1996), Productivity and the Density of Economic Activity, *American Economic Review*, 86: 54–70.

Combes, P.-P., G. Duranton, and L. Gobillon (2008), Spatial Wage Disparities: Sorting Matters!, *Journal of Urban Economics*, 63(2): 723–42.

Combes, P.-P., G. Duranton, and L. Gobillon (2012), *The Costs of Agglomeration: Land Prices in French Cities*, CEPR Discussion Paper 9240, London; revised in 2018. See http://real.wharton.upenn.edu/~duranton/Duranton_Papers/Current_Research/UrbanCosts.pdf.

Combes, P.-P., G. Duranton, L. Gobillon, and S. Roux (2010), Estimating Agglomeration Economies with History, Geology, and Worker Effects, in: E. L. Glaeser (ed.), *Agglomeration Economics*, NBER, University of Chicago Press, Chicago.

Combes, P.-P., and L. Gobillon (2015), The Empirics of Agglomeration Economies, in G. Duranton, J. V. Henderson, and W. Strange (eds.), *Handbook of Regional and Urban Economics*, Vol. 5, Elsevier (North Holland), Amsterdam.

Combes, P.-P., T. Mayer, and J.-F. Thisse (2008), *Economic Geography: The Integration of Regions and Nations*, Princeton University Press, Princeton.

De La Roca, J., and D. Puga (2017), Learning by Working in Big Cities, *Review Of Economic Studies*, 84: 106–42.

Desmet, K., and E. Rossi-Hansberg (2013), Urban Accounting and Welfare, *American Economic Review*, 103(6): 2296–2327.

Dhingra, S., H. Huang, G. Ottaviano, J. Pessoa, T. Sampson, and J. Van Reenen (2016), *The Costs and Benefits of Leaving the EU*, London School of Economics Centre for Economic Performance, London. See VOXeu: http://voxeu.org/article/economic-consequences-brexit; full paper: http://cep.lse.ac.uk/pubs/download/pa016_tech.pdf.

Duranton, G. (2011), California Dreamin': The Feeble Case for Cluster Policies, *Review of Economic Analysis*, 3: 3–45.

Duranton, G., and D. Puga (2004), Micro-foundations of Urban Agglomeration Economies, in: J. V. Henderson and J.-F. Thisse (eds.), *Handbook of Regional and Urban Economics*, Vol .4, Elsevier (North Holland), Amsterdam.

Florida, R. (2002), *The Rise of the Creative Class: And How It's Transforming Work, Leisure, and Everyday Life*, Basic Books, New York.

Florida, R. (2006), *The Flight of the Creative Class*, Basic Books, New York.

Garretsen, H., and Marlet, G. (2017), Amenities and the Attraction of Dutch Cities, *Regional Studies*, 51(5): 724–37.

Garretsen, H., J. I. Stoker,D. Soudis,R. L. Martin, and P. J. Rentfrow (2019), The Relevance of Personality Traits for Economic Geography: Making Space for Psychological Factors, *Journal of Economic Geography*, 19(3): 541–65.

Garretsen, H., J. I. Stoker,D. Soudis,R. L. Martin, and P. J. Rentfrow (2018), Brexit and the Relevance of Regional Personality Traits: More Psychological Openness Could Have Swung the Regional Vote, *Cambridge Journal of Regions, Economy and Society*, 11 (1): 165–75.

Gaubert, C. (2018), Firm Sorting and Agglomeration, *American Economic Review*, 108 (11): 3117–53.

Gerber, A. S., G. A. Huber, D. Doherty, and C. M. Dowling (2011), The Big Five Personality Traits in the Political Arena, *Annual Review of Political Science*, 14: 265–87.

Glaeser, E. L. (2008), *Cities, Agglomeration and Spatial Equilibrium*, Oxford University Press, Oxford.

Glaeser, E. L. (2011), *Triumph of the City: How Our Greatest Invention Makes Us Richer, Smarter, Greener, Healthier And Happier*, Penguin Press, New York.

Glaeser, E. L., and J. D. Gottlieb (2009), The Wealth of Cities: Agglomeration Economies and Spatial Equilibrium in the United States, *Journal of Economic Literature*, 47 (4): 983–1028.

Glaeser, E. L., H. D. Kallal, J. Scheinkman, and A. Shleifer (1992), Growth in Cities, *Journal of Political Economy*, 100: 1126–52.

Glaeser, E. L, J. Kolko, and A. Saiz (2001), Consumer City, *Journal of Economic Geography*, 1: 27–50.

Heblich, S., S. J. Redding, and D. M. Sturm (2018), *The Making of the Modern Metropolis: Evidence from London*, CEPR Discussion Paper 13170, London.

Henderson, J. V. (1974), The Sizes and Types of Cities, *American Economic Review*, 64: 640–56.

Henderson, J. V. (2003), The Urbanization Process and Economic Growth: The So-What Question, *Journal of Economic Growth*, 8: 47–71.

HM Treasury (2016), *The Long-Term Economic Impact of EU Membership and the Alternatives*. See https://www .gov.uk/government/publications/ hm-treasury-analysis-the-long-term- economic-impact-of-eu-membership- and-the-alternatives.

John, O.P., L. P. Naumann, and C. J. Soto (2008), Paradigm Shift to the Integrative Big Five Trait Taxonomy, *Handbook of Personality: Theory and Research*, 3: 114–58.

John, O.P., and S. Srivastava (1999), The Big Five Trait Taxonomy: History, Measurement, and Theoretical Perspectives, *Handbook of Personality: Theory and Research*, 2: 102–38.

Kaufmann E. (2016), *It's Not The Economy, Stupid: Brexit as a Story of Personal Values*. London School of Economics and Political Science; see http://blogs .lse.ac.uk/politicsandpolicy/personal- values-brexit-vote.

Kemeny, T., and M. Storper (2010), Urban Growth and Change in the USA: Production and Jobs, or Amenities and Consumer Utility?, mimeo, University of North Carolina at Chapel Hill.

Krueger, J. I. (2016), *The Personality of Brexit Voters: Openness Predicts Best, Psychology Today* blog (after Bastian Jaeger). See https://www .psychologytoday.com/blog/one-among-many/201606/the-personality-brexit-voters.

Lee, N. (2017), Psychology and the Geography of Innovation, *Economic Geography*, 93: 106–30.

Los, B., P. McCann, J. Springford, and M. Thissen (2017), The Mismatch between Local Voting and the Local Economic Consequences of Brexit, *Regional Studies*, 51(5): 786–800.

Marshall, A. (1920[1891]), *Principles of Economics*, 8th edition, MacMillan, London.

Melo, P., D. Graham, and R. Noland (2009), A Meta-Analysis of Estimates of Urban Agglomeration Economies, *Regional Science and Urban Economics*, 39(3): 332–42.

Moretti, E. (2012), *The New Geography of Jobs*, Houghton Mifflin Harcourt, New York.

Partridge, M. (2010), The Duelling Models: NEG vs Amenity Migration in Explaining US Engines of Growth. *Papers in Regional Science*, 89(3): 513–36.

Rappaport, J. (2006), Moving to Nice Weather, Working Paper, Research Division, Federal Reserve Bank of Kansas City.

Redding, S. J., and D. M. Sturm (2016), *Estimating Neighborhood Effects: Evidence from War-Time Destruction in London*, mimeo, see http://www .princeton.edu/~reddings/papers/ LWW2-9Mar16.pdf.

Rentfrow, P. J., S. D. Gosling, and J. Potter (2008), A Theory of the Emergence, Persistence, and Expression of Geographic Variation in Psychological Characteristics, *Perspectives on Psychological Science*, 3: 339–69.

Rentfrow, P. J., M. Jokela, and M. E. Lamb (2015), Regional Personality Differences in Great Britain, *PLOS ONE*, 10(3): e0122245.

Roback, J. (1982), Wages, Rents, and the Quality of Life, *Journal of Political Economy*, 90: 1257–78.

Rosenthal, S. S., and W. C. Strange (2004), Evidence on the Nature and Sources of Agglomeration Economics, in: J. V. Henderson and J.-F. Thisse (eds.), *Handbook of Regional and Urban Economics*, Vol. 4, Elsevier (North Holland), Amsterdam.

Stuetzer, M., D. B. Audretsch, M. Obschonka, S. D. Gosling, P. J. Rentfrow, and J. Potter (2018), Entrepreneurship Culture, Knowledge Spillovers and the Growth of Regions, *Regional Studies*, 52(5): 603–18.

Stuetzer, M., M. Obschonka, D. B. Audretsch, M. Wyrwich, P. J. Rentfrow, M. Coombes, L. Shaw-Taylor, and M. Satchell (2016), Industry Structure, Culture, and Entrepreneurship. An Empirical Assessment Using Historical Coalfields, *European Economic Review*, 86: 52–72.

Thünen, J. H. von (1826), *Der Isolierte Staat in Beziehung auf Landwirtschaft und Nationalökonomie*, Perthes, Hamburg.

Chapter 7 References

Anderson, J., and E. van Wincoop (2004), Trade Costs, *Journal of Economics Literature*, 42: 691–751.

Baldwin, R. (1999), The Core–Periphery Model with Forward-looking Expectations, Working Paper, no. 6921, National Bureau of Economic Research, Cambridge, MA.

Brakman, S., H. Garretsen, and C. van Marrewijk (2009), *The New Introduction to Geographical Economics*, Cambridge University Press, Cambridge, UK.

Brakman, S., and B. J. Heijdra (eds.) (2004), *The Monopolistic Competition Revolution in Retrospect*, Cambridge University Press, Cambridge, UK.

Brakman, S., and C. van Marrewijk (1998), *The Economics of International Transfers*, Cambridge University Press, Cambridge, UK.

David, P. (1985), Clio and the Econometrics of QWERTY, *American Economic Review Papers and Proceedings*, 75: 332–7.

Disdier, A.-C., and K. Head (2008), The Puzzling Persistence of the Distance Effect on Bilateral Trade, *Review of Economics and Statistics*, 90: 37–41.

Dixit, A., and J. Stiglitz (1977), Monopolistic Competition and Optimum Product Diversity, *American Economic Review*, 67: 297–308.

Donaldson, D. (2018), Railroads of the Raj: Estimating the Impact of Transportation Infrastructure, *American Economic Review*, 108(4–5): 899–934.

Feenstra, R. C. (2016), *Advanced International Trade: Theory and Evidence*, Princeton University Press, Princeton.

Fujita, M., P. R. Krugman, and A. J. Venables (1999), *The Spatial Economy: Cities, Regions, and International Trade*, MIT Press, Cambridge, MA.

Fujita, M., and J.-F. Thisse (2013), *Economics of Agglomeration: Cities, Industrial Location, and Globalization*, Cambridge University Press, Cambridge, UK.

Harris, T. F., and Y. M. Ioannides (2000), *History versus Expectations: an Empirical Investigation*, Discussion Paper 200014, Department of Economics, Tufts University.

Head, K., and T. Mayer (2014), Gravity Equations: Workhorse, Toolkit, and Cookbook, in: G. Gopinath, E. Helpman, and K. Rogoff (eds.), *Handbook of International Economics*, Vol. 4, Elsevier (North Holland), Amsterdam.

Krugman, P. R. (1979), Increasing Returns, Monopolistic Competition, and International Trade, *Journal of International Economics*, 9: 469–79.

Krugman, P. R. (1980), Scale Economics, Product Differentiation, and Pattern of Trade, *American Economic Review*, 70: 950–59.

Krugman, P. R. (1991), Increasing Returns and Economic Geography, *Journal of Political Economy*, 99: 483–99.

Krugman, P. R. (1999), *Was it All in Ohlin?*, mimeo, MIT, Cambridge, MA. See http://web.mit.edu/krugman/www/ohlin.html.

McCallum, J. (1995), National Borders Matter: Canada–US Regional Trade Patterns, *American Economic Review*, 85: 615–23.

Melitz, M. J. (2003), The Impact of Trade on Intra-industry Reallocation and Aggregate Industry Productivity, *Econometrica*, 71: 1695–1725.

Neary, J. P. (2001), Of Hype and Hyperbolas: Introducing the New Economic Geography, *Journal of Economic Literature*, 39: 536–61.

Neary, J. P. (2004), Monopolistic Competition and International Trade Theory, in S. Brakman and B. J. Heijdra (eds.), *The Monopolistic Competition Revolution in Retrospect*, Cambridge University Press, Cambridge, UK.

Puga, D. (1999), The Rise and Fall of Regional Inequalities, *European Economic Review*, 43: 303–34.

Radelet, S., and J. Sachs (1998), *Shipping Costs, Manufactured Exports, and Economic Growth*, mimeo, Harvard.

Redding, S., and E. Rossi-Hansberg (2017), Quantitative Spatial Economics, *Annual Review of Economics*, 9(1): 21–58.

Redding, S. J., and M. A. Turner (2015), Transportation Costs and the Spatial Organization of Economic Activity, in: G. Duranton, J. V. Henderson, and W. Strange (eds.), *Handbook of Regional and Urban Economics*, Vol. 5, Elsevier (North Holland), Amsterdam.

Samuelson, P. A. (1952), The Transfer Problem and Transport Costs: The Terms of Trade When Impediments are Absent, *The Economic Journal*, 62: 278–304.

Schelling, T. C. (1978), *Micromotives and Macrobehavior*, Norton, New York.

Tirole, J. (1988), *The Theory of Industrial Organization*, MIT Press, Cambridge, MA.

Chapter 8 References

Ades, A., and E. L. Glaeser (1995), Trade and Circuses: Explaining Urban Giants,*Quarterly Journal of Economics*, 110: 195–228.

Baldwin, R. (2006), *Globalisation: The Great Unbundlings*, Prime Minister's Office-Economic Council of Finland.

Baldwin, R. (2016), *The Great Convergence: Information Technology and the New Globalization*, Belknap Press of Harvard University Press, Cambridge, MA.

Baldwin, R., R. Forslid, P. Martin, G. I. P. Ottaviano, and F. Robert-Nicoud (2003), *Economic Geography and Public Policy*, Princeton University Press, Princeton.

Behrens, K., and J. F. Thisse (2007), Regional Economics: A New Economic Geography Perspective, *Regional Science and Urban Economics*, 37: 457–65.

Black, D., and V. Henderson (1999), A Theory of Urban Growth, *Journal of Political Economy*, 107(2): 252–84.

Bosker, M., S. Brakman, H. Garretsen, and M. Schramm (2006), A Century of Shocks: The Evolution of the German City Size Distribution 1925–1999, *CESifo Working Paper* No. 1728.

Brakman, S., H. Garretsen, R. Gigengack, C. van Marrewijk, and R. Wagenvoort (1996), Negative Feedbacks in the Economy and Industrial Location, *Journal of Regional Science*, 36: 631–52.

Brakman, S., H. Garretsen, C. van Marrewijk, and M. Van Den Berg (1999), The Return of Zipf: Towards a Further Understanding of the Rank–Size Curve, *Journal of Regional Science*, 39: 183–215.

Carroll, G. (1982), National City-Size Distributions: What Do We Know After 67 Years of Research?, *Progress in Human Geography*, 6: 1–43.

Combes, P.-P., T. Mayer, and J.-F. Thisse (2008), *Economic Geography*, Princeton University Press, Princeton.

Córdoba, J.-C. (2008), On the Distribution of City Sizes, *Journal of Urban Economics*, 63(1): 177–97.

Crafts, N. F. R., and A. J. Venables (2003), Globalization in History: A Geographical Perspective, in: M. D. Bordo, A. M. Taylor, and J. G. Williamson (eds.), *Globalization in Historical Perspective*, University of Chicago Press, Chicago.

Dicken, P., and P. E. Lloyd (1990), *Location in Space*, Harper & Row, New York.

Dobkins, L. H., and Y. M. Ioannides (2001), Spatial Interactions Among US Cities, *Regional Science and Urban Economics*, 31: 701–31.

Duranton, G. (2006), Some Foundations for Zipf's Law: Product Proliferation and Local Spillovers, *Regional Science and Urban Economics*, 36(4): 543–63.

Eaton, J., and Z. Eckstein (1997), Cities and Growth: Theory and Evidence from France and Japan, *Regional Science and Urban Economics*, 27: 443–74.

Eeckhout, J. (2004), Gibrat's Law for All Cities, *The American Economic Review*, 94: 1429–51.

Forslid, R., and G. I. P. Ottaviano (2003), An Analytically Solvable Core-Periphery Model, *Journal of Economic Geography*, 3: 229–40.

Fujita, M., P. Krugman, and T. Mori (1999), On the Evolution of Hierarchial Urban Systems, *European Economic Review*, 43(2): 209–53.

Fujita, M., P. R. Krugman, and A. J. Venables (1999), *The Spatial Economy: Cities, Regions, and International Trade*, MIT Press, Cambridge, MA.

Fujita, M., and T. Mori (2005), Frontiers of the New Economic Geography, *Papers in Regional Science*, 84(3): 377–407.

Fujita, M., and J.-F. Thisse (2002), *Economics of Agglomeration: Cities, Regions, and International Trade*, MIT press, Cambridge, MA.

Fujita, M., and J.-F. Thisse (2013), *Economics of Agglomeration: Cities, Industrial Location, and Globalization*, Cambridge University Press, Cambridge, UK.

Gabaix, X. (1999a), Zipf's Law and the Growth of Cities, *American Economic Review, Papers and Proceedings*, 89: 129–32.

Gabaix, X. (1999b), Zipf's Law for Cities: an Explanation, *Quarterly Journal of Economics*, 114: 739–66.

Gabaix, X., and R. Ibragimov (2011), Rank-1/2: A Simple Way to Improve the OLS Estimation of Tail Exponents, *Journal of Business and Economics Statistics*, 29(1): 24–39.

Gabaix, X., and Y. M. Ioannides (2004), The Evolution of City Size Distributions, in: J. V. Henderson and J.-F. Thisse (eds.), *Handbook of Regional and Urban Economics*, Vol. 4, Elsevier (North Holland), Amsterdam.

Head, K., and T. Mayer (2004), The Empirics of Agglomeration and Trade, in J. V. Henderson and J.-F. Thisse (eds.), *Handbook of Regional and Urban Economics*, Vol. 4, Elsevier (North Holland), Amsterdam.

Helpman, E. (1998), The Size of Regions, in: D. Pines, E. Sadka, and I. Zilcha (eds.), *Topics in Public Economics*, Cambridge University Press, Cambridge, UK.

Henderson, J. V. (1974), The Sizes and Types of Cities, *American Economic Review*, 64: 640–56.

Kooij, P. (1988), Peripheral Cities and Their Regions in the Dutch Urban System until 1900, *Journal of Economic History*, 48: 357–71.

Kratz, M., and S. I. Resnick (1996), The QQ-Estimator and Heavy Tails, *Communications in Statistics. Stochastic Models*, 12: 699–724.

Krugman, P. R. (1991a), Increasing Returns and Economic Geography, *Journal of Political Economy*, 99: 483–99.

Krugman, P. R. (1991b), History Versus Expectations, *Quarterly Journal of Economics*, 106: 651–67.

Krugman, P. R. (1996a), *The Self-organizing Economy*, Blackwell, Oxford.

Krugman, P. R. (1996b), Confronting the Mystery of Urban Hierarchy, *Journal of the Japanese and International Economies*, 10: 399–418.

Krugman, P. R., and R. Livas Elizondo (1996), Trade Policy and Third World Metropolis, *Journal of Development Economics*, 49: 137–50.

Krugman, P. R., and A. J. Venables (1995), Globalization and the Inequality of Nations, *The Quarterly Journal of Economics*, 110: 857–80.

Nitsch, V. (2005), Zipf Zipped, *Journal of Urban Economics*, 57: 86–100.

Ottaviano, G. I. P. (2007), Models of 'New Economic Geography': Factor Mobility vs. Vertical Linkages, in: B. Fingleton (ed.), *New Directions in Economic Geography*, Edward Elgar, Cheltenham.

Ottaviano, G. I. P., and F. Robert-Nicoud (2006), The 'Genome' of NEG Models with Vertical Linkages: a Positive and Normative Synthesis, *Journal of Economic Geography*, 6: 113–39.

Ottaviano, G. I. P., T. Tabuchi, and J.-F. Thisse (2002), Agglomeration and Trade Revisited, *International Economic Review*, 43: 409–35.

Ottaviano, G. I. P., and J.-F. Thisse (2004), Agglomeration and Economic Geography, in: J. V. Henderson and J.-F. Thisse (eds.), *Handbook of Regional and Urban Economics*, Vol. 4, Elsevier (North Holland), Amsterdam.

Parr, J. B. (1985), A Note on the Size Distribution of Cities Over Time, *Journal of Urban Economics*, 18: 199–212.

Pflüger, M. (2004), A Simple, Analytically Solvable, Chamberlinian Agglomeration Model, *Regional Science and Urban Economics*, 34: 565–73.

Pflüger, M., and J. Südekum (2007), *On Pitchforks and Tomahawks*, IZA Discussion Paper 3258.

Pflüger, M., and J. Südekum (2008), A Synthesis of Footloose-Entrepreneur New Economic Geography Models:

When Is Agglomeration Smooth and Easily Reversible, *Journal of Economic Geography*, 8(1): 39–54.

Puga, D. (1998), Urbanization Patterns: European Versus Less Developed Countries, *Journal of Regional Science*, 38: 231–52.

Puga, D. (1999), The Rise and Fall of Regional Inequalities, *European Economic Review*, 43: 303–34.

Puga, D. (2002), European Regional Policy in light of Recent Location Theories, *Journal of Economic Geography*, 2(4): 372–406.

Redding, S., and A. J. Venables (2004), Economic Geography and International Inequality, *Journal of International Economics*, 62(1): 53–82.

Robert-Nicoud, F. (2005), The Structure of Simple New Economic Geography Models (or, On Identical Twins), *Journal of Economic Geography*, 5: 201–34.

Rossi-Hansberg, E., and M. L. J. Wright (2007), Urban Structure and Economic Growth, *Review of Economic Studies*, 74(2): 597–624.

Simon, H. (1955), On a Class of Skew Distribution Functions, *Biometrika*, 42(3–4): 425–40.

United Nations Population Division (2014), *World Urbanization Prospects: The 2014 Revision*, United Nations, New York.

United Nations Population Division (2016), *The World's Cities in 2016 – Data Booklet*, United Nations, New York (ST/ESA/ SER.A/392).

Venables, A. J. (1996), Equilibrium Locations of Vertically Linked Industries, *International Economic Review*, 37: 341–59.

Vries, J. de (1984), *European Urbanisation 1500–1800*, Methuen and Co, London.

Chapter 9 References

Ahlfeldt, G., S. Redding, D. Sturm, and N. Wolf (2015), The Economics of Density: Evidence from the Berlin Wall, *Econometrica*, 83(6): 2127–89.

Allen, T., and C. Arkolakis (2014), Trade and the Topography of the Spatial Economy, *Quarterly Journal of Economics*, 129: 1085–1140.

Allen, T., and D. Donaldson (2018), *The Geography of Path Dependence*, mimeo, MIT. See https://dave-donaldson.com/research/#tab-id-1.

Anderson, J., and E. van Wincoop (2004), Trade Costs, *Journal of Economics Literature*, 42: 691–751.

Baldwin, R., R. Forslid, P. Martin, G. I. P. Ottaviano, and F. Robert-Nicoud (2003), *Economic Geography and Public Policy*, Princeton University Press, Princeton.

Baldwin, R., and T. Okubo (2006), Heterogeneous Firms, Agglomeration and Economic Geography: Spatial Selection and Sorting, *Journal of Economic Geography*, 6: 323–46.

Baum-Snow, N., and F. Ferreira (2015), *Causal Inference in Urban and Regional Economics*, in: G. Duranton, J. V. Henderson, and W. Strange (eds.), *Handbook of Regional and Urban Economics*, Vol. 5, Elsevier (North Holland), Amsterdam.

Bayer, P., F. Ferreira, and R. McMillan (2007), A Unified Framework for Measuring Preferences for Schools and Neighborhoods, *Journal of Political Economy*, 115: 588–638.

Behrens, K., and F. Robert-Nicoud (2015), Agglomeration Theory with Heterogenous Agents, in: G. Duranton, J. V. Henderson, and W. Strange (eds.), *Handbook of Regional and Urban Economics*, Vol. 5, Elsevier (North Holland), Amsterdam.

Bernasek, A. (2005), Blueprints from Cities that Rose from Their Ashes, *New York Times*, 9 October.

Black, S. (1999), Do Better Schools Matter? Parental Valuation of Elementary Education, *Quarterly Journal of Economics*, 114: 577–99.

Bosker, E. M., S. Brakman, H. Garretsen, and M. Schramm (2007), Looking for Multiple Equilibria when Geography Matters: German City Growth and the WWII Shock, *Journal of Urban Economics*, 61: 152–69.

Bosker, E. M., S. Brakman, H. Garretsen, and M. Schramm (2008a), A Century of Shocks: The Evolution of the German City Size Distribution, *Regional Science and Urban Economics*, 38(July): 330–47.

Bosker, E. M., S. Brakman, H. Garretsen, H. de Jong, and M. Schramm (2008b), Ports, Plagues and Politics, Explaining Italian City Growth 1300–1861, *European Review of Economic History*, 12(1): 97–131.

Bosker, E. M., S. Brakman, H. Garretsen, and M. Schramm (2010), Adding Geography to the New Economic Geography, *Journal of Economic Geography*, 10(6): 793–823.

Bosker, E. M., and E. Buringh (2017), City Seeds: Geography and the Origins of European Cities, *Journal of Urban Economics*, 98: 139–57.

Bosker, E. M., Buringh, E., and J. L. van Zanden (2013), From Baghdad to London: Unravelling Urban Development in Europe and the Arab World 800–1800, *Review of Economics and Statistics*, 95–4: 1418–37.

Bosker E. M., and H. Garretsen (2010), Trade Costs and Empirical New Economic Geography, *Papers in Regional Science*, 89(3): 485–511.

Bosker E. M., and H. Garretsen (2012), Economic Geography and Economic Development in Sub-Saharan Africa, *World Bank Economic Review*, 26(3): 443–85.

Bosker, E. M, H. Garretsen, G. Marlet, and C. van Woerkens (2019), Nether Lands: Evidence on the Price and Perception of Rare Natural Disasters, *Journal of the European Economic Association*, 17(2): 413–53.

Brakman, S., H. Garretsen, and M. Schramm (2004a), The Spatial Distribution of Wages: Estimating the Helpman-Hanson Model for Germany, *Journal of Regional Science*, 44(3): 437–66.

Brakman, S, H. Garretsen, and M. Schramm (2004b), The Strategic Bombing of German Cities During WWII and its Impact on City Growth, *Journal of Economic Geography*, 4(2): 201–18.

Brakman S., H. Garretsen, and M. Schramm (2006), Putting New Economic Geography to the Test: Free-ness of Trade and Agglomeration in the EU Regions, *Regional Science and Urban Economics*, 36(5): 613–36.

Brakman, S., H. Garretsen, and C. van Marrewijk (2015), Regional Resilience Across Europe: On Urbanisation and the Initial Impact of the Great Recession, *Cambridge Journal of Regions, Economy and Society*, 8(2): 225–40.

Combes, P.-P., G. Duranton, and L. Gobillon (2008), Spatial Wage Disparities: Sorting Matters!, *Journal of Urban Economics*, 63: 723–42.

Combes, P.-P., G. Duranton, L. Gobillon, D. Puga, and S. Roux (2012), The Productivity Advantages of Large Cities: Distinguishing Agglomeration from Firm Selection, *Econometrica*, 80(6): 2543–94.

Combes, P.-P., G. Duranton, L. Gobillon, and S. Roux (2010), Estimating Agglomeration Economies with History, Geology, and Worker Effects, in: E. L. Glaeser (ed.), *Agglomeration Economics*, NBER, University of Chicago Press, Chicago.

Combes, P.-P., and L. Gobillon (2015), The Empirics of Agglomeration Economies, in: G. Duranton, J. V. Henderson, and W. Strange (eds.), *Handbook of Regional and Urban Economics*, Vol. 5, Elsevier (North Holland), Amsterdam.

Costinot, A., D. Donaldson, M. Kyle, and H. Williams (2016), *The More We Die, The More We Sell? A Simple Test of the Home Market Effect*, mimeo, MIT.

Crozet, M. (2004), Do Migrants Follow Market Potentials? An Estimation of a New Economic Geography Model, *Journal of Economic Geography*, 4: 439–58.

Dachis, B., G. Duranton, and M. A. Turner (2012), The Effects of Land Transfer Taxes on Real Estate Markets: Evidence from a Natural Experiment in Toronto, *Journal of Economic Geography*, 12(2): 327–54.

Davis, D. R. (1998), The Home Market, Trade and Industrial Structure, *American Economic Review*, 88: 1264–77.

Davis, D. R., and D. E. Weinstein (1996), *Does Economic Geography Matter for International Specialization?*, mimeo, Harvard University.

Davis, D. R., and D. E. Weinstein (1997), *Increasing Returns and International Trade: An Empirical Confirmation*, mimeo, Harvard University.

Davis, D. R., and D. E. Weinstein (1999), Economic Geography and Regional Production Structure: An Empirical Investigation, *European Economic Review*, 43(2): 379–407.

Davis, D. R., and D. E. Weinstein (2001), An Account of Global Factor Trade, *American Economic Review*, 19: 1423–53.

Davis, D. R., and D. E. Weinstein (2002), Bones, Bombs and Breakpoints: The Geography of Economic Activity, *American Economic Review*, 92: 1269–89.

Davis, D. R., and D. E. Weinstein (2003), Market Access. Economic Geography and Comparative Advantage: An Empirical Assessment, *Journal ofInternational Economics*, 59(1): 1–23.

Davis, D. R., and D. E. Weinstein (2008), A Search for Multiple Equilibria in Urban Industrial Structure, *Journal of Regional Science*, 48: 29–65.

De La Roca, J., and D. Puga (2017), Learning by Working in Big Cities, *Review Of Economic Studies*, 84: 106–42.

Donaldson, D. (2018), Railroads of the Raj: Estimating the Impact of Transportation Infrastructure, *American Economic Review*, 108(4–5): 899–934.

Donaldson, D., and R. Hornbeck (2016), Railroads and American Economic Growth: a 'Market Access' Approach, *Quarterly Journal of Economics*, 131(2): 799–858.

Duranton, G., and M. Turner (2012), Urban Growth and Transportation, *Review of Economic Studies*, 79(4): 1407–40.

Eaton, J., and S. Kortum (2002), Technology, Geography and Trade, *Econometrica*, 70: 1741–79.

Ellison, G., and E. L. Glaeser (1997), Geographic Concentration in U.S. Manufacturing Industries: A Dartboard Approach, *Journal of Political Economy*, 105: 889–927.

Ellison, G. and E. L. Glaeser (1999), The Geographic Concentration of Industry: Does Natural Advantage Explain Agglomeration?, *American Economic Review, Papers and Proceedings*, 89: 311–16.

Fingleton, B., H. Garretsen, and R. Martin (2012), Recessionary Shocks and Regional Employment: Evidence on the Resilience of UK Regions, *Journal of Regional Science*, 52(1): 109–33.

Fingleton, B., H. Garretsen, and R. Martin (2015), Shocking Aspects to Monetary Union, the Vulnerability of Euroland, *Journal of Economic Geography*, 15(5): 907–34.

Fujita, M., and T. Mori (2005), Frontiers of the New Economic Geography, *Papers in Regional Science*, 84(3): 377–407.

Garretsen, H., and R. Martin (2010), Towards More Credible (New) Economic Geography Models: Taking Geography and History Seriously, *Spatial Economic Analysis*, 5(2): 127–60.

Gibbons, S., S. Machin, and O. Silva (2013), Valuing School Quality Using Boundary Discontinuities, *Journal of Urban Economics*, 75: 12–28.

Glaeser, E. L., H. D. Kallal, J. Scheinkman, and A. Schleifer (1992), Growth in Cities, *Journal of Political Economy*, 100: 1126–52.

Glaeser E. L., and J. M. Shapiro (2002), Cities and Warfare, *Journal of Urban Economics*, 51: 205–24.

Hanson, G. H. (2005), Market Potential, Increasing Returns, and Geographic Concentration, *Journal of International Economics*, 67(1): 1–24.

Harris, C. (1954), The Market as a Factor in the Localization of Industry in the United States, *Annals of the Association of American Geographers*, 64: 315–48.

Head, K., and T. Mayer (2004), The Empirics of Agglomeration and Trade, in J. V. Henderson and J.-F. Thisse (eds.), *Handbook of Regional and Urban Economics*, Vol. 4, Elsevier (North Holland), Amsterdam.

Head, K., and T. Mayer (2006), Regional Wage and Employment Responses to Market Potential in the EU. *Regional Science and Urban Economics*, 36(5): 573–94.

Helpman, E. (1998), The Size of Regions, in: D. Pines, E. Sadka, and I. Zilcha (eds.), *Topics in Public Economics*, Cambridge University Press, Cambridge, UK.

Hering, L., and S. Poncet (2010), Market Access and Individual Wages:

Evidence from China, *The Review of Economics and Statistics*, 92(1): 145–59.

Holmes, T. J., and H. Sieg (2015), Structural Estimation in Urban Economics, in: G. Duranton, J. V. Henderson, and W. Strange (eds.), *Handbook of Regional and Urban Economics*, Vol. 5, Elsevier (North Holland), Amsterdam.

Krugman, P. R. (1980), Scale Economics, Product Differentiation, and Pattern of Trade, *American Economic Review*, 70: 950–59.

Krugman, P. R. (1991), Increasing Returns and Economic Geography, *Journal of Political Economy*, 99: 483–99.

Krugman, P. R. (2001), An Injured City, *New York Times*, 3 October.

Krugman, P. R. (2011), The New Economic Geography, Now Middle-aged, *Regional Studies*, 45(1): 1–7.

Krugman, P. R., and A. J. Venables (1995), Globalization and the Inequality of Nations, *The Quarterly Journal of Economics*, 110: 857–80.

Malanima, P. (1998), Italian Cities 1300–1800. A quantitative approach, *Rivista di Storia Economica*, 14(2): 91–126.

Matsuyama, K. (2015), *The Home Market Effect and Patterns of Trade Between Rich and Poor Countries*, mimeo, Northwestern University.

Miguel, E., and G. Roland (2011), The Long Run Impact of Bombing Vietnam, *Journal of Development Economics*, 96(1): 1–15.

Neary, J. P. (2001), Of Hype and Hyperbolas: Introducing the New Economic Geography, *Journal of Economic Literature*, 39: 536–61.

Puga, D. (1999), The Rise and Fall of Regional Inequalities, *European Economic Review*, 43: 303–34.

Puga, D. (2002), European Regional Policy in Light of Recent Location Theories, *Journal of Economic Geography*, 2(4): 372–406.

Redding, S., and E. Rossi-Hansberg (2016), Quantitative Spatial Economics: A Framework for Evaluating Regional Policy and Shock in the Real World, *VOX EU*, 27 October. See https://voxeu.org/article/evaluating-regional-policy-and-shocks-real-world.

Redding, S., and E. Rossi-Hansberg (2017), Quantitative Spatial Economics, *Annual Review of Economics*, 9(1): 21–58.

Redding, S., and D. M. Sturm (2008), Costs of Remoteness: Evidence from German Division and Reunification, *American Economic Review*, 98(5): 1766–97.

Redding, S., D. M. Sturm, and N. Wolf (2011), History and Industry Location: Evidence from German Airports, *Review of Economics and Statistics*, 93(3): 814–31.

Redding, S., and A. J. Venables (2004), Economic Geography and International Inequality, *Journal of International Economics*, 62(1): 53–82.

Rossi-Hansberg, E. (2019), Geography of Growth and Development, *Oxford Research Encyclopedia of Economics and Finance*. https://oxfordre.com/economics/view/10.1093/acrefore/9780190625979.001.0001/acrefore-9780190625979-e-273, accessed on 16 August 2019.

Stelder, D. (2005), A Geographical Agglomeration Model for Europe, *Journal of Regional Science*, 45: 657–79.

Thomas, A. (1996), *Increasing Returns, Congestion Costs and the Geographic Concentration of Firms*, mimeo, International Monetary Fund, Washington.

Thünen, J. H. von (1826), *Der Isolierte Staat in Beziehung auf Landwirtschaft und Nationalökonomie*, Perthes, Hamburg.

Venables, A. J. (1996), Equilibrium Locations of Vertically Linked Industries, *International Economic Review*, 37: 341–59.

World Risk Report (2014), United Nations University – Institute for Environment and Human Security and Bündnis Entwicklung Hilft.

Chapter 10 References

Acemoglu, D., S. Johnson, and J. Robinson (2001), The Colonial Origins of Comparative Development: An Empirical Investigation, *American Economic Review*, 91(5): 1369–1401.

Acemoglu, D., S. Johnson, and J. Robinson (2002), Reversal of Fortune: Geography and Institutions in the Making of the Modern World Income Distribution, *Quarterly Journal of Economics*, 117(4): 1231–94.

Acemoglu, D., and J. Robinson (2012), *Why Nations Fail: Origins of Power, Poverty and Prosperity*, Crown Publishers, New York.

Ades, A., and H. B. Chua (1997), Thy Neighbor's Curse: Regional Instability and Economic Growth, *Journal of Economic Growth*, 2: 279–304.

Anderson, J., and E. van Wincoop (2004), Trade Costs, *Journal of Economic Literature*, 42: 691–751.

Au, C.-C., and J. V. Henderson (2006a), Are Chinese Cities Too Small?, *Review of Economic Studies*, 73: 549–76.

Au, C.-C., and J. V. Henderson (2006b), How Migration Restrictions Limit Agglomeration and Productivity in China, *Journal of Development Economics*, 80: 350–88.

Baldwin, R. (2016), *The Great Convergence: Information Technology and the New Globalization*, Belknap Press of Harvard University Press, Cambridge, MA.

Baldwin, R. E., and R. Forslid (2000), The Core–Periphery Model and Endogenous Growth: Stabilizing and Destabilizing Integration, *Economica*, 67: 307–24.

Baldwin, R., and P. Martin (2004), Agglomeration and Regional Growth, in: J. V. Henderson and J.-F. Thisse (eds.), *Handbook of Regional and Urban Economics*, Vol. 4, Elsevier (North Holland), Amsterdam.

Baldwin, R., P. Martin, and G. I. P. Ottaviano (2001), Global Income Divergence, Trade and Industrialization: The Geography of Growth Take-offs, *Journal of Economic Growth*, 6: 5–37.

Barro, R., and X. Sala-i-Martin (2004), *Economic Growth*, 2nd edition, MIT Press, Cambridge, MA.

Baum-Snow, N., L. Brandt, J. V. Henderson, M. A. Turner, and Q. Zhang (2017), Roads, Railroads and Decentralization of Chinese Cities, *Review of Economics and Statistics*, 99(3): 435–48.

Bosker, E. M., S. Brakman, H. Garretsen, H, de Jong, and M. Schramm (2008), Ports, Plagues and Politics, Explaining Italian City Growth 1300–1861, *European Review of Economic History*, 12(1): 97–131.

Bosker, E. M., S. Brakman, H. Garretsen, and M. Schramm (2012), Relaxing Hukou: Increased Labour Mobility and China's Economic Geography, *Journal of Urban Economics*, 72: 252–66.

Bosker, E. M., E. Buringh, and J. L. van Zanden (2013), From Baghdad to London: Unravelling Urban Development in Europe and the Arab World 800–1800, *Review of Economics and Statistics*, 95(4): 1418–37.

Bosker, E. M., U. Deichmann, and M. Roberts (2018), Hukou and Highways: The Impact of China's Spatial Development Policies on Urbanization and Regional Inequality, *Regional Science and Urban Economics*, 71: 91–109.

Bosker, E. M., and H. Garretsen (2009), Economic Development and the Geography of Institutions, *Journal of Economic Geography*, 9: 295–328.

Bosker, E. M., and H. Garretsen (2012), Economic Geography and Economic Development in Sub-Saharan Africa, *World Bank Economic Review*, 26(3): 443–85.

Brakman, S., H. Garretsen, and C. van Marrewijk (2016), Urban Development in China, *Cambridge Journal of Regions, Economy, and Society*, 9: 467–77.

Brakman, S., and C. van Marrewijk (2008), It's a Big World after All, *Cambridge Journal of the Regions, Economy and Society*, 1(3): 411–37.

Breinlich, H. (2006), The Spatial Income Structure in the European Union – What Role for Economic Geography?, *Journal of Economic Geography*, 6: 593–617.

Breinlich, H., G. Ottaviano, and J. R. W. Temple (2013), Regional Growth and Regional Decline, in: P. Aghion and S. Durlauf (eds.), *Handbook of Economic Growth*, vol. 2, Elsevier, Amsterdam.

Chan, K. W., and W. Buckingham (2008), Is China Abolishing the Hukou System?, *The China Quarterly*, 195: 582–606.

Desmet. K., D. K. Nagy, and E. Rossi-Hansberg (2018), The Geography of Development, *Journal of Political Economy*, 126: 903–83.

Easterly, W., and R. Levine (1998), Trouble with the Neighbours: Africa's Problem, Africa's Opportunity, *Journal of African Economics*, 7: 120–42.

Easterly, W., and R. Levine (2003), Tropics, Germs and Crops: How Endowments Influence Economic Development, *Journal of Monetary Economics*, 50: 3–40.

Eaton, J., and S. Kortum (1996), Trade in Ideas Patenting and Productivity in the OECD, *Journal of International Economics*, 40: 251–78.

Faber, B. (2014), Trade Integration, Market Size, and Industrialization: Evidence from China's National Trunk Highway System, *Review of Economic Studies*, 81(3): 1046–70.

Frick, S. A., and A. Rodríguez-Pose (2018), Big or Small Cities?: On City Size and Economic Growth, *Growth and Change*, 49(1): 4–32.

Giannone, E. (2018) Skill-Biased Technical Change and Regional Convergence, working paper, University of Pennsylvania. See https://sites.google.com/view/elisagiannone/research.

Glaeser, E. L., and J. V. Henderson (2017), Urbanization for the Developing World: An Introduction, *Journal of Urban Economics*, 98: 1–5.

Grossman, G. M., and E. Helpman (1991), *Innovation and Growth in the Global Economy*, MIT Press, Cambridge, MA.

Hall, R., and C. I. Jones (1999), Why Do Some Countries Produce So Much More Output Per Worker Than Others?, *Quarterly Journal of Economics*, 114: 83–116.

Hanson, G. H. (2005), Market Potential, Increasing Returns, and Geographic Concentration, *Journal of International Economics*, 67(1): 1–24.

Harris, J., and M. P. Todaro (1970), Migration, Unemployment & Development: A Two-Sector Analysis, *American Economic Review*, 60(1): 126–42.

Helpman, E. (2004), *The Mystery of Economic Growth*, Belknap Press, Cambridge, MA.

Helpman, E., M. Melitz, and Y. Rubinstein (2008), Estimating Trade Flows: Trading Partners and Trading Volumes, *The Quarterly Journal of Economics*, 123(2): 441–87.

Henderson, J. V. (2003), The Urbanization Process and Economic Growth: The So-what Question, *Journal of Economic Growth*, 8: 47–71.

Henderson, J. V. (2009), Cities and Development, *Journal of Regional Science*, 50: 515–40.

Henderson, V., T. Squires, A. Storeygard, and D. Weil (2018), The Global Distribution of Economic Activity:

Nature, History, and the Role of Trade, *Quarterly Journal of Economics*, 133(1): 357–406.

Krugman, P. R. (2011), The New Economic Geography, Now Middle-Aged, *Regional Studies*, 45: 1–7.

Krugman, P. R., and A. J. Venables (1995), Globalization and the Inequality of Nations, *The Quarterly Journal of Economics*, 110: 857–80.

Lakner, C., and B. Milanovic (2016), Global Income Distribution: From the Fall of the Berlin Wall to the Great Recession, *The World Bank Economic Review*, 30(2): 203–32.

Lucas, R. E. (1988), On the Mechanisms of Economic Development, *Journal of Monetary Economics*, 22: 3–42.

Maddison, A. (2007), *Contours of the World Economy 1–2030 AD: Essays in Macroeconomic History*, Oxford University Press, Oxford.

Malanima, P. (1998), Italian Cities 1300–1800. A quantitative approach, *Rivista di Storia Economica*, 14(2): 91–126.

Malanima, P. (2005), Urbanisation and the Italian Economy During the Last Millenium, *European Review of Economic History*, 9(1): 97–122.

Marrewijk, C. van (1999), Capital Accumulation, Learning and Endogenous Growth, *Oxford University Papers*, 51: 453–75.

Marrewijk, C. van (2012), *International Economics: Theory, Application and Policy*, Oxford University Press, Oxford.

Marrewijk, C. van (2017), *International Trade*, Oxford University Press, Oxford.

Milanovic, B. (2006a), Economic Integration and Income Convergence:

Not Such a Strong Link?, *Review of Economics and Statistics*, 88: 659–70.

Milanovic, B. (2006b), *Global Income Inequality: What It Is and Why It Matters*, Policy Research Working Paper no. 3865, World Bank, Washington, DC.

Milanovic, B. (2016), *Global Inequality: A New Approach for the Age of Globalization*, Harvard University Press, Cambridge, MA.

Moretti, E. (2012), *The New Geography of Jobs*, Houghton Mifflin Harcourt, New York.

Murdoch, J. C., and T. Sandler (2002), Economic Growth, Civil Wars and Spatial Spillovers, *Journal of Conflict Resolution*, 46(1): 91–110.

Nunn, N., and Puga, D. (2012), Ruggedness: The Blessing of Bad Geography in Africa, *Review of Economics and Statistics*, 94(1): 20–36.

Poncet, S. (2006), Provincial Migration Dynamics in China: Borders, Costs and Economic Motivations, *Regional Science and Urban Economics*, 36: 385–98.

Puga, D. (1999), The Rise and Fall of Regional Inequalities, *European Economic Review*, 43: 303–34.

Puga, D., and A. J. Venables (1996), The Spread of Industry: Spatial Agglomeration in Economic Development, *Journal of the Japanese and International Economics*, 10: 440–64.

Redding, S., and A. J. Venables (2004), Economic Geography and International Inequality, *Journal of International Economics*, 62(1): 53–82.

Roberts, M., U. Deichmann, B. Fingleton, and T. Shi (2010), *The Impact of Infrastructure on Economic Development: Using the New Economic Geography to Evaluate China's Highway Expansion*, mimeo, University of Cambridge/World Bank.

Rodríguez-Pose, A. (2018), The Revenge of the Places that Don't Matter, *VOX EU*, 6 February, https://voxeu.org/article/revenge-places-dont-matter.

Rodrik, D., A. Subramanian, and F. Trebbi (2004), Institutions Rule: The Primacy of Institutions and Integration in Economic Development, *Journal of Economic Growth*, 9: 131–65.

Romer, P. M. (1990), Endogenous Technological Change, *Journal of Political Economy*, 98(5), part 2: S71–S101.

Rossi-Hansberg, E. (2019), Geography of Growth and Development, *Oxford Research Encyclopedia of Economics and Finance*. https://oxfordre.com/economics/view/10.1093/acrefore/9780190625979.001.0001/acrefore-9780190625979-e-273, accessed on 16 August 2019.

Rougoor, W., and C. van Marrewijk (2015), Demography, Growth, and Global Income Inequality, *World Development*, 74: 220–32.

Sachs, J. D. (2003), Institutions Don't Rule: Direct Effects of Geography on Per Capita Income, NBER Working Paper 9490, Cambridge, MA.

Sala-i-Martin, X. (2006), The World Distribution of Income: Falling Poverty and ... Convergence, Period, *Quarterly Journal of Economics*, 121: 351–97.

Santos Silva, J. M. C., and S. Tenreyro (2006), The Log of Gravity, *The Review of Economics and Statistics*, 88: 641–58.

Simmons, B. A., and Z. Elkins (2004), The Globalization of Liberalization: Policy Diffusion in the International Political Economy, *American Political Science Review*, 98(1): 171–89.

Spence, M., P. Clarke Annez, and R. Buckley (eds.) (2009), *Urbanization and Growth*, World Bank, Washington, DC.

Spolaore, E., and R. Wacziarg (2013), How Deep Are the Roots of Economic Development?, *Journal of Economic Literature*, 51(2): 325–69.

Whalley, J., and S. Zhang (2007), A Numerical Simulation Analysis of (Hukou) Labour Mobility Restrictions in China, *Journal of Development Economics*, 83: 392–410.

World Bank (2009), *World Development Report 2009*, Washington.

Zhang, J., and Z. Zhao (2011), *Measuring the Income–Distance Trade-off for Rural–Urban Migrants in China*, mimeo, Clark University USA.

Chapter 11 References

Ahlfeldt, G., and E. Pietrostefani (2017), The Economic Effects of Density: A Synthesis, *SERC Discussion paper*, no. 210.

Austin, B. A., E. L. Glaeser, and L. H. Summers (2018), Jobs for the Heartland, Place-Based Policies on 21st Century America, NBER Working Paper, no. 24548, Cambridge, MA.

Baldwin, R. (2016), *The Great Convergence: Information Technology and the New Globalization*, Belknap Press of Harvard University Press, Cambridge, MA.

Baldwin, R., Forslid, P. Martin, G. I. P. Ottaviano, and F. Robert-Nicoud (2003), *Economic Geography and Public Policy*, Princeton University Press, Princeton.

Baldwin, R., and P. R. Krugman (2004), Agglomeration, Integration and Tax Harmonization, *European Economic Review*, 48: 1–23.

Baldwin, R., and F. Robert-Nicoud (2007), Entry and Asymmetric Lobbying: Why Governments Pick Losers, *Journal of the European Economic Association*, 5(5): 1064–93.

Barba-Navaretti, G., and A. J. Venables (2004), *Multinationals in the World Economy*, Princeton University Press, Princeton.

Barca, F., P. McCann, and A. Rodríguez-Pose (2012), The Case for Regional Development Intervention: Place-based versus Place-neutral Approaches, *Journal of Regional Science*, 52(1): 134–52.

Baum-Snow, N., L. Brandt, J. V. Henderson, M. A. Turner, and Q. Zhang (2017), Roads, Railroads and Decentralization of Chinese Cities, *Review of Economics and Statistics*, 99(3): 435–48.

Bhagwati, J. (1982), Directly-Unproductive, Profit-Seeking (DUP) Activities, *Journal of Political Economy*, 90: 988–1002.

Bosker, E. M., S. Brakman, H. Garretsen, and M. Schramm (2012), Relaxing Hukou: Increased Labour Mobility and China's Economic Geography, *Journal of Urban Economics*, 72: 252–66.

Bosker, E. M., and H. Garretsen (2012), Economic Geography and Economic

Development in Sub-Saharan Africa, *World Bank Economic Review*, 26(3): 443–85.

Brakman, S., H. Garretsen, and C. van Marrewijk (2008), Agglomeration and Government Spending, in: S. Brakman and H. Garretsen (eds.), *Foreign Direct Investment and the Multinational Enterprise*, MIT Press, Cambridge, MA.

Brakman, S., H. Garretsen, and C. van Marrewijk (2011), References Across the Fence: Measuring the Dialogue Between Economists and Geographers, *Journal of Economic Geography*, 11(2): 371–85.

Brakman, S., and C. van Marrewijk (2013), Reflections on Cluster Policies, *Cambridge Journal of Regions, Economy and Society*, 6: 217–31.

Brülhart, M., S. Bucovetsky, and K. Schmidheiny (2015), Taxes in Cities, in: G. Duranton, J. V. Henderson, and W. Strange (eds.), *Handbook of Regional and Urban Economics*, Vol. 5, Elsevier (North Holland), Amsterdam.

Brülhart, M., M. Jametti, and K. Schmidheiny (2012), Do Agglomeration Economies Reduce the Sensitivity of Firm Location to Tax Differentials?, *Economic Journal*, 122(563): 1069–93.

Combes, P.-P., and L. Gobillon (2015), The Empirics of Agglomeration Economics, in: G. Duranton, J. V. Henderson, and W. Strange (eds.), *Handbook of Regional and Urban Economics*, Vol. 5, Elsevier (North Holland), Amsterdam.

Criscuolo C., R. Martin, H. Overman, and J. Van Reenen (2012), The Causal effects of an Industrial Policy, NBER Working Paper 17842, Cambridge, MA.

Criscuolo C., R. Martin, H. Overman, and J. Van Reenen (2019). Some Causal Effects of an Industrial Policy, *American Economic Review*, 109(1): 48–85.

Crouch, C., and H. Farrell (2001), Great Brittan: Falling Through the Holes in the Network Concept, in: C. Crouch, P. Le Gales, C. Trogilia, and H. Voelzkow (eds.), *Local Production System in Europe: Rise or Demise?*, Oxford University Press, Oxford.

Dachis, B., G. Duranton, and M. A. Turner (2012), The Effects of Land Transfer Taxes on Real Estate Markets: Evidence from a Natural Experiment in Toronto, *Journal of Economic Geography*, 12(2): 327–54.

Desmet, K., D. K. Nagy, and E. Rossi-Hansberg (2018), The Geography of Development, *Journal of Political Economy*, 126: 903–83.

Donaldson, D. (2018), Railroads of the Raj: Estimating the Impact of Transportation Infrastructure, *American Economic Review*, 108(4–5): 899–934.

Donaldson, D., and R. Hornbeck (2016), Railroads and American Economic Growth: a 'Market Access' Approach, *Quarterly Journal of Economics*, 131(2): 799–858.

Duranton, G. (2007), Urban Evolutions: The Fast, the Slow, and the Still. *American Economic Review*, 97(1): 197–221.

Duranton, G. (2011), California Dreamin': The Feeble Case for Cluster Policies, *Review of Economic Analysis*, 3: 3–45.

Duranton, G., and D. Puga (2004), Micro-foundations of Urban Agglomeration Economies, in: J. V. Henderson and J.-F. Thisse (eds.), *Handbook of Regional and Urban Economics*, Vol. 4, Elsevier (North Holland), Amsterdam.

Duranton, G., and A. Rodríguez-Pose (2005), Guest Editorial, *Environment and Planning A*, 37: 1695–1705.

ECPG (2010), *European Cluster Policy Group: Final Recommendations – A Call for Policy Action*, Brussels.

European Commission (2003), *Final Report of the Expert Group on Enterprise Clusters and Networks*, European Commission, Brussels.

Faber, B. (2014), Trade Integration, Market Size, And Industrialization: Evidence From China's National Trunk Highway System, *Review of Economic Studies*, 81(3): 1046–70.

Feser, E. J. (1998), Old and New Theories of Industrial Clusters, in: M. Steiner (ed.), *Clusters and Regional Specialization: On Geography, Technology and Networks*, Pion, London.

Fujita, M., P. R. Krugman, and A. J. Venables (1999), *The Spatial Economy: Cities, Regions, and International Trade*, MIT Press, Cambridge, MA.

Gardiner, B., R. Martin, and P. Tyler (2010), Does Spatial Agglomeration Increase National Growth? Some Evidence from Europe, *Journal of Economic Geography*, 11(6): 979–1006.

Garretsen, H., and G. Marlet (2017), Amenities and the Attraction of Dutch Cities, *Regional Studies*, 51(5): 724–37.

Gaubert, C. (2018), Firm Sorting and Agglomeration, *American Economic Review*, 108 (11): 3117–53.

Glaeser, E. L. (2005), Reinventing Boston: 1630–2003, *Journal of Economic Geography*, 5: 119–53.

Glaeser, E. L. (2008), Cities, Agglomeration, and Spatial Equilibrium, Oxford University Press, Oxford.

Glaeser, E. L. (2011a), Which Places are Growing? Seven Notable Trends from Newly Released Census Data, Harvard Kennedy School Policy Briefs, March, Boston.

Glaeser, E. L. (2011b), *Triumph of the City*, MacMillan, London.

Glaeser, E. L., and J. D. Gottlieb (2008), The Economics of Place-Making Policies, *Brookings Papers on Economic Activity*, Spring 2008: 155–239.

Greenstone M., R. Hornbeck, and E. Moretti (2010), Identifying Agglomeration Spillovers: Evidence from Winners and Losers of Large Plant Openings, *Journal of Political Economy*, 118(3): 536–98.

Heblich, S., S. J. Redding, and D. M. Sturm (2018), *The Making of the Modern Metropolis: Evidence from London*, CEPR Discussion Paper 13170, London.

Hellerstein, J. K., M. Kutzbach, and D. Neumark (2014), Do Labor Market Networks Have an Important Spatial Dimension, *Journal of Urban Economics*, 79: 39–58.

Hoogendoorn, S., J. van Gemeren, P. Verstraten, and K. Folmer (2019), House Prices and Accessibility: Evidence from a Quasi-experiment in Transport Infrastructure, *Journal of Economic Geography*, 19(1): 57–87.

Iammarino, S., A. Rodríguez-Pose, and M. Storper (2017), Why regional development matters for Europe's economic future, European Commission, DG Regional and Urban Policy, working paper 07/2017.

Kline, P., and E. Moretti (2014a), People, Places, and Public Policy: Some Simple Welfare Economics of Local

Economic Development Policies, *Annual Review of Economics*, 6: 629–62.

Kline, P., and E. Moretti (2014b), Local Economic Development, Agglomeration Economies and the Big Push: 100 years of Evidence from the Tennessee Valley Authority, *The Quarterly Journal of Economics*, 129: 275–331.

Krugman, P. R. (1991), Increasing Returns and Economic Geography, *Journal of Political Economy*, 99: 483–99.

Krugman, P. R. (2011), The New Economic Geography, Now Middle-aged, *Regional Studies*, 45(1): 1–7.

Leslie, S. W., and R. H. Kargon (1996), Selling Silicon Valley: Frederick Terman's Model for Regional Advantage, *Business History Review*, 70(2): 435–82.

Lorenzen, M., and R. Mudambi (2013), Clusters, Connectivity and Catch-up: Bollywood and Bangalore in the Global Economy, *Journal of Economic Geography*, 13(3): 501–34.

Marshall, A. (1890), *Principles of Economics*, Macmillan, London.

Martin, R. (1999), The 'New' Geographical Turn in Economics, Some Critical Remarks, *Cambridge Journal of Economics*, 23: 65–91.

Martin, R. (2008), The 'New Economic Geography': Credible Models of the Economic Landscape?, in: R. Lee, A. Leyshon, L. McDowell, and P. Sunley (eds.), *A Compendium of Economic Geography*, Sage, London.

Martin, R., and P. Sunley (2003), Deconstructing Clusters: Chaotic Concept or Policy Panacea, *Journal of Economic Geography*, 3(1): 5–35.

Melo, P., D. J. Graham, and R. B. Noland (2009), A Meta-Analysis of Estimates of Urban Agglomeration Economies, *Regional Science and Urban Economics*, 39: 332–42.

Menzel, M.-P., and D. Fornahl (2009), Cluster Life Cycles – Dimension and Rationales of Cluster Evolution, *Industrial and Corporate Change*, 19: 205–38.

Moretti, E. (2010), Local Labor Markets, in: D. Card and O. Ashenfelder (eds.), *Handbook of Labor Economics*, Vol. 4b, Elsevier (North Holland), Amsterdam.

Neary, J. P. (2001), Of Hype and Hyperbolas: Introducing the New Economic Geography, *Journal of Economic Literature*, 39: 536–61.

Neumark, D., and J. Kolko (2010), Do Enterprise Zones Create Jobs? Evidence from California's Enterprise Zone Program, *Journal of Urban Economics*, 68: 1–19.

Neumark, D., and H. Simpson (2015), Place-based Policies, in: G. Duranton, J. V. Henderson, and W. Strange (eds.), *Handbook of Regional and Urban Economics*, Vol. 5, Elsevier (North Holland), Amsterdam.

Ottaviano, G. I. P. (2003), Regional Policy in the Global Economy: Insights from the New Economic Geography, *Regional Studies*, 37(6–7): 665–73.

Porter, M. E. (1990), *The Competitive Advantage of Nations*, Free Press, New York.

Porter, M. E. (1998), Clusters and the New Economics of Competition, *Harvard Business Review*, 76(6): 77–91.

Porter, M. E. (2000a), Location, Competition, and Economic

Development: Local Clusters in a Global Economy, *Economic Development Quarterly*, 14(1): 15–34.

Porter, M. E. (2000b), Locations, Clusters, and Company Strategy, in: G. L. Clark, M. P. Feldman, and M. S. Gertler (eds.), *The Oxford Handbook of Economic Geography*, Oxford University Press, New York.

Prager, J.-C., and J.-F. Thisse (2012), *Economic Geography and the Unequal Development of Regions*, Routledge, London.

Redding, S., and E. Rossi-Hansberg (2016), Quantitative Spatial Economics: A Framework for Evaluating Regional Policy and Shock in the Real World, *VOX EU*, 27 October. See https://voxeu.org/article/evaluating-regional-policy-and-shocks-real-world.

Redding, S. J., and E. Rossi-Hansberg (2017), Quantitative Spatial Economics, *Annual Review of Economics*, 9(1): 21–58.

Redding, S. J., and D. M. Sturm (2016), *Estimating Neighbourhood Effects: Evidence from War-Time Destruction in London*, mimeo. See http://www.princeton.edu/~reddings/papers/LWW2-9Mar16.pdf.

Roelandt, T., and P. Den Hertog (1999), Cluster Analysis and Cluster-Based Policy Making in OECD Countries: An Introduction to the Theme, in: OECD, *Boosting Innovation: The Cluster Approach*, Paris.

Saxenian, A. (1994), *Regional Advantage: Culture and Competition in Silicon Valley and Route 128*, Harvard University Press, Cambridge, MA.

Scott, A. J. (2006), Handbook of Regional and Urban Economics, vol. 4, *Journal of Economic Geography*, 6: 104–7.

Stiglitz, J. E. (1977) The Theory of Local Public Goods, in: M. S. Feldstein, and R. P. Inman (eds.), *The Economics of Public Services*, MacMillan, London.

Storper, M. (2003), *Institutions, Incentives and Communication in Economic Geography: Hettner-Lecture 2003*, Franz Steiner Verlag, Heidelberg.

World Bank (2009), *World Development Report 2009*, Washington.

Index

Printed in the United States
by Baker & Taylor Publisher Services